THE
TAKING
OF
GETTY OIL

THE TAKING OF TAKING OF GETTY OIL

PENNZOIL, TEXACO, AND THE
TAKEOVER BATTLE THAT MADE HISTORY

STEVE COLL

OPEN ROAD
INTEGRATED MEDIA
NEW YORK

Cover design by Ian Koviak

978-1-5040-4953-5

This edition published in 2017 by Open Road Integrated Media, Inc.
180 Maiden Lane
New York, NY 10038
www.openroadmedia.com

For the Colls from Coll Island—
Shirley, Robert, Geoff, Dan, and Dorothy

CONTENTS

OWNERSHIP OF GETTY OIL COMPANY—MAY 1982

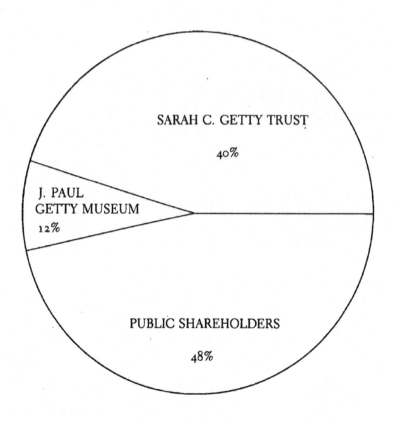

SARAH C. GETTY TRUST

40%

J. PAUL
GETTY MUSEUM
12%

PUBLIC SHAREHOLDERS

48%

CAST OF CHARACTERS

Sarah C. Getty Trust
>Gordon P. Getty, Trustee
>Ann Getty, Gordon's wife
>Moses Lasky, Gordon's attorney
>Charles "Tim" Cohler, Gordon's attorney
>Thomas Woodhouse, Gordon's attorney
>Marty Siegel, Investment Banker, Kidder, Peabody & Co.
>J. Paul Getty Jr., Gordon's brother and a beneficiary
>Vanni Treves, J. Paul Jr.'s Counsel
>J. Ronald Getty, Gordon's half-brother and a beneficiary
>Anne Catherine Getty, Gordon's niece and a beneficiary
>Claire Eugenia Getty, Gordon's niece and a beneficiary
>Caroline Marie Getty, Gordon's niece and a beneficiary
>Tara Gabriel Galaxy Gramaphone Getty, Gordon's nephew and a remainderman
>Seth Hufstedler, Guardian for Tara

J. Paul Getty Museum
>Harold Williams, President
>Harold Berg, Chairman of the Board of Trustees
>Martin Lipton, Outside Counsel
>Patricia Vlahakis, Outside Counsel
>Jay Higgins, Investment Banker, Salomon Brothers

Getty Oil Company
> Sidney R. Petersen, Chairman and Chief Executive
> Dave Copley, General Counsel
> Barton J. Winokur, Outside Counsel
> Robert Miller, President
> Geoff Boisi, Investment Banker, Goldman, Sachs & Co.
> Henry Wendt, Director
> John Teets, Director
> Laurence Tisch, Director
> Harold Stuart, Director
> Chauncey Medberry III, Director
> Herbert Galant, Outside Counsel

Pennzoil Company
> J. Hugh Liedtke, Chairman and Chief Executive
> Baine Kerr, President
> James Glanville, Investment Banker, Lazard Freres & Co.
> Arthur Liman, Outside Counsel
> Perry Barber, General Counsel
> Moulton Goodrum, Outside Counsel
> Joe Jamail, Trial Counsel
> John Jeffers, Trial Counsel
> Irv Terrell, Trial Counsel

Texaco Inc.
> John McKinley, Chairman and Chief Executive
> Al DeCrane, President
> James Kinnear, Vice Chairman
> William Weitzel, General Counsel
> Bruce Wasserstein, Investment Banker, First Boston Corp.
> Joseph Perella, Investment Banker, First Boston Corp.
> Morris Kramer, Outside Counsel
> Richard Miller, Trial Counsel
> Richard Keeton, Trial Counsel

Others
> Corbin J. Robertson, Jr., Quintana Petroleum
> T. Boone Pickens, Mesa Petroleum
> Kurt Wulff, Oil Industry Analyst

William Tavoulereas, President, Mobil Oil
Richard Lawler, Jury Foreman
James Shannon, Juror
Theresa Ladig, Juror
Shirley Wall, Juror
Laura Johnson, Juror
Anthony Farris, Judge
Solomon Casseb, Judge

THE
TAKING
OF
GETTY OIL

PART ONE

AN EMBARRASSMENT OF RICHES

1

THE BURGLAR'S DILEMMA

For months, C. Lansing Hays had known that he was dying, but he refused to discuss the fact openly with anyone, as if by sheer obstinacy he might defy mortality. His stubbornness did not surprise his family, even during those last, difficult days in the hospital in Monterey. They knew Lansing well enough. They knew that he could not tolerate frailty or weakness in himself or in others, this despite his own obvious, human fallibility. For his wife and children, who knew him best and loved him most, there was in Lansing's final, often cantankerous last stand an important, ambivalent truth. Lansing died the way he had lived, with audacity and contempt and drama, and that was as it should be. But by pretending that he would survive during those final days, he had also cheated them a little, deprived them of a chance finally to touch him.

In late April 1982, knowing that he could not last much longer, the children had all flown out to Carmel, California, where their parents owned a winter home. Spencer, the middle son and the one who had so closely imitated his father's life, attending the same college and law school and now practicing in New York City as Lansing had done, spent a full week hanging about the hospital, convinced that his father would die at any time. He wanted to be there for his passing. But the old man refused to let go, refused even to admit his time was near, so Spencer returned to New York and to pressing business at his office. Just a few days later, on May 10, 1982, his father was gone.

It took a week or so to arrange for a memorial service. The body was cremated, an appropriate act since Lansing Hays paid scant attention to his physical self while he was alive. He had been an imposing man, of average height but with extremely broad shoulders and a solid barrel chest. His head was large, and its most distinctive feature was a jutting chin that Lansing cocked and tilted aggressively if he found himself in an argument. Until 1979, when his lungs finally rebelled, he smoked three or four packs of cigarettes a day, and there always seemed to be one hanging from his lips or burning steadily in his ashtray. When, following a silent heart attack, the doctors finally ordered him to quit, he grew a silver mustache, which nicely complemented his thinning white hair and made him look distinguished, if also somewhat like a rascal. He said he would not shave the mustache off for fear the act might somehow cause him to take up smoking again. He held his whiskey well, but did not drink to excess because to do so would interfere with work.

And work, particularly work for Getty Oil Company, his principal client, was without question the most important thing in the world to Lansing Hays. It was not just that he worked hard. There was a ferocity about him, as if he believed that success in the practice of law depended not mainly on wit or judgment, but on stamina and unbridled animal aggression. He was a bellower, a ranter, an intimidator, a bully. He had a flash-powder temper, and once provoked, he would scream until his face reddened and the veins protruded from his neck. He was demanding and domineering, and he justified his abuse of others through the example of self-abuse. No one could work harder than he did. No one could care more about the client than he did.

Some of his partners, and even some of his clients, lived in fear of his outbursts. There were those, including his family and several of the younger partners at his firm, who loved Lansing despite his tyrannies, who regarded his bellowing as mere noise, and who accepted his abusive screaming and accusations as the price of his exceptional devotion. These few even found amusement in Lansing's wild, angry tirades. There was a hilarious story his son Spencer told, for example, about the time the family vacationed on a dude ranch in Montana and his father tried with terrible sound and fury to master a reluctant horse. But by the end of Lansing's life, there were many others, law partners and clients alike, who felt weary and bitter and even spiteful toward him. They had taken enough. Too many times they had been loudly, profanely accused of incompetence or imbecility. Too often they had been embarrassed in front of their colleagues. These people were frankly relieved when Lansing Hays was gone.

A powerful man who is disliked will nonetheless receive a proper tribute, and so they came from all across the country to the memorial service. It was held on a clear, warm day in Riverside, Connecticut, at St. Paul's Episcopal Church, a large and modern building. The church was not far from the Hays house, which was hidden in the Riverside woods on a private lane and commanded a breathtaking view across Long Island Sound. For the family, who of course were aware that Lansing had risen to the top of his profession, the turnout at the service was nonetheless touching and impressive.

Sidney Petersen, the chairman and chief executive of Getty Oil Company, for years Lansing's principal client, had flown the corporate jet in from California to attend. Other top company executives had come along with him. From Philadelphia, a contingent of partners from Dechert Price & Rhoads, the big law firm Lansing had merged with in 1979, came to pay their last respects. Other lawyers who had worked with Lansing for decades in the small firm of Hays & Landsman, and who were now partners in Dechert Price's New York branch, consoled Lansing's wife and children, whom they had known in the days before Lansing achieved his great success. And from San Francisco arrived the most impressive mourners of all, Gordon Getty and his beautiful wife Ann. The fourth son of J. Paul Getty, the renowned president of Getty Oil who died in 1976, Gordon was now one of the richest men in America, heir to approximately $25 million a year in income from his father's fortune.

It was that fortune which had bound Gordon Getty to Lansing Hays. Since J. Paul's death six years before, the two had been cotrustees of the Sarah C. Getty Trust, which owned 31.8 million shares of Getty Oil stock, or 40 percent of the company. The Sarah Getty Trust constituted the largest portion of J. Paul Getty's financial legacy. Gordon, his brother J. Paul Jr., and several of his nieces shared the dividend income from the trust's stock, but Gordon and Lansing, as trustees, controlled the rights of ownership. Both sat on the Getty Oil board of directors, and both earned more than a million dollars a year as a special fee for their trusteeship. When an issue was put to a shareholder vote, the two consulted together and decided which way to vote the trust's stock. In theory, they were equal partners in management of the trust, although in practice Lansing dominated Gordon, as he did almost everyone. Still, Gordon respected Lansing, and he had felt compelled to travel to Connecticut for the memorial service.

For all of those gathered in St. Paul's Episcopal Church that day, there was no escaping Lansing's potent and aggressive personality, even on the occasion of its expiration. Bluster had been the essence of him, and his intensity provoked deep and often conflicting reactions in those who knew him. Some at the memorial service wept uncontrollably. Some sat stiffly, feeling no mournfulness, thinking to themselves that this was one man whose passing would not draw their tears. Lansing's youngest son began the service by talking about his father and mother, and he described how theirs was a relationship that succeeded. Then an old friend and classmate of Lansing's at Williams College, who was himself not in very good health, stood and said a few kind words. And lastly, Spencer Hays came to the front of the sanctuary, unfolded a sheet of yellow legal paper on which he had made some notes, and delivered a remarkable eulogy.

"First, a brief story," he began. "A few years ago, my father and mother were spending the night alone in our summer house on Fire Island. It was during the off-season, so there were not many people about and the house was dark. My father woke up thinking he had heard someone in the house. He got out of bed and stood by the closed bedroom door and listened. He heard footsteps coming up the creaking wooden stairs, then coming down the hall to the bedroom. As he watched in the moonlight, he could see the bedroom doorknob beginning to turn. So he grabbed the doorknob, yanked open the door, and emitted what must have been a thunderous uproar of bellowing—without, I am sure, any expletives deleted.

"The hapless intruder must have had a stout heart indeed, for he did not drop dead on the spot. Instead, he turned tail, leaped down the stairs, probably without touching them, and burst out right through the closed screen door. He went screeching off into the night.

"I like to think that encounter with my father was enough to deter the intruder from a further life of crime."

A wave of laughter rolled through the church. Even those who had attended the service more from obligation than sentiment laughed easily and warmly. That was Lansing Hays exactly, the man they had known and dreaded.

Spencer went on. "My father was not much of one for speeches, eulogies, public statements, and the like. Respecting that thought, but wanting to say some words about my father, I decided to avoid a speech and simply list some words, single adjectives, that I think describe him. Having composed the list, I was struck by two things.

"First, the adjectives cover a very wide range of characteristics, some seemingly contradictory. One would think they could not all apply to the same man. Hence, his ability to keep one constantly on one's toes. My second thought on reviewing the list was that every single adjective applies to my father tenfold. Each word could, without overstatement, be modified by an 'extremely' or at least a 'very' and in certain cases an 'incredibly.' Here is the list:

"My father was shy. He was circumspect. He was *noisy*. He was private. He was complicated. He was honest—he was fond of recalling that a respected business associate once said to him, 'Lansing, you're so honest it's painful.' He was lawyerly—I'm sure he hated that word. He was hardworking—we have witnesses here. He was strong-minded. He was respected. He was loyal—to his clients, to his school, to his friends, and to his family. He was short-fused—to everyone. He was fair. He was independent. He was feisty—he loved the word. He was steadfast. He was courageous. He was sensitive. He had heart. He had great humor.

"And he could," Spencer Hays concluded, "send you right through a closed screen door. He shall be missed."

After the service, a small group from Lansing's immediate family drove to a nearby grave site for a brief private ceremony. Then the family returned to the house on Leeward Lane where the other mourners were gathering for a reception. By late afternoon, there was a throng of guests, and a drone of conversation possessed the house. The visitors paid their condolences to Nancy, Lansing's widow, and they talked among themselves about how their own lives might change now that Lansing was gone.

Ever since J. Paul Getty died, Lansing Hays had functioned as a kind of surrogate for the old man, as J. Paul was called, controlling both the direction of Getty Oil Company and the power of the Sarah Getty Trust's stock. Lansing's bombastic personality had, in effect, postponed the impact on the company and the trust of J. Paul Getty's death. From the early sixties on, J. Paul had lived at his mansion, Sutton Place, outside of London, England, and in fact did not set foot on American soil during the last fifteen years of his life. He had managed to retain firm control of Getty Oil, which was headquartered in Los Angeles, through the tenacious force of his own personality and also through Lansing, his eyes and ears in America. Lansing was, J. Paul once remarked, "my great friend and attorney par excellence," and that endorsement endowed Lansing with extraordinary power for a man who had never been an officer or employee of the company.

For many years, Lansing's only official connection to Getty Oil was his role as chief outside counsel, based in New York. Later he joined the board of directors and became cotrustee of the Sarah Getty Trust. But Lansing's power at Getty Oil had never been exercised through official channels. It depended not on title but on intimidation. If Lansing Hays wanted something done at Getty Oil, or if he did not like something that had been done by the company's executives, he would scream and bully and ridicule until he had his way. And since the old man, ornery but secluded in England, had made clear his trust in Lansing, there was no recourse except resignation for company executives who could not tolerate Lansing's tyranny. When J. Paul died, some expected Lansing's power to diminish because the old man would no longer be quietly behind him, but in fact his power only grew, mainly because he ascended to control of the Sarah Getty Trust. Now if the Getty Oil executives dared challenge his authority, they would not merely be battling J. Paul's lawyer and mouthpiece, but a man in charge of 40 percent of the company— although nominally he served as cotrustee with Gordon. And so Lansing had his way. He often treated Sid Petersen, the chairman of the board, with open contempt. He publicly humiliated Ralph David Copley, the company's vice-president and the man ostensibly in charge of Getty Oil's legal strategy. Copley, who had endured perhaps more abuse than anyone from Lansing, did not travel to Connecticut for the memorial service.

And then there was Gordon Getty. Of them all, it was Gordon's position that would be most profoundly affected by Lansing's death, although the Getty Oil executives and lawyers gathered at the Hays house in Riverside that day did not suspect how great the change would be. For the last six years, ever since he had joined the Getty

Oil board of directors at Lansing's insistence, Gordon had been an inscrutable and occasionally distracting presence at the company. When, after J. Paul Getty's death in 1976, Lansing had demanded that Gordon be appointed as a director, he had said it was because there should be a Getty on the board now that J. Paul was gone. The company's executives and some of the other directors suspected that Lansing's real aim was to secure an easy vote, because they believed that Gordon would do whatever Lansing told him. Their assessment had proved more or less correct, although sometimes, despite Lansing's screaming and his calling Gordon a fool in front of the other directors, the Getty scion went his own way. But Gordon's occasional independence—he would abstain from voting on important issues or sometimes cast the only negative vote—seemed to the Getty Oil executives more a kind of adolescent rebellion against Lansing's authority than a true, reasoned dissent.

And as anyone could see, though he was now in his mid-forties, there was still much of the adolescent in Gordon Getty. He was a tall, gangly man, six feet five inches, with a floppy, curly mop of brown hair that draped over his brow, contributing to the general impression of an oversized Muppet. Graying sideburns added years to his otherwise boyish face. His nose and fingers were gracefully long and thin. Overall, his appearance, clothes, and manner combined to create an image that Gordon himself enjoyed, and perhaps even cultivated: the absent-minded professor. Especially distinctive were his gestures and facial expressions. In serious conversation, he would adopt an exaggerated, scrutinizing pose, his eyebrows knit, his forehead furrowed like a bulldog, his mouth drawn tightly in a half-smile. His expression could change as suddenly as a flashing sign, however, and then his eyebrows would flex up and down while his long hands waved dramatically to make a point.

Gordon's disposition contrasted vividly with Lansing's. Gordon was a fundamentally sweet, easy man, though in his own way he was just as unpredictable as his explosive partner. In board meetings, Gordon would tilt his head back, shut his eyes, and appear to doze off, though afterward Gordon would say that he had only been thinking to himself. High-ranking company executives remarked that when you met Gordon, sometimes he acted as if you were his dearest, oldest friend, but the next time he would seem not to remember your name. He was often late to meetings, and seemed to the Getty

Oil executives and directors to have no familiarity with the ordinary protocols of business. Sometimes Gordon seemed to act arrogantly, as if he thought the world turned by his clock, but mostly he seemed lost and confused. Once at a board meeting, he had gone into a side room to make a call on one of those new credit-card telephones. After a few minutes, when he had not returned, a Getty Oil executive looked in, and there was Gordon with half a dozen consumer and department-store credit cards strewn on his lap, complaining that he couldn't figure out how the damn phone worked.

The most widely circulated stories about Gordon's absent-mindedness concerned his erratic relationship with automobiles. Getty Oil board meetings were normally held in Los Angeles, and Gordon would fly down to attend from his home in San Francisco. He would rent a car at the airport and drive to the company's head-quarters building near downtown. But after the meeting, Gordon sometimes couldn't remember where he parked his car, or even what make and model it was, and so a company executive would have to escort him through the underground garage, searching for a car with a rental sticker on the windshield. At one meeting, Gordon forgot about his car altogether and took a cab back to his hotel, then called frantically over to the company the next morning, worried that his rental had been stolen.

He had been an awkward boy, intimidated and degraded by his miserly, philandering father, and overshadowed by his charming, self-destructive older brother J. Paul Jr., and also by his half-brother George, the only one of J. Paul Getty's sons to succeed in the family business. Gordon was quiet, introspective, and something of a dreamer, particularly when it came to the principal passion of his life, music. He had been an opera enthusiast from an early age and began to compose classical music in his late teens. But his father, who married five times and saw his sons only a few times a year, urged Gordon to pursue a career in business. Gordon was eager for his father's approval, which J. Paul Getty hoarded as tightly as he did his money.

For eighteen years, beginning in 1962, Gordon abandoned his composing. His attempt to find a place in his father's oil company was disastrous, however. His first assignment, as an aide in the so-called Neutral Zone at the head of the Persian Gulf, led to a minor international incident. Gordon ignored local laws by refusing to turn over two Getty Oil employees being sought by authorities for questioning. He was placed under house arrest and soon had to leave the country. His father angrily ridiculed him for his incompetence. Gordon bounced from position to position, trailed by criticism from a wide variety of Getty Oil executives who found him immature, selfish, stubborn, and poorly qualified for business. Unable to hold a regular job in the company, Gordon began to do ad hoc consulting work at his father's request, analyzing Getty Oil's far-flung operations in the United States and around the world. His proposals were often dismissed as impractical by company managers. Yet he insisted that he be treated very seriously, and he came in conflict with company employees and even his own half-brother, George, J. Paul's eldest son, who was then rising steadily through the executive ranks. Fed up, George wrote his father in England to tell him that Gordon would never become a "well-rounded and seasoned business executive" and he even began to insinuate that Gordon was not really J. Paul's son. "Your musical compositions are very good," J. Paul wrote Gordon, but "you are not sufficiently mature." Even Gordon's mother, now divorced, complained to J. Paul that her son was growing up far too slowly.

Then in 1964, Gordon eloped to Las Vegas with Ann Gilbert, a willowy, red-haired, small-town girl from Wheatland, California. For a young man universally derided for lacking judgment, it was a remarkably successful decision. Through Ann, Gordon achieved what no Getty had in nearly half a century: a stable family life. Together they had four children, and as the years passed, Ann began to display all the gumption and solidity and poise seemingly absent in her husband. She defended Gordon in family battles, encouraged him socially, supported his music, and in San Francisco built a household with both traditional roots and a presence in the community.

Raised on a working ranch in the desolate plains of north-central California, Ann grew more and more socially ambitious in San Francisco, but she was demure and possessed of sufficient elegance that few resented her climb. She had done what millions of American girls growing up in small towns in the 1950s had dreamed of: she had married a rich, faithful man, raised his children, and surrounded herself with all the clothes and jewelry and beautiful possessions befitting her station. Most important, she had managed to carry it all off without pretension. She was newly rich, but she was not *nouveau riche*. There were those at Getty Oil Company who believed that Ann dominated Gordon in the same way that his father did and, later, Lansing Hays. But unlike J. Paul and Lansing, Ann persuaded gently, and over time Gordon began to grow up a little, until by the late 1970s it seemed that he had changed some. He took up his music again, composing a song cycle for female voice and piano based on a book of Emily Dickinson poems. Perhaps it was not a work of genius, but it was a spare, arresting piece, and it suggested authentic talent. In no small part because of Ann's ever-widening social connections, it was premiered at the National Gallery of Art in Washington in 1981. There were those who believed that underneath the surface, Gordon was the same petulant, selfish, adolescent rich kid who had so plagued his half-brother and his father during the 1960s. But by the early 1980s, Gordon Getty was now well into his forties, and it seemed to some that, at least partly because of Ann, he was finally coming into his own.

Ann Getty was ambitious, but she was also careful not to get ahead of her husband. She wanted respect for Gordon, both in music and in business, but there were sharp limits to her role. She knew that as time went on, the Getty Oil Company executives in Los Angeles began to see her as the power behind her husband, as a kind of puppeteer who controlled Gordon's very movements. This was not the case, she said. She advised Gordon on a few occasions, yes, and once in a while she even negotiated for him, but she was only a facilitator, not a decision-maker. Gordon was his own man. He was a man nearly bursting with ideas, and Ann's role was merely to help him turn those ideas into accomplishments.

Yet after J. Paul Getty's death in 1976, there had been one impediment to Gordon's maturation that even Ann could do nothing about: C. Lansing Hays. Lansing was such a forceful personality, and his ties to the company and the family were so deep, that as long as Lansing was alive Gordon would always be a kind of second-class citizen, despite his cotrusteeship and board of directors membership. There were those in the company who believed that Gordon preferred relationships with powerful, dominant people. His father had been that way, certainly, and Gordon liked affectionately to compare his father to a formidable lion with a deep growl and a ferocious appearance. Lansing was the same way; his roar was his most distinctive characteristic, and he acted sometimes as if he were Gordon's stepfather. Despite the abuse he endured, Gordon felt a deep respect for

Lansing Hays. He felt, as nearly everyone did, that Lansing could be surly, boisterous, and disagreeable, but he also believed that Lansing was less rude to him than he was to others. As cotrustees of 40 percent of Getty Oil's stock, Gordon and Lansing were allies. They had mutual interests to protect, and they shared a skepticism of Getty Oil's management, led by chairman Sid Petersen. Shortly before Lansing's death, Lansing and his wife Nancy had come to dinner at Gordon's San Francisco mansion. Before the meal was served, Lansing and Gordon were sitting alone in the opulent living room. Lansing turned to Gordon and, for the first time, confessed indirectly that he might not live forever.

"You know," he said, "You're going to have to go it alone sometime as sole trustee. And you might, eventually, have to get rid of Sid Petersen."

It was the first time Gordon had heard Lansing say such a thing. "What is that all about?" he asked.

"Well, Sid's an accountant. He doesn't think in broad terms."

Gordon wasn't sure what Lansing meant by that remark, and he did not try to draw the lawyer out. He was uncomfortable with Lansing's implication that he was dying. "Oh, Lansing," Gordon said, "you'll outlive us all. Let's not sound funereal."

Even if they had known that Gordon and Lansing had had such a conversation only weeks ago, it would have been hard for Sid Petersen and the other Getty Oil executives gathered in Riverside, Connecticut, on that spring afternoon in May 1982 to imagine what Gordon would do now that Lansing Hays was gone. After all this time, Gordon remained a mystery to them, despite the fact that he was near their age. Gordon's wealth, family history, and erratic demeanor all contributed to his inscrutability. By and large, the Getty Oil executives felt they could control Gordon. They had seen Lansing do it, and there was no reason to believe they couldn't do it themselves. But as to Gordon's plans, they were totally in the dark.

At the reception after the memorial service, Gordon offered a hint of his feelings and intentions, though none of the Getty Oil executives and lawyers in the crowd overheard his remark. Gordon was off in a corner of the house, speaking to Spencer Hays about the eulogy he had delivered earlier at church.

"You left one word off your list of adjectives," Gordon said sympathetically to Lansing's son.

"What was that?"

"Lansing was a *trustee.*" Gordon spoke with emphasis, his eyebrows knitted, his bony hand gesturing urgently.

The idea was an important one to Gordon Getty. At this moment, for the first time, Gordon was the sole trustee of the bulk of the Getty family fortune. The value of the Sarah Getty Trust was something over $1.5 billion. Until now, Gordon had relied on Lansing to perform the essential duty of a trustee: to preserve the value of the trust's stock, prudently to make that value rise, and to protect the trust from any threats to its holdings. Now, suddenly, Gordon was alone in charge. It was, by anyone's standards, an awesome responsibility, but for Gordon it was especially so, since his experience in finance and the oil business was limited. Gordon might be a flake, as the Getty Oil Company executives always put it, but he was a man who took his responsibilities seriously, even if he had not quite shed his immature outlook on matters of business.

It was not entirely clear that afternoon at the Hays home whether Gordon was indeed sole trustee of the Sarah Getty Trust, but Gordon certainly believed that he was, and that was perhaps all that really mattered. The history of the trust was long, litigious, and warped by family intrigue. The trust had been created in 1934 in the midst of fierce warring between J. Paul Getty and his eighty-year-old, deaf, partially crippled mother, Sarah. It was then four years since the death of George Getty, J. Paul's father and the founder of Getty Oil Company, and Sarah was suspicious and skeptical of the way her son J. Paul was running the family business. It was the middle of the Great Depression, and instead of drilling for oil, J. Paul was feverishly buying stocks in oil companies, many of which were in shaky financial condition. J. Paul kept pressing his mother for more money, but Sarah, who still had her wits about her, feared that if she turned the entire family fortune over to J. Paul, he would blow the bundle on penny stocks. In fact, J. Paul was pursuing a sound business strategy that would lead him to such wealth as Sarah could never contemplate, but since his strategy involved buying stocks, and since the collapse of stocks in 1929 had caused so much hardship, Sarah was intractably skeptical. In a hasty compromise over Christmas 1933, she created the trust as a mechanism to pass control of the family wealth to future generations.

The trust document itself, executed early in 1934, was deeply convoluted and contained a variety of strange and restrictive provisions, most of which reflected Sarah's concerns about her only son's lack of prudence. In essence, cash income from the trust's holdings—dividends, interest, and so on—would be divided in fixed portions between J. Paul and his sons: George, Ronald, J. Paul Jr., and Gordon. (A fifth son, Timothy died young. There were no daughters.) Control of the trust's stock would pass solely to J. Paul, but he was prohibited from investing the trust's assets in companies other than those already in the Getty Oil group. After 1934, a number of disputes and several family lawsuits arose over the issue of precisely what J. Paul could and could not do as sole trustee. After his mother's death, however, J. Paul did what he pleased, and he fought off all his challengers.

The question of who would succeed to control of the trust when J. Paul died had been an issue of some contention between father and sons, but as a practical matter it was clear that George Getty II, J. Paul's son and only child by his first marriage, was the favorite. By the late 1960s, George had risen to the top rank of Getty Oil Company. His official title was executive vice-president, since J. Paul wanted to be called president even though he never left England. But in the United States, where the company was based and where most of its business was conducted, George was clearly in charge. He was a moody man, but he was a competent executive and was well liked by the company's employees. It was assumed by all that when the old man died, George would run both the Sarah Getty Trust and the company. Gordon and his brothers would receive income from the trust, but George would be in control, just as his father had been throughout his life.

Instead, in 1973, George preceded his father to the grave, dying in Los Angeles from an overdose of barbiturates. The coroner ruled it suicide. The death shook J. Paul and led him to reconcile with Gordon; for all his insensitivity to his family, the old man decided in the end that his bloodline was important to him. He drew up a new document to govern control of the trust after his death. There were to be three equal cotrustees: Gordon, Lansing Hays, and the Security Pacific National Bank, an enormous financial institution headquartered in Los Angeles and long one of Getty Oil's bankers. But by the time of the old man's death in 1976, Security Pacific had still not agreed to accept the position of cotrustee. This was not a pressing issue at the time. As long as Lansing was around, Lansing was in charge, and if a representative of the bank joined him as a third cotrustee, it would just be one more person in the irascible lawyer's sphere of influence.

In fact, as the time passed and Security Pacific still refused to become cotrustee, some executives at Getty Oil suspected that Lansing was stonewalling the bank, unwilling to share his power and his trustee fees. There always remained some doubt about Lansing's intentions toward the bank, but it later became clear that Security Pacific had decided on its own not to serve as cotrustee. The bank was afraid that if it accepted the position, it might somehow get caught in all the family battles among the Gettys. There was a dispute in England about whether J. Paul's residency at Sutton Place made his estate subject to stiff British inheritance taxes, and it was legally possible that if Security Pacific became a cotrustee, its own assets might be tied up by British courts. Then, too, there were so many strange provisions in the trust document itself, and such a long history of disputes about its meaning, the cautious bankers at Security Pacific felt it would be imprudent to get involved, despite the millions the bank would earn in fees.

Toward the end of his life, Lansing Hays became concerned about what could happen to the trust and Getty Oil Company if he were to die and the bank refused to accept a cotrusteeship with Gordon. Then Gordon, whom Lansing so frequently ridiculed, would alone control 40 percent of the company's stock and a $1.5 billion fortune. On February 9, 1981, just over a year before his death, Lansing met with three top executives of Security Pacific in downtown Los Angeles in an attempt to persuade them to accept the cotrustee position.

"Gordon is going to be around for a long time and obviously will run things by himself if you choose not to participate," Hays told the bankers. "I can control Gordon. I think that if it were to be Gordon and Security Pacific as trustees, you could control him, too. He would have little choice."

When the bank's officers still refused to change their minds, despite Hays' pleading, Lansing asked if at least the bank would hold the matter open. He was afraid that if the bank filed with the court formally declaring that it would not serve, great turmoil would erupt at Getty Oil Company because the executives and investors would realize that Gordon was sole heir to 40 percent of the company's stock. The bank agreed not to file, and by the time of Lansing's death, the issue of whether Gordon would be sole trustee was still open, at least in the minds of some Getty Oil Company executives.

And so in addition to the sorrow and sympathy that pervaded the Hays home on the afternoon of the memorial reception, there was also an air of uneasiness and uncertainty. What would Gordon Getty do, now that he was suddenly possessed of so much power and wealth, now that he was free from the ghost of his father, which had been manifested in Lansing Hays? Even before Lansing's death, there had been whispers in the corridors of Getty Oil Company's sleek Los Angeles headquarters. It was rumored that at the most recent quarterly board meeting, during a brief remission of Lansing's illness, the dying lawyer had taken board chairman Sid Petersen aside and told him, "If you think I've been tough on you, wait until you have to deal with Gordon." Petersen said later that rumors of such a conversation were unfounded, but still, the story spread quickly through Getty Oil's top floors. As it was repeated that spring, the point was always the same: coming from Lansing Hays, who was so proud of his own fearsome reputation, there could be no more ominous a warning about the company's future.

A LETTER FROM RONALD

After the funeral, Gordon and Ann Getty returned home to their six-story, twenty-five-room mansion overlooking San Francisco Bay. In some ways, Lansing's death had changed their world dramatically. There was a host of questions to be answered now, new responsibilities to be managed, and suddenly Gordon was at the center of things. He would have to make his own decisions, and for the first time, those choices would hold direct consequences for both Getty Oil Company, one of the largest corporations in America, and for the extravagantly rich Getty family, whose wealth depended on the stock Gordon now controlled. And yet, despite these important changes, Gordon and Ann Getty did not intend to alter the basic rhythms of their life. Why should they? To their wealth they had now added power, and that meant the world would have to come to them.

Specifically, the world would have to come to their house on Broadway, a place that reflected both the extravagance of their riches and the odd contrast in their personalities. For Ann, the house was a manifestation of social position and luxury, and she paid close attention to the details of its opulence. There was a butler and a footman and five other full-time servants, including a French chef. Some of the staff had worked for J. Paul Getty at his Sutton Place mansion, and had been imported to San Francisco after his death. As it had been at Sutton Place, the ambiance at 1500 Broadway was decidedly old-world. There was no electricity in the dining room, for example, only candlelight. Antique and ornate, the furniture and design blended European ostentation with the simpler styles of Asia and California. In all, it was the sort of house that might properly be the center of society for the more artistic, pretentious factions of San Francisco's upper class, and that was precisely what Ann Getty wanted. She was becoming a charming and frequent hostess to San Francisco's rich, and to the musicians, artists, and writers who amused them.

While Gordon gladly accommodated Ann's taste for luxury, he did not share his wife's enthusiasm for society. For him, the mansion on Broadway was a kind of sanctuary, a refuge where he could indulge the passion of his middle age, music. Often, while the upstairs parlors of his home hummed with the conversation of Ann's guests, Gordon retreated to the basement and the privacy of his sound-proofed study and music room. There he kept a Yamaha grand piano, a stereo system, and on shelves lining two walls, thousands of classical recordings, some of them rare and old. He had begun the collection at age fifteen, and he prized his records more than any other of his possessions. Every day he was home, Gordon spent several hours alone in the basement, composing or singing in his booming, operatic baritone or just listening to music. He seemed at times ambivalent about the materialism so visibly pursued by his wife. While Ann drove a Porsche, for example, Gordon preferred a Jeep Wagoneer, and he kept a mid-sized Chrysler and a 1979 Pacer parked on the street outside the mansion—there was no garage. Once, a television interviewer asked Ann Getty what was the principal luxury of her husband's life. "Music," she answered.

"What is your luxury?" the interviewer asked her.

"All the rest of this, I guess," Ann said, waving vaguely at the splendor of her living room.

And now, with Lansing's death, that luxury was at the center of attention in the Getty family. For years, Gordon himself, as well as his older brother, J. Paul Getty, Jr., a registered drug addict living in England, and his only surviving half-brother, J. Ronald Getty, had focused their material ambitions on their father, who alone controlled the family fortune. Before the old man's death, they had fought J. Paul Sr. over income from the family trust and over the right to control that trust after he passed away. When the old man died in June 1976, the field of battle shifted to his will, and disputes over that testament were settled only after four years of lawsuits and negotiations. Now, with Lansing Hays dead and Gordon ascendant to sole control of the Sarah Getty Trust, the field had shifted again. When they returned to San Francisco from Lansing's funeral in May 1982, Gordon and Ann Getty knew that their mansion on Broadway would inevitably become the nucleus of a new round of family feuding over money.

They did not have long to wait. Only days after their return, Ronald, who lived in Los Angeles but traveled frequently around the country and in Europe, wrote Gordon asking that he consider appointing him as a cotrustee of the Sarah Getty Trust. It was a letter Gordon should have expected. Ronald was a bitter, cantankerous man whose resentment seemed only to increase with age. He had good cause to be caustic about the family; at age six, he had been the victim of an arbitrary and quite costly act of revenge by his father. Ronald was the only child born to the marriage of J. Paul Getty and his third wife Adolphine Helmle, the daughter of a German industrialist. When J. Paul and Fini, as he called her, were divorced, Fini's father extracted a painful alimony settlement from Getty, who was by then renowned in European society for his art-buying sprees and his philandering lifestyle.

"In Dr. Helmle, I encountered a businessman who was most certainly my equal," J. Paul admitted ruefully in his autobiography. And so to take revenge on Helmle for the divorce settlement, J. Paul arranged the Sarah Getty Trust documents to provide that Ronald would never receive more than three thousand dollars in annual income from the trust. During the 1970s, when the trust distributed tens of millions annually to Gordon, J. Paul Jr., and the late George Getty's three daughters, Ronald received virtually nothing. To compound the spite, J. Paul provided that when the trust dissolved upon the death of the last of his four surviving sons, its corpus would be divided equally among all of his grandchildren, including Ronald's offspring. For decades, then, Ronald had endured not only the status of poor relation in one of the world's richest families, but he had also lived with the knowledge that his children would become immensely wealthy after his own death. Such circumstances would try any man's patience, but in Ronald, who seemed to those who knew him a naturally acrimonious person, they produced a stubborn, alienating anger that rarely subsided.

If Ronald, like Gordon, had spent most of his adult life disaffected from his father, unlike his brother, Ronald evidenced none of the sweetness or charm that might have led to a reconciliation. He, too, had tried his hand in the family business. As a vice-president for marketing at Tidewater Oil in Tulsa, Oklahoma, then in J. Paul Getty's control, he had so infuriated his successful half-brother George that the old man was forced to intervene. Ronald was sent to Hamburg, Germany, to oversee Tidewater's European marketing subsidiary. His tenure was disastrous. Like his father, Ronald refused to fly, and he traveled by cruise ship, maddening Getty Oil executives in Los Angeles by charging around-the-world voyages to the company. In France, he was prosecuted for improperly enticing employees of another company to join his own, was found guilty, and received two suspended prison sentences. Finally quitting the oil business, Ronald moved to Los Angeles to try his hand first as a movie producer, then as a restaurateur—and finally as a litigant against his family. When he moved with his wife and children into his mother's Los Angeles home, Fini filed suit to have them thrown out. When he tried to use the family name to establish the Getty Financial Corporation, an enraged George Getty threatened to sue him, and finally registered the name in every state but California to prevent Ronald from expanding. In both the film and restaurant businesses, Ronald failed to earn the fortune denied him by his father, producing only a handful of poor B-movies and a chain of Don the Beachcomber eateries. He shifted his attention from business to the courtroom.

In the years leading up to J. Paul Getty's death, a great deal of family gossip and speculation centered on the provisions of the old man's will. The future of the Sarah Getty Trust was not in question; Gordon, Lansing Hays, and the Security Pacific Bank had already been appointed successor cotrustees, and all but three thousand dollars of its tens of millions in annual income was earmarked for equal division between Gordon, J. Paul Jr., and the late George Getty's daughters—the Georgettes, as they came to be known. But J. Paul Getty, in his own name, also owned another 12 percent of Getty Oil's stock; this block, combined with the control of the Sarah Getty Trust's 40 percent, put the old man in charge of a majority of Getty Oil's shares while he was alive. The question was, who would get the old man's personal estate when he died? Since the trust controlled 40 percent of the company's stock, whoever inherited J. Paul's 12 percent would own a "control premium"; enough stock, that is, to take control of Getty Oil in combination with the trust. It was Ronald's hope that his father would right his past wrongs and leave his personal estate to him. Then, not only would Ronald be restored to wealth roughly equal to his half-brothers, he would be a power to be reckoned with at Getty Oil. Again, however, Ronald was disappointed by his father. The old man left virtually his entire estate to the J. Paul Getty Museum Trust, based in Malibu, California. The trust operated an art museum which housed paintings, sculpture, and eighteenth-century French furniture collected by J. Paul in Europe. The bequest, valued at more than $400 million, instantly made the museum, a somewhat gaudy replica of a Roman villa situated on a bluff above the Pacific Ocean, one of the richest art institutions in the world. Ronald was not entirely shut out by his father's will: he was appointed executor of J. Paul's personal estate, a position that would earn him some $6 million in fees, and he also inherited a house in Italy which he later sold for about $1 million.

Seven million dollars might be enough for some men, but it was not enough for Ronald Getty. He sued the museum for $28 million more, claiming that he had found documents among his father's personal belongings which suggested that J. Paul had intended to rescind the Sarah Getty Trust and then establish a new one in which Ronald would be an equal beneficiary with his half-brothers. The museum believed that Ronald's claims were baseless, but it could not receive its own fortune until the lawsuit was out of the way, and so a settlement was reached by 1980 in which Ronald was paid close to $10 million. Still, Ronald continued to press his half-brothers for an equal share of the trust income.

So for Gordon, the letter from Ronald that arrived soon after Lansing's funeral was yet another salvo in what had by now become a long, grinding campaign of family lawsuits. It was a campaign in which Gordon had himself participated not too long before. In the late 1960s, Gordon had sued his father in California, demanding more money from the Sarah Getty Trust. The issue was whether "share dividends," or shares of Getty Oil stock issued to current stockholders, should be considered part of the income generated by the Sarah Getty Trust or part of the trust's principal, or corpus. The question was important to Gordon because of the way his father ran the trust and the company. It was J. Paul's ambition to accumulate wealth, not distribute it, and so he plowed nearly all of Getty Oil's huge profits back into the company and into the trust. It was that

philosophy which had caused the value of the trust to grow from several million dollars when it was established in 1934 to nearly a billion dollars by the 1960s. One consequence, however, was that precious little cash was distributed to J. Paul's sons. Until age twenty-five, Gordon received nine thousand dollars annually from the trust; after that, he was supposed to receive 20 percent of its income until his father's death, when he would get one-third. But since J. Paul was paying out share dividends, not cash dividends, there was no money to be had.

"I would be very pleased if you would follow the example of your brothers and work for a living," J. Paul wrote to Gordon when his son threatened a lawsuit over the issue. J. Paul pleaded with Gordon not to sue. The Rockefellers do not sue the Rockefellers, nor the Kennedys the Kennedys, he told his son. It would cause him great personal embarrassment. To stave off the suit, the old man instructed George to declare a cash dividend of ten cents per Getty Oil share, enough to give Gordon a fifty-thousand-dollar annual income.

Gordon said later that a lack of extreme wealth during his young adulthood had helped to build his character, but at the time he apparently could not see the value in such wisdom. He decided instead to press his case despite the ten-cent dividend, and he sued his father in California. Lansing Hays was instructed by J. Paul to supervise the litigation. To try the case, Hays hired a San Francisco trial attorney named Moses Lasky, then head of the litigation department at the large Bay Area law firm Brobeck, Phleger & Harrison. Lasky, a combative, ornery litigator and one of the few men around Getty Oil willing and able to stand up to Lansing Hays, beat up unmercifully on Gordon in court. So badly did it go for Gordon that at one point during the trial, Ann Getty called her father-in-law in England to tell him that Lasky was "killing" her husband on the stand and to urge him to instruct Lasky to ease up. J. Paul responded by telephoning Lasky and telling him, "Keep hammering Gordon. Keep hammering." In the end, on October 30, 1970, the judge ruled that Gordon was entitled "to have and recover nothing whatever from the trust estate or from J. Paul Getty."

Fortunately for him, Gordon was not the sort to harbor a grudge. Not only did he reconcile with his father after George's 1973 suicide, resulting in his being named cotrustee of the Sarah Getty Trust. He also became friendly over the years with Lasky, who had split from

Brobeck, Phleger to start his own small litigation firm in San Francisco, called Lasky, Haas, Cohler & Munter. Indeed, Gordon was so impressed with Lasky's performance against him in court back in the late 1960s that he began to talk with the aging trial lawyer about representing the trust after Lansing Hays died and Gordon became sole trustee. Lasky was more than willing. The trust would be a gold mine for his small firm. Gordon was heir not only to billions of dollars but to a tortuous family history of expensive lawsuits and infighting. What better client on which to build a law firm? By the time Gordon and Ann returned from Lansing's funeral that May, the engagement was official. Lasky and two of his younger partners, Charles "Tim" Cohler and Tom Woodhouse, would represent Gordon in all matters pertaining to his own fortune and to the Sarah Getty Trust.

That meant, first off, they had to deal somehow with Ronald Getty's threatening letter. Earlier that month, immediately after Lansing's death, Gordon had spoken with Ronald by telephone and had told him that he had no intention of accepting a cotrustee, whether it be Security Pacific Bank or a member of the family. Ronald's letter made it clear that he did not regard Gordon's decision as satisfactory. Gordon turned the letter over to Lasky, who drafted an unyielding reply for Gordon's signature. Now approaching eighty, Lasky remained every inch the formidable trial lawyer who had so badgered Gordon more than a decade before. Neither he nor his client saw any reason to be soft on Ronald. On May 28, Gordon and Lasky sent the stiff answer to Gordon's half-brother, telling him that a cotrusteeship was out of the question. Ronald was in Europe when the letter arrived, so he replied through his advisor in New York, one Horst Osterkamp.

"Ron's letter was not intended to be a legal matter and did not wish to solicit an attorney's reply," Osterkamp wrote to Gordon. "Ron was very disappointed in not receiving any further response from you after your telephone conversation in early May. He wanted to reemphasize his concern about a sole trustee and his desire to be appointed as a joint trustee. He strongly feels that you should share the same concerns. . . . As Ron is continually on the move, I would be happy to forward a letter or supply you with a current telephone contact."

Gordon turned Osterkamp's letter over to Lasky and asked him what he should do about it. A few days later, Lasky wrote Gordon at his mansion on Broadway. "My advice is to ignore Osterkamp's suggestion that you telephone Ronald. Instead, I would write Osterkamp a letter about as follows: 'Dear however you address him, In your letter you state that Ronald's letter was not intended to be a legal matter and that he did not wish an attorney's reply. So far as there may be nonlegal aspects, it seems to me that my father had his reasons as to why he did not appoint Ronald as one of the successor trustees, and I would be unfaithful to his wishes and to my duties as trustee if I were now to consent to have someone appointed as trustee whom my father had not designated.'"

Such was the spirit of Getty familial relations. It was a family in which every issue was a potential lawsuit, in which the threatening language of lawyers substituted for the patter of brothers. There was no other way to treat Ronald, of course; he had many times before demonstrated a willingness, even an eagerness, to take the family's problems to court. Besides, Ronald's challenge to Gordon's sole trusteeship had implications beyond relations between the two of them. Gordon believed that control of the Sarah Getty Trust should lead to control of Getty Oil Company, even though the trust did not own a full majority of the company's shares. He had seen Lansing Hays exercise such control through the force of his personality. Though he lacked Lansing's bombast, Gordon was determined that May to imitate the lawyer's example and assume control of Getty Oil—not of its day-to-day operations, which even Gordon conceded he was not qualified to supervise, but of its policies and strategies. It seemed logical, he said later, that a trust controlling 40 percent of a company's stock, even a company as large and complex as Getty Oil, should control policy. And Gordon did not want Ronald or anyone else to thwart his ambitions. Already the Lasky firm was researching the legal aspects of Gordon's rights as sole trustee, preparing to fend off any challengers. Frustrated by Gordon's unresponsiveness to his request, Ronald might well sue to gain a cotrusteeship, but Lasky believed such a suit had no basis in the trust document itself and could be beaten back. A more difficult issue was how Getty Oil itself would respond to Gordon's ascent to power and his aim—which he kept largely to himself—to control the company's destiny. For the last six years, Getty Oil's executives had endured Lansing Hays' tyrannical reign. They might not easily accept a new bid for control from Gordon.

Moses Lasky understood this problem well enough. On and off, he had served as a trial lawyer for Getty Oil for more than ten years.

He had developed friendships with several of Getty Oil's key executives, including Sid Petersen, the chief executive officer, and Dave Copley, the general counsel, who Lasky regarded as an uncle might a nephew. Moses Lasky knew Gordon, too. At the trial against him, he had emphasized Gordon's perceived immaturity and erratic habits. And though he said that Gordon had matured considerably in the years since then, his client was still the same man, the same whimsical "Gordo," as his father had sometimes called him—a dreamer who had spent much of his life in the shadows of tougher, more practical men. There had been his father, then Lansing, and now, perhaps, Moses Lasky. If anyone could pave the way for Gordon at Getty Oil, it would be Lasky. Certainly, most everyone believed, Gordon could not take control of Getty Oil on his own. He needed a proxy, someone to fight and argue and negotiate as Lansing had done.

And that was why, that May, Moses Lasky called Sid Petersen and arranged to have dinner with the Getty Oil chairman in Los Angeles. He wanted to talk, he said, about Gordon's new role at the company.

3

COMPANY MAN

It was with feelings of both apprehension and relief that Sidney R. Petersen made a dinner reservation at the Los Angeles Club for the evening of Tuesday, May 18, 1982.

When Lasky had called the chairman's office to say that his firm was now representing Gordon Getty and the Sarah Getty Trust and to suggest that perhaps they should meet to discuss these new circumstances, Petersen had thought to himself that this was a positive development indeed, perhaps the first good news since the death of Lansing Hays a week before. Petersen had first met Lasky back in the early 1970s when Petersen was a rising young executive in Getty Oil's financial and corporate planning departments and Lasky was litigating on Getty Oil's behalf a long, complex antitrust suit that had been filed against the company. Petersen had worked with Lasky then, and he had come to regard the trial lawyer as a friend. They did not spend much time together socially; there was a twenty-year difference between them, and Lasky lived in San Francisco while Petersen was in Los Angeles. But Petersen had spent time socially with Lasky's younger partner, Tim Cohler. In 1979, Petersen, Getty Oil general counsel Dave Copley, Cohler, and their wives had gone on a vacation cruise together in Greece. They had all stayed in touch since then, exchanging Christmas cards and other pleasantries and occasionally working together on Getty Oil business. Now that Lasky was representing Gordon, his firm could no longer work for the company; it would be a conflict of interest. But that did not really bother Petersen. As he awaited their dinner meeting, Petersen regarded Lasky's new association with Gordon as a potential breakthrough. They both knew Gordon. In the past, they both had endured his petulance and his lack of business sophistication. Petersen had been George Getty's executive assistant during the time when Gordon had tried his hand at the family business, and he knew all the stories about Gordon's feuds with his half-brother, his erratic habits, and absent-mindedness.

More recently, Petersen had witnessed Gordon's behavior in the Getty Oil boardroom, where the Getty scion seemed to him completely out of sync with the other directors, unable to articulate even the basic issues faced by the company. One incident that stuck in Petersen's mind was the directors' vote on the acquisition of the ERC Corporation, an insurance company Getty Oil bought during the late 1970s in an effort to diversify from the oil business. It was an important deal—the price tag was more than $500 million—and Petersen had invested a great deal of time and effort negotiating the purchase and explaining it to the directors. Gordon had never once voiced an objection to the deal. But when it came time to approve it, Gordon cast the only negative vote. His dissent was not much of a problem because all of the other directors were strongly in favor of the deal, but the vote so surprised and annoyed Petersen that he had turned to Gordon across the table and asked him why he voted against the proposal.

"Well, everybody else voted yes, and I thought someone should vote against it," Gordon had answered.

The arbitrariness, the silliness of that answer had stayed with Petersen. He regarded Gordon as a man simultaneously indecisive and stubborn. He was encouraged by Lasky's engagement now because Lasky, too, knew this story about his client, and no doubt knew other stories as well. Petersen hoped that Lasky would understand the dilemma he faced as the chairman of a Fortune 100 company with tens of thousands of public stockholders who were now potentially at the mercy of the whims and idiosyncrasies of a man such as Gordon Getty. It was important that Gordon and the company find a way to work together now that Gordon was in control of 40 percent of Getty Oil's stock. Perhaps Lasky could bridge the gulf between Petersen and Gordon.

It was a gulf rooted in time, culture, and social standing. In demeanor, background, and experience, Sidney Petersen had little in common with Gordon Getty. He had grown up in Oakland and San Leandro, across the bay from the glamorous San Francisco society in which Gordon and his wife moved so easily. His father was a small businessman who owned a speedometer repair shop where Sid worked during the summers. The company had been started in the midst of the Depression, and the vast majority of its business came from used-car lots that wanted the speedometers on their cars turned back. Petersen was the youngest child, and the only son, in a stable, stoical Danish family that emphasized hard work and showed little emotion. Sid was the first in his family to finish college, and for all the success he achieved in school and later in corporate life, his parents never expressed much surprise or pleasure over his accomplishments.

Petersen worked hard despite his parents' outward indifference. He attended the University of California at Berkeley, and after graduation served in the army for twenty-one months. At the time of his release, he was married and the father of a young child, so he returned to the Bay Area to search for a job. It was the 1950s, an era of prosperity and corporate conformity in America, and Petersen chose a secure career with the giant Tidewater Oil Company, then just newly under the control of J. Paul Getty after a decades-long takeover campaign. Petersen was placed in an administrative training program and landed in the transportation department. When Tidewater's headquarters were moved to Los Angeles as part of a consolidation with Getty Oil, Petersen went with the company reluctantly after his search for a new job in San Francisco yielded no offer more promising than the job he already had. In time, he came to enjoy Los Angeles, at least partly because he began to succeed professionally.

Tidewater had been notorious for its penny-pinching corporate policies, and the company had hired only a handful of young executives in the twenty years since the Depression. The result was that Petersen moved rapidly through the corporation's ranks because there were few contemporaries around to block his ascent. By the 1960s, because of the twenty-year informal hiring freeze, when an executive retired at age sixty-five, there was no one fifty-five years old working in a job one notch below, waiting to replace the retiree. Someone such as Petersen—young, smart, and aggressive—could move quickly into the vacuum. Moreover, when Tidewater's name was changed to Getty Oil, its culture was altered, too. The company began to expand aggressively, making up for the time lost by the old Tidewater management's frugal caution. New service stations were erected across the country, a fleet of tankers was built, and a plethora of new oil wells were sunk in Texas, Oklahoma, California, and elsewhere. In this atmosphere of growth, it was Petersen's facility with numbers and his talent for budgets and planning, not his knowledge of the oil patch, that led to his rise. The planners were ascendant in the new Getty Oil; in a company experiencing such rapid change and expansion, they had to be, J. Paul Getty believed. By the mid-1970s, Petersen was positioned for Getty Oil's chairmanship, and in 1979, three years after the old man's death, he was voted to the post by the company's board of directors.

There were those in and around Getty Oil company who thought that Sid Petersen had changed for the worse when he became chairman. Before, they said, he had been a quiet, nervous, almost shy man, whose solid professionalism distinguished him from the coarser, less articulate executives who surrounded him. The board had chosen Petersen because since George Getty's death in 1973 the company had been led by executives "with mud still on their boots," as the saying at the company went, men from the oil patch who, while knowledgeable about bits and drills and wells and pipelines, lacked the sophistication necessary to lead Getty Oil into the modern corporate era. Or so the board believed. Certainly, the company was no longer the Getty family's private empire—it was a visible, publicly owned, sprawling and complex enterprise. The company could benefit from a higher profile on Wall Street, in the Los Angeles community, and in the corporate oil fraternity.

Sid Petersen, the board felt, was the man who could lead the way. He had never gotten mud on his boots; so far as anyone knew, he didn't even have boots. In more than twenty years with the company, he had worked outside of corporate headquarters for only nine months. Sid Petersen was a numbers man, a spokesman, the sort of CEO who might just as easily lead a food company or a diversified conglomerate. And yet, some of Getty Oil's executives thought, he had taken his new, public role too seriously since becoming chairman. It was little things that annoyed them, trappings of power and ambition absent in his predecessors. For years, Getty Oil's top executives had driven company Cadillacs to and from the office, but that wasn't good enough for Petersen, they said—he had to have a Jaguar for himself. Some increasingly perceived his shyness as arrogance. Socially, he became openly ambitious, joining the Los Angeles Philharmonic board and hosting dinner parties for Los Angeles' artistic cognoscenti. In this realm, the contrast between Petersen and his immediate predecessor, Harold Berg, a large, burly man who had spent nearly all of his life in the Texas oil fields, was especially vivid. There was a story about how after his retirement Berg had joined Petersen at a glittering fund-raising party for the Philharmonic. While Petersen mixed comfortably with the symphony's directors and musicians, Berg stood off by himself. Finally, a woman who worked with the symphony approached him and, expecting to initiate a discussion about Mozart or Handel or Chopin, asked him, "Mr. Berg, what kind of music do you enjoy?"

"Well," Berg drawled, "I'm kind of partial to barbershop quartets."

It seemed to some that after Petersen became chairman, he snubbed his old friends. He was a handsome man, square-jawed, with graying temples and thin, fashionable silver glasses. With his $460,000 chairman's salary, not including bonuses and benefits, now in hand, he seemed increasingly to pay close attention to his clothes and personal appearance. Petersen's wife, Nancy, irritated a few company executives and their wives with previously suppressed pretensions—she used the company limousine to take herself on shopping sprees, for example, and stopped talking to wives who felt they had helped "cultivate" Nancy socially while her husband climbed the Getty Oil ladder.

The grievances against the Petersens were on their face petty, but they reflected a deeper cultural and social divisiveness in corporate headquarters. For years, Getty Oil's managers and executives had shared the same life-style. They had been a kind of family. They lived in the less glamorous sections of Los Angeles County—sleepy, suburban Glendale, mainly—and they played golf together at the Wilshire Country Club a few miles from downtown. They were part of the old Los Angeles business establishment, which included the downtown banks and the oil companies and a handful of other industrial concerns. Petersen, in perhaps subtle ways, was seen to be leaving that orbit and moving into the glitzy, more socially self-conscious ranks of new Los Angeles: Hollywood. His house in Studio City, a large

corner Tudor in a plush neighborhood, had once been occupied by
Bing Crosby and was right next to Bob Hope's block-long estate. The
most talked-about symbol of Petersen's ambitions, though, was the
new office building he had announced soon after becoming chairman. It would be a large, elaborate building across the Hollywood
Hills from downtown and near Universal City. Sharing the building
with Getty Oil, Petersen hoped, would be a large movie company.
Nancy was helping with the interior design decisions, or so it was
rumored among company managers. Some of the executives at Getty
Oil felt that what Petersen was really doing in Universal City was
building a monument to himself and to the new Getty Oil he was
fashioning in his own image.

Gordon Getty, whose world was far removed from the gossip and
intrigue at Getty Oil's headquarters, did not feel that the new office
building represented a physical incarnation of Sid Petersen's ego, nor
was he uncomfortable with the chairman's visible social aspirations.
After all, Gordon Getty was well accustomed to the prerogatives and
perquisites of wealth and power. What bothered Gordon about Sid
Petersen was that he seemed to think he could push the Getty scion
around. Whether Sid's attitude was a by-product of the personal
power he now felt as chairman of a huge Los Angeles oil company
hardly mattered to Gordon. What mattered was that Gordon did not
like the way he was being treated.

The friction between them had arisen quickly after Lansing's
death. Hays had died only a few days before Getty Oil's annual shareholders meeting in 1982, where stockholders gathered to hear about
the company's performance and future plans, and to ratify proposals
submitted by the management. That year's meeting was being held
at the Beverly Hills Hotel, a sprawling pink-stucco compound at the
center of monied Hollywood society. In order for the annual meeting
to take place, a quorum had to be established—a certain percentage
of company shares had to vote "present."

With Lansing suddenly gone, there was a question about how the
Sarah Getty Trust's large block of stock would be handled. If Gordon was now sole trustee, then he would have to submit his proxy
to establish the quorum. In the past, when Lansing and Gordon
together controlled the trust, there had been times when Gordon
refused to sign the quorum proxy until the very last minute before
the annual meeting began. Such occurrences had been extremely

aggravating to Petersen because it would be a huge personal embarrassment if an annual meeting had to be canceled for lack of a quorum. Petersen and other Getty Oil executives had regarded Gordon's
past refusals to sign the proxy as a kind of adolescent rebellion by
Gordon against Lansing. By postponing his signature, Gordon was
reminding Lansing that, for all his bluster and authority, the lawyer
could do nothing if Gordon did not go along. Lansing handled the
rebellion in his usual manner: he confronted Gordon, loudly berated
him for his imbecility, and obtained his signature. After Lansing's
death, Gordon against postponed signing the proxy until the last
minute—he stayed in his room at the Beverly Hills Hotel, Petersen
said later, until thirty seconds before the meeting's commencement.
Petersen interpreted the postponement as a personal message to him
from Gordon, a reminder that if he chose to, Gordon alone could
grind even the most routine Getty Oil shareholders meeting to a
halt. Gordon finally signed the proxy, but he did not apologize for
his delay.

Petersen's fears had been compounded by a private meeting he
had with Gordon the day before the annual shareholders gathering
convened. Gordon had flown down from San Francisco and had
come to the chairman's office on the eighteenth floor of the Getty
Oil headquarters building near downtown Los Angeles. Petersen felt
that he should talk briefly with Gordon before the annual meeting
began.

"Those of us in management, and more particularly the other
directors of the company, will be looking to you for some signal
or indication about what you feel your role will be at Getty Oil,"
Petersen said.

"I'm not going to make any changes in management—yet," Gordon answered. "And the present slate of directors is okay for now."

Gordon did not elaborate. Petersen was chilled by the response.
He was unaware that Lansing had talked with Gordon about a
change in management before the lawyer's death. For his part,
Gordon believed that he was simply communicating to Petersen
the decision he had arrived at in recent days, that as a 40 percent
stockholder in Getty Oil he intended now to control the company's
policies. Ever since he had come on the board of directors in 1976,
after his father's death, Gordon had regarded Getty Oil's management with some suspicion. He sensed their hostility toward him, and

he resented the manner in which they addressed him. As the most prominent surviving son of J. Paul Getty, and as cotrustee of so much of the company's stock, he felt in those years that he deserved far more deference and respect than he received. Gordon felt that Sid Petersen, particularly, had been rude to him over the years. So he was not bothered by the thought that his new power as sole trustee made the Getty Oil chairman uneasy.

"I'm aware that forty percent is forty percent," Gordon had told Petersen before the annual meeting. "It's not the same as fifty-one percent. I'm also aware that even if I have a ninety-nine percent controlling interest, I still have to control the company according to the best interests of all the stockholders, not just the ninety-nine percent controlling interest."

Such caveats and assurances from Gordon about the importance of "all the stockholders" did not comfort Sidney Petersen. He hoped that over dinner with Moses Lasky that Tuesday evening, May 18, he would obtain a more concrete understanding of Gordon's intentions as well as assurances that Lasky would help Petersen keep Gordon under control in the months ahead. By the time their dinner meeting was over, however, Petersen was more concerned than he had ever been before.

The evening began with an inauspicious conversation between Lasky, Tim Cohler, and Dave Copley in Copley's office at Getty Oil headquarters. A worried, white-haired man who had spent nearly his entire career as a Getty Oil lawyer, Copley had spent years as the company's top in-house lawyer, but he had been denied the dignity of his new title, general counsel, because Lansing Hays did not want any confusion about who was Getty Oil's most important attorney. A graduate of the Colorado School of Mines and the University of Denver Law School, Copley had spent far too much time, he felt, at the mercy of Lansing's bullying. Now that Lansing was gone, Copley was finally in a position to direct the company's legal strategy.

Tim Cohler had flown down from San Francisco to accompany Lasky to dinner with Petersen; Lasky was already in Los Angeles, since he was then trying the Oakland Raiders' antitrust suit against the National Football League on the Raiders' behalf. Before joining Petersen for dinner at the Los Angeles Club, which was on the top floor of the Getty Oil headquarters building at the corner of Wilshire and Western, Cohler and Lasky decided to drop in on Copley to talk about Gordon Getty's new role at the company.

"It might be appropriate if Mr. Getty was named chairman of the company," Lasky said not long after they got under way. "It would be more of an honorary title—Gordon is not interested in running the company day-to-day. But the title would be helpful in relations with management." Lasky went on to say that Gordon might also consider assignment to some of the board of directors' important committees, such as the nominating committee and the executive compensation committee.

Copley was surprised by Lasky's suggestion—Getty Oil already had a chairman, Sid Petersen. "It's my view," Copley said, "that if Mr. Getty presses to be chairman of the board, I anticipate there might be some resignations on the board. Our board members are by and large men of independent means and have successful careers and are truly independent board members."

Lasky countered. "It is both Mr. Getty's and Mrs. Getty's view that Gordon should assume a role of more significance at the company. More respect should be given to his position now that he is sole trustee."

"The directors are courteous to Gordon," Copley answered. "But it presents problems at times. Gordon will make proposals that catch them by surprise. Also, Mr. Getty's punctuality leaves something to be desired at times."

"I hope the board members will not show or reflect their feelings about Mr. Getty's proposals. If they don't think the proposals are prudent, I hope they won't respond to him in a manner where he would sense disrespect. That might cause friction," Lasky said.

"I think the Getty Oil directors are gentlemen, and they conduct themselves as such. But Mr. Getty's apparent lack of concern for business routine and etiquette can cause problems, too. That can lead to friction itself."

Lasky agreed with Copley that Gordon didn't have much appreciation for what Lasky called "the day-to-day routine of business." But the lawyer emphasized to Copley that really, the issue with Gordon was not control of Getty Oil's operations, but one of respect. If Petersen and Copley and the company's directors would just treat Gordon carefully, deferentially, and not be rude to him, then Gordon would not become a problem. The tone of the conversation was collegial and professional; they were all friends. The implication from Lasky was that if the company would only cooperate, he could help them manage Gordon.

The meeting ended cordially, and Lasky and Cohler rode the elevator up to Petersen's office. Unaware of the suggestions that had been made to his general counsel just moments before, Petersen accompanied the two lawyers upstairs to the Los Angeles Club. The restaurant commanded a striking view of the city: to the north was the Hollywood sign resting in the hills, to the east was downtown's clump of steel-and-glass skyscrapers, and to the west, hidden in the haze, lay the Pacific Ocean.

The dinner lasted two hours, and through its courses Lasky repeated to Petersen the message he had just delivered to his general counsel, Copley. The company now had to be very, very careful about its manner and attitude toward Gordon, and somehow, it had to recognize Gordon's new power. For one thing, Lasky said, Getty Oil had to find a new title that would satisfy both Gordon and Ann. Chairman of the board was one possibility. Though it was not the case at Getty Oil, in some companies the chairman's title was considered more decorative than authoritative. If Gordon was named chairman under this scheme, then Petersen, who was now called chairman and chief executive officer, would have his title changed to president and chief executive officer. Robert Miller, now Getty Oil's president and chief operating officer and the executive second in command to Petersen, would surrender the title of president to Petersen. But there were other possibilities, too, Lasky said. Certainly, Gordon needed to have his board committee assignments changed as a gesture of respect—he was now on the unprestigious employee benefits committee, and he wanted off that one. Perhaps they could call him chairman of the executive committee of the board of directors. At the least, Lasky indicated, Petersen should shift Gordon to whatever new board committees he wanted to serve on.

"Look, if you fellows just drop these ideas that you have about Gordon, recognize that he does represent ownership of a large part of the company, and if you don't treat him with disdain, you're going to have no trouble at all," Lasky said. "Mr. Getty is not interested in running this company day-to-day, but he does own the company. Gordon does not want your job, Sid. In my judgment, that shouldn't even cross anybody's mind."

At one point, Petersen asked Lasky, "Don't you think appointing a cotrustee to serve with Gordon would be a good idea? If something were to happen to Gordon, the whole future of the trust would be in doubt."

"No," Lasky answered. "If you tried to appoint a cotrustee, you'd just be inviting Ronald to seek the appointment. That's the last thing anybody wants."

Petersen, of course, did not have Ronald in mind. He was thinking about Security Pacific National Bank as a possible cotrustee. Petersen was not convinced that Lasky's "be afraid of Ronald theory," as he later characterized it, was really such a frightening specter. His general counsel, Copley, had told him, as Lasky himself had told Gordon, that Ronald had no legitimate right to be cotrustee and no sound basis for a lawsuit seeking an appointment. Still, Petersen did not press his cotrustee proposal; Lasky's dismissal of the idea was insistent.

As it had been in the meeting with Copley earlier, the tone of the conversation over dinner that evening was cordial and relaxed. There was an affinity between the three of them. As they watched Petersen, listened to his comments, and answered his questions, Lasky and his partner Cohler thought that Sid understood their message, that Gordon posed no threat to Getty Oil so long as management treated him properly. When the meal was concluded, they left the table confident that their mission had been successful.

In fact, as the dinner went along, Sid Petersen became more and more alarmed. As he listened and watched, he thought he saw the wheels turning in Moses Lasky's head: Lasky, Petersen believed, was out to be the new power behind the throne at Getty Oil. He was going to try to replace Lansing Hays as the man who controlled Gordon's wealth and power and, through Gordon, controlled the company. Whereas he had first regarded Lasky as a potentially positive force, someone who could help management restrain Gordon's erratic impulses, by the time dinner was over, Petersen looked on Lasky and his partner Cohler with suspicion and concern. At the same time, though, Petersen was not in a panic about Gordon Getty's new role. Like Lasky himself, Petersen believed that with patience and diplomacy and a little toughness, he could work with Gordon. It might be an exasperating, aggravating effort, Petersen thought, but it could be done. Gordon Getty could be controlled, neutralized. Lansing had done it. Lasky was suggesting that he would do it. Sid Petersen believed that he, too, could control Gordon Getty on his own.

And for a time at least, it seemed that Petersen was right. Spring yielded to summer, and the confusion, concern, and confrontation that had followed Lansing Hays' death subsided. Lasky went on trying the Raiders case in Los Angeles. Cohler returned to San Francisco to attend to other business. In the first weeks after the dinner with Lasky, an effort was made to shift Gordon's committee assignments. There was a bit of discomfort over that, but no more than Petersen would expect from Gordon. The board committees rotated annually in September. There was no problem with adding Gordon to more prestigious committees before then. But Petersen hoped that in addition, Gordon would stay on the employee benefits committee until new assignments were drawn up in the fall. That way, none of the other directors would be affected by the moves. But Gordon wouldn't have it—he wanted off of benefits immediately. So Petersen had to call Norman Topping, the retired chancellor of the University of Southern California and a longtime Getty Oil director, to ask if he would mind switching to the benefits committee out of turn. Petersen suspected that the real reason Gordon wanted off the benefits committee was that it met at eight o'clock in the morning before the quarterly board meetings and that Gordon disliked rising early for business meetings. Still, Topping was agreeable to the switch if Petersen thought it was necessary, and the changes were made without incident.

That summer, Gordon and his family rented a beach house in Malibu, just north and west of Los Angeles. He called Petersen and told him that he would like an office at Getty Oil headquarters, some place where he could begin to learn about the company's finances and operations. Petersen agreed immediately—it was a perfectly reasonable request on its face, though the Getty Oil chairman was a little nervous about what Gordon's actual intentions might be. An appropriate office was quickly located and secretarial service was arranged. Petersen told several of the company's top financial executives about Gordon's plans. He said that they should provide Gordon with whatever documents he needed and answer any questions he had. To Gordon himself, Petersen even suggested that instead of just looking at the company on paper, he might want to tour some of its oil field operations and meet the managers in Bakersfield, Houston,

Tulsa, and elsewhere who were responsible for drilling, producing, and processing the company's vast oil reserves.

"You're the only one of us with your name on the company," Petersen said to Gordon. "Why not go out and meet some of the people?"

But Gordon rejected that suggestion. He was on vacation with his family, and besides, he was primarily interested in Getty Oil's finances, about which he knew and understood very little. He wanted to get a firm grasp that summer of just where the company's money was invested and what it was invested in. He wanted to look at the cost of drilling, he said, and where the reserves were, and whether the company's oil operations were "wise," as he put it later. As for Petersen, Gordon felt that summer an increasing tension between himself and the Getty Oil chairman. He could not understand why Petersen did not make more of an effort to get along with him. Bob Miller, the company's chief operating officer, a rough oilman who had been bred in the Texas fields, got along with him well, Gordon thought. So had Harold Berg, the oilman who preceded Petersen as chairman. From time to time, it seemed to Gordon that Miller and Berg would blow their stacks and just clear the air with him. But Petersen, he thought, so cold and reticent and calculating, was the sort of man who would just "simmer and fester, fret and fume," as Gordon said later.

So while Petersen watched apprehensively, Gordon drove into Los Angeles from Malibu each day to learn about the Getty Oil Company. To the Getty Oil finance executives who worked with him, it seemed that Gordon did not have the faintest idea about what he wanted to examine. In a way, they felt some sympathy for him. They would select what they thought might be helpful documents, and then sit in his office and try to explain the company's operations to him. But Gordon was starting from ground zero, and the executives were surprised at how little he knew about the company or about basic corporate finances. Perhaps someone should have provided Gordon with an outline, a kind of syllabus for learning about the operations of so large a corporation, they thought. But Gordon might not have tolerated such condescension, and anyway, he kept insisting that he wanted to delve into the most complex and arcane aspects of Getty Oil's finances—cash-flow models, comparative rates of return among oil wells, tax-basis models, and so on. He seemed to grasp little of the material that was presented to him, but he often insisted that the documents he saw weren't the ones he had wanted in the first place, and that was the cause of his frustration. To the finance executives who endured this tormenting process, Gordon seemed to be floundering. To them, he seemed like a boy who had lived his life in a bubble and now suddenly had been released into harsh, complex reality.

And certainly, Getty Oil was a sprawling and complicated corporation to understand. Though its principal business was oil and natural gas, the company also owned gold and uranium mines in the American West, a copper deposit in Chile, vineyards, orchards, grazing lands, timberlands, refineries, and chemical plants. Besides these natural resource holdings, Getty Oil had acquired in the late 1970s both ERC, the insurance company, and ESPN, a cable network that offered twenty-four hours per day of sports programming. The company's oil and gas reserves were scattered around the globe in Indonesia, the Neutral Zone, Kuwait, Algeria, Spain, and the North Sea. But nearly two-thirds of its reserves were in the politically secure United States—a fact that distinguished Getty from most other large oil companies. Of its American oil, most lay in the Kern River field of California, near Bakersfield, which was the second-largest known oil deposit in the state. It was a patulous, dusty field where jackhammer wells stretched as far as the eye could see across rolling, barren brown hills. When analysts and oilmen described the Getty Company, they turned their attention quickly to the Kern field and talked about it in a covetous tone. Not only was the field deep and rich, its profit margins were exceptionally high. It was projected that the Kern River field would have a long life, well into the twenty-first century, and in 1982 it was one of the most prized oil properties in America.

Gordon Getty was especially interested in the Kern field, as anyone would be, and he asked the Getty Oil executives who worked with him that summer to explain the financial aspects of the field's operations. The executives tried, but when the summer waned and Gordon prepared to return to San Francisco, they did not believe that they had succeeded.

Sid Petersen was uncertain whether Gordon's exercise in learning had been satisfying to the Getty scion, but by the time Gordon left Los Angeles, Petersen had another, more important problem to worry about. At the summer board of directors meeting, which was held in Texas, Petersen met with Gordon privately to see where things stood. There were a number of things that Gordon wanted to talk about, including his committee assignments ("Everyone should understand that I have to be on the executive committee," he mentioned), and the possibility of selling Getty Oil's insurance subsidiary, ERC, whose acquisition Gordon had opposed.

"I think we should look at selling ERC and then redeploying the money to avoid high debt levels," Gordon said. Debt was something of an obsession with Gordon; he disliked it greatly and often suggested unusual plans to avoid debt levels other large corporations would regard as small. To Petersen, Gordon's views about debt were just another example of his lack of sophistication.

Then, out of the blue and in a casual tone, Gordon mentioned that he had met recently with Sid Bass, the immensely rich Texas oilman and corporate takeover specialist. Gordon said that he had talked with Bass about Getty Oil, and particularly about the company's plan to repurchase its own Getty Oil shares in the open market, thus increasing, in all likelihood, the value of all the other shares not purchased.

"Sid Bass owns two hundred fifty thousand shares of Getty Oil stock, and he thinks the repurchase plan is a great idea," Gordon said. "I think we really should accelerate our repurchase program. Spending our money on stock—ours or somebody else's—is better than spending it on finding and developing oil reserves."

Gordon's remark was appalling to Petersen. That Gordon would try to sell the chairman on the repurchase plan was itself not surprising, since any open market buy-back of company stock would increase the percentage of the Sarah Getty Trust's holdings, already at forty percent. Indeed, the trust could conceivably be pushed into a majority, fifty-one percent position if the company bought back and retired enough shares. Naturally, Gordon would be in favor of such a program. But that Gordon would use Sid Bass's endorsement to sell the plan to Petersen was hard to believe. Bass made his living trying to take over other companies—the fact that he already owned 250,000 shares of Getty Oil was something to be alarmed about, even though it represented only a tiny fraction of the company's ownership. Why was Gordon, a director of Getty Oil, talking to him about private company business, such as the repurchase of shares?

Petersen thought that Gordon simply didn't understand the implications of such a conversation: in his innocence, Gordon might give Bass the impression that he would not oppose a takeover run on Getty Oil stock by the Bass family. Then, too, Gordon might inadvertently disclose confidential, inside company information to Bass. Apart from the potential legal problems associated with such disclosure, it was strategically disastrous for a company such as Getty Oil to share information with an outsider, especially a known takeover specialist. Here was Gordon, sitting all summer in a Getty Oil office examining company documents, and then running off to talk about the company's operations with an outsider. What was Gordon telling Bass? The possible answers were almost too disquieting for Petersen to contemplate.

Of course, while Petersen had his suspicions, he had no proof that Gordon had done anything wrong. Sid Bass was a patron of the arts and a leading light of the high society that Gordon and Ann Getty now moved in. Perhaps Gordon had just met Bass casually at the opera and had talked innocently in the lobby with him during intermission. Petersen didn't know, and he had no way to find out. With all the delicacy now surrounding his relationship with Gordon, and taking into account Lasky's admonitions at their dinner meeting, he was not about to start grilling Gordon for details.

"Gordon, you really should be careful about talking with an outsider like Sid Bass," Petersen said.

Petersen later regretted the tone of his remark. He should have screamed at Gordon, he said, maybe jumped up and down and stamped on Gordon's toes. At the time, however, the Getty Oil chairman felt that Gordon understood him sufficiently. "Enough said," was the tone of Petersen's response. There was no need to spell it out and risk a confrontation. After all, Petersen thought, if Gordon had said too much to Sid Bass, it wasn't really his fault. Gordon was naïve. He wouldn't knowingly do something to hurt Getty Oil—after all, the company's interests and his own were fundamentally the same, since the trust's wealth derived from the company's success. Gordon Getty may be a rich and powerful man, Sid Petersen thought, but he knows not what he does.

Petersen's view of Gordon was reinforced by the company executives and directors with whom he frequently spoke. After the July board meeting in Texas, at which no action was taken on Gordon's informal proposals about the sale of ERC and his own appointment to the executive committee, one of Getty Oil's outside directors, pharmaceuticals executive Henry Wendt, had called Petersen to talk about Gordon. Wendt had flown down to Texas for the board meeting in his own company's plane, and afterward, he had taken the jet on to San Francisco for the weekend. Wendt had volunteered to give Gordon and Ann a ride home, and he talked with them for several hours along the way.

"This is a classic case of the paranoia of the rich," Wendt told Petersen when he called to report on the flight two days later. "Gordon is just sure that everyone is out to get him—including Getty Oil management.

"I tried to talk with him about implementing a new bonus and stock-option program for the executives," Wendt continued. "I told him that the stock-option program was especially important because it makes "management's interests the same as the shareholders'. But Gordon feels that the problem with big salaries and bonuses for executives is that everyone starts to upgrade his living standards, probably unwisely."

In other circumstances, they might have laughed about it—Gordon Getty, one of the richest men in the country, jetting home to his Broadway mansion, lecturing that corporate executives had to learn to live within their means. But as Sid Petersen contemplated that airborne conversation, and as he thought about the future of his relationship with Gordon Getty, he could not find the humor in it all.

4

THE INNOCENT ON WALL STREET

For more than an hour, Sid Petersen and Bob Miller sat together in the Phoenix airport terminal waiting for Gordon Getty to arrive. This time, it was not Gordon's fault that he was late; Petersen and Miller had gotten the time zones confused, so when they flew Getty Oil's Falcon corporate jet in from Los Angeles that bright September afternoon, they arrived in Phoenix an hour earlier than planned.

Gordon was flying in by commercial plane from New York, where he and his wife had been staying for the past two weeks. It was not unusual for Gordon to spend time in Manhattan these days. In recent months, Ann had become increasingly involved in New York's gilded high society—museum and gallery shows, black-tie fund-raisers, exclusive luncheons and dinner parties—and she was even contemplating the purchase of an apartment in the city. Gordon preferred the more relaxed pace of life in California, and he did not relish being away from his basement music room in the Broadway mansion. When they were in New York together, he rarely accompanied Ann out on the town, preferring to spend his evenings in his suite at the Pierre Hotel on Central Park. In Gordon's absence, Ann traveled the city on the arm of Alexander Papamarkou, a Greek-born stockbroker and social gadfly whose independent brokerage had been built on personal service to the obscenely rich. While Ann fluttered about Manhattan with Alecko, as he was known familiarly,

Gordon stayed home to work on music or attend to the business of the Sarah Getty Trust.

As he waited in Phoenix that September afternoon, Sid Petersen had no idea what Gordon had been doing on his most recent sojourn in Manhattan. Much as he might be tempted to do so, it was not the Getty Oil chairman's prerogative to keep track of Gordon Getty's every movement. Some days earlier, he had reached Gordon at the Pierre and arranged to meet him at the Phoenix airport so they could ride together to Greyhound Corporation headquarters nearby. Petersen hoped to recruit Greyhound's chairman and chief executive, John Teets, to join the Getty Oil board of directors. Gordon was now on the board's nominating committee and he had insisted that he accompany Petersen to any interviews with prospective directors.

Gordon's plane arrived without incident, and he, Petersen, and Miller walked together through the modern terminal, making small talk. Outside, they hailed a cab. And then, as they rode through Phoenix to the Greyhound offices, Gordon began to talk about his recent adventure in New York.

It was an odd conversation, one typical of the increasingly strained relations between Getty Oil's chairman and its largest stockholder. Gordon's tone was casual, conversational, even enthusiastic. Petersen, by contrast, was tense, anxious, and laconic.

"I had a very interesting meeting with Bill Tavoulareas," Gordon said early on during the cab ride, referring to the iconoclastic president of giant, New York-based Mobil Oil. "He made a number of interesting suggestions about what we should be doing."

Suggestions? Visited by a 40 percent stockholder of a rich, rival oil company, and asked for his opinions about what that rival company should do in the future, the shrewd, acquisitive Tavoulareas—Tav, as he was known in the industry—had made a few suggestions? Petersen could imagine the dollar signs dancing before the Mobil president's eyes as he sat with Gordon Getty in his New York office. What a preposterous scene! What had Gordon been doing there? What could he have been thinking?

But Petersen said nothing yet, and as Gordon talked, it became clear that Tav was not the only one the Getty scion had asked for advice during his recent trip to Manhattan. Gordon said that he had also met with some investment bankers on Wall Street and had asked them what strategies Getty Oil should be pursuing to raise the value of its stock. This news was nearly too much for Petersen to bear. It was bad enough that Gordon had talked to Tavoulareas. Still, at least Tav would be smart enough to keep what he learned from Gordon to himself. But investment bankers—some of those people would sell their grandmothers to get a merger or takeover deal underway. That September, 1982, Wall Street's investment banking houses were at the center of an unprecedented merger mania encouraged by lax antitrust enforcement and the Reagan administration's free-market policies. The merger fever was washing over industries like an irresistible tidal bore, shifting from sector to sector as Wall Street's fashions turned. Media companies, food companies, paper companies, entertainment companies—each industry became "hot," as the Street put it, as if the destiny of American business was like hem lines or tennis shoes. Now oil companies were hot—indeed, scorching hot. T. Boone Pickens, Jr., was fast on his way to national celebrity by launching hostile takeover raids against the oil giants. And for every deal that took place, no matter which company won or lost, the investment bankers on the Street earned millions in fees. For Gordon Getty, a 40 percent stockholder in one of America's largest oil companies, to wander through the investment houses soliciting "advice" on how to raise the value of Getty Oil stock—well, he might as well have hung a for-sale sign around his neck. All those bankers think about is deals, Petersen fumed as he listened to Gordon, and now Gordon has stirred their interest in Getty Oil.

But Petersen did not lecture Gordon. Instead, as the cab rolled through Phoenix, he and Bob Miller tried desperately through gestures and whispers to silence him. They pointed quietly to the cab driver. He might be listening, Gordon, they tried to indicate. Who can tell about cab drivers? Maybe this fellow is a business student earning his tuition. Gordon's discussions with Tav and the New York investment bankers were clearly "insider" information; if the cab driver understood its significance, he might illegally buy or sell Getty Oil stock on the basis of knowledge unavailable to other shareholders. Worse, he might spread rumors about Gordon's meetings in New York. Whether he did or not, in New York such rumors were no doubt issuing from investment bankers' lips at this very moment.

Through their gestures and curt comments, Petersen and Miller convinced Gordon that it would be better to postpone their discussion until after they were out of the cab. The meeting with Teets went well, and the Greyhound chairman agreed to join the Getty Oil board. Afterward, Petersen, Miller, and Gordon secluded themselves at the Phoenix airport and concluded their conversation.

Again, as he had done before the board meeting in July, Petersen admonished Gordon that it was unwise to discuss Getty Oil business with outsiders, but again, the Getty Oil chairman adopted a moderate tone. He was firm, but he did not scream or rant or dwell on the point. Petersen was tense. He understood all too well that he was walking a tightrope with Gordon. If he said anything to anger him, Gordon might respond by allying himself with some raider or financier and making an immediate bid to takeover the company. That was the last thing Petersen wanted—his career, his position, his salary, and his future were on the line. At the same time, he had to find some way to make it clear to Gordon that these meetings with outsiders could not continue.

Petersen still believed, as he had in July, that Gordon simply didn't appreciate the consequences of his actions. How could he? The sophisticated, ruthless world of investment banking and corporate takeovers was alien to Gordon; there was something almost touching about the naïveté that would lead him to wander the halls of the Street's major investment houses seeking advice about the future of his company. When he explained his New York meetings to Petersen, Gordon said that he was simply asking a variety of Getty Oil stock-holders—owners, such as himself—what they thought about how the company was being run. Petersen later decided that Gordon had visited the investment houses because, when he looked at the list of Getty Oil shareholders, he didn't understand that many stockholders list their ownership through their brokerage house—thus, Gordon had erroneously concluded that the houses themselves owned Getty Oil stock. There was a certain innocent logic about that mistake. To Petersen, Gordon was like an ancient Christian asking the hungry lions what sort of food they'd like for supper.

In their discussion at the airport, though, Gordon indicated that he had in fact learned a few things about the oil industry while back in New York. "I've heard some very interesting things about royalty trusts," Gordon said. "I really think we should investigate them and see if they make sense for Getty Oil."

Royalty trusts were all the rage in the oil business that September. Advocated most prominently by Boone Pickens, they were a complex, tax-oriented restructuring device designed to raise the value of a company's stock. Obviously, somebody had been giving Gordon Getty an education.

"Yes, we've heard about royalty trusts," Petersen said. "In fact, we recently developed an internal study about them and whether they'd be right for the company. I'll show you that memo when we get back to Los Angeles."

Gordon was satisfied. Throughout the afternoon, even during the cab ride, his air of genuine excitement over the discoveries he had made in New York never waned. He simply wanted to share his information with Sid Petersen. There was no fear in Gordon Getty's eyes, as there was in Petersen's. There was only eagerness, enthusiasm.

Gordon Getty said later that throughout this period he at all times understood and accepted the implications and consequences of his actions. That claim did not always seem credible. But whether accidentally or not, Gordon's trip to New York and his conversation with Petersen in Phoenix did serve to further the two goals he had articulated repeatedly since the death of Lansing Hays the previous May: to control Getty Oil's policies through the ownership of 40 percent of its stock, and to raise the value of the trust's holdings.

It was this latter goal that led Gordon Getty to an interest in royalty trusts in the fall of 1982. The price of Getty Oil stock, and thus the value of the Sarah Getty Trust, was languishing. That fall, the company's stock was selling for between $50 and $60 a share. When Gordon visited with industry analysts on Wall Street, however, they told him that the value of Getty Oil's underlying assets—what the company's oil and gas reserves, land, refineries, and mines would be worth if they were sold on the open market—was more than $100 a share, and perhaps even as much as $200 a share, or four times the current stock price. John S. Herold Inc., one of the best-known oil industry consulting firms, estimated that a share of Getty Oil stock was actually worth $182.45, not $50 or $60 dollars. Another analyst in Houston, whose own company held a large number of Getty Oil shares, had said recently that Getty Oil's "politically secure" oil and gas reserves alone had a "present value of $15.6 billion, or $190 per share." Everyone Gordon Getty talked to that fall said the same thing: Getty Oil's shares were vastly undervalued by the stock market. As the analysts put it, the company was worth more dead than alive. The stock price had drifted so badly, it was calculated, that if you adjusted for inflation, the stock market value of Getty Oil had actually declined in the six years since J. Paul Getty's death, and this during a period when the oil industry experienced a huge windfall because of OPEC and rising world oil prices.

Yet while everyone agreed that Getty Oil was the victim of a so-called "value gap" between the price of its stock and the worth of its assets—on this issue, the numbers spoke compellingly for themselves—there was little agreement about the causes of this gap or about its implications. For one thing, Getty Oil was not alone in its predicament; nearly every large oil company in America was undervalued by the stock market in the fall of 1982. Indeed, the value gap was at the center of a raging debate within the oil industry and on Wall Street.

The gap was the essential economic impetus for all the corporate takeovers then in fashion: if a raider could acquire control of a company's stock at a price far below the company's actual value, then he could profit immensely by later selling off its assets. There were many in the oil industry, including nearly all the managers of companies threatened by raids, who regarded such takeovers as the unscrupulous and irresponsible exploitation of a stock market quirk. In 1982, OPEC, faced with declining oil consumption in the West and buffeted by internal dissension, lowered its formal per-barrel prices. Investors responded to the price drop by selling off oil stocks, causing the price of those stocks to decline markedly.

Many oilmen regarded this fall in stock prices as simply a temporary market aberration inevitable in a cyclical industry whose profits depended on the whims of an international cartel. Besides, these industry executives said, current stock price was not the only way to measure the long-term value of a company. A company's stock price might be depressed for a variety of reasons, some quite desirable: management might be investing money in long-term programs, it might be "writing off" past mistakes in order to clean its slate for the future, or it might simply be in the trough of a short-term business cycle—and the oil industry was indisputably cyclical. Besides, these takeover critics said, a large oil company should not simply be defined by the numbers on its balance sheet. Any company has constituencies beyond its stock owners: its employees, its community, its suppliers, and even its consumers, who benefit from the competition a company provides. Raiders in the oil industry and elsewhere were just despicable, opportunistic "liquidators," the critics said. They used cheap stock prices to acquire companies and then destroyed them by selling off their valuable assets, leaving tens of thousands unemployed and whole towns wasted in their wake.

Convincing as such arguments might be, to men such as Sid Petersen, men who after all had their salaries and careers and life-styles at risk in any takeover attempt, there was another side of the debate, a side especially striking to Gordon Getty that September. Why, after all, was Getty Oil's stock price so low—not just a little bit depressed, but two or three or even four times less than the company's actual value? Who was responsible? Boone Pickens and his allies on Wall Street said unequivocally that it was Sid Petersen's fault.

Pickens might be an opportunist, but he was also a brilliant, articulate oilman, and the critique he proffered of large, publicly held oil companies such as Getty was persuasive. The domestic oil industry, Pickens said, was already in a state of liquidation; corporate raiders such as himself were only accelerating an inexorable trend. For more than ten years, the largest American oil companies had been unable to replace their domestic reserves as fast as they produced and sold them. That meant the companies were living on borrowed time—eventually, their reserves would run out and there would be no oil in the United States to replace them. American soil had been thoroughly picked over for oil; no major field had been discovered since Prudhoe Bay, in Alaska, back in the 1960s, and there was no reason to believe that any major discoveries were left to be made. For decades, the only large fields found were under the ocean, in the Gulf of Mexico and off the coasts of Alaska and California. Such oil was difficult and expensive to drill and produce, and besides, even the ocean floors surrounding the United States were by now pretty well explored.

The inability of giant oil companies such as Getty to replace their domestic reserves had important political and national security implications. More and more, the oil companies relied on reserves in politically volatile areas overseas, often in countries whose governments were hostile to American foreign policy. The failure of the big oil companies to anticipate the nationalization of foreign-owned oil properties in Arab countries during the early 1970s, for example, had led to profound industrial shocks in the West when the OPEC nations organized an embargo in 1973. By 1982, it was widely appreciated that the United States was dangerously dependent on imported oil because its own reserves were running dry. Some government officials felt that hostile takeover raids in the oil industry such as those masterminded by Boone Pickens only exacerbated an already serious problem. But Pickens was a capitalist, not a statesman, and to him the national security concerns expressed by oil executives were a canard. Those men were worried about their salaries and perquisites, not the future of the United States, he said. To Pickens and his intellectual brethren on Wall Street—particularly a prominent oil analyst named Kurt Wulff and the aggressive, pro-takeover investment bankers at Drexel Burnham Lambert Inc.—the important aspects of declining American oil reserves were financial, not political. Pickens argued, not illogically, that it was capitalism which had made America an industrial power in the first place, and it was capitalism which would save it from the oil crisis. Let the free market rule, he declared.

From Pickens' vantage, the depressed stock prices of companies such as Getty Oil in 1982 were easy enough to explain. In sum, the problem was bad management. The job of an oil executive such as Sid Petersen was to serve his stockholders, his owners, not to pontificate about national security. And Petersen and his like in the executive suites of the country's largest oil companies had done their jobs poorly, Pickens believed. During the late 1970s, when deregulation and the Arab cartel drove world oil prices nearly through the roof, companies such as Getty Oil were the happy recipients of billions of dollars in windfall profits. For Sid Petersen and other oil executives, the question then had been, what should we do with all the money?

There were several choices. They could hand the money directly over to their stockholders as a kind of bonus. They could plow it back into the oil business, exploring for new reserves to replace the ones currently depleting. Or, they could diversify out of the oil business altogether. The conventional wisdom in the industry was that the oil business was finite—sometime in the twenty-first century, the world would run out of oil. By then, it was hoped, the West would have shifted its dependence on oil to other, preferably renewable sources of energy. Consumption of oil was already declining because of higher prices. Shouldn't the oil giants use their cash windfall to prepare for the future? it was asked. Shouldn't the companies protect their stockholders by investing in new industries, ones that would be still be viable thirty or forty years from now?

The other alternatives—plowing the windfall back into the oil business or giving it directly to stockholders—seemed short-sighted if one accepted the premise that the oil industry would soon go the way of the dinosaurs. For one thing, with all the billions in cash the oil companies suddenly possessed, it was simply impossible to use that money prudently to explore for new fields of oil. Companies such as Getty devised their oil and gas exploration projects on the basis of strict "rate of return" formulas. That is, the companies tried to balance their exploration spending between projects that were certain to succeed and those that were more risky. The safer projects yielded less profits but were more likely to turn up oil; the riskier ones promised big payoffs but also potentially large losses. The problem was that there were many more risky exploration projects available for funding than safe ones. If the companies simply threw their newfound billions into exploration, they would have to spend a disproportionate amount on high-risk projects. If those projects failed, they would have blown the bundle on the most expensive dry wells in history. The other choice, that of distributing the money directly to shareholders, seemed irresponsible to oil executives such as Petersen. They had to think about the future of the company, they said. If they indulged stockholders now, what would be left of the company in twenty years?

To that intriguing question, Boone Pickens and his allies answered: "Nothing, perhaps, and that's fine with us. Give us the cash. If we want to invest in high tech or insurance or entertainment, we'll buy stock in companies that specialize in those businesses." Pickens' argument was disarmingly simple. If one accepted that the domestic oil industry was doomed, then why not give stockholders the benefit of a liquidation sale? Why not let them profit directly from rising oil prices? While higher prices partly ensued from international politics, they were also, in part, the natural result of a declining world oil supply. As supply declined, price went up. Why not pass the profits along before there was no oil left? Stockholders such as Gordon Getty owned companies such as Getty Oil, Pickens said. Executives like Sid Petersen served at the stockholders' pleasure; they had no absolute or divine right to their companies.

But the large oil companies defied their critics in the late 1970s. They chose to diversify out of the oil industry. Mobil bought Montgomery Ward. Exxon acquired Reliance Electric and tried to move into the office products business, in competition with IBM and Xerox. And Getty Oil, under the impetus of Sid Petersen, bought—in friendly deals, not hostile takeovers—ERC and ESPN. It was exciting for executives such as Petersen to be involved in a diversification program. It moved them out of the oil patch, onto the front pages of the financial press, and finally into heady new worlds of technology, electronics, finance, and entertainment. At Getty Oil, for example, the acquisition of the cable sports network ESPN had been sponsored by an executive named Stuart Evey, who had built his reputation in the company through his personal friendship with George Getty.

Evey was the ultimate embodiment of the "new" Getty Oil; he had the spirit of Hollywood in his bones. Evey was a fixer, a facilitator. He maintained a box at the beautiful Santa Anita Racetrack and parceled out passes to those Getty Oil executives currently in his favor. He also had season tickets to Dodger Stadium. For years, Evey and his wife had been close to Sid and Nancy Petersen, and Evey had supported Petersen's rise to chairman at the expense of the muddy-boots oilmen in corporate headquarters. Evey had never worked in the oil patch; he supervised Getty Oil's real-estate holdings and at one point ran a company-owned hotel in Acapulco, Mexico. He was a tanned, handsome man who wore his shirts unbuttoned to expose the gold chains around his neck. He knew actors and actresses by their first names, and he fancied himself something of an entertainment mogul. Through his personal connections, he brought ESPN to Petersen's attention and helped shepherd the acquisition through Getty Oil's board of directors.

By 1982, however, when Gordon Getty traveled to Wall Street, it was clear that the exhilarating, ambitious diversification programs embarked upon by oil executives such as Sid Petersen—programs to save their companies in the face of declining reserves—had failed. Actually, Getty Oil did better than some. Exxon's foray into office products was an unmitigated disaster, and the company lost hundreds of millions of dollars before finally bailing out. Mobil had only marginally better luck in the department-store business. For Getty Oil, ESPN was a similar albatross around the company's neck, losing tens of millions each year without any near prospect of a turnaround. ERC, however, proved a sounder investment, though company critics argued nonetheless that it represented an unnecessary diversion of cash and resources. After all, oil was still the company's primary business, and Getty Oil's reserves continued to drain away without any discernible benefit to shareholders; ERC's profits were not nearly enough to make up the difference in the long term or even the short term.

When Gordon Getty visited Wall Street in September 1982, he heard both sides of the debate over the oil industry's recent past and uncertain future. To him, the case sponsored by Boone Pickens and his aggressive, takeover-minded allies made the most sense because it explained the poor recent performance of Getty Oil stock, as evidenced by the failure of management to properly invest the late 1970s windfall, and laid the blame at the feet of Sid Petersen, whom Gordon doubted for his own reasons. Actually, Petersen was not as hostile to the Pickens movement as some other executives of large oil companies. He, too, was distressed by Getty Oil's value gap and the company's foundering stock price. He was distressed above all because the value gap meant that Getty Oil was a prime takeover target for Pickens or some other like-minded corporate raider.

What Petersen appreciated better than Gordon Getty did, however, was that the debate on Wall Street and in corporate boardrooms over the oil industry's past errors and future policies had two distinct aspects. On the one hand, there was sometimes a scholarly, academic atmosphere about it all, a sense among industry analysts of reasonable men disagreeing over complex business issues. In that context, Petersen was willing to examine the Pickens "theory" of the oil business, and even, after thorough study, to implement its principles at Getty Oil if it would benefit stockholders. The problem was that Boone Pickens was not a university professor, and neither were the financiers, investment bankers, and oil men who had adopted his views and strategies. They were tough, bloodied, ruthless businessmen out to profit from the value gap in the oil industry. They might sound like intellectuals, like well-spoken dissenters who had taken a fresh look at a fraternal, in-bred industry and then seized upon some innovative solutions—but the record did not support such a view, Petersen believed. Boone Pickens was after one thing: money. Pickens always said that what he wanted was to run a big oil company and to operate it for the benefit not of management, but of its owners, the stockholders. But when push came to shove in a takeover fight, he was willing to take the money and run. "Greenmail," they called it, and the nefarious tone was appropriate enough. Pickens or Sid Bass or some other raider would accumulate stock in a company, announce a takeover attempt, and then quickly reach a special "settlement" with management that involved the target company buying the raider's stock at a premium over the market price, enough to make the raider tens of millions of dollars in instant profits.

The point was, Petersen thought, that for all the nicely dressed arguments about diversification and exploration and liquidation, the oil industry was just as wild, ruthless, and dangerous as it had been at the gushing Spindletop well in Texas eighty years before. Gordon Getty, the self-styled absent-minded professor, was attracted to the intellectual aspects of Wall Street's critique, but Petersen believed he failed to appreciate that those arguments disguised some very ungentlemanly intentions. For example, the wisdom among merger experts on the Street offered that when a raider approached an executive "just to talk" about a value gap or a possible takeover offer against the executive's company, any answer from the executive short of "Fuck you, get out of my office" was an indication that he might be willing to entertain a bid by the raider. That was because executives in such situations had diverse loyalties and could not appear to be too friendly to the raider even if they wished to receive a takeover offer. Not only had Gordon Getty failed to say "Fuck you" during his visit to Wall Street, he had actually told them all, "Come see me sometime."

And they had taken him at his word. Almost as soon as Gordon returned to San Francisco, a secret plan to take control of Getty Oil was set in motion by Corbin Robertson, Jr., head of Texas-based Quintana Petroleum. Robertson was the front man for the conservative, sober, private, and immensely rich Cullen family, which had billions in cash at its disposal. It was hard to know exactly how large the Cullen fortune was, since none of the family companies, including Quintana, was publicly owned and thus subject to federal disclosure requirements. But since the family wealth was the legacy of oil tycoon Hugh Roy Cullen, who was considered one of the world's richest men during the 1950s, the fortune was no doubt formidable. Quintana Petroleum was the largest of several closely held family companies. Its chief executive was Robertson, who had married into the Cullen family. As such, he was the man who negotiated its deals and often represented the family, when necessary, in political and social forums. Through contacts in New York, he had heard about Gordon's curious meetings on Wall Street. Days later, Robertson contacted Gordon in San Francisco. He told him that he shared Gordon's befuddlement over Getty Oil's depressed stock price, and said that he had a plan to correct the situation. Without consulting Petersen, Gordon agreed to a meeting.

There was later some dispute over who knew what and when about the Cullen family's plans, but it may well have been that Sid Petersen learned about Gordon's intention to meet with Robertson before Gordon's own lawyers did. One day early in October, Petersen received a call from Chauncey Medberry III, retired chairman of behemoth Bank of America and long a member of the Getty Oil board of directors. Now approaching seventy, Medberry had always been one of Petersen's most enthusiastic supporters.

"I just got a call from a banker friend of mine down in Texas," Medberry said. "He wanted to know if I could arrange a meeting or set up a telephone call or something between Corby Robertson and Gordon. I wanted to know how you think I should handle it."

Petersen was stunned; he knew that Robertson and the Cullens were both rich and aggressive. "They're going to get to Gordon one way or the other," Petersen sighed. "You might as well be the vehicle."

With Medberry's assistance, then, Corby Robertson flew to San Francisco on Thursday, October 14. To demonstrate to Gordon that he was serious about his takeover proposal, the Quintana chief brought along John McGullicuddy, chairman and chief executive of Manufacturers Hanover Trust, one of the nation's largest banks. Manny Hanny, as the bank was known in financial circles, was there to persuade Gordon that Robertson had billions at the ready if Gordon was willing to make a deal.

That day at the Broadway mansion, Gordon was presented with a document typed on plain paper entitled "Confidential Presentation." Lest it fall into the wrong hands, the proposal made no specific mention of Getty Oil, referring instead to "Old Company" and "New Company." Gordon was referred to as "Stockholder I" and the J. Paul Getty Museum, with its 12 percent holding in Getty Oil, as "Stockholder II." The Cullen family was described in the document as "an investor group."

"Stockholder I and an investor group will each form a partnership and enter into a joint venture arrangement to take Old

Company private by buying out Stockholder II and then the public for cash. Old Company will be then liquidated to flow oil and gas reserves directly to the partners. A management company will hire existing employees and manage assets under the existing organization structure," the proposal said. On page 2, under a heading labeled "B. Bottom Line," the document said simply, "Everybody wins!"

Everybody, perhaps, but Sid Petersen. In fact, it was not clear at this stage what price the Cullens would be willing to pay for Getty Oil—that was a "detail" to be worked out later if Gordon wished to go forward. Under Robertson's plan, Gordon would not take control of the company; he would likely have less influence over its operations than he did presently. Robertson and the Cullens would control 60 percent of the new, privately held Getty Oil. The advantage for Gordon, Robertson argued at the Thursday meeting, was that instead of owning stock in a publicly traded company, the Sarah Getty Trust would have direct ownership, through a partnership arrangement, of the profits from 40 percent of Getty's oil fields. Gordon and the trust would put up no cash—that would all come from Robertson and Manufacturers Hanover.

"If you're satisfied with the general concept, then we'll proceed with further investigations," Robertson told Gordon. "We'll formulate a business plan, a management plan, and look into the legal, tax, and government implications. Then we'll hire the investment bankers and determine a price for the public stockholders and the museum. The timing and sequence of events are essential. The security of information is a top priority. We can inform only those who need to know."

It was not until after that Thursday meeting with Robertson that Gordon decided his own lawyers at the Lasky firm had a need to know; Gordon had met with Robertson without legal counsel present. It may actually have been Petersen who first told Lasky about Gordon's flirtation with the Cullens—the Getty Oil chairman called Lasky soon after he heard from Medberry and asked the lawyer what Gordon was doing. Petersen had now also learned from a friend in the investment business that Manny Hanny had a $8 billion line of credit arranged should a takeover campaign be launched by Gordon and the Cullens. In any event, it was not until a week after Gordon's meeting with Robertson, on Thursday, October 21, that Petersen,

Lasky, and Gordon finally talked directly about Quintana's takeover proposal.

Petersen was in his office at Getty Oil headquarters in Los Angeles; Lasky, Gordon, and Tim Cohler were on the speakerphone together in Lasky's office in San Francisco.

"There was a visit from Corbin J. Robertson and a Manufacturers Hanover banker representing the Cullen family interests," Petersen was told. "They proposed a buy-out of the public shareholders—i.e., they want to take the company private. The scheme would then be to sell off some of the company's assets, including refineries and so on, to pay back the money borrowed."

Petersen was stunned. He had feared the worst when Gordon told him about his trip to Wall Street in September. Now, perhaps, the worst was about to occur.

Gordon, however, tried to reassure the Getty Oil chairman. "I'm not very sympathetic to it," he repeated several times, referring to Robertson's proposal.

"Instead," Gordon went on, "I've hired the Lasky firm to help me consider the establishment of a royalty trust at Getty Oil. I have a new wrinkle. I'd like to meet with you next Tuesday, if we can, to begin the study, and I'd like to bring along Tim Cohler and Tom Woodhouse."

Petersen was relieved that Gordon was "not very sympathetic" to the Cullens' takeover plan, but there was no way to be sure how Gordon had left things with Robertson. Perhaps Gordon had merely decided to think about Robertson's ideas while he studied a royalty trust, the restructuring device first raised by Gordon at the Phoenix airport in September. Petersen said that Getty Oil would certainly cooperate with any internal studies that Gordon wished to undertake. He also expressed his concern that any detailed royalty trust study would require access to some of the company's most sophisticated and confidential financial information. It was important, Petersen indicated, that the study be kept secret from Getty Oil managers; the chairman did not want wild rumors about Gordon Getty's intention to possibly restructure the company spreading through headquarters. Petersen told the Lasky lawyers that only a handful of Getty Oil's top executives would be involved—mainly Steadman Garber, a former investment banker now in charge of planning, and Duane Bland, the chief financial officer. Gordon would have to keep his lips sealed.

Also, Petersen said, the company would have to suspend its stock buy-back program, the one Gordon had urged Petersen to pursue at the Texas board meeting in July. The company could not legally purchase its own shares in the market while contemplating a major royalty trust restructuring that would affect the price of company stock—such purchases would surely invite a shareholder lawsuit against management alleging insider trading. Gordon's lawyers agreed to Petersen's conditions. As a legal matter, there was no question that the buy-back should be suspended, and as for the chairman's concerns about confidentiality, well, Gordon's lawyers said they would defer to Petersen's judgment about who should be informed. What Gordon wanted was a detailed royalty trust study. He did not much care how it was produced.

Privately, Petersen felt ambivalent about the idea of a royalty trust. As an intellectual issue, as a business structure to be explored and evaluated, he was all for it, he said later. But a royalty trust was also a tactical device—it was Boone Pickens' weapon of choice in the bloody oil industry takeover wars, where careers and whole companies were at stake. In that context, Petersen was hardly inclined to embrace the idea. Simplified, a royalty trust was a restructuring program that would transfer ownership of specific oil properties from the corporation, Getty Oil, directly to shareholders such as Gordon Getty's family trust. The rich Kern River field in California, for example, might be an attractive candidate for conversion into a royalty trust. That way, Getty Oil stockholders would own the field directly through the trust, and the profits from its production would flow directly to them, rather than through the corporation.

Advocates of royalty trusts argued that there were both tax and economic benefits to this arrangement. For one thing, a trust eliminated the so-called double taxation of dividends. Ordinarily, the profits from the Kern field flowed first to Getty Oil, where they were taxed as corporate profits. Then, after those taxes were paid, some of the remaining money was distributed to shareholders in the form of quarterly stock dividends, where the money was taxed again as personal income. With a trust in place, the Kern River profits would be taxed only once each year when they were distributed directly to shareholders of the Kern royalty trust. By the same logic, the overall stock price of Getty Oil should rise if a royalty trust was established. Because large oil companies such as Getty were so vastly undervalued

by the stock market, it was calculated that the combined price of a
royalty trust and the shares of surviving Getty Oil would be significantly higher than the company's current stock price (the trust was
a structural, paper-shuffling change; employees would be technically
reassigned to the trust but not fired).

It was this possibility—that the creation of a royalty trust at Getty
Oil might quickly and dramatically raise the price of the company's
stock—that attracted Gordon Getty. The principles involved were
similar to those underlying Corby Robertson's "partnership" takeover proposal, except there would be no change in ownership or
control if Petersen went along with the royalty trust. Since the Sarah
Getty Trust controlled by Gordon owned some thirty-two million
shares of Getty Oil stock, even a small price rise could have a profound effect on the value of the Getty family's holdings. If Gordon
could close the value gap completely by raising Getty Oil's stock
price above $100 a share, then he would virtually double his family's
wealth in just a short time.

As he had promised Gordon in Phoenix, Sid Petersen had indeed
sent him a copy of an earlier study of royalty trusts prepared by Getty
Oil's corporate planning department. Gordon, however, was disappointed by the memo he received. It had been prepared by Steadman
Garber, and it did not express nearly the enthusiasm Gordon did
about royalty trusts. "I have completed a review of royalty trusts and
I believe that neither of the previously used methods of distribution
are appropriate for Getty," Garber had declared in the first sentence
of his August 18, 1982, report.

The memo, which was only a few pages long, went on to list the
drawbacks of a trust. It might be difficult to finance; it might raise
the company's debt level; its full tax consequences were difficult to
determine; and, of course, there was the problem that implementing a royalty trust would be like admitting that Getty Oil was in a
state of liquidation, that it was having a last white sale for shareholders. "While liquidation may be seen as a way to increase the shareholder's wealth near term, it is management's objective to ensure
that the organizational value as a going concern is greater than its
liquidation value," Garber wrote. Management's *objective*—yes. But
it was an objective unmet. It had been years now, and still Getty Oil
was worth more dead than alive. After his meeting with Robertson
on October 14, Gordon had discussed the Garber memo with Tim

Cohler and Tom Woodhouse at the Lasky firm. He did not feel that Petersen had explored the issue thoroughly enough; even Garber's own report indicated that there was more that could be done. It was Gordon's desire for more studies that led to the October 21 phone call with Petersen, where the meeting with Robertson was finally disclosed and a new demand was made for an in-depth company study of royalty trusts.

After that telephone conference, and all through the fall of 1982, Cohler and Woodhouse traveled between San Francisco and Los Angeles, ferrying questions and documents and computer analyses between their client, ensconced in his mansion on Broadway, and the company, represented now mainly by Garber and Bland. Relations between them were basically cordial. Like Petersen, Garber and Bland were curious about the ideas so forcefully propounded by Boone Pickens, and they were willing to examine the ideas in detail. They tended to doubt that a royalty trust would withstand close scrutiny, but they were willing to keep an open mind. In his August memo, Garber had rejected the essential Pickens premise that companies such as Getty Oil should accept the fact they were in a state of liquidation. Even so, it was possible that some form of royalty trust would raise the price of Getty Oil stock, and that was an objective all the company's top executives shared, not least because they feared a takeover raid by Gordon or the Cullens. So, maintaining tight secrecy about the nature of their work, Garber and Bland dug through the company's files and operating reports to assemble the detailed financial information necessary for their studies.

It seemed to them, however, that whenever they presented their findings to Gordon, it was like they slipped backward on a treadmill. Gordon seemed to ignore their conclusions and drift off on tangents. After a few weeks, for example, the finance executives discovered that the tax consequences of a royalty trust for Gordon might well be disastrous—it was a problem unforeseen by Boone Pickens because Gordon's situation was so unusual. When the royalty trust was established, each Getty Oil shareholder would have to pay a one-time tax on those Getty shares converted into the trust. The amount of that tax depended on how much the shareholder had paid for his stock in the first place—his so-called "basis." In Gordon's case, the stock held by the Sarah Getty Trust had been acquired decades before by his father and his grandfather. The trust's basis was close to zero. That meant if a royalty trust was established, the Sarah Getty Trust's one-time tax bill would be enormous, perhaps as much as a billion dollars or more. For Garber and Bland, that was enough to kill the idea altogether. But Gordon seemed not to accept this conclusion and instead tinkered with the numbers and asked additional questions. So back they went to the files, digging for more information to satisfy Gordon. After a time, Gordon abandoned his interest in royalty trusts, and he told the Getty Oil finance men that he was now interested in studying limited partnerships, the structure proposed to him by Corby Robertson.

A partnership was conceptually the same as a royalty trust, but it had different tax consequences. Garber and Bland's frustration began to build—after weeks of hard work, they had managed only to start all over again. Petersen, too, grew increasingly frustrated by Gordon's questions and demands. By late fall, the Getty Oil chairman wanted these studies behind him. He wanted to return to the stock buy-back plan that had been authorized by the board earlier in the year, but which was now suspended pending the outcome of Gordon's studies. Petersen had not told any of the board members about the studies or the buy-back suspension, and he was worried that soon he would be forced to make an explanation as to why the company had stopped buying its own shares in the market.

"I never thought it was going to be like this," Petersen muttered to his top executives as the fall wore on and still Gordon's questions about trusts and partnerships persisted.

There was some consolation, at least. The studies might be frustrating and distracting, Petersen thought, but they seemed to have turned Gordon away from the takeover proposal made by the Cullens in October. Petersen assumed that Gordon had stopped talking to Corby Robertson. Surely, Gordon understood that it would not be appropriate to talk with Robertson about Getty Oil now that Gordon had regular access, through his studies, to the company's most closely guarded financial information.

In fact, Gordon had kept up regular contacts with the Cullens, and he even disclosed to Robertson some of the sensitive data passed along to him by Garber and Bland. In kind, Robertson tried his best to stimulate Gordon's interest in a takeover. On October 21, October 29, November 11, November 22, November 30, December 2, and December 7, Robertson wrote letters to Gordon at his Broadway mansion, sometimes enclosing analyses or newspaper articles he thought might be of interest. If Gordon was indeed "not very sympathetic" to the Cullens' proposal, Robertson himself seemed not to get the message. He continued to press Gordon about a deal, and Gordon continued to correspond and to receive his calls. Anything was possible, Gordon said later. And he meant it—Gordon Getty was a man nearly bursting with enthusiasm for change. Precisely what sort of change, he could not say. Precisely where that change would lead, he was not sure. But he *was* certain about one thing: when he finished, things would not be the same at Getty Oil Company.

About that much, Gordon Getty was absolutely right.

AT THE BONAVENTURE

Friday, December 24, 1982, the day before Christmas, was cool and blustery in San Francisco, but the Getty mansion on Broadway was warm and bright with holiday cheer. There were no less than fourteen Christmas trees in the sprawling house, each one distinctively decorated and illuminated. Among them was the family's traditional "teddy bear tree," hung with a variety of specially dressed toy bears. Amid such splendor and radiance, a sentimental man such as Gordon Getty might feel a certain glow of satisfaction about the world he inhabited.

Certainly, that was the tone of the letter Gordon wrote that day to Sid Petersen in Los Angeles. The day before, Thursday, Petersen had been in San Francisco for a meeting with Gordon at the Lasky, Haas offices, situated on the twelfth floor of a steel-and-glass office building near the Transamerica tower in the downtown financial district. The purpose of the meeting had been to present to Gordon the latest studies about limited partnerships and royalty trusts conducted by Steadman Garber and Duane Bland. The Getty Oil contingent had hoped that this presentation would mark the end of Gordon's inquiries. Bland, Garber, and Petersen had concluded weeks before that there were too many tax and financing problems associated with trusts and partnerships, and that the best course would be to end all the studies and return to the stock buy-back program originally established by the board of directors. Petersen had been sorely disappointed at the meeting on Thursday at Lasky, Haas. Not only had Gordon refused to end the studies, he declared that there was much work still to be done on the question of limited partnerships. There had been a nearly audible sigh in the Lasky conference room when Gordon made his pronouncements. Petersen had seemed tense and defensive to some of those at the meeting, but he had ended the day on a cordial note with Gordon, trying his best to show the deference and respect that was so important to the Getty scion.

"The meeting yesterday was really helpful," Gordon wrote to Petersen from his mansion on Christmas Eve. "I am convinced that you and I both have the same objectives—the best interest of all the stockholders—and that we both have open minds. We all want to resolve the uncertainties as quickly as we can. . . . It will save time if Getty Oil Company's people and the trust's remain in close contact, since each discovery may suggest a shift of emphasis. What we want first is 'enough' detail sufficient to warrant either disclosure of the studies to shareholders or suspension of the studies. We don't know yet how much is enough. At some point, we'll decide we're there. . . . The idea we were studying before the current one, by the way, shouldn't be pronounced dead. If the current one fails, the other one might be revived. But we can give it a low priority for now. Thanks again for the time and trouble taken away from your holidays. Merry Christmas to you and Nancy. Best Regards, Gordon P. Getty."

The contrast between Gordon Getty's happy, easy, open-ended attitude and Sid Petersen's tense, tight-lipped concern was growing wider as the days passed, and perhaps nothing captured the contrast better than Gordon's letter. Here was Gordon, the day after a meeting at which he had aggravated Petersen to no end, writing as if the Getty Oil chairman was his firm ally. In part, this gulf of misunderstanding was a result of Petersen's distant demeanor around Gordon, his unwillingness to raise his voice, his attempts to show Gordon the respect urged by Moses Lasky the previous May. Also, however, it was a reflection of Gordon's own naïveté, his inability to sense that Petersen's deference was insincere and that the Getty Oil chairman was harboring deep anger and anxiety behind his respectful veneer. Later, Gordon and his advisors would call Sid Petersen "two-faced," and it was in some ways a just accusation, since Petersen felt deeply angry and concerned about Gordon Getty and yet showed him little of his brewing emotion. Petersen festered, as Gordon himself put it.

But after all, Lasky had told Getty Oil general counsel Dave Copley in May that if the company directors thought poorly of Gordon and his ideas, Lasky hoped they would not show their feelings and by doing so provoke the Getty scion to rash action. Petersen, then, was merely following Lasky's advice.

By that December, however, Gordon Getty seemed to be acting rashly despite the executives' careful approaches. The contact with Corby Robertson was beyond the pale, Petersen thought. It was not just that Gordon was conspiring with an outsider who was poised to make a hostile bid for control of Getty Oil. It was that Gordon was using, in all likelihood, the highly confidential company information being developed for the Garber and Bland studies to act against the company itself. Nearly every week, detailed, sophisticated, highly secret analyses of Getty Oil's reserves, operations, and finances were being shipped by Garber and Bland up to Gordon in San Francisco. Was he then turning these studies over to Robertson and other outsiders? Petersen had no way to know for certain, but he suspected that Gordon was sharing information in the studies. If so, Gordon was likely violating the law; at the very least, he was moving into a precarious legal gray area. Gordon was a director of Getty Oil. In that position, he had certain legal obligations to protect the company's shareholders. Turning over secret company documents to a competitive, aggressive corporate raider was hardly consistent with those obligations.

What Gordon Getty did not realize when he wrote his hopeful, friendly letter to Sid Petersen on December 24 was that only a few days before, concerned about Gordon's behavior, Petersen had met with his lawyers at Getty Oil headquarters to discuss how they might launch a legal challenge to Gordon's control of the Sarah Getty Trust. At that meeting, Petersen was not yet convinced that an all-out war between Getty Oil and the company's largest stockholder was necessary or desirable. But he was willing to consider the possibilities. Apart from what he described as Gordon's outrageous conduct—the trip to Wall Street, the meeting with Robertson, his probable misuse of confidential company information—Petersen was driven by his own instincts and frustrations. *It wasn't meant to be this way*, he thought. There was a reason that J. Paul Getty had not named Gordon sole trustee of the Sarah Getty Trust in the first place. The old man knew his son. That's why he wanted Lansing and Security

Pacific Bank as cotrustees, so that Gordon would never be alone in charge. *How right the old man was,* Petersen believed. At the meeting in his office that December afternoon, the Getty Oil chairman had asked his lawyers if there was anything they could do to thwart Gordon Getty's unchecked power over the family trust.

With Sid Petersen in his office that day were Dave Copley, the company's white-haired general counsel, and Barton J. Winokur, partner in the Philadelphia law firm of Dechert Price & Rhoads. From that afternoon forward, Bart Winokur would play a role of increasing importance in the affairs of Getty Oil and, eventually, in the fortunes of several other large corporations as well.

In demeanor and background, Winokur differed from his clients, company men such as Petersen and Copley who had grown up in the West, in middle-class families, and who attended public universities known more for their pragmatism than their panache. For Petersen and Copley, the credentials of success came slowly. They rose at Getty Oil Company not because of some blinding, raw talent or intelligence, but because they were loyal, committed, smart, patient, and stable. Bart Winokur, by contrast, was the sort of man who made an immediate impression, often favorable, always indelible. He looked boyish, with a hint of red in his hair and freckles on his face, and although he was now in his forties he retained the energetic confidence—some said cockiness—of a younger man. He had grown up in Philadelphia, the son of a highly successful lawyer. His Jewish family emphasized education and achievement, and Winokur had met their expectations, attending Cornell University as an undergraduate and then Harvard Law School. He graduated from Harvard in 1964, clerked briefly in the U.S. Court of Appeals, and then joined the large, corporate Dechert firm as an associate.

In some respects, it was a surprising choice. Dechert was a "white shoe" firm, conservative and Protestant, which served the downtown banks as well as Philadelphia's old, wealthy Main Line families. The Main Line was an insular, elite society whose families traced their roots to Pennsylvania's colonial Quakers. Theirs was a world of debutante balls, high manners, and inflexible traditions—the Main Line was the closest thing in America to a European-style aristocracy. The major law firms in Philadelphia were divided into two classes: those, such as Dechert Price & Rhoads, which served the Main Line, and those which served the Jewish business community, specializing not

in banking or estate law, but in labor, real estate, and commercial litigation. By the 1980s, this essential distinction between Philadelphia's
elite law firms had begun to blur, but in 1964, when Bart Winokur
joined Dechert, the ethnic and class divisions were pronounced.
Because of both his talent and his charisma, Winokur never seemed
terribly burdened by his status as an outsider to the Main Line. By
1972, he was a full partner specializing in mergers, acquisitions, and
corporate finance, and he was respected not only for his impressive,
articulate legal work but for his smooth, ingratiating manner with
clients—he was known as a clients' man, and in a large firm such
as Dechert Price that was perhaps the most important thing of all.
A smart lawyer who did not attract clients might go nowhere in a
large firm, but an attorney such as Winokur could rise quickly by
cultivating corporate executives in need of Dechert Price's various
legal services. By age forty, Winokur was earning as much money
as partners twenty years his senior—a fact Winokur himself was not
reluctant to point out—and he was regarded as one of the firm's most
promising young lawyers.

It surprised no one, then, that Winokur was asked by his partners
to cultivate the Getty Oil account for Dechert Price when Lansing
Hays and his handful of New York partners merged with the firm in
1979. In Lansing's view, his merger with Dechert was a way to build
a more secure future for his young partners and to broaden the legal
services available to his principal client, Getty Oil, although it was
also clear that Lansing did not for a moment intend to relinquish his
own dominant role at the company. Dechert Price's motivations in
the deal were clear. The firm hoped to preserve Getty Oil as a client
after Lansing was gone, and even in 1979 it was clear to most who
knew him that Lansing Hays would not live much longer. If Dechert
could keep Getty Oil after Lansing's death, it would mean millions of
dollars in annual billings.

Winokur, the client's man, was the ideal partner to attempt to
forge this transition. Soon after the merger, he and Hays began to
work together on Getty Oil legal matters. Unlike some of Hays'
own partners, Winokur was brash enough to stand up to the aging,
cantankerous lawyer, and Winokur's independent manner began
quickly to offend Hays. Winokur hardly cared about that; he disliked
Lansing thoroughly. His mission was not to curry Lansing's favor, it
was to win over the executives of Getty Oil. And after years of loud,

ranting abuse from Hays, Winokur's smooth and confident manner was a refreshing change indeed—here was a lawyer who actually was nice, even gracious to his clients. While Hays was alive, Winokur tried at every turn to disassociate himself and even his law firm, of which Hays was now a member, from Lansing's domineering manner. For example, once, at a Getty Oil board meeting in Colorado Springs, Colorado, Winokur returned to his hotel room late at night and found two messages: one from Dave Copley, requesting a meeting at 7:15 the next morning, and one from Hays, asking to meet Winokur at 7:00 A.M. Promptly at seven, Winokur met Hays in the hotel lobby. They shook hands, and Hays said immediately, motioning toward Dave Copley across the way, "Don't pay any attention to him."

A few minutes later, chairman Sid Petersen approached Hays and Winokur and attempted to join their conversation about the upcoming board meeting. "You don't need to be here," Hays said abruptly to his client. "We'll call you when we need you." Petersen turned angrily and left.

At breakfast an hour later, Winokur pulled Petersen aside and told him, "I'm humiliated by what Lansing did. I want you to know that this kind of behavior does not represent the views of Dechert Price & Rhoads."

By such whispering in his client's ear, Winokur managed over time to distance himself from Hays. Still, when Lansing died in May 1982, Winokur and his firm were unsure about where Getty Oil would look for outside legal counsel. After all, Dechert Price was headquartered in Philadelphia, while Getty Oil was in Los Angeles. Then, too, the company had never really had a choice before about its outside lawyers—Lansing had been forced upon the company by J. Paul Getty, and the company might now want to shop around. As the summer passed, Dave Copley occasionally called Winokur and asked him to handle some small legal problems for Getty Oil. Still, it was unclear whether Dechert Price would be retained. By fall, when the rumors about Gordon's trip to Wall Street began to spread, Winokur began to talk directly with Sid Petersen. He flew to Los Angeles and consulted with the chairman and general counsel. Not only was Winokur the sort of lawyer who instilled confidence in his clients, he seemed to have the specific expertise necessary to devise strategy against Gordon that fall. Winokur, understood the ruthless world of corporate takeovers—both its technical, legal aspects and its broader, warlike strategic imperatives. There were those at Getty Oil who were put off by Winokur's youth and cocky manner. He had an Ivy League swagger, it was said, a powerful arrogance about his credentials and his abilities that did not blend well with the practical, middle-class backgrounds of many Getty Oil executives. Some wondered whether Winokur was loyal to the company the way Lansing had been; after all, for all of Lansing's capacity to offend and irritate, his loyalty to his client was never in question. Winokur, one top Getty Oil executive put it later, seemed to some a "very flexible human being." But he did not seem that way to Sid Petersen, who by December had decided that Winokur was to replace Lansing Hays as the company's chief outside counsel and top legal strategist.

It was Winokur, then, in late December, who helped devise the idea for the remarkable meeting with Gordon Getty at the Bonaventure Hotel in Los Angeles in early January.

They had talked about it that afternoon together in Sid Petersen's office. Petersen had asked Winokur that day to research ways in which the company might challenge Gordon's authority as sole trustee of the Sarah Getty Trust, in light of his contacts with outsiders such as Corby Robertson. But Petersen also thought that Gordon's actions were perhaps not entirely his fault. Petersen believed that Gordon simply didn't understand how the world worked. And he realized that despite several opportunities to do so, he had failed to forcefully explain to Gordon the dangers of his behavior. Petersen and Winokur agreed that if only they could explain it to Gordon, if only they could make him understand all the implications of his actions, then by sheer force of logic Gordon would be persuaded, he would come around. They had to make Gordon appreciate that he, too, was vulnerable in a takeover attempt. The trust only owned 40 percent of Getty Oil, not, as Gordon himself had pointed out to Petersen months earlier, 51 percent. If a raider acquired the 60 percent not controlled by Gordon, he could "squeeze" the trust by either locking Gordon in as a minority owner or forcing a merger at an unfavorable price. If Gordon would only understand this, if he would see that his best hope was to align with management, that his and management's interests were really the same here—well, they *had* to make him understand. And perhaps most important, they had to stop Gordon from disseminating confidential company information to outsiders.

Here, at least, Petersen and Winokur had some clout. There was no room for debate on this issue. Ethically, morally, and legally, Gordon was wrong, they thought. Even Gordon's own lawyers would have to agree about that.

Gordon himself continued to display a stubborn indifference to management's concerns; he seemed to project more and more the attitude that Sid Petersen was just a hired hand who had no right to tell a stockholder such as Gordon Getty what to do. Around the first of the year, for example, Gordon called Petersen at Getty Oil headquarters to tell him that Corby Robertson had just offered, if Gordon would cooperate, to buy out all of Getty Oil's stock for $80 a share, about 50 percent above the current market price.

"I called Corby and told him that I wasn't interested in the deal," Gordon said to Petersen. "Then I brought him up to date on what we had been doing at the company, with the studies—but only in general terms. I sort of rambled around."

Petersen was taking notes during the phone call, and he jotted down Gordon's phrase, "I sort of rambled around." Beside it, he made a large exclamation mark. It was frightening to think that while discussing Getty Oil's internal business with a potential hostile raider, Gordon had discussed freely his thoughts and perceptions—Petersen was well acquainted with Gordon's ramblings and he knew they could lead anywhere. But the exclamation mark also reflected Petersen's shock that Gordon would admit openly that he "sort of rambled around" while discussing highly sensitive, confidential company studies. It suggested to Petersen the unfathomable depth of Gordon's naïveté.

"This was my final rejection to him," Gordon said. "But Corbin called back in thirty minutes to ask if I would object if they bought the museum's twelve percent. I immediately told him no, and later my lawyers agreed with that position. I told him, though, that if they went for more than fifty percent of Getty Oil's stock, I might have to compete. He told me that he wouldn't do anything that I objected to. He also proposed just making a tender offer, open to all shareholders, for ten percent of Getty Oil's stock."

"If he does that, it will create a decision for you, as to whether or not you should sell some of your stock to the Cullens," Petersen pointed out. "It will probably result in a lawsuit against you from the beneficiaries, no matter what you decide. Let me ask you, Gordon:

have you decided to do something?" Gordon was always using that phrase, "do something." No one was ever certain what it meant, but here Petersen was referring to the royalty trust studies, and he was asking if Gordon had finally made up his mind to stand behind a single course of action.

"Yes, I darned near have decided to do something," Gordon answered. "Darned" was another of Gordon's favorite words.

"We have got to tell the board of directors something about what is going on between us," Petersen said.

"I agree. I'm ready to tell all. I like to be candid with everyone, including the Cullens."

"Well, I would suggest we be somewhat circumspect about what we tell the board," Petersen said. "But we shouldn't lie. At the very least, we have to tell them about the Cullen offer."

"I agree. I have been candid with everyone. When I talked to Tavoulareas at Mobil a few months ago, I said that even with a premium over the market price, such as the $80 proposed by Corbin, the prices being talked about for Getty Oil stock are too low. Tavoulareas said that was true, but other stocks were too low, too. You can buy at the market price and sell at the asset value price, which is much higher." This, of course, was the basic economic incentive underlying all the oil industry takeovers.

"I'd point out, though, that the Cullens are basically borrowing the money for their buy-out of Getty Oil by using the company's own assets," Petersen responded. "I think management could do that, too." In other words, Petersen thought, if the company is going to be taken over because of its undervalued assets, why shouldn't it be management, rather than an outsider, that profits by the deal? On his notepad, Petersen jotted a note to himself: "Of course, management doesn't have $500 million" in seed money. Sid Petersen could not match the Cullens' wealth.

"If it comes down to it, will you give management the first chance to buy the company?" Petersen asked Gordon.

"Oh, of course. You can count on it."

That was an interesting possibility, but it hardly solved the problems at hand. Despite Gordon's assurances about a "final rejection," Petersen knew that an alliance between Gordon and the Cullens was still possible—if the Cullens bid for 60 percent of Getty Oil's stock, they could force Gordon to join with them because if he refused, the trust might be locked permanently into its 40 percent minority position. Gordon still seemed unable to understand this basic reality, that as a 40 percent stockholder, he was vulnerable to an outside raid.

In the aftermath of his conversation with Gordon, Petersen wanted to arrange a meeting with Gordon as soon as possible—a private meeting, away from company headquarters, where the Getty Oil chairman could lay out, forcefully and directly, the admonitions, pleas, and warnings that he had failed to make in Phoenix or at the board meeting in Texas the previous July. Now Petersen would lay his cards on the table. That did not mean he would scream or shout at Gordon; such confrontation would only distort the issues. But Petersen would make himself clear, as respectfully as possible. Winokur, too, could play a role; with his expertise in mergers and acquisitions, he could explain to Gordon the dangers of the trust's position and why it was important that the trust and the company try to build an alliance against outsiders.

The timing of this meeting was important. Petersen had heard through Lasky and other sources that Gordon was going to meet again with Corby Robertson in late January, and the Getty Oil chairman wanted to intervene before then, to stop Gordon from handing Robertson new studies compiled by Bland and Garber. Petersen had wanted to meet even before the first of the year, but vacation schedules around the holidays made that difficult to accomplish. Later, in fact, there would be some dispute over exactly how and why the Bonaventure Hotel meeting was arranged for the evening of Wednesday, January 12, 1983. Gordon's attorney, Tim Cohler, would remember that it was he who suggested the meeting, casually, as a chance for Gordon and Sid to discuss anything on the chairman's mind before the regular January board meeting. Petersen and others would recall it differently; this was not an open-ended meeting, they said, with a vague agenda. It was a confrontation with Gordon Getty, an attempt to end his dalliances with corporate raiders and royalty trust analysts, all those outside encounters that Winokur described facetiously to Getty Oil executives as "Gordon Getty's Odyssey of Discovery."

They gathered in the Bonaventure's lobby that Wednesday evening after nightfall. The hotel was a cylindrical, splashy, mirrored building in the heart of Los Angeles's revived downtown center. Petersen, Copley, and Winokur drove over from Getty Oil headquarters, only a mile or two west on Wilshire Boulevard. Tim Cohler, of the Lasky firm, flew down with Gordon from San Francisco and then drove downtown with him from the airport. When he entered the lobby, Cohler spotted his old friend Dave Copley, said hello, and then registered for the room. Cohler and Gordon were introduced to Winokur, whom they had never met and about whom they knew little. Then the five of them—Petersen, Copley, Winokur, Gordon, and Cohler— rode the elevator together up to their suite. Inside, there were several couches in the outer room, and a number of comfortably appointed armchairs. The men arranged themselves casually, in something like a circle. A tense mood was beginning to rise among them.

In Cohler's mind, the purpose of the meeting was to address whatever concerns Sid Petersen wanted to raise with his client, and he expected the Getty Oil team to take the lead. But Cohler wanted first to establish some ground rules. He sensed that this meeting might later be of interest to outsiders, and he wanted to know whether Copley and Winokur agreed with him that the attorney-client privilege would apply. A discussion among the lawyers ensued. The issue was whether Gordon and Sid Petersen shared a "mutuality of interests," in which case, they could all five claim attorney-client privilege about the meeting.

"This is a chief executive officer meeting with a director in advance of a directors meeting, with counsel for the company and counsel for the director present," Cohler said. "There is no reason to believe that there is anything but mutuality of interest here, and so perhaps we can agree that there is a sound basis for claiming attorney-client privilege if the question should ever arise."

"I'm not sure that Gordon is here in his capacity as a director of Getty Oil," Dave Copley responded. The implication was clear—Gordon had other loyalties besides the company, not the least of which was his family trust.

"Well, I think what you're suggesting, Dave," Cohler responded, "is that somebody might later urge that Gordon was not here as a director if they were trying to challenge a claim of privilege." The point could be argued, Cohler was saying, but there was no reason for the five of them to disagree.

Gordon intervened, contradicting his own lawyer. "I'm not here solely as a director. I'm also here as a trustee of the Sarah Getty Trust and as a trustee of the J. Paul Getty Museum. I'm wearing three hats."

There was some more arguing among the lawyers about whether they had a mutuality of interest, and it became clear that the problem would not be easily resolved.

"Look, we don't know what Sid's going to talk about," Cohler finally said. "So I guess we ought to proceed on the theory that if it's appropriate and it ever arises, we would consider claiming the privilege, but everybody speaking here should recognize that such a claim might fail and proceed in their best judgment."

Attention then turned to Sidney Petersen. Gordon and Cohler later recalled that Petersen seemed especially tense that evening; his jaw seemed locked shut and his lips were tightly pursed. But Cohler and Gordon both recognized immediately, as Petersen began to speak, that the Getty Oil chairman was doing his best to be gracious, cautious, and polite, however difficult it might be for him. It was not a soliloquy that Petersen delivered, but over the next half an hour, he began to repeat several themes to Gordon Getty, interrupted and augmented from time to time by Copley and Winokur. At first, Gordon said little. He watched Petersen closely. He watched Winokur. And he listened.

"You know, Gordon, your father, Mr. Getty, was a very patient man," Sid Petersen said. "He took his time accumulating an equity position in the various companies that ended up becoming Getty Oil. He started buying Tidewater stock back in the 1930s and he did not gain control until twenty years later. I just think that such patience, in accumulating a control position over time, has proven itself in the past by the experience of your father."

Cohler listened carefully to Petersen. This was the Getty Oil chairman at his most poised, he thought. But he wondered where Petersen was headed with this line of thought.

"By the same token, Gordon, it might be appropriate for the company to consider getting back into the market, continuing the stock buy-back program that was authorized by the board, which we've suspended because of all these studies, as everyone knows. If we did that, if we kept buying the stock, that course might ultimately lead the trust to be in a majority position. Your percentage would increase from forty, and you could creep into control."

Soon Petersen was carrying his point further, making it stronger. Gordon had yet to respond. "We need a flat assurance that these studies are at an end, Gordon," Petersen declared. "We have an alert board of directors. They know they've authorized the buy-back in the open market. The stock price has been in the range where they would expect that we would have been buying back. The information available to them will show them that we have not been in the market. And I expect somebody's going to ask me why. What am I supposed to say, Gordon?"

The heat of that question, which for the first time challenged Gordon directly, alarmed Cohler. He shot a glance at Copley, hoping to indicate that perhaps Sid should cool down a little, lest Gordon erupt in anger. There were a lot of concerned, questioning looks being passed privately around the room. They were trying to measure Gordon's response, to gauge his silence.

Whether in response to Cohler's eye contact or not, shortly after Petersen's accusatory question, Copley interjected, "You know, Gordon, it doesn't necessarily have to be a commitment that, in the future, no studies would ever be resumed. It would just be a statement that no further studies were presently necessary."

"I appreciate everyone's views," Gordon finally responded. "I'm glad that the views have been exchanged. I think it's my duty to listen to all the good thoughts that people might have. My father always welcomed people to Sutton Place and listened to their views and then made up his mind as to what was best. And I think that's a way of conducting yourself that can't be criticized. I'm an ethical guy and I know what my duties are, and I'm responsible. But I cannot in good conscience say to you that there have been a complete set of studies made. I cannot yet be sure that the shareholders as a whole would not benefit from further studies."

In his inimitable fashion, Gordon Getty had said no. He would not end the studies. The mood began to shift. Bart Winokur began to speak up more forcefully. He had been introduced by Petersen as a brilliant lawyer highly experienced in mergers and acquisitions, and now he began to tell stories from his legal career, stories about hostile takeovers that had arisen in situations similar to this one. He used some of the wild metaphors popular in his trade: by meeting with outsiders, Gordon was spreading "blood in the water," Winokur said. Gordon was demonstrating to Wall Street that the company was bleeding, and once that blood hit the water, sharks would be sure to gather.

"You should not be doing anything that anyone outside the company could interpret as encouraging them to make their proposals for control of the company," Winokur said to Gordon. "You should not be talking to Corby Robertson at all."

It was Bart Winokur's first meeting with Gordon Getty. As he spoke, it seemed to Tim Cohler and indeed to Gordon Getty himself that Winokur did not appreciate the delicacy of the situation. Gordon felt that Winokur was rude and abrasive, this in contrast to his view of Petersen, who had tried to present his points with some statesmanlike caution. But Winokur was aggressive. He described in vivid terms a variety of scenarios in which Gordon and the trust could be "squeezed" by an outsider like Robertson who could gain control of those Getty Oil shares not owned by the trust. Over and over, Winokur emphasized the squeeze.

"Don't you realize, Mr. Getty, that you could be the juice?" he asked Gordon.

"I've had further conversations with Mr. Robertson about his buying the rest of the Getty Oil shares. We could run the company together," Gordon said. "What Robertson proposed was a deal where he would buy sixty percent of Getty Oil stock, then we would run the company as partners. We didn't discuss exactly how that would work."

"Have you been giving Robertson company information?"

"Yes, I have been reviewing information with him. I have given him some documents. But I don't think it will be used improperly. Mr. Robertson is a gentleman."

"What documents have you given him, exactly?"

"Oh, some general things."

Copley, Petersen, Winokur, and even Cohler all told Gordon that this was not an issue he was entitled to decide on his own. "A director, if he's acting as a director and not as a shareholder, doesn't have the unilateral right to decide what company information should be made public. The board and management have to deal with that. You have to work through those institutional forums, Gordon," one of the Getty Oil trio said.

"I don't agree with that."

"You have obvious conflicts, Gordon. You're a trustee of the museum, and you've told us that Robertson might want to buy the museum's shares, and yet you're giving him company information as a Getty Oil director—and a shareholder. You've got a lot of conflicts."

"Well, it's a real conundrum," Gordon conceded. "It presents moral and ethical dilemmas."

Cohler asked Gordon if he could talk to him privately. It seemed clear to Petersen and Winokur that Cohler was uncomfortable with his client's statements; any lawyer would be, they thought. Cohler and Gordon stepped into the bedroom and shut the door. When they returned to the living room a few moments later, Gordon seemed transformed—but not for the better. Instead he was more stubborn than ever. He now absolutely *insisted* that he had the right to determine what was confidential company information and what was not.

Petersen had been encouraged by Cohler's earlier comments on the issue—surely Gordon would listen to his own lawyer, and Cohler was saying now that it would be a grave mistake to turn over confidential documents to an outsider such as Robertson. This was a turning point, Petersen thought.

"I feel an ethical obligation," Gordon responded, referring apparently to a perceived obligation to Robertson.

The tension began to rise; voices were growing louder and more taut. An ethical obligation! What did that mean? The ethics of the situation were clear: Gordon was misusing confidential Getty Oil information and perhaps was violating the law. What other ethics could prevail? They began to divide themselves in the hotel suite now, Gordon on one side of the room, Winokur, Petersen, Copley, and Cohler on the other, facing him, arguing urgently that Gordon had gotten it wrong, that he was not free to make up his own rules about the confidentiality of company financial data.

But the more the others pressed him, the more defiant Gordon Getty became. They had touched a streak in him, it seemed—he simply would not concede their point, or any other point that implied that he was wrong. He argued intractably, insisting that he answered only to himself, and that he was a better judge of ethics and responsibilities than they were.

"I answer to a higher morality," Gordon said at one point after he returned to the living room with Cohler, and he was including the morality of his own lawyer in that judgment. Perhaps Gordon was referring to his various responsibilities—to the trust, to the Getty family, to the company, to the board of directors. But at that moment in the hotel suite, in the heat of the debate, it sounded as if he meant he was better than everyone else, possessed of a clearer moral vision.

To Sid Petersen, that moment, that statement, was the turning point. He looked across the room at Gordon Getty and what he saw was selfishness, churlishness, blind rebellion. Gordon was out of control. He was wild. He was like a very rich and powerful child throwing a temper tantrum. Petersen felt sorry for Tim Cohler; the lawyer was clearly trying his best to serve his client, but Gordon was beyond anyone's advice. Cohler and Gordon said later that it was not legal advice Gordon had rejected from Cohler that evening, with his references to higher morality, but rather it was business advice—Cohler thought the trust would be hurt by contacts with outsiders, whereas Gordon didn't, and so they had a reasonable disagreement. But that was not Petersen, Copley, and Winokur's interpretation. To them, Gordon was out on a limb, possibly violating federal laws against insider trading, and here he was telling Cohler, his own attorney, that he didn't need his advice—he'd make his own laws. Was this the side of Gordon Getty that had caused him to be tossed out of the Neutral Zone by angry local government officials two decades earlier? The full details of that incident had never been revealed, but they suspected that it was.

After about two hours, the meeting ended. Gordon had made his position starkly clear. They would have to trust his own judgment on matters of confidentiality. This Sid Petersen was not prepared to do. He had decided now that his own hopes were misplaced; there was no way he could work with Gordon Getty, it was impossible. On the tactical front, they had at least made some small progress by the end of the Bonaventure meeting; it was agreed that Copley and Cohler would draft a letter to Corby Robertson for Gordon's signature, in which Gordon would ask for appropriate confidentiality assurances from Robertson and the Cullens.

"During our conversation two days ago," Gordon wrote to Robertson in the letter dated January 12, the day of the Bonaventure meeting, "you informally broached several of your ideas of possible transactions involving the stock of Getty Oil Company. In light of your statements to me, I felt ethically obliged to describe very generally to you a number of ideas about which I had been ruminating relative to Getty Oil Company. I shall greatly appreciate your confirming to me by your countersignature at the foot of this letter that you have not on Monday or since then and will not in the future . . . engage in the purchase, sale, or exchange, directly or indirectly, of Getty Oil Company stock."

In some ways, then, Robertson's dealings with Gordon had back-fired on Quintana and the Cullens. Because Gordon had disclosed company information, Robertson was now being forced to agree to stop privately buying company stock, or else risk violating the insider trading laws.

So concerned were Gordon's attorneys now about their client's attitude toward confidential information that just four days after the Bonaventure meeting, Moses Lasky, appraised by Cohler of what had occurred the previous Wednesday in Los Angeles, sat down on a Sunday afternoon and wrote an eight-page, double-spaced letter to Gordon about the laws governing confidential information and insider trading. The Lasky, Haas firm itself had been placed in a pre-carious position by Gordon's statements at the Bonaventure. If Gor-don was now going to answer to a "higher morality," if he was going to make up his own rules about what company information could be disclosed and what could not, then the Lasky firm was flirting with a malpractice predicament. They had to make it clear, if the need should later arise, that they had advised Gordon strongly and properly about the law. Early in Lasky's letter that Sunday, the lawyer set down in writing, as much for his firm's own protection as for Gor-don's edification, a brief history of his and Cohler's advice to Gordon on the topic of insider trading.

"I take this opportunity to put down in succinct writing some cautions and information about the state of the law which Tim, Tom, and I have told you about orally from time to time," Lasky wrote. "For obvious reasons, I am not willing to entrust this letter to the mails. As Tim lives just around the corner from you, he has agreed to drop it by. As you know, we as lawyers do not presume to volun-teer advice on business decisions or what would be a sound course of action financially. You therefore will find nothing in this letter that bears on the wisdom or prudence of any course of action. But business decisions have to be made in light of applicable law. . . . One of the most sensitive and trickiest aspects of the law has to do with inside information and insider trading. Class actions have been brought claiming multimillions in damages or profits on behalf of persons claiming that if they had known what the insiders knew, they would have bought or sold and thus made big profits or avoided big losses. Heretofore, we gave you legal advice about a proposal by a Mr. Robertson of Texas. . . .

"The business world," Lasky's letter continued, "particularly the world of investors, is full of people seeking 'tips' or even bits of information that they can add together or add to publicly known facts to give them a basis of prediction that others do not have. In a grosser sense, there are 'sharks' and 'barracudas.' One court described the problems of an insider who talks to investment analysts as that of a person fighting a duel on a tightrope. . . . Specifically, I think it is imprudent to have *any* communications with security analysts *at all*. They seek to hear from you not to benefit you but themselves. Security analysts are notorious for trying to see hints in what they are told, and they and a jury could misconstrue your communications as giving them a subtle tip. If you are seeking an investment banker's advice to engage his services, there is no reason why you may not do so. But otherwise, it is imprudent to talk to investment bankers unless they have been engaged as part of a serious discussion looking toward a transaction under serious consideration. I do not advise that you not talk to someone with whom you seriously have in mind to negotiate. But I am dubious about your telling any of these people about what discussions you have with Getty Oil Company management or about other possibilities of reorganization you have in mind. . . . No law prohibits you from doing that, but the law may then require Getty Oil to make all the information public, thus giving publicity to ideas that might in fact not jell. The effect on the company and its stockholders could be injurious. . . .

"It takes a great foresight to thread one's way through these thickets and because of that fact most people in like situations proceed cautiously, and many do not even engage in discussions in the absence of counsel," Lasky concluded, referring unsubtly to the fact that his firm had not been consulted by Gordon during his meetings with Robertson, Bass, and other outsiders. Lasky and Cohler had been as much in the dark as anyone else about those meetings. By talking and sharing company information with the outsiders, Gordon had placed himself "under the obligation to make the legal determination of whether the facts must be disclosed to the public. I do not see how you can make that determination without legal advice from specific case to specific case," Lasky wrote.

But four days earlier, at the Bonaventure, that was precisely what Gordon had said he would do. He would make his own determinations about ethics and morality and legality. Business, Gordon Getty believed, was a matter of intuition, like music. You just sensed what deal was possible, what was good, what was progress, what was a blind alley, what was proper, what was improper. Business evolved through inspiration, the way melodies came into your head. Ever since Lansing's death, Gordon had felt himself pushing forward to some inevitable goal, what he described later as the light at the end of the tunnel. He did not know the exact form or direction of this goal, but he was driven by his own personal instincts—certainly not by the inflexible rules of those around him, including his lawyers. Gordon's "rule," he said, was that anyone in the room with him could pipe up with business advice, but generally, he listened to lawyers strictly for their legal opinions, and even then, he felt free to make his own decisions. After all, it was his responsibility. It was his trusteeship. It was his money.

Or was it, really? Did the Getty family fortune now belong to Gordon, as sole trustee, as the Lasky firm contended, or did it really belong to the Getty family beneficiaries, the brother, half-brother, nieces, and nephews who shared the trust's income and stood someday to inherit portions of its corpus? That was a theoretical and legal question long debated within the Getty family. That January, however, when Sid Petersen returned to company headquarters after his confrontation at the Bonaventure, the Getty Oil chairman decided he should test the issue once and for all. If Petersen had his way, the question of who owned the Sarah Getty Trust's stock would no longer be a matter for abstract debate; it would become, in the months ahead, the center of a struggle for power within the Getty family itself.

6

FRIENDS OF THE FAMILY

Shortly after the Bonaventure meeting, Bart Winokur returned home to Philadelphia, but he stayed in touch with Petersen and Copley by telephone virtually every day. When the three of them talked now, the subject was almost always the same. How could they stop Gordon Getty? It wasn't so much a debate over technique as it was a question of strategy, judgment, diplomacy. It would be easy enough to initiate a sudden, open, and quite dangerous corporate and legal war with Gordon. The company could sue him on behalf of the public shareholders, for example, alleging that Gordon was disclosing confidential information and violating his fiduciary duties as a director. Or, Petersen and the other top executives could try to buy the company out from Gordon, using Getty Oil's rich assets to borrow the money to purchase 60 percent of the company's stock. Then they could put the kind of squeeze on Gordon that had been described by Winokur at their hotel meeting.

These were radical, risky ideas, however. They would be sure to provoke a bitter, chaotic, highly publicized contest for control of Getty Oil. The facade of cooperation between the trust and the company so long preserved by Petersen's public silence would be shattered. Gordon would be forced to scramble to protect both himself and the value of his family trust; he might form any number of hasty alliances with outsiders interested in taking the company. In such a battle, which would inevitably involve lawsuits and publicity campaigns and proxy fights and shareholder votes, it was quite possible that Getty Oil would somehow be lost, either to Gordon and his allies or to a neutral, so-called "white knight" who might step in to buy the whole company out of its distress for cash. In either event, Sid Petersen's long career would be finished. The challenge in his mind early that winter, then, was to find a way to restrain Gordon without setting off a full-scale war. It was like the challenge faced by the West during Hitler's rise in the 1930s, one lawyer involved put it later. You didn't want to be Neville Chamberlain, but you didn't want to start World War II, either.

So Petersen, Winokur, and Copley turned to the 1934 Sarah Getty Trust document, and to the tortuous history of the Getty family and its wealth. Surely, through the Getty family itself, there was a way to challenge Gordon indirectly. After all, Petersen thought, the company and the family beneficiaries were now really in the same position: both were at the mercy of Gordon Getty's caprice. If Gordon fouled things up, not only would Getty Oil be lost, but the family fortune would be jeopardized as well. As Winokur had tried to explain at the Bonaventure—rudely, Gordon felt—if the trust was squeezed, or locked in as a 40 percent minority holder in some newly configured company, there would be nothing Gordon could do about it. For one thing, the Sarah Getty Trust document provided that the trust's shares could only be sold if the trust faced the prospect of a "substantial loss." For another, the trust's premium value as an independent, large, potentially controlling block of shares would vanish if a single outsider owned 60 percent of the company. The trust would then be just a minority shareholder at the mercy of new ownership. As Winokur had tried to convey at the Bonaventure, there were hundreds of conceivable scenarios in which the trust could be hurt by outsiders bidding for control of Getty Oil.

And if the trust were hurt, it was not only Gordon who would be affected; it was his family as well. Gordon's brother, J. Paul Jr., chronically ill and dependent on heroin and other drugs in a London hospital, received millions annually from the trust. What would he think of Gordon's sojourn in Wall Street and his urgent talk of company restructurings? The Georgettes, George Getty's three daughters—Claire, Anne, and Caroline—were smart, sophisticated women who had known "Uncle Gordo" as the unpredictable man who warred with their father when George was Getty Oil's executive vice-president. The Georgettes now lived in Los Angeles. Two of them were married, and while they did not lead publicly extravagant lives, they were highly protective of their fortune—approximately $8 million each in annual trust income, plus a portion of the corpus when the last of the Getty brothers died. Indeed, when rumors about Gordon's adventures in the fall of 1982 began to spread, the Georgettes had contacted Sid Petersen through their lawyer to ask what their uncle was doing. Petersen had then declined to answer their inquiries, knowing he would offend Gordon if he did, and he told the sisters to direct their questions to Gordon, who was in the best position to provide answers. When the Georgettes responded that Gordon would not answer their questions on the grounds that he might inadvertently disclose confidential company information, Petersen had to laugh a little at Gordon's selective caution, but he nonetheless had decided not to provoke Gordon by talking with his nieces.

Now, after the Bonaventure, Petersen changed his mind. The only way to control Gordon without provoking open warfare was through his family, who could sponsor the appointment of a corporate cotrustee to serve with Gordon as Lansing Hays had done. In a series of four or five conversations that January, Petersen, Winokur, and Copley devised a clandestine, two-track strategy that, if it succeeded, would shift the forum of dispute with Gordon to the courts, and would widen the intrigue to include the entire Getty family. As a legal matter, Winokur pointed out in those January conversations, Gordon's right to be sole trustee of the family fortune was still technically unresolved.

The trust instruments provided for Security Pacific National Bank to serve with Gordon and Lansing after J. Paul's death, but even after Lansing's death the bank had yet to either officially decline or accept the position. And thus, the Lasky firm had taken the position that by default Gordon was the rightful sole trustee. But didn't the Getty family, the trust's beneficiaries, have the right to challenge that position if they wished? And didn't the bank have the right to make up its mind and finally accept a corporate cotrusteeship? If Security Pacific would accept the position, then Gordon would have to persuade a designated bank officer, the new cotrustee, to go along with his restructuring schemes and his attempts to control company policy through the trust's stock ownership. Such an officer, conservative

and cautious by training and inclination, would be unlikely to side
with Gordon against the professional corporate managers now running Getty Oil. Gordon would not personally be hurt by such an
arrangement, Petersen believed; he and Ann would still receive their
millions in annual trust income. But the era of Gordon's business fol-
lies would be finally ended.

While a team of Dechert Price lawyers in Philadelphia began
to investigate the detailed legal history of the Sarah Getty Trust to
determine the various ways a legal challenge to Gordon's sole trusteeship might be launched, Winokur flew back to Los Angeles for a
meeting on Thursday, January 20, with an attorney named Edward
Landry. Landry was an estate and tax lawyer with the Los Angeles
firm of Musick, Peeler & Garrett, which had drafted J. Paul Getty's
personal will and had been involved in a variety of disputes involving the trust, the J. Paul Getty Museum, and Security Pacific Bank.
At one point years earlier, Landry had advised the bank on the dangers it faced if it accepted a corporate cotrusteeship. Those dangers
mainly involved the potential for litigation among Getty family
members, which might tie up bank assets or lead to financial liability.

Because of his firm's history with the Getty family, Landry had
come to know Dave Copley, Getty Oil's general counsel, and Copley regarded Landry as an important source of information about
Security Pacific's current thinking about the trust. Landry would also
be a useful contact, Copley thought, because he sometimes worked
personally with the lawyers for the Georgettes and J. Paul Getty Jr.,
whom Sid Petersen now hoped to involve in his campaign against
Gordon. Ronald was out of the question as a potential participant—
he was fighting his own battles against Gordon over his paltry three-
thousand-dollar annual income, and besides, he was not well liked
by the Getty Oil executives. Petersen's frustration with Gordon was
born at least in part from his conviction that Gordon's father had not
intended for Gordon to run the trust by himself; certainly, the old
man had never intended for Ronald to be in charge. But J. Paul Jr.
and the Georgettes had much more at stake than Ronald, and were
regarded by Petersen as reasonable, intelligent people, regardless of
their much-publicized foibles and family tragedies.

The meeting with Landry in Los Angeles that Thursday, only eight
days after the confrontation with Gordon at the Bonaventure, included
Copley, Winokur, and another lawyer from Dechert Price's Philadelphia

offices, who specialized in trust matters. Copley asked Landry to give
the group a "composite picture" of Security Pacific's position regarding
a corporate cotrusteeship. Little had changed from the bank's point of
view, Landry said. Security Pacific remained convinced that serving as
cotrustee with Gordon posed more problems than it would be worth.
But if Getty Oil had new information to present, or new ideas about
how to solve the bank's problems, Landry was confident that Security
Pacific's top executives would be willing to listen.

For Copley and Winokur, it was a start, at least. At best, they
hoped that if they could sit down with the bank's chairman of the
board and explain the situation, Security Pacific would agree to initiate a court action by petitioning for its right to serve as cotrustee
with Gordon. At worst, Winokur hoped the bank would go to court
and officially decline to serve, thus opening a case about whether
another bank should be appointed to serve in Security Pacific's place.

After hearing about the meeting with Landry, Sid Petersen called
the chairman and chief executive of Security Pacific, Richard Flamson, on Wednesday, January 26. Petersen knew Flamson socially; as
chief executives of mammoth, downtown-based corporations, they
moved in the same circles.

"Dick, I'm calling basically because the legal advice I'm getting as
to the risks the bank might face if it became a cotrustee with Gordon
seems to be significantly different from the legal advice that you are
getting. I think if we sit down, and have everybody talk about it, with
the two of us there, we might be able to resolve it."

"I'd be agreeable to that. I've heard about your meeting with
Landry."

"I just think you're getting bad advice, Dick. The chances of the
bank getting in trouble are not even a million to one—they're nonexistent. We can even arrange for insurance, if that will help. We
think five hundred million dollars in liability insurance is possible
to arrange.

"Back in 1973," Petersen went on, "your bank signed a fee agreement with J. Paul Getty to serve as cotrustee. He relied on at least the
implied acceptance that you gave. I think you now have a moral, if
not a legal, duty to serve."

"How can we get such different legal advice?" Flamson responded.
"I'm willing to make one more effort to have our attorneys reconcile
their views."

A meeting was arranged for Wednesday, February 9, at Security Pacific's corporate headquarters in a mirrored-glass skyscraper in downtown Los Angeles. Flamson would attend, as would Petersen; Winokur; Copley; Robert Smith, head of Security Pacific's trust department; two other bank executives; and a bank lawyer. It would be a kind of corporate summit meeting, a last chance for Petersen to persuade the bank to challenge Gordon Getty's right to control his family's fortune.

"We'll be happy to hear what you have to say and to discuss all these matters with you," Security Pacific's chairman said as the meeting began that sunny, hazy Thursday morning.

"What are the specific reasons that Security Pacific has not gone forward with the cotrusteeship?" Bart Winokur asked immediately. "Perhaps if we hear them, we can address your concerns."

Robert Smith, the bank's top trust executive, did most of the talking in the wide-ranging discussion that ensued. "There are several ambiguous provisions in the trust document," he said. "There's the provision restricting the sale of Getty Oil stock unless the trust is faced with substantial loss, for example. That provision might put the bank in a position where in attempting to follow the trust document, the bank might be challenged as to whether it was violating the securities laws. If you know that Getty Oil Company is about to experience a substantial loss, and so you sell the trust's stock, then it could be argued that you should have disclosed your knowledge to the public before selling. But if you did that, then the stock price would collapse and you would have the substantial loss you were trying to avoid." In other words, if Getty Oil experienced some internal catastrophe—an oil spill that left the company exposed to hugely expensive lawsuits, for example—the bank could do nothing to protect its position.

"I don't think the trust document, any trust document, would require a trustee to violate a federal law," Winokur responded, and the Dechert Price trust expert he had brought along agreed. Winokur and Smith went back and forth on that issue, but they could not come to terms.

"The trust is huge," Smith said, "billions of dollars. The bank faces large risks of exposure if it deals in any way with the trust—just because of the trust's size. What would happen to the bank if it made an error of some kind, or an omission? We could lose a substantial portion of our assets in a lawsuit."

"But isn't handling large trusts the business of a bank like Security Pacific?" Winokur asked pointedly. The implication was clear: risk is a part of business. Security Pacific, after all, was a bank willing to lend billions to Third World debtor nations like Mexico, Brazil, and Argentina. Could supervising the Getty family fortune be any more risky than that?

Smith only repeated himself, however. "The trust is just too large."

"What if insurance could be obtained to protect the bank's liability if there were errors or omissions in your trust management? Getty Oil has an insurance subsidiary and we could make the arrangements. Would that satisfy the bank's concerns?" Winokur asked.

"Well, that is something to think about," Smith answered.

The statements from Smith and from the other bank executives at the meeting made it clear to Winokur, Copley, and Petersen, that the trusteeship was something the bank had been studying for years, and that the very length and depth of Security Pacific's internal inquiry now made it nearly impossible for the bank to shift direction. Over the years, there had accumulated in the bank's files a substantial pile of memos outlining all the risks Security Pacific might face if it accepted a corporate cotrusteeship; even if those risks were one in a million, a certain bureaucratic inertia had now taken hold within the trust departments. If Security Pacific was ever sued in a dispute over its management of the trust, the memos written about its potential risks would be certain to haunt the bank in litigation. The executives at the meeting just kept repeating the worries they had been dwelling on for years.

"That clause about not selling except in the face of substantial loss is just a huge concern," one of them said. "I can easily imagine a scenario in which the bank as trustee would try to sell its Getty Oil stock in order to avoid a loss because of events at the company, but is forced because of federal securities laws to disclose the information it has. Then the market is ruined, and the bank is sued by the beneficiaries. It's a no-win situation."

"I just feel that a corporate cotrustee would afford benefits to all shareholders in relation to the large block of stock the trust has in the company," Sid Petersen told the bank executives. "That's my main concern."

As the meeting concluded, Flamson, the bank's chairman, made it clear that Security Pacific was not going to change its course simply because Getty Oil now found itself in an uncomfortable dispute with Gordon Getty, however much the bank might sympathize with Petersen's plight.

"If we had to make the decision today, I don't know if we would make the same decision we made before," Flamson said, referring to the bank's refusal to accept a cotrusteeship even while Lansing Hays was alive. "But the decision is behind us. Although we have not filed an official declination, I cannot see the bank accepting the trusteeship at this time."

Disappointed but still determined, Petersen, Copley, and Winokur returned from downtown to Getty Oil headquarters. If Security Pacific was unwilling to serve, that only meant the three of them would have to push harder into the Getty family for help. In recent weeks, the battle with Gordon had transformed the three Getty Oil leaders into a secretive triumvirate, planning and strategizing outside normal company channels. Secrecy was imperative now, both within the company and with regard to the Lasky firm and Gordon, who of course had no idea what course was being plotted by Getty Oil management. Despite the extraordinary demands of his battle with Gordon, Petersen still had to supervise the ordinary business of Getty Oil, but increasingly he became a remote, secluded figure on the executive floors, distracted by the intrigue he carried on with Copley and Winokur.

And within days after the meeting with Security Pacific, the triumvirate was busy with a fresh strategy. The team of lawyers at Dechert Price in Philadelphia had drafted a "Petition for Appointment as Successor Trustee" that Winokur had hoped would be filed in court by Security Bank. But if not by them, why not by some other bank? Indeed, there was a logical, credible candidate: California-based Bank of America, an institution even larger than Security Pacific, and whose retired chairman sat on the Getty Oil board of directors. Like Security, Bank of America had performed wide-ranging services for Getty Oil over the years. It was regarded as a bank relatively willing to take risks—if those risks promised lucrative rewards. And here was a chance, as cotrustee of the Sarah Getty Trust, to earn millions of dollars in trust fees every year, perhaps more from this one client than from all the bank's other trusts combined. Petersen himself made direct contact with the bank's executives, who said they would be glad to consider whatever the Getty

Oil chairman had in mind. On Friday, February 18, Copley mailed a copy of the company's draft petition to Harris Taylor, Bank of America's vice-president and assistant general counsel in Los Angeles.

And while Bank of America mulled its options, Getty Oil's attempts to contact family members through attorney Edward Landry finally yielded a response. In March, Landry telephoned Dave Copley and told him that he had been talking with Vanni Treves, J. Paul Jr.'s solicitor in London, about the growing tensions between Gordon and the company. Landry told Copley that Treves had indicated a desire to talk with somebody high up in Getty Oil, and Landry wondered if perhaps Copley would like to fly with him to London to meet with Treves and discuss the situation. If Treves could be convinced that something was amiss, then perhaps J. Paul Jr. would sponsor a lawsuit challenging the sole trusteeship of his brother Gordon.

Paul Jr. was regarded by company executives as the most intelligent of the old man's surviving sons, but there was no doubt that any dealings with him would have to be channeled through his London attorney, Treves. Paul had only lately been released from his most recent hospital stay, which had lasted more than four months, from August 7, 1982, until December 22, just before Christmas, when the heir had returned temporarily to Tudor House, his London mansion. Apart from his dependency on heroin, Paul suffered from numerous circulatory problems and related ailments. He could walk only a few yards under his own power. He was in his fifties now, disheveled, overweight, reclusive, dependent on his doctors to relieve his physical pain and discomfort. Cirrhosis and pneumonia had left his liver and lung functions impaired, and he was able to stay away from the hospital for only weeks at a time.

His decrepit condition was the legacy of a wild, self-indulgent, decadent youth and early middle age that wasted his potential, once considered brighter than any other of the old man's sons. In youth, he was charming, handsome, and intelligent, though even then he did not abide convention. He dropped out of San Francisco State University to educate himself in literature, music, and the arts, and then married Gail Harris, who produced the first of J. Paul Getty, Sr.'s grandsons, J. Paul Getty III. Paul ingratiated himself to his father from the start; christened Eugene Paul, he changed his name to J. Paul Jr. in 1958. "I am proud of my little family," the old man wrote of his son and grandchildren in his diary—Gail had by now born three other children. But as the years passed, Paul Jr.'s idyllic world atrophied. As it had been for his younger brother Gordon—Paul Jr. and Gordon were the only full brothers among the old man's sons—his stint in the family business was disastrous. After a short internship in California, Paul Jr. became head of Getty Oil's refining and marketing operations in Italy. He floundered, and by the mid-1960s was fired by his father, who blamed him for a $2 million annual loss in the operation.

Spun off into the hedonistic society of European aristocracy, Paul underwent a radical transformation, and certainly not for the better, in his father's view. The marriage to Gail Harris ended in 1964 and Paul began to drink heavily. Through his close friendship with Claus von Bülow, who would later achieve his own special notoriety in the United States, the young Getty heir met Talitha Pol, from the island of Bali, an exotic daughter of a Dutch painter and a friend to the most celebrated hippies of Europe. Paul and Talitha became friends with the Rolling Stones, and were seen gallivanting through European capitals with lead singer Mick Jagger and his wife, Bianca. They had a son, and in keeping with the spirit of the times, they named him Tara Gabriel Galaxy Gramaphone Getty. The family appeared in European magazines, with Paul often wearing, as his father put it, "a tie-dyed velvet outfit that would make any genuine hippie green with envy." By the end of the decade, Paul's marriage to Talitha was disintegrating, and there were rumors of divorce. When she came to Rome in 1971 to discuss a reconciliation, however, Talitha died in Paul's apartment of a massive heroin overdose.

From there, it all went from bad to worse. In 1973, Paul's oldest son by his first marriage, J. Paul III, was kidnapped in Rome and held for ransom. He was returned only after losing his ear to the kidnappers while his family debated paying the $3.2 million demanded. As Paul's health deteriorated, he moved to London, where he argued from time to time with his father and rarely saw anyone, including his own children. Gail Harris, his first wife, returned to California with disfigured J. Paul III and the others, while Tara Gabriel Galaxy Gramaphone enrolled in an English boarding school under the general supervision of his grandparents on Talitha's side, who lived in France. Gail Harris also took an interest in Tara, certainly more interest than the boy's father, who was proving himself a rather despicable parent. In 1981, for example, J. Paul III lapsed into a paralyzing coma after an alcoholic binge. Confined to a wheelchair, his medical bills began to run twenty-five thousands dollars a month, a tiny sum given his father's income, but one Paul Jr. nonetheless refused to pay—Gordon had to take care of Paul III until a court action forced Paul Jr. to fork over the money, While the family controversy raged, Paul donated millions to British art museums. As Gail Harris became more and more estranged from her former husband, she came to admire Gordon both for his generosity to her family and for the relative stability and sweetness that seemed to prevail in his life at the Broadway mansion in San Francisco.

All these intimate, convoluted Getty family conflicts, deaths, disasters, and resentments were now of crucial importance to Sidney Petersen and his counselors at the highest rank of the billion-dollar Getty Oil corporation. Persuading Paul Jr. to join the company in its campaign to neutralize Gordon depended not only on business and financial imperatives, but on the strange, labyrinthine alliances that had taken hold within the family over the years. Paul Jr. now held his own family's purse strings because he was an income beneficiary of the trust, but his children by Gail Harris would inherit a portion of the corpus when Paul and his brother and half-brother were dead. His children, then, were "remaindermen" and were also, in a legal sense, beneficiaries of the trust, even though they would not receive any money for years, perhaps decades. They, too, had a stake in the dispute with Gordon, Petersen believed.

Dave Copley's hope in meeting with Vanni Treves, Paul Jr.'s London solicitor, that spring of 1983, was that Treves would persuade Paul that everyone involved would benefit by the appointment of a corporate cotrustee to serve with Gordon. If a representative of Security Pacific or Bank of America could be persuaded to serve with Gordon, Petersen and Copley thought, then the old man's original intentions would be fulfilled. The trust would be stabilized, Getty Oil would remain independent, and Paul and his family would receive the appropriate portions of their wealth without interruption caused by Gordon. Paul might have his own views about Gordon's qualifications to direct the family fortune, but he certainly would be concerned about any of his brother's actions that affected Getty Oil Company, since Paul depended on company dividends for the lifestyle he maintained in his London mansion and hospital rooms.

Copley asked Landry to fly with him to London, at Getty Oil expense, to meet with Treves. Copley had never met the man, but Landry was becoming an important intermediary between the increasingly desperate executives at Getty Oil and the Getty family. Landry was someone to be cultivated. So it was Landry who called Treves and arranged for a dinner meeting at the solicitor's private gentlemen's club in central London on Thursday evening, April 7, 1983.

Landry had already told Treves that in his view, as one of the lawyers responsible for the old man's will and estate, it was never J. Paul Getty, Sr.'s intention that Gordon should serve as sole trustee. Once they arrived in London, it was up to Copley to convince Treves that unless Paul Jr. helped the company do battle with his brother in San Francisco, grave consequences might ensue for everyone.

"Ever since Lansing Hays' death, there has been less stability and cohesiveness in the trust's representation in relation to Getty Oil," Copley told the solicitor over supper at the gentlemen's club that night. "We have concerns that information is getting to the market. There have been security analyst reports out of Wall Street that indicate Gordon is continuing to talk to people in New York about the company. We think it would be beneficial to all the shareholders, including the beneficiaries of the family trust, if there was a cotrustee appointed with Gordon—a corporate cotrustee experienced in handling large trusts."

"In my judgment," Treves answered, "any trust the size of the Getty trust would benefit by having more than one trustee. A cotrustee with Gordon would be desirable, particularly a corporate one. I would feel that way regardless of who the sole trustee was. At the same time, I know about Gordon Getty and his personality, and I can understand the concern."

"The problem now, with Gordon in charge, is that we're having difficulty finalizing decisions, so that the company can make long-term plans," Copley said.

"I'm quite familiar with Gordon Getty. I can understand what you're saying about a lack of stability," Treves emphasized.

"One problem is that Security Pacific has declined to act. I don't think they will accept an appointment. But there probably will be another bank that would agree to accept such an appointment. We think that if one of the beneficiaries, such as your client, was interested in moving ahead with this, then another bank would probably be interested also. But everyone would have to agree that it is appropriate."

"Again, I think a corporate cotrustee would be highly desirable. If something specific is available from Getty Oil, in the way of a proposal, I would be willing to examine it and make my own decision, at that time, about whether to recommend it or not recommend it to Paul."

The supper ended cordially; Copley was encouraged. He felt that the next step would be to present Treves with a detailed package of documents—a proposed lawsuit, drafted by Getty Oil's lawyers and ready to be filed in California court, including the precise arguments to be made and a decision on which family members would be named in the lawsuit as the plaintiffs officially challenging Gordon in the case. Getty Oil would not actually file the suit, even though it was orchestrating the case; Paul Jr. or his children or possibly the Georgettes and their children would serve as proxies for the company in court, arguing that Gordon had abused his trusteeship by jockeying for power at Getty Oil Company.

The next day, Copley and Landry flew back to Los Angeles from London. Copley reported on his dinner meeting to Petersen and Winokur. This was good news indeed, a potential breakthrough. It was essential now to move as quickly as possible, to neutralize Gordon before he did any real damage to the company. Each week, it seemed, there were fresh rumors about Gordon's plans and, as Winokur liked to describe it, about the hungry sharks swimming feverishly toward blood in San Francisco Bay. Describing their predicament with such violent metaphors lent a certain urgency and importance to the Getty Oil executives' work. It made their pulses quicken. Hostile takeover battles were raging in the oil business and in other sectors all across the country; now they, too, were being drawn into the vortex of modern finance and industry, where executives proved themselves not by their ability to make and sell products, but by their courage and stamina and wit in a warlike exigency. They did not ask for this, they did not want it, but they were willing to meet the challenges—indeed, by now they were moving aggressively on new fronts, stirring up new combatants. The odd thing about it was that their opponent in this campaign seemed utterly oblivious to the culture of modern industrial warfare. Gordon seemed unmoved, uncomprehending. There seemed to be a shell around him; he was impenetrable. He was like a boy wandering through the raging battlefield, pulling a red wagon, selling apples to the soldiers, Was he genuinely innocent? Were those apples in that wagon, or grenades? The triumvirate at Getty Oil had decided they could wait no longer to find out.

7

THE PUPPY AND THE SLEDGEHAMMER

None of it seemed to matter to him. He would have been angry, of course, if he had known the company was trying to stir up mutiny within his family. He listened closely, he said, to all the frightened, angry admonitions against contacting outsiders and disclosing company information and leaving a trail of blood in the water. But none of it really took hold. The Bonaventure Hotel meeting, the letter about insider trading from his lawyer, Moses Lasky, the now explicit demands by Getty Oil financial executives that all these studies on royalty trusts and limited partnerships be ended—these seemed to have no impact on Gordon Getty during the early weeks of 1983. As he always had, as he always would, Gordon answered to his own muse. That was, he implied, a prerogative of his wealth and position.

So while Sid Petersen and his company lawyers regarded the Bonaventure confrontation as a turning point, one forcing them to pursue drastic new strategies, Gordon saw the event as merely another unsettling spat with Getty Oil's rude managers. It certainly would not slow his drive to control the company's policies and to raise the price of its stock through some kind of restructuring. He concluded simply that Sid Petersen and Bart Winokur were being unwise to provoke him, that they should know better than to treat him disrespectfully. For his part, Petersen wished—as he told Copley and Winokur one afternoon that winter in his office—that Gordon would just go back to singing opera. "And he isn't much good at that, either," Petersen added.

No matter what they said or thought about him, however, Gordon Getty was still a 40 percent stockholder. Gordon understood, he said later, that his actions that winter might lead eventually to the loss of his family-controlled company to some aggressive outsider or to Sid Petersen's management. But he was not sentimental about Getty Oil. Like his father, he viewed companies as merely the means to an end: money. And toward that end he was now in unbridled pursuit.

It was no longer feasible for Getty Oil itself to conduct the royalty trust and other studies he desired. That much was clear to Gordon after the Bonaventure meeting. There was just too much hostility; the studies could no longer be presented objectively. Shortly after he returned to San Francisco, then, Gordon decided that he would hire an independent outside firm, an investment banker, to finish what he and the Getty Oil financial executives had begun. (Of course, the Getty Oil finance men thought they *had* finished, that the ideas simply wouldn't work and there was nothing more to examine.) A Wall Street investment bank, Gordon thought, would be sure not only to crunch the numbers thoroughly and objectively, it would also lend its prestigious imprint to any conclusions reached, thus making it easier for Gordon to press the ideas on his reluctant adversaries in Getty Oil management. So only a few days after the Bonaventure meeting, Gordon telephoned one of his lawyers at the Lasky firm, Tom Woodhouse, and told him to prepare for a trip to New York on which Gordon intended to hire an investment banker. Gordon did not know which investment house he wished to engage; he would leave it to Woodhouse to make some recommendations. Like law firms, Wall Street's investment banks varied in size, specialty, and reputation. It would be important to choose the right firm.

It was on a Friday evening that Woodhouse called Dave Copley at Getty Oil headquarters in Los Angeles. "Gordon is not satisfied with the studies the company has been doing," Woodhouse said. "He wants to have an independent investment banker look at it. So Gordon and I are going to New York on Monday to hire an investment banker. Do you have any suggestions about who we should interview?"

The question was relayed to Petersen—they were both appalled by the inquiry. To them, it was an indication that Gordon's small, litigation-oriented law firm was in over its head in matters of corporate intrigue, strategy, and finance. In a trial or lawsuit, Petersen and his advisors thought, Lasky and Cohler and even Woodhouse would be fine lawyers, perhaps some of the best around. But when it came to what Winokur liked to call "deal counsel"—the intangible blend of courage, aggression, wit, and savvy that made the difference between winning and losing in a takeover battle—Woodhouse, at least, seemed to be treading water.

What would he and Gordon be thinking? If Gordon Getty went back to Wall Street, lawyer in tow, and paraded through half a dozen major investment banking firms in search of someone to tell him what was wrong with his company, Getty Oil would be "in play," as the Street described corporations ripe for a takeover attempt, before Gordon's head hit the pillow at his beloved Pierre Hotel that evening. If Gordon made a display of himself, the firm he hired would be busy not with investigations of royalty trusts, but with defenses against a hostile bid launched at the instigation of the firms that Gordon interviewed but chose not to engage. Besides, it would probably be against the law for Gordon to hire an investment banker in the manner Woodhouse seemed to be proposing. In order for an investment house to conduct the studies that Gordon wanted, it would need access to all the company financial data and oil field statistics compiled by the Getty Oil finance men for the earlier studies. Gordon did not have the right to independently disclose such confidential information to his own investment banker; he could only do it with the company's permission and cooperation.

Quickly and somewhat desperately, Petersen and Copley tried that weekend to talk Woodhouse out of his proposal. They succeeded by offering a compromise: if Gordon really wanted an investment banker to repeat the same studies Getty Oil had already finished, that was all right with the company, Petersen said. But it should be Getty Oil, not Gordon or the Sarah Getty Trust, that hired the banker on Wall Street. That way, it would appear to the Street that Gordon and Petersen were in complete agreement about the need to study a company restructuring; there would be no rumors about problems between management and the trust, no trail of blood in the water. Also, the investment house could then have access to whatever company information it needed to perform a thorough and objective study. Such a study might be expensive—investment bankers charged about a million dollars for the sort of inquiry Gordon wanted—but if that was the price of peace, Petersen thought, so be it. He could use the time bought by the study to find someone in the Getty family willing to sue Gordon over his control of the trust. By Monday, they had agreed that representatives of both the company and the trust would travel to New York to hire an investment firm. After making separate lists and talking back and forth several times, they had also agreed on who that firm would be: Goldman, Sachs & Company.

It was an interesting choice for several reasons, but most importantly, it was a strategic victory for Sid Petersen. Headquartered on Broad Street, across from the New York Stock Exchange in lower Manhattan, Goldman, Sachs was one of the largest and most prestigious firms in the ascendant realm of Wall Street investment banking. It was a firm of many contradictions. For decades, it had been considered one of the Street's most aggressive trading houses—that is, a firm that specialized in stock, bond, and commodity trading for its own account and for clients. It was a traditionally Jewish firm, an unapologetic contrast to the staid, cautious WASP establishment represented by houses such as Smith Barney and Morgan Stanley. Since the 1950s, Goldman, Sachs had been dominated by two of the Street's canniest, fiercest traders, Gus Levy and Sidney J. Weinberg. Levy, especially, had been a major force in American finance, serving as director of numerous large corporations and raising millions for Republican politicians and Jewish philanthropies. He was indefatigable, intense, and deeply attracted to the power of money. He loved nothing better than to trade for profit; his particular specialty was arbitrage, an arcane, fast-paced field wherein success depends on guts, speed, and stamina. Weinberg, too, was a natural trader, and though less well known than his partner Levy, he was an equal force on Wall Street, where he churned out huge profits for his firm.

Both these titans died suddenly, Weinberg in 1969, and Levy of a stroke in 1976. By then, Goldman, Sachs had begun to grow and change. The takeover boom was under way, and hundreds of large corporations were under siege. Investment houses were expanding rapidly in size and scope, and nearly all wanted a place in the highly lucrative mergers game, where fees were based not on an hourly charge for advisory service, but on a percentage of the deal—in some takeovers, investment bankers could make millions in just a few days. For a firm like Goldman, there was a clear choice: should it help those companies on offense, the hostile raiders, or those on defense, the targets?

After Levy's death, control of the firm had passed to John L. Weinberg, Sidney Weinberg's son, and John C. Whitehead, who had been the younger Weinberg's friend and partner at Goldman for twenty-five years. These two had the attitude of second-generation bankers—more cautious, more part of the establishment, less ruthless and aggressive. They decided that in the mergers field, the firm's future lay in defense, in protecting the managers of large corporations, men such as Sid Petersen, from unwanted attacks by outsiders. Alone among prominent investment bankers on Wall Street, Goldman, Sachs established a formal policy that as a matter of principle it would never work for anyone engaged in a hostile takeover bid. It was a profitable pronouncement since it attracted to the firm all those companies worried about a potential hostile bid but afraid that consultations with a banker would only aggravate their predicament by planting takeover ideas in the bankers' heads.

There were some on Wall Street who regarded Goldman, Sachs' policy as a hypocritical ruse, a marketing trick, because Goldman instigated hostile deals directly and indirectly despite its policy, and because nearly every other investment house provided defenses against raiders without making a moral issue out of it. But it was precisely Goldman's moral tone, the fact that defending corporations was not just a business but a matter of principle, that attracted executives like Petersen to the firm in times of crisis. As a result, Goldman was earning many tens of millions annually from the hostile takeover boom while at the same time declaring publicly that it opposed the phenomenon. In parallel, it had secured its reputation as an establishment firm dedicated to the interests of its huge, blue-chip corporate clients.

That February, 1983, Tom Woodhouse, representing Gordon and the trust, Steadman Garber and Bart Winokur, representing Getty Oil, visited the Goldman, Sachs headquarters on Broad Street to discuss the firm's engagement with Weinberg, Whitehead, and other partners. For Goldman, landing a client the size of Getty Oil was a happy occasion, especially since the company was the subject of swirling takeover rumors on Wall Street. Later there would be some dispute about exactly what was communicated when Woodhouse and Garber met with the Goldman, Sachs partners, but at the time everyone seemed to understand why the firm was being hired. Though it was being officially engaged by Getty Oil, Goldman was to undertake an objective study, supported jointly by the company and the trust, into royalty trusts, limited partnerships, stock buy-back programs, and any other gimmicks or devices that might raise the depressed price of Getty Oil stock. When the study was completed, Goldman would present its findings to Gordon, Petersen, and the Getty Oil board of directors. Goldman was to have no preconceived ideas about any of the issues it would address, Woodhouse said, and it was not to favor either the company or the trust in its analysis—it was to help decide what would be best for all stockholders. For reasons no one quite understood, Gordon was adamant that Goldman not pay any special attention to the trust's position in a restructuring. This vague, even illogical admonition seemed to be another of Gordon's private ethical imperatives.

To assist Goldman's effort, the Getty Oil finance executives in Los Angeles who had worked on these same issues for Gordon earlier sent boxes of their detailed financial data and tables back to New York. To the Getty Oil finance men, this was an absurd exercise. The only potential positive result, they thought, was that Goldman, Sachs, by virtue of its unassailable reputation, would convince Gordon of what the finance men had failed to persuade him, namely, that Gordon's ideas about the oil business were worthless. *Let Goldman try to explain it to him*, they thought.

But there was a certain defensiveness in the financial executives' attitude toward the Goldman, Sachs study. After all, the corporate analysts at Goldman were regarded as the best in the business. They were young, brilliant Ivy Leaguers, financial blue bloods, confident to the point of arrogance. The Goldman analysts were especially proud of their credentials, their degrees and titles, it seemed to the Getty Oil executives. The Getty Oil men were older than the investment bankers and felt they had done much to earn their high positions at the company—hard work had gotten them ahead, not impressive sheepskins. So the finance men took a certain pleasure, during those first weeks after Goldman, Sachs was hired, as they watched the young, smug analysts struggle desperately to understand what Gordon Getty wanted. The Goldman bankers would call the Getty Oil finance men and say, in effect, "Well, you've got the numbers together here. But you don't seem to know what Gordon's *objectives* are. That's the most important thing in a situation like this. You must know what the client's *objectives* are." The Getty Oil finance men rankled at this sort of lecture—"objectives" was a buzz word at the Ivy League business schools, they knew—and they tried to explain that it wasn't that they were stupid, it was just that Gordon didn't know what his objectives were, or if he knew, he wasn't saying. When the young Goldman, Sachs analysts would pass this frustration on to their superiors at their firm, they would hear the same lecture from Weinberg or Whitehead: "Well, you've got to figure out what Gordon's *objectives* are. Then you can do the study."

It was Whitehead, finally, who decided that he would personally determine what it was that Gordon Getty wanted. As part of Goldman's engagement, it had been stipulated that one of the firm's two cochairmen would fly to San Francisco to meet personally with Gordon and to pay homage to him. The task fell to Whitehead, and with Sid Petersen he arranged a day in February when the two could talk with Gordon at his Broadway mansion. Whitehead began the meeting by telling Gordon what he thought the scope of the assignment was. He tried to press Gordon about his objectives. "What, exactly, do you want to accomplish in a restructuring, if in fact a restructuring is one of your objectives?"

Gordon did not really answer. Instead, he talked a great deal about the tax consequences of limited partnerships. Whitehead was not following Gordon, and he tried to shift the discussion to a more philosophical level. He wanted a broader sense of Gordon's plans. "Do you want cash—income from the trust—or do you want long-term growth?" Whitehead asked.

"Yes," Gordon answered, curling his lips into an inscrutable smile.

Then Gordon began to talk. In his characteristic fashion, he rambled on to the Goldman, Sachs cochairman about fiduciary duties and value gaps and debt ratios and mutual funds—sometimes coherently and cogently, but more often stringing wild *non sequiturs* behind him. At one point, Gordon and Petersen took up their long-standing debate about diversification.

"I really don't think diversification makes much sense. A company should stick to what it knows, and stockholders can diversify by choosing the companies they own," Gordon said.

"Well, timing is the important factor to consider," Petersen countered. "We did diversification during one period and now we are in

fact doing other things and not diversifying because other invest-
ments look more attractive now. But the present situation may
change, and diversification may look attractive again in the future.
Business is not static. It's dynamic and you make decisions within
that. You can't just liquidate the company, Gordon."

"Yes, I can," he answered.

After two hours or so, Petersen, Whitehead, and Gordon moved
to the dining room for lunch. They continued their discussion, but
Gordon's tone began to shift. Whereas before he had said things
like "We ought to be looking at" or "The company is considering,"
he now began to use the personal pronoun: "I will do this" and "I
might do that." Petersen and Whitehead both became increasingly
uncomfortable.

When the meeting concluded, Petersen and Whitehead agreed to
share a limousine ride to San Francisco International Airport, some
twenty minutes from Gordon's mansion.

As soon as the chauffeur had closed the door, Whitehead turned
to Petersen and said, "I'm glad he's your director and not mine.
You've got a loose cannon on the deck."

The Goldman, Sachs partner was at a loss. How could they deal
with Gordon?

"Should we play to his ego?" Whitehead asked. "What should our
role be?"

"Play it straight," Petersen answered. It was important, he thought,
that Goldman not get the impression that there was deep dissension
at Getty Oil. If that happened, the investment banker might put the
company in play on Wall Street, knowing it would earn huge fees
from any takeover deal.

"None of this makes sense," Whitehead concluded.

Petersen often repeated Whitehead's remarks in the limousine
that afternoon to other Getty Oil executives. The Goldman chief
had validated Petersen's own view of Gordon as a flake, a problem
child meddling in affairs beyond his grasp. People might not take Sid
Petersen's word that Gordon was irresponsible, but John Whitehead
was a well-known and well-respected corporate financier, a man
who would soon take a high-ranking position in President Reagan's
Department of State. Surely, his opinion counted for something.

Petersen emphasized the point because increasingly that winter,
Gordon was allying himself with respectable, intelligent critics of the

oil business—analysts and takeover specialists and oil men whose opinions might be radical but whose credentials were impeccable. Though Petersen and Bart Winokur were doing all they could to prevent it, Getty Oil was becoming more and more a topic of public comment and speculation; the company's destiny was being debated in the financial community. For Petersen, a large and aggravating problem was that the financial analysts took Gordon at face value— they took him seriously. They seemed to respect his ideas and his position as a 40 percent stockholder in Getty Oil, as Petersen did not.

The worst blow had come on Tuesday, February 1, when the oil analyst Kurt Wulff published a special report about Gordon and the future of Getty Oil. A member of the Wall Street brokerage firm of Donaldson, Lufkin & Jenrette, Wulff was regarded as a maverick analyst, brilliant but radical and iconoclastic. His job was to analyze oil companies for his firm's clients, and to recommend stocks for purchase. Friend and intellectual ally of Boone Pickens, as Pickens rose to influence in the oil business, so did Wulff. Donaldson, Lufkin did not finance or participate in Pickens' raids, but Wulff provided a kind of intellectual cover for the Texan when the going on Wall Street got tough. In his analyst reports, which enjoyed wide circulation on the Street and in the oil industry, Wulff propounded Pickens' views nearly to the letter. He described large oil companies like Getty as "obsolete oil megacorporations" and argued that they should be taken over and dismantled into as many as ten separate corporations. Providing detailed financial analysis to support his claims, Wulff said, as Pickens had earlier, that the oil giants were worth more dead than alive. Getty Oil, for example, was valued by Wulff at about $240 a share, more than four times its stock price. He advocated that large stockholders such as Gordon Getty take militant action to force company managements to restructure in order to realize such underlying value.

For months during the fall of 1982, Wulff had been like a fly buzzing around Sid Petersen's ear, annoying and elusive. The reports Wulff published and the questions he asked at industry gatherings irritated the Getty Oil chairman because they criticized his style of management, but also because Petersen disagreed with Wulff's premises—the Getty Oil chairman argued that there was more to a company than its raw assets. But Petersen had assumed that Wulff was just parroting Pickens, and that he had no inside information about Getty Oil. That all changed on February 1, just three weeks after the Bonaventure meeting, when Wulff issued a special report entitled "Oil and Gas Valuation" to his clients.

The report made clear that Kurt Wulff had been talking directly to Gordon Getty, and that discussions between them had occurred even after the warnings to Gordon by Lasky about contact with outsiders. The report included a flattering biography of Gordon and some general descriptions of the powerful stock position of the Sarah Getty Trust. And then Wulff dropped what Petersen and Winokur regarded as a bombshell: "Mr. Getty is clearly most intrigued with eliminating double taxation by the technique of a royalty trust or limited partnership. It would be presumptuous to say that he has reached any conclusions on that subject, but there is no doubt he has investigated the issues thoroughly. . . . Mr. Getty is impressed that Boone Pickens was able to form his royalty trust without incurring any initial taxation."

That same Tuesday, Wulff released another report, a "research bulletin," that included a transcript of a breakfast Wulff had recently attended. Wulff was quoted as saying at the breakfast, held at a Manhattan hotel: "My thesis on Getty Oil is that there has been a major change in the ownership of the company and that the new owners want something different from their investment. The major change in the Sarah Getty Trust is that it is now managed by a single trustee, Gordon Getty. Up until last May there were two trustees. . . . The major stockholders ought to be dissatisfied that the stock market is saying that the company can't reinvest its money profitably or that something else is wrong. I was greatly encouraged to see that Mr. Getty is strongly interested in enhancing value for shareholders."

Wulff was telling all the world what Petersen already knew—Gordon was a loose cannon at Getty Oil. The analyst was also disclosing publicly what for months had been a tightly guarded secret even at Getty Oil headquarters, namely, that Gordon was interested in a restructuring involving royalty trusts or limited partnerships. The disclosure would have an effect on morale at Getty Oil headquarters, Petersen knew. What Petersen and Winokur could not anticipate, however, was the effect of Wulff's report on T. Boone Pickens, Jr., the dreaded scourge of the corporate oil industry.

Boone Pickens once remarked that attempting a takeover raid of Getty Oil Company by currying Gordon Getty's favor was like "going after a puppy with a sledgehammer." Gordon was the puppy, Pickens the hammer. The comment was suggestive of the ways in which ego and personal power figured in the oil industry takeover wars, which were so often described by men like Pickens and Wulff in the abstract language of economic theory. The plain fact was that Boone Pickens was smarter and hungrier than most of his adversaries in the executive suites or the behemoth oil corporations—that had as much to do with his success as value gaps or the perceived genius of his restructuring ideas. He was articulate, charming, smooth, and savvy—an oilman in pin stripes. He was a child, literally, of the 1928 Seminole oil boom in Oklahoma, where his lawyer-trained father was wildcatting his way to fortune in the fields. His father traded leases and royalties successfully for a number of years, then began investing directly in wells during the mid-1930s. Five years later, he was broke—"He kept missing" was how Boone liked to describe his father's predicament. During the war, Boone the elder got a job in a defense plant, and then in 1944 he went to work in Amarillo, Texas, for Phillips Petroleum, a company his son would try unsuccessfully to raid some forty years later. Boone Jr. was an only child. "All the attention was focused on me," he said later when asked to identify the sources of his intense competitive urges. There was discipline, he said of his early life, and encouragement and love and high expectation. He always felt that he was as good or better than anyone else. He had to win, he said.

At age fifty, as the chairman and chief executive of a huge independent oil company, Mesa Petroleum, Pickens still felt that way. Acquainted with his father's misfortunes as a wildcatter, he trained himself not as a lawyer but as a geologist, and he began quickly to drill wells without missing. By the time he launched his takeover raids during the 1970s, Pickens was a confident, experienced oilman, a product of the Texas oil patch, and the wealthy chief executive of a large independent company. But unlike the good old boys, the oilmen like Getty's former chairman, Harold Berg, who ran the large corporations, Pickens remained ambitious, lean, and aggressive into his middle age. It was a personal edge that set him apart from his peers and colleagues, a sense of leadership and composure.

Pickens himself liked to talk about it. He liked to make fun of the oil executives he played golf with, men so fat and lazy they couldn't bend over to tie their golf shoes, he said, men who would wander around the course with their shoestrings flapping at their ankles. By contrast, Pickens was in peak physical condition. He could not abide the Texas provincialism of the good old boys, their muddy snakeskin boots and Stetsons and silver buckles, and the way they seemed deliberately to cultivate an ignorance of Wall Street and sophisticated modern finance. Pickens wore immaculate, tailored suits and black wing tip shoes, and he traveled by corporate jet and limousine. He embodied the new, confident Texas so much in fashion during the 1970s and early 1980s. He was articulate and equally at ease with investment bankers and refinery workers. Although there were important economic aspects of the takeover wars Pickens initiated, and he raised important issues in the oil business, most who met him agreed that, for Boone Pickens, a takeover was first about winning. It was about proving that he was better than the entrenched, slothful, self-indulgent corporate executives who opposed him. Boone Pickens thought he was smarter than those executives. He thought he was better. His trick was to get very, very rich proving himself right.

After he read Kurt Wulff's report of February 1, Pickens began his run at Sid Petersen, a man Pickens regarded as a mediocrity, and at Petersen's company, Getty Oil. Pickens knew the gossip in Texas about Gordon's meetings with the Cullens, but he also knew from Wulff that Gordon was not yet contemplating any direct move against Sid Petersen and the rest of Getty Oil management. Pickens called Gordon in San Francisco.

"Gordon," he began, "I've never met you, but I appreciate the nice things you said about me to Kurt Wulff."

"Well, I'm a big fan of yours," Gordon replied. "We should get together and talk sometime."

"Sure," Pickens replied. "Let's do."

On Thursday, February 24, Pickens flew his jet into Los Angeles and rode by limousine to the Beverly Wilshire Hotel in Beverly Hills, where Gordon was staying for a few days. Lunch began at 1 P.M. in Gordon's suite. Pickens brought along one of the top executives from his oil company; Gordon had no lawyers or advisors with him. Pickens considered himself to be in an unusual situation. Normally, if he was interested in taking over a large oil company like Getty, he would just purchase a large block of stock and then launch a hostile raid to buy the rest. That was not possible with Getty Oil, Pickens and his Mesa executives believed. They regarded Gordon as a majority owner of the company, even though he controlled only 40 percent of the stock. Any raid would require Gordon's cooperation; without it, the attempt would be too risky. Gordon might be a puppy, but he was a very important puppy. The way Pickens and his executives talked about it, they were treating Gordon's position exactly as Sid Petersen should, acknowledging explicitly that Gordon, not management, was in charge of Getty Oil Company. They were not going to make the same mistake as Petersen, they said, by underestimating Gordon's power.

The meeting in Gordon's room lasted about two hours. "How can we get Getty Oil going?" was Gordon's question. "What should we be doing?" It was the same question he had been asking all across America.

"The first thing you've got to do, you've got to get Sidney on board," Pickens answered. "Once you have Sidney on board, you can do something with the undervalued assets. You have to advise a plan first as to how you're going to capitalize on this."

Gordon said that what concerned him was the diversification pursued by Petersen and the fact that Getty Oil's reserve base was rapidly depleting—the base had been built up over decades by Gordon's father, and now it was disappearing. Gordon also told Pickens that while he was getting tens of millions in annual dividends out of the company currently, that seemed to him only a fraction of the cash he should be receiving. If he had direct access to 40 percent of the profits flowing from Getty Oil's rich fields, Gordon said, the trust's income would be something over $700 million annually.

"Something is haywire at the company," Gordon said.

"Something *is* haywire," Pickens echoed.

Pickens told Gordon that he understood his frustration. Gordon was a 40 percent stockholder and yet the company was being run "totally for the management."

"You've got one of the biggest problems in the business with depleting reserves," Pickens said. "The company is replacing only a percentage of what it's producing, and it's throwing away its cash flow on things like ESPN."

Gordon agreed. He told Pickens about his interest in limited partnerships. Pickens responded by saying that he thought royalty trusts were a superior restructuring vehicle. They talked about taxes and the trust's "zero basis" problem, the fact that if a deal took place, Gordon would have to pay tax on the entire value of the trust's stock.

"You know, there's an opportunity here if we can come up with a good idea," Pickens said.

Pickens was subtle and eloquent. He never brought out the sledge-hammer. In fact, Pickens would later regard his dealings with Getty Oil as one of the few strategic failures of his corporate raiding career. When he returned to his headquarters in Amarillo, Texas, after his lunch with Gordon, Pickens was so excited about his restructuring ideas for Getty Oil—ideas he asked his staff to develop into detailed proposal books for Gordon and Petersen—that he began to deceive himself a little. He began to think that the restructuring he would propose to Gordon and Petersen was so attractive, so profitable for everyone involved, that the company would be actually excited and pleased to accept. The proposal was called a "reverse triangular merger" and it was a kind of friendly takeover in which Getty Oil and Pickens' company would be combined into a new, restructured organization designed to elude some of the taxes on oil field profits. Pickens would run the new company, and Petersen would lose his job, but nearly everything else about Getty Oil would remain secure, including its thousands of employees.

Pickens, however, was not so naïve that he thought Petersen would be pleased to lose his job to the infamous Pickens, so he devised a "golden parachute" severance package for the Getty Oil chairman that was so lucrative, he thought, Petersen would be a fool to pass it up. If he left the company peacefully under Pick-ens' plan, Petersen would receive millions in cash, stock options, and shares in the newly formed company—in all, more money than Petersen was likely to make in all his career at Getty Oil. In the weeks after his meeting with Gordon, Pickens consulted with his Mesa executives and met with his lawyers at Baker & Botts in Houston, preparing to make a formal pitch to Petersen and Gordon Getty. Pickens was ebullient. It would be a pleasant change to take control of an oil giant without the pain of a protracted, vitriolic, hostile takeover battle.

When the proposal was ready, Pickens flew secretly to San Fran-cisco to meet with Gordon at the Broadway mansion. He reviewed his ideas with Gordon and explained the financial benefits of the restructuring for the trust. Again, Gordon did not invite his own lawyers to the meeting with Pickens. He was intrigued by Pickens' plans and told the raider that he would be interested in pursuing the merger further. Of course, Pickens did not appreciate that for months Gordon had been interested in pursuing a great many things further, but he had yet to arrive at any conclusions.

Days after his return from San Francisco, Pickens wrote to Petersen at Getty Oil headquarters, briefly describing his merger proposal and asking for a meeting as soon as possible. Petersen was stunned—after all the struggles and strategies and headaches involving Gordon, now he had to contend with the country's most successful takeover artist. It was not, Petersen felt, what he needed at this time. But Petersen was prepared to do battle; there was no other choice. He consulted with Winokur, whose merger expertise was reassuring, and they decided to inform Pickens that Getty Oil would only consent to a meeting if Pickens agreed to sign a "standstill" prohibiting him from buying Getty Oil stock for several years. Petersen naturally feared that far from wanting to discuss a "friendly merger," Pickens was actually preparing to launch a hostile takeover raid. If Pickens was serious about what he said in his letter, if he really wanted to discuss a friendly deal, Petersen said, then he would agree to the standstill. The Getty Oil chairman also insisted that Morgan Stanley & Company, Pickens' Wall Street investment banker, agree to the standstill.

There were days of telephone negotiations back and forth, and Pickens finally agreed to sign. It was a decision very much out of character for the Texas raider, who frequently used the threat of a hostile raid as leverage in negotiations. But Pickens genuinely believed in his restructuring proposal; he was convinced that Petersen would be sold on the idea once the Getty Oil chairman understood it. Also, Pickens was reluctant to raid Getty Oil under any circumstances because of Gordon's huge 40 percent block of stock. Morgan Stanley, however, did not share Pickens' optimism about the deal, and it refused to go along with the standstill—it wanted to reserve its right to help raid Getty Oil at some future date. Pickens responded by cutting his investment banker out of the deal, and he told Petersen that he would meet with him on his own.

Petersen selected the luxurious Century Plaza Hotel, just south of Beverly Hills, as the site of his secret summit meeting with Pickens; the last thing he wanted was to have Pickens parading through the halls of Getty Oil headquarters. Pickens flew out from Texas with one of his executives and a tax lawyer from Baker & Botts. Petersen brought along Winokur, Copley, and two of his top finance men. The meeting began around 11 A.M. in a two-room private suite in the hotel's central wing.

The tension and fear of the Getty Oil executives was palpable, Pickens thought as the meeting began. Petersen and his advisors watched the raider's every move as he entered the suite and sat down beside a coffee table. Pickens never carried a briefcase, but he had brought an apple with him from his private jet, in case he wanted a light snack during the day-long meeting. Not having any place to store the fruit, Pickens took the apple from his pocket and set it on the table in front of him just as the meeting began. The Getty Oil executives looked at the apple. What did it mean? they wondered. Was Pickens going to take out a knife and carve it up as a demonstration of his intentions? All through the afternoon, the apple just sat there, and when the meeting was concluded, Pickens retrieved it from the table and put it back in his pocket. Long afterward, the Getty Oil executives remembered the apple and they pondered its significance—was this part of the subtle psychological warfare for which Pickens was renowned? Hardly, Pickens said later when asked about the fruit. He just wasn't hungry.

Sid Petersen's first question as the meeting began was simple and direct. "Have you talked to Gordon Getty?" he asked Pickens.

"Yes, I have."

"When?"

"A couple of times, recently. He is totally supportive of my approaching the company with these ideas."

"Does Gordon have a copy of the proposal you're presenting us?"

"Yes."

"What's the date on his book?"

"It's dated earlier than yours. I'm not sure exactly."

That was all Sid Petersen needed to hear. For the rest of the afternoon, he never asked another question. His worst suspicions had been confirmed; Pickens was in cahoots with Gordon. Who knew what confidential company data Gordon had given Pickens? Gordon had said nothing to Petersen about his meetings with the Texas raider. Petersen was anxious and concerned. If Pickens was working with Gordon, he thought, then this was not a friendly proposal. This was just a new episode in the widening war between the company and Gordon Getty.

As he talked to Petersen, and as his advisors described the details of his proposal, Pickens realized that he had miscalculated. He could see immediately that Petersen would never go along; it was written on the Getty Oil chairman's face. As Pickens watched Petersen that afternoon at the Century Plaza, he was reminded of his own son. When Pickens' boy got in trouble, when he earned poor grades or violated some household rule, Boone and his son would sit down on the couch and have a face-to-face. Pickens' boy would clench his jaw during those talks, and his cheeks would begin to twitch with tension. Petersen's cheeks were twitching, too, that afternoon, and his mouth was tightly shut. It was funny, Pickens thought to himself, that the chief executive of a huge oil company would respond to him like a boy who'd just bashed up the family car.

The substantive discussion that day centered on the details of a reverse triangular merger. The Getty Oil finance men thought that Pickens' proposal was deceitful and possibly illegal. It was a two-state deal and required certain filings with the federal Securities and Exchange Commission. But as the Getty finance executives saw it, the proposal required the company to lie about its intentions to investors during the first stage of the deal in order to get certain tax benefits during the second stage. Pickens' people disagreed with this opinion, and the Baker & Botts lawyer tried to persuade them that they were wrong. Later, the Getty Oil executives would say they turned down the deal because of its potential legal irregularities. Pickens thought that was patently absurd; this was a fine-print issue, he said, and no matter what the Getty Oil executives' concerns, the problems could be solved through negotiation and compromise. They could even ask the SEC what it thought about the deal. The real problem, Pickens thought, was that Sidney Petersen was scared of him and of Gordon Getty and of any meaningful change at Getty Oil Company. There was nothing he could do to overcome that fear.

"I'll tell you one thing," Boone Pickens said disgustedly to one of his advisors as they walked through the lobby of the Century Plaza after the meeting had ended in failure. "Petersen and those guys are not going to be around that company for very long."

It was the sort of prophecy that had made Pickens a very rich man. Ordinarily, he would have enforced his own prediction by launching a hostile takeover raid against Petersen. This time, however, he had outsmarted himself. For once, his intuition wasn't worth a dime to T. Boone Pickens, Jr.

FOR THE OLD MAN'S SAKE

The race was on now.

Sid Petersen could no longer entertain any illusions about his or Getty Oil's future. It was clear now that the dam was breaking—so clear, in fact, that as soon as Pickens made his overtures to Getty Oil management, the company's board of directors authorized new employment contracts for Petersen and Copley. The contracts provided for the very "golden parachutes" contemplated by Pickens, lucrative salary and severance agreements that would yield Getty Oil's top executives more than $1 million each in cash and stock in the event they lost their jobs in a takeover or restructuring. The rationale for the contracts was that if the executives knew they would become rich even when their careers were ended, then they would have less incentive to protect themselves at the expense of stockholders during a takeover battle. But the contracts did not lessen Petersen's drive to save his career and his company that spring; there was more than money at stake for a man like Petersen, who had worked long and hard to reach the top of one of America's largest corporations. The parachute was only a reminder that he had a long way to fall. His efforts were redoubled. The trust had to be neutralized before a hostile raider made a bid for control of the company. Somehow, a lawsuit challenging Gordon's sole trusteeship had to be instigated, and quickly. Copley's April meeting with Vanni Treves in London had been encouraging, but Petersen realized now that he had to explore other possibilities as well.

J. Paul Jr. was six thousand miles away, but in Los Angeles there were other family members who might be willing to take Gordon to court: the Georgettes. George Getty's three daughters and their children clearly had a stake in the future of the Sarah Getty Trust. Wouldn't they agree with Petersen that the company and the trust would both benefit by the appointment of a corporate cotrustee to serve with Gordon? Petersen asked Dave Copley to see if he could arrange a meeting. Copley enlisted the aid of Edward Landry, the lawyer who had been so helpful in arranging meetings with Security Pacific and Treves. Landry called James Isaacs, a Los Angeles attorney who represented two of the Georgettes, Caroline Getty and Claire Getty Perry. Isaacs told Landry that on behalf of his two clients, he would like to talk to someone high up in Getty Oil about Gordon. Landry relayed the message to Copley. On Wednesday, April 27, 1983, a meeting was held at Isaacs' office.

Winokur, Landry, and Copley arrived on behalf of Getty Oil. Winokur did most of the talking; he was spending more and more time in Los Angeles now, and the strategic counsel he offered Petersen was increasingly important. Winokur was hardly Getty Oil's new Lansing Hays—he was a clients' man, smooth and political, not domineering—but his influence was nonetheless strong.

"We really think there should be a corporate cotrustee appointed," he urged Isaacs. "This would give Getty Oil a sense of continuity, and we hope the new trustee would be a harmonizing influence. That would be of benefit to all the shareholders, including the beneficiaries of the trust. Gordon changes his mind about what he wants all the time."

"I know Gordon and his personality," Isaacs said. "But my clients are fond of their uncle. I, myself, can see that a lawsuit would be a good idea. I don't know what my clients would think. If you develop the idea in specific form, I would be willing to recommend it to my clients."

Isaacs left Dave Copley, for one, with the impression that if Getty Oil submitted a proposed lawsuit, Isaacs would recommend it to his clients. But until then, the lawyer was unwilling to discuss the matter with the Georgettes. In the weeks ahead, the Getty Oil lawyers and executives would begin to wonder whether Isaacs was serious about what he said. Whenever they fed him information about Gordon's behavior, the lawyer seemed to do nothing with it.

When Winokur and Copley returned to Getty Oil's headquarters building at Wilshire and Western, they called over to Security Pacific Bank to arrange a meeting for early the next morning. The idea now was to pursue every possible channel. Perhaps Security Pacific could be persuaded to file a petition seeking the appointment of Bank of America as a cotrustee in Security Pacific's place; that possibility had been raised at the summit meeting with Petersen in February, and Bank of America had subsequently agreed to serve as cotrustee if it was appointed by a court.

"What standing do we have to file a lawsuit?" one of Security Pacific's lawyers demanded at the meeting the next morning. It was a hot, sunny day and acrid smog hovered over the Southern California basin; the view from Security's tall headquarters building downtown was obscured by haze.

"It would be embarrassing to go into court and petition for B of A's appointment if we have no legal standing to file a suit," the bank's lawyer said. Security Pacific and Bank of America were the two cornerstones of the downtown financial community; their skyscrapers were like marble pillars, symbols of stability.

One of the Getty Oil lawyers suggested that the embarrassment could be avoided by the appointment of a "guardian ad litem." That is, the Georgettes or J. Paul Jr. would agree to have one of their children file the lawsuit against Gordon. But then, since the child was under eighteen, a special guardian would have to be appointed by the court to handle the suit on the child's behalf. Getty Oil and the bank would agree in advance on who that guardian would be—a well-known, experienced lawyer, if possible, someone who could do battle in court against Gordon and the Lasky firm. The central idea was that the lawsuit technically would be filed by one of Gordon's nieces or nephews, but in reality it would be handled by an attorney hand-picked by Getty Oil and Security Pacific Bank. The lawyer would argue in court that a cotrustee should be appointed to neutralize Gordon and that Bank of America should be selected to do the job. The attorney's fees would be paid out of income from the trust, since the lawyer would argue that he was trying to protect the trust from abuse by Gordon. The child who filed the suit would have to pay nothing. He might not even have to meet his "guardian."

"Now, how do we accomplish that?" one of the Getty Oil lawyers asked, pleased that he had identified a solution.

They bandied about names of respected Los Angeles lawyers who might be willing to join their scheme. Someone suggested Robert Warren, a partner with the large and prestigious Los Angeles firm of Gibson, Dunn & Crutcher. Warren had a great deal of experience handling contentious, sometimes bitter family lawsuits over wills and estates.

"Would you have any problem if Warren was the guardian?" Bart Winokur asked the Security Pacific executives.

"No."

Encouraged, the Getty Oil lawyers—Copley, Winokur, and Wesley Nutten, a Los Angeles attorney recently retained to help devise a legal strategy that would unseat Gordon—concluded the meeting and walked over to Nutten's nearby office. Nutten knew Bob Warren, and he called him immediately.

"Bob, we've got a matter over here that I think is of some importance. We'd like to talk with you about it. Could you come over and meet with us?"

"I've got a tough schedule today," Warren answered.

"It's important."

"Well, if I did it right away, I could see you for a little while."

"Great. We'll be here."

Warren had never met Copley or Winokur, so Nutten introduced them when the Gibson, Dunn partner arrived. Winokur and Nutten did most of the talking; because of Warren's schedule, they had to move quickly. They explained the background of the Sarah Getty Trust and of the Getty family as best they could in the short time available, editorializing liberally about the quirks and character of various family members, particularly Gordon. They explained Getty Oil's urgent desire to have a corporate cotrustee appointed in order to put a halt to Gordon's activities. They told Warren about the meeting just concluded with high-level Security Pacific Bank executives. They said that Warren's name had come up during their discussions, and that he was acceptable to the bank.

"Would you be interested in acting as a guardian ad litem for one of Gordon's relatives if that could be arranged? Would you be willing to handle the lawsuit?" Warren was asked.

"Yes, I'm interested."

"We don't really have any time to waste," Nutten said. "This has got to be handled in a short time."

"I'd like to bring Ron Gother into the discussions," Warren answered. Gother was one of his partners.

"That's fine," Nutten said. "We'll get in touch with him and bring him up to date."

Nutten met that same afternoon with Gother and laid out the same pitch they had given to Warren. Gother indicated that he was interested, but he and Warren would have to review some of the files at their law firm. Gibson, Dunn did a lot of legal work for Security Pacific, as did most of the large downtown law firms in Los Angeles. There might be a conflict of interest involved. If Warren were to become a guardian ad litem on behalf of one of the Getty children, he might find himself opposed to Security Pacific in court, or he might have to argue about issues he had previously discussed with the bank while acting as its attorney. Gother also wanted to discuss the matter with Bank of America, to make sure there were no conflict problems that would jeopardize his firm's lucrative business representing that bank.

"Obviously, we'll give you time to make a decision about whether you want to serve and whether you can," Nutten told Gother. "But this isn't something that we want to drag on for a couple of years. The whole thing is imminent and we need to get your prompt attention."

Gother indicated that he would move as quickly as possible. A few days later, he called Nutten.

"Our thinking is that maybe it would be better to get a retired judge, or some such person, to be the actual guardian ad litem," he said. "Then Gibson, Dunn would represent the judge in court instead of actually having Warren serve as the guardian himself. That would make the whole thing look more prestigious, and it would free us from any situation where one of our lawyers would have to represent himself."

Nutten didn't think Gother's worries about a lawyer representing himself were justified, but he said that if finding a retired judge would make Gibson, Dunn more comfortable, that was fine with him. Arthur Marshall, a retired Los Angeles judge with considerable experience in probate law, was a name the Getty Oil lawyers had discussed before. Nutten would look into that, and he would begin drafting a lawsuit. He mentioned to Gother that it would be helpful if one of the Getty family members would agree to go into court to petition for Warren's appointment as guardian. So far, despite all the meetings and drafting and planning, nobody had actually asked any of the Gettys if they would be willing to sue their Uncle Gordon. Petersen and his Getty Oil lawyers were plotting on their own.

It wasn't until Thursday, June 9, that Ron Gother delivered Gibson, Dunn's bad news to Wesley Nutten and the Getty Oil executives.

Gother had called Nutten the day before and said, "There have been some new developments I think you'll be interested in. Can I meet with you tomorrow?" A time had been arranged and when Gother arrived, he was carrying a thick stack of files obtained from Security Pacific Bank.

"The new development is that Security Pacific is seriously reconsidering getting involved in this thing at all. They've hired our firm to produce an analysis of three different options as to what they should do next. One option would be to do nothing. A second option would be to go along with your plan and help file a petition requesting that Bank of America be appointed as a cotrustee with Gordon. A third option would be for Security Pacific to go to court and petition for its own appointment as cotrustee. If they did that, it would have to be on the condition that some of the trust provisions would be changed. We've already made some recommendations to Security about what provisions in the trust document should be altered."

Gother went on—his news was only going to get worse. "Now that Gibson, Dunn is working for Security Pacific, we can't act as guardian ad litem in a lawsuit. It would be a conflict."

Nutten asked why the firm had so dramatically changed its mind about their plan to sue Gordon.

"We had a meeting with Security Pacific," Gother answered. "The bank's executives are worried about the meetings they've had with Getty Oil, with Petersen and you and the rest of the lawyers. They're afraid that if this thing ends up in court, the fact that they met with you would be disclosed. They think that might be compromising and embarrassing."

Gother said that this concern applied not only to Security Pacific but to his own law firm.

"My senior partners are worried about the conspiracy aspects of this," Gother said.

He told Nutten that his firm and the bank were now working together to find a way to protect themselves and to make the "right decision." Gibson, Dunn had assigned a team of five lawyers to the problem and intended to recommend a course of action to the bank by the end of the month. Moreover, if Gibson, Dunn and Security did eventually decide to go into court, they now wanted to meet with Gordon beforehand to clear the air.

"If we do decide to go with reformation of the trust's provisions, I suggest we initiate a dialogue with Gordon," Gother said.

But a dialogue with Gordon Getty was impossible, Petersen and Winokur and the rest of them believed. If Gibson, Dunn was afraid to get its hands dirty, if it was willing to pass up the huge fees available from the trust, which for decades had been a kind of legal honey pot, then Getty Oil would just find another firm to do the job.

Five days after the meeting between Gother and Nutten, the Getty Oil lawyers arranged a telephone conference call with two senior partners at O'Melveny & Meyers, another large Los Angeles firm headquartered downtown. Again, Copley and Nutten explained the background of the trust and of the company's problems with Gordon since he became sole trustee. They said that they had met with James Isaacs, the attorney for two of the Georgettes, and that one of the Georgettes' children might be persuaded to petition for the appointment of a guardian ad litem in a suit against Gordon. The call lasted about an hour. Afterward, the Getty Oil lawyers sent over copies of the trust documents by messenger, and some correspondence between Gordon and Lansing Hays dating back to 1973, which concerned the appointment of successor trustees after J. Paul Getty's death. Two days later, on Thursday, June 16, the O'Melveny & Meyers partners called to say that they could not take on the case; the firm had advised Security Pacific some years back about whether or not it should accept a co-trusteeship. The partners felt they faced a conflict of interest if they were to become involved in a new lawsuit at Getty Oil's instigation.

Undaunted, Copley and Winokur telephoned Seth Hufstedler, a renowned Los Angeles criminal and civil trial attorney, and arranged a meeting for the following week, on Wednesday, the twenty-second, in Hufstedler's downtown office. Again, the Getty Oil lawyers brought along the trust documents and the correspondence between Gordon and Lansing Hays, and again, they presented their version

of the Getty family history and the company's recent problems with
Gordon Getty. Copley did most of the talking. He described the size
and form of the Sarah Getty Trust's assets, the value of its stock in
Getty Oil, and he explained the peculiar circumstances by which
Gordon had come to control the family fortune. He talked about
Lansing Hays, what kind of influence he had been on Gordon, and
about the consequences of Hays' death a year before. He recounted
George Getty's history at Getty Oil and said that it had always been
J. Paul's hope that George would run things after his death, but that
George had died unexpectedly, making it possible for Gordon to reconcile with his father. Finally, Copley ran through the list of Getty
family members who were in a position to file a lawsuit against Gordon, commenting as he named them on their relative likelihood to
do so, given their feelings about Gordon and the family's tortuous
history.

"Gordon has taken an active interest in the business," Copley
said. "He's asked for various kinds of studies of our executives and
of others. He's been interested in a royalty trust or some sort of limited partnership or some other means of getting more income for
the stockholders. But he's inconsistent and erratic about his positions
and we're uncertain from time to time what his positions are, even
though we discuss it with him."

Hufstedler listened closely. At last, Copley asked him, "Would
you be available or interested in serving as guardian ad litem should
one of the members of the family nominate you?" "I'll consider it,"
Hufstedler answered noncommittally. "I'll have to look at the documents and see if our firm has any conflicts of interest, and then I'll let
you know what I think."

Two days later, Hufstedler called Copley with the good news: he
was interested in pursuing the matter. They arranged another meeting for the following week.

"Everyone in this room should realize that he's going to have his
deposition taken," Hufstedler announced when they were reassem-
bled. "We're not going to be able to hide the fact that there have been
contacts with the company. Once a lawsuit is filed, Gordon is certain
to allege that something improper has gone on here."

The Getty Oil lawyers did not seem terribly concerned about that.
Their first objective was to get the lawsuit against Gordon rolling;
they'd worry about his hurt feelings once they had a means to control

him. At the meeting, Hufstedler emphasized that he was not going to contact any Getty family members himself. They would have to come to him. The morality Hufstedler later described drew a distinction between conspiracies undertaken by Getty Oil Company and those undertaken by himself. If the lawsuit was going to proceed, the Getty Oil executives would have to come up with the plaintiff. They reviewed the list of Getty offspring who might be willing to ask for Hufstedler's appointment.

"Maybe we should go over this afternoon and talk to Isaacs again," Copley said.

After all, this was a major new development: a well-known and respected Los Angeles attorney was now willing to serve as guardian ad litem in a challenge to Gordon. Also, the company now had drafted petitions and complaints and lawsuits they could show Isaacs. Perhaps that would convince him to recommend the scheme to his clients, Claire and Caroline.

When they finally met with Isaacs at his office, the Getty Oil lawyers were well prepared. They brought not only the proposed lawsuit drafts, but also a stack of oil analyst Kurt Wulff's reports, which detailed his contacts with Gordon. They went over the material and explained all that they had learned about Gordon's dealings with outsiders, including his recent, foiled flirtation with T. Boone Pickens, Jr.

"I'll take these with me when I meet with Caroline and Claire," Isaacs said. He gave the Getty Oil lawyers the impression that he was very interested in participating in their lawsuit. Isaacs indicated, however, that he was not due to see his clients at all until early August, and he suggested—without saying so directly—that the Georgettes were not presently in Los Angeles, that they were somewhere in northern California or the Pacific Northwest on vacation.

"If it's an emergency, I can go up and see them," Isaacs told Copley and Winokur. "But I'll be seeing them in the early part of August, in the normal course of things."

The Getty Oil lawyers had to be careful. They did not want to alienate Isaacs by pushing too hard. But they could not allow their problems to linger indefinitely, and Isaacs seemed unable or unwilling to follow through on their discussions. Isaacs said that he supported a lawsuit. He said he would recommend it to his clients. Why wouldn't he then *do* something about it?

"We can't tell you that there's any drastic emergency," one of the Getty Oil lawyers said. "But we would like to get Claire and Caroline's earliest indication as to whether they would be interested in pursuing the lawsuit." They tried their best to make it clear: no one's life was at stake, but this was a very urgent matter.

"Well, if Gordon makes any attempt to take over the company, I'd want to know about that," Isaacs said. "If Gordon did something like that, I would immediately recommend that my clients take some action."

"There's nothing we know about that would require anyone to jump on an airplane to go see his clients. But, then, we don't know about anything that Gordon does."

"If he tries to take over the company," Isaacs repeated, "I want to know about it."

What more could they do? They had laid the matter on Isaacs' desk, and it was now up to him to consult with the Georgettes. Hufstedler was ready. Bank of America was ready. Getty Oil Company was ready. Now all they needed was for someone in the Getty family to agree with them that Uncle Gordon should be sued.

It was a strange, even perverse situation. Later, just as the Gibson, Dunn & Crutcher lawyers had feared and as Seth Hufstedler himself had predicted, Getty Oil's executives and lawyers would have to explain the reasons for the "conspiracy" against Gordon secretly arranged in those plush downtown law offices that May and June of 1983. It was not as easy to explain away as perhaps some of them expected. They said later that they had no choice. They said that they were trying to protect all the public stockholders from Gordon Getty's wild caprice. And certainly, they believed as much. But the desperation of their effort, its secrecy, and the presumptions they made about the private affairs of the Getty family belied such protestations. *Why did you think it was any of your business?* Sid Petersen and Bart Winokur and Dave Copley were asked later. *Why did you try so hard to hide what you were doing from Gordon? Wasn't it because you knew that you were being deceitful and underhanded?* They tried to answer such questions. They said that Gordon had defined the morality of their predicament. Gordon said at the Bonaventure that he alone would decide what was ethical. Were they simply to surrender to that selfish, perverse ethic? Petersen, particularly, said that once he learned about what Gordon had been doing behind his back, about

the meetings with outsiders and the disclosures of company information, he no longer felt any ethical obligation to share Getty Oil's
private strategies with Gordon.

Then, too, there was a sense of desperate frustration. It was difficult to describe accurately the feeling that pervaded among the triumvirate at Getty Oil headquarters during those months—the sense
of pressure and unraveling. It was one thing to feel that a twenty-five-
year career was ending for reasons beyond one's control: the power
of Wall Street, the value gap in the oil industry, the greed of a corporate raider. But it was another thing to feel that everything one
cherished—career, power, position, community, the lifelong realization of work and ambition—was slipping away because of events that
were not meant to be, events that had been anticipated and guarded
against years before.

Perhaps it was presumptuous, perhaps it was even a little disingenuous, but Sidney Petersen did believe that he knew what the
old man had wanted. J. Paul Getty's life had been dedicated to the
growth and control of Getty Oil Company. He had died some seven
years earlier believing that his legacy would be preserved. And now
his son, Gordon, was destroying it all—Gordon was a nice man, a
good man, yes, they all knew that, but they also knew that he was not
qualified to control a giant oil company, and with it the destinies of
its executives, shareholders, and employees. By the summer of 1983,
there was a palpable aggravation bubbling in Petersen's gullet. When
he hinted about his problems to people who knew the company and
the family, he always received the same knowing, sympathetic look.
"Oh, yes, I know about Gordon. He's an interesting man." That was
the way one said it. Interesting. Or "unpredictable," that was another
word people used. This was not a mom-and-pop business, it was a
giant international corporation. Was it so much to ask that order be
restored to Sid Petersen's universe, to the stockholders and workers
and executives at Getty Oil Company? Was it so much to ask that
Gordon Getty be required by some judge to return to the serene
riches of his Broadway mansion, away from matters of business and
finance, back to the music and composing he so clearly enjoyed?

Those who sympathized with Gordon Getty and despised
Petersen for the deceits he practiced that spring said that Gordon
was only trying to claim his rightful place in the family company. He
had been ridiculed by his father, humiliated, told he was a failure in

business, and now he was trying to prove himself. Morally, they said, he had that right. Legally, through his sole control of the family trust, he had that power. What right did Sid Petersen have to stop him?

When it was all over, when there was time for the actors to sort out their motivations and justify their actions, Gordon himself put it this way: "Of course, it was a challenge for me to see if I could step into my father's shoes. Obviously, I could no more be as good a businessman as he was, or as good an oilman as he was, than he could write music like I do. Still, I felt that I could be a pretty good trustee. Now, I didn't think I had a bit of his talent to run Getty Oil as a chief executive. I thought that I could run it as a controlling stockholder. You say, what about ambitions, the desire to satisfy and please your father even after he's gone—sure, I think it's a good, healthy thing for any individual to please his parents and to please himself and to be a success and to meet challenges. That kind of ambition is a darned good thing. I think I felt some of it."

And so that summer they swam ahead, Petersen and Gordon, buoyant on a sea of moral certitude. For all the billions of dollars at stake, the barrels of oil, the copper mines and farms and refineries, their causes seemed at times oddly immaterial.

PART TWO

IN PLAY

ON THE FENCE

As heat and haze settled viscidly over Los Angeles that first week in July 1983, steeping the city in a kind of opaque summer lethargy, so, too, did the layers of intrigue surrounding Getty Oil Company thicken and coagulate.

The plots and counterplots now afoot were each designed to clear away the company's problems, but taken together they seemed only to compound its predicament. There were so many tangled strands now: the secret effort by Petersen, Winokur, and Copley to instigate a family lawsuit against Gordon; the negotiations with Pickens; lingering concerns about the Cullens and other corporate raiders; the million-dollar restructuring study undertaken by Goldman, Sachs, now nearing completion; and the continued thinking and tinkering by Gordon at his Broadway mansion, from where new ideas and plans seemed to issue weekly.

For more than a year, the shifting schemes had been largely confined to small, closely guarded circles at Getty Oil headquarters and around the Broadway mansion. The company's board of directors, for example, knew virtually nothing about Petersen's dealings with Gordon and the Lasky firm; the board had not been consulted even when Petersen authorized the huge payment to Goldman, Sachs for the stock price study. Neither had the board been fully informed about the overtures by Pickens and the contacts by Gordon with other potential corporate raiders. For his part, Gordon continued to act in similar isolation as sole trustee, receiving phone calls and reviewing documents in his basement study, never consulting with the family beneficiaries about his plans, and often relying on the Lasky firm for only the narrowest legal advice.

A widening of the intrigue to include at least the Getty Oil board was now inevitable. The company's quarterly directors meeting was scheduled for Friday, July 8, and Petersen knew he could no longer postpone an explanation. That he had waited so long was questionable; to continue to make decisions solely through his cabal with Winokur and Copley was no longer viable. Petersen did not intend to tell the board everything—the plot to instigate a family lawsuit through attorney Seth Hufstedler would remain secret, for example. So, too, would the full extent of management's battles with Gordon. But the dealings with Pickens and Goldman, Sachs would have to be disclosed to the board. The Goldman corporate analysts had finished their five months of work and were ready to present the confidential "black books," as they were called, which contained analytical details and conclusions. Petersen would have to tell the directors why the study had been commissioned in the first place. He did not intend to say that Goldman had been hired to placate Gordon; that would make Petersen look foolish, since the investment banking firm had cost so much to hire. He still had an open mind about the study, he would tell the board. With all the takeovers and restructurings now raging in the oil industry, and with the company's stock price so depressed, it was sensible for Getty Oil to see whether the ideas advocated by critics such as Pickens and Kurt Wulff made any sense, and also to examine steps that might defend the company against a takeover attempt. That, at least, was what the board would hear at their meeting early in July.

It was curious that Petersen had waited so long to bring the board into his confidence, and that even when he did so, it was with less than total forthrightness. To be sure, it was the prerogative of a chief executive to run his company as he saw fit; if the board didn't like Petersen's methods, it could discharge him. Still, the board of directors was the base of Sid Petersen's power at Getty Oil. It was the board that had boldly chosen him, a finance man, over the traditional oil patch operating man, Robert Miller, for the chairmanship. It was the board that had welcomed the era of a "new" Getty Oil under Petersen, an era of diversification and leadership in the oil industry and the Los Angeles community. The directors, too, knew Gordon Getty. They had served with him for years. And yet, as Petersen plotted against his company's largest stockholder, he kept his schemes and strategies mainly to himself.

One problem was that while the board supported Petersen, the Getty Oil chairman felt ambivalent about his directors. He liked them individually. He thought they were good, smart men. But overall, he was uncomfortable with the kind of board he had inherited. J. Paul Getty and the oilmen who ran the company for him in Los Angeles had always appointed certain kinds of directors—"insiders," was the way they were described. There was Chauncey Medberry III, the retired chairman of Bank of America, who had been appointed in 1971 at the suggestion of George Getty. Medberry's bank was, of course, a major supplier of credit and other services to Getty Oil. Similarly, a representative of Security Pacific Bank, Fritz Larkin, had been on the board for many years. There had been a seat reserved for the late Lansing Hays, the company lawyer; one for Willard Boothby, managing director of Blyth Eastman, Getty Oil's longtime investment banker; and one for Harold Stuart, who owned a large number of Getty Oil shares by virtue of his marriage into the Skelly family, whose Tulsa-based oil company was acquired by J. Paul Getty during the 1930s. In addition, there was Harold Berg, the former Getty Oil chairman, Norman Topping, an old friend of J. Paul Getty's, Gordon, Petersen, and Miller. All of these directors had some financial connection with Getty Oil. They were not objective outsiders, corporate executives who would speak without encumbrance for the public shareholders. They were company men.

Petersen wanted to change the board—"professionalize" it, as he would say—by appointing chief executives from large corporations that had no connection with Getty Oil. Such "outsiders" were common on the boards of most large, publicly owned American corporations. With its heavily "inside" board, Getty Oil was lagging behind the times. That was why in the previous September Petersen had recruited John Teets, the chief executive of the Phoenix-based Greyhound Corporation. Besides Teets, Petersen had also appointed Henry Wendt, chairman and chief executive of the giant SmithKline Beckman Corporation, the Philadelphia-based pharmaceutical conglomerate; and Dr. Clayburn La Force, dean of the UCLA Graduate School of Management. Teets and Wendt, particularly, were forceful, articulate, independent executives who had no personal interest in the fate of Getty Oil Company, or even in the fate of Sid Petersen, whom they had not known before their recruitment. On the one hand, Teets and Wendt supported the modernization of Getty Oil being conducted by Petersen. After all, they were part of the plan. On the other hand, the two executives had said adamantly that they were loyal to the public shareholders, not to Petersen's career or to some sentimental view of Getty Oil's past. For Petersen, then, the Getty Oil board was partly a mystery of his own making. It was hard to predict what someone like Henry Wendt or John Teets would think of the secret dealings with Gordon Getty. It was hard even to be sure that they shared Petersen's view of Gordon and the trust. For that and other reasons, Petersen had closely confined knowledge about the extent of his plotting against Gordon.

The turning point, as it happened, came that sunny, smoggy Friday, July 8, when the directors assembled in the company board room on the executive floor of the Getty Oil headquarters building in central Los Angeles. There was a feeling on all sides, as the meeting began, that this would be a pivotal event.

For weeks, the groundwork had been laid by both Petersen and Tim Cohler, Gordon's lawyer. Ever since February, Cohler had been awaiting the Goldman, Sachs study. He knew nothing about the plot to foment a family lawsuit challenging Gordon's control of the trust. To him, the six months since the Bonaventure confrontation had been a kind of intermission. There had been meetings with Pickens and Wulff, yes, but Gordon had excluded his attorneys from those discussions. Besides, Gordon himself was eagerly awaiting Goldman's verdict, which would be delivered at the July directors meeting. If the firm supported his ideas about royalty trusts, limited partnerships, or stock buy-backs, then the study might lead to a major Getty Oil restructuring involving Gordon and the trust. In the weeks before the July board meeting, Cohler had met with the Goldman, Sachs corporate analysts to review the progress of their work and to be sure the firm had fulfilled its promise to conduct an objective study.

Just a few days before the Friday directors meeting in Los Angeles, however, Gordon had thrown his attorney a curve ball.

Gordon was a member of the J. Paul Getty Museum board of trustees, which was chaired by Harold Berg, Petersen's predecessor as Getty Oil chief executive. The museum owned 12 percent of Getty Oil's stock. Its president was Harold Williams, a former corporate executive, dean of the UCLA Graduate School of Management (he was replaced by Clayburn La Force, the Getty Oil director), and chairman of the Securities and Exchange Commission under President Jimmy Carter. Sometime in late June, Gordon had traveled to Malibu to attend a museum trustees meeting, and there he had talked casually with Williams about the business of Getty Oil, in which Williams had an intense interest because of the 9 million shares he controlled.

The way Gordon had always figured it, the museum would sell its stock in any restructuring or takeover plan he devised. There was no reason for an art museum to own so much stock in an oil company, Gordon thought. The J. Paul Getty Museum owned its 9 million shares only by the fluke of its patron's legacy, and it would probably be wise to diversify the wealth in order to generate income for art acquisitions. Besides, there was a tax law that applied to the museum which seemed to require that the institution sell its stock by 1988 or thereabouts. Naturally, then, Gordon had assumed that "the museum was a seller," as he always put it.

That June evening at the museum offices, however, Williams had hinted in casual conversation that he might like to "stay in" if some deal could be arranged to raise the price of Getty Oil stock or wrest control of the company from Petersen. Gordon was surprised and excited. Between the trust and the museum's holdings, Gordon and Williams controlled 52 percent of Getty Oil; they could snap their fingers and take control if they wished. It was the same 52 percent that had been owned by J. Paul Getty while he was alive. Gordon's mind began to reel with the possibilities.

Just a few days before the July directors meeting, then, Gordon called Cohler and told him about his conversation with Harold Williams. Gordon said he might now like to pursue a "leveraged buyout" of the entire Getty Oil Company in cooperation with Williams. Actually, the deal Gordon had in mind was known as a "leveraged buyout with a fence." In structure, it was a fairly simple transaction. Gordon and Williams would do nothing with their stock. Using 48 percent of Getty Oil's assets as a kind of collateral, they would borrow enough money to buy the 48 percent of the company's stock owned by the public. Then Gordon and Williams would own the entire company. Williams would become chief executive, perhaps; Gordon would be named chairman; and Petersen probably would be fired. The Sarah Getty Trust and the J. Paul Getty Museum would share the company's profits—and there would be no more public stockholders to worry about.

It was a neat trick. Leveraged buy-outs had become that year a popular device by which corporate "insiders" such as executives or directors could obtain ownership of their companies without putting up any cash. It worked like this: since the analysts said Getty Oil was worth as much as $240 a share, and since the stock was selling for about $60, Gordon thought that he and Williams could buy out the public stockholders for some premium above the market price—$80 or $90 a share, maybe—and profit enormously from their bargain. What distinguished Gordon's plan from the most common leveraged buy-outs was that he wanted to erect a "fence" around his and Williams' stock and around 52 percent of Getty Oil's assets. In other words, not only would Gordon not ante up a dime of his or the trust's or the museum's wealth, he would protect 52 percent of the assets, the oil, "their" oil, from the perils of debt. For a man so often derided for lacking business sense, it was a sophisticated, even savvy idea. Gordon told Cohler that he wanted to explore the notion further with Harold Williams.

That instruction, delivered on Tuesday evening, July 5, in San Francisco, put Cohler in something of a bind. On Friday, the directors would consider Goldman, Sachs' restructuring study, which had been ordered in the first place at Gordon's insistence. Now Gordon was off in a different direction; he had outrun his own study. It was important, then, that the directors take no votes about Goldman's recommendations at the Friday board meeting. Cohler wanted all the restructuring plans left open. That way, he and Gordon would have time to discuss a leveraged buy-out—or LBO, as it was called—with Williams.

Cohler telephoned Petersen in Los Angeles and asked if he would object to Harold Williams' attending a briefing that Goldman, Sachs was going to provide Gordon on Thursday, the day before the board meeting, in Los Angeles. The purpose of the briefing was to explain the contents of the black books before they were shown to all the directors.

Petersen regarded Harold Williams with acute suspicion. They served together on the board of directors of the Los Angeles

Philharmonic Association, but the museum president was an enigma to Petersen. Williams clearly possessed the credentials to run Getty Oil as its chief executive—he had the credentials Gordon lacked. Ever since he had been named museum president in 1981, Petersen had wondered whether Williams coveted the title of Getty Oil chief executive, his title. He knew, of course, that if Williams and Gordon became fast allies in a takeover bid, the fight would be over in an instant, since together they controlled 52 percent of the company. Petersen had never been able to read Williams. The museum president seemed to have had a distinguished career, but he had moved around, from corporate life to academia to government and now to an art institution. As SEC chairman, Williams had been moderately active, but he was viewed by his commission staff just as he was seen by Petersen—as a mystery. For example, he had been known at the commission for burying his most important announcements deep in the texts of his speeches. In person, there was a settled, relaxed manner about him. He was a slumped, soft-spoken man with a full head of silver hair and thick metal-framed glasses. In conversation, he sometimes spoke so quietly as to be inaudible. The words drifted from his small, narrow mouth carrying no weight or urgency. One Getty Oil executive said that Williams seemed like an aging, somewhat overweight, highly elusive elf.

"I met with Harold last week," Petersen told Cohler on the telephone when the lawyer asked if Williams, who was aware that Goldman had been retained, could attend Gordon's Thursday briefing. "I got the impression that Harold really is not up to speed as to what Goldman, Sachs has been doing, what the analyses are, what kinds of studies are being undertaken."

Cohler said that he had no reason to doubt Petersen about that. Still, the chairman's assessment seemed to support the idea that Williams should attend the Goldman briefing.

"Greg Robertson—the Goldman partner in charge of the studies—is concerned that Gordon doesn't really have a lot of confidence in what Goldman is doing," Petersen answered. "Robertson wants some time on Thursday where he can just be alone with Gordon, just to get his confidence up. He doesn't want a big meeting with management people or outsiders present as well."

"Well, I would like to give Harold the Goldman black books, the ones they finished in June," Cohler said. "Is there a problem with that?"

"That's fine, if it will help to get Harold up to speed. But I don't want you to give him anything before the directors have seen Goldman's presentations at the board meeting on Friday."

"No problem," Cohler answered. "Tom Woodhouse and I will go see Harold at the museum offices at the same time you're having your board meeting. So there won't be any problem of diplomacy with Harold getting the books before the directors do."

"That's great," Petersen said.*

Cohler also telephoned Dave Copley to get assurances that there would be no votes taken at the Friday board meeting. The plan was for Cohler and Woodhouse to meet with Williams at the museum's offices in Century City while Gordon attended the board meeting at Getty Oil headquarters across town. Then, if all went well, they would arrange a face-to-face meeting between Gordon and Williams and they would inform Petersen and Copley about Gordon's plans for an LBO takeover.

Cohler's strategy succeeded. Gordon's briefing on Thursday went well, although there was a moment of discomfort when Gordon discovered that Goldman, Sachs had included a hypothetical case study in its black books that analyzed the effects of various deals on a "zero basis" shareholder, that is, one who had acquired his stock in Getty Oil back in the 1930s, when it was worth very little. To Gordon, this seemed a thinly disguised analysis of the Sarah Getty Trust's position. He said that he had explicitly requested that no special attention be paid to his family fortune—this was supposed to be a study for all shareholders. Gordon announced forcefully at the briefing that he wanted these case studies removed before the black books were presented to the Getty Oil directors. The outburst seemed to unnerve Greg Robertson, the Goldman vice-president making the presentation, and it certainly did not contribute to Robertson's goal of building Gordon's confidence in his firm's work. But no one in the room believed that

---

*   Tim Cohler said in an interview three years later that his recollection of this conversation was "very clear and strong." In the course of a lawsuit, he produced contemporaneous, handwritten notes which support his recollection. Sid Petersen, however, said in an interview that he does not recall the conversation described by Cohler at all. The conversation may have occurred, Petersen said, but he does not remember it. Petersen said that he was suspicious of Williams and thus it was unlikely he would have allowed the confidential Goldman studies to be disclosed to the museum president.

Robertson personally was at fault, so the briefing concluded amicably. Meanwhile, Cohler and Woodhouse flew down to Los Angeles from San Francisco carrying a set of black books for Harold Williams.

Friday morning, as Gordon drove from his hotel to Getty Oil headquarters for the board meeting, Cohler and Woodhouse arrived at the museum offices on the twenty-third floor of the prominent Century Park East Tower. They would spend the day reviewing with Williams the confidential details of Getty Oil's finances and discussing Gordon's idea for an LBO takeover "with a fence." Moses Lasky was back in San Francisco; Gordon would be on his own at the directors meeting across town.

As they filed into the board room on the eighteenth floor of Getty Oil headquarters that Friday morning, the directors were confronted by indelible images from the company's long history. On the walls were pictures of the Gettys who had served on the board over the years: George Getty I, J. Paul, George Getty II, and finally, the only survivor among them, Gordon. The windowless interior room was dominated by a long, winged conference table, which was surrounded by deep, studded-leather chairs. At the center of the table, where its parallel wings converged, was a seat sometimes called the "cockpit," from where Sid Petersen, the chairman, always presided. This morning, Petersen knew, he would have to pilot his board as never before.

"As I indicated in my letter of June 15, we have retained some consultants to study strategic planning issues for the company," Petersen began after some routine, preliminary business was dispensed with. "The purpose of the study was to identify ways the company might enhance shareholder wealth. Ever since 1979, when Boone Pickens issued the first royalty trust in the oil industry, I have followed the development of royalty trusts both as a financing tool and as a means of distributing cash to shareholders. Similarly, I have also followed the development of limited partnerships as a way to raise money and reward stockholders."

Petersen paused. He was going to lay out some version of the past year's events to his directors now, but he had to be very careful. Gordon was sitting right there at the table. Petersen did not want to provoke him.

"Late in September, 1982," he said, "Gordon Getty requested

that the company undertake additional studies about the desirability of using a royalty trust for the purpose of enhancing shareholder wealth. Those studies were undertaken, and in addition, we performed a series of in-house analyses on limited partnerships. All of these studies were furnished to and reviewed by Mr. Getty and his lawyers. The in-house studies were essentially completed by year-end. In January, however, Gordon Getty said that he felt it was desirable that the company's studies be reviewed by an independent investment banking firm, and that the firm give consideration to the liquidation of Getty Oil Company—in whole or in part—into limited partnerships. Gordon said that he was willing to undertake such a study, and to retain the investment banker, on behalf of the trust.

"In my judgment, having Gordon undertake the study independently from the company and its management might well be disruptive. Also, that procedure did not readily adapt itself to permitting Getty Oil to furnish the investment banker the confidential and proprietary information required to perform the studies. Because of that, I agreed to have the studies desired by Mr. Getty performed at the request and expense of the company."

Then Petersen mentioned the price tag—the studies had cost in excess of $1 million.

He explained that Goldman, Sachs had been retained in February by mutual agreement with Gordon, and that the firm had been chosen by virtue both of its reputation and the fact that it had never worked for Getty Oil before. The studies had proceeded as planned, Petersen said, and Goldman had examined both the royalty trusts and partnerships identified by Gordon as well as other restructuring ideas suggested by Getty Oil management and the investment firm itself. Now Goldman was ready to make its presentation to the board, Petersen said.

The chairman asked someone to call the advisors into the board room. Greg Robertson, Robert Hurst, and Peter Barker of Goldman, Sachs stepped inside, as did Bart Winokur and Steadman Garber, who had worked closely with Goldman in recent weeks on Petersen's behalf. Hurst, a young, lean, smartly dressed man who looked very much the part of the modern Wall Street banker, distributed the black books and prepared to make an introduction.

"You'll notice," he said as the directors began to open their books, "the items referred to in the presentation outline as '9.C' and '10.C' are not in the books you have been supplied. This was done at Mr. Gordon Getty's request."

Petersen intervened. "The removal of those pages is subject to reconsideration." It was not clear whose reconsideration—his or Gordon's.

"Why were they taken out?" asked John Teets, the Greyhound chairman. Teets was a blunt, plain-spoken man. As he listened to Petersen's cautious, winding speech moments before, he had wondered what the hell was going on at Getty Oil Company.

"The sheets that were taken out referred to the Sarah Getty Trust," Gordon answered. "I wanted the trust to be considered just as any other shareholder."

As Hurst began his presentation, he suggested that this had been part of Goldman's problem all along. "The objective of our assignment was easy to state but hard to define in many respects," he said carefully. "The 'enhancement of shareholder wealth' depends on the position of each shareholder—such as the shareholder's objectives, his price basis in the stock, and the tax consequences of any specific course of action to that shareholder. We approached the assignment with the idea that there should be an affirmative, long-term impact in any restructuring, not a one-shot impact."

Hurst began to review the thick black books in detail. There were a number of things that Goldman had specifically not studied, he quickly pointed out, such as the size of the company's value gap and the impact of any restructurings on company employees or on the cities and communities where Getty Oil was a major employer. The firm had also been forced to make a number of assumptions, most importantly about the future world price of oil and gas. Accepting these caveats, however, Hurst went on, Goldman had completed a thorough evaluation of all the alternatives suggested by Gordon and Petersen.

"Some of the alternatives you see outlined could present serious structural problems if you tried to actually implement them," Hurst said. "Sometimes an alternative which might appear attractive in the abstract is actually impractical. For example, you could not turn all of Getty Oil into a six-billion-dollar limited partnership—a partnership so large could not be absorbed by the market, even if it was possible to assemble it properly. At the present time, the total of all royalty trust and limited partnership interests available on the market is estimated to be something less than two and a half billion dollars. You would oversaturate the market." Hurst's point was clear: Goldman believed there were sharp limits to the ideas advocated by Kurt Wulff and Boone Pickens for a company the size of Getty Oil. There was some question as to whether Gordon had ever considered these elemental practical problems.

"Others of the alternatives would leave the company with serious credit problems," Hurst went on. "Getty Oil's stock price is quite volatile—it's picked up thirty percent in value since Goldman began its work.

"Of course," Hurst added, pointing out what Sid Petersen knew all too well, "there have been some analysts commenting for some months on the possibilities of the company creating a royalty trust or a limited partnership, and also on the possible takeover of the company. There could be a touch of 'merger premium' in the current price of the stock."

That was one way to put it. There was another way: Gordon's meanderings on Wall Street had caused the value of his family fortune to rise by nearly one-third, largely due to speculative trading in Getty Oil's stock.

For hours, the board room presentation dragged on. Hurst and Greg Robertson reviewed the technical details of their various analyses, answered questions, explained their methods, and otherwise attempted to justify the fees their firm commanded. They were eloquent, articulate, intelligent; the success of their work depended on an ability to personally impress the directors of large corporations.

Finally, Hurst offered his summary and conclusions.

"From a financial perspective, on a longer-term basis, a stock buy-back program appears to create more enhanced value for shareholders than any of the other alternatives we looked at.

"If you consider the impact on Getty Oil itself, a buy-back program is the least onerous alternative. It gives each shareholder the maximum flexibility to make individual investment decisions. It's also quite straightforward and simple to execute, and it permits the board to determine and redetermine from time to time the number of shares to be brought back—in light of market conditions or other factors. If you pursued a buy-back program, you could still consider some of the other alternatives—the royalty trust, limited partnership, and so on—at some later date."

That was it. A stock buy-back plan, where Getty Oil would repurchase its own shares in the market, thus raising the value of all the remaining shares, including those controlled by Gordon. It was, of course, exactly what the company's directors had authorized way back in April 1982, before Lansing's death, before Gordon's insistence on new studies had forced Petersen to suspend the program.

As Chauncey Medberry now put it angrily, speaking directly to Gordon across the table, "You mean, we spent one million dollars to find out that something we decided more than a year ago was right?"

Petersen was in a precarious position. There was an opening here, a chance to alert the board to the full extent and nature of his problems with Gordon. But he could not take the lead; the directors would have to draw their own conclusions about what Gordon had done. Petersen knew, too, that he could take no votes today; that had been agreed to beforehand with Cohler. So he suggested that if there was a consensus among the directors that a buy-back program should be reinitiated, then he would order an internal Getty Oil management study to determine what the most beneficial program would be. For one thing, Petersen knew, any buy-back would have to stop short of raising Gordon's stock holdings to a majority percentage. Gordon now had 40 percent; if the company repurchased and retired more than 10 percent of its outstanding stock, Gordon would suddenly own 51 percent. He would instantly have control.

But the directors were not thinking so far ahead. This was their first chance to speak with Gordon about his actions during the last six months. Most of them knew about the Kurt Wulff reports. A few had heard in more detail about the tension between Gordon and Petersen. The directors thought, nearly to a man, that so far as they could tell, this whole charade with Goldman, Sachs had been an appalling waste of time and money. Some of them were upset at Petersen, who had gone along with it, but they were even more angry at Gordon, who clearly had insisted that Goldman be retained.

Teets, the newcomer, took the lead, grilling Gordon about what Hurst had said. The board could not authorize any buy-back program until Gordon agreed that all of the studies about royalty trusts and limited partnerships and other financing tricks were finished, done, completed, *finito*.

"Gordon, there can be no more," Teets insisted. "Do you agree?"

But Gordon was in a difficult position. He knew, as he listened to Teets, that his lawyers were across town meeting with Harold Williams, discussing a possible LBO takeover of Getty Oil. But he did not know yet whether Williams favored the deal or not. He could hardly disclose his plans openly to the board before he knew what Williams thought. Besides, Gordon was in fact still tinkering, still thinking that July afternoon. He relied on his instincts, and his intuitive feeling was that not enough had yet been done to explore a restructuring or an LBO takeover.

"I think that additional alternatives should be considered," he told Teets.

The Greyhound chairman continued to press. "Gordon, what is it you *want*? What are your goals? Tell us, so we can understand what you're doing."

Gordon paused, and then answered philosophically. "What I really want to do is find the optimum way to optimize values."

Teets leaned on the board table. "Gordon, you may know what you just said, but nobody else in this room does."

Other directors began to join in, men such as Harold Stuart, who had sat on the board with Gordon for more than six years. Their comments were addressed mainly to Gordon, but the message was aimed at Sid Petersen as well. There was no screaming or profanity; that was Lansing Hays' style, now behind them. But the directors said unequivocally, and in firm tones, that this studying and tinkering had to end. Immediately. The studies were too expensive, they said, they were unnecessarily disruptive, and they prevented management from carrying out sensible programs such as the stock buyback or a restructuring of Getty Oil's debt. If Gordon had ideas for any other alternatives, the board would consider them if and when Gordon was prepared to make a full presentation. Gordon said little in response.

Capitalizing on the board's disgruntlement, Petersen shifted the topic to Gordon's dealings with Boone Pickens and to the meeting Petersen had held with Pickens at the Century Plaza Hotel. Calmly, without explicitly criticizing Gordon, the Getty Oil chairman described the sequence of Pickens' proposals—first to Gordon, then to management—and the details of his proposed "reverse triangular merger." Quickly and directly, Petersen told the board that he had personally decided that "no consideration should be given" to the deal, and that he had told Pickens as much. Casting a few sidelong glances at Gordon, the directors told Petersen they supported his position.

With that, the meeting adjourned. The directors gathered their things, stood to chat casually, and began to drift into the hallway on the executive floor. Gordon approached Petersen and asked if they could speak privately in Petersen's office.

When the door was closed, Gordon said: "I have a list of three things that I am interested now in studying. The first priority is a possible leveraged buy-out—with a fence—of the entire Getty Oil Company. This would be done in conjunction with the museum— we would be partners, in control of fifty-two percent of the stock. I would like Goldman, Sachs to undertake a study of whether this would be feasible."

Gordon launched into an enthusiastic speech on the potential attractions of an LBO. He displayed no hostility or defensiveness about what had just passed in the board room. He was the same Gordon, the idea man—his long, thin hands gestured in emphasis, his eyebrows flexed up and down, his brow furrowed in professorial seriousness. He said that if a leveraged buy-out didn't work, then he wanted to dissolve the company into a partnership. If that didn't work, he said, his final alternative was a simple liquidation of Getty Oil Company.

Petersen did not argue. It was clear that Gordon's sudden alliance with the museum was more than just another of his vague, casual suggestions. An LBO was really a takeover. Gordon said later that he had not firmly decided that July afternoon whether Sid Petersen would stay or go if and when he controlled all of Getty Oil Company, but Petersen himself believed that he had no real future in a company run by Gordon. As he listened to Gordon, he was in a mild state of shock. He had heard of leveraged buy-outs before, but frankly, he said later, he didn't know what the hell a fence was.

His ignorance lasted only briefly, but the irony of that moment in his office lingered for years. Sid Petersen, the finance man, the chief executive who had risen to the top because of his savvy with numbers and budgets and financial strategy, was about to lose his $6 billion oil company in a takeover deal he didn't even understand.

10

GOLDEN HANDCUFFS

When they later tried to describe the shift in mood at Getty Oil headquarters in the days following the July 8 board meeting, the lawyers, executives, and bankers involved said things like "We moved into deal mode" or "Now we knew the game was afoot." In some ways, it *was* a game—a deadly serious, very expensive one. At times, though, it seemed as if there were two games going on at once, and two categories of players. One category included Sidney Petersen, Gordon Getty, Dave Copley, and the other high-ranking Getty Oil career men who were involved in the strategies and intrigue that summer. For them, the game was Life. It was their careers, or their money, or their families at stake. Whether they won or lost, they were never going to play again. Surrounding these central actors, however, was a rather different group of players: the advisors. For them, the battle for control of Getty Oil was more like playing Monopoly with someone else's money. Yes, they were under personal stress themselves, and yes, they felt a genuine, empathetic loyalty to their clients, but theirs was a fundamentally different situation. If Bart Winokur, for example, lost Sid Petersen and Getty Oil as clients because of a takeover, it might set him down a notch at Dechert Price & Rhoads, but it would hardly change his life. There were other clients, other deals for him. Indeed, his career might acquire a certain panache for having brushed against so large a corporate happening, even if he ended on the losing side.

He would then have sailed the big ocean and seen the big whale, even if his ship and captain were lost along the way.

It was in July that the advisors, the Monopoly players, began to dictate the flow of the action. It really started that moment in Sid Petersen's office when Gordon mentioned the fence. What was a fence? Petersen had wondered. The Goldman, Sachs investment bankers would know; they built fences all the time. They had to be mobilized now; they had to explain what Gordon might do. More fundamentally, the idea of a leveraged buy-out shattered the fragile facade of unity at Getty Oil. It was no longer plausible to pretend that Sid Petersen and Gordon Getty had the same basic long-term interests at the company. In an LBO, with or without a fence, Gordon would buy the 40 million shares of Getty Oil stock owned by the public. It was Petersen's responsibility, as a matter of both law and principle, to protect the interests of his shareholders. For the first time, he and Gordon were indisputably on opposite sides.

Also for the first time, a potential takeover of the company was imminent. While the board met that Friday at Getty Oil headquarters, Cohler and Woodhouse had spent several hours talking with the museum's Harold Williams about a joint bid with Gordon for ownership and control.

"This is not a 13D group," Cohler had joked at the start of that meeting in Century City, referring to the SEC rule which required anyone who owned 5 percent of a company's stock and was launching a takeover to disclose publicly his intentions toward the company. They had laughed loudly at that remark because Williams, the former SEC chairman, presumably knew that they each had to be careful about what they said and how they said it. Otherwise, they could be accused of misleading Getty Oil's public shareowners.

"Gordon told us that on the basis of a conversation he had with you last month, he thought the museum might not necessarily want to sell its shares in any possible deal or restructuring," Cohler told Williams. "If Gordon was right, if you might be willing to consider staying in during a deal, then it probably would make sense for you and Gordon to get together and talk."

Cohler mentioned the LBO with a fence and Williams responded favorably. It was definitely an idea that should be considered and investigated, Williams said, and he complimented Gordon's creativity. Williams might be a threatening enigma to Sid Petersen, but to Gordon and his lawyers there was no mystery about him. He might be soft-spoken, almost sleepy, but he was clearly possessed of unusually sharp intelligence. After all, he had graduated Phi Beta Kappa from college at age eighteen and completed Harvard Law School by twenty-one. He was also independently wealthy; before he was forty, Williams had been named chairman of the $2 billion Norton Simon conglomerate, and he had made a fortune in the job. During his tenure at the SEC, he lived in a $750,000 home in fashionable Georgetown amid opulence unusual for a Washington official. He was a man, then, who shared a certain wealth and experience, as well as a fondness for fine art and classical music, with Gordon Getty. He might be just the partner Gordon needed. Like Petersen, Williams was qualified to manage Getty Oil day-to-day, but unlike Petersen, he seemed to have no qualms about working closely with Gordon.

At the conclusion of their Friday session, Cohler and Woodhouse arranged a meeting for the next morning between Williams and Gordon. They met in Gordon's room at the Beverly Wilshire Hotel for several hours. Gordon told Williams that if they did agree to make a bid for Getty Oil together, he didn't care how the titles were dispensed once they gained control. Gordon made it clear that he thought Williams had the necessary experience to run the company if he wished, but that Williams should also feel free to bring in some new outsider to be chief executive. In sharp contrast to Gordon's dealings with Sid Petersen, the mood that Saturday morning was relaxed, easy, almost brotherly. There were still some very important questions to be answered—whether the fence was economically feasible, whether the money could be borrowed, how their legal responsibilities as museum trustees came into play if they joined forces—but the feeling at the end of the meeting was that they should definitely go forward. The first step, they both agreed, was to have Goldman, Sachs perform a detailed study of their LBO proposal to determine if it was economically viable—that is, whether 48 percent of Getty Oil's assets could be used to finance the purchase of 48 percent of the company's stock. Petersen had not objected to such a study during his short encounter with Gordon after the Friday board meeting. Cohler said he would talk to Winokur and Copley, too, and make certain that Goldman understood precisely what it was that Gordon wanted the firm to study.

"I think the board of directors might be of the view that Goldman has made enough studies," Winokur objected when Cohler spoke with him.

"Well, that's because they didn't know anything about this. Look, it's up to Sid to decide what he wants to do with it," Cohler said. The implication was clear: the company could continue to cooperate with Gordon, or it could force him to take action on his own.

"Well, we'll talk to Sid," Winokur answered.

When he did, Winokur found Petersen disheartened. The chairman had thought at the board meeting that the studies were finally behind him. Now there was yet another. Moreover, it seemed to him—and this was a depressing realization—that Gordon now had no doubt in his own mind that Petersen would do whatever he was told. That perception had to be changed, Petersen thought. But the chairman decided over the weekend, as he had in similar situations all during the past year, that this was not the time to provoke Gordon Getty. Petersen was just beginning, in the aftermath of the Friday meeting with Gordon in his office, to organize a special team of takeover advisors. Until that team was in place, it would be useless to challenge Gordon openly. Besides, with Seth Hufstedler now on board, the secret plan to sue Gordon over his trusteeship seemed more promising than ever. So Petersen relayed a message to Cohler that Goldman could proceed as requested and study the viability of an LBO takeover with a fence.

Geoff Boisi was dispatched by Goldman, Sachs to assist Bart Winokur with the LBO study and the negotiations with Gordon. Boisi's entrance marked a major shift in strategy by Goldman and Getty Oil; it meant the game was indeed now afoot. For the past six months, Petersen had been working with partners and associates in Goldman's corporate analysis department, the side of the firm that crunched numbers and evaluated long-term corporate planning strategies for its blue-chip clients. Boisi was the chief of a very different department at Goldman: mergers and acquisitions, or M&A, as Wall Street's shorthand described it. The partners in M&A were not planners, they were deal-makers. They were the central players in—some said the cause of—the merger mania sweeping American industry in the early 1980s. They were the brokers of the country's largest corporations. Their jobs involved not simply buying and selling companies, however. Their role was more akin to a general's

wartime headquarters staff: they devised tactics, mapped out strategies, and devoted themselves entirely to the goal of victory. There
was no rest for an M&A partner like Geoff Boisi; he was always on
alert, jetting from city to city as the battles shifted, sometimes advising four or five clients at the same time. A banker like Boisi, who
was at the top of his profession, the head of M&A at one of the most
important investment banking firms, was drawn to takeovers where
there was the most at stake. This was not only because the big deals
were most exciting; they were also the most lucrative.

M&A advisors routinely contracted for a small, flat retainer fee
plus a percentage of any future transaction involving their client. The
bigger the client, then, the more expensive was the transaction and
the higher was Boisi's potential fee. That July, Getty Oil looked like
it might end up in one of the biggest deals of all time. The company
was so large and so rich that even a 48 percent LBO takeover would
generate millions in banking fees. There were those, including Gordon Getty himself, who questioned the fee structure prevalent in the
merger area of investment banking. These critics wondered whether
bankers like Geoff Boisi weren't driven to cause *any* deal to happen,
regardless of its merit or consequences, because that was the central incentive in their fee arrangements. Certainly, it seemed to be
a problem some of the time, especially in deals where the bankers
themselves instigated a hostile takeover. But that was not the situation at Getty Oil in July. It was Gordon who threatened to put the
company in play, and Goldman, in keeping with its policy, was man-
ning the defense on management's behalf. Also, while Boisi himself
was considered to be a rising star on Wall Street, he was not regarded
as one of the most aggressive M&A bankers, comparable, say, to the
fast-talking Bruce Wasserstein at First Boston or the highly visible
Martin Siegel at Kidder, Peabody & Company, bankers who seemed
to thrive in the most hostile and bitter takeover deals.

Rather, Goldman, Sachs' conservative reputation and Boisi's own
temperament led him to cultivate a lower profile. He was a tall, bony,
tense man with long fingers that often rested against his cheek, grip-
ping it nervously. His hair was coal black, his shoulders high and
broad, and large ears protruded from the sides of his head. Like many
of the bankers in his field, he was very young, in his mid-thirties, and
the pressure of work had not yet aged his boyish face. There was an
air of serious intelligence and concentration about him. He was not a

playboy, like many of his colleagues, or a connoisseur of fast cars and exotic travel. He was a family man, and when he was home, he commuted between Wall Street and Long Island by train. He had grown up in New York, attended Boston College and then the University of Pennsylvania's Wharton School of business and finance. He was a vice-president at Goldman, Sachs before he was thirty and a partner three years later. By 1979, barely into his thirties, he was running the firm's M&A department and was earning more than a million dollars per year in salary and bonuses.

In the weeks ahead, Boisi and attorney Bart Winokur would become fast allies in the affairs of Getty Oil Company. They were two of a kind—young, Ivy League-smart, wealthy and successful way beyond their years, and privy to the most stimulating intrigues of American finance. They shared a certain distance from the experiences of a lifelong company man like Sidney Petersen, a man who had grown up setting back speedometers at his father's tiny auto repair shop, but they also shared a fierce competitiveness and loyalty to their client. There were those at Getty Oil who regarded Winokur and Boisi as too smart, too sharp, too much taken with themselves; but whether such resentments were born of class and social differences or reflected actual experience was hard to tell. In some respects, Boisi and Winokur were men apart at Getty Oil that July. Yet, in the management cabal that included Petersen and Copley, they wielded extraordinary power.

On Gordon's side, too, the advisors were becoming more important. For part of every summer, Gordon and Ann vacated their Broadway mansion and flew to Europe to travel and attend a series of classical music festivals, particularly the Vienna Festival, where the emphasis is on opera. In the Gettys' absence, Cohler and Woodhouse found that they had to take more responsibility for their client's dealings with Getty Oil. Gordon had left the country enthusiastic about an LBO takeover with Harold Williams, but there was much still to be done; it wasn't clear, for one thing, whether Petersen would ever support the idea. After all, in all likelihood, the takeover would result in the loss of his job.

The new focus on Williams, the museum, and Getty Oil meant the Lasky firm, which had been largely excluded from the dealings with Pickens (who following his rebuff by Petersen was now turning his attention to a raid on Gulf Oil) and Corby Robertson and the

Cullens (whom Gordon continued to string along in his casual sort of way), was again at center stage. Cohler was the point man, since Lasky himself, nearing eighty years of age, did not relish the constant travel between San Francisco and Los Angeles and was busy with other cases. Woodhouse, while technically Cohler's equal, did not share his partner's penchant for deal-making or his aggressive, articulate personality. That July, in fact, some of the executives at Getty Oil headquarters began to describe Tim Cohler as a "mini Lansing Hays" because of his increasingly prominent and forceful representation of Gordon Getty. He was a litigator by training and nature, and he began to display a tough, swaggering posture in negotiations with Winokur and Boisi. He seemed to cultivate the aura of a hard-boiled California detective drawn from the novels of Raymond Chandler and Dashiell Hammett. He was a bit like Sam Spade, attorney at law. His face was sallow and unexpressive, his hair closely cropped, and he smoked unfiltered Camel cigarettes. When he took one from the pack, he liked to tap it meaningfully on the face of his gold watch, compressing the tobacco. Then, with flair, he struck a wooden match and lit the end, exhaling billows of smoke through his nose. He was a Harvard Law graduate, but he had lived in California for more than a decade, and he lacked the manners of Eastern privilege exuded by Winokur and Boisi.

For several weeks, beginning with a day-long meeting at Getty Oil headquarters on Wednesday, July 20, Cohler, Winokur, and Boisi began to feel each other out. They knew a takeover match was on now, and each had to take the other's measure. Cohler had flown down to Los Angeles expecting that Goldman, Sachs would present to him the full, detailed results of their LBO study—with all the data Goldman had assembled for the earlier studies, it would only have taken the firm days to analyze an LBO. But when Cohler arrived at the conference room on the eighteenth floor, there were no books, charts, or slides. There was only Winokur and Boisi and two of Getty Oil's in-house finance men. Cohler had never met Boisi before, but he understood the implications of the M&A partner's presence. Getty Oil was readying for a fight.

"There is no way an LBO takeover with a fence will fly," Winokur announced flatly as soon as they were seated. "It's just not even close—there's no way to do it." Gordon's proposal was something bankers referred to as a "100 percent leveraged transaction." In other words, since 48 percent of the company's stock was being financed by 48 percent of its assets, there was no room for error. If Gordon and the museum wanted to buy out the public stockholders, they would have to pay a fair price. Although Goldman had not yet done a formal study, the firm would conclude in just a few weeks that $120 per share was the minimum fair price for the public shares. The actual value of Getty Oil's assets was estimated by Goldman to be between $120 and $150 per share. A banker financing a fenced buy-out, then, would have to lend $120 cash based on collateral assets worth roughly the same amount. Bankers rarely made that kind of loan under any circumstances. For example, a homeowner whose equity in a house was worth $100,000 on the open market could not borrow the full $100,000 from a bank, using the house as collateral. The bank insisted on a cushion. It might lend $50,000, or even $75,000, but it would not loan the full amount. On a much larger scale, that was the problem Gordon faced with his proposal for a leveraged buy-out with a fence.

Cohler was surprised by Winokur's sudden pronouncement that the deal could not work, but he accepted the conclusion—Goldman, Sachs, after all, was a reputable firm. Later Cohler discovered that Winokur was correct. The debt required to buy out the public stockholders without touching the assets behind Gordon's "fence" was too great. Without a fence, that is, using all the company's assets to finance the purchase of 48 percent of the stock, a buy-out might work. Even then, it would be risky for both the banks and the buyer. Cohler made it clear that Gordon was not interested in an LBO without a fence. If he did that, he would be using his family trust's assets as collateral—assuming the risk of the purchase. And with a fence in place to protect the family trust, the deal was untouchable.

"The directors last Friday did favor a stock buy-back plan, however," Winokur went on, without pausing long to explain his dismissal of the LBO. "In fact, the company and Goldman, Sachs have been giving further thought to that idea. Geoff is here because he's an expert not only on mergers but on stock buy-back programs, and I think he could be a help to all of us."

Winokur and Boisi then began to outline in detail a proposal for a dramatic 16-million-share stock buy-back. If implemented, they said, the company would purchase from public stockholders, in the near future, some 15 percent of Getty Oil's outstanding stock.

Gordon would do nothing, but when the buy-back was completed, the percentage holdings of his trust's 32 million shares would rise from 40 to more than 50 percent. That meant, obviously, that Gordon would control Getty Oil Company. He could fire executives, replace the board of directors, change the business strategy, do whatever he pleased. Cohler listened closely. On its face, this new proposal was a great victory for his client. But why would Winokur and Boisi support, even initiate, a buy-back plan that put Gordon in control? What was going on here? Certainly, a large stock repurchase such as the one suggested would benefit public stockholders by paying those who sold out a premium over the market price and by indirectly raising the value of those shares the public chose to retain. But Cohler was not naïve. Had Petersen suddenly decided to sacrifice his career for the benefit of the public stockholders? There had to be a catch.

Winokur, finally, explained it. He asked a question. "Speaking philosophically, what do you think Gordon's reaction would be, Tim, if there were structural changes in the company that would permit Gordon to hold a majority of Getty Oil's stock—but with certain safeguards for protecting the minority shareholders, the public shareholders, and also safeguards for preserving an independent board of directors?"

"Bart, will you tell me what you mean by that?" Cohler responded. "That's just a bunch of words. What do you mean, protecting the minority shareholders' and 'preserving an independent board of directors'?"

Winokur did not want to get more specific. He was just exploring the question, he said, almost as a matter of business philosophy. He and Cohler began to have the sort of conversation lawyers have when they are speaking for absent clients: long-winded, vague, abstract, filled with caveats. Cohler pressed Winokur for specifics; Winokur avoided him.

Cohler kept saying: "Look, if you make the proper disclosures required by the SEC, and you've got a publicly owned company, a majority owner is a majority owner. There isn't anybody who's ever bought a share of Getty Oil stock who didn't know that the trustees owned forty percent, and that there was always the potential for that to become a controlling block. What do you mean, 'protect the minority shareholders'? The law protects them."

Winokur responded, "That's not the issue. The issue is, what are the interests of the public shareholders? State law is inadequate in most cases like this—you're using the company's money to put an individual shareholder in control. Look, I don't want to get into the specifics right now—I don't want to talk about the mechanics. We just have this concern about protecting the minority shareholders. Getty Oil would use its own money, through the buy-back, to put Gordon in a majority position, and so naturally the company would have concerns about protecting the minority shareholders and the independence of the board. These would only be safeguards."

Carefully and somewhat vaguely, Winokur was proposing placing what would later be called, in the shorthand of the advisors, "handcuffs" on Gordon Getty. The idea was that the company would repurchase 16 million shares from the public stockholders, raising the numerical percentage of Gordon's holdings above 50 percent. Before the company began the buy-back, however, Gordon would agree to rules prohibiting him from actually exercising majority control. Gordon would own a majority of Getty Oil's stock, but he would be allowed to vote only 40 percent, the same percentage he currently held. At one level, the company's rationale for such handcuffs was defensible: in its own business judgment, Getty Oil management believed that Gordon was not qualified to run the company, and they wanted to be sure that he did nothing to harm the public stockholders who came under his sway after a buy-back. At another level, however, the plan was deceitful. Winokur and Boisi were asking Cohler to consider handcuffing his client while the company secretly arranged a family lawsuit that would permanently undermine Gordon's power. Cohler, of course, knew nothing about the meetings with Seth Hufstedler and other Los Angeles attorneys or about the contacts with lawyers for the Georgettes and J. Paul Getty, Jr.

Moreover, at that Wednesday meeting Winokur seemed reluctant to admit that it was Getty Oil management's personal feelings about Gordon, their strong belief that he was erratic and unqualified to run the company, that led them to propose the handcuffs. Instead, Winokur implied that their sole motivation was the "protection of the minority, public shareholders" and that these "safeguards" would be necessary regardless of who was in control of the Sarah Getty Trust. There was a certain moral tone to Winokur's general statements about protecting the minority shareholders. Cohler kept pressing for specifics because he wanted Winokur to acknowledge that the issue was really Gordon, not the public shareholders. Then Cohler could argue that Winokur had no right to pass judgment on Gordon's qualifications—Gordon owned Getty Oil, or at least a large part of it, and he had the right to run the company as he saw fit, regardless of management's opinions about his personality. But Winokur refused to be drawn into a discussion about Gordon's personal qualifications. He insisted that his and Petersen's aim was merely to protect the public stockholders—increasingly, he referred to them as "minority stockholders" as if to emphasize that Petersen had a moral obligation to handcuff Gordon.

"I just want to get a sense of what Mr. Getty's view would be, philosophically, about these kinds of safeguards," Winokur said.

It was the soft-spoken Tom Woodhouse, of all people, who finally cut through the thick layers of legal posturing. "I think that Mr. Getty would be highly offended by any suggestions that he would not be able to exercise his lawful rights and power, owning whatever stock he held as trustee," Woodhouse declared emphatically. "He would own exactly the same shares of stock before and after any buy-back—it would be the company that would be buying stock and changing his percentage holding. As a trustee, Mr. Getty has a fiduciary obligation and he couldn't possibly agree to changing the rights that the law gives him."

Even Cohler was uncomfortable with the strength of Woodhouse's declaration. He tried immediately to soften his partner's assertion that Gordon would never agree to handcuffs, that all this talk about protecting the minority stockholders was just so much bullshit.

"Look, Tom's expressing more confidence in what Mr. Getty would think than I am," Cohler said. "I happen to agree with all the things Tom said, as far as his basic instincts, but I'm not going to sit here and tell you what Mr. Getty thinks." No one could predict the state of Gordon Getty's mind from day to day.

It was now lunchtime, and the advisors decided to break for sandwiches. In just a few hours, the LBO takeover had been declared dead by Winokur and Boisi. Cohler had implied that he would bring the handcuffs proposal to Gordon's attention, but it was impossible for him to go further before he talked to his client.

There was an alcove beside the conference room, and the advisors wandered over to a table where a catered lunch had been laid out. They stood casually, eating their sandwiches; the atmosphere was relaxed. Cohler stepped over beside Geoff Boisi. They had never met, and they decided to get acquainted.

"What are Gordon's goals here?" Boisi asked, voicing the question that had been so often repeated around Getty Oil headquarters in recent months.

Cohler went through his usual speech: Gordon was interested in exploring ways to "maximize value for all shareholders." He wanted to close the "value gap" between the price of Getty Oil's stock and the worth of its underlying assets. Cohler was not specific, although he did mention that the LBO takeover was the sort of thing that Gordon had been very interested in, but now, apparently, that idea was dead.

Boisi swallowed a bite of his sandwich, looked at Cohler, and asked him what Cohler later described as "the $64,000 question."

"Is Gordon trying to put the company in play in order to attract a hostile, front-end-loaded, two-tier tender offer so that he'll be free to sell his stock under the trust instrument?"

Boisi meant, borrowing Winokur's metaphor from the Bonaventure Hotel meeting: Does Gordon actually want to be squeezed? Does he *want* to be the juice?

Because of the strange provisions of the 1934 Sarah Getty Trust documents, Gordon could only sell his 32 million Getty Oil shares for cash to prevent a loss. Boisi was describing a particular brand of hostile takeover that would put Gordon in such a position. If Boone Pickens, say, made a tender offer—that is, an official, openly declared offer to purchase stock—for 60 percent of Getty Oil's shares, then he could squeeze Gordon out. Suppose Getty Oil's shares were selling for $60 on the stock market. Pickens could offer $80, all cash, for 60 percent of the shares. Each stockholder could then decide: should I sell to Pickens for $80, or hold on to my stock? Because Pickens was offering $20 per share more than the market price, many would sell. Once Pickens gained a majority, he could squeeze Gordon out. He might offer the trust less money than his first $80 tender offer, or he might offer a less attractive $80 "face value" package of cash and debt securities that was actually worth much less than $80. Or Pickens could simply force Gordon to sell his shares for, say, $70. Then Gordon would have to go to court, exercising his "appraisal rights" and ask a judge to determine how much a share of Getty Oil stock was really worth. If the judge decided it was worth more than $70, then

Pickens would have to pay the difference. But if the judge decided $70 was fair, Gordon would be stuck. Either way, exercising appraisal rights was a long and expensive process. Gordon and the trust would be facing a loss. They would be free to sell to Pickens at his original price: $80 cash.

The point of Boisi's "$64,000 question" was this: Perhaps it was Gordon's secret goal to sell the 32 million Getty Oil shares owned by the trust. Perhaps his wanderings on Wall Street, and his friendly, seemingly naïve meetings with Pickens and the Cullens, were really just a clever ruse, an effort to provoke a hostile tender offer that would put him in a position to sell out for cash. A "front-end-loaded, two-tier" hostile bid was the most onerous form of takeover because it put tremendous pressure on shareholders. They had to decide, very quickly, whether the "front end"—$80 cash, in the Pickens example—was a fair price for their shares. If they felt it was not, if they decided to hold on to the stock because they believed it was worth more than $80, they faced the prospect of a court fight after a forced merger. Takeover critics in Congress and on Wall Street often used the front-end-loaded, two-tier takeover as an example of abusive practices when they pressed for regulatory restrictions on hostile mergers.

Cohler was impressed that Boisi had seen this possibility in Gordon's actions over the last six months. Clearly, Boisi was a very sophisticated player. But the fact was that Gordon was not nearly as savvy as Boisi's question implied. If Gordon had put Getty Oil Company in play, it was not by design. It was a result of his intuitive feelings about business strategy, his instinctive push toward "the light at the end of the tunnel."

"That is absolutely not the strategy," Cohler told Boisi flatly. "That is absolutely not what Gordon is doing." Cohler believed that Boisi had taken him at his word. But he knew, too, that his dealings with Getty Oil had been elevated to a new level of sophistication.

As they stood together in the alcove, finishing their sandwiches, Cohler and Boisi began to talk openly about the gamesmanship now overtaking the negotiations between Petersen and Gordon. Specifically, they talked about the role of museum president Harold Williams and the suspicion with which he was regarded by Petersen. During the morning session in the conference room, there had been a lot of speculation about whether Williams was interested in controlling Getty

Oil, and whether the museum itself could be "squeezed" if Gordon and the company agreed on a buy-back plan. At the center of these discussions had been the mystery of Williams' intentions.

"You know, you can over game-play," Cohler remarked to Boisi as they finished their sandwiches.

"Yes, you can," Boisi agreed.

Nonetheless, the games persisted. All through Wednesday afternoon and again on Thursday, the advisors discussed "handcuffs" for Gordon Getty, sometimes jokingly referring to them as "golden handcuffs" or "platinum handcuffs" because a buy-back plan might raise the trust's wealth even as it restricted Gordon's personal power. By the end of Thursday, though, there was still no agreement. Cohler and Woodhouse made it clear that in their view the next step was to proceed with the 16-million-share buy-back—without handcuffs—that would put Gordon in the majority; that was, after all, what Goldman had seemed to recommend at the July 8 board meeting. But Winokur and Boisi insisted on the handcuffs, golden or otherwise.

"This is not going to fly," Tim Cohler said as the two-day session ended on Thursday afternoon. "We've got legal problems with any handcuffs, and Woodhouse has a very strong sense as to what Mr. Getty's personal reaction will be."

Cohler continued to insist that Winokur was being disingenuous, that the issue was not the minority shareholders but management's view of Gordon's personality and qualifications. "Look, you're just not willing to admit that the board of directors is flatly refusing to let Mr. Getty into a majority position because they don't like him," Cohler said.

"That's not true," Winokur answered. "The board is simply concerned with carrying out its fiduciary obligations to maintain its independence and protect the minority shareholders. It doesn't matter whether it's Mr. Getty or anybody else—or any combination of people."

Cohler and Woodhouse said that despite their pessimism about his reaction, they would discuss the handcuffs issue with Gordon. They flew back to San Francisco that evening. Early the next week, they reached Gordon in Europe and explained what had happened at the two-day meeting in Los Angeles. When Cohler heard Gordon's reaction, he called Winokur and arranged for another two-day summit in Los Angeles, on Thursday and Friday, July 28 and 29.

"Tom was absolutely right," Cohler announced when the advisors reconvened at Getty headquarters that hot, smoggy Thursday morning. "Gordon was deeply offended by the suggestion that he be handcuffed."

The tone of the meeting, which had earlier been cool and rational, if also tense, began to change. A freewheeling discussion about the handcuffs ensued, with Winokur insisting again that they were necessary to protect the public shareholders, and with Cohler and Woodhouse now adamantly opposed to the concept. They broke for lunch and went at it again. By afternoon, tempers were beginning to fray.

Cohler finally pushed it over the edge. For three full days, they had sat in this conference room discussing the buy-back and the handcuffs. It had gone far enough—there could be no agreement. They were at an impasse.

"Look," Cohler said with exasperation. "This whole two-day meeting idea has been awkward for me anyway because I'm getting married on Saturday. I told you that I have to be back tonight in San Francisco for the bridal dinner. And frankly, I'm not sure there's any point in coming back to L.A. tomorrow. This is a week that's difficult for me for personal reasons. I'd always let professional obligations take precedence over personal needs, but frankly guys, we're not getting anywhere."

Cohler actually began to shout at Winokur. He was out of control. "I just don't think you're playing straight with me! I do not think that the reasons you're giving for the handcuffs are the real reasons. You've got people in management and on the board who just plain won't deal with Gordon because they don't like him. This is a personal thing, and it's totally contrary to the board's fiduciary obligations, which you so nicely invoke. The board of directors is supposed to do its job, and it's not supposed to have a personality contest! You're not even following your own investment banker's advice, to go ahead with the buy-back."

Cohler didn't stop; he continued to press Winokur in a virtual tirade. "Analytically, this thing just doesn't stand together, Winokur! If you guys mean what you say about the minority shareholders, then—well, what if there *were* no public shareholders? What if they were bought out? You'd probably *still* say the same garbage—anything to keep Gordon from getting control! You're just trying to blackmail us! You're just insisting on handcuffs in order to protect Sid Petersen's job!"

"We're not trying to protect anybody's job," Winokur countered. "Do you know what you're talking about? You're contradicting yourself. *You* are the one who said last week that Gordon would only buy out the public if he could build a fence around 'his' assets. We're perfectly willing to let Mr. Getty take control of this company if he's willing to pay a fair price. We would require no conditions, no handcuffs, no restrictions. If Gordon will pay a fair price, fine. But he can only pay a fair price if he's willing to take the risk himself, if he's willing to take down the fence. If Gordon will use his own assets to borrow the money, he could probably pay a fair price."

Cohler began to calm down; Winokur's suggestion seemed to intrigue him. Perhaps Cohler had spoken too soon when he insisted the week before that Gordon would never consider an LBO without a fence. Perhaps Gordon had told him in the interim that he *would* be willing to risk his family's fortune to take control of Getty Oil. Whatever the reason, Cohler now said that he was impressed by Winokur's commitment to a takeover proposal that might well result in the loss of Sid Petersen's job. Cohler said that he would return to Los Angeles after his bridal dinner in San Francisco that evening. The discussions could continue.

On Friday, the meeting was restored to its earlier mood of civility. Gordon was indeed willing to consider an LBO takeover without a fence, Cohler reported. He, Winokur, and Boisi agreed that Goldman, Sachs should study the proposal. It would take some time, they also agreed. August was approaching, Cohler was going off on his honeymoon, and the rest of them had summer vacations scheduled. Boisi would return to New York, and with the help of his firm's corporate analysts, he would produce another detailed study. For the first time, Goldman would have to decide exactly how much it thought Getty Oil Company was worth, and it would have to declare an official, minimum fair price for the public shareholders. Meanwhile, Cohler said, the Lasky firm would begin to draft the legal papers necessary to implement the takeover. When they reconvened in a month's time, he said, they should be prepared to move quickly. An LBO takeover had to be consummated swiftly; otherwise, outside raiders might try to jump in at the last moment and snatch the company away.

Cohler was pleased. Gordon's success was in some ways linked to his own. If Gordon took control of Getty Oil, Cohler might well become one of the company's leading executives—certainly, Gordon would need good advice more than ever. Encouraged, Cohler returned to San Francisco and to his wedding. The game was on, yes, and Winokur and Boisi were still on the opposite side, but they had all agreed now to try a deal together. If the LBO without a fence worked, Boisi could help Gordon fend off unwanted outsiders. And if all went well, Gordon Getty would own the giant Getty Oil Company by Labor Day.

11

BLOOD ON THE FLOOR

In time, intrigue acquires its own momentum. Complexity accumulates in layers, like grime on a windshield, until finally, the road ahead is obscured from view. At Getty Oil Company that summer, it was not merely that the contest for control depended increasingly upon arcane financial analysis and the advice of sophisticated specialists, whose training and intelligence permitted them to justify plausibly even the most outrageous course of action. The problem was also that the delicate balancing act so long sustained between Sid Petersen and Gordon Getty had suppressed the most basic of personal resentments. The advisors, and even at times Petersen and Gordon, preferred to speak in a neutered, passive, pedantic language. They talked about "facilitating a transaction" and about "preserving the independence of the board" and about the importance of behaving like "gentlemen." In part, this inertness reflected the sterile culture of a large American corporation. In part, too, it was an issue of class—Gordon, more than any of them, valued the polite refinement of manner he associated with wealth and high position. Moreover, the lawyers controlled the words that were spoken and the tone of negotiation, and they rightly suspected that the events unfolding at the company would later be subject to the scrutiny of litigation. They hoped their clients would not say or do anything that was indefensible in a courtroom.

Most important of all, however, was a kind of unspoken understanding that bound most of them together. They were very much like family. They had known each other for decades. They knew each other's marriages, and divorces, and illnesses, and weaknesses, and triumphs. They had all served the old man, J. Paul Getty, and they were bound not only by his money but by his vision of legacy: a company, a family, a museum, all intertwined. The old man had intended for tens of thousands of Getty Oil employees, several generations of the Getty family, and one of the richest art museums in the country somehow to share the same destiny. For Sid Petersen, Moses Lasky, Dave Copley, and some of the others, there was always a strong impulse to settle their problems "between friends," to close the door on the outsiders and hammer out a compromise, a "family solution," as it was later described by the daughters of George Getty. They shared a reluctance to confront each other or to overstep the bounds of family propriety. Petersen, for example, refused to talk directly with the Georgettes about instigating a lawsuit against their Uncle Gordon; he insisted that the approach be made through their attorney, Isaacs. And even though Isaacs appeared to do nothing about the company's reports on Gordon, Petersen declined to "take advantage" of his relationship with the Getty family by meeting directly with the Georgettes. That would be unseemly, he thought. Similarly, the Lasky firm was willing to negotiate for month after month with Petersen and the company because it was convinced that permanent harmony could be established—Lasky had never wavered from the view he expressed to Petersen over dinner back in May 1982, that through diplomacy and decorum Gordon Getty could be controlled. Indeed, Lasky and Cohler often seemed willing to go further than Gordon in negotiations with Petersen.

All these intricate elements informed that moment in Moses Lasky's San Francisco offices on the afternoon of Thursday, September 1, 1983, when the relationship between Gordon Getty and the Getty Oil Company was irrevocably changed.

They had been talking for the better part of an hour in the main conference room—Lasky, Cohler, Woodhouse, Gordon, Petersen, Winokur, Boisi, Copley, and a couple of analysts from Goldman, Sachs. They had met to discuss the LBO takeover by Gordon which Goldman had studied all during August. The numbers had been crunched, the asset values analyzed, and the debt ratios calculated. Boisi had told the group that an LBO without a fence was possible, but risky. It was Goldman's view that the minimum value of the company's stock was near $120 per share. If Gordon borrowed the money to buy out all the stock at that price, using Getty Oil's assets as collateral, he would incur an enormous debt load. The debt was not prohibitively high, but it was a gamble. Hearing this, Gordon had announced that despite his earlier enthusiasm for an LBO takeover, he was not willing to assume so great a risk—he was concerned about his fiduciary obligations as trustee of the family fortune. While Gordon personally might be willing to take a chance on an LBO takeover, his brothers and nieces and nephews might not be, and they could sue to prevent the deal. Gordon was pleased that Goldman had studied the matter so thoroughly, he said, but now that he saw the numbers, particularly those pertaining to debt, he was unwilling to go forward. He told the group his plans for an LBO takeover were off.

So there they were, returned again to the original impasse. What were they supposed to do now? They could talk again about the stock buy-back program that would put Gordon in a majority position, but Cohler had already made it clear that "handcuffs" were unacceptable and Winokur had been equally adamant that Getty Oil would not be handed to Gordon without "protections" for the minority shareholders. Something had to give.

At that moment, Moses Lasky looked across the conference table at Sid Petersen. In Lasky's view, Petersen had been promoted to chairman and chief executive in no small part because of Lasky's support and recommendations over the years. They shared a kinship. They shared a common purpose.

"Sid, don't you think it would be useful if you and I went into my office and just had a chat about where we are?" Lasky asked.

"I think that might be a very constructive idea," Petersen answered. "But I'd better check with my lawyers about it first."

Petersen, Winokur, and Copley stepped out of the glass-walled conference room and huddled together in the hallway. After a few minutes, they returned.

"That's just fine, Moses, but I'm advised that I shouldn't meet with you, because you're counsel for Gordon, unless I have my own counsel present," Petersen said.

"So, Sid, it has come to this, has it? Well, okay."

It was hard to say whether Lasky was hurt or angry or surprised, or all three. But he clearly was changed. On its face, Petersen's request was perfectly reasonable; he and Lasky were on opposite sides of a business problem, and the Getty Oil chairman simply wanted the advice and protection of his lawyer, Winokur. But to Lasky, Petersen's refusal to meet privately was a personal affront, and it was an indication that a "family" solution was now out of the question. It was time to take the gloves off.

So they moved around the corner to Lasky's private office—Petersen, Winokur, Copley, Cohler, Woodhouse, and Lasky. Gordon was not invited; Lasky said he thought that more could be accomplished without him.

"It's clear that Gordon isn't going to do an LBO takeover. He's clearly rejected that. The real solution now, then, is to get the trust in a control position," Lasky began.

"The company is unwilling to do that," Winokur answered, speaking for Petersen as he increasingly did.

"If the company and the trust can find a way to reach an agreement, putting the trust in a majority position, then you've solved the problem of an outside raider trying to take Getty Oil over. The trust would own fifty percent and no one could touch the company," Lasky said.

"The issue is not so much the trust as it is Gordon," Winokur finally declared.

"You're acting as if Gordon has to come to you on bended knee, as if you're the only people who have the right to exercise judgment as to what is appropriate for all the shareholders—nobody else gets to have any thoughts," Cohler said. "Let's not forget here that Mr. Getty owns forty percent of the stock. There are any number of things that he can do unilaterally, which we are trying to find a way to avoid. But the gentleman is not powerless if you drive him to exercise his rights under the law."

"What exactly do you have in mind?" Winokur asked.

"You can't play dumb with me, Bart. You know exactly what can be done." Cohler was forceful.

"Well, you're a lot smarter than I am, then. I haven't figured out anything he can do. He only owns forty percent."

"Well, then, I guess there's no point in discussing this."

"Obviously, Gordon could launch a proxy fight against management," Lasky pointed out. "He would only need ten percent, at most, of the shareholders' votes to get control of the company on his own."

"You should understand that management is determined not to permit that," Winokur answered. "We'd rather put the company up for sale than risk Gordon getting control."

Tempers were flaring; this was the direct confrontation over power and control that had been so studiously side-stepped during the past six months. Petersen had wanted to avoid such open warring with Gordon and the Lasky firm precisely because it might lead to a sale of Getty Oil, voluntary or involuntary. It would be a Pyrrhic victory indeed if the company was desperately sold to prevent Gordon from taking control. None of them wanted that to happen.

"Look, it's better to have the blood on the floor in this room, among ourselves, to see where we are, than to have it spread out in public, on the financial pages. At least we should see if we can't avoid having the blood spill out there," Cohler said.

"The company would feel differently about taking Gordon into a majority position if we could get an institutional cotrustee appointed," Winokur ventured. He made no mention of the company's contacts with Bank of America and Seth Hufstedler; no family member had yet come forward to sue Gordon over the issue.

"That's totally out of the question," Lasky said. "You can't have a bank as a trustee."

A few minutes later, Winokur raised the idea again; it was the only way to break the impasse, he said. The company was unwilling to put the trust in control unless there was some way to restrain Gordon once he gained majority power.

"Look, Bart, if we're going to try to do something constructive to solve the company's problems, we shouldn't try to solve the company's problems at the trust level," Lasky said. "And besides, you know that the minute anybody suggests the possibility of a cotrustee, Ronny would come running in and say that he was a candidate and we would be all the way back into those problems again."

"We don't want Ronald. We want a bank, an institution."

"It wouldn't be good to have a bank as trustee because they aren't any good at dealing with or standing up to the management of big companies," Lasky answered.

"Well, what if there were two additional cotrustees, besides Gordon, each with half a vote. Gordon would have one vote. So that way, if Gordon had an idea that was genuinely appealing, all he would have to do is persuade one of the two cotrustees. It would only be if his idea is so off the wall that both of the others are against him that they could veto him."

"If we can find a way to get Gordon into a majority position, then Gordon could have another seat on the board. I would join the board and that could address some of your concerns about Gordon," Lasky responded.

"If we got an extra one or two cotrustees to serve with Gordon, we would be willing to have you come on the board," Winokur said.

Lasky asked to speak with Winokur alone, and they stepped out of the office and into the hallway.

"If we're going to make an accommodation," Lasky said when the office door was closed, "Gordon is going to have to be made chairman of the board. He's going to need an office in Los Angeles and he'll have to be treated with respect. He's not going to run the company day-to-day; Sid will still be in charge. But he needs that title. I'd appreciate it if you could convince Petersen to accept this. It's the only way to move forward."

"I'll talk to him," Winokur said.

For a few moments, they broke into smaller groups, wandering through the law firm. Winokur spoke privately with Petersen. When he was finished, the group reconvened in Lasky's office.

"Sid will agree to step down as chairman if we can get the two cotrustees appointed, each with a half vote, to serve with Gordon. If you can convince Gordon to accept the two cotrustees, then the company will take Gordon to fifty-one percent, Gordon will become chairman, and Moses will become an additional director," Winokur proposed. Despite the hyperbole of their negotiations, the Getty Oil leaders respected Lasky's judgment.

"I don't know if the directors will go for that plan, but I'd be willing to present it to them," Petersen said.

"Look, you've made the suggestion about cotrustees often enough in this meeting. We are trying to find something that will work, I know. So I will take the proposal to Gordon. But I will tell you this: I will not recommend cotrustees to him, or anything like that. I'm absolutely opposed to it. I'm confident that Gordon will agree that co-trustees would be a huge mistake."

On that discouraging note, the meeting ended. Petersen and his Getty Oil advisors arranged for a limousine to take them out to the San Francisco airport; they would be flying back to Los Angeles that

evening. Lasky said that he would meet with Gordon as soon as possible and inform them of his client's response.

That evening, only hours after Petersen and his advisors had
departed, Lasky and Cohler sat down with Gordon in Lasky's office
to discuss Winokur's proposal. On Lasky's recommendation, Gordon rejected the idea of cotrustees; he was unwilling to share control
of the family fortune with anyone. But Lasky proposed a compromise
to his client. Perhaps they could address the company's concerns about
the caprice of Gordon's power through a different mechanism. Under
Lasky's plan the company would buy back enough stock to put Gordon in control. Gordon would be named chairman and Lasky would be
appointed a director. Then, the corporation's by-laws would be amended
to create a new "supermajority" of the board to approve major policy
decisions, such as mergers, acquisitions, royalty trusts, or other substantial restructurings. It would take three directors to veto any proposal.
Gordon alone could not stop a deal, and neither could Gordon and
Lasky acting together. They would have to persuade one other director,
whose appointment would be approved by management, to go along.

Lasky continued, "This way, I can put it to Sid, 'Look, if you want
to do something of a large magnitude at the company, then Gordon can't block it unless he can persuade one other person besides
myself. And if you're not comfortable with that, if you can't have a
board of responsible people where this arrangement doesn't pose
problems for you, then you don't have the independent board you're
always talking about.'"

After discussing Lasky's plan into the evening, Gordon finally
agreed. If the company would put him in control, he would go along
with the restrictions proposed by Lasky.

The next morning, Lasky called Dave Copley.

"We've talked with Gordon and we think there would be some
value in having another meeting. If you and Sid and Bart will come
up here today, we think it would be worthwhile."

The Getty Oil triumvirate flew up to San Francisco that Friday
afternoon in a company plane. Winokur, for one, assumed that Gordon had accepted the idea of cotrustees. Instead, when they arrived
at Lasky's office, they were told about the plan for a "supermajority."

They talked about it for hours, well into the night, and most of the
discussion centered on the number of directors required to veto any
major policy proposal. Lasky insisted that the total number should

be three. The company wanted to consider a larger number, so that if Gordon proposed a major change at the company he would have to persuade three or possibly four other directors that his plans were sound. There was also a question about how new directors would be nominated when the current board members began to retire. By the end of the meeting, they seemed to be close to an agreement.

"This is not just some wild, wide-eyed idea of the lawyers," Cohler emphasized. "Gordon is on board."

The earlier ambience of comity had been partially restored; they were beginning to mop up the blood on Lasky's floor. That night, Petersen, Copley, and Winokur flew back to Los Angeles, agreeing that they would attempt to hammer out the details in the next few days. Over the weekend, Cohler spoke with Copley by telephone several times. On Monday, they spoke again.

"There are only two problems I can think of at this point," Copley said. "One is that Mr. Lasky is older than our age requirements for board members allow. I don't think that will be a problem, but we shouldn't completely overlook it, either. There have been some small diplomacy problems with a couple of our directors over age, and that could conceivably be a hang-up."

"Look, Dave, if that's the only thing that stands in the way after all of this, that's not going to be a problem."

"You and I know it's not going to be a problem. I'm just alerting you to the diplomacy of it. The other thing, though, is the exact number of the supermajority of the board. You and Lasky kept insisting on an eighty percent figure for the supermajority, which would require Gordon to enlist one other director besides Mr. Lasky. I think maybe seventy-five percent would be better. Then he'd have to persuade two other directors."

"Dave, don't make a mistake. Sid used that eighty percent number in our conversation on Friday. He seemed to accept it."

"I don't remember that."

"I distinctly remember it because the logic of the whole thing is wrapped up in that number. This is what you guys call a deal-breaker. Let's not let the thing get screwed up on that basis. I think we've got something that's going to fly here."

Copley emphasized that he was speaking only for himself, but he left Cohler with the strong impression that he understood and agreed. Finally, this was a deal that could work, Cohler thought.

Later that Monday, and all through the week, Cohler talked with Winokur, who had returned to Philadelphia, about the kinds of papers they would have to draft in order to implement the plan. Geoff Boisi, too, joined these conversations—his expertise on corporate by-laws and reorganizations was useful, and it would also be important to have Goldman, Sachs help sell the plan to the Getty Oil board of directors. Petersen was expressing some skepticism about how the directors would react to Lasky's plan. He said that he couldn't promise anything.

The September quarterly board meeting was coming up in just a few days, beginning Friday, the ninth. It was the annual "resort" meeting, the one held each year at a luxurious locale where management and the directors could bring along their wives for a weekend of golf, tennis, shopping, dining, and somewhat incidentally, a board meeting. The gathering this year was to be held at Pebble Beach, the golfing resort on the Pacific Ocean just south of San Francisco. Cohler hoped that Winokur and Petersen would agree to present the new buy-back and supermajority plan when the meeting began on Friday. But Winokur was reluctant. He said that he didn't want to present the directors with a "half-baked cake," and that he wanted to be sure that all the details of the agreement were final before it was disclosed.

As he talked with Winokur about Pebble Beach, Cohler's concerns began to grow. Winokur said that he was thinking about inviting Geoff Boisi to the meeting. Cohler thought that was a bad idea. Boisi's presence would only raise the directors' worries about infighting between Petersen and Gordon. At the "blood on the floor" session in Lasky's office the previous Thursday, the company and the trust had come close to declaring open warfare. Now they seemed to be moving again toward compromise. Boisi was a merger specialist, a game-player. He could only give the directors the wrong impression.

"Look, if the plan is going to be presented at Pebble Beach, then Geoff should be there because he's key to the presentation," Cohler said. "But if it's not going to be presented, and you're telling me that you don't think it will be, then you are holding back from the board something that is very close. You want us to work out all the fine points. If you have Geoff there, that is going to invite questions about the status of relations between the company and the trust. And you have almost no chance, in my view, of getting through a board meeting without trickling the thing out, rather than presenting it in an orderly way. I think we're close enough to having this thing actually done so that it can be recommended by management. I don't see why we're screwing around with all this stuff. Let's just do it."

"Geoff's going to be on the West Coast," Cohler was told. "We'll see then if his presence at the meeting is desired by Sid."

"Look, it's not up to me. I just simply expressed my opinion. I believe we're all working toward the same goal."

"I just want to be sure that we have some piece of paper that can be agreed upon before it goes to the board," Winokur said. "Geoff will be flying with Sid and me in the company plane to Pebble Beach. We'll decide en route whether he should attend."

When he heard that, Cohler thought to himself, *That ain't what's going on here.* He said nothing, but he suspected that management was far less interested in the Lasky plan than they seemed to profess. He feared that Petersen intended to use the Pebble Beach meeting to launch some new assault on Gordon.

They arrived at the resort on Friday from all across the country. Many of the directors brought their golf clubs with them, expecting innocently that the weekend would be easy and relaxed. They were soon disappointed. As the board meeting dragged on and on, some of them gazed wistfully through the hotel windows at the spectacular vista of manicured, verdant fairways winding along the rugged, windswept California coastline. Years later, what they remembered most clearly about the Pebble Beach meeting was the feeling that an exceptional golfing opportunity had been wasted.

Inside the lushly appointed hotel conference room where the board gathered on Friday, the mood was tense. Later there would be contradictory recollections about what was said at the meeting, and by whom. This much was agreed upon by nearly everyone who attended:

Shortly after the meeting was convened and after some routine preliminary business was dispensed with, Sid Petersen asked Gordon Getty, Harold Berg, and their advisors to excuse themselves. Petersen said that the board was going to consider the nomination of Harold Williams to be a director—Williams had been pressing for a seat on the board, and Petersen had earlier told the Lasky lawyers that the directors would consider the request at Pebble Beach. Since Gordon and Berg were trustees of the museum, of which Williams was president, it would be inappropriate for them to participate in the discussion. So Gordon and Berg returned to their rooms at the hotel. They were absent during most of the meeting.

When they were gone, Sid Petersen apparently decided that an important opportunity was at hand. For more than a year now, he had been fighting and negotiating and arguing and jockeying with Gordon Getty, and yet he had never once informed his board about the extent of Getty Oil's problems with its largest stockholder. With some directors, such as Henry Wendt and Chauncey Medberry, Petersen had been more open than with others. But no one besides himself, Winokur, Copley, and perhaps Boisi knew the full story. At the July board meeting in Los Angeles, Petersen had tried to suggest the flavor of his dealings with Gordon, but he had been in a difficult position. For one thing, Gordon had been present in the room. For another, the Goldman, Sachs studies were under discussion and Petersen did not want to reveal to Goldman the nature of management's contentious relationship with the chief stockholder, for fear the information might put the company in play. Now, finally, Petersen was prepared to reveal everything to the board. He had no choice. All of the plans and plots now afoot—the Lasky proposal for a supermajority, the Winokur proposal for a buy-back with handcuffs or cotrustees, the maneuverings to launch a family lawsuit against Gordon—were coming to a head. Petersen had to know where his directors stood, what they would permit.

He presented a kind of chronological monologue, interrupted by questions and occasionally by comments from Winokur and Boisi, who did attend the meeting at Petersen's request. He began back in May 1982, with the death of Lansing Hays and the ominous dinner meeting with Moses Lasky. He told them almost everything: Gordon's flirtation with the Cullens, the meeting at the Bonaventure, the visit by Whitehead to Gordon's Broadway mansion, the possibility of launching a family lawsuit seeking the appointment of Bank of America as a cotrustee. In greater detail, he described what had occurred since the last directors meeting in July: Gordon's proposal for an LBO takeover with a fence, the concern about Harold Williams' ambitions, the handcuffs negotiations, the discussion of an LBO takeover without a fence, the blood-on-the-floor meeting with Lasky and Cohler, and finally, the most recent proposals for a supermajority on the board and a stock buy-back that would put

Gordon in control. It was hardly the objective and "orderly" presentation of the supermajority plan that Cohler had hoped for.

Years later, trying to explain his board's deeply furious reaction
to the history he recited, Petersen said that perhaps he had lost some
of his perspective about the intrigue at his company by the time of
the Pebble Beach meeting. Looking back, he said, he could understand how it happened. He was involved so closely in the negotiations and battling with Gordon and the Lasky firm that he lost sight
of the big picture. The compromises and negotiations, the plots and
counterplots, had built up incrementally, slowly, pushed along by
the seemingly logical imperative that the independence of Getty Oil
Company should be preserved. The directors, however, had not been
in the trenches. They had not seen the give-and-take. They only saw
the end result that day in Pebble Beach: a proposal that would give
Gordon Getty control of their company. This they could not abide.
They were furious. They could not even imagine, several of the directors told Petersen when he was finished with his monologue, how he
could have allowed things to go so far. What was all this nonsense
about supermajorities and handcuffs and what have you? What was
Petersen talking about? *Gordon Getty is not going to run this company*, they said. *He is not going to take control. We will not have it.*

At the July meeting, the directors had expressed frustration about
Gordon and the million dollars Petersen had spent on the Goldman
studies, apparently to placate him. The directors thought that they
had made it very clear that no further studies were to be undertaken,
that too much money had been wasted on Goldman already. Now
they were being told not only that studies had continued, but that
management had actually contemplated handing the company to
Gordon in an LBO takeover. The directors' earlier frustration was
transformed to anger. *This is absurd*, they said.

"You'll never be able to make a deal with Gordon Getty," one of
the outside directors told Petersen. "You'll never do it. Forget it."

"If Gordon wants to put this company up for sale, then at least
let's do it right," Henry Wendt said. "If you want to protect the minority shareholders, then you must be prepared to sell the company in
an orderly fashion—through some kind of controlled action."

Most of the vitriol was aimed at Gordon. The directors cursed
him, called him a fool, a plague, a menace. But they were angry, too,
at Petersen. He had been much too soft on Gordon, they said. The

implication was clear: there was only so far Petersen could go to protect his career. No one was accusing the chairman of putting his own interests ahead of Getty Oil's, but the directors were reminding Petersen sharply that he had to accept reality. Whether by design or by inadvertent bumbling, Gordon was putting the company into play. Petersen had to accept that some kind of sale was now a strong possibility. Certainly, he had to understand that the directors would rather sell than let Gordon take control.

Gordon, of course, had no idea what was passing behind the conference room doors. He had been asked to leave while the directors considered Harold Williams' nomination to the board. But hours passed, and still the discussion on this seemingly narrow issue did not end. (The board decided eventually to postpone the question indefinitely). One executive in attendance said later that anyone other than Gordon would have stormed back to the conference room and demanded an explanation. "But Gordon wasn't aware of it," the executive said. "He was a little frustrated that he had been out of the meeting so long. But he didn't get it."

Indeed, when Gordon returned to his Broadway mansion from Pebble Beach that weekend, he still believed that Lasky's plan for a supermajority would prevail, and that some of the directors, at least, would welcome his ascension to the chairmanship of Getty Oil. The irony was that Gordon regarded as his staunchest allies on the board two outside directors who had most vociferously opposed him at Pebble Beach, Henry Wendt and Chauncey Medberry III. The latter had even indicated at the Pebble Beach session that he would resign if Gordon ever became chairman. But Gordon didn't understand. He believed that while they were sometimes rude to him, the company's managers and directors at least retained some basic respect for his talent and intelligence. Nothing he observed at Pebble Beach had changed his mind about that.

On Monday, after the meeting had ended and everyone had scattered home, Bart Winokur called Moses Lasky in San Francisco. "There's a lot that has to be said about what happened at Pebble Beach," Winokur reported. "It's going to affect our negotiations. I think that you and Tim should come back here to Philadelphia and meet with us as soon as possible." They struggled to find a date when everyone was free, but it was difficult, and Winokur finally suggested the coming Sunday, September 18, the day after Yom Kippur. Lasky said that he objected to traveling on Saturday, the holy day. Winokur answered that it was a holy day for him, too, and he understood Lasky's feelings. But this was important, he said, and he urged Lasky to come anyway. Lasky agreed.

By different routes, Lasky and Cohler arrived in Philadelphia on Saturday evening, September 17. They ate dinner together at Bookbinders restaurant and rode over the next morning to Winokur's offices at Dechert Price & Rhoads, directly across the street from Philadelphia's historic City Hall.

Winokur met them in the reception area and escorted them to an airless, windowless conference room. When they stepped inside, Lasky saw that Geoff Boisi had come down from New York for the meeting. Lasky stopped dead in his tracks.

"What is he doing here?"

Like Cohler, Lasky had grown increasingly suspicious of Boisi's role. He thought that Goldman, Sachs had been hired with the explicit understanding that the firm would remain neutral in matters involving Gordon and the company. Now, he thought, Goldman and Boisi had decided to throw their weight behind Sid Petersen and management.

"I don't think I'll talk while he is here," Lasky said defiantly. "Mr. Boisi, what you're trying to do is precipitate the sale of the company so that Goldman, Sachs can pick up some easy fees."

Boisi denied the accusation and responded that it was Lasky's client who had put the company in a precarious position.

Diplomatically, Winokur tried to persuade Lasky that Boisi should be allowed to join the meeting; he had come down all the way from New York, and he understood the issues facing them very well. Finally, Lasky relented. They took their seats at the conference table.

"Your proposal for a supermajority was presented to the board at Pebble Beach," Winokur began. "But we're facing a runaway board now. The board was absolutely angry at Sid. They told him that it was their view that in July they had instructed him to end the Goldman studies. The board feels that management has been much too yielding in dealing with Gordon all during the past year. They feel very strongly about not taking Gordon to fifty-one percent without strong assurances that the integrity of the company and the interests of the public shareholders can be protected. Some of the directors felt that not even a new cotrustee or some of the handcuffs we've discussed would be adequate.

"The board is extremely hostile," Winokur concluded. "But Sid still feels that it would be best if we can come up with some solution that would allow the company to continue in business. He wants to try it one more time. And there is some chance, if we can work something out together, that Sid might be able to persuade the board to consider it."

As Cohler and Lasky listened to Winokur, they suspected that he was exaggerating the board's reaction at Pebble Beach. But they had not been present. They had no evidence with which to contradict Winokur's adamant assertions that the directors opposed any concessions to Gordon.

Winokur said that he, Boisi, and some other Dechert Price lawyers had been working on a new proposal all week long. It was a complicated proposal—so complicated, Lasky said later, that he wasn't sure that he ever understood it. They talked about it for more than an hour. The company would buy enough shares to put Gordon in a majority position, but he could not vote any shares over 40 percent, and the company had dozens of mechanisms to protect itself if Gordon should ever attempt to exercise power through a proxy fight or other means. The proposal would neutralize Gordon effectively and indefinitely. To Cohler and Lasky, it was like taking "five million steps" backward.

"This is just a bunch of rigmarole," Lasky finally declared angrily. "This is just a piece of paper designed to end any discussion."

"That's not what it is at all," Winokur answered emphatically.

"You are trying to pull something over on me, Mr. Winokur. You deceived me when you said it was important that I come to Philadelphia." Lasky complained that he had traveled on a religious holiday only to find himself in an airless room talking about a worthless proposal.

Again, Winokur denied Lasky's accusations. It was time to break for lunch, but Lasky now declared that he wasn't coming back. He and Cohler were going to head for the airport and try to catch an earlier flight back to San Francisco, he said.

"Why don't you at least think about it over lunch, and come back and see if there isn't any way you can consider this. Perhaps you're just overreacting a little. I'm sorry that you're uncomfortable in the conference room—we'll do something about that—and I'm sorry that you had to travel on Saturday."

They met again after lunch, but the mood did not change.

"Can't you come up with something better?" Lasky asked. "If I go back to San Francisco empty-handed, it's going to hurt my credibility with Gordon."

"I feel bad about that. But I think we've given you something reasonable and we're willing to work on it," Winokur said.

"Why don't you put your proposal in writing," Lasky suggested.

Winokur agreed to do that. "The problem with your supermajority proposal is that it focuses an enormous amount of pressure on a single individual—Gordon, or the one director he tries to persuade. That idea is contrary to the whole concept of the board of directors as a decision-making body," he said.

Lasky yielded no ground, however, and the meeting ended that Sunday afternoon on a note of pessimism. Lasky said he would talk to Gordon. Winokur said he would talk to Petersen. There was nothing else they could do.

What bothered Tim Cohler as he flew back to San Francisco that evening was the realization that Bart Winokur had seized the initiative in their negotiations. It was Pebble Beach that had changed things, or more precisely, Winokur's version of what happened there. Lasky's supermajority proposal was dead now because Winokur insisted that the board would not accept Gordon as a majority shareholder without very tight, almost absurd limitations on his authority. Was Winokur telling the truth about the board, or was he just using Pebble Beach as a negotiating ploy? Cohler had no way to know, but he had a powerful instinct that what he called the "Winokur-Boisi combine," the outsiders, the game-players, were distorting the facts. Perhaps now was the time for Gordon to approach the board directly, to begin searching for a "family" solution that excluded the posturing and manipulation of the advisors.

Cohler and Lasky discussed these ideas with Gordon when they returned to San Francisco. Within days, Gordon had contacted Getty Oil directors Chauncey Medberry and Henry Wendt by telephone. On Friday, Gordon called Lasky to say that he had arranged a dinner with Medberry in Los Angeles for the following Monday, September 26. Gordon wanted Lasky to attend, and Lasky agreed to come along.

That Monday, Lasky was in Los Angeles attending to other business. Gordon reached him by phone at 11:25 A.M. and said that dinner with Medberry was set for that evening. Gordon wanted Lasky to meet him at the Beverly Wilshire Hotel, where Gordon was staying, at six o'clock. Lasky said that was fine.

Just a few minutes later, Gordon spoke by telephone with Medberry and said that he was no longer available for dinner, but wanted to meet him immediately for lunch. Medberry was surprised, but said that he would come to the Beverly Wilshire as soon as possible. He arrived at Gordon's room shortly after noon. Gordon invited him in for a talk.

"I am interested, in some form or other, in acquiring control of Getty Oil. I want to know whether you would agree to stay as a director should I obtain control," Gordon said.

"I would not serve on the board if you were the sole trustee and in control of the company," Medberry answered bluntly.

Gordon, apparently, was shocked. They talked some more, but there was nothing else to say: Medberry was adamant. If Gordon ever took control of Getty Oil, he would resign from the board. After a time, Medberry asked Gordon if he was interested in eating lunch, as they had planned. Gordon answered that he wasn't hungry, but that he would accompany Medberry to the restaurant. While Medberry ate, Gordon sat with him, sipping water. When the check came, Gordon allowed Medberry to pay it, which struck Medberry as peculiar, since Gordon had invited him to the Beverly Wilshire in the first place.

At five o'clock, Lasky arrived at the hotel and checked in. He found a message to call Tim Cohler at their offices in San Francisco.

"I had a phone call this afternoon from Gordon telling me that there was some mix-up, that Medberry had insisted on seeing him at noon," Cohler reported. "They met, and Medberry told Gordon that there was no way he would consent to the trust obtaining a majority of the stock." At six, Lasky stopped by Gordon's room to hear what had happened. Gordon repeated what Medberry had said earlier. Gordon was very upset.

"The directors are a bunch of snakes," Gordon said. "They're trying to loot the company."

Lasky said that he didn't think that was true, but there was little he could do to calm his client. As for the confusion over the scheduling of lunch, Lasky wrote in a confidential memo to file a few days later, "I have not pursued with Gordon this discrepancy."

The next day, in San Francisco, Gordon telephoned Lasky to say that he had devised an entirely new plan for dealing with his problems with the Getty Oil board of directors. He made an appointment to discuss it on Wednesday in the Lasky offices.

"I'm considering five possibilities," Gordon told his lawyers. "First is accepting the immediate resignations of all or most of the board of directors and replacing them with my designees. Second is to do nothing, maintain the status quo. Third would be to make a proposal to the museum for an immediate joint takeover of the company. Fourth, we could continue to work on the proposals from Winokur presented in Philadelphia. And last, I might launch a proxy fight against management and the company."

After talking with his client on Wednesday, Lasky wrote a letter to Gordon at the Broadway mansion. He urged Gordon to consider only the third and fourth of his enumerated plans. His first idea, accepting the resignations of the "snakes" on the Getty Oil board, "cannot be accomplished for it would constitute a complete and abject surrender by the directors." The other two possible courses, maintaining the status quo or launching a proxy fight, Lasky dismissed because they "would arouse the immediate interest of raiders and neither you nor the present board of directors would have control of what happens. . . . The only proxy fight that would have a chance of success would be one mounted shortly before the annual meeting and we do not believe that events will wait that long."

Thus there were two choices, Lasky wrote: Gordon could continue to negotiate with management toward the realization of some stock buy-back plan that would put Gordon in a majority position, or he could make a proposal to Harold Williams and the museum for an immediate joint takeover of Getty Oil. "My judgment, shared by Tim and Tom, is that the wisest course is this [negotiated buy-back] deal," Lasky wrote. The lawyer listed several reasons why a takeover in combination with the museum was a bad idea: it would cost too much; it would probably lead to a lawsuit against Gordon by the family beneficiaries; and finally, "it would constitute a coup. In the eyes of the financial and business public, it would constitute an upheaval at Getty Oil Company—either a condemnation of the present management or a threat of unpredictable future conduct by the company. I would not minimize that consideration. . . . There are at least four players in the game: you, Getty Oil Company, the museum, and the outsiders or raiders. These four can make various permutations or combinations and no one of them has control of what may happen. Having started down the course of effecting a change in the status quo, I do not see how you can stop midstream, even though one cannot predict the outcome."

They met again at Gordon's Broadway mansion to discuss the letter. Gordon told his lawyers that despite Lasky's advice, he favored a joint takeover with the museum and he intended to approach Harold Williams with a proposal. At his lawyers' urging, however, Gordon agreed simultaneously to pursue negotiations with Winokur for a stock buy-back plan. Such a deal would have to be concluded in a matter of days, however, Gordon said. Otherwise, he would meet with Williams.

"Bart, Mr. Getty intends to attend a meeting of the board of trustees of the J. Paul Getty Museum next Tuesday in London," Lasky told Winokur that Friday by telephone. "He intends to make a proposal for joint action with the museum. It's an attractive offer and I don't see how the museum can refuse it.

"You have only one chance to choose another course of action," Lasky went on. "We will send you a set of papers which we think have some chance of being considered by Mr. Getty as an alternative to his making this proposal to the museum. If the company has accepted in writing the materials that we are sending you by a deadline we will specify, that will be considered by Mr. Getty as an alternative to his museum proposal. And I should tell you that there is no room for subsequent discussion."

Lasky hung up the phone. He had succeeded, at least, in presenting his client's unpredictable impulses as a reasoned, tough negotiating stance toward management. Winokur understood well enough what an "offer the museum can't refuse" might mean. Between them, Gordon and the museum controlled 52 percent of Getty Oil's stock. If Gordon offered to make Harold Williams chief executive, to give him a free hand to run Getty Oil Company as he pleased, the two of them might combine immediately to take control. They could do it, quite literally, in seconds. They could sign a piece of paper, called a "consent," declaring that Petersen, Winokur, Copley, and the entire board of directors were fired instantly and that Gordon and the museum were now in charge. If Harold Williams privately longed to control Getty Oil, he would have his chance—on Tuesday, six thousand miles away, in the unlikely environs of London, England.

12

LONDON

On Sunday, Lasky was at home in San Francisco when Winokur telephoned.

"Moses, you've got to go over to London. You're the only person we can work with. We can't make a deal without you there."

"I don't know. Cohler and Woodhouse are already over there. You can work with them."

"Please."

"Well, I'll see if I can find them in London and I'll see what they think."

Winokur was in Philadelphia that afternoon at the Dechert Price offices. A light rain was falling and the city was enshrouded by heavy fog. Winokur, Petersen, Copley, Boisi, and several other Getty Oil lawyers had reservations to fly to London that evening; they could only hope the fog would lift. Meanwhile, they were all huddled in a conference room on the thirty-fourth floor. An emergency meeting of the Getty Oil board of directors had been called on Friday as soon as Winokur heard about Gordon's plans to approach the museum with a takeover proposal. Gordon was already on his way to England; he never received notice about the emergency board meeting. When Winokur talked to Lasky that day, he did not mention that Getty Oil's directors were all assembled in Philadelphia.

The board had been convened to ratify a plan devised by Winokur, Boisi, and two Wall Street lawyers recently retained by the company, Herbert Galant and Stuart Katz. Fearing that Gordon and Williams might use their combined 52 percent position to sign a "consent" takeover, the Getty Oil advisors had decided to prepare for the worst. There were presently about 80 million shares of Getty Oil stock outstanding. Gordon's trust owned 32 million, the museum 9 million. Together, their 41 million shares were a majority. But the company also had another 9 million shares in the bank, so-called treasury shares, which had not been issued to the public. The treasury shares were a kind of stand-by reserve of stock. If the board of directors suddenly decided to issue all of the treasury stock, they would increase the total number of outstanding Getty Oil shares from 80 million to 89 million. Then the 41 million shares controlled by Gordon and the museum would only constitute about 46 percent, not enough to take control through a consent. There were a variety of technical mechanisms by which the 9 million treasury shares could be issued, and there were a number of complex legal questions that might eventually snag the plan. But at the least, issuance of the treasury shares would buy the company time by making it impossible for Gordon and the museum to sign a consent firing management and board.

That Sunday afternoon at Dechert Price in Philadelphia, at Sid Petersen's urging, the directors agreed to support the plan, and they authorized issuance of 9 million shares to dilute the position of the trust and the museum. The treasury shares were not actually issued that day; management was given a kind of blank check to issue the shares whenever it desired. A bundle of stock certificates was prepared by the Wall Street lawyers, ready for signature. The battle with Gordon might well come down to an Old West "draw," only it would be pens, not guns, whipped from the lawyers' holsters. Gordon, Williams, and Petersen might find themselves in the same room in London, negotiating a new compromise. The deal might suddenly fall through. If Gordon and Williams signed their consent takeover firing Petersen before the Getty Oil chairman signed his treasury share certificates, then Gordon would control the company. On the other hand, if Petersen signed first, then Gordon's power would be diluted. The question would be, who could draw his pen the fastest?

This scenario and many others were discussed with the directors that Sunday afternoon at Dechert Price. Dave Copley reported on the progress of the family lawsuit against Gordon; he said that he hoped to meet with Vanni Treves, J. Paul Jr.'s solicitor, the next week in London. Surely, if Paul Jr. was ever going to authorize a lawsuit against his brother, he would do it now. Gordon was careering out of control. He was endangering not only the company, but his family's wealth, Copley believed. Sid Petersen explained the status of the buy-back negotiations with Gordon. They would not give the company to Gordon, he said, but they had to be prepared to compromise, to buy as much time as possible.

The meeting recessed and again Winokur called Lasky at home in San Francisco. The company's best hope, Winokur thought, was not to play dueling pens with Gordon Getty, but to negotiate a realistic buy-back plan with Lasky. Winokur had studied the "ultimatum" proposal sent to Philadelphia by Lasky earlier in the week. It was unacceptable to management. But Winokur had sat down with Lasky's plan and with his own and had drawn up a list of differences, trying to identify ground for a potential compromise. He was encouraged by that effort. Winokur somewhat naïvely believed that by dint of inspiration and hard work, any problem could be solved, even the problem of Gordon Getty's personality.

"I've talked to Cohler and Woodhouse in London," Lasky told Winokur. "They said they'd like me to come over. I'm leaving on a five-thirty Pan Am flight this afternoon."

"That's great, Moses. We'll see you over there."

Winokur reported the news to Petersen and Boisi: there was still hope that Gordon could be stopped, or at least slowed, in London. None of them really wanted to issue the 9 million treasury shares. That would dilute the value of the company's outstanding stock, inviting lawsuits, and it would certainly make clear to Wall Street that Getty Oil Company was beset by serious internal dissension. The blood, as Winokur would put it, would be everywhere.

Still, as they flew to London that night, none of them knew about the museum. What would Harold Williams do? What did he want? Ever since Pebble Beach, Petersen and Gordon had been acting on the assumption that Williams wanted to control Getty Oil as much as they did. But they had not spoken to Williams about it directly. Gordon had not talked at length with the museum president since their meeting in July, when they discussed an LBO takeover with a fence. Petersen, too, had been extremely cautious during his few telephone conversations with Williams. Not only did he suspect that Williams wanted his job, he also knew that if Getty Oil and Gordon ever reached an agreement on a stock buy-back plan, they might try to force the museum to sell its shares in a "squeeze" in order to raise the Sarah Getty Trust's stock position above 50 percent. It was important, then, that details about the company's negotiations with Gordon be kept from Williams. At one point in July, fearing that Williams would accuse them of improper secrecy, Winokur and Cohler had drafted a written statement about the status of the buy-back negotiations and Cohler had read the declaration to Williams over the telephone. Since then, they had told the museum president little about the progress of their talks.

One thing they did know that Sunday night was that Harold Williams had finally hired a lawyer to help him protect the museum's stock position should open war erupt between Gordon and the company. And not just any lawyer—Williams, they learned, had retained Martin Lipton, Wall Street's premiere takeover lawyer, a man of singular reputation in American finance. Both Getty Oil and the Lasky firm assumed that Lipton had been playing a significant role behind the scenes that summer, advising Williams about how the museum should respond to Gordon's LBO takeover offer and to the growing suspicion and hostility expressed by Sid Petersen about the museum.

In fact, it was not until that weekend, when Petersen, Winokur, Boisi, and the rest convened the emergency board meeting in Philadelphia and then flew on to London, that Marty Lipton actually became involved in the tangled affairs of Getty Oil Company. Lipton had met with Williams in Los Angeles a couple of times during the summer, but the visits had been mainly social. Lipton and Williams were friends; they had met when Williams was chairman of the SEC and Lipton served on a special advisory committee to the commission made up of Wall Street securities experts. They sustained their friendship even after Williams left the East Coast to become president of the J. Paul Getty Museum Trust. Lipton served on the board of the Los Angeles Museum of Contemporary Art, so when he flew to L.A. for his monthly board meeting, he would arrange to have breakfast or lunch with Williams in Beverly Hills. It had been at one of those casual lunches in July that Williams asked if Lipton would help him protect the museum's huge stock position in Getty Oil. Lipton agreed to help. It was a favor for a friend, he said later. He did not regard the engagement as a paying matter for his law firm. When he left for London from New York on October 3, spurred by unexpected, urgent phone calls from Tim Cohler and Harold Williams, Lipton had not even opened an office file on the museum case. Suddenly, Gordon was going to make an offer the museum could not refuse, the lawyer was told. But Lipton was barely acquainted with the personalities involved.

He was a lawyer well qualified to learn as he went along, however. Indeed, by that October, 1983, the mere mention of Martin Lipton's name in connection with a takeover proposal was enough to change the entire course of negotiation. In less than two decades, Lipton and his law firm, Wachtell, Lipton, Rosen & Katz, had risen to a position of profound influence over American industry and finance. Lipton himself was considered to be one of the two leading merger lawyers in the country, along with Joseph Flom, of the large Wall Street firm Skadden, Arps, Slate, Meagher & Flom. Lipton and Flom formed a kind of traveling legal exhibition: in numerous hostile takeover battles during the early 1980s, Lipton was retained by one side, Flom by the other. They developed a comfortable, competitive relationship that earned each of them millions per year in fees and established their firms as the leaders in merger and acquisition law. Lipton had invented the famous "poison pill" defense for corporations under attack by a hostile raider—it was a complex stock issuance device that could be quickly "swallowed" by a company's board of directors, making the company instantly unattractive to a hostile bidder. Flom, similarly, had devised innovative attacking techniques to avoid the perils of Lipton's poison. They did battle again and again, each time becoming stronger, smarter, and above all, richer.

It was a dazzling ride that had carried Martin Lipton to success, and to the East Side apartment where he lived in October 1983. He was born and raised across the Hudson River from Manhattan, in Jersey City, New Jersey, the only son of first-generation Jewish immigrants from Poland. His mother was a housewife, his father an insurance salesman and erstwhile entrepreneur. The elder Lipton had arrived poor in America as a teenager during the First World War, and had saved his money to bring others in his family out of Poland. Those who were left behind perished in the Holocaust; only the Liptons who came to America survived the 1940s. The family emphasized education; though Marty Lipton's father had no schooling at all, he was remembered by his son as a "brilliant man, very well read, with the typical attitude that the key to success was education." There was a year or more during the Depression when Lipton's father did not work, and the family suffered, but during World War II he joined a family business making parachutes and uniforms, and he prospered modestly. Young Martin played stickball and touch football in the streets of Jersey City, and studied assiduously to please his parents. Lipton would do anything to please his father, and since his father wanted him to become an investment banker, he enrolled at the University of Pennsylvania's Wharton School as an undergraduate. But finance bored him. In the spring of 1952, he decided to apply to law school, took the entrance exam, and was accepted by New York University in Manhattan.

It was in law school, Lipton said later, that he found himself. Looking back, he had been a relatively immature and unsophisticated young man before he began his legal education. His relationship with the law was "love at first sight and it just got better." He graduated first in his class and was editor in chief of the school's law review. For six years, he worked for a small Wall Street firm specializing in bankruptcy, securities, and corporate litigation. When the firm dissolved in 1964 because of internal bickering, Lipton and a few young friends decided to go it alone. They started with just a few basic concepts: they would all be equal partners, no matter what, for as long as the firm survived. When they parceled out salaries, they would never pay attention to who got the clients or who did the most work—the only objective was to do superior legal work. The clients would come, and so would the money, they thought. Their egalitarian precepts allowed them to be flexible, to form cooperative client teams. They began to grow, from seven to twenty to thirty-five and finally, by the 1980s, to nearly one hundred lawyers.

The turning point came in 1975, when Lipton represented the Loews Corporation, which was run by Laurence and Robert Tisch, in a contentious, hostile takeover against an insurance company, CNA. Lipton's side won, and suddenly he and his firm were hot—they were the only ones who stood a chance in a takeover battle against Joe Flom, it was said. Flom's principal client was Robert Greenhill, the renowned merger specialist at the old Wall Street investment banking firm of Morgan Stanley & Company. Lipton began to represent the other major investment houses opposed to Morgan in takeovers, particularly Goldman, Sachs & Company and Salomon Brothers. By 1982, Lipton was at the vortex of what he called "the hostile-tender-battle period in American finance."

His success was manifested not only in professional prominence and personal wealth. It was evidenced, too, by his position in Manhattan's ascendant society of privilege and power during the early 1980s, a society bolstered by an unprecedented bull stock market and the growing influence of Wall Street over mainstream American industry. On weekday mornings, Lipton, a bulky man with an oblong nose and extremely thick tortoise shell spectacles, could be seen at the "Regency power breakfast," as the magazines called it, which was held at the Regency Hotel on Park Avenue. There lawyers, investment bankers, and corporate takeover specialists discussed greenmail and poison pills over coffee and eggs Benedict. In the evenings, Lipton was in demand as a speaker and fund-raiser at gala benefits for art museums, Jewish philanthropies, universities, and other charities. He was renowned, too, for the annual New Year's Day party he threw at his apartment, where Wall Street's leading cognoscenti gathered to celebrate another year of unbridled prosperity. Theirs was a close-knit circle bound not only by the raging takeover wars but by the city of New York. During the 1970s, Lipton had been prominently involved in the Municipal Assistance Corporation, a quasi-governmental agency led by Lazard Frères merger banker Felix Rohatyn and formed to save New York from bankruptcy. Since then, the elite bankers and lawyers had pledged an informal allegiance to New York Mayor Ed Koch, and they occasionally served on special city commissions at his request.

All of this history, its potency and flair, hung over Martin Lipton like a halo. Any deal he touched was imbued with the power of his reputation. He was regarded, to say the least, as a formidable opponent. Getty Oil's management was bolstered by the energy and skill of young Winokur and Boisi; Gordon could boast about the Lasky firm's shrewd toughness; but Harold Williams and the museum, well, they had an emerging legend in their corner.

Indeed, it was Lipton's reputation that exacerbated the fears of Sid Petersen and the others as they flew to London that Sunday night early in October 1983. Harold Williams *must* be serious about a bid for control of Getty Oil; why else would he hire Marty Lipton? Boisi, at least, had worked on Lipton's side in a number of deals where both

Lipton's law firm and Goldman, Sachs had been retained to help a company fight off a hostile takeover bid. Boisi trusted Lipton and was not intimidated by him. The two were bound by both friendship and economics; Goldman, Sachs was one of Lipton's most important clients. Still, there was no question, either, that Marty Lipton was relentless and at times unforgiving in the service of his clients. Getty Oil was a rich prize—one of the largest companies ever put in play by Wall Street. If Harold Williams wanted to take the company, Marty Lipton would be sure to deliver the quarry.

They spent the early hours of Monday morning sleeping off the jet lag in a dumpy motel near Heathrow Airport in London. The rooms were like dungeons. It was as if they had landed in Europe to take the Continent from the Germans and were sleeping on mattresses before shipping out to the front, one of the lawyers on the trip said later. It was an amusing scene: all these high-powered investment bankers and corporate attorneys, as well as the chief executive of one of the world's largest oil companies, sprawled out in the dimly lit motel rooms, trying to refresh themselves with a nap. They checked out early in the afternoon and took a cab to more appropriate quarters, Claridge's, a luxury hotel in central London.

It was early evening before they gathered in the basement conference room of Dechert Price & Rhoads' small London office at 52 Bedford Square. Sid Petersen was asked to remain in an office on the second floor; detailed negotiations would be left to the advisors. For the company, there was Winokur, Copley, Boisi, Galant, Katz, and Dan O'Donnell, a Dechert partner who often worked closely with Winokur. For Gordon, there was Lasky, Cohler, and Woodhouse.

"We're here to try and come up with an agreement that will forestall Gordon's presentation to the museum tomorrow," Winokur said. Lasky concurred. He continued to believe, as he had told Gordon the previous week, that a negotiated stock buy-back plan was preferable to a joint takeover with the museum. For the first time, all of the advisors faced an imminent, concrete deadline. If there was no deal by Tuesday, Gordon would go his own way. He would make an offer to Harold Williams.

Thus, a new, urgent atmosphere of cooperation and compromise pervaded in the basement conference room that evening. There was no time to moralize or play games. They had to make a deal.

Winokur and Lasky began by drawing up a list of some ten points where there was disagreement between the company and the trust on a stock buy-back plan. Systematically, methodically, they attacked that list, giving some here, taking some there, searching for the middle ground. When the company had to make a major concession, Winokur and Boisi would walk up to the second floor and consult with Petersen. When it was Gordon who was forced to compromise, Lasky made his own decisions. His client was in London, but Lasky did not want to speak with Gordon about a buy-back deal until there was some final agreement.

The goal of the negotiation was to find a way to put Gordon in a majority position without handing him immediate control of Getty Oil Company. Over the last three months, they had tried a number of formulas. In late July, Winokur had proposed "handcuffs" that would prevent Gordon from voting more than 40 percent of the company's stock, even if he owned 51 percent. Then at the September meeting in San Francisco, Lasky had suggested his supermajority plan that would have forced Gordon to compromise with other directors once he gained control. At the same time, Winokur had suggested two institutional cotrustees be appointed to restrain Gordon's power. From there, the two sides had moved into a seemingly unbreakable deadlock. Now they decided to return to the beginning, to the idea of handcuffs.

They introduced a new element: a time limit. The idea was that Getty Oil would buy back 16 million shares of its own stock, raising Gordon and the trust to fifty-one percent. The company would agree never to issue the 9 million treasury shares secretly authorized in Philadelphia on Sunday, thus guaranteeing that Gordon would control a permanent majority. In exchange, Gordon would accept handcuffs for a period of three or four years—Lasky wanted three, Winokur more than that. During that time, Gordon could only vote 40 percent of the company's stock. The rest would likely be controlled by management. Gordon would be named chairman of the board, and there would be no restrictions on his ability to sell his trust's shares to outsiders, though Gordon would have to guarantee a fair price to the public in the event of a full outside takeover attempt. Moreover, Gordon would retain the power to launch a stockholders' proxy fight against management, using his 40 percent as a base to recruit other shareholders to his cause. After two or three years,

Gordon would have the right to end unilaterally the handcuffs on his voting power, thus gaining total control of the company, so long as he gave Getty Oil management two years' notice of his intentions.

This last point was of great significance to Winokur and Petersen, and later it would become the basis of bitter acrimony between the company and the Lasky firm. Winokur referred privately to the two-year notice provision as Getty Oil's "out." That is, once Gordon told Getty Oil management that he planned to exercise majority control in two years' time, Petersen and the board could arrange a sale of the company before Gordon took control. In fact, the board had made it clear at Pebble Beach that it would never serve Gordon Getty or allow him to take the reins of the company. Moreover, the time provisions negotiated that Monday evening in London would allow the company to pursue a family lawsuit challenging Gordon's control of the Sarah Getty Trust. Gordon would have to wait at least three years before declaring his intention to take majority control, then another two years before the handcuffs would be unlocked. That meant Petersen and Winokur had fully five years to win a family lawsuit seeking the appointment of a bank to serve with Gordon as cotrustee. None of this, of course, was explained to Lasky, who was totally unaware of management's contacts with the Getty family. Lasky believed that Winokur and Petersen were sincere about letting Gordon eventually gain control of Getty Oil.

And certainly, all of them were nearly bursting with sincerity and good cheer when the meeting ended in London at two-thirty Tuesday morning. They had done it—they had made a deal. Lasky, particularly, was effusive in his praise for Winokur and Boisi, the company advisors he had so angrily attacked two weeks before in that airless conference room in Philadelphia.

"I'm extremely happy with what we've accomplished," Lasky said that night as he prepared to return to his hotel from Bedford Square. "You were true to your word, Winokur, and you did everything you conceivably could have done to try and reach an agreement. I'm elated. You all brought imagination and understanding to the resolution of the problems.

"I am confident—not certain—but confident that Gordon will accept this agreement," Lasky concluded. "We will call you in the morning as soon as we have spoken with him."

When Lasky and his partners had departed, Winokur, Petersen,

Boisi, and the others congratulated themselves heartily. By skillful negotiation and compromise, they had stopped Gordon's proposal to the museum. They had averted the loss of Getty Oil Company, they thought. They were exhausted, but also too excited to sleep, so they wandered about London searching for a restaurant that was open all night. They finally found a Chinese place and shared a meal before returning to their hotel.

At ten minutes before ten the next morning, Gordon met with Lasky, Cohler, and Woodhouse in Lasky's room at the John Howard Hotel, not far from Claridge's in central London. Lasky began the meeting by handing Gordon a copy of the long letter he had written the previous week, which compared the merits of a joint museum takeover with a compromise buy-back deal with Getty Oil. Lasky described the negotiations that had taken place the night before at Bedford Square, and he listed for his client the provisions of the agreement he had reached with Winokur.

"The provisions granting you the power to terminate the restrictions, or handcuffs, are much better for you than even the possible deal I described in my letter," Lasky said.

Gordon listened. He looked over Lasky's letter. And then he flatly rejected his lawyer's recommendation.

"I'm not willing to make any deal with Getty Oil," he declared. "I'd rather make my takeover proposal to the museum."

Lasky told Gordon that if he did so, the company would surely issue its 9 million treasury shares to dilute Gordon's stock position. Lasky did not know exactly what the directors had done in Philadelphia, but he knew the 9 million treasury shares existed and he assumed the company was smart enough to authorize their issuance.

"If Harold Williams is not interested in my proposal, I'd rather maintain the status quo," Gordon said.

"You can't maintain the status quo, because the nine million shares will change everything," Lasky insisted.

"Well, my idea of the status quo is that I would immediately launch a proxy fight or make a tender offer to take over the company and replace the board of directors," Gordon answered.

"But, Gordon, if you want to launch a proxy fight, you'd be better off under the deal we negotiated last night. Besides, if you try to start a proxy fight or a tender-offer takeover, the plan will not succeed because management will move immediately to sell the company.

Winokur told us that himself last night. In our judgment, you're better off with the compromise we negotiated. That is the best solution. The alternative can only be litigation, and litigation is both very difficult and very expensive. It could involve millions of dollars in expenses and unquestionably there would be a tax on you personally. If you decide to go to the museum, your decision could result in lawsuits by the beneficiaries to the trust."

Despite Lasky's pleading, Gordon would not move. "I am not going to enter into any deal with the company," he said. "You should tell Winokur that his proposed agreement is unacceptable."

The lawyers did not yet give up. As Lasky put it in a memo to file he dictated later that afternoon, "In every possible way short of using the word 'mistake' we told Gordon that his decision was a mistake."

Lasky emphasized again that the compromise negotiated at Bedford Square the night before was more favorable than any proposal previously considered by Getty Oil management. It was even more favorable than proposals made by Lasky himself in September.

"Well, I never authorized you to make that supermajority proposal in the first place," Gordon said ominously.

All three of the lawyers jumped in. They reminded Gordon that at a Saturday meeting at his Broadway mansion, he had "distinctly authorized" Lasky's supermajority proposal.

They continued to argue, but Gordon became increasingly stubborn. Lasky was even unable to explain all of the details of the agreement he had reached with Winokur at two-thirty that morning because Gordon refused to consider any restrictions on his voting power at all. Gordon said that after his conversation the previous week with Med-berry, he was not about to make any accommodation with the "snakes" on the Getty Oil board of directors.

"The decision is yours," Lasky finally said. "We can only give you our opinion. As your attorneys, we will necessarily follow your instructions."

Gordon then told his lawyers to call Winokur and tell him the deal was off.

Tim Cohler telephoned Claridge's at 11:41 A.M. Winokur, Boisi, Petersen, Copley, Galant, and the others were in the hotel dining room, eating a late breakfast. Winokur was summoned to a telephone in the hallway.

"We presented the proposal to Mr. Getty, Bart," Cohler said. "He flatly rejected it. We are proceeding now to make the proposal to the museum."

Winokur was stunned. "You're going to do that right now?"

"Yes."

"Well, can we talk about what the problems were that you had with Mr. Getty? Why did he turn it down?"

"I'm not free to tell you that. Mr. Getty flatly rejected the proposal."

"Does Mr. Getty understand that if he goes and makes the proposal to the museum, that the company will be forced to act in a way that will ensure the sale of Getty Oil?" Winokur asked.

"I understand from our discussions last night that that's the company's position. I transmitted that to my client," Cohler answered. It seemed to Winokur that Cohler's voice was tight, choked.

"Is that what your client wants?" Winokur demanded. "Does he want to sell the company? Because if he wants to sell the company, we've told you repeatedly in the past that there are better ways to sell Getty Oil than in a war. In a war, you're not going to get the best price. We'll have a much better chance if we do it in a friendly manner. If he's going to take a step which is going to lead inevitably to the sale of the company, then we should all agree to just sell the company."

"I understand your position on that and I have transmitted it to my client," Cohler answered. "I can't discuss my client's reasons, just as you refused to discuss the nine million treasury shares and what you plan to do with them."

"Well, what we've done with those shares is not irrevocable."

Winokur hung up the phone and returned to the dining room to finish what was left of his breakfast. He reported his conversation with Cohler to Petersen, Boisi, and the others. They discussed what they should do next. They had to prepare immediately to issue the 9 million treasury shares, in case Gordon and Williams tried to sign a consent firing the board of directors that very afternoon. They decided to return to the Dechert Price & Rhoads offices to establish a base of operations.

It was shortly after they arrived at Bedford Square that Marty Lipton telephoned and asked to speak to his friend Geoff Boisi.

Boisi stepped into an unoccupied office to take the call. Winokur and Galant followed him in. During the conversation, Boisi repeated what Lipton was saying to the other Getty Oil lawyers.

"There has been a meeting between Gordon and Williams," Boisi reported. "Gordon has proposed a joint consent takeover. Marty thinks that we are in an absurd situation. He wants all of us, including Sid, to come over to Claridge's and meet with Harold Williams."

"Tell him that we don't think it's a good idea for Sid to come over," Winokur instructed. "Tell him that the advisors will come over and meet with him."

Boisi repeated Winokur's instructions, and Lipton agreed. A few minutes later, Lipton, Winokur, Boisi, Galant, and Patricia Vlahakis, a Wachtell, Lipton associate, gathered in Lipton's hotel room.

"I have just undergone one of the most exceptional and curious experiences of my career," Lipton began. "I had a meeting with Gordon and his lawyers that was patently absurd. They made an absolutely absurd proposal. It was truly outrageous, it involved firing the entire board of directors, and obviously it is totally unacceptable to the museum.

"In the course of that discussion," Lipton continued, "I was also told that Getty Oil held a board meeting over the weekend and that some action has been taken to issue treasury shares and threaten the status quo. I am quite upset about that, too. I can't understand how we can be in a situation like this. I cannot understand how the company could have done something like that."

"We did it because we received a telephone call from Moses Lasky indicating that Mr. Getty was going to make a proposal to the museum, and that in Lasky's view, it was a proposal which was so attractive that the museum could not possibly refuse it," Geoff Boisi said. "Not knowing what the proposal would be, we were unable to make an independent judgment on whether or not the museum would or would not refuse it. So we had to take action to protect against the possibility that the museum would accept it."

"That's absolutely ridiculous," Lipton responded. "How anyone with a sense of responsibility could think that a responsible man like Harold Williams or a lawyer like Marty Lipton would ever enter into an agreement with Gordon Getty like this is just inconceivable. Mr. Williams is a responsible businessman. He is respected in the business community and he obviously would always act responsibly. It's just inconceivable that he would ever enter into an agreement like this."

"Well, that may or may not be true," one of the Getty Oil advisors said. "And we're certainly happy to hear that you don't find the proposal acceptable, but we don't even know what the proposal was. We don't know why you found it unacceptable, and we have no way to know whether, if that proposal was modified in some way, you might find it acceptable in some different form."

"The proposal is totally absurd and there is no redeeming feature about it," Lipton declared.

"I understand that you've said that," Geoff Boisi answered, pressing Lipton. "But that might well have been because it was ill conceived in terms of structure. And knowing your genius and brilliance, we're afraid that perhaps you will be brilliant enough to figure out a proposal yourself which the museum might not be able to refuse. Maybe you haven't had the time to do that yet. Maybe you ultimately will be able to do that, and maybe then you'll reach an agreement with Gordon to take over the company."

"Geoff, it's just outrageous to think that a man of Harold Williams' stature would ever endanger his reputation by entering into an agreement conceived like this with Mr. Getty, someone like Mr. Getty. I had never met Gordon Getty before this morning, and frankly, I've heard a lot of stories about him. But I was unprepared for what I actually met with a few moments ago.

"I really think the solution here is just to tone everybody down," Lipton went on. "There ought to be a standstill agreement, a truce, a three-way standstill between the company, the museum, and Gordon. The standstill ought to give everybody enough time—eighteen months or so—so that everyone can calm down and try to approach these problems in a more rational, businesslike way."

"Without having talked with our client, I would think the idea of a standstill would have some appeal," Winokur answered. "But at the same time, that has some dangers to it because at this moment, the company is in a position to defend itself by forcing an auction sale in the event there is action by the museum and Mr. Getty."

"I think the company ought to take down its defenses, including whatever you did with the nine million shares—which was probably illegal anyway," Lipton said.

"What does the company have to gain by an eighteen-month standstill?" Boisi asked. "Our concern is that during the truce the company will have no defense, but Gordon will have time to ally himself with an outsider, maybe the museum, maybe somebody else."

"Well, I think the company could use the standstill period to attempt to neutralize Gordon Getty as trustee of the Sarah Getty Trust," Lipton answered. Unbeknownst to Lipton, of course, that was precisely what the company was attempting to do through the family lawsuit yet to be executed, challenging Gordon's right to be sole trustee.

They talked about it some more and finally agreed that a standstill truce would be sensible. But before the meeting ended, Winokur raised another issue.

"There has been a failure of communication, at the very minimum, between Williams and Petersen," he told Lipton. "We still have a concern that Mr. Williams has other objectives here, including involving himself more fully and heavily, in some direct way, in the day-to-day affairs of Getty Oil or its board of directors."

"Harold Williams has no such intent of involving himself," Lipton said. "He is interested only in being a shareholder. In fact, what he is interested in is cooling things down and not causing embarrassment for the museum. He is not looking to sell his shares at this point. He's happy with his investment." Williams might eventually sell his shares for tax reasons but he was in no hurry.

"Perhaps Mr. Williams ought to speak directly to Mr. Petersen and tell him directly his views about the company and his role in the company, so that they can have a very frank discussion and get out on the table all these issues that have so far been boiling below the surface," Winokur suggested.

"That would be a good idea," Lipton agreed.

Winokur then telephoned Sid Petersen at Bedford Square and asked him to come over to Claridge's.

"I'll go down the hall and see if Mr. Getty's lawyers, or Mr. Getty himself, would be willing to enter into a standstill," Lipton said.

He found Tim Cohler and Tom Woodhouse with their client in Gordon's two-room suite. Lasky had not bothered to attend the earlier meeting where Gordon presented his proposal to Harold Williams. Lipton explained to Gordon and his two lawyers that he had met with Getty Oil's advisors and that the company had agreed to enter into a standstill.

"You have one hour to agree to a standstill," Lipton said. He had decided to play hardball with Gordon. The "or else" attached to his deadline was the implication that Getty Oil would immediately issue its 9 million treasury shares, diluting Gordon's position. It was an empty threat, since the company's lawyers were still suspicious of Lipton, but it was effective nonetheless.

Cohler telephoned Lasky at the John Howard Hotel. He explained that Williams and Lipton had flatly rejected Gordon's proposal, that Lipton had subsequently met with Winokur and Boisi, and that now he was proposing a standstill agreement. Gordon had one hour to accept, or the company would likely issue its 9 million treasury shares, Cohler said. He urged Lasky to hasten over to Gordon's suite at Claridge's.

Fifteen minutes later, Lasky arrived. Gordon, Cohler, Woodhouse, Lipton, and Vlahakis were there. Lipton repeated to Lasky the ultimatum he had previously delivered to Cohler.

"Would you like to hear my views as to whether you should enter into this standstill agreement?" Lasky asked Gordon.

"I would," his client answered.

Lipton and Vlahakis stepped into the adjoining room so that Gordon could talk privately with his lawyers.

Lasky did everything in his power to persuade Gordon to accept the standstill. "In my opinion, Gordon, you've done what you were required to do as a fiduciary after you became sole trustee of the family trust more than a year ago. You explored all possible avenues of improving and protecting the value of your shares in Getty Oil Company.

"Now that you've done that, it is apparent that if you don't enter into the standstill agreement, the company will be put on the block and sold," Lasky went on. "This morning, you said that you wanted to maintain the status quo. If the museum proposal is not going to work, the standstill comes as close as anything to maintaining the status quo."

"I am not going to make a decision about the standstill before Lipton's deadline," Gordon announced when Lasky was finished with his speech. "One thing I learned from my father is that whenever somebody gives an ultimatum that something has to be done immediately, the thing to do is to refuse to act immediately."

"But it's not a matter of being able to avoid a decision," Lasky insisted. "By refusing to make a decision to enter into a standstill, you would in fact be making a decision to sell the company."

"I will not meet Lipton's deadline," Gordon repeated stubbornly.

Exasperated, Lasky called Lipton back into the room. "Perhaps you could go back to the company's representatives and see if the deadline can be postponed twenty-four or forty-eight hours or even until we all get back to the United States," Lasky suggested. "It seems absurd that a matter concerning a company in Los Angeles should be determined by rush proceedings in London."

"I will try," Lipton said.

Lipton and Vlahakis walked back to the suite where Winokur, Boisi, and the others were waiting. Sid Petersen had arrived from Bedford Square and was meeting in the adjoining room with Harold Williams. They were talking about their mutual suspicions.

"I tried to give Gordon a time deadline and I got no response to that," Lipton reported. "The answer was not 'Yes,' and it was not 'No.' It was 'I don't know.' He doesn't know what he is going to do, and he doesn't know when he is going to know what he is going to do."

"Since we don't know when or what Mr. Getty is going to do," Lipton continued, "we ought to consider signing a two-party standstill between the company and the museum, in case they decide not to join us."

They talked for a while about whether a two-way standstill was even worth signing, with Winokur questioning its value and Lipton insisting it was a sound idea. Lipton even drafted a few sentences on a Claridge's notepad.

"Maybe we should draft a standstill document right here and sign it," Winokur suggested at one point during the discussion.

"That really isn't necessary," Lipton said. "What we ought to do is all go back to the United States and draft a document in an atmosphere where we're capable of doing it properly."

"That's all fine to say," Winokur responded. "But the fact is that World War III has just about broken out here. And even though you've assured us that there is no way that you're going to set off the bomb, there is no way that we can know that for sure. What is there to prevent a signing tomorrow, where you and the trust act to take over the company?"

"It's absurd to think we would do that," Lipton said. "Look, I am in this business, this merger and acquisition business. This is my life. My word is what I live and survive on. If I break my word, I will be out of the business."

Herb Galant, the Wall Street lawyer recently retained by Getty Oil, accepted Lipton's protestations. "That's right," he said. "If he breaks his word, he will be out of the business."

"I've known Marty for a lot of years and I agree with that," Geoff Boisi added. "He could never afford to break his word."

"I give you my word on behalf of me and the museum that under no circumstances will the museum sign a consent with Gordon and the trust to take over the company," Lipton declared.

"Marty's word is good enough for me," Galant said.

And with that, Martin Lipton and the Getty Oil advisors agreed that their adventure in London was concluded. The next day, they would fly back to the United States to begin work on a formal, eighteen-month standstill agreement.

Down the hall, in Gordon Getty's suite, Moses Lasky was once again meeting with his client. Gordon had summoned his lawyers back to his room because, he said, he had now made a decision.

"I suppose you think I'm out of my mind for rejecting your recommendation this morning and again for refusing to enter into the standstill," Gordon told Lasky, Cohler, and Woodhouse. "But I will not enter into the standstill agreement. I have decided that I must sell the shares of Getty Oil owned by the family trust. I would like the three of you to accompany me to New York tomorrow morning so that we can consult an investment banker on this subject."

"I'm scheduled to go to Los Angeles tomorrow," Lasky said quietly.

"Well, it's really not necessary for you to be in New York. Tom and Tim can take care of it."

"Yes, they can," Lasky answered. He was laconic, withdrawn.

"What do you think of Gordon's decision to sell the trust's shares, Moses?" Tim Cohler asked his partner.

"I have nothing to say," Lasky answered. "The decision is his to make, and he has made it."

13

A NEGOTIATED PEACE

Vanni Treves, J. Paul Getty, Jr.'s solicitor, had been trying to reach Dave Copley while he was in London, but it was not until late Tuesday that the two attorneys finally spoke by telephone. Treves asked for a meeting with Copley and Sid Petersen. He wanted to know if there was any new information about Gordon's activities at Getty Oil. Copley assured him that there was. They tried to find a time for a meeting, but by now it was getting late in the evening, and Petersen and Copley had reservations on a flight back to Los Angeles the next morning. Copley suggested that if Treves could come to Claridge's early Wednesday, then perhaps he could join them for a cab ride out to Heathrow Airport. They could talk about Gordon in the car.

Treves was agreeable, and so the next morning they all piled into one of London's distinctive black taxicabs: Treves, Petersen, Copley, and Winokur. As they rolled through central London and then west on the highway toward Heathrow, they talked about Gordon Getty's latest escapades. In earlier discussions with the solicitor, Treves had emphasized that Paul Jr. would almost certainly take action against his brother if Gordon did anything to jeopardize management's control of Getty Oil. Copley had tried earlier to make the case that Gordon was doing just that by visiting with Wall Street analysts and insisting on restructuring studies by Goldman, Sachs. As recently as September 14, Copley had met with Treves in Los Angeles over dinner at the Biltmore Hotel; Treves had been in California on a brief stopover on his way to Hong Kong on unrelated business. After dinner, while walking back to Treves' hotel, Copley had handed the solicitor a draft petition for a lawsuit against Gordon. Treves agreed to examine the document, but it was still not clear to Copley whether the solicitor felt a family lawsuit against Gordon was really necessary. Now, at least, the company's case against Gordon was compelling. In London, Gordon had crossed the line. He had made a direct, hostile proposal for control of the company in combination with the museum.

"We understand from Martin Lipton, the museum's attorney, that Gordon's proposal involved immediately throwing out the entire board of directors and replacing them with Gordon's designees," Bart Winokur told Treves in the taxi. "According to Lipton, the museum rejected the proposal because they considered it absurd and outrageous."

Winokur, Petersen, and Copley each described their hurried, harried two days in London. They said that Gordon seemed now to be rejecting even the advice of his own lawyers. And while they were pleased that they had seemingly averted disaster on Tuesday afternoon, they remained concerned that anything could happen when they returned to the United States. After all, Gordon had refused to sign a standstill truce.

"I can't picture Gordon in control of Getty Oil," Treves commented. "I'll be in touch with you as soon as possible," he added. Treves was cautious about discussing his reclusive client, Paul Jr. He gave no firm indication about whether Paul was prepared to go forward with a company-sponsored suit against his brother.

Exhausted, the Getty Oil lawyers, bankers, and executives flew back to the United States that afternoon, some to New York, others to Philadelphia and Los Angeles. For the lawyers, the game-players, there was a self-conscious awareness that the London episode had raised the battle for control of Getty Oil to a new plane of exotic interest.

"Who do you think will play Gordon in the movie version?" one lawyer asked his partner on the flight back.

"I don't know. Maybe Dudley Moore."

They laughed deeply and began to pretend that they were casting directors. Who could they sign to play Sid Petersen? Moses Lasky? Marty Lipton? If they had overheard this exchange, it is doubtful that Petersen, Copley, and the other Getty Oil career men would have shared the lawyers' easy amusement. Increasingly, the company executives were like actors in a script produced not in Hollywood, but on Wall Street. And if that script was true to its genre, the executives knew, they would likely lose their company, their careers, and their professional identities in the final scene.

That same day, but on a different flight, Tim Cohler and Tom Woodhouse were discussing a man who could easily play himself in any Hollywood version of Getty Oil's troubles. His name was Martin Siegel, the investment banking whiz kid with the Wall Street firm Kidder, Peabody & Company. The night before, at the John Howard Hotel in London, Cohler and Woodhouse had tried to draw up a short list of investment bankers who might ably serve Gordon if he went ahead with his decision to sell the family trust's 32 million shares of Getty Oil stock. They had discussed several names, but Woodhouse had been particularly enamored of Siegel, who was one of the best-known merger deal-makers in the country.

One thing that distinguished Marty Siegel from, say, a Geoff Boisi, was his personal style. He was only thirty-five years old, possessed of stunning good looks and a brash, confident manner. He was regarded as one of the most aggressive merger bankers on Wall Street, renowned for what some bankers considered to be his unseemly, unsolicited approaches to large corporations. Siegel would contact a company's chief executive, tell him that his corporation appeared to be vulnerable to a hostile raid, and then would offer a "defense" consultation against unwanted takeovers at the rate of about $125,000 per year. If the executive turned Siegel down, he had to worry that Kidder, Peabody would somehow make good on its warning by quietly putting his company into play on Wall Street. Siegel defended his consults as a perfectly legitimate marketing device, but to some the program smacked of a protection racket. Siegel took on dozens of defense clients at a time and Kidder earned $8 million annually from the program. More important, the defense consultations put Siegel on retainer at companies which, by Siegel's own calculation, were likely to face a takeover bid. If a raid emerged, then Siegel was in a perfect spot to handle the deal and reap some of its huge transaction fees.

Siegel earned more than $2 million annually in salary and bonuses and he lived lavishly and visibly. From his spectacular cedar-and-glass home on Long Island Sound in Greenwich, Connecticut, complete with swimming pool, tennis courts, gymnasium, and a private beach, he commuted daily to Manhattan by helicopter. He drove an Alfa Romeo, and before settling down with his second wife in the early 1980s, he was regarded as a kind of *enfant terrible* in Manhattan's gilt-edged bachelor society. He talked eagerly to the press about his deals and his career—he was a prolific source for financial reporters at the major newspapers. When not reading about himself, Siegel preferred science fiction stories. As his friend Stuart Shapiro, a Wall Street lawyer, put it, Siegel was partial to tales with "a particular type of hero. They are young men of tremendous ambition and dashing looks who, by dint of their own efforts and the luck of the Lord, restructure the universe and change the course of history in some way."

It was an odd archetype for a man of Marty Siegel's upbringing. He was raised in Massachusetts in a decidedly middle-class family; his father was in the shoe business. From an early age, he wanted to be an astronaut, and he figured that by the time he was old enough to qualify, the country would be looking not for test pilots, but for scientists to send into space. So, precociously brilliant, Siegel earned a bachelor's degree in chemical engineering at the age of nineteen. After deciding that finance was more interesting than science, and having abandoned his plans to be an astronaut, he graduated as a Baker Scholar from the Harvard Business School at age twenty-three. Just ten years later, he was earning millions as the leading partner in Kidder, Pea-body's merger division.

Flying into New York from London that Wednesday afternoon, Cohler and Woodhouse agreed that Siegel would be their first choice to be Gordon Getty's investment banker. Not only was Siegel regarded as one of the best merger bankers on the Street, he also possessed a reputation nearly equal to Martin Lipton's and certainly comparable with Boisi and Goldman, Sachs'. In London, the big takeover guns had been hauled onto the deck. Gordon had decided to shop for one himself.

Once in Manhattan, it took a series of urgent, cryptic telephone calls before Woodhouse and Cohler could gain an audience at Kidder, Peabody on Wednesday evening. Woodhouse told the firm that he could not reveal his client's name over the phone, but he assured the Kidder bankers that it would be worth their while to grant a meeting. Finally, Cohler and Woodhouse were invited to see Peter Goodson, who was ostensibly Siegel's boss in the Kidder merger division, but who earned significantly less money than his better-known subordinate.

Cohler and Woodhouse sat down in Goodson's office, located in Lower Manhattan's dense financial district. Goodson was cordial but hardly ebullient. He had no idea what Cohler and Woodhouse wanted.

"We asked for a meeting because we represent Gordon Getty," Woodhouse began. "As you probably are aware, Mr. Getty owns about forty percent of Getty Oil Company's stock, and—"

Goodson held up his hand. "Excuse me for just a minute," he said politely.

He stood up and walked casually out of his office. Once safely around the corner, Goodson broke into a frantic half-sprint down the hallway. He reached Marty Siegel's office, flung the door open, and announced "Siegel! Get out here! They're Gordon Getty's lawyers! Come on!"

The sweet fragrance of wealth was all around them. Siegel scrambled out from behind his desk and trotted eagerly back down the hall with Goodson. As they approached his office, they slowed to a casual walk, wiped the excitement from their faces, and then stepped back in.

"This is Marty Siegel," Goodson said, making introductions. "I thought that he should join us."

Cohler and Woodhouse recounted the long, complicated history of Gordon's relationship with Getty Oil management and the museum. They described the occasion of their visit—the negotiations in London, and the entrance of Martin Lipton. Siegel knew Lipton well; they had worked together frequently in hostile takeover battles. The two lawyers asked Siegel if he would be willing to work with Gordon Getty, possibly on the sale of his stock, possibly on some other course of action that Mr. Getty might devise. Siegel said that he would be pleased to do so. They worked out a fee arrangement under which Kidder would be paid several hundred thousand dollars cash immediately, for consulting and advising by Siegel, plus three-eighths of 1 percent of any future transaction involving the trust's shares. Under that formula, if the entire company was sold, Siegel would garner more than $10 million for his firm.

Siegel also agreed to meet briefly with Gordon while he was in New York. At that meeting, asked about his objectives, Gordon did not instruct Siegel to sell the trust's shares, the course he had apparently decided upon in London. Instead, he told Siegel the same thing that he had told everyone else who asked him what he wanted.

"I want to maximize the trust's value," Gordon said.

Siegel replied that he would quickly analyze Getty Oil's assets and the restructurings considered earlier that year by the company, and then he would fly to San Francisco to present Mr. Getty with his findings. Siegel also said that he would like to review the "black books" on Getty Oil's finances prepared by Goldman, Sachs earlier in the year, and he asked Gordon's lawyers if they could make the arrangements with Goldman. They said they would try.

It was not until the following Monday that Tim Cohler finally spoke with Bart Winokur about the retention of Marty Siegel and Siegel's request to see the earlier Goldman studies.

"We assume that you would think hiring Siegel is a good idea," Cohler said.

"Has Gordon made up his mind about whether he's going to sign the standstill?"

"He has not made a final decision," Cohler replied. "At this point, he is not signing the standstill, but he might decide to later. You should be assured, however, that Mr. Getty is not going to take any precipitous action until after he has reviewed the situation fully with Mr. Siegel and has had his advice."

Soon after hearing from Cohler, Winokur traveled by train to New York for a meeting with Geoff Boisi and Marty Lipton. When they had left London the previous Wednesday, the three of them agreed to negotiate a two-way standstill agreement between the company and the museum, even if Gordon was unwilling to go along. Winokur and his partners in Philadelphia had already begun to draft a formal document—their version was long, complex, and filled with detailed clauses. It was lawyerly. Lipton had seen a copy of the draft, and he had told Winokur that he thought it was "unseemly." There was too much fine print, Lipton said. A truce, by nature, must be basic and simple. Winokur, in his draft, seemed to anticipate every possible nefarious move that his opponents might conceivably make, Lipton said. Winokur replied that he was only trying to be thorough. They scheduled a meeting in Lipton's Midtown offices to talk things over.

Inevitably, the conversation turned from Winokur's drafted agreement to Gordon's decision to retain Kidder, Peabody. Geoff Boisi had by now spoken with Siegel about the Goldman, Sachs black books.

"Marty is busy reviewing all the materials," Boisi told Lipton and Winokur. "He told me that they were trying to figure out what it was that Gordon was interested in and that they have not figured that out yet, what his objectives are. So they're going to explore some alternatives, including some of the alternatives we already studied, and then present their conclusions to Gordon.

"My impression is that Marty might be in contact with outsiders who might be interested in acquiring Getty Oil," Boisi continued. "I think Marty might be trying to build some alliances with outsiders. That might be a great threat not only to the company, but to the museum, too. The museum could find itself out in the cold. But I don't know that for sure. I just got that feeling from Marty.

"Marty, as you know, has a tendency, when he gets involved in these things, to look for the deal and the fee on the deal," Boisi concluded.

"I know that, but that doesn't mean he's going to do that here," Lipton said.

"Yes, but we certainly have to be concerned about that," Boisi replied.

"I agree," Lipton said.

Even among friends, Marty Siegel's aggressive reputation preceded him. Siegel was a deal-maker, an instigator, Boisi and Lipton knew. Of course, Boisi and Lipton were not exactly reluctant to pick up multimillion dollar merger fees for themselves. But in their own minds, Siegel was dangerously aggressive. They had to be careful about what Marty might do.

Over the next two weeks, then, a new level of gamesmanship took hold. It was no longer simply that the advisors were ascendant over the affairs of Getty Oil Company. Now, with the entrance of Lipton and Siegel, the company's destiny had passed irretrievably to Wall Street. Not even the contentious negotiating between Winokur and the Lasky firm was consequential anymore; the important talks now involved Boisi, Lipton, and Siegel, the merger men, the mercenary warriors in New York who had battled each other before over companies long forgotten, and who would contend again when the Getty Oil deal was done.

There was a collegial feeling among those three that outsiders might not understand, a sense perhaps not of arrogance, but at least of potency and confidence. The era of the hostile takeover in American finance was nearing a stage of maturity; the game was no longer fresh, and prominent players like Lipton, Boisi, and Siegel had shed their early exuberance. Lipton, for example, now expressed doubts about the effects of merger mania on the long-term health of the country's economy, this despite the personal fortune he had made during its halcyon days. He even drafted legislation and testified before Congress, urging that restrictions be imposed on corporate raiders such as Boone Pickens, Carl Icahn, and Irwin "The Liquidator" Jacobs. Lipton's critics, and there were plenty of them, decried the hypocrisy of his sudden moralizing about takeovers. At a more personal level, merger maestros such as Lipton, Boisi, and even the ambitious Siegel, had by the fall of 1983 settled into a steady, quiet professional routine. Siegel and Lipton were recent fathers, Boisi a family man of longer standing. In comparison to the average corporate manager, all three still worked grueling, stressful hours, but they were no longer quite so excitable, so driven as they had been during those wild, trailblazing takeover campaigns during the 1970s. With experience had come confidence and also friendship. Now, if a problem such as the dissension and uncertainty at Getty Oil arose, they could sit down together and talk about it, rationally, calmly. There was no need to start a war preemptively.

And so the three of them, and Bart Winokur, too, began to feel each other out about the problems at Getty Oil and how they ought to be resolved. In the two weeks following the London meetings, Lipton was in the middle, talking freely with Siegel on the one side and Boisi and Winokur on the other. To all of them, he insisted that an eighteen-month standstill was the only sensible course, and he hoped that Gordon and the company would agree to join the truce. With Winokur, Lipton continued to discuss the long standstill draft prepared by Dechert Price & Rhoads. Lipton insisted that Dechert's approach was too complex. Besides, he said, Gordon would never go for Winokur's draft. By Monday, October 17, Lipton began to talk with Siegel about a trip to San Francisco where all the parties could meet to negotiate a standstill. With Siegel's assistance, an all-day meeting was set for Wednesday, the nineteenth, at the Lasky firm's offices. Lipton suggested that he and Siegel fly to California together so they could spend a few hours on the plane discussing the provisions of a new, three-way standstill document.

Despite Lipton's speeches in London about the "absurdity" of Gordon's takeover proposal to the museum, and despite the heart-to-heart at Claridge's between Williams and Petersen, which had been designed to clear up the suspicions between them, Getty Oil's management and advisors remained dubious about the seemingly benign intentions professed by Marty Lipton. When Winokur, Boisi, and Petersen heard that Lipton and Siegel were flying to California together, they were concerned. The presence of Siegel might make a joint takeover between Gordon and the museum more palatable to Lipton and Williams. The company advisors could imagine the two Martys, Lipton and Siegel, stepping off the plane in San Francisco, shaking hands, and then advising their clients that they had agreed to take control of Getty Oil. There was a comity between Lipton and Siegel, a long history of treacherous deals skillfully negotiated. Petersen and his advisors decided that they had to proceed with caution.

On Wednesday, the nineteenth, Petersen flew to San Francisco from Bakersfield, California. Since his return from London, the Getty Oil chairman had been immersed in a series of annual company budget and planning meetings that were held at regional headquarters around the country. In fact, because of his intercontinental travel, Petersen had missed a couple of important sessions, and Bob Miller had been forced to chair the meetings. After returning from London, Petersen rejoined his top executives in Salt Lake City, offering no explanation for his highly unusual absence. From Utah, he had moved on to the regional headquarters at Bakersfield. On Wednesday, he was again forced to skip an important budget meeting because of the negotiations in San Francisco. Increasingly, Petersen was slipping away from involvement in the day-to-day affairs of his company.

Morning broke warm and clear across San Francisco Bay that Wednesday. Siegel arrived early at the Lasky offices on Sansome Street in order to meet with Gordon and his lawyers before Williams, Petersen, and their advisors arrived.

"My conversations with Marty Lipton on the flight out were very productive," Siegel reported to Gordon, Cohler, Woodhouse, and Lasky. "We agreed on an outline for a possible standstill agreement. Marty is going to recommend it to Harold Williams.

"I think there is a very substantial identity of interests between the museum and the Getty family trust," Siegel went on. "I think Williams and Lipton are of the same view as Gordon on most of the important matters. Lipton thinks that the attitude of the company's lawyers is high-handed, and he is willing to go pretty far to work around that and to keep management from screwing things up some more."

"I'm not surprised to hear that," Gordon said. "I have great confidence in Mr. Williams. I've been confident throughout this that Harold and I would see eye to eye on the important points."

There were two conference rooms among the Lasky firm's twelfth-floor offices. When Petersen, Williams, and their advisors arrived early that afternoon, separate camps were established. Petersen, Winokur, Boisi, and Galant were shown to one conference room; Williams, Lipton, and the Lasky lawyers to the other. Over the next few hours, a number of small negotiating caucuses convened.

First off, Gordon and Sid Petersen met privately in an unoccupied office. It was their first face-to-face encounter since Pebble Beach.

"Now that we're talking again, Sid, I think we should just have an oral agreement not to do anything, to have a truce," Gordon suggested when they were alone.

Petersen said that he didn't think that was a very realistic idea. He was thinking, but he did not say, *I can't trust you, Gordon, you schlemiel. You'll change your mind tomorrow or forget what you said. We can't make any oral agreement.*

A few minutes later, Harold Williams joined their private caucus. It was the first time that all three principals had been alone together, with no advisors present. Gordon repeated his suggestion that the three of them make an oral agreement not to sell Getty Oil or attempt a takeover.

"That might be all right with me," Williams said. Petersen was stunned. He couldn't believe that Williams would accept an oral agreement with Gordon.

The Getty Oil chairman said that he would talk about Gordon's idea with his company lawyers.

A short time later, Petersen, Winokur, Boisi, Galant, Lipton, and Williams met in the glass-walled conference room where Getty Oil management was stationed. Lipton summarized his discussions thus far with Gordon.

"Mr. Getty is unwilling to sign any piece of paper, but he is willing to have an informal agreement, where everyone would say orally that they wouldn't do anything for some period of time, perhaps sixty days."

"Gordon told me the same thing when I met with him a few minutes ago," Petersen said.

"As far as I'm concerned, an oral agreement would be all right," Williams reiterated. "I think it would be preferable to have a three-way standstill of some kind, even oral, rather than just a two-party agreement between the company and the museum."

"I told Gordon that as far as I am concerned, it is not satisfactory to have an oral agreement," Petersen said. "People have enough trouble figuring out what something means when they write it down, but at least then you have the words to refer to. If you don't write them down, then nobody can even remember the words that were used, because everybody has a different recollection. I don't want to do that. If there's going to be an agreement, we have got to write it down."

"Well, Harold is uncomfortable with some of the provisions in the two-way standstill that the company has proposed," Lipton said, referring to the elaborate document drafted by Winokur the previous week. "It might tie the museum's hands at a time when Gordon might be taking some action which would be detrimental to the museum. If that happened, the museum would want to protect itself. The point is, we would have to make some changes in that agreement if we're going to sign it. My client feels very strongly that he wants to have a three-way truce."

"Well, we're not willing to accept an oral agreement," Winokur said strongly. "So if there's going to be any agreement at all, it's going to have to be in writing."

"All right. We'll go talk with Gordon and his lawyers," Lipton said.

For hours, Petersen and his Getty Oil lawyers and bankers were alone in their conference room; they neither heard from nor saw Lipton, Williams, Gordon or the Lasky attorneys. They had made their position clear. If there was to be a truce, it had to be in writing. There was nothing to do now but wait.

On the other side of the floor, Lipton was trying desperately to persuade Gordon Getty to sign the simple, handwritten standstill agreement that he and Marty Siegel had drafted during their flight to California. At Siegel's insistence, the length of the proposed truce had been reduced from eighteen to twelve months. They had negotiated a number of important provisions. The company would rescind its action at the emergency board meeting in Philadelphia authorizing the issuance of 9 million treasury shares. Management would agree, additionally, to the election of Moses Lasky and Harold Williams as company directors, as well as to the appointment of three other directors selected by Gordon and approved by management—the board would be expanded from twelve to seventeen to accommodate the new members. In exchange, Gordon and the museum would agree not to act by consent or to attempt a joint takeover of Getty Oil. All three parties—Gordon's trust, the museum, and the company—would be prohibited from joining with any "group" to attempt a takeover or to independently seek the sale of the company. No major corporate changes would be undertaken during the year covered by the truce. There could be no buy-backs or issuance of stock, no restructurings, reorganizations, liquidations, or recapitalizations. Getty Oil's basic structure and operations would be frozen in place. Finally, all three sides would agree not to launch any stock proxy fights challenging management or the board of directors.

All of this was covered in only two pages, handwritten in Lipton's distinctive block-capital printing style. They talked about it over and over, and still Gordon was reluctant to sign.

At dinnertime, someone ordered in Chinese food. It was, several of those present said later, the worst Chinese food they had ever eaten. Whether for that or other reasons, Gordon Getty began to grow pale. He said that he didn't feel well. He was nauseous. But they continued to talk and negotiate, all of them urging Gordon to sign the truce. Finally, around eight-thirty, Gordon gave in. He and Harold Williams both signed and dated the three-way, handwritten truce.

Suddenly, Gordon Getty looked positively ashen. "I feel very sick and I have to go home," he declared.

Tim Cohler said that he would drive Gordon to his Broadway mansion immediately. They left.

Lipton took the signed truce over to the company's conference room across the floor. "We spent hours with Gordon trying to convince him to sign an agreement," he announced. "In the course of that, we finally convinced him that he should sign a three-way agreement."

Lipton handed the two-page standstill to Winokur and Boisi, and they looked it over.

"This is a substantial change from the discussions we had last week," Winokur said.

"Look, this was the only way we could get Gordon to sign anything," Lipton said. "Mr. Williams and I think it is not a bad idea to have additional board members, because hopefully, if they are responsible people—and Gordon has assured us that he will only name responsible people—they might have a positive influence on Mr. Getty and his relationship with the rest of the directors."

"Well, this outline is obviously ambiguous in many respects," Winokur said. "It is purely an outline, and there are a whole series of questions we addressed in our draft that we worked on together as lawyers. We worked out what the language meant." Winokur went through some examples. He was concerned, among other things, that the company had now apparently lost its "out," its ability to sell Getty Oil rather than let Gordon take control. Moreover, the brief paragraph in Lipton's draft prohibiting "fundamental corporate changes" such as reorganizations or liquidations struck Winokur as highly ambiguous. What exactly is a fundamental corporate change?

"I recognize all that, but I think we have found a moment in time here, a brief moment in time, when the trustee was willing to sign something," Lipton said. "I'm afraid that moment might never appear again if we attempt to clarify or redraft anything. We have to take whatever we can get tonight. You might not think it is perfect, or even satisfactory, but the fact is that it is better than nothing."

"Sign it as it is or don't sign it at all," Lipton concluded.

Feeling that he had no choice, that Lipton was right—even an imperfect truce was better than no truce at all—Sid Petersen finally agreed. He told Lipton, however, that he did not have the power to sign such a document in the company's name. He would have to write "Subject to approval of the board of directors" beneath his own name. Lipton thought that was reasonable, and he talked about it with Gordon's lawyers, who agreed.

Around nine o'clock, Sid Petersen finally signed the standstill truce on behalf of Getty Oil.

Marty Lipton, Moses Lasky, Tom Woodhouse, and Tim Cohler were nearly ecstatic after the summit meeting broke up that night in San Francisco. After stepping to the brink in London, they had managed in just two weeks to pull back, to restore "rationality," as Lipton liked to put it, to the affairs of Getty Oil. Now they had twelve long months to negotiate a sensible, long-term solution. Gordon was appeased; he could busy himself with the selection of his new directors. Williams, meanwhile, could return peacefully to his expansive art-acquisition program and his elaborately ambitious plans to build a large new museum facility on a barren bluff overlooking the San Diego Freeway, near Beverly Hills. There would be no danger of embarrassment or disruption to the J. Paul Getty Museum because of infighting at Getty Oil.

Sid Petersen, however, did not feel so sanguine as he flew south to Bakersfield late that night, preparing to attend the next day's round of company budget meetings. Despite their acquiescence to Lipton's handwritten truce, Petersen and his advisors still believed that Getty Oil Company could only be saved if Gordon's control over his family trust was somehow undermined. By signing the standstill that night, Petersen thought, he had agreed not to sell the company or to implement any major restructurings. But he had not agreed to end his sponsorship of a family lawsuit challenging Gordon's right to be sole trustee—the issue had not even been discussed at the Lasky offices, of course, because neither Gordon nor Williams knew anything about Petersen's plans. The standstill agreement had bought Petersen some time, the Getty Oil chairman knew. But it would hardly preserve a lasting peace.

14

"SNOOKERED"

Even before Gordon Getty signed the truce with management and the museum, there were signs that his own family was preparing to rebel against him.

It was a terribly frustrating time for Gordon. He had been betrayed, he felt, by Chauncey Medberry and the "snakes" on the company board who had said they would resign before they permitted Gordon to take control of Getty Oil. His proposal to Harold Williams and the museum had been flatly rejected. Marty Lipton had described Gordon's thinking as "absurd." Moreover, Gordon's own attorneys had made it clear to him in London that they thought he was wrong, mistaken. In the face of all this disapproval and disappointment, there was a part of Gordon Getty that seemed to say, *The hell with them.* In the weeks after his return from London, he became increasingly churlish and stubborn. Shortly after the day-long truce negotiation in San Francisco, for example, Gordon received a bill for services from the Lasky law firm. It totaled more than $1 million. The bill pushed Gordon into a rage; it was excessive, outrageous, he declared. *Everyone thinks they can get something from me, take advantage of me,* was the message he delivered to the Lasky lawyers through Laurence Chazen, his friend and financial advisor in San Francisco. Cohler and Lasky were told by Chazen that Gordon was so upset that he was thinking about retaining new attorneys. Further, Gordon had decided that despite the provisions of the standstill document he signed, he was not going to permit Moses Lasky to become a company director. He instructed Tom Woodhouse to immediately inform Getty Oil that Lasky's name should not be included in any press release announcing the nomination of new directors at the company.

"My relationship with Gordon is gone," Lasky told Bart Winokur by telephone just a few days after the standstill negotiations in San Francisco. "Gordon isn't confiding in me or looking to me anymore."

It was amid this atmosphere of isolation, anger, and frustration that Gordon began to hear from members of his family about his activities at Getty Oil and about his status as sole trustee of the family fortune. The first contact came on Monday, October 10, when Paul Jr., in London, telephoned Gordon at the Broadway mansion. Paul spoke with both Ann and Gordon, and to both of them he expressed his deep concern that Gordon was fouling things up at Getty Oil Company, and that he would lead the family into a new round of internal dissension and lawsuits if he did not accept a corporate cotrustee to help manage the family stock. Gordon and his wife both tried to assure Paul that there was no need to worry, that everything was in hand. But Paul was unconsolable. At one point, he burst into tears over the prospect that Gordon's refusal to accept a cotrustee would lead to family in-fighting.

Shortly thereafter, Paul wrote to Gordon in San Francisco. "It was Father's clear intention that there should be a corporate cotrustee," his letter said. "I don't want to threaten you or even appear to, but I'm afraid that litigation will be inevitable if you don't quickly agree to another trustee and I'm sad to think that I, too, would be sucked into it."

At virtually the same time, Gordon began to hear from the Georgettes. "I have heard from several sources that you are attempting to make some major changes that concern Getty Oil, the museum, and the Sarah Getty Trust," Caroline wrote on October 21. "I am concerned that you are continuing to act as sole trustee. . . . Since as trustee you act in a fiduciary capacity on my behalf, and since any changes at Getty Oil or the trust affect me directly, I am interested in knowing what your reasons are for trying to change the company and what your ultimate goals for the trust are."

Gordon was uncertain what the impetus was for these ominous letters from his brother and nieces, but he did not suspect that Getty Oil management was behind them. There had been a few sketchy newspaper stories about Gordon's takeover proposal to the museum in London, and news about fresh dissension at the company was circulating on Wall Street. After the standstill agreement was signed on the nineteenth, the company itself was forced to issue a press release describing the provisions of the truce. That a truce was necessary at all, and that it contained specific language prohibiting the sale of the company or alliances by the museum and the trust with outside "groups" made it plain that Getty Oil had been buffeted by serious internal hostilities. It was not terribly surprising, then, that Gordon's relatives had contacted him to express their concern about his role in the company's troubles.

Gordon moved quickly to assuage his nieces. Shortly after he received Caroline's letter, he flew to Los Angeles for a meeting with the Georgettes and Mark Harris (who also used his given name, Mark Getty), Paul Jr.'s son by his first marriage. Caroline, particularly, pressed Gordon about his meddling at Getty Oil and asked why he felt it necessary to challenge Sid Petersen's management decisions. From her stockbroker and her attorneys, she had heard about Gordon's dealings with the Cullen family and Boone Pickens, and she had been told that Gordon had disclosed confidential information to the potential raiders.

"Since the trust has so much money already, why are we trying to get more?" Gordon was asked.

"A very interesting philosophical question," Gordon answered with typical professorial enthusiasm. "But it is my fiduciary duty to maximize the wealth and income of the trust and to prevent it from falling into a weak minority position."

A few days after that meeting, Gordon wrote to Caroline, Anne, and Mark, with carbon copies to Claire, Ronald, and Paul Jr. "It was good to talk with all of you recently," Gordon told his family. "Your views and questions on the 1934 trust are welcome anytime. . . . The trust by itself doesn't control the company since forty percent isn't a majority. What the company does is up to its directors, of which I am only one. I think it should stick to the oil business and keep debt low. Getty Oil, like many other companies, has been called 'worth more dead than alive.' In other words, our appraised asset value is far larger than the current stock price. . . . I personally believe that if Getty Oil does not solve this problem it will sooner or later be taken over and on terms which the trust may not have the power to control.

"I am convinced that a solution is possible," Gordon went on. "The tripartite [standstill] agreement will give us time to achieve it. (I'm afraid I can't say much more without revealing private company information). A corporate co-trustee would probably mean a passive and neutralized trust just when it most needs to take the lead in working for a solution. Love, Gordon."

It was vintage Gordon Getty—carefree, affectionate, sincere, and naïve. But on November 3, only two days after writing that appeasing missive, Gordon sat down in his basement study at the Broadway mansion and signed a much tougher letter to his brother Paul Jr. in London.

"Your recent telephone call to me and your letter of October 28 lead me to write you now," Gordon began. "There is no basis on which anyone has any legal standing to seek the addition of another trustee, and any attempt to do so would be opposed. There is, moreover, nothing to favor a corporate trustee. A corporate trustee, such as a bank, operates through underlings and their judgment about how the company should be operated has nothing to commend it. . . .

"You say that Father intended that there be a corporate trustee, but we know that in the 1948 designation of successor trustees, he stated that the corporate trustee should act only if individual trustees were dead. And in the 1971 designation, Father appointed George alone and designated a bank to act only if George should fail to act. The history shows that Father 'covered the bases' by making provisions for contingencies when he wished to do so. In the 1973 designation he did not designate a substitute corporate co-trustee if Security Pacific should fail to act.

"Your letter deplores another round of dissension in the family," Gordon continued. "No one would deplore that more than I. But there can be no such dissension after Ronald's current litigation comes to an end unless someone in the family takes it on himself to create dissension by instituting litigation. Ronald wants to be a trustee. He has already broached that idea to me and I turned him down. If anyone should institute litigation seeking an additional trustee, that would be an invitation for Ronald to come into the suit and seek appointment of himself.

"And speaking of Ronald, you might wish to consult your own attorneys about the risks you would be taking should you involve yourself in litigation in California about the appointment of a

trustee. You might find yourself subject to the jurisdiction of California's courts in Ronald's litigation against the trust and the other
beneficiaries. . . .

"Let me put you at ease by assuring you that I am always willing
to give you information about the 1934 trust so far as you, as a beneficiary, have any interest, but always short of revealing private Getty
Oil Company information. I cannot abdicate my duties and responsibilities by acceding to efforts to dilute my position. The relationship
between the trust and the company is now amicable, perhaps more
so than at any time since Father's death. Management and I are coop-
erating to the common good of everyone. I hope you will not try to
upset this amity. Love, Gordon."

It was an extraordinary letter, perhaps most of all because of what
it revealed about Gordon's perception of his relationship with Sid
Petersen. Gordon believed that Thursday morning in early November that relations between himself and management were perhaps
better than at any time in the previous seven years. Yet, virtually as
he wrote those words, Getty Oil management was taking its final
steps to undermine Gordon's authority as sole trustee of the Getty
family's wealth.

Petersen's attempt to find a family member who would file suit
against Gordon had languished since the recruitment of Seth Hufstedler the previous June. While Caroline and the other Georgettes
seemed concerned about Gordon, their lawyer, Isaacs, apparently
was unwilling or unable to spur his clients to action against Gordon. After the near fiasco in London, and their conversation with
Vanni Treves on the way to Heathrow, Petersen and Dave Copley
had focused their attention on Paul Jr. Informed by Treves of Gordon's actions in London, Paul had tried at first to solve the problem
directly, through his telephone conversation with Gordon and Ann,
and then through an exchange of letters. But Gordon was unyielding, and so Paul had finally indicated to Treves that he was willing
to consider the sponsorship of a lawsuit. During the first week of
November, just as Gordon was writing Paul to ask him not to "upset
this amity" between himself and the company, Treves contacted
Dave Copley and said that he would fly to Los Angeles on Monday,
the seventh, to meet with Hufstedler and discuss his appointment as
guardian ad litem for one of Paul's children. Copley arranged a two-
day meeting between Hufstedler and Treves, as well as a number of

other attorneys now involved, for Tuesday and Wednesday, November 8 and 9, at a law office in downtown Los Angeles.

On Monday, the day before the meeting between Treves and Hufstedler, Moses Lasky called Dave Copley at Getty Oil headquarters. Lasky had heard about the telephone call and letter from Paul to Gordon asking about the appointment of a corporate cotrustee.

"Have you talked to Paul Getty about what's been going on at the company?" Lasky asked Copley.

"No, I haven't," he answered.

In the narrowest sense, Copley told the truth; he had not talked to Paul Jr. directly. But two days later, when Lasky's partner Tom Woodhouse spoke with Bart Winokur, Winokur decided that he should answer the question about Paul somewhat more honestly.

"I know there was a conversation between Dave and Mr. Lasky about this," Winokur said when Woodhouse asked if the company's lawyers had been talking to Paul Jr. about Gordon. "And Dave gave a narrow answer. To my knowledge, and to Dave's knowledge, nobody from the company has met with Paul Getty. But there has been some contact between representatives of the company and Paul Getty's counsel."

Beyond that, Winokur said, he could not elaborate.

Meanwhile, the two-day meeting between Treves and Hufstedler in Los Angeles was progressing smoothly. Early on, the crucial decision as to which minor child would actually be the sponsor for the lawsuit had been made: it would be Tara Gabriel Galaxy Gramaphone Getty, 15, Paul's only son by the late Talitha Pol, who was living at a boarding school in England. Though he knew nothing at all about the plans now afoot, Tara was now the obvious choice to file the suit against Gordon. The rest of Paul Jr.'s children, those born to his first wife, Gail Harris, had been living in California with their mother for years. It was not clear whether Gail Harris would even permit a guardian ad litem such as attorney Seth Hufstedler to be appointed for one of her four children in a lawsuit against Gordon. After all, Gordon had supported Harris and her children when Paul refused to pay his paraplegic son's medical bills. Tara Getty, on the other hand, had no particular loyalties to Gordon, and no mother to intervene against Paul Jr. if he decided to sponsor a lawsuit against his brother. So Treves and Hufstedler drafted a consent form for Paul Jr. to sign, authorizing Hufstedler's appointment as Tara's guardian ad litem in

California. In addition, they prepared other documents, including the lawsuit petition itself, so that all would be ready when Paul's signature was obtained. Satisfied, Vanni Treves flew back to London on Wednesday, the ninth. He said that he would return the signed documents as soon as he was able to present them to his client.

The next evening, Thursday, Treves met with J. Paul Getty, Jr. Treves showed him the documents he had drafted with Hufstedler and explained that if Paul signed them, a lawsuit would be filed against Gordon in Tara Getty's name. Paul agreed to the plan, and he signed the documents.

Earlier that same day, Mark Harris, Tara Getty's half-brother, had been in London for a visit with his father. Paul told him that based on the information supplied to him by Getty Oil management, he wished to impose a corporate cotrustee on Gordon. He said that he was prepared to engage in litigation to that end and that he was going to meet with Vanni Treves that night to discuss it. When Mark Harris himself met with Treves two days later, concerned that alternatives to a lawsuit had not been fully explored, Treves told him: "You must realize that I hate litigation. Everybody on this floor hates litigation. And everyone in this building hates litigation. We do everything possible to avoid litigation."

Still worried, Mark Harris spoke with Tara's maternal grandparents in France and even rode out to visit with his half-brother at his boarding school. Tara said that he had never met Seth Hufstedler, had never even spoken or corresponded with him. All Tara knew, he said, was that his father had told him that his interests were being looked after and that he should not be concerned if his name began to appear in the newspapers during the next few weeks.

Six thousand miles to the west, on the eighteenth floor of Getty Oil headquarters, the tangled web was being spun with increasing speed and urgency. On Friday, November 11, the company's quarterly board meeting was scheduled to convene at Getty Oil's regional headquarters in Houston, Texas. If Seth Hufstedler was now ready to file his lawsuit, then the company's board of directors had to be informed. Petersen and Copley had indicated to Hufstedler all along that Getty Oil would officially "intervene" in the lawsuit against Gordon and argue that everyone would be better off if a corporate cotrustee was appointed. For Petersen to take such action when Hufstedler filed his suit, he would need board approval. Petersen spoke with Winokur, Boisi, and Copley and told them that they should fly to Houston and be ready to assist with a presentation to the board about the lawsuit.

In time, much would be said and written about the Getty Oil board meeting that began that Friday morning in one of downtown Houston's clumped steel-and-glass skyscrapers. There would be a great deal of moralizing about the conduct of management, the directors, and particularly their chief outside counsel, Bart Winokur, who carried the presentation that day about Hufstedler's lawsuit against Gordon. A number of Getty Oil executives and advisors would privately express regret about the decision undertaken at the meeting. But at the time, they felt they had little choice. They had come this far down the road. It seemed to them that it was impossible now to turn back. "You get to the point where you're up against the wall," one company executive at the meeting said later. "You end up fighting like the other guy."

Sid Petersen, at the head of the conference table, called the session to order. The minutes of the Pebble Beach board meeting, which had been distributed to the directors in advance, were quickly approved. And then, by prior agreement, Gordon Getty and Harold Berg were asked to leave the conference room. The board, Petersen said, was about to consider approval of the standstill agreement signed some three weeks earlier in San Francisco. Gordon could not participate in that discussion because he was a party to the truce, and neither could Berg, since he was chairman of the museum's board of trustees, and the museum was also a party to the agreement. Gordon had traveled to Houston without his lawyers; Gordon had told his attorneys that there was no need for them to attend the board meeting.

As Gordon and Harold Berg left the conference room, Bart Winokur, Geoff Boisi, and Herbert Galant stepped inside. There would later be some dispute over precisely how this occurred. Some recalled that when Gordon and Berg left, the company advisors came into the conference room through a side door, out of Gordon's view. Others, including Winokur, Boisi, and Galant themselves, remembered it differently; they recalled going in the same door through which Gordon exited. As a matter of substance, the point was hardly important. But the image of that moment, its suggestion of "back door" duplicity and deceit by the company advisors, lingered for years.

As Gordon had been promised, the directors did discuss the standstill truce in his absence. But they spent more time debating an apparently contradictory topic: intervention in the Tara Getty lawsuit against Gordon. Winokur and the others said later that in their minds, the standstill agreement signed in San Francisco did not preclude Getty Oil from intervening in the Hufstedler suit. If they had believed it did, they would never have signed the document, they said. Indeed, the discussion about the lawsuit that afternoon in Houston did not center on whether company intervention was legally permissible under the standstill. Instead, the debate focused on the morality of Getty Oil's involvement in the affairs of the Getty family.

According to three sources who attended the meeting, several company directors, including Henry Wendt, John Teets, and later Harold Berg—who was allowed to rejoin the session when the topic shifted from the standstill to the lawsuit—expressed serious doubts about the propriety of management's proposed intervention in the lawsuit. This is not the sort of thing a large, publicly owned corporation ought to be involved in, they said. Berg and others said that this was not the way Getty Oil used to conduct itself when the old man, J. Paul Getty, was alive. Winokur was asked whether there was some alternative to formal intervention, which was certain to raise charges of treachery and double-dealing. After all, not only had the company signed a standstill truce with Gordon, it had in London made "handcuff" proposals to restrict Gordon's power for a limited time. Now, if the company intervened in the Hufstedler lawsuit, those proposals would appear hypocritical to Gordon, to say the least. The directors asked if there was a less onerous method than formal intervention to assist Hufstedler. Perhaps the company could file simple affidavits about Gordon's behavior over the past eighteen months, it was suggested. Perhaps it could do nothing at all, and simply let Hufstedler disclose Getty Oil's clandestine role while answering questions at some future deposition.

Winokur and Petersen, however, were firm. The company had to intervene in the suit. They had raised this issue with Hufstedler, they reported, and Hufstedler insisted that they were in this together. Without the united front raised by Getty Oil's formal intervention, Hufstedler was reluctant to file the lawsuit on Tara Getty's behalf.

"Intervention is the best alternative," Winokur told the board. "The company has to intervene in the lawsuit."

Finally, the directors gave their approval. Gordon had pushed the company too far in London, they said later. Henry Wendt said that by making a takeover offer to the museum, Gordon had pointed a gun at the company's head and pulled the trigger. It turned out that the gun wasn't loaded, Wendt continued, because Harold Williams and Marty Lipton rejected Gordon's proposal. But the important point was that Gordon had pulled the trigger. To stop that from happening again, even intervention in a family lawsuit challenging Gordon's right to be sole trustee was justified, Wendt argued. Others, such as Bart Winokur, felt there was nothing to apologize about. Gordon Getty had set the rules of the game. He had declared at the Bonaventure that the morality of it all was his to determine. The company was only responding in kind.

And so Gordon was invited back into the conference room, and the meeting continued. He was told nothing about the board's decision to intervene in a lawsuit against him. He was informed, however, that the directors had approved the standstill truce, and with it, the appointment of Harold Williams and three of Gordon's nominees as directors, effective at the next board meeting. Gordon was pleased to hear it, and the directors moved on to discuss their regular agenda of routine company business.

Informed over the weekend about the board's decision in Houston, Seth Hufstedler walked from his office to the downtown Los Angeles County Superior Court Building on Monday morning to file a lawsuit on behalf of Tara Getty seeking the appointment of Bank of America as cotrustee of the Getty family trust. *For the Matter of the Declaration of Trust of Sarah C. Getty Dated December 31, 1934*, was the suit's appropriately Dickensian title. Hufstedler showed the lawsuit to a probate judge before filing it, and there was some discussion between them about whether Hufstedler had the legal right to serve as Tara's guardian ad litem in California. Finally, later that morning, Hufstedler reached one of Paul Jr.'s attorneys in San Francisco, who had previously served as Tara's guardian in California, and the lawyer assured the probate judge that Hufstedler was on the level. With that, the suit was filed. The next day, Getty Oil sent one of its own lawyers to the courthouse and filed a formal intervention in support of Hufstedler's allegations against Gordon Getty.

All along, Sid Petersen, Bart Winokur, and the rest of them had assumed that Gordon would not be pleased to learn that Getty Oil had intervened in a lawsuit seeking the appointment of Bank of America as cotrustee. But Petersen and his advisors had consoled themselves with the belief that they were only doing what was necessary to protect the company's public stockholders from Gordon's whimsical exercise of power. What they had not anticipated, to their deep and lasting chagrin, was the reaction of Harold Williams and Martin Lipton.

When the company's intervention was filed publicly in Los Angeles, they heard from Lipton almost immediately, and it was not a pleasant experience. The violence of Lipton's reaction, his outrage at what he called Getty Oil's "duplicity and deceit" shocked Winokur, Boisi, and Galant. It also frightened them. Until now, the camaraderie of the Wall Street merger advisors—Siegel, Lipton, Boisi, Galant—had helped to stabilize the fulminating atmosphere at Getty Oil. Now, suddenly, the fearsome Lipton, the man of a thousand takeovers, was on the rampage.

They tried unsuccessfully to calm him. That week, they arranged a conference telephone call between Lipton, Boisi, Galant, and Winokur to explain to Lipton why the company had filed the intervention and why it believed it had not violated the letter or the spirit of the San Francisco truce agreement. But Lipton did not want to hear about it—he was morally outraged, he said. He simply could not believe the company had done such a thing. It violated even the most rudimentary notions of fairness and ethical behavior.

They tried to move Lipton away from his talk about morality. They wanted him to understand that the lawsuit was an expression of strategy, not principle. *Forget about the ethics of it*, they told Lipton. *What does this do to hurt the museum? Why are you so mad about it?*

"Supposing we are as dirty and nasty as you say we are," Galant told Lipton during the conference call that week. "Supposing everything you say is true. What does this do to you? Why doesn't this just preserve the museum's position? I mean, are you going to deny the fact that the trust requires two trustees? Are you going to deny the family its legitimate rights?"

"We got snookered," Lipton answered.

"Maybe Gordon should feel snookered," Galant countered. "But you guys—what have we done to you? This is what you wanted, remember? You said in London that the reason a standstill was in our interest was that we could use the time to neutralize Gordon and the trust. We told you this was going to happen."

"You never said anything about this in London. You never said anything about a lawsuit," Lipton replied forcefully. "This is a complete violation and repudiation of the standstill agreement."

The conversation ended without any prospect of accommodation or agreement between them. Lipton and the museum were now on the loose. Winokur, Boisi, and Galant, who had never shed their suspicions about Harold Williams' desire to run Getty Oil himself, feared that the museum president would seize this opportunity to "grasp for power."

All during the next two weeks, they talked back and forth by telephone in nearly every conceivable combination. Lipton spoke with the Lasky firm lawyers, who had been reconciled with Gordon partly because of the emergency presented by Hufstedler's lawsuit, about what they should do next. Gordon spoke with Harold Williams, and once, very curtly, with Sid Petersen. Tim Cohler "put on his litigation hat," as he liked to put it, and began to fight the Hufstedler suit by arranging to take the depositions of Winokur, Petersen, Copley, and others. Late in November, Gordon traveled to New York to meet with the three new Getty Oil directors he had nominated, and to inform them of this new phase of trouble with management. The new directors were Larry Tisch, a close friend of Marty Lipton's and chairman of the Loews Corporation; Alfred Taubman, a Detroit real-estate developer who had recently acquired control of Sotheby's, the art auction house; and Graham Allison, dean of Harvard University's John F. Kennedy School of Government. (All three had been recruited to join the Getty Oil board not by Gordon, but by his wife Ann. She met with each of them in New York and agreed to join Sotheby's board in exchange for Taubman's promise to serve as a Getty Oil director with her husband). Meanwhile, the company's executives and advisors tried to calm Harold Williams by talking to his boss, museum trustee chairman Harold Berg, to see if he could help. But it seemed that nothing would placate Williams. Through both Berg and Lipton the company's executives learned that the museum president was absolutely furious about the lawsuit.

Finally, the game was beyond anyone's control. In those first weeks after the Hufstedler lawsuit filing, it was impossible for the advisors even to know where their opponents were, much less what they were thinking and planning. There was a great deal of anger and confusion. Late in November, Harold Williams was in Europe on museum business, while Gordon was in New York to attend his fiftieth birthday party and a performance of his Emily Dickinson song cycle. Despite all of the distractions and concerns, Gordon was still composing music every day—he said later that the business and legal pressures that fall seemed only to increase his artistic capacity. His intuition flowed from music to business, then back to music again, he said.

By the first week in December, Gordon and Williams had reached a tentative agreement: they would combine to sign a majority stockholder consent, forcing Getty Oil to withdraw from the Hufstedler lawsuit. Gordon wanted them to go further—he wanted to return to his proposal in London and use the consent to fire the entire board of directors because of their action. But despite his anger at Petersen and the board, Williams refused to take such a drastic step, which would inevitably draw Wall Street's rapt attention to the struggle for power at the company. Getty Oil was suffering enough from publicity about its troubles, Williams believed; the last thing it needed was a coup against the entire board.

Williams and Lipton were nonetheless willing to consider other enforced changes at the company. On Monday, December 5, Gordon and Williams met at Marty Lipton's Manhattan law offices to draft a document. Williams had just flown in from Europe. They spent most of the day working on the language and provisions—any sudden exercise of majority stockholder power, no matter how justified by management's behavior, was a legally delicate proposition. Williams, particularly, was concerned about protecting his and the museum's reputations. He agreed, finally, to a provision establishing a "super-majority" of fourteen out of sixteen directors which would be required to approve any major corporate transaction, such as a stock buy-back, merger, or restructuring. Since Williams, Gordon, and three of Gordon's nominees were now on the Getty Oil board, the new super-majority would give them effective control over the company's major policies. Late that night, Gordon and Williams signed the consent, and the next day it was delivered to Sid Petersen at Getty Oil headquarters in Los Angeles.

Nineteen months after the death of Lansing Hays, then, Gordon Getty had finally exerted formal control over the policies of his family's business, the giant Getty Oil Company. It had not been easy, nor had Gordon's ambitions been fully realized. There was still work to be done, he believed. What he did not realize that wintry Monday evening in New York when he signed the consent with Harold Williams, what he apparently could not understand, was that the destiny of Getty Oil was now beyond the influence of any one man. "The events had overtaken us," was the way Harold Williams described it later. Or, to borrow the metaphor so enthusiastically employed by Bart Winokur at the Bonaventure Hotel eleven months earlier: the blood was in the water now, and it was spreading irretrievably. The sharks would come now. They always did.

PART THREE

WHEN THE FAT LADY SINGS

THE BULLDOG

For some, a face is just a mask. Who could look at the drooping, boyish visage of T. Boone Pickens, Jr., for example, with its eyes so modestly averted, its jaw slack and withdrawn—the face of a small-town high school principal—and suspect its owner was a ruthless, indefatigable corporate raider, a man intensely driven to acquire not only wealth, but to achieve recognition, political power, and sweeping reform of American industry? And yet it was precisely the modesty of Pickens' face, its softness, that lent credibility to his insatiable ambition. Other faces, by contrast, say too much about the men who possess them. When it mattered, no one could believe Richard Nixon; his face betrayed his deceits, as if he were Pinocchio. And then there is the ideal face, the countenance that carefully reflects the essence of its host but does not divulge his secrets. Such a face belonged to John Hugh Liedtke, the chairman and chief executive of the Pennzoil Company, the man who decided in December 1983 that he would like to take control of Getty Oil.

It was the face of a bulldog, all jowls and jaw and power, carved into a head bigger than a pumpkin. Its skin folded and creased below the ears, like the flaps of a hunting hat, lending the impression of a retired football lineman whose brawn has softened into flaccidity. Still, there was an undeniable strength in Liedtke's pleated cheeks; there wasn't anything puffy about him. In the center of his face was a large, bulbous nose, like the anchor of a ship. When Liedtke squinted, his blue-gray eyes disappeared entirely behind the folds of his skin, but when he stared ahead in anger or determination, they beamed like fog lights on an ocean liner.

Still, the face concealed Hugh Liedtke's own arcana. It was the face of a plain-speaking oilman, a good old boy, a Texan with mud still on his boots. That was the image of himself that Liedtke liked best, the one he cultivated in public, the one that made him feel relaxed, at home. But it was hardly a full picture of the man. And it did not explain why, that December of 1983, Hugh Liedtke was planning to launch a hostile takeover against Getty Oil Company.

Hugh Liedtke was a child of the Southwestern oil patch, to be sure, but he was also well schooled in the means and methods of the Eastern elite. He was born in 1922 in Tulsa, Oklahoma, then the center of the world oil industry His father was a scholarly attorney known locally as "Judge," a magistrate in the Indian Territory and the youngest delegate to Oklahoma's constitutional convention before becoming regional general counsel for the giant Gulf Oil Corporation. Young Hugh worked summers as a laborer in the Tulsa oil fields, but he also attended private schools and lived in a spacious, luxurious house filled with books. He was an extremely bright student, fascinated by history and philosophy, but he was also something of a prankster, skilled at cards and magic tricks. When it was time for college, Liedtke moved to New England, majoring in philosophy at Amherst and earning a master's degree in business from Harvard University. In 1943, he joined the navy and served on an aircraft carrier in the Pacific. Twice during the war, he met up with his younger brother Bill, once at Saipan and another time at Okinawa. They shared a few beers and talked about what they would do if the war ever ended and they could return to civilian life. They talked about high finance and the oil business.

When the opportunity finally arrived in 1946, they decided to go to law school together. They enrolled at the University of Texas, renting rooms from a young congressman named Lyndon Johnson. One of their fellow tenants in Austin that year was a law student named John Connally—in the years ahead, the Liedtke brothers experienced some hard times, but they never knew a poverty of social and political connections. When the brothers graduated, they followed the migrating Texas oil boom to Midland, near the recently discovered Permian basin, where they hung a shingle and began to look for ways to make money. They used their family connections to get started—their father had a friend in Tulsa who had sold his business and was looking to reinvest the proceeds in oil. Hugh and Bill Liedtke agreed to handle the purchases for 5 percent of the price; not a bad beginning for a fledgling law practice. Soon the brothers were making deals all across Texas and Oklahoma, investing in oil well royalties, leases, and finally buying whole groups of producing properties.

By 1953, the Liedtkes were ready to go it alone, and they formed a partnership, called Zapata Petroleum, with a young, rich, and well-connected Texan named George Bush. They pooled their money and used every penny to buy a six-thousand-acre tract that had on it six producing oil wells, widely dispersed and generally considered to be unconnected beneath the soil. As it happened, the general wisdom was flawed; Bush and the Liedtkes drilled 127 wells on their plot without a dry hole. They were rich now—within two years Zapata was earning $12 million in profits on $86 million in revenues—but they were also heavily indebted because of all their drilling, and so they turned to Bush's family friends and to the Liedtke's own rich connections to raise more money. The new funds begat new projects, many of them tied together by innovative, sophisticated tax and financing vehicles. By the late 1950s, Bush was pushing to enter the nascent off-shore drilling industry and he asked to take his share of the company public. A friendly divorce was negotiated; the Liedtkes and Bush remained close friends for the next twenty-five years.

Hugh Liedtke agreed to the separation from Bush because his ambition was not to experiment with off-shore drilling, but to build an American oil company large enough to rival the huge, international conglomerates such as Texaco, Gulf, Shell, and Getty. He pursued this goal assiduously over the next twenty years. The key to his growth was not technical expertise in the oil business, or even exceptional luck as a wildcatter; his success was built on shrewd, sophisticated financial and legal maneuverings—on the application of skills acquired at Harvard and the University of Texas Law School. He pioneered the structural and analytical principles later adopted by others: takeovers based on undervalued assets, financial restructurings to raise stock prices, asset spinoffs to shareholders, and so on.

It began in 1962, when Liedtke was in Midland, Texas, flipping through Moody's guide to publicly owned corporations, looking for

something in which to invest his profits. He came across an entry
for the South Penn Oil Company, based in Pittsburgh, which manu-
factured the popular Pennzoil motor oil and owned vast reserves in
the old Bradford, Pennsylvania, oil field, the first major oil basin discovered in America. South Penn's shares were then trading for about
$28, but its underlying assets, Liedtke figured, were worth far more
than that. The problem, he thought, was lackadaisical management.
He decided to invest his money and turn things around himself.
With his brother and the usual coterie of family-connected outside
investors, he formed a partnership and began to buy up South Penn
stock. The company was controlled by J. Paul Getty, who owned just
under 10 percent of its shares, but who had taken no active interest
in its management. Through a mutual acquaintance in Tulsa, Liedtke
contacted Getty and asked him for the chance to run South Penn.

"You don't have much to lose," Liedtke said, referring to the
depressed price of South Penn's stock.

After some initial reluctance, J. Paul agreed, and Liedtke was
installed as president in 1962. He moved to Pittsburgh, implemented
dramatic new management and restructuring programs, and more
than doubled the price of South Penn stock in just a few years. By
1964, it was clear that South Penn would be Hugh Liedtke's company for as long as he wished to run it. Homesick for Texas, Liedtke
changed South Penn's name to the Pennzoil Company and moved its
headquarters to Houston.

In 1965, Liedtke shocked Wall Street with his most ambitious
gambit yet: a virtually unprecedented $130 million hostile takeover
of sleepy United Gas, a company many times larger than Pennzoil.
The ploy worked, and it set off a fountain of complex, paper-shuffling
deals involving Pennzoil and the Liedtke brothers: stock swaps, asset
spin-offs, royalty restructurings, company splits, mergers, and takeovers. In one of the deals, Hugh and Bill Liedtke went their separate
ways, Bill taking a piece of United Gas with him and Hugh holding
on to Pennzoil, a company devoted solely to oil drilling and marketing. There was talk about a falling out between the brothers, and they
did have some differences, but really the cause was Hugh Liedtke's
soaring ambition.

Through all the deals and manipulations, Hugh had never
wavered from his goal to build a major American oil company;
and over the next fifteen years, Pennzoil grew and grew. Unlike the

salaried managers of the behemoth, publicly owned oil corporations such as Exxon and Getty, Liedtke was not seduced by the glamour of diversification during the 1970s. In a word, he thought the idea was stupid. Hugh Liedtke knew what business he was in—the oil business. That business meant everything to him; he was especially proud of his membership in the All-American Wildcatters Club in Houston, a club whose motto read, "My word is my bond." Liedtke had absolutely no interest in programming sports television or selling office products, even if such ventures would attract publicity and allow him to circulate in a new, glittering financial society. He did not much care for Wall Street or Hollywood; he preferred Arkansas, razorback country, where he owned a four-thousand-acre ranch for fishing and deer-hunting. When not at his large, waterside estate down on the Houston bayou, Liedtke could often be found parked in a motorboat on one of the lakes at his ranch, his feet propped on the runner, his line trolling behind, his large pumpkin face tucked into his chest. It was the image of a man contented, a wealthy Texan in his element.

The two sides of Hugh Liedtke—the candid good old boy and the shrewd, connected financial manipulator—always raised questions about Liedtke's essential integrity and motivations. Most people took Liedtke at face value and praised his uncanny ability to manage growth in the oil industry for the benefit of his stockholders—of which Liedtke himself was the largest with some 358,000 Pennzoil shares, worth $25 million by 1983. It was said that Hugh Liedtke was the sort of oilman who should be running the international giants; he managed a lean, clear-eyed company and did not protect management perquisites at stockholders' expense. Though it was now a huge, sprawling, publicly owned corporation, Pennzoil retained the culture of entrepreneurship. Its top managers were its owners and they shared the risks of business; not only did Liedtke own a large amount of stock, so did most of the members of his board of directors. Liedtke did not accept Boone Pickens' liquidation theory of the American oil industry—he desperately pursued growth, not shrinkage—but in nearly every other way he was a model of the styles and strategies advocated by Pickens, and in fact Pickens and Liedtke were friends and sometimes even industrial allies.

At the same time, however, there were some who questioned Liedtke's methods. Federal regulators investigated a number of his complex, paper-shuffling deals, and the SEC once forced Liedtke, his brother, and several others to pay back a hundred thousand dollars in profits from stock trading the commission alleged was improper. During Watergate, Pennzoil's name arose when investigators questioned the use of a company plane to fly seven hundred thousand dollars in Nixon campaign money from Texas to Washington two days before a new disclosure law was to take effect—part of the money was traced to the account of one of the Watergate burglars. Hugh and Bill Liedtke were closely involved in Nixon's 1972 reelection effort in Texas. Of the decision to let the jet be used, Hugh merely shrugged and drawled, "It seemed like the neighborly thing to do." No criminal charges were ever brought as a result of any investigation, and most chalked the incidents up to the loose mores of Texas politics and Hugh Liedtke's unusual enthusiasm for enriching himself and his Pennzoil shareholders.

By early December 1983, when news of the consent decree giving Gordon Getty and Harold Williams effective control over Getty Oil's destiny appeared in the financial press, Hugh Liedtke and his Pennzoil Company had reached a kind of plateau. Liedtke was now sixty-one, four years from his official retirement date as Pennzoil chief executive. Over the past twenty years, he had achieved extraordinary success in the oil business, and he had amassed great personal wealth, but he had fallen short of his goal of building a rival to the largest American oil companies. Pennzoil owned some 350 million barrels of oil, enough to rank it eighteenth or thereabouts in size. Exxon, by comparison, owned some 8 billion barrels of oil. Pennzoil had more than eight thousand employees, it ranked first or second in sales of consumer motor oil, and it had sizable sulphur, copper, gold, and other mineral holdings. But the company sold virtually no gasoline, and it had no prospect of increasing its basic supply of oil reserves through exploration: like everyone else in the American oil industry, Pennzoil was selling more reserves each year than it could replace. It was, Boone Pickens would say, in a state of liquidation.

On December 11, 1983, just six days after Gordon Getty and Harold Williams signed their consent, there appeared in the *New York Times* a lengthy article about the recent troubles at Getty Oil. Hugh Liedtke read the story with interest. Ever since the standstill agreement was announced in October, Liedtke had been trying to stay abreast of Getty Oil's affairs. Now, for the first time, the

Pennzoil chairman glimpsed the depth of animosity extant among Gordon, Williams, and Sid Petersen. The *Times* article reported generally about Gordon's growing disenchantment with Petersen and it included some details of their defiant confrontation in London early in October. The story made clear that reconciliation between Gordon and Petersen was an unlikely prospect. Even before he read the article, Liedtke had been considering the idea of a hostile takeover attempt against Getty Oil. When he was finished, he felt he understood something about the poisonous atmosphere pervading his target company. He was more certain than ever that Getty Oil was ripe for a takeover raid. If he succeeded, Hugh Liedtke knew, Pennzoil would finally become the oil giant he had long wanted to create.

Early in December, Liedtke assembled a small team of top Pennzoil executives for a meeting in the thirty-third-floor conference room of Pennzoil's downtown Houston headquarters. It was the same brain trust that had devised so many of Liedtke's sophisticated financial deals in the past. Three of them were lawyers: Liedtke; Baine Kerr, Pennzoil's president and former head of the corporate law department at Baker & Botts, a large and prestigious Houston firm; and Perry Barber, Pennzoil's general counsel and also a former Baker & Botts corporate partner. The other two, Norman Luke and Clifton Fridge, were accountants and corporate finance experts.

Fridge presented a number of hypothetical "pro forma" takeover proposals that he had been instructed to prepare. One assumed that Pennzoil would try to buy 20 percent of Getty Oil's publicly owned stock at $100 per share; Liedtke said that he would then try to make a deal with Gordon Getty to take full control of the company. Other documents assumed that Pennzoil would bid for all of Getty Oil's publicly owned stock, 48 percent of the total, at $90 a share. Then Liedtke and Gordon would meet and try to split Getty Oil's rich assets between them, Liedtke said.

Fridge handed Liedtke another hypothetical takeover proposal, one for 20 percent of Getty Oil's stock at $120 a share. Liedtke had not asked for a pro forma at that price—it was much higher than what he wanted to pay for Getty Oil's shares.

"I don't want anything with $120 on it walking around," Liedtke snapped. "I am looking at a $90 purchase." Liedtke knew that lawsuits attended any hostile takeover attempt, and that any documents prepared by Pennzoil before a bid would later fall into enemy hands.

He did not want it known that anyone at Pennzoil had considered a $120 offer—that might be grounds for a Getty Oil shareholder lawsuit alleging that Pennzoil had bought the company at too low a price.

Liedtke wanted the $120 pro forma destroyed. Before it was, however, he looked over the numbers in the document: how much Getty Oil's assets were worth on the open market, how much money Pennzoil would have to borrow, what debt ratios it would have after the deal, and so on.

"This is still a good deal," Liedtke told the Pennzoil executives in the conference room. "This is still a very good deal at this price." The Pennzoil chairman was beaming with pleasure. If buying Getty Oil at $120 a share was a good deal, then taking control at $90 was a financial coup.

After that meeting in the thirty-third-floor conference room, while the company lawyers and finance experts continued to refine their takeover documents, Liedtke began to widen the circle of knowledge about a possible takeover attempt against Getty Oil. He flew to New York and met on Monday, December 12, with his longtime Wall Street investment banker, James Glanville, of Lazard Frères. Liedtke and Glanville had worked together for years on a plethora of complex financial deals. Though he sometimes decried Wall Street's unquenchable thirst for transaction fees, Liedtke had respect and even affection for a number of Wall Street bankers and lawyers with whom he worked closely, and Glanville was chief among them. Liedtke's relationship with the Street was ambivalent. On the one hand, he expressed discomfort about the slick, monied, rapacious culture of Manhattan finance, where no one ever seemed to say what he was really thinking; Liedtke preferred the candid greed of Texas. On the other hand, Liedtke was at least as sophisticated about modern corporate law and finance as many of his Wall Street advisors—manipulations of Pennzoil's stock and structure had been a key to his remarkable success.

In Glanville's Wall Street office that Monday afternoon, Liedtke began to develop the details of his takeover strategy. A hostile bid for Getty Oil was fraught with peril. Because of Gordon's huge block of stock, and because of the deep distrust between Gordon and Petersen, Liedtke's success would depend on his ability to forge an alliance with one side or the other. He had to take sides. Liedtke told

Glanville that he intended to pursue the same strategy earlier devised by Pickens and Corby Robertson: he would try to make a deal with Gordon. It was the strategy Pickens described as "going after a puppy with a sledge hammer," and surely Liedtke, with his financial savvy and Texas charm, had as much chance as anyone to hammer a deal with Gordon. Liedtke said later that as he planned his takeover raid against Getty Oil that December, he believed that he would never be able to make a deal with Sid Petersen: the chief executive was the problem, not the solution. Getty Oil had been ruined by Sid Petersen, Liedtke said, by his ill-advised attempts at diversification, by his disrespect for Gordon Getty, and by his bid for glamour and recognition in Los Angeles society.

"Getty Oil's troubles began when Petersen took over," Liedtke said. "Getty Oil had been run by people who were operating people, oilmen. Petersen was not. He was a financial man, and when he took over, the whole focus of the company changed. He wanted to madly diversify like some of the other companies and I think that began the decline in morale at the company. . . . Even Lansing Hays was in the oil business. He wasn't off getting into bedsprings and widgets."

As Liedtke laid out his thinking to his investment banker, he began to conclude that there was only one sensible way to make a hostile takeover attempt. Pennzoil would announce a surprise tender offer for 20 percent of Getty Oil's stock at a premium above the market price. Perhaps the offer would be $90 a share, perhaps $100—whatever price was high enough to ensure that stockholders would sell. Liedtke had already made clear, however, that he was not interested in paying as much as $120; even though that still might be a "good deal," as he had put it, it was too expensive. Getty Oil, with its billions of barrels of oil, was there for the taking at $100 a share. Why pay more?

Then, having secured his 20 percent, Liedtke would approach Gordon Getty and offer to combine with him to take control of the company and throw out Petersen and the board of directors; this was the step Harold Williams and the museum had been unwilling to take. Depending on how it all went, Liedtke might then become chief executive of a combined Getty Oil and Pennzoil, allowing Gordon the title of chairman, or they might decide to simply split up Getty Oil's assets, allowing Gordon to carry off a piece of the company for himself and permitting Liedtke to integrate some of Getty

Oil's reserves into Pennzoil. Regardless of the details, the key to the strategy was Hugh Liedtke's ability to negotiate with and control Gordon Getty. Liedtke had no appreciation of how many people had tried and failed to master Gordon. He might be a puppy, but thus far, every time someone had attacked him with a sledge hammer, Gordon yapped and danced and dodged the blows.

Hugh Liedtke was a man of confidence and ambition, however, and by the end of that week he had decided to go forward with his plans. Speed was critical; if Getty Oil's vulnerability was now apparent to Liedtke, then it must also be apparent to other corporate raiders as well. Liedtke's investment bankers at Lazard Frères advised that a good time to make a surprise hostile takeover announcement was over the Christmas holidays—under federal law, Pennzoil would have to wait about twenty days from the time of its announcement before it could begin to actually purchase Getty Oil shares. The waiting period was designed to give a target company's management time to devise a response. By bidding over the holidays, when Getty Oil executives and their advisors would likely to be scattered around the world on vacations, Pennzoil's "Christmas surprise," as it would become known, could provide Liedtke with a precious strategic advantage.

On Monday, December 19, a clear and bitterly cold morning in Houston, Liedtke arrived at the Pennzoil Place skyscraper downtown and began to prepare for a meeting of his board of directors. If the board could be persuaded to endorse a bid for Getty Oil—and there was little doubt in Liedtke's mind that he could convince his directors that the idea was a good one—then the final hurdle would be cleared.

The meeting in the boardroom lasted most of the day. Predictably, the directors were easily and quickly convinced that Getty Oil was an alluring target. Liedtke ran through a list of the company's rich assets: its vast oil and gas reserves, most of them "politically secure" in the United States or Canada; its unrivaled Kern River oil field near Bakersfield, California; its gold and copper and mineral holdings; its agricultural land and timberland; and finally, its diversified subsidiaries, ERC, ESPN, real estate, and hotels. Liedtke said that if he gained control, he would move quickly to sell off the subsidiaries—he told his board that ERC, for example, could fetch at least $750 million cash within months after an acquisition. Next,

Liedtke passed out the "pro forma" documents secretly prepared by his top staff. They showed what a combined Getty Oil and Pennzoil Company would look like. It was, to say the least, a pretty picture.

But as the discussion moved on, the directors, perhaps to their credit, began to express one serious reservation about Hugh Liedtke's ambitious proposal: the problem of Gordon Getty. Some of the directors had known J. Paul Getty and his family during his days as an oilman in Tulsa, Oklahoma. All of them had read about the terms of Gordon's proposal to the museum in London. Could a man like that be trusted?

"Gordon is flaky," one of the directors said. "He has very little, if any, business experience."

"We don't know what Gordon's position will be about our offer. We don't know if he will even meet with us," another added.

Hugh Liedtke was prepared for these doubts; he harbored some of them himself. He told the board that he had talked about this problem with some of his lawyers. They had arrived at a possible solution. Moulton Goodrum, a corporate partner at the Baker & Botts firm, was asked to explain.

"We need a chance to test the water after we make our offer," he said. "If the water feels too cold, we don't want to dive in. We have to see if there is anyone interested in working with us. If we make a tender offer, there is an out, an escape hatch. Under the law, if you think that the value of the shares you are proposing to buy would be diminished because of your purchase—whether because you felt you couldn't work with Gordon Getty or whatever—then you don't have to go through with it. We could make that determination during the three-week waiting period after our announcement. Then, if Gordon or no one else will make a deal, we can abandon the tender and be left only with the cost and expenses from the offer."

The "out" was critical—no one on the Pennzoil board was yet prepared to commit the company to a working relationship with Gordon Getty. Even if they were able to quickly negotiate a deal with Gordon to take control of Getty Oil, Liedtke and his advisors would negotiate an escape hatch. After one year of joint control, say, Pennzoil would have the option to split off its portion of Getty Oil's assets and walk away. Gordon would be left on his own with the rest of the reserves. It would later be alleged that this plan was the only one Liedtke harbored seriously, that his goal all along was merely to use

Gordon. He would make a deal with the Getty scion to take control and throw out Petersen, negotiate a one-year "divorce" clause with Gordon, and then, when the year was up, walk away with a huge chunk of Getty Oil's assets. Liedtke denied that he was so devious; anything was possible after he made his hostile bid, he contended, even a negotiated arrangement with Sid Petersen. Still, at the board meeting in Houston that Monday, Liedtke made a point to emphasize the escape hatch he would seek from Gordon.

"Any part of any plan we would enter into with Gordon would have to include some way for us to get out," Liedtke told his directors. "We'll attempt very quickly to get with Gordon and/or the museum and/or the company and see if we can't play a constructive role in putting together a restructuring to resolve this dispute. But Gordon is the one we'll have to deal with."

After hours of discussion about Gordon's changeable character and about the ways Pennzoil might be able to protect itself in any deal with him, the board finally authorized Liedtke to proceed with a hostile takeover. The directors granted their chief executive wide latitude in any future negotiations with Gordon, the museum, or Getty Oil's representatives. Liedtke's best judgment was good enough for the board. So many times in the past, the Pennzoil chairman had pushed his company into dangerous, complex takeovers and restructurings, and nearly every time, he had won handsomely.

Of course, he had never before played a game with Gordon Getty.

BUYERS AND SELLERS

A chill rain was falling in San Francisco on Tuesday, December 27, but once again Gordon Getty's Broadway mansion was basking in holiday warmth. The Christmas trees had been raised, including the traditional family teddy bear tree. One year before, when he retreated to his basement study and wrote a glowing letter to Sidney Petersen, Gordon had seemed infected by the spirit of the holidays; his good will extended even to his adversaries at Getty Oil, who were at the time formulating secret plans to launch a family lawsuit against him. To Gordon, the future of Getty Oil had seemed bright with promise. Now so much was changed. Gordon felt little but disgust and contempt for the company managers and advisors in Los Angeles. He wanted very much to overthrow Sid Petersen and the board of directors. Only the reluctance of Harold Williams prevented him from doing so.

Gordon was not terribly distraught, therefore, when Moses Lasky telephoned him that Tuesday afternoon to say that the Houston-based Pennzoil Company had announced a hostile tender offer for 20 percent of Getty Oil's outstanding stock. Gordon believed that hostile takeovers were good for the nation's economy; they kept entrenched managers like Sid Petersen on their toes. His initial reaction was that Pennzoil's bid was perhaps less a threat than an opportunity. This was not because he knew very much about Pennzoil. He had never heard of Hugh Liedtke. Indeed, what Gordon knew about Pennzoil was confined to impressions gleaned from the company's television commercials for motor oil, which featured the golfing legend Arnold Palmer and his tractor. Gordon said later that he did not believe Arnold Palmer was Pennzoil's chief executive, but beyond that, he had no real knowledge about the company. He was surprised to learn that Pennzoil owned hundreds of millions of barrels of proven oil reserves, and that its holdings ranked it in the top twenty among American oil companies.

Shortly after he heard from Lasky that Tuesday afternoon, Gordon received a call from Marty Siegel, who was vacationing with his family in the Virgin Islands. So far as Siegel was concerned, Pennzoil's holiday offer had been a Christmas surprise indeed—Siegel was staying in a hotel room with no telephone, and when Pennzoil's announcement came over the ticker tape in New York, Siegel's partners at Kidder, Peabody had been forced to employ a messenger in the Virgin Islands to transmit the news. When he got the message, Siegel found a public telephone and called his client in San Francisco.

"If there's going to be a Pennzoil tender offer at $100 per share, and if no other alternatives become available to the public stockholders, then I think it will be a successful offer—Pennzoil will get the full twenty percent," Siegel told Gordon. "There is a considerable danger that this could lead to Pennzoil somehow assuming a majority position and locking out you and the trust. But we can also look on it as a promising development, an opportunity."

Gordon agreed that there was reason to be optimistic about the hostile bid. His family might not see it that way—in the pending lawsuit they had filed against him, with Getty Oil management's assistance, the trust's beneficiaries alleged that Gordon's behavior might lead precisely to his present dilemma, with the family fortune mired in a takeover war with an outside raider. But after all, Gordon had said all along that his goal was merely to "maximize" the value of his family trust's stock holdings. A year before, that stock had been worth only $50 or $60 per share. Now, apparently, Pennzoil was willing to pay $100.

Gordon instructed his investment banker to return to New York as quickly as possible. Siegel said that he would cut his vacation short and catch the next plane out of the islands. The largest company ever put into play on Wall Street was now effectively on the auction block and Siegel had a contract for a percentage of the deal. For the sake of his client, and for the sake of his firm, there was no time to waste.

By late that Tuesday afternoon, all of the Wall Street advisors had been fully mobilized. There was a new player now, Pennzoil, represented by Jim Glanville of the Lazard Frères investment banking house. Glanville was an experienced merger partner who specialized in the oil business, and was considered as capable and aggressive a banker as any. His senior partner in the Lazard merger division was Felix Rohatyn, perhaps Wall Street's most celebrated investment banker. Rohatyn had made his reputation working for the trailblazing conglomerate ITT during Wall Street's so-called go-go years, the 1960s. In that era, ITT bought and sold subsidiary companies in unrelated businesses as if they were interchangeable parts of some great industrial kaleidoscope. Rohatyn earned millions shepherding the deals. During the 1970s, through his stewardship of the Municipal Assistance Corporation, Rohatyn gained equally prodigious fame by rescuing New York City from bankruptcy. Later he took charge of the Lazard merger division and began to contribute long essays to the intellectual press about the terrible dangers of merger mania, even as he continued to broker deals for his firm.

Naturally, because of their places in Manhattan's financial society, both Rohatyn and Glanville had developed close professional and personal relationships with Marty Lipton. Glanville had figured that since Lipton's client, the museum, owned 12 percent of Getty Oil, and since it was caught precariously in the middle of warring between Gordon and Petersen, Lipton and Williams might be willing to sell their shares to Pennzoil once its hostile tender offer was announced. That Tuesday morning, December 27, Glanville had telephoned Lipton and asked him to lunch.

At the restaurant, Glanville told Lipton that he had something "very important" to discuss with him, but that he was not quite ready to talk about it yet. To the two old merger hands, Glanville's cautious statement was a familiar kind of code: a big deal was in the works, he was saying, and Lipton would be involved, but Glanville could not identify the companies until an announcement went over the ticker tape. Lipton asked if perhaps Glanville would be ready to discuss the matter in the evening, after the stock market closed—major takeover announcements were often made around five o'clock New York time, so that chaos would not erupt on the trading floor. Glanville answered that yes, he might well be ready by evening, and so Lipton invited his friend to dinner at his luxury apartment.

Glanville arrived at Lipton's place at about seven-fifteen; news of Pennzoil's tender offer was already on the wire.

"I think the most appropriate thing to do would be to call Mr. Williams and tell him immediately about Pennzoil's offer," Lipton told Glanville. "I could put you on the phone with Williams right now."

Glanville said that he had a strong desire to talk with Mr. Williams about Pennzoil's intentions.

Lipton telephoned his client, quickly transmitted what he knew about Pennzoil's bid, and then handed the receiver to Glanville.

"Pennzoil would like very much to have the museum sell its shares to us—either pursuant to the tender offer or in some other way," Glanville said. They talked about price. Williams wanted to know how high Pennzoil would be willing to go if it could buy all of the museum's shares separately from the tender offer.*

Glanville indicated to Williams that Pennzoil might be willing to pay as much as $110 or more per share if the museum would sell its stock in one fell swoop.

"At $120 a share, I am certain that the museum would want to sell," Williams responded.

Glanville said that he would take that under advisement. He was encouraged by this opening in the negotiations. For the past eighteen months, the museum's 12 percent swing block of Getty Oil shares had been a kind of linchpin at the company—the museum played Gordon and management off against each other and managed to wield great control over Getty Oil's affairs. By bidding for 20 percent, Pennzoil was hoping to become a kind of swing block itself, owning enough stock to combine with Gordon and take control. If Pennzoil

---

* In a partial tender offer, as Pennzoil's 20 percent takeover bid was called, the number of shares any single stockholder could sell depended on the total number of shares submitted, or tendered, for sale to Pennzoil. If, after the twenty-one-day waiting period, all of Getty Oil's shareholders offered to sell to Pennzoil, then the purchase would be "prorated"—that is, each stockholder would be allowed to sell 20 percent of his shares for $100. If less than 20 percent of Getty Oil's shares were tendered for sale to Pennzoil, then all the shares tendered would be purchased by Pennzoil if it went ahead with the deal.

could take the museum out of the picture altogether by purchasing its shares, Hugh Liedtke would have moved a long way toward his goal of total control over Getty Oil's rich assets.

It was not until the following morning, Wednesday, that Liedtke himself finally got in touch with Gordon Getty at the Broadway mansion. Ever since the Pennzoil board meeting on December 19, Liedtke and his advisors had been trying to find a way to reach Gordon privately once their takeover bid was announced. Liedtke wanted to assure Gordon as quickly as possible that he intended nothing hostile toward the Getty family trust. The trouble was that no one on the Pennzoil board knew Gordon personally, except perhaps by reputation, and so Liedtke was concerned that he would have to work through Gordon's lawyers, which he did not want to do. One of Pennzoil's directors, William Wilson, who was the American ambassador to the Vatican and a longtime California friend of Ronald Reagan, told Liedtke that he might be able to reach Gordon through a friend of a friend in San Francisco. On Tuesday, when the Pennzoil offer was announced, Wilson went to work on the telephone. Just before noon the next day, Liedtke received a message at Pennzoil headquarters in Houston that Gordon would be willing to take his call.

"His reaction was cool," the message from Liedtke's secretary read, referring to Gordon.

There was a telephone number, and Liedtke put the call through.

"We're prepared to work with you, Mr. Getty," Liedtke said. "I want to cooperate with the trust—I think I share many of your objectives in terms of Getty Oil management and restructuring. For one thing, I think we could eliminate the corporate shell at the company and then you'd be able to stop paying the double tax on your dividends."

Gordon said little, but he was polite and friendly. He was receptive to Liedtke's ideas; with his talk of shared goals and eliminating the corporate shell, the Pennzoil chairman had pushed the right buttons.

"I am planning to call Mr. Williams," Liedtke said. "I'd be happy to do that, but if you would prefer to do it, why, you can do it. But I'd like to sit down with you at the earliest possible time."

Gordon said that he thought that might be a productive idea. He added, however, "I'd prefer to talk to Mr. Williams myself."

"That's fine," Liedtke answered.

The call ended cordially. Liedtke said that he would be available virtually anytime to meet with Gordon. Gordon thanked him and said that no doubt they would be in touch.

That Wednesday afternoon, the telephone calls volleyed around the country like Ping-Pong balls in a wind tunnel. Liedtke telephoned Harold Berg at his home near Austin, Texas, and repeated the message he had delivered to Gordon. Berg called Dave Copley at Getty Oil headquarters and passed on the substance of his talk with Liedtke. Harold Stuart, the Getty Oil director from Tulsa, called Hugh Liedtke's brother Bill to discuss Pennzoil's offer.

In Los Angeles, a shaken Sid Petersen spent nearly the entire day on the phone, talking to Bart Winokur in Philadelphia, Geoff Boisi in New York, and also with various members of his board, who were scattered about the country. The consensus was that if nothing was done, Pennzoil's 20 percent bid would succeed—Boisi said that $100 per share was high enough to cause a full subscription to the offer. Petersen, Winokur, Boisi, and the directors also agreed that $100 was too low a price for them to approve on behalf of the public shareholders.

Back in August, when Gordon had been talking about combining with the museum to launch a leveraged buy-out takeover against the company, Goldman, Sachs had for the first time studied the actual, underlying value of Getty Oil's shares. The firm had concluded that the minimum value for the company's stock was about $120 per share—twenty dollars more than Pennzoil was now offering. Goldman had even put its $120 valuation on paper in connection with a presentation to Gordon in San Francisco. If Boisi now advised the Getty Oil board that Pennzoil's $100 offer was fair to shareholders, he would be contradicting his earlier advice. Then, if Goldman was sued by Getty Oil shareholders—and in any hostile takeover lawsuits were a virtual certainty—Boisi would be confronted with his August opinion and asked to explain why his firm had declared that something near $120 was the minimum value in August, while $100 was an acceptable price in December. That was an untenable position for both Goldman, Sachs and the Getty Oil board of directors. None of them wanted to lose their jobs and their company to Gordon Getty and Pennzoil. But if Getty Oil had to be sold, they at least wanted it to go at a fair price for the public stockholders—one high enough to protect them from the expense and liability of class-action share-holder lawsuits.

And still, as Petersen, Winokur, Boisi, and the rest of them talked about it that Wednesday afternoon, there was the question of what Gordon Getty wanted. None of them had talked to Gordon since the Pennzoil bid was announced. What did he think about it? What was he planning? For months, they had discussed with Gordon the very possibility that was now upon them. They had warned him that his family trust might be squeezed out, that Gordon might be the juice. If Gordon was willing, Petersen and his advisors thought, the company and the trust could forge an alliance to beat back Pennzoil's takeover bid. For more than a year now, the company had discussed a self-tender that would put Gordon in a majority position. If Getty Oil now tendered for 20 percent of its own stock at a price higher than Pennzoil's $100 per share—say, $120, the Goldman, Sachs minimum—it could "make Pennzoil go away," as Petersen put it, and buy enough time to either sell the company or negotiate a long-term power-sharing agreement with Gordon. As they talked that Wednesday afternoon, they asked each other: Would Gordon be willing to negotiate with the company to fight off Pennzoil? Or, did he have his own agenda, his own plans to unite with Liedtke and take the company? None of them knew. And none of them had any sure way to find out.

Since the filing of the family lawsuit challenging Gordon's right to be sole trustee, relations between the company and Gordon had been virtually nonexistent. The poison ran too deep. To the Lasky lawyers, Petersen's instigation of a family lawsuit against their client seemed an unconscionable deceit. Now aware of the lawsuit, when Cohler, Lasky, or Woodhouse looked back on their long year of negotiations with Winokur, Boisi, and the rest—a year of arduous struggle to reach an accommodation between Getty Oil and Gordon—they saw the whole process in a different light. Petersen was never seriously interested in allowing Gordon to share power at the company, they believed. All those negotiations about handcuffs and self-tenders and LBO takeovers were just a sham, a filibuster to buy time for the family lawsuit, they thought. It was now hard for the Lasky lawyers to believe that any good could ever come from negotiations with Sid Petersen and his advisors.

As they had been ever since his decision that Getty Oil's directors were "a bunch of snakes," Gordon's hopes for power at the company lay with Harold Williams and the museum. And so, confronted by a bid for control from an outsider, Pennzoil, Gordon turned not to Petersen, but to Williams. Shortly after his conversation with Liedtke on Wednesday, Gordon telephoned Harold Williams in Los Angeles and invited him to the Broadway mansion for a meeting the next day. Gordon said that in the wake of Pennzoil's hostile tender offer, he had a new proposal to make to the museum.

Williams agreed to fly up the next morning. His views of Gordon Getty were quite different from those of Sid Petersen and the Getty Oil advisors. He said that he considered Gordon to be an intelligent, talented, and capable man, though he did not believe that Gordon was qualified to be chief executive of a company the size of Getty Oil. Still, it was hard for Petersen and his advisors to be sure what Williams believed from one moment to the next. In London, his lawyer, Lipton, had described the idea of a joint consent takeover between Williams and Gordon as utterly absurd. Two months later, after the company's complicity in the family lawsuit was disclosed, Williams had indeed signed a majority stockholders' consent with Gordon, though he had stopped short of throwing out the board of directors. Now, in the face of a threatening bid by an outsider, who knew what Harold Williams would resort to?

At the Broadway mansion that Thursday morning, Gordon laid out his plan to the museum president: the Pennzoil tender was potentially dangerous for both of them, he said, but there was one way to stop it cold.

"Our response to the Pennzoil offer should be to act by consent and assume control of the company," Gordon said. "I believe that we should immediately remove the board of directors. I would be installed as chief executive and you would become chairman of the finance committee. We would control fifty-two percent of the stock and there would be nothing Pennzoil could do." Because of the consent they signed in December, Gordon and Williams wielded virtually absolute control over Getty Oil's major policy decisions. Management could mount no defenses such as their threatened issuance of treasury shares in October.

Williams listened to Gordon and then told him that he did not think the plan was sound. Gordon did not possess adequate experience to be Getty Oil's chief executive, Williams said. Williams himself did not want the job. Gordon suggested that if his own credentials were the problem, then perhaps they could take joint control of the company and then conduct a search for a new chief executive to replace Sid Petersen. Williams said that he didn't think that would work because after they fired Petersen and the directors, there would be an interim period with no one really in charge, this while Getty Oil was trying to fight off a hostile takeover from Pennzoil.

"At $100 per share or higher, the museum is a seller and not a buyer," Williams told Gordon.*

The museum president wanted no part of Gordon's plan. In fact, the audacity of Gordon's proposal to fire the board and name himself chief executive had persuaded Williams that there was no longer any good reason for the museum to remain a shareholder in Getty Oil. When he telephoned Marty Lipton that afternoon to report on what Gordon had said, he told his lawyer that he wanted out. The museum would sell its shares to the highest bidder. Lipton was instructed to pass the word to the Getty Oil advisors.

In fact, while Williams was talking with Gordon Getty at the Broadway mansion in San Francisco, Lipton had been meeting in his own office with Winokur, Boisi, Galant, and other advisors. By the time Williams called to say that he wanted to sell, that he wanted nothing to do with any company in which Gordon Getty had a role, Lipton had concluded a day of productive negotiations with the company designed to forge a united front against the Pennzoil bid. They had talked about launching a 20 percent self-tender at some price above $100 per share, then signing a document that would establish peace at the company. The proposal under discussion guaranteed that Gordon and Harold Williams would remain company directors with important committee assignments for at least three years. It even contemplated the forced retirement of Sidney Petersen as a means to acquire Gordon's support for the deal. As Dave Copley's handwritten notes about the meeting put it: "Query role of Sid Petersen. Company understands he does not have the confidence of Gordon Getty. Gordon Getty likely to insist on Petersen's retirement as condition to agreement with the company." There had been some telephone discussions with Getty Oil directors, including Henry

---

*   Gordon later testified that he recalled Williams' remark clearly because it "was a rhyme. Put me among a circle of poets for that. That's the lowest circle in hell, by the way."

Wendt, about the possibility of Petersen's forced retirement. No decision had been made, but Wendt, for one, did not believe it was a sensible idea.

Regardless, Lipton announced that Thursday afternoon, the deal was now off. He told Winokur and Boisi about Williams' meeting with Gordon in San Francisco that morning. Winokur and Boisi were not exactly surprised; nothing about Gordon could shock them anymore. But they were discouraged. Williams' decision to get out of Getty Oil, to sell his shares as quickly as possible, meant that Petersen and his advisors could only ward off Pennzoil through an alliance with Gordon. And they knew that it would be much more difficult to make a deal with Gordon than it would be to forge one with Marty Lipton and the museum.

As the Getty Oil advisors discussed in New York that afternoon how they might persuade Gordon to join them in a battle against Pennzoil, Gordon himself was winging toward them. After his morning meeting with Williams, Gordon rode to the airport with his wife Ann and boarded a plane to New York. Along with Ann, Gordon was accompanied on the flight by Mark Leland, his personal financial advisor and a former assistant secretary of the treasury under President Reagan, and two of his Lasky firm lawyers, Cohler and Woodhouse. That same day, Dave Copley had issued notice by telegram of an emergency Getty Oil board meeting to be convened in Manhattan on Monday evening, January 2; the board was to formally consider its response to Pennzoil's tender offer. Gordon had decided that since Williams was unwilling to fire the board, the best place for him to conduct his negotiations with Getty Oil and Pennzoil was in New York. Late that night, he checked into a two-room suite at the Pierre Hotel on Fifth Avenue, overlooking Central Park. Over the next week, he would only rarely leave the hotel. As it had been all along, those who wished to control the future of Getty Oil Company would have to come to him.

Ever since his initial phone call to Gordon on Wednesday, Hugh Liedtke had been pressing for a face-to-face meeting. By Friday, December 30, he had succeeded only in arranging a meeting of the advisors for Pennzoil and the trust in New York. The meeting convened early Friday afternoon in the Manhattan offices of Lazard Frères; Liedtke was still holding the fort at Pennzoil headquarters in Houston. Representing him were Glanville and Arthur Liman, a well-known partner at the New York law firm of Paul, Weiss, Rifkind, Wharton & Garrison. Liman had made his considerable reputation in both corporate work and criminal law. His specialty was defending white-collar criminals. Like Marty Lipton and Felix Rohatyn, Liman was a member of New York City's "shadow government" of Manhattan lawyers and financiers; he served on a number of special mayoral commissions that investigated municipal corruption. Liman knew Lipton and Rohatyn well. With the similarly well-connected Glanville, he would become over the next week a point man for Hugh Liedtke's dealings with the Wall Street lawyers and bankers now in control of Getty Oil's destiny. Representing Gordon at the meeting that Friday afternoon were his investment banker, Marty Siegel, and his lawyers, Cohler and Woodhouse.

It was Siegel who began the discussion. "Gordon Getty is prepared to join with Pennzoil in acquiring Getty Oil," Siegel announced to the group. "But he will do so only if Pennzoil is prepared to make the acquisition on a basis in which Gordon Getty would end up owning four-sevenths. That's a nonnegotiable condition. Gordon Getty would never permit himself to be in a minority position.

"And there can be no negotiating about the make-up of a new board of directors," Siegel continued. "The board would also have to be divided four-sevenths, three-sevenths, between Mr. Getty's nominees and Pennzoil's.

"There is also no way that the company can be acquired at the $100-per-share price Pennzoil is offering. I've been in touch with Marty Lipton. He tells me that the museum is a seller. But I'd like to get your reaction to a number. What do you think your reaction would be if I floated a number like $120?"

"You're taking all of the fun out of it at $120," Glanville answered.

"Well, there certainly is no sense in pursuing this unless Pennzoil is prepared to go at least to $110."

"What protection is Pennzoil going to have if Gordon Getty is going to end up with control of the board and four-sevenths of the company?" Arthur Liman asked. There was some discussion of the "divorce clause" that Hugh Liedtke had talked about with his own board of directors—Pennzoil wanted some kind of "out" if it ended up owning a company controlled by Gordon.

"The only protection that Pennzoil can have is a divorce clause," Siegel answered. "If the partnership doesn't work out after a year,

Getty Oil's assets could be divided proportionately, four-sevenths to Gordon Getty and three-sevenths to Pennzoil."

Glanville and Liman indicated that the basic terms of Siegel's proposal sounded like something that Hugh Liedtke would be willing to entertain—so long as the divorce clause was a part of the package.

"We'd like all of these terms and conditions to be the subject of a summit meeting between the two principals, Liedtke and Gordon," Liman said.

"A summit meeting can take place after all the conditions have been agreed on, but Mr. Getty prefers that the matter be negotiated by the bankers and not by the principals. We would be better served if we conducted the negotiations that way," Siegel responded.

Liman said he would pass that along to Liedtke. He used a phone in the Lazard meeting room to telephone the Pennzoil chairman at his Houston office. Liman and Glanville outlined the deal proposed by Siegel and explained that Siegel insisted that the terms be finalized and agreed upon by the bankers and lawyers before Liedtke met directly with Gordon.

"Mr. Getty's people want to have a structured meeting," Glanville told Liedtke.

"Well, what on earth is that?" Liedtke demanded.

"They want to present to you an outline of what they think you ought to talk about with Mr. Getty, and then they'll go up and review it and take it up and review it with Mr. Getty."

"Like hell they will," Liedtke answered forcefully. "I'm going to deal directly with Mr. Getty and I'm not going to deal with third parties. I don't want them telling Mr. Getty what I think or what I'm offering. I want to sit right across the table from him and tell him myself so there won't be any question. And if they can't arrange that, then I'm not going to have any 'structured' meeting."

Glanville passed Liedtke's message on to Siegel. Siegel asked if he could speak directly with Liedtke, and Glanville handed him the phone. They talked for about twenty minutes, and Liedtke was no less adamant: he was not going to have this deal negotiated by bankers and lawyers. Either he was going to sit down with Gordon Getty or there was going to be no deal at all.

They had reached an impasse. Neither Siegel, Cohler, nor Woodhouse was willing to agree to a face-to-face meeting between their client and Hugh Liedtke. The basic terms of an alliance between

Gordon and Pennzoil had been agreed upon, but there was no consensus on how the deal could be negotiated. As the meeting ended, Liman telephoned Liedtke and told him that they could not arrange a summit.

Hugh Liedtke decided that he would try to arrange a meeting with Gordon Getty himself. He telephone Fayez Sarofim, a stock fund manager and investment advisor based in Houston who specialized in the oil business. Sarofim's fund owned a large block of Getty Oil stock. Shortly after the Pennzoil tender offer was announced, Sarofim had telephoned Liedtke to report on a call he had received from Ann Getty. Sarofim told the Pennzoil chairman that Mrs. Getty had wanted to know "what kind of people" the Pennzoil executives were. Now Liedtke thought that perhaps Sarofim could get a message to Gordon through, Mrs. Getty—without it being filtered by Gordon's lawyers and bankers.

"I think we're getting the run-around," Liedtke told Sarofim. "I want to meet at the earliest possible date with Gordon Getty himself and I don't want to talk through third parties."

Sarofim said that he might be able to help. He said that he knew Alexander Papamarkou, Ann Getty's stockbroker and social escort, and that perhaps through him a message could be passed to Gordon.

The next morning, Saturday, Liedtke heard back from Sarofim. "The meeting is going to take place," Fayez confided. Liedtke thanked him. And he waited to hear from Gordon through more official channels.

That same morning in Manhattan, however, it seemed to the advisors of Getty Oil Company management that Gordon Getty was far from ready to enter into any agreement with Hugh Liedtke and Pennzoil. Indeed, it seemed to Bart Winokur and Geoff Boisi that Gordon was on the verge of signing an entirely different deal: a temporary truce with Sid Petersen that would raise a united front against Hugh Liedtke's takeover bid.

It was not Gordon himself who conveyed this impression to Winokur and Boisi. Rather, it was the same trio of lawyers and bankers who had negotiated with Arthur Liman and Jim Glanville at the Lazard offices the day before—Marty Siegel, Tim Cohler, and Tom Woodhouse. They had come that morning to the Park Avenue offices of Wachtell, Lipton, Rosen & Katz to meet with

Winokur, Boisi, and Lipton and to negotiate a self-tender plan that would ward off Pennzoil's 20 percent bid. They had discussed the same idea the day before, after the meeting at Lazard with Liman and Glanville. After hours of complex negotiations, the plan had become fairly simple: Getty Oil would announce a 20 percent self-tender offer at some price above Pennzoil's $100 per share—exactly what price had not been decided, but Winokur assumed it would be $120 or more—and it would simultaneously announce that the entire company was up for sale if a buyer would come forward within ninety days. Gordon, the museum, and Petersen's management team would each agree that if a buyer came forward and proposed to purchase the entire company for a price greater than the Getty Oil self-tender, all three parties would sell their shares outright. If no buyer for the whole company made an offer during the ninety-day period, then Getty Oil would execute its self-tender for 20 percent of the public's shares. As a result, Gordon's family trust would be moved into a majority position and Gordon could do whatever he pleased with the company. There would be no handcuffs, no supermajorities on the board, nothing. Until that ninety-day "auction period" was up, however, Gordon would have to agree not to exercise power at the company in combination with the museum.

Winokur and Boisi were saying to Gordon, in effect: "We think Getty Oil is worth a lot more than $100 a share if we can only arrange a controlled auction and shop the company to interested buyers. If we're wrong, you get the company. If we're right, then you get to sell your shares for billions of dollars, at more than $120 per share."

That Saturday morning in Marty Lipton's office, Siegel reported that on Friday night he, Gordon, Cohler, and Woodhouse had discussed this idea at some length. Siegel said that he personally believed that this was the best plan available to Gordon, his client. He could not, of course, vouch for what Gordon might do once he was presented with a document for his signature. At the moment, Siegel said, there were two sticking points.

First was the question of who would be in charge of Getty Oil during the ninety-day auction period. Was Sid Petersen willing to resign? This had seemed to be one of Gordon Getty's principal objectives ever since he learned about the family lawsuit against him. It had been the key to his proposal to Harold Williams at the Broadway mansion earlier in the week. Now came the crunch point: would Petersen sacrifice himself to buy a ninety-day auction period for the company?

The answer was no. Petersen himself was willing to consider the idea, but his board of directors had made it clear in telephone conversations that they refused to throw him overboard simply to please Gordon Getty. After all they had been through, the directors refused to give in to this last and most egregious of Gordon's whims, Winokur and Boisi made clear.

Siegel himself did not greatly care whether Petersen resigned. They were not talking about the future of Getty Oil now—they were discussing a ninety-day auction period. If the company was sold, Petersen's career would likely be over. If the auction failed and a self-tender was executed, then Gordon would be in charge and Petersen would be fired. With all that was at sake, ninety days hardly seemed so important.

But to both sides it was a matter of principle and neither would concede the ground. So they moved on to the second problem: the price of the company's 20 percent self-tender offer. Boisi and Winokur had been talking about a price of at least $120 per share, and perhaps as much as $130. That way, the company's offer to its shareholders would be much higher than Pennzoil's, and Goldman, Sachs could stick to its official opinion that $120 was the minimum fair price for Getty Oil's stock.

Now, however, Gordon was expressing some doubt about the $120 price. As the meeting progressed that Saturday at Lipton's office, he sent yet another emissary to express his views. The messenger was Laurence Tisch, one of the best-known and most respected corporate financiers in New York. Larry Tisch was then the chairman of the multibillion-dollar Loews Corporation, a diversified conglomerate with hotel, entertainment, and insurance holdings. With his brother Robert, Tisch had built his companies from scratch—he had grown up on the streets of New York and had worked his way through night school—and by December 1983, he was regarded as one of the shrewdest, most determined corporate executives in the country. Indeed, just three years later, when he acquired control of CBS Inc. Tisch made the cover of *Time* Magazine. But now, through no particular ambition of his own, he was a director of Getty Oil

Company. Back in October, when the three-way standstill truce was signed in San Francisco, Gordon had been empowered to nominate four new directors of his own choosing. He had decided then that he wanted to choose "entrepreneurial" men who were nonetheless highly experienced in the management of large corporations. Gordon's thinking was that such entrepreneurs would share his perspective as an owner of a huge block of Getty Oil stock; they would know what it was like to be a major shareholder in a large corporation. Such directors, Gordon hoped, would understand the dangers posed by Getty Oil's entrenched, professional managers—its "club of chief executive types," as one lawyer involved described the cadre of Petersen, Henry Wendt, Chauncey Medberry, John Teets, and the rest. Lacking social connections himself, Gordon dispatched his wife Ann to recruit Tisch, who agreed to join.

Until that Saturday in December, however, Tisch had played little role in Getty Oil's affairs. His nomination to the board had only been approved at the November meeting in Houston; he had yet to attend a directors meeting. In the course of things, however, he had talked with Gordon Getty and had learned something about his tangled relationship with Sid Petersen, Harold Williams, Marty Lipton, and the rest. Tisch was very close with Lipton; their luxury apartments were nearby on the upper East Side and together they had pioneered the "power breakfast" at the Regency Hotel during the 1970s, when Lipton represented Loews in its landmark takeover of the insurance company CNA. Now Tisch, trading on his friendships and his widespread reputation for business acumen, hoped to help negotiate a solution to Getty Oil's problems. The effort was not purely philanthropic: when he accepted Gordon's nomination to the board, Tisch acquired for his corporation between sixty and seventy thousand shares of Getty Oil stock. He figured that the company's shares were vastly undervalued by the market.

At the Saturday meeting in the offices of his friend Marty Lipton, Tisch told the assembled lawyers and bankers that Gordon Getty was "definitely a seller" and that Gordon was willing to accept a ninety-day auction period to see if Getty Oil could be sold. Tisch added, however, that Gordon felt the $120-per-share price contemplated for the company's self-tender was too high.

"Gordon is willing to sell at any price above $110," Tisch announced.

Winokur and Boisi were incredulous. Here they were willing to establish an auction at which the minimum price for all of Getty Oil—including the 32 million shares controlled by Gordon—would be $120 per share. And now Gordon was saying that he would prefer the minimum price to be $110.

"It's not often that you ask somebody to be willing to sell at $115 or $120 and he comes back and says, 'Yes, I'll agree, but I'll agree to sell at a lower price,'" Winokur told Tisch.

"Don't look a gift horse in the mouth," Tisch replied.

To Geoff Boisi, however, Gordon's offer was more like a Trojan horse. Gordon wanted the self-tender price lowered to $110 because if the ninety-day auction failed to turn up a buyer, Gordon would own Getty Oil. Suddenly, Gordon would be a buyer of Getty Oil stock, not a seller. And if that was the case, he would rather buy at $110 than at $120. The problem for Boisi was that Goldman, Sachs believed the company was worth at least $120—probably much more. If the company executed a self-tender at $110, it would be contradicting Goldman's assessment. Despite this problem, Boisi and Winokur agreed to Tisch's suggestion. They agreed for two reasons. They were under tremendous pressure because of Pennzoil's bid, and $110 was better than letting Pennzoil buy 20 percent of the company for $100. And second, Boisi was extremely confident that once the ninety-day auction was announced, a buyer for the entire company would be found. Then the public shareholders would be well rewarded, the bankers would all earn millions in fees, and Gordon's bid for control would be thwarted. Only Sid Petersen and the other top Getty Oil executives would be the losers, and by now there was virtually no hope that their careers could be salvaged.

Winokur told Gordon's representatives that he would immediately begin to draft a three-way agreement between Gordon, the company, and the museum. The document, which was completed by 10 P.M. that night, New Year's Eve, provided for a $110 self-tender and a ninety-day auction period. Winokur said that he would deliver the document to Gordon's suite at the Pierre Hotel as soon as possible, and he did so, before midnight. The Getty Oil advisors assumed that Gordon would sign it the next day. Then the self-tender would be announced and the public auctioning of Getty Oil would begin.

After the meeting with Tisch, however, while Winokur and his partners were hurriedly drafting an agreement, Marty Siegel returned to the Pierre to speak with Gordon Getty. He explained the terms that had been negotiated with Winokur and Boisi. A short time later, Siegel telephoned Hugh Liedtke in Houston.

"Mr. Getty will meet with you tomorrow afternoon at the Pierre Hotel," Marty Siegel said.

17

AT THE PIERRE

After packing, Hugh Liedtke located a pilot to fly Pennzoil's corporate jet, rode to the airport, and flew that New Year's Eve to New York City. He did not arrive in Manhattan until the wee hours of 1984. The empty streets were littered with broken glass and debris from the city's annual Times Square celebration; it was an eerie scene. Since Pennzoil policy prohibited the company's chairman and president from flying on the same airplane, Liedtke was alone—Baine Kerr would travel to New York in the morning. Exhausted, Liedtke rode to the copper-domed Waldorf-Astoria on Park Avenue, where Pennzoil maintained a two-bedroom executive apartment on the thirty-eighth floor, and went to sleep.

It was not until noon on Sunday, January 1, that the rest of Pennzoil's Houston contingent arrived at the Waldorf. Kerr, general counsel Perry Barber, and Baker & Botts partner Moulton Goodrum had flown up together that morning, and their landing in New York had been inauspicious: the wheels of their airplane would not lock into place. The pilot circled the airport trying to fix the problem and eventually he touched down on the runway without incident. But the Pennzoil executives were late arriving in Manhattan and they were a little bit shaken from the ordeal.

Marty Siegel had said the day before that the summit meeting between Liedtke and Gordon would take place at 4 P.M. at the Pierre. In the interim, Liedtke's New York advisors—attorney Arthur Liman and banker Jim Glanville—arrived at Pennzoil's Waldorf suite to help plan for the event.

"I want to be certain that if I am going to make a deal with Gordon Getty that I will also be able to make a deal with the museum," Liedtke told his advisors.

The Pennzoil chairman wanted somehow to include more than 50 percent of Getty Oil's voting power in any agreement he struck that afternoon. That way, Sid Petersen and his directors could do nothing to block the deal. If Pennzoil, Gordon, and the museum were all part of the same alliance, they could dictate terms to the Getty Oil board. But if the museum held out, then Pennzoil would have the support only of Gordon's 40 percent. The Getty Oil directors were convening Monday evening to consider their response to Pennzoil's takeover bid. Liedtke wanted to leave them little room for debate.

"I'm willing to live with the four-sevenths, three-sevenths ratio and with Gordon controlling the board provided that there is an understanding on how the company will be operated," Liedtke told his executives and advisors. "Gordon Getty does not know how to operate an oil company. Our people would have to operate it. And if this arrangement doesn't work out, then we would divide up the assets proportionately."

It was decided that Liedtke, Kerr, Barber, and Glanville would attend the meeting with Gordon at the Pierre. Goodrum would await instructions at the Waldorf. And in an effort to enlist the museum's cooperation, Arthur Liman would walk up to Marty Lipton's apartment. Liman had been invited to Lipton's annual New Year's Day party, a catered affair where Manhattan's legal and financial cognoscenti gathered to usher in another year of unbridled prosperity. It was unclear what Lipton thought about Pennzoil's bid. He had said that the museum was a seller, and the day before he had agreed to the three-way self-tender and auction plan proposed by Getty Oil management. But Lipton was in a bind. If Pennzoil and Gordon forged an alliance without the museum, they would be very close to gaining majority control of Getty Oil. Because of the consent agreement signed by Harold Williams and Gordon in December, it now took fourteen out of sixteen directors to approve any major change of ownership. Williams and Harold Berg were the museum's only representatives on the Getty Oil board—the two of them alone could not block a deal. If Pennzoil and Gordon took control together, they might squeeze the museum out at an unfavorable price, or lock its shares in as a permanent minority block. Marty Lipton, then, had a powerful incentive to negotiate with Pennzoil to protect the museum's position. Arthur Liman figured that the attorney's New Year's Day party would be a good place to begin the discussions.

Of course, Liman's talks with Lipton that afternoon depended entirely on the success of the summit meeting between Hugh Liedtke and Gordon Getty. Gordon had received many suitors over the past eighteen months, including such monied oil men as Corby Robertson and Boone Pickens, but he had yet to accept a proposal from any of them. The circumstances were more favorable this time: Gordon was deeply angry at Sid Petersen. In addition, Liedtke had put pressure on the Getty family trust by launching his hostile 20 percent tender offer. But not even Gordon's lawyers and bankers could be certain what their client would do when confronted with a final decision.

At the appointed hour, Liedtke and his Pennzoil team arrived at the Pierre, a large and ornate limestone tower on the eastern edge of Central Park decorated by American and Canadian flags. It was a clear and bitterly cold afternoon. When they entered Gordon's suite, they found that the Getty scion was surrounded by his usual coterie of advisors: Siegel, Woodhouse, Cohler, and Mark Leland. Ann was in the bedroom and at one point during the two-hour meeting she emerged, was introduced to the Pennzoil executives and advisors, and then left.

The mood at the beginning of the meeting was watchful and expectant; Hugh Liedtke had demanded this summit and it was now up to him to charm Gordon Getty. This Liedtke proceeded to do with great aplomb. When they had all shed their coats, the Pennzoil chairman sat down and began to talk with Gordon about the history of his association with the Getty family. Liedtke talked about his wildcatting days in Texas and Oklahoma, and about his encounters with J. Paul and Jack Roth, who was second to George Getty at the company after J. Paul moved to England.

"Our interest in coming into the picture is an attempt to be constructive," Liedtke said. "We could see from the outside that Getty Oil has very, very serious problems. We can see the conflict between the three different parties and we can see the breakdown in morale at the company. I'm aware from other sources that the company has

lost a number of its really good explorationists." Liedtke was referring to the geologists whose search for oil was the nearest thing to an
intuitive art in the oil industry.

"I think the record is fairly clear that we did a good job for your
father," Liedtke told Gordon. "We doubled the value of his invest-
ments in South Penn in a year. Then he offered to sell it out to us in
1963 and we accepted. Your father even sent me a congratulatory
telegram. I think we might be able to do the same thing for Getty
Oil. We have a public record of straightening out situations which are
in difficulty and making them viable, profitable, growing concerns.

"Mr. Getty," Liedtke continued, "I think you should assert yourself. I think that the performance of Sid Petersen is outrageous, and
if I were in your shoes, I would assert myself in various ways. This is
one way to do it: to work out a plan which would put Getty Oil back
in the oil business and try to build a company that your late father
and grandfather spent some hundred years trying to build. When
you own forty percent of a company, you have the right to be treated
halfway decent, and if you are not, why, then I think you should take
action to assure yourself that you are given a fair hearing and not
jacked around by somebody who seems to be bent on destroying you
and your family."

As Marty Siegel sat in the hotel room and listened to Hugh
Liedtke's speech, he thought to himself, *This fellow is pretty smooth.*
It was Siegel's first encounter with the Pennzoil chairman, whom he
knew by reputation as an excellent oilman and a hard-nosed negotiator. *He is doing a very nice job of making Mr. Getty feel at home and
relaxed*, Siegel thought.

And the young investment banker was right—Gordon Getty was
taken by Hugh Liedtke's presentation. Liedtke said that Pennzoil's
role was "to maximize value for the large stockholders" in Getty Oil.
That was precisely the idea that Gordon had been trying to articulate to Sid Petersen for eighteen months. Gordon talked with Liedtke
about eliminating Getty Oil's "corporate shell" and trying to find a
way to avoid double taxation of Gordon's dividends. They were on
the same track. Gordon appeared to be excited.

"I'm a buyer and not a seller," Gordon finally declared.

That remark threw off the Pennzoil executives for a moment;
they weren't sure what Gordon meant. No one had ever contemplated that Gordon or his family trust would actually buy any shares

in a deal with Pennzoil. The idea behind the four-sevenths, three-sevenths plan was that Gordon would stand pat, Pennzoil would use its money to buy three-sevenths of Getty Oil's stock, and then Getty Oil's assets would be used to borrow enough money to put Gordon's family trust in a four-sevenths position. That, actually, was what Gordon meant when he said that he was a buyer: that he would take control of Getty Oil.

Even though Gordon expressed his willingness early on to join with Liedtke, there were still a number of important points to be discussed at the Pierre that afternoon. Marty Siegel joined the conversation and outlined in detail the provisions of a four-sevenths, three-sevenths plan: Gordon would be named chairman, Liedtke would be president and chief executive, Baine Kerr would be chairman of the executive committee. There was some discussion that Gordon's lawyer, Tim Cohler, might become general counsel of the new company. In addition, appointments to the board of directors would be made in proportion to the four-sevenths, three-sevenths arrangement. Both sides agreed to what Liedtke called the "split the blanket clause" providing for a division of Getty Oil's assets after one year if the new arrangement didn't work out.

There was a discussion, too, about what would happen if the Getty Oil board of directors refused to go along with the plan. Liedtke was concerned that Petersen and his board might try to block the deal simply to spite Gordon. The directors were to meet at the Inter-Continental Hotel in Manhattan the next evening; they knew nothing about Liedtke's talks with Gordon. Liedtke, Kerr, Gordon, and his representatives discussed signing a second agreement, besides the one covering their four-sevenths, three-sevenths deal: they would all sign a letter among themselves saying that if the Getty Oil board refused to approve the joint takeover between Gordon and Pennzoil, they would try to immediately fire all of the directors. That plan had a certain appeal to Gordon Getty, who had been trying for so long to overthrow the "snakes" on the board. The trouble was that such an agreement would have no teeth unless the museum, too, signed on. Gordon controlled only 40 percent of Getty Oil; he could not unilaterally fire the directors. But if the museum would cooperate, then Pennzoil would have signed up more than 50 percent of the company's stock and an agreement to throw out the board would be enforceable.

Gordon said that he would be willing to sign such a letter and the Pennzoil executives said they would try to enlist the museum's cooperation.

Finally, however, there was the matter of price. On this point, Hugh Liedtke was exceptionally stubborn—he did not want to raise his offer above $100 per share.

"Our tender offer is progressing very well. It will probably be oversubscribed at $100," Liedtke said. "No one thinks that anyone will offer more than $100 and I even wonder if we should have been so bold as to go that high in the first place. I would take a very dim view of any price over a hundred. Our offer is very heavily subscribed by the public shareholders at this price, so there's no need to go higher."

"There is a need," Marty Siegel countered. "I can tell you that the Getty Oil board will never approve a deal at $100 per share. The minimum price that the directors are going to be willing to accept as a fair price for the public stockholders is $110." Siegel had attended the meeting with Boisi, Winokur, and Lipton the day before, where all three had agreed to a self-tender auction plan at $110.

"How about $105?" Liedtke asked.

"It has to be $110. I can tell you that the board won't accept anything lower."

Liedtke was uncomfortable—it felt to him like he was bidding against himself. Who was now offering more than Pennzoil? Who was ever going to offer more than Pennzoil? But Siegel continued to argue that the problem was not some abstract notion of what was a "fair price," it was a fundamentally practical difficulty: the Getty Oil board would not approve a price lower than $110. The extra ten dollars was not going to benefit Siegel's client—Gordon was not selling. It was necessary to overcome the Getty director's inevitable resistance to a takeover by Gordon and Pennzoil, Siegel said. At the Pierre that afternoon, Liedtke never explicitly said that he would accept the $110 figure, but he made it clear that he was enthusiastic about the agreement he had reached with Gordon, and that he would do what was necessary to consummate the deal.

It was about six o'clock when the meeting ended. Liedtke said that his lawyers would spend the night drawing up the necessary papers and that he would return to sign them with Gordon the next day. Meanwhile, the Pennzoil executives said, they would do what they could to sell their takeover deal to Marty Lipton and Harold Williams.

While Hugh Liedtke, Baine Kerr, and Perry Barber returned to Pennzoil's apartment at the Waldorf, Marty Siegel and Jim Glanville walked one block from the Pierre to Marty Lipton's luxury apartment building. They joined the lawyer's New Year's Day party. Siegel quickly corralled Lipton and Arthur Liman, who had been at the party since four o'clock—Siegel said that he had to speak with them privately. The trio stepped into a hallway outside Lipton's kitchen, away from the other guests.

"Liedtke and Gordon have met and they have reached an understanding subject to the agreement of the museum," Siegel began. "Liedtke has agreed to a four-sevenths, three-sevenths split, with Gordon controlling the majority of the board. Gordon has agreed that Liedtke will be president and chief executive and that Gordon will be chairman. Pennzoil has agreed that it will acquire the shares of the museum and I think Pennzoil is prepared to offer $110 a share, but it will do that only if the museum is ready to sell at that price."

Lipton was surprised by Siegel's declaration. He had been told earlier, when Liman arrived at the party, that Liedtke and Gordon were meeting face to face, but he thought that Gordon had accepted the self-tender auction deal negotiated in Lipton's office on Saturday—they were just waiting for the papers to be signed, Lipton had thought. Now, that deal was apparently off and a new one seemed on the verge of completion. The museum had no choice but to negotiate: together, Gordon and Pennzoil could squeeze Harold Williams out if he refused to cooperate.

"Either I or my investment banker will get in touch with Pennzoil at the Waldorf tonight," Lipton said.

Liman left the party and returned to the Waldorf to confer with Liedtke. Lipton's banker, Jay F. Higgins of Salomon Brothers, arrived a short time later. He stayed only ten or fifteen minutes—he said that he had no authority to make a deal and his servile manner seemed to irritate Liedtke greatly. When he saw Higgins floundering, one of the other bankers in the room hustled him out of the Pennzoil apartment. Glanville then telephoned Marty Lipton at his apartment.

"Higgins was here, but he doesn't have the authority to act for the museum in making a deal," Glanville said. "I am prepared on behalf of Pennzoil to increase the offer from $100 per share to $110 and to buy the museum shares at $110, provided the museum is prepared to accept the $110 price."

"Ridiculous," Lipton said. "I'll call you back in five minutes. I've got to talk to Williams."

Glanville hung up and repeated what Lipton had said to the others in the room. They waited. The phone rang, and Glanville answered. He listened for a moment and then cupped the receiver.

"Marty says he accepts. There are some terms, and Arthur, you'd better get on the phone so that we get them straight."

Liman picked up an extension. Lipton was there.

"The museum is prepared to accept the $110 provided that the same offer is made to all other Getty shareholders, so that the museum will not be receiving a premium over anyone else," Lipton said. "I want the museum treated the same as everyone else. At the same time, we want price protection, a top up." A "top up" or "most favored nations" clause would provide that if Pennzoil or anyone else ever offered to pay more than $110 for a share of Getty Oil stock, the museum would automatically receive the same price.

Liman repeated Lipton's terms to everyone in the Waldorf apartment.

"Tell him yes," Liedtke said.*

Liman and Glanville, who were still on the phone, then both asked Lipton whether, in addition to selling the museum's stock, he would sign a consent agreement to remove the Getty Oil board of directors if the board did not agree to the $110 deal.

---

* There is no serious disagreement that this "Lipton accepts" conversation took place, but there is some dispute about when it occurred and what it meant. Liman and the Pennzoil executives contend the phone calls took place on the night of January 1, after their meeting with Gordon. Lipton insists that it was not until the next day that he accepted, after he received a "fairness opinion" from Salomon Brothers on the $110 price and after Harold Williams had arrived in New York for the Getty Oil board meeting. Whether the conversations occurred Sunday night or Monday afternoon has no bearing on their substance. More important is the disagreement over what the conversations meant. Lipton contends that he did not really "accept" anything, that he was merely saying the museum would help Pennzoil and Gordon present the $110, four-sevenths, three-sevenths proposal to the Getty Oil board of directors at their emergency meeting on January 2. Subsequent events make clear that this was what Lipton intended to do; whether it was what he said he would do is still in dispute.

"I'm not authorized to agree to that," Lipton said.

"The Pennzoil people are concerned that they have raised their bid from $100 to $110, and they now want to make sure that this isn't simply frustrated by the board, given the fact that the board members could do that," Liman responded. "They are very, very edgy. The trustee, Gordon, is prepared to sign a consent to remove the board. Wouldn't you be willing to do the same?"

"It's not part of the bill. I'm not authorized to give that and I won't give that," Lipton insisted.

"Well, what good is your acceptance at $110 if the Getty Oil board can kill the deal, not accept it, and just try to negotiate Mr. Liedtke up from $110 to a higher price? He's already gone from $100 to $110."

"It's not part of the deal," Lipton repeated. "But if this board acts to obstruct this transaction, then Mr. Williams will recommend to the board of the museum that they sign a consent and remove the board. We're not going to let the board stand in the way of a transaction. There will be a deal at the board meeting. It's going to come to a head and be resolved at the board meeting tomorrow."

The conversation concluded and Liman reported Lipton's position to Liedtke and the other Pennzoil executives and advisors. Liedtke was worried.

"I don't understand how, if Lipton has the authority to accept the $110, then he doesn't have the authority to sign the consent and remove the board if they block the deal," the Pennzoil chairman said. "That doesn't make any sense. I'm concerned that I'm being set up here—they've got me bidding against myself. They got me to go from $100 to $110, and now they'll try to get me to go beyond that, this time using the board's reluctance as a pretext. I don't like the feel of this. Can I trust Lipton?"

"I trust Marty Lipton," Liman answered.

"I trust him, too," Glanville concurred.

Liedtke was not fully satisfied, but there was nothing more he could do. The Waldorf apartment emptied of advisors and the Pennzoil executives retired for the night.

As they flew from Los Angeles to New York in a Getty Oil jet that Sunday night, Sid Petersen and Dave Copley were totally unaware of the deal for control of Getty Oil that had been struck between

Gordon, Pennzoil, and the museum that afternoon. The last they had heard was that on Saturday, Winokur, Boisi, Lipton, and Gordon's representatives had agreed to draw up a self-tender auction plan that would beat back Pennzoil's bid. Petersen had high hopes that the auction agreement would be signed before the emergency board meeting convened Monday evening. That way, the directors could devote their discussion to the best way to conduct an orderly sale of Getty Oil in the ninety-day time period available. Sid Petersen's long career at the company was finished, he suspected. But it was still quite possible, if the auction plan went forward, that the company would be sold to someone who would require his services as chief executive.

Those faint hopes had been considerably dampened by three o'clock the next afternoon. After straggling to his hotel late Sunday night and sleeping a few hours, Petersen spent the morning conferring with Winokur and Boisi at Dechert Price & Rhoads' New York offices, on Madison Avenue. As they talked, snow began to fall on Manhattan. They were still waiting to obtain Gordon's signature on the self-tender, ninety-day auction documents; they had no idea that Gordon was preparing to sign a rather different agreement with Pennzoil that same day. Early in the afternoon, however, they were all summoned to a meeting at Marty Lipton's offices on Park Avenue. They were told by Marty Siegel that a few things needed to be explained before the emergency Getty Oil board meeting began.

In a conference room at Wachtell, Lipton, Rosen & Katz, they all convened: Petersen and his lawyers and bankers; Lipton and his associate, Patricia Vlahakis; and Gordon's advisors, Siegel, Cohler, and Woodhouse. Cohler and Siegel did most of the talking. They described the terms of a joint takeover that had been agreed to by Liedtke and Gordon the day before, and they said that a written, signed proposal would be presented to the board that evening.

Petersen and his advisors were stunned by the news. Had Gordon finally won? Had he finally taken Getty Oil away from them?

Cohler announced that apart from the ownership provisions of the four-sevenths, three-sevenths plan, Pennzoil would receive an option to buy 8 million Getty Oil shares. Added to the 24 million shares it had already agreed to acquire from the public and the museum, the option would provide Pennzoil with a way to acquire a total of 32 million shares in the event of a dispute with Gordon during the weeks ahead. Since Gordon already controlled 32 million shares, the partners would be in a deadlock position and neither could take shareholder action without the other. Cohler also told Petersen that he could expect personal lawsuits to be filed if the board took action to block Gordon's takeover.

Siegel mentioned the price of the deal: $110 per share. Boisi and Winokur pounced on him.

"You know we think that's inadequate. The board is not going to accept that price. Goldman, Sachs has already said that $120 is the minimum fair price."

"Well, yesterday, we were all willing to agree to $110 and so we obviously thought it was a fair price," Siegel countered.

"We never thought that was fair and you know it," Winokur said.

"Well, Mr. Liedtke is a very tough negotiator."

"He may well be, but in this situation he's a buyer and you're a buyer. And with all due respect to how good a negotiator you are, Marty, it's hard to expect two buyers to agree on a fair price that the seller wants to sell at," Winokur insisted.

"We did the best we could," Siegel said.

"Well, I would feel a heck of a lot better if we had an opportunity to negotiate with Pennzoil directly."

It was now less than three hours before the board meeting was scheduled to begin at the Inter-Continental Hotel. Winokur, Boisi, and Galant decided that they would walk immediately over to the Waldorf to see if they could meet with the Pennzoil executives and try to persuade them to pay a higher price. When they reached the Waldorf's elaborately decorated lobby, they called up to Liedtke's apartment.

"The man for you to talk to is Mr. Glanville," the Getty Oil advisors were told.

So they called Pennzoil general counsel Perry Barber's suite, where Glanville was stationed, and asked for an audience. Glanville called over to Liedtke, received permission, and then agreed to meet.

"We have no problem dealing with Pennzoil," one of the Getty Oil advisors said when they arrived at Barber's Waldorf suite. "Our only concern is that we obtain a fair price. It's clear from what we heard about the agreement that Pennzoil's interest in this matter is in getting assets, oil reserves, and we're prepared, on behalf of Getty Oil management, to discuss and negotiate a transaction where you would acquire the assets you're interested in. But we would want to do that at a fair price."

Glanville and Barber made it clear that they were in no mood to deal with the emissaries from Getty Oil management. "We've had discussions with Gordon Getty, we're satisfied with our arrangements, and we don't see any productive purpose in negotiating with you."

Winokur, Boisi, and Galant tried to convince them that there was no such thing as a firm deal where Gordon Getty was involved. They briefly enumerated all of the times over the past year when they, too, thought they had made a deal with Gordon only to find that Gordon had changed his mind twenty-four hours later. They tried to impress on Pennzoil's representatives the importance of negotiating with Getty Oil management, which would not change its mind or its mood once an agreement was reached.

"Besides, we don't believe the board of directors will approve a $110 price. Goldman, Sachs has done valuation studies that indicate the company is worth far more than $110. The directors will not approve such a transaction."

"We have made our deal with Gordon Getty and we think the board of directors will come around to our point of view," the Pennzoil advisors countered. They did not mention, of course, the letter Gordon had agreed to sign declaring that he would try to fire the board if it did not accept his takeover approval.

The discussion began to go around in circles; Glanville and Barber remained uninterested in negotiation. After less than thirty minutes, Boisi, Winokur, and Galant took their leave, discouraged. Pennzoil was sticking to its guns—that was a metaphor employed frequently by the Getty Oil advisors. Pennzoil had a gun at their heads, they liked to say. The point was, Hugh Liedtke would not abandon his alliance with Gordon.

By five o'clock that Monday, darkness had fallen on Manhattan; traces of the morning's snow still lay on the sidewalks. Winokur, Boisi, and Galant returned to the Dechert Price offices on Madison Avenue and reported to Sid Petersen the failure of their overture to Pennzoil. Getty Oil directors were beginning to arrive from around the country—Wendt from Philadelphia, Medberry from Los Angeles, Teets from Phoenix. Some of them dropped by Dechert Price & Rhoads, where they learned the details of Gordon Getty's latest and most audacious bid for control of their company. An angry mood began to settle in. The emergency board meeting would be convening in less than an hour. Somehow, Gordon had to be stopped. Somehow, in the next few hours, eighteen months of bitter warring at Getty Oil Company had to be ended. On that chilly evening, it did not seem that either side was willing to go peacefully.

AFTER MIDNIGHT

By all accounts, the Getty Oil board meeting which began that Monday evening in Manhattan was unlike any in the company's long and sordid history; indeed, those who attended said later it was unlike anything they had heard described in their careers in corporate governance. The meeting would later be intricately dissected by lawyers, judges, and jurors. It would be difficult for those outside advocates and arbiters to comprehend the swirling anger and confusion which pervaded the Inter-Continental Hotel that night and well into the following day. So much had passed between the participants before the meeting began—an indelible, bitter poison had seeped into their relations. Gordon Getty's long, sometimes irrational bid for control of the company; the attempt by Sid Petersen and his advisors to instigate a family lawsuit against Gordon; the increasingly cantankerous negotiations between the plethora of lawyers and investment bankers; the shifting role of Harold Williams and the museum—all of this had infected the executives, directors, and advisors who gathered in Sutton Room II on the third floor of the Inter-Continental Hotel. It was like a fever. In the hours ahead, the eminent industrial leaders struggling for final control of Getty Oil's rich reserves would seem torn by two competing instincts. On the one hand, they were professionals, trained in judicious caution and deeply concerned about their reputations. Somehow, they had to do the right thing, the proper and legal thing. But on the other hand, they were only human beings—tired, angry, vindictive, even childish. Judging by what they said to each other, there were times at the Inter-Continental when this reputable elite of American finance might have liked to physically attack one another, to settle their disputes by wrestling vigorously on the meeting room floor. Perhaps, in the end, that would have been the best solution.

What everyone remembered about the setting was its cramped size. After the Pennzoil tender offer, there had been insufficient time to make more luxurious arrangements for the Getty Oil board's emergency meeting. The meeting room booked at the Inter-Continental in midtown was stately enough; there were red tasseled drapes, walnut-stained paneling, gilded mirrors, and Edwardian chairs surrounding the oblong table. But the room was airless and narrow. There were thirty of them crammed inside by 6 P.M., when the meeting began. Sid Petersen, the chairman, was at the center of the table. To his left were his advisors: Winokur, Boisi, Galant, and half a dozen other Wall Street lawyers and bankers. At the same end of the table was the museum's contingent, led by Harold Williams and Marty Lipton. On the opposite side, appropriately, sat Gordon Getty, Tim Cohler, Marty Siegel, and Tom Woodhouse. The Getty Oil directors were interspersed among them. There were not enough places at the table, so many of the advisors sat in chairs pushed against the walls; they would sometimes lean forward to whisper in the ears of their principals. As time wore on, the formality of these arrangements broke down: whispers turned to shouts; the directors stood and wandered about; informal caucuses gathered in corners and outside in the hotel hallways. Through it all, Dave Copley, Getty Oil's general counsel, sat stoically near the center of the table with a pen and a green writing tablet, scribbling furiously to record what was said.

There was confusion from the first moment. At Marty Lipton's offices that afternoon, Tim Cohler had said that the deal signed between Gordon, the museum, and Pennzoil to take control of Getty Oil would be presented to the board at their emergency meeting. But when the meeting began, a written proposal had not yet been delivered for presentation. The delay was a result of continuing negotiations with the museum: Marty Lipton insisted that before Williams would sign any final agreement with Gordon and Pennzoil, changes had to be made in the wording so it would be clear the deal was subject to the approval of the Getty Oil board. Lipton wrote the changes on the document by hand and then passed it to Williams at the board table, where he signed it. Lipton's changes provided that if the takeover agreement was not approved by the board, the deal would not be binding.

While they waited for copies of this new agreement, Geoff Boisi delivered a long monologue to the directors about the provisions of Pennzoil's 20 percent tender offer—despite Liedtke's new takeover deal with Gordon, that offer was still outstanding, and the Getty Oil board was legally required to respond on behalf of its public shareholders. If they did nothing, Boisi told the directors, Pennzoil would soon own 20 percent of the company. What was more, he said, "It is Goldman's judgment that the offer of $100 per share is grossly inadequate." The implication was clear: in Boisi's opinion, if the board allowed Pennzoil's tender to go through, it would be permitting Hugh Liedtke to steal a large piece of Getty Oil. During their frantic telephone conversations with Petersen the previous week, the directors had assured Getty Oil's chairman that they would do what they could to prevent Liedtke from succeeding.

When Boisi was finished, Bart Winokur reviewed the self-tender, ninety-day auction negotiations that had taken place between himself, Boisi, Lipton, and Gordon's advisors. Winokur told the board that this deal, which Gordon had now apparently rejected in favor of a takeover with Pennzoil, would "permit the orderly disposal of the company at the highest possible price." Winokur said pointedly: "It's my understanding that we have arrived at an agreement to these terms. Today, however, I have come to understand that Mr. Getty and his trust will not agree to such an arrangement."

Harold Williams intervened. "The museum is ready to go ahead with that plan. Is it correct, Gordon, that you will not proceed on that basis?"

All eyes turned to the Getty scion. Most of the directors had heard about his deal with Hugh Liedtke, but they had not yet seen it. Perhaps Gordon was still keeping an open mind. Perhaps he would be willing to consider an auction sale of Getty Oil Company.

"Yes, it is correct that I will not proceed," Gordon said. "There is a better proposal available for all shareholders." He was referring, of course, to his own plan to finally gain control of the family business.

"Well, then why don't you or your advisors describe this new proposal that's been made by Pennzoil?" Petersen asked.

Before Gordon or anyone else could respond, however, Marty Lipton jumped in. "Actually," he said, "the museum has just signed the new proposal by Pennzoil. But the museum will not be bound by the proposal unless the board approves it."

For the beleaguered Petersen, this was a most demoralizing development. He had not known that Williams and Lipton were now allied with Gordon and Hugh Liedtke. Harold Williams continued to confound the Getty Oil chairman. After all the museum had been through with Gordon, why would it now join with him against Getty Oil management?

"Look, the museum is a nonprofit, eleemosynary institution," Williams explained to the angry, befuddled directors. "We have to protect our funding. At $110 per share or better, we're a seller. I hope the company and the trust can reach an agreement so that the company can take the action that is best for all shareholders. The museum wants all shareholders treated equally. We signed the new Pennzoil proposal so that it would be considered by the board—if the proposal isn't approved, the museum will not be bound by my signature. I think, however, that the proposal is a reasonable approach and the museum is prepared to support it."

"Given this new development, I think we should break for fifteen minutes so the company's advisors can discuss it," Petersen responded.

Winokur, Boisi, Petersen, and some of the other Getty Oil lawyers and bankers stepped out of Sutton Room II and gathered in a nearby conference room. If the museum's position was that a $110 takeover by Gordon and Pennzoil constituted "a reasonable approach," then the Getty Oil directors were now under tremendous pressure. It was no longer merely the erratic Gordon who backed the takeover deal; now the proposal had the support of Marty Lipton's considerable reputation.

"What problems do you see with Pennzoil's proposal other than price?" Sid Petersen asked his advisors. It was no longer a question of Petersen protecting his job—they had to be sure now that whatever transpired, the directors could defend their actions during the inevitable lawsuits that would follow a change in control at Getty Oil.

"In our view, there are a whole series of problems besides price," Winokur volunteered. He ticked off three or four: that despite its apparent agreement with Gordon, Pennzoil was unwilling to drop its

20 percent tender offer immediately; that the agreement apparently called for the company to buy the museum's shares, which immediately would alter the balance of power at Getty Oil by removing the museum from its "swing" position; that Pennzoil had an option for 8 million shares exercisable at any time; that there were a lot of other complex issues that had not even been discussed.

"Since there are all these complex issues that will require extensive negotiation with Pennzoil, rather than dealing with these at the board meeting, when we get back, we think you should see whether the directors are willing to let Gordon and Pennzoil take the company private, and also the threshold issue of price—whether the board will approve a deal at $110 per share," Winokur urged.

Petersen agreed that this was the only sensible course. A few minutes later, at five before seven, he reconvened the directors in Sutton Room II.

"I'd like to suggest that before we move on to this new Pennzoil proposal, the board should consider dealing with the $100 tender offer," the chairman began.

Retired Bank of America chairman Chauncey Medberry, who would later describe his state of mind at the meeting as one of near apoplexy, responded: "I move that the board recommend against Pennzoil's $100 tender offer for twenty percent of the shares." Harold Stuart seconded the motion.

A vote was called: the verdict was unanimous. Pennzoil's $100 offer was rejected. Even Gordon joined the directors in voting against the tender offer. After all, it was Gordon's banker, Marty Siegel, who had managed the day before to persuade a reluctant Hugh Liedtke to raise the price of their joint takeover to $110. To Gordon, Pennzoil's original $100 offer was no longer relevant.

When the vote was recorded, Tim Cohler passed out the new takeover proposal. It was signed by Gordon, Hugh Liedtke, and Harold Williams, though next to Williams' signature appeared Marty Lipton's handwritten caveat that the museum's signature was for purposes of presentation to the board only. The document was titled "Memorandum of Agreement." Four pages long, single-spaced, it described the terms of the four-sevenths, three-sevenths takeover formula agreed to at the Pierre on New Year's Day by Gordon and Hugh Liedtke. In the third numbered paragraph, the agreement provided that the museum would sell all of its shares to Getty Oil for $110 per share "subject to adjustment before or after closing in the event of any increase in the offer price." In the sixth and final numbered paragraph, the document read, "This Plan is subject to approval by the Board of Directors of the Company at the meeting of the Board being held January 2, 1984. Upon such approval, the Company shall execute three or more counterparts of the 'Joinder by the Company' attached to the Plan and deliver one such counterpart to each of the Trustee, the Museum, and Pennzoil."

Marty Siegel read the document aloud to the directors. When he was finished, Harold Stuart asked, "Does this require approval by fourteen board members?"

"That depends on whether the consent agreement signed by Mr. Getty and Mr. Williams in December is still in effect," Bart Winokur answered. "If it is, the answer is yes. If it isn't, the answer is no."

"I think we should break again so that the directors can read the new proposal," Sid Petersen said. "Before we do that, are there any questions the directors would like to ask?"

"I have a question for Goldman, Sachs," director Henry Wendt responded. "What's the adequacy of the $110 price?"

This was the heart of the matter, so far as the Getty Oil board was concerned. If Goldman, Sachs, their investment banker, would provide a "fairness opinion" stating that in the firm's expert opinion $110 was an adequate selling price for all the company's shareholders, then the directors would be well protected from any lawsuits arising from the deal. If Goldman would not provide such a fairness opinion, then the directors would be in a very difficult position. If they wanted to approve the deal, they would have to defy their own expert advisor's opinion.

"In our opinion, the $110 price is inadequate," Geoff Boisi answered. "Given time and the indications of interest by others in acquiring the company that we've already received, and also given our own study of the value of the company's assets, we cannot provide a fairness letter at the $110 level."

As Marty Siegel listened to Boisi, he was struck by the Goldman banker's predicament. A "fairness opinion" was just that—only an opinion. The easiest thing for a banker in Boisi's position to do would be to simply declare that $110 was fair and be done with it. The financial wizards down at Goldman's Wall Street offices could certainly come up with appropriate numbers to justify that opinion. Despite

Goldman's indications the previous summer, during the LBO takeover and stock buy-back negotiations, that $120 was the minimum
value of Getty Oil's stock, the firm had also said that the "range" of
values for Getty Oil began at $105 per share and rose perhaps as high
as $140 or $150. Thus, it would not be totally unreasonable for Boisi
to declare that $110 was a fair price. But the banker refused to do
it. Despite all of the pressure now faced by the Getty Oil directors,
Boisi was insisting that if Gordon and Pennzoil wanted to take the
company, they had to pay a higher price. There were two ways to
view Boisi's stubborn insistence that $110 was not a fair price. Per-
haps, as Boisi himself insisted, it was simply a matter of integrity;
Goldman had a reputation to look out for, and its bankers had to
be true to their beliefs, no matter how sticky the consequences. But
there was also the undeniable issue of Goldman's financial motives as
Getty Oil's principal broker. Because of the way Goldman's retainer
deal was structured, if the Pennzoil takeover went through, Goldman, Sachs would earn about $9 million in fees. But if a buyer for the
entire company could be found at a higher price, then Boisi might
easily double his take to $18 million.

"I have a question for Gordon Getty," Henry Wendt now said. "I
have heard that you were considering offering the entire company
for sale, but that you rejected that idea in preference for the new
Pennzoil offer."

"I have considered and rejected many things," Gordon said with
rare understatement. "None of them was better than this." None of
them, that is, put him in control of the company and empowered
him to throw out the "snakes" now gathered around him.

"Why did you reject selling the whole company?" Wendt pressed.

"I am certain that this is the best approach," Gordon answered.

"You have had discussions with other companies, as we know.
Have you considered other prices?" Harold Stuart asked.

"I have not had any discussions with other companies," Gordon
said. "Some of my advisors have." His demeanor, even in this most
intense environment, was unchanged. The mop of curly hair, the furrowed eyebrows, the dramatic, squinting expressions—it was like
sharing a board room with Amadeus.

"Well, will Mr. Siegel comment on these discussions?"

"There have been no discussions with anyone regarding a specific price," Siegel said. "The $110 price gives you a feel for my firm's

opinion about what's fair." Siegel, like Boisi, would be required to issue a "fairness letter" on behalf of Kidder, Peabody stating that the price of the deal was proper. Siegel, whose client was a buyer, thought $110 was fair. Boisi, whose client was a seller, thought $110 was too low.

"How did you arrive at that price? Do you think it's the best price available?"

"I never said that. I have looked at the Goldman data. I don't know if anyone would pay more than $110 for this company or not. I only know that right now, you have someone willing to take all the public shares at $110 and it appears fair to me. . . . The fact is that no one can guarantee that the company can do better than $110 per share."

"Can you guarantee that we *can't* do better than $110?" Henry Wendt demanded.

Siegel conceded that he could not.

"I've been approached by an oil company that's financially capable of buying Getty," Petersen told the board. He did not disclose the name of this suitor. "I think a price well above $110 is potentially available. Besides, there are other alternatives than the sale to some third-party buyer." Petersen was referring to the self-tender, ninety-day auction talks that would have bought the Getty Oil directors time to find a solution to their conundrum. The chairman was hoping that somehow he could revive Gordon's interest in a self-tender. He knew nothing, of course, about the letter Gordon had signed with Liedtke promising to try to fire the entire board if they failed to go along with the $110 takeover proposal.

"Is it correct, as I understand it, that on Saturday Gordon was a seller at $110 and today the trust is a buyer at $110?" Henry Wendt asked.

"We never asked Gordon Getty to be a seller at $110," Winokur answered. "That was his idea, to set the bottom price for an auction at $110. What surprises me is that the company has said repeatedly that we could do better than $110 and yet this doesn't seem to be what the trust wants."

Tim Cohler piped up to challenge Winokur. Ever since he found out about his role in the family lawsuit against Gordon, Cohler had regarded Winokur as a duplicitous menace. "What's been said is that some of your bankers have a hope that there would be a better price than $110. The agreement you have proposed for a self-tender and auction would require the trust to sell its shares at $110 plus one penny."

"That's just not true," Winokur countered forcefully. "*You* proposed that Mr. Getty would sell at $110. If you had said the trust would sell at $115 or more, the company would have agreed to that price."

"*Would* the trust sell at $115?" Petersen asked.

"I want to discuss all of these proposals in order," Cohler answered. "I don't want to do this twice." It was the Pennzoil takeover proposal at $110 that was now on the table. The directors had to make a decision about that deal, one way or the other. Cohler was not about to take the pressure off of them by discussing a different plan.

"I am very uncomfortable with the way the proposal has been brought in, with the directors being placed in the position of having to make a decision in three or four hours on a take-it-or-leave-it basis, involving enormous sums of money and complex issues," said Clayburn La Force, dean of the UCLA Management School and one of Petersen's more recent recruits to the Getty Oil board.

That was precisely the point, Geoff Boisi added. Time was on Pennzoil's side. Boisi and the company's other Wall Street advisors began to sling the metaphors of their trade about the crowded room. The directors were faced with "a gun at their heads." Pennzoil, Boisi said, was "giving this company a bear hug. It is using speed and pressure to get a good deal for itself—that's the tactical reason behind the short time for consideration. The directors are here to figure out what is best for the company, not what is best for Pennzoil."

As the meeting dragged on, the anger and frustration of the Getty Oil directors focused increasingly on Gordon Getty. He had brought them here, they felt. He was responsible for their predicament. If they voted to approve his $110 takeover proposal without a fairness opinion from Goldman, Sachs, they would be sued. If they voted not to approve the proposal, they would be sued. If they did nothing, they would be sued. It was not a comfortable situation. Over and over, they tried to persuade Gordon that there was only one sensible course, only one way for them all to walk away from Getty Oil Company with their hands clean: the sale of the company to some third party at a price above $120 per share. Then Gordon and his family trust would receive billions in cash, the public shareholders would be

happy, Petersen and his cohorts would retire on their golden parachutes, the advisors would pocket millions in fees, and all would
be right with the world. Yes, Hugh Liedtke would be upset, but the
Pennzoil chairman had known that he was taking a risk when he
entered the fray. Yes, rank-and-file Getty Oil employees might suffer
under new, outside ownership, which would be eager to consolidate,
but perhaps they could find a buyer who would agree not to implement drastic layoffs. Why, Petersen and his advisors asked again and
again, was Gordon unwilling to sell to the highest bidder? Why did
he insist on pressing this $110 joint takeover with Pennzoil?

But all of the questions, all of the anger and threatening bluster,
had no apparent effect on Gordon Getty.

"Everyone has been working for months and then a paper is laid
on the directors and we are told we have four hours to react," Harold
Stuart told Gordon at one point. "It's unreasonable to expect us to act
on that proposal with good business judgment within that time. This
is a seven-billion-dollar deal. The trust and the museum are pushing
the board to take or leave the Pennzoil offer tonight, and I cannot
personally assimilate the facts required to make a decision in that
time."

"We only saw Pennzoil's proposal yesterday ourselves," Cohler
answered.

"The trust's advisors are professionals. You are familiar with the
situation."

"The new Pennzoil offer exists and it is $110," Cohler insisted.

"On the $110 self-tender that we worked out yesterday, if the
price was higher, would the trust still turn that down?" Sid Petersen
asked.

"We've been close to a deal a lot of times, but it hasn't happened.
You are now confronted with what is a contract signed by the trust
and the museum," Cohler said.

Petersen had no choice: he had to take a vote. Gordon moved
that his joint takeover with Pennzoil be adopted by the board. Alfred
Taubman, the Detroit real-estate developer recruited to the board by
Ann Getty in November, seconded.

"How many directors are needed to pass it? Fourteen?" Harold
Stuart asked.

"It is the trust and the museum's position that fourteen votes
are necessary," Winokur answered. Another company lawyer

volunteered that with less than fourteen votes they could all be sure that the deal would wind up in court if it was implemented.

The directors were polled. Gordon, Taubman, and Graham Allison, dean of Harvard's Kennedy School and another of Gordon's recent nominees, voted yes. Petersen, Boothby, Teets, Wendt, and Bob Miller voted no. It was Larry Tisch's turn.

"I don't want to vote until I know more of the consequences involved. If nothing happens, the shareholders could end up with $50 a share, with Pennzoil working with the trust and there being no other offer by anyone."

"I think the company is worth much, much more than this," Bob Miller responded. "Gordon Getty would rather buy than sell at $110, which in my view means that $110 is a low price."

"We have to hit the road and get more than $110 for the public shareholders," Wendt added.

"With time, the company could do better," Tisch conceded. But Tisch then voted for the $110 Pennzoil proposal anyway. Harold Williams followed with another yes vote. The rest of the board, however, voted no. There was some question later as to which way Harold Berg went—most people remembered that he voted yes, though it was recorded that he voted no. Either way, it didn't matter—Gordon's proposal to take Getty Oil with Pennzoil for $110 per share was defeated. The final tally was either 10–5 or 9–6 depending on how Berg's vote was counted.

Petersen now turned to Tim Cohler. "You said earlier that the group had to deal with things as they are. The Pennzoil proposal has now been turned down by the board. Is there any possibility that the trust will now go back to the other proposal we have discussed?"

Geoff Boisi summarized the alternative advocated by Petersen: the board would approve a self-tender offer for 20 percent of its stock at $110 per share or higher, then spend ninety days searching for a buyer for the entire company.

"Do the directors understand the various proposals?" Petersen asked.

"No," Gordon answered. "What are they about?"

"The purpose of the self-tender would be to ward off Pennzoil while an effort is made to sell the company at a higher price for the benefit of all shareholders," Petersen explained. He went on to describe how the self-tender could be financed.

"Why can't we all go back to the proposal for a three-way self-tender, including Gordon, that was considered on Saturday?" Henry Wendt asked.

"Because of Gordon Getty," Larry Tisch answered.

Again, they had reached a stalemate. It was now ten-thirty, four and a half hours into the meeting. The directors were tiring. Some of them were hungry. All of them were edgy. Petersen suggested that they take a break.

For two hours, they wandered in the hallways of the Inter-Continental Hotel, caucusing, negotiating, persuading. Petersen, Boisi, and Winokur continued to press for the self-tender proposal that would buy the company time to hold an auction. They needed fourteen votes. Talking individually with his directors, Petersen took a straw poll and then reported to Winokur that he had ten votes: all of the directors who had voted against the Pennzoil take-over, including Harold Berg. Somehow they had to line up four more votes. Petersen, Winokur, and Boisi fanned out, talking privately with Tisch, Williams, Taubman, and Allison, Gordon's supporters on the board. Williams agreed fairly quickly to support the proposal—his goal now was simply to sell the museum's shares as quickly and with as few complications as possible. Tisch said that, if necessary, he would cast his vote against Gordon and for the self-tender and he agreed to persuade Taubman and Allison. Petersen and Winokur watched as Tisch drew the two directors aside in the hallway and talked with them. A few moments later, Tisch returned.

"They've agreed to support the self-tender and auction proposal. But we have to get back in the board room and vote."

Just as Petersen and Winokur began to gently herd the directors back into Sutton Room II, however, telling them that it was time to reconvene their meeting, a caterer arrived with a chocolate cake. The famished directors gathered around it and began to eat. Petersen watched helplessly as Taubman and Allison, holding their plates, began to talk with Gordon's advisors about their plan to support Getty Oil management on the self-tender vote. There was a vigorous discussion between them, out of Petersen's earshot. Some minutes later, Tisch reported back to the Getty Oil chairman that Taubman and Allison had changed their minds—they would not support the self-tender. Sidney Petersen had been foiled by a cake.

Gordon Getty, meanwhile, had retreated to a two-room suite around the corner which he had rented for the evening. Mark Leland, his personal financial advisor, was there to man the phone while Gordon was in the board meeting. Arthur Liman, Pennzoil's attorney, had also been stationed in the suite, prepared to advise Liedtke, who was across the street in his Waldorf apartment, of any new developments. When the board recessed at ten-thirty, Gordon and his advisors told Liman that the vote on Pennzoil's takeover proposal had gone against them. Liman had called Liedtke to report the bad news. Then he decided to wander into the hallway to talk with the mingling Getty Oil directors.

Larry Tisch quickly sought Liman out. He explained that the root of the directors' dilemma was Goldman, Sachs' refusal to issue a fairness opinion for any price below $120.

"Arthur, get your client to go up the extra ten dollars and we can close the deal tonight," Tisch said. "It doesn't have to be ten dollars in cash. It can be a subordinated debenture [a kind of corporate IOU] with a face value of ten dollars. But the cost to your client would be less. You go and persuade them that they should go up the ten dollars and we can all go home tonight and have the deal done. Please speak to Boisi, of Goldman, Sachs, about the detailed terms."

Liman found Boisi and pulled him aside. He repeated what Tisch had said about an extra ten dollars, which would bring the price of a joint takeover by Gordon and Pennzoil to $120 per share. "My impression from my conversation with Tisch is that while the face amount of this debenture would be ten dollars, its market value might be less."

"That's not what I meant when I talked about this possibility with Tisch," Boisi said adamantly. The Goldman banker made it clear to Liman that any debenture would have to be worth exactly ten dollars, nothing less, and that a shareholder who received it as compensation over and above the base price of $110 would have to be able to sell it on the market immediately for ten dollars.

"So we're talking about Pennzoil really going up from $110 to $120," Liman said.

"That's absolutely right." Boisi was still unwilling to compromise on price.

Liman returned to the two-room suite around the corner, informed Gordon and his advisors about the discussions now under way, and then telephoned the Waldorf. He spoke first with Jim Glanville, Liedtke's investment banker. "They got Liedtke to go from $100 to $110 on the understanding that it would be accepted, and that the museum and Gordon would push for it if there was no better offer on the table," Glanville said. "There is in fact no better offer on the table and now they are doing what we all feared—they just want us to go to $120 on our own." Liedtke had said all along that he hated to bid against himself and now, for the second time, he was being asked to do exactly that.

"Tell them we'll get back to them tomorrow," Liedtke said when Liman finally spoke with him that night. "Why don't you come back over here to the hotel and meet me tomorrow for breakfast at eight o'clock?"

Liman reported the news to Larry Tisch: they would think about it, but Liedtke did not sound agreeable.

It was well after midnight when the chocolate cake was gone and the exhausted directors reconvened in Sutton Room II.

"The board feels very put upon," Larry Tisch said with sweeping understatement. "We're being asked to decide the true value of the company. It may be that the board could never decide the true value. I think that Mr. Getty and Pennzoil should enhance the $110 offer to $120 in some form so that Goldman can give a fairness opinion and the board can go forward with a transaction with Pennzoil."

There was more discussion about Petersen's proposal for a self-tender and auction sale. The chairman said that he had tried to round up enough votes in favor, but had only managed to secure eleven commitments, not enough to call a formal vote. The impasse remained. Finally, the directors asked all of the advisors to leave the room. Something had to be done. Perhaps if the lawyers and bankers were absent, the directors could speak their minds and reach a decision.

"We're in a very difficult position," Harold Williams began when the door was closed. "I don't think the board can do nothing. With the existing Pennzoil tender offer for twenty percent at $100 per share, the prospect is that Pennzoil will acquire twenty percent and then it could take control with Gordon and his trust. At the same time, the board is faced with Goldman's advice that the present offer is not adequate. And the time element is preventing us from taking other action."

"We're talking about a difference of $400 million, cash and paper, between the $110 and $120 proposals," Tisch said. "That amount should not break a deal of this size. If Pennzoil says no to the $10 increase, then the board would feel very comfortable that it had tried to make a fair deal."

"I think a vote should be taken," Henry Wendt said. He wanted the board to approve Petersen's self-tender proposal, the one earlier thwarted by the arrival of a chocolate cake.

"I don't think the votes are there," Harold Williams sighed.

"It is time for a vote," Chauncey Medberry urged. "Management and the board must take a position. We should each speak our minds and get on the record about all of this."

"From an executive's view, I would be hard-pressed to vote for a self-tender," Larry Tisch said. Earlier, when Taubman and Allison had considered supporting the proposal, the idea had seemed a tangible way out of the board's dilemma. Now, however, when it was clear that there were not enough directors willing to back the proposal, a vote on a self-tender would be only symbolic—a chance, as Medberry put it, to "get on the record" about the $110 takeover proposal being pressed by Gordon and Pennzoil.

Tisch went on to explain his reservations. "First, it would require more money than the company has been able to commit. Second, I don't know what would happen: Pennzoil might buy enough shares and vote with Gordon Getty and squeeze out the public. That's not a valid reason to vote for a self-tender—just because the directors are angry at Pennzoil and Gordon Getty."

Larry Tisch then turned to Gordon. With his hairless head, protruding ears, and commanding gaze, Tisch was an intimidating man. He had come on the Getty Oil board at the request of Gordon and Ann, but he did not need Gordon Getty. He did not want anything from him, except to extract himself from his ill-advised directorship with a minimum of pain and embarrassment.

"There is no question that you may be facing lawsuits if you do this takeover by threat," Tisch said. "You should discuss this with your attorneys. All of the directors are in an embarrassing position. The way to avoid the problems is to get something more—ten dollars more—so Goldman can say 'The deal is fair.' I think you, Mr. Getty, as much or more than any of the others, want this. If someone challenges the transaction, we will say you forced us, Mr. Getty. You might speak to your attorneys about that."

"I have done nothing unethical," Gordon replied defiantly.

"This is not ethics," Tisch said. "You have not given the board the opportunity to seek a fair price."

"If there is no agreement, the market decides."

"The market does not decide: you have barred us from the market. I think that is worth your considering, Mr. Getty. A small ten-dollar sweetener. Something to satisfy this board."

"When I became sole trustee, Getty Oil stock was selling for $50 a share and if I had not been the sole trustee, it still would be," Gordon answered. In his mind, the debate was not about a ten-dollar sweetener. It was about his own character, his credibility. This was not an unreasonable assessment. Only a stone would not feel the hostility toward Gordon Getty that was rising in the narrow conference room.

"You should go back and bargain," Tisch urged him.

"This company is not looking for a white knight so that it can protect its management," Harold Williams said, still arguing for the self-tender and ninety-day auction. "It is management itself that is looking to sell the company."

"If we do nothing, Pennzoil might come in and get enough shares to put Mr. Getty in control," Petersen added. "What we need is time."

"The board is at the mercy of Mr. Getty and Pennzoil," Tisch agreed. "If the board is not given time, Mr. Getty might get sued."

"The board might get sued, too," Henry Wendt said. A few moments later, the SmithKline chairman added, "The only way to tell whether $110 is fair is to place the company on the market. I don't think a self-tender cripples the company."

"Pennzoil has been very clever and it's putting tremendous pressure on the board," Petersen said.

"This whole thing is an attorney's dream," Wendt answered disgustedly. "The board has got to maximize value for small shareholders. I think that either $120 has to be obtained from Pennzoil or else the situation has to be opened up to the market."

Harold Stuart, the aging Oklahoman who had married into a fortune in Getty stock, now turned on Gordon angrily. "You said that you brought the stock price up from $50. I don't think you did that at all. When Getty's stock was at $50, all oil company stocks were at an all-time low. The board and management had a great deal to do with the increase—as well as Pennzoil's tender offer."

"You, in effect, have put the company on the block," chimed in Chauncey Medberry. There was a group of them now—Medberry, Stuart, Wendt, Teets—all beginning to lose their tempers, all directing their outrage at Gordon.

"Gordon is forcing the board by signing the agreement with Pennzoil," Tisch said. "Without that agreement, the board would approve a self-tender offer for twenty percent at $110, which would give ninety days to solve the problems we're facing."

"That arrangement for the opportunity to sell the company has only been discussed," Gordon replied. "It is not my fault that I didn't follow Mr. Tisch's advice on that."

"How can the company get bids if the trust and Pennzoil own fifty-five percent of the stock between them?" Tisch demanded of Gordon. "No one could buy the company under those circumstances."

"Is it reasonable to ask Pennzoil to go over $110 per share when a major investment banker—Salomon Brothers, the museum's banker—has said that $110 is OK?" Gordon asked in reply.

"Getty Oil's investment bankers have not said that," Teets answered.

Gordon remained adamant in the face of the directors' anger. "There is no proposal that should be voted for that I have seen this evening other than the Pennzoil proposal. I think the Pennzoil proposal is more attractive. The directors are responsible to all the shareholders, including large ones like myself."

"I don't think that's true, in that you agreed to buy at $110," Tisch said. Tisch meant that the directors were responsible to shareholders who were selling their stock, not to those trying to buy the company.

"Gordon is willing to liquidate at $110 and therefore, in effect, he is a buyer—and Goldman said that $110 is an inadequate price," Bob Miller added.

"Maybe I'm buying, you could say. Maybe I'm standing pat. The Pennzoil deal is best for the minority. I might withdraw my offer and do nothing," Gordon said.

"If you would withdraw your offer, the board would vote for a self-tender," Tisch responded.

"I've done a lot for the shareholders," Gordon insisted.

Sid Petersen interrupted this debate. "We've *got* to do something about the Pennzoil tender offer." That was the problem with doing nothing—Pennzoil's 20 percent, $100 bid would go forward, and it would be successful.

"I don't think it's possible to get the Pennzoil offer increased," Harold Berg volunteered. "Liedtke told me that if the board doesn't approve the $110 offer, the deal is off."

"That might be a negotiating ploy," Medberry said.

"The board could put the company on the market anytime and wait for the phone to ring," Gordon said, still defending his refusal to support the self-tender, ninety-day auction plan.

"You need board action to do that," Wendt replied.

"I don't think so," Gordon said.

Petersen returned to his earlier theme: "We have got to act by a week from this coming Tuesday to protect the company from the Pennzoil offer."

Gordon, however, was not interested in Petersen's mounting fears. "The board is crazy if it thinks I am buying at $110 a share. I am protecting my position and doing a favor for the shareholders."

Tisch tried again to persuade him. "Look, Gordon, the board is willing to *give* the company to you at $110 per share. All it asks is ninety days to beat that price."

"That's not what the board is doing, either," Gordon answered.

"Under the proposal talked about on Saturday, the board would put the trust over fifty percent at the end of ninety days and you can do anything you want if the company isn't sold for more than $110," Tisch pressed.

"When that proposal was discussed and considered, it was only negotiations," Gordon answered. "I did not agree to it."

"The only difference from the Pennzoil deal is that the company gets a chance to get a better price for the shareholders. All of the directors but you are in favor of that."

Gordon said nothing. Someone asked if he was willing to withdraw the consent he signed with Harold Williams in early December. Then it would no longer be necessary to round up 14 votes to adopt the self-tender auction plan.

"I would under certain circumstances, including the reconstitution of the board," Gordon replied.

"Will you explain what you mean by that?" Medberry asked him.
"I don't care to."

"The company has to block the Pennzoil tender offer to get an offer that is better," Wendt told Gordon.

"If the Pennzoil offer is low, bigger fish will come in," Gordon answered.

Harold Stuart, for one, could not understand Gordon's attitude. He had known Gordon for years now, had sat through countless meetings with him, endured his stubborn defiance, his questioning of management, his vaguely articulated quest for maximized values. And yet, Stuart now felt, there was something very peculiar about Gordon's present refusal to consider the self-tender, ninety-day auction plan now that the board had rejected his joint takeover with Pennzoil. It simply made no sense. Gordon, it seemed to Stuart, had everything to gain by an open auction for Getty Oil, and nothing particularly to lose, apart from his ambition to be chairman of the company, an unlikely prospect at best, in Stuart's view. Why was he being so intractable? Harold Stuart had a notion, and he turned directly to Gordon: "Do you have any agreement or other arrangements with Pennzoil other than what you've told the board about?" he asked.

Gordon paused. He knitted his furry eyebrows. He pursed his lips. He folded his long, bony hands before him. And then he said, "I would have to talk with my advisors about that."

Someone stepped into the hallway and summoned the mass of lawyers and bankers back into the room. It was now ten minutes before two in the morning. Harold Stuart repeated his inquiry. Did Gordon have some sidebar arrangement with Pennzoil which he had not disclosed to the board?

Tim Cohler said that he would answer that question. From his briefcase he produced a one-page document, which would come to be known by its salutation as the "Dear Hugh" letter. Cohler read the agreement aloud. It was addressed to Pennzoil, and it said, in simple language, that if the Getty Oil directors refused to approve the Pennzoil takeover, Gordon would do everything in his power to have them immediately and summarily fired.

There was a hailstorm of profanity and accusation.

"Gordon, you fucking asshole," director John Teets said. "I'd like to wring your fucking neck." The Greyhound chairman did not act on this sudden impulse.

"Very bad form," Larry Tisch conceded about the man who had named him to Getty Oil's board. "Very bad form."

In one corner of the room, Fritz Larkin, the retired Security Pacific banker, turned to Harold Stuart and said simply, "The old man is rolling over in his grave."

At the far end of the table, Gordon Getty sat impassively. He felt no regret. It was these same directors, after all, who had fomented the lawsuit challenging his right to be sole trustee of the Getty family trust. It was these directors who had treated him so rudely over the years. It was they who had blocked his effort to control the company over the last eighteen months. The snakes were only getting what they deserved.

19

DEAL-MAKERS

At that moment of final collapse in Sutton Room II when the directors of Getty Oil began to curse Gordon Getty and his heritage, it was Martin Lipton, the consummate deal-maker, who offered a way out.

While the lawyers and bankers were exiled from the board room, Lipton had been talking again with Arthur Liman and Jim Glanville about a formula that would increase Pennzoil's takeover offer to $120 a share. At first, Lipton was told that Hugh Liedtke would offer "not a penny more" than $110, but later Glanville reported that he would be speaking about the matter with Pennzoil's chairman in the morning, and that Pennzoil would be willing to consider a new proposal from Getty Oil's board at that time. Lipton, Liman, and Glanville proceeded to devise a complex formula, based on the sale of Getty Oil's ERC insurance subsidiary, to raise Pennzoil's takeover price to $120. Moments later, when Tim Cohler read the "Dear Hugh" letter to the embattled directors and the board room erupted in volcanic anger, Lipton tried to calm the scene by outlining the new proposal, which might solve everyone's predicament. The directors turned their attention away from Gordon and began to listen. In his deliberate, articulate manner, the bespectacled Lipton described a new debenture formula that would raise the Pennzoil offer by ten dollars.

"Are there other provisions of the Pennzoil offer presently before the board that would be applicable?" Harold Stuart asked when Lipton was finished. Stuart was referring to the "Memorandum of

Agreement" signed by Gordon, Liedtke, and Williams, which the board had earlier voted down.

"Who cares?" Lipton asked.* From the beginning of the meeting, the problem had been price. Now there was a plausible formula to raise the offer to $120. Nothing else mattered, Lipton was saying.

"Goldman could give a fairness opinion on the terms Marty outlined," Geoff Boisi volunteered. Those were the magic words. For the first time all night, Boisi was willing to write a fairness letter.

"What's the trust's view?" Sid Petersen asked Gordon.

"I'll sleep on it," he said.

"You can't do that with the time deadlines we're facing," Petersen insisted.

For twenty minutes, they wandered about the narrow conference room, informally discussing what they should do next. There was consensus on one issue: everyone needed to sleep. Finally, just before two-thirty, a vote was called. Gordon said that he would not stand in the way if the board wanted to recommend Lipton's $120 proposal to Pennzoil. But he made it clear that he was not endorsing the idea and he said that he could not guarantee how he might vote "as a shareholder" in the future. The tally was counted. All of the directors voted in favor of recommending the $120 formula to Pennzoil, except Chauncey Medberry, who voted no as a matter of principle. Medberry indicated that he was too upset by the circumstances of Pennzoil's alliance with Gordon to recommend an offer to them, despite the $120 price.

With that, Sid Petersen suggested that the emergency meeting of the Getty Oil board of directors be recessed until the following afternoon. By then, Pennzoil would have responded to Lipton's $120 debenture proposal. The directors would be well rested. The fate of Getty Oil Company might finally be decided.

The weary board members gathered their belongings and began to disperse.

---

* Lipton said later that he believes he asked "Who knows?" rather than "Who cares?" in response to Stuart's question. It was a point of potential significance in subsequent litigation. Under oath, Lipton said that he could not be absolutely certain which was accurate, but said that he would "defer" to the "Who cares?" version in Dave Copley's notes of the meeting.

~

It was sometime after three o'clock that morning when Geoff Boisi and Bart Winokur pushed through the Inter-Continental Hotel's revolving door and stepped into Manhattan's chilly, abandoned streets. They walked a short distance together to the Waldorf-Astoria Hotel on Park Avenue, walked through the lobby, and rode the elevator up some thirty floors. They located the room occupied by Jim Glanville, who lived in Connecticut but stayed in Manhattan when a rich deal such as this was in full bloom. Boisi slipped a two-page note, handwritten on yellow legal paper, beneath Glanville's door.

The note began: "Jim, The attached is the transaction the Getty board approved. After you have had a chance to review this with your client or if you have questions please contact me at the Helmsley Palace or Dechert Price & Rhoads' office." Boisi signed his name below two telephone numbers. On the second page, there was a handwritten outline of the terms of Marty Lipton's new $120 formula. It read in part: "The Getty board has approved the following transaction. PZ [Pennzoil] will withdraw its tender. PZ & Getty will enter into a merger agreement. . . . PZ will contribute $2.64 billion to the capital of the surviving corp." That was enough to give Hugh Liedtke the three-sevenths position he had negotiated with Gordon on New Year's Day. The question remaining was whether Liedtke would bid against himself and raise his price to $120 in order to achieve his goal.

After the note was delivered, Geoff Boisi and Bart Winokur walked from the Waldorf to their respective hotels and went to bed. It had been a long night.

Neither of them, however, could afford to sleep late. They had reached the vortex of a multibillion-dollar hostile takeover, and this was the milieu in which the performance of a merger expert was measured. The romanticization of takeovers, promoted not only by the media but by Wall Street bankers and lawyers, was at its pinnacle that January, 1984. Prominent players such as Boisi, Lipton, and Siegel had developed an acute self-consciousness about the urgent importance of themselves and their profession. Financial reporters tracked their deals like sportswriters covering a pennant race. Triumphs and fiascos alike were chronicled—a single here, a home run there, a strike-out with the bases loaded. Wall Street was at the center of the national, Reagan-era consciousness. Earlier, flying back to New York from London, one of the lawyers involved had talked about who would be cast as Gordon Getty in the movie version of Getty Oil's travails. That attitude, that giddy sense of self-awareness, had only increased in recent weeks. So much was at stake, the Wall Street advisors felt. So much depended on what they did next.

It was just before seven on Tuesday morning when an exhausted Geoff Boisi arrived at Goldman, Sachs' stately offices on Broad Street, down from the New York Stock Exchange. The Getty Oil board was not scheduled to reconvene at the Inter-Continental for another six hours. Boisi had a great deal to do before then. He had a lot of phone calls to make.

His first, promptly at seven, was to Jim Glanville at the Waldorf.

"I just wanted to be sure that you found my note under the door," Boisi said.

"I found it and I was surprised by it," Glanville replied. "My understanding last night was that the board was going to come back with some changed optics. I thought we were talking about optics. What you've asked for here is real money."

"You bet," Boisi said.

The $120 formula devised by Lipton was indeed "real money," in the sense that it would actually be worth $120 on the market. But it was different from the straight debenture proposal discussed earlier on Monday by Liman and Tisch in that it depended on the sale of Getty Oil's ERC subsidiary. If ERC commanded a high price, as Boisi expected it would, then the Lipton formula would cost Pennzoil less than $120 from its own pocket. But if ERC fetched a modest offer, then Pennzoil would have to pay the full $120.

Glanville said that he would discuss the proposal with Liedtke over breakfast. He did not sound optimistic.

Geoff Boisi now decided to place a few more telephone calls. The night before, during the confused caucuses at the Inter-Continental Hotel, Boisi had talked with Sid Petersen about whether it was possible to quickly find a third-party buyer for Getty Oil, without the formal ninety-day auction sought by Petersen. The Getty Oil chairman had encouraged Boisi to see what he could do. Directors such as Henry Wendt, Chauncey Medberry, and even Larry Tisch had argued repeatedly during the board meeting that the company could fetch an offer above $120 if only it had time to hold a formal auction. Boisi felt that even without an auction he might be able to quickly find a buyer, a "white knight" willing to step in and pluck Getty Oil from the outstretched arms of Gordon Getty and Hugh Liedtke. It was the business of a merger banker like Boisi to pull off such a coup, even under tremendous time pressure. It was a chance for him to hit a home run.

So after speaking to Glanville early that Tuesday morning, Boisi met with John Weinberg, Goldman, Sachs' cochairman. Weinberg, Boisi knew, played golf occasionally with John McKinley, the chairman and chief executive of mammoth, New York-based Texaco Inc. Boisi had been told that McKinley was the sort of chief executive who preferred to deal with people with whom he was well acquainted. So Boisi asked Weinberg if he would telephone McKinley to explore Texaco's possible interest in acquiring Getty Oil.

Weinberg and Boisi shared a speakerphone. When they reached McKinley's office, however, they learned that the Texaco chairman was not in—he was spending the holidays at his home in Alabama. Weinberg asked to be transferred to the office of Al DeCrane, Texaco's president. DeCrane accepted the call.

"I'm going to put Geoff Boisi on the phone," Weinberg said after some preliminary pleasantries. "He is the head of M&A at Goldman, Sachs. We're representing Getty Oil management and the original board in this situation."

DeCrane, like nearly everyone else in the oil fraternity, had been closely following, through the financial press, the events surrounding Pennzoil's tender offer for 20 percent of Getty Oil. He knew what Weinberg meant by "the original board"—those directors adamantly opposed to Gordon Getty. DeCrane was not aware, of course, that Liedtke and Gordon had made a new arrangement for a full takeover of the company; the New Year's Day deal had not been publicly disclosed.

Boisi told DeCrane that the Getty Oil directors were in the midst of a board meeting recess. "The sense of the board is that if there was an attractive offer for the entire company, they would sell," Boisi said. "The museum is a definite seller. Gordon may be a seller or a buyer—he's probably a seller at some price. He doesn't want to be a minority party."

DeCrane was taking notes as Boisi spoke, and he underlined this last sentence. If a third party were to buy the 12 percent owned by the museum and the 48 percent owned by the public, then Gordon would be left in a 40 percent minority position. He might have no choice but to sell. Otherwise, as Winokur had put it nearly a year before at the Bonaventure, Gordon would be squeezed, he would be the juice.

"Is Texaco interested, in principle, in making an offer?" Boisi asked.

"We are."

"If the board came to Goldman and concluded that they wanted to sell, to contact people, would Texaco want to be on that list? If the board reached the conclusion that it would like to see who was interested, would Texaco like to have its name presented?"

"Yes," DeCrane answered. The Texaco president wanted to know how much information about Getty Oil's finances would be available to prospective buyers if a sale was undertaken. "If the company goes through some formalized procedure for the sale, would you anticipate that a data room would be established?" DeCrane asked. A so-called data room was commonplace in the auction of a large company. A center containing detailed financial information was established by the seller so that interested buyers could examine materials not publicly available in federal regulatory filings.

"Yes, that might be a possibility," Boisi replied. "Is there anything you can say through me to the Getty Oil board about your interest in this?"

"Just that we would like to be included in a group that might receive information to evaluate the company," DeCrane answered.

When the phone call was concluded, Boisi was encouraged, though hardly overwhelmed. DeCrane was clearly interested, but the Texaco president had expressed no urgent enthusiasm. The lanky, nervous Boisi returned to his telephone. All morning and afternoon he placed urgent phone calls, "shopping," as the merger bankers put it, for a $7 billion customer. He spoke with an officer of Standard Oil of California, known variously as Chevron or Socal. Boisi made essentially the same pitch he had delivered to DeCrane. He got the impression that Chevron was significantly more interested in acquiring Getty than Texaco was, and that the California-based giant would move quickly to study Getty Oil's finances and line up Wall Street advisors. Boisi also spoke with representatives of Shell, who expressed interest in Getty Oil's rich Kern River field, and General Electric, who said they might like to buy the ERC insurance subsidiary. There was also a flurry of conversations between Boisi and

a number of rival Wall Street investment bankers, all of them eager
for information about Getty Oil's status, all searching themselves for
clients who might step in and buy the company, thus generating millions in quick transaction fees. And throughout the day, Boisi spoke
frequently with Bart Winokur, who was stationed at the Dechert
Price offices in Midtown. Boisi updated Getty Oil's lawyer about the
prospects of a white knight rescue.

So busy was Geoff Boisi with his shopping spree, in fact, that he
was late arriving at the Inter-Continental Hotel for the second session of Getty Oil's marathon emergency board meeting.

The scene that greeted him was again one of chaos and confusion.

The problems had begun even before all of the directors assembled for the three o'clock start. Arthur Liman, Pennzoil's attorney,
was one of the first to arrive. He had spent the day at the Waldorf,
discussing with Liedtke, Siegel, and Glanville the $120 proposal
slipped under Glanville's door by Geoff Boisi the night before.

When he read the proposal, Liedtke had declared simply that it
was "outrageous." The Pennzoil chairman had then made a series of
profane remarks comparing New York lawyers and bankers to certain predatory animals. Finally, after a long discussion, Liedtke had
agreed to a counterproposal: Getty Oil shareholders could take their
choice between $110 in cash and $90 in cash plus a note whose value
depended on the price fetched for ERC in an open sale. If Goldman,
Sachs' high estimate of ERC's worth was correct, shareholders who
selected the second option would receive about $115 per share. If
Goldman was wrong, they might receive as little as $100. Just before
three, Liman arrived at the Inter-Continental carrying a written version of Liedtke's proposal. He spotted Marty Lipton and handed the
paper to him.

Lipton read it over. "It won't sell," the bespectacled attorney
declared when he was finished. "It's too cute. I won't present it to the
board."

"Liedtke didn't even want to make this proposal because he
thought the time had come to see whether you and Williams could
be counted on to remove the board, since the $110 is the best pro-
posal," Liman said. "But Glanville, Siegel, and I got him to do this.
If Goldman is right in its estimate of what ERC is worth, then the
shareholders are going to get $115 to $120 per share. And if Goldman is wrong, the shareholders will take the $110."

"I will not present this," Lipton repeated. "Go back to Mr. Liedtke and get a stub—some kind of debenture or note—plus the $110."

They had moved into Gordon Getty's two-room suite around the corner from Sutton Room II. People were moving in and out; there was a great deal of commotion. Liman picked up the telephone. He called Liedtke and told him what Lipton had said about the new proposal from Pennzoil.

There were some expletives on the other end of the line.

"Look," Liman said to Liedtke. "There is no way that we are going to get acceptance of a proposal today unless you come up with a sweetener. You may not like it, but that's what they're doing to us."

"Okay. Offer them on top of the $110 a stub, a right for all the shareholders to receive an interest in whatever we get in selling ERC above a billion dollars after taxes." Goldman, Sachs had estimated that ERC was worth between $1 billion and $1.5 billion.

"What about some guarantee, in case ERC doesn't go for more than one billion?" Liman asked.

"Okay, if it doesn't yield more than three dollars extra for the shareholders, then at the end of five years, we will make up the difference. So the shareholders will get $110 immediately plus a guarantee that within five years they will get at least another three dollars. You are authorized to present that to Lipton and tell him that if this isn't good enough, then I expect him to live up to what he said before." Liedtke was referring to Lipton's statement two days earlier that he and Williams would not let the Getty directors stand in the way of a transaction. If the board did not go along with this new plan, Liedtke wanted them summarily removed.

Liman hung up and turned to Lipton, who was standing just a few feet away. Liman repeated what his client had just said. Lipton did some quick arithmetic.

"You know, if you discount the three-dollar, five-year guarantee to its present value, you get something worth less than two dollars on the open market. Why don't you get Liedtke to make a guarantee of five dollars in five years, which would have a present value of about two dollars fifty cents?"

"Martin, I value my life now," Liman replied. "I'm not going back to Hugh Liedtke and ask him to bump this again. If you come back to me and the board has approved the whole plan and the only thing it wants is to move the three-dollar guarantee to five dollars, I will undertake to recommend it and sell it to Mr. Liedtke. But I'm not going back and ask him to keep raising it without having a firm deal with you."

"I will try," Lipton said. "It will be very questionable whether Goldman, Sachs will give a fairness opinion at this level." He wrote down a short note describing the basic terms outlined by Liman and Liedtke.

Lipton walked down the hall to Sutton Room II. The directors were reconvening. When the door was closed, Lipton described his negotiations with Liman and outlined the terms of the new proposal. The present value of the deal for public shareholders and the museum would be $112.50—$110 in cash plus a guaranteed $5 in five years' time. Gordon would stand pat and take control of Getty Oil in combination with Pennzoil.

Speaking for Gordon, Marty Siegel said, "The trust has advised Pennzoil that such a proposal is acceptable to the trust." A brief discussion ensued about the prospects for a sale of ERC and the prices that might be obtained for the subsidiary. Finally, someone asked Geoff Boisi whether Goldman, Sachs would be willing to issue a fairness letter sanctifying the $112.50 takeover.

"I'm not prepared to commit as to whether the proposal is fair," the banker declared.

Petersen called for another recess, and again the directors wandered through the hallways and adjoining conference rooms. Almost immediately, Marty Lipton asked to speak with Boisi. The two of them, as well as Larry Tisch and Harold Williams, found a place away from the crowd.

Lipton and Williams argued strongly with Boisi, attempting to persuade him that Goldman, Sachs should issue a fairness opinion for Liedtke's $112.50 proposal. "Salomon Brothers, the museum's investment banker, is prepared to give the museum an opinion at that level. We want Goldman, Sachs to do the same," they said.

Still, Boisi refused to give in. He said that Goldman had made some preliminary contacts with other companies and had obtained expressions of interest, which he felt would yield a significantly higher price. The young banker was adamant. He would not issue a fairness letter.

Deeply worried about what might happen if the present impasse persisted, Lipton began to negotiate again with Pennzoil's advisors.

He tried to use Boisi's refusal to issue a fairness opinion as lever-age with Liman, urging the lawyer to persuade Liedtke to raise his offer beyond the five-dollar, five-year guarantee. But Liman, too, was intractable. Liedtke had gone as far as he was going to go, Liman said. It was time for the board to make a decision. Still, Lipton continued to argue and negotiate. He was afraid that if the deadlock was not broken, Pennzoil would simply tender for its 20 percent, combine with Gordon, and squeeze out the museum. Somehow, Lipton felt, a negotiated solution had to be reached.

After more than an hour of futile talks, the "original" Getty Oil directors—those allied with Sid Petersen against Gordon—assem-bled in a nearby conference room for a private briefing from Bart Winokur. Geoff Boisi joined the group. Winokur reviewed the dire circumstances faced by the directors. He described the corporate law that governed their power and their decisions, and he listed some of the actions he felt they could and could not take, in each case outlin-ing the board's "exposure" in future lawsuits. Winokur reiterated the terms of the deal described earlier by Marty Lipton and he updated the directors on the last hour's negotiations.

"There are substantial items which we have been unable to clarify and therefore are not going to be able to clarify before we go back into the board meeting," Winokur said.

"Based on the information we have, I am unwilling to give a fair-ness opinion on this transaction," Boisi added. "I am not ruling out that possibility if we are able to negotiate satisfactory terms in the future." The banker went on to describe some of his contacts with prospective buyers, such as Chevron and Texaco, and said that he expected to receive proposals from some of them. He could not, however, predict how soon the proposals would come. Even after his arrival at the Inter-Continental that afternoon, Boisi had continued to place and receive calls on the courtesy phones scattered about the hotel's third floor.

At one point during this caucus meeting, Winokur and the direc-tors asked Sid Petersen, Dave Copley, and Bob Miller—the three Getty Oil officers present—to leave the room. They complied. Winokur told the remaining board members that he wanted to talk with them about employment contracts and legal indemnities for the company's top executives. Winokur was concerned about threats Gordon Getty had made against Petersen and Copley. He thought Getty Oil's executives should have both legal and financial protection—amended "golden parachutes"—in case Gordon gained control of the company. The directors agreed, and they asked Winokur to discuss the matter with Lipton. Winokur did, and Lipton said that he would speak with Gordon and the other directors to secure their agreement.

Just after six, the Getty Oil board members and their coterie of advisors returned to Sutton Room II. Marty Lipton, who had been thrust—or who had thrust himself—to the center of the negotiations, reviewed in detail the terms of the $112.50 offer by Pennzoil and Gordon Getty. When Lipton was finished, several questions were asked about the mechanics of the deal. And then, finally, more than twenty-four hours after they had begun, the directors decided to vote on the $112.50 proposal by Pennzoil and Gordon Getty.

"I have concerns," Chauncey Medberry said before the poll was taken. "I have a different opinion as to values. Major shareholders are making it impossible for us as directors to perform our duty as well as we might. I think more is to be obtained for the shares."

"Most of us feel that the real value of the company under normal circumstances is greater, and our investment bankers have so stated, but under the circumstances we cannot obtain it," Harold Stuart replied.

Alfred Taubman, the Detroit shopping-mall magnate recruited to the board by Ann Getty, interrupted to recount a tale from the Midwest.

"There's the story about the Michigan boy that dated the girl with a pimple on her nose," he told the directors. "After he married her, he said, 'If you marry a girl with a pimple, you can't divorce her for acne.' If public shareholders bought stock in a company with two large shareholders—Gordon and the museum—they should be aware of the potential problems. It's like dating the girl with the pimple on her nose."

"Except in this case, she didn't used to have the pimple," Harold Stuart quipped. Stuart was referring to the company's long era of calm before the deaths of J. Paul Getty and Lansing Hays.

On that unusual note of levity, Harold Williams moved that the board accept Pennzoil's proposal, provided that Liedtke could be persuaded to go to a five-dollar guarantee—a present value of $112.50. All of the directors voted in favor, except Chauncey Medberry, who again voted no.

The $112.50 proposal had passed. Gordon Getty, apparently, would become the chairman of Getty Oil.

Sid Petersen asked if there were any other items to be brought before the board. At Harold Stuart's suggestion, there was a unanimous acclamation praising "the splendid job done by the chairman in handling the meeting under difficult conditions." Thus flattered, Petersen was then enriched. The directors, including Gordon, unanimously approved a proposal by Henry Wendt to indemnify Getty Oil's top executives against future lawsuits arising from their actions during the previous eighteen months, and to favorably amend the employment contracts, or golden parachutes, of "key executives of the company whose careers were likely to be affected by the change in management."

What remained was to persuade Hugh Liedtke to formally raise his offer to $112.50—at the moment, he had not actually authorized anything above the three-dollar ERC guarantee, with a present value of just over $111. Marty Lipton told Petersen that he would carry the news of the directors' vote to Arthur Liman and attempt to get a final confirmation from Liedtke. As Lipton left the room, the board meeting temporarily recessed.

Liman was stationed in Gordon's two-room suite around the corner. After twenty-five hours, Liman had begun to feel like a hostage. He kept asking, "Can I go home? Can we get it over with?" and always the answer was no, there was still more to be negotiated.

Now, just before seven, the advisors came streaming out of Sutton Room II and into Gordon's suite. Lipton led the way; behind him came Marty Siegel, Tim Cohler, Bart Winokur, and Geoff Boisi.

Liman was told about the 15–1 vote. It was now necessary for Liedtke to formally raise his offer to $112.50. Liman said that he would immediately telephone the Pennzoil chairman at his Waldorf apartment. The others reminded him that Goldman, Sachs was as yet refusing to issue a fairness opinion, that they would have to be persuaded to do so in the final negotiations. Someone mentioned that the board had voted to indemnify Getty Oil's top executives and to provide them with lucrative golden parachutes.

Liman picked up the phone and called Liedtke.

"Hugh, they've come back. They voted fifteen to one in favor, but I'm sorry, they want five dollars guaranteed in five years."

"Is that it?"

"I've asked them about it. That's it except for two little things."

"What are those 'little things?'" Liedtke's cynicism was evident.

"One is they've indemnified the management on any actions involving what they did to Gordon Getty and the museum and so on."

"That's no problem," Liedtke said.

"Second, they want the executive compensation committee to be able to give golden parachutes."

"How many people?"

Liman cupped the phone and turned to the advisors in the suite. "How many people?" he asked.

"Something like seven to nine," was the answer, and Liman repeated the figure to Liedtke.

"That's okay, too. Do we have a deal at this juncture?"

"That's it."

"You can tell them yes," Liedtke said.

Liman turned to Marty Lipton. "My client accepts."

"We have to go back into session," Lipton replied.

"Why do you have to go back in session?" Liman demanded. "I thought you told me that the board had voted this and it was done."

"No, they voted the counterproposal. Now I have to communicate to them that you have accepted the counterproposal."

"Fine," Liman replied.

"You can come and wait outside the room," Lipton said. "This is only going to take two seconds."

The directors inside Sutton Room II were now standing, putting on their coats, gathering their briefcases and papers. When the door was closed again, Marty Siegel announced that Pennzoil had accepted the board's counterproposal. The meeting was adjourned. Bart Winokur tried to ask about the details of the final negotiations with Pennzoil and whether a document would come back to the board for approval. Lipton cut him off, saying that normally a final, written takeover agreement would come back to the directors for ratification.

There would later be serious dispute about precisely what happened next. This much was agreed upon by everyone: The door to Sutton Room II opened. The directors and their advisors began to wander out. Arthur Liman was standing in the hallway outside the room. He was waiting to hear what had happened inside.

Liman later testified under oath that either Marty Lipton or Marty Siegel, or perhaps both of them, stepped into the hallway and said, "Congratulations, Arthur, you've got a deal." Lipton testified that he did not remember saying any such thing, and that he was in no mood to congratulate anyone, principally because Goldman, Sachs had not yet agreed to provide a fairness letter sanctifying the transaction. Siegel's memory about the incident was vague. Unlike Lipton, however, Siegel represented Gordon Getty and thus was on the same side of the deal as Liman, who represented Pennzoil. Conceivably, Siegel would have more reason to be pleased about the board's action than Lipton. In any event, Liman testified that after this initial round of congratulation, he asked permission to enter Sutton Room II to thank the Getty Oil directors for their arduous and diligent efforts. Liman said that he shook hands with a number of the board members, who made remarks to him such as "Congratulations" and "Congratulations to you." However, a number of directors and advisors present at the board meeting testified later that they did not recall seeing Liman in the room after the final vote. None of them remembered shaking hands with the Pennzoil attorney.

The issue of who was in a congratulatory or celebratory mood at seven o'clock that Tuesday evening would eventually become a critically important one. At the time, however, there were no pictures taken of smiling or drooping faces, no notes made about the facial expressions of the participants. When the time came to sort the matter out, there was only memory, with all of its conveniences.

About this much, too, there was no dispute: In the first hours following the conclusion of Getty Oil's emergency board meeting that Tuesday, January 3, Gordon Getty and Hugh Liedtke were both ecstatic. They believed that they had won, that they had taken control of Getty Oil for $112.50 per share. For Gordon particularly, it was the triumphant end of a long and difficult campaign against Sidney Petersen.

Soon after he heard the good news from Arthur Liman, Hugh Liedtke, who was still at his Waldorf apartment, telephoned Gordon's suite at the Pierre. Ann picked up the phone; Gordon had stepped out for a moment, she said.

"I've heard the news and I'm delighted," Ann told the Pennzoil chairman. "We're going to have a champagne party here to celebrate." She invited Liedtke to join them. The Pennzoil chairman thanked her but asked for a rain check, saying that he was "running awfully late" to his own celebration dinner with his company's top executives. They were all dining at the "21" Club.

"I understand," Ann Getty said. "Congratulations."

And with that, Hugh Liedtke went on his way, secure in the belief that in the space of just a week, he had managed, with Gordon Getty's cooperation, to transform the modest Pennzoil Company into one of the largest oil corporations in the world.

AN AGREEMENT IN PRINCIPLE

The immediate question on the lips of the lawyers and bankers as they gathered up their belongings at the Inter-Continental Hotel that Tuesday evening was this: what should we do next?

They congregated and talked in the third-floor hallway; no simple answers were forthcoming. It was fine for Gordon Getty and Hugh Liedtke to sip champagne and toast their success over gourmet cuisine. Such were the prerogatives of victory. It was fine, even, for the ashen, exhausted Getty Oil directors to return to their hotel rooms, sleep, pack their bags, and prepare for their journey home. The directors had done what they could. But for the advisors, the game-players, the ordeal was far from over. There were documents to be drawn up, points to be negotiated, financial arrangements to be made, and press releases to be issued. The latter problem—disclosure—was an especially tricky and important one. In the week since Pennzoil's original 20 percent tender offer—Liedtke's "Christmas surprise"—neither Getty Oil nor anyone else had made a formal public announcement about the progress of negotiations. There had been some leaks, and some sketchy reporting in the financial press about a possible alliance between Liedtke and Gordon, but no official confirmations. Under the law, companies involved in a takeover were required to inform the public if any significant agreement was reached, the theory being that public stockholders had the right to make fully informed investment decisions. The Getty Oil board's

15–1 vote approving the $112.50 proposal, whatever its ultimate significance, was certainly a meaningful event. It had to be disclosed to the public—and quickly. As they talked about it, the lawyers and bankers for all the parties involved decided that a press release should be their first priority. Even if it took them all night, they had to get something out before the stock market opened in the morning. Then, with their obligations to the public met, they could begin negotiations to produce a final, detailed merger agreement.

Phone calls went out from the Inter-Continental and a new bevy of advisors was summoned: the financial public relations experts. Pennzoil had hired a New York firm, as had Getty Oil. Each party to the deal designated one or more advisors to help write the press release, to explain precisely the agreement defined by the board's final 15–1 vote. For the museum, Marty Lipton, who was exhausted from the marathon negotiations, asked his associate, Patricia Vlahakis, to handle the matter. Lipton wanted to get some rest. Ordinarily, in a deal of this size and complexity, Lipton would have assigned a battery of experienced partners from his firm to supervise the preparation of a press release, but because of the odd circumstances of Lipton's involvement—the fact that he had regarded representation of the museum as a personal favor to Harold Williams, not as a major paying matter for his firm—there was no one but Vlahakis who understood the issues. For Gordon, Marty Siegel indicated that he would take charge; Siegel had helped write hundreds of takeover press releases in the past. For Getty Oil itself, there was Bart Winokur, Geoff Boisi, and several other Wall Street lawyers. Dave Copley, too, said that he would go along as an officer of the company, to approve any release in Getty Oil's name. Finally, for Pennzoil, there was Arthur Liman and his partners at Paul, Weiss, Rifkind, Wharton & Garrison. Liman volunteered his firm's offices on Third Avenue as the site for all-night preparation of the press release.

It was eight o'clock by the time all of the advisors arrived at Paul, Weiss. At first, they all crowded together in a conference room and tried to decide who should do what, when, and in what order. There was a great deal of confusion and competing conversation. There were questions about who was representing whom and in what capacity. Only the museum, represented by Patricia Vlahakis, who was just a couple of years out of law school, had but one retainer at the meeting. Pennzoil, for example, was represented by two law firms—the New Yorkers from Paul, Weiss and the Texans from Baker & Botts—as well as an investment banker and a public relations firm. For Gordon, there were Cohler and Woodhouse from the Lasky firm, as well as Marty Siegel and Siegel's own Wall Street lawyers. Similarly, Getty Oil was represented by two different law firms, one based in Philadelphia and another on Wall Street, plus an investment banker, the investment banker's law firm, and a public relations outfit. None of the principals was present, except for Dave Copley. It was like a zoo—and since most of the advisors were being paid by the hour, it was a very expensive zoo.

It became quickly clear to them all that responsibilities had to be delegated, or else nothing would be accomplished. It was decided that the public relations experts should take the first crack at a press release. At the same time, it was suggested that Pennzoil's attorneys should write the first draft of a final merger agreement—the protocol of the merger game provided that the winner presented the first version of a final document, with all the details in place. The idea was that while the press release was finalized, Pennzoil's lawyers would spend all night preparing their draft. Then, in the morning, lawyers for the company, the museum, and Gordon Getty would join the negotiations.

This much decided, the advisors dispersed from the central conference room and began to roam about the Paul, Weiss offices, waiting.

Hank Londean, the Getty Oil executive in charge of public relations, bumped into Richard Howe, a Pennzoil executive with similar responsibilities, in the corridor.

"Congratulations," Londean told him. "You're stuck with Gordon Getty now."

"Thanks," Howe replied.

Such lighthearted comity did not extend to others of the advisors. In groups to two or three, they began to bicker with each other about what should be said, or not said, in the press release. At one point, Patricia Vlahakis, who was feeling frightened by the responsibility thrust upon her by Lipton, her firm's most senior partner, spotted Marty Siegel speaking on the telephone in one of the Paul, Weiss offices. She listened—it was clear that Siegel was talking to a newspaper reporter, explaining what had happened at the Inter-Continental. Vlahakis, a petite, attractive woman with a capacity for strident outburst, became livid. She demanded that Siegel hang up the phone immediately. A public relations man representing Gordon intervened and explained to Vlahakis that Siegel was only trying to be sure that the *Wall Street Journal* got its story right for the next day. (This in itself was not unusual, since Siegel cultivated relationships with a wide variety of financial journalists.) But Vlahakis would have none of it—they had not even agreed on the terms of a press release, and Siegel was already gabbing with a reporter, she said.

Vlahakis stepped into the office. "If you don't get off the phone, I'm going to reach over and hang it up," she said.

Siegel concluded his conversation.

From there, relations between the advisors continued to deteriorate. Shortly after nine, a draft press release prepared by the public relations experts was passed around. Vlahakis took her copy to the law firm's reception area and sat down to read it. The very first line of the release stated that the Getty Oil directors had voted to "accept" a plan that would provide for the merger of Pennzoil and Getty Oil. In the third paragraph, it read, "The agreement provides. . . ." Vlahakis stopped reading—this was totally unacceptable, she thought. No such agreement yet existed; there had only been a vote by the board. One of the lawyers for Gordon Getty wandered by and the two of them decided that they should start from scratch. In his own hand, and with Vlahakis' assistance, the lawyer wrote: "Getty Oil Company, Pennzoil Corporation, the J. Paul Getty Museum, and Gordon P. Getty as trustee for the Sarah C. Getty Trust, dated December 31, 1934, announced today that they had agreed in principle. . . ." Perhaps it was not Hemingway, but to Vlahakis the key point was "agreed in principle," a term of art in the merger business. Everyone had his own idea about what an "agreement in principle" actually was. At the very least, the phrase implied that a final document had yet to be drafted, and thus it accurately reflected the state of affairs at Paul, Weiss that evening.

While Gordon Getty's lawyer finished the drafting, Vlahakis was called aside by Bart Winokur. Winokur, too, had seen the press release drafted by the public relations experts, and he was unhappy. The draft contained a paragraph stating that Getty Oil would immediately purchase the museum's 9 million shares, before the public's shares were bought by Pennzoil.

"There is no way the company is going to buy back the museum's shares," Winokur insisted. To do so would change the balance of power at Getty Oil before the public shareholders received their compensation.

"That's unacceptable," Vlahakis retorted. "The company has to buy them."

"There were statements made at the board meeting and in the various caucuses that the museum was going to be treated no differently than anyone else," Winokur said. "There's no way the company is going to be in a position where the museum's shares are bought first because then there would be a possibility that Pennzoil would not go through with the deal."

Vlahakis was vehement. "If you're not going to agree on that, then there's no deal."

"So be it," Winokur said.

They agreed that, given the chaos around them, they should agree to disagree, to set the issue aside and be certain that any reference to the museum's shares was removed from the final press release. The pair walked back into the main conference room where most of the lawyers and bankers were gathered, now arguing about the draft by the public relations experts.

Finally, the lawyer who had scribbled a new draft with Vlahakis in the reception area entered the conference room and read his version aloud. Everyone agreed that it was an improvement. Almost immediately, however, Moulton Goodrum, the Baker & Botts attorney representing Pennzoil, announced that his client's name would have to be removed from the release.

"I've looked at the new draft, and I have no basic problem with it, but as a result of all the squabbling between the parties, and because I can't reach my client at the restaurant, I myself have no authority to authorize the release," Goodrum said. "I want Pennzoil's name off of it."

Patricia Vlahakis, concerned now that events were careering wildly and that she was steering the museum's course without any guidance from her senior partner, decided to call Marty Lipton at home. She told him about her argument with Winokur over the purchase of the museum's shares. "In light of the fact that there's no way we are going to work through that issue tonight, as I can see it, the only way the press release can go out is if it makes no reference to the museum's shares."

"I agree," Lipton said.

Reassured, Vlahakis returned to the central conference room and announced, "We are not going to hold up issuance of a press release so long as the language about the museum's shares is deleted. But everybody in this room should understand that there is no agreement as to how the museum's shares are to be treated in any transaction. I want everyone to understand that there are absolutely no agreements on that issue." The young lawyer spoke emphatically and repeated her message several times to be sure that there would be no misunderstanding.

With Pennzoil and the museum now both out of the process, Stuart Katz, one of Getty Oil's Wall Street lawyers, took charge of the drafting. Sitting at the conference table, he began to write out yet another draft based on a volley of comments from the lawyers, bankers, and public relations executives in the room. It was after midnight before the one-page release was completed and turned over to the PR firms for distribution to the wire services and major news organizations first thing in the morning.

The final press release said: "Getty Oil Company, the J. Paul Getty Museum and Gordon P. Getty, as trustee of the Sarah C. Getty Trust, announced today that they have agreed in principle with Pennzoil to a merger of Getty Oil and a newly-formed entity owned by Pennzoil and the Trustee.

"In connection with the transaction, the shareholders of Getty Oil, other than Pennzoil and the Trustee, will receive $110 per share cash plus the right to receive a deferred cash consideration in a formula amount. The deferred consideration will be equal to a pro rata share of the net after tax proceeds in excess of $1 billion from the disposition of ERC Corp., the Getty Oil insurance subsidiary, and will be paid upon the disposition. In any event, under the formula each shareholder will receive at least $5 per share within five years.

"Prior to the merger Pennzoil will contribute approximately $2.6 billion in cash and the trustee and Pennzoil will contribute the Getty Oil shares owned by them to the new entity. Upon execution of a definitive merger agreement, the December 28th, 1983 tender offer by a Pennzoil subsidiary for shares of Getty Oil stock will be withdrawn. Following consummation of the merger the trustee will own four-sevenths of the outstanding common stock of Getty Oil and Pennzoil will own three-sevenths.

"The trustee and Pennzoil have also agreed in principle that following consummation of the merger they will endeavor in good
faith to agree upon a plan for restructuring Getty Oil on or before
12/31/84 and that if they're unable to reach such an agreement then
they will cause a division of the assets of the company."

The advisors to Sid Petersen's management team and to Gordon
Getty, as well as Getty Oil general counsel Dave Copley, approved
this version of the press release and authorized its issuance. It was
the language of an armistice—in the view of both parties, the release
accurately described the meaning of the directors' final 15-1 vote
at the Inter-Continental Hotel. The key phrase was "agreement in
principle." Apart from its legal definition or its utility in the insular,
specialized world of Wall Street merger-making, there was an irony
about the use of "principle" to describe an agreement between two
parties whose very lack of moral accord had been the cause of eighteen months of anger and turmoil. By whose principles was there
now an agreement between them? The principles of Sid Petersen and
Bart Winokur, whose drive to protect the public shareholders and
themselves had led them to secretly instigate a family lawsuit against
Gordon? Or the principles of Gordon Getty, whose desire to protect
his power over the family trust and to increase its already monstrous
wealth had caused him to undermine the stability of a decades-old
enterprise? Each side believed that its principles, its morality, was
superior to the other's and had behaved accordingly. Now, suddenly,
they were relying on an objective definition of motive and intent.
And yet they continued to view the destiny of Getty Oil through sub-
jective, fiercely partisan eyes.

Was the deal done? Had Gordon Getty and Hugh Liedtke won
out? Or was the game still on, was final control of the company still
in doubt? That depended, obviously, on how one interpreted the
phrase "agreement in principle." If one assumed the perspective of
the merger game-player, if one subordinated the objective meaning
of language to the rules of the game, then an agreement in principle
was no agreement at all. To Geoff Boisi, the Getty Oil banker who
had played this game hundreds of times before, an agreement in
principle meant simply that nothing was final, that everything was
up for grabs. This was not his personal definition; it was a convention of the game he played. In the card game of bridge, for example,
one bids for control of a hand through coded declarations that bear

no relation to the objective meaning of language. One says, "Two clubs," when one means, "I have no spades." Those players at the table familiar with the convention understand. But clearly there are risks attached to the appropriation of language, especially when the conventions of a game are not universally comprehended. Words, finally, convey objective meaning. Throughout the battle for control of Getty Oil, references were constantly made to the "public investor," and the image conjured was of a common man, a real-estate broker in Omaha, Nebraska, or a car salesman in Indianapolis, Indiana, who invested his family's hard-earned money in stocks in the hope that he might modestly increase his stake in the world.

As it happened, that image was largely misleading, since most of the "public" investors in Getty Oil were large institutions—pension funds, mutual funds, other corporations, and so on. These institutions and their managers were game-players, too. But there were plenty of individual, middle-class investors in the company as well; people whose contact with Wall Street was limited to the advice of a small-town stockbroker. To such an investor, armed with a dictionary and reading Getty Oil's press release on the morning of Wednesday, January 4, the phrase "agreement in principle" would hardly have indicated that everything was up for grabs. It would have suggested, to the contrary, that an agreement had been reached. If he wondered at all about the words "in principle," and if he was possessed of an exceptionally sophisticated and subtle mind, the investor might have assumed that only the essential, fundamental terms of the deal had yet been negotiated, and that the parties would now bargain in good faith to hammer out the details of a final document. But even that conclusion was far from self-evident. The phrase "in principle" might also refer to the theoretical, moral certitude of the transaction, to the parties' unyielding determination to conclude a deal. This latter and perfectly plausible interpretation, of course, was precisely the opposite of the Wall Street game-players' definition. To them, "in principle" was a convention, a signal to the bankers and lawyers on the Street that Getty Oil was still in play.

Geoff Boisi, therefore, was burdened by no self-doubt when at eight o'clock on Wednesday morning, at the very moment when the press release was being issued to the public, he arrived at Goldman, Sachs' offices on Broad Street and began to place a new round of telephone calls, searching for someone to step in and buy Getty Oil Company.

Boisi later described his contacts that morning as "courtesy" calls intended to alert those executives with whom he had discussed Getty Oil on Tuesday that nothing had been finalized by the directors, despite what they might read in the newspapers. He placed his calls first thing in the morning because he wanted to reach the prospective suitors before they saw their papers and were confused by the reports of a 15–1 vote. As it happened, most of the executives he spoke to had already heard the news.

His conversation with Al DeCrane early that Wednesday morning was typical.

"What is the status of things?" DeCrane wanted to know.

"At this point, the board has commented on the price of the Pennzoil offer—the $112.50—but the definitive merger agreement has not been executed and discussions are still going on. There is no binding agreement," Boisi answered.

"If someone came in, would that offer be heard by the Getty Oil board?" DeCrane asked.

"The board has agreed on price, but there are a number of substantive matters that have to be discussed and ultimately reflected in a definitive merger agreement, if indeed they can be agreed on, and then they will have to go back to the board," Boisi said. "Until you have a signed, definitive agreement, you don't have anything. The directors of Getty Oil have a fiduciary responsibility to consider a higher offer. If one comes in, they will have to consider it."

All through that day and the next, Boisi worked the telephone, reiterating to executives of Chevron, Texaco, and other interested buyers—including, at one point, the government of Saudi Arabia—that nothing was final. Boisi's view of the fifteen-to-one vote was that it reflected the board's opinion on the price of $112.50 only, that it did not address other important issues in the deal, such as those contained in the "Memorandum of Agreement" originally signed by Gordon, Liedtke, and Harold Williams. The directors of Getty Oil would welcome an offer that would take the company from the grasp of Gordon Getty and Pennzoil, Boisi said. This view was confirmed, when necessary, by Sidney Petersen, the chairman of the board himself. At one point, Petersen was called by an investment banker in New York who was jockeying to line up Texaco as a client. The banker wanted to know, once and for all, whether Getty Oil had a firm contract with Pennzoil and Gordon.

"We do not," Petersen answered. "The fat lady has not yet sung."

And yet there was evidence that even Boisi's firm, Goldman, Sachs, was confused about the issue. On the same day that Goldman's senior merger partner, Boisi, was assuring buyers that no deal was done, the firm sent Getty Oil a bill for $6 million, the fee due it under the terms of the Pennzoil takeover.

Meanwhile, negotiations to produce a final merger agreement with Pennzoil had suddenly stalled. The night before, at the Paul, Weiss offices, it had been agreed by everyone that Pennzoil's attorneys would write the first draft of a final document and present it to the other lawyers on Wednesday morning. But while Boisi placed his calls from his Broad Street office, the attorneys uptown did nothing. There was nothing they *could* do—the Pennzoil lawyers had failed to deliver their draft. Morning passed to afternoon, and still there was no word from either Baker & Botts or Paul, Weiss. Patricia Vlahakis, Bart Winokur, and other lawyers for both the company and the museum called several times to find out what was causing the delay. Each time they were told that the draft would be delivered by messenger shortly, and each time they waited in vain. It was not until eight-thirty in the evening, fully twenty-four hours after the board meeting at the Inter-Continental was concluded, that the Pennzoil lawyers finally delivered a draft.

By the standards of the merger game, this was an unusual delay; ordinarily, the bidding party tried to negotiate a final document as quickly as possible to prevent outsiders from stepping in. Sometimes the final contracts were even prepared in advance. The delay by Pennzoil's attorneys was never satisfactorily explained. There were some who questioned the experience of Liedtke's outside attorneys—Baker & Botts and Paul, Weiss, while universally regarded as excellent law firms, were not noted for their merger expertise. Perhaps it was this absence of experience in large-stakes mergers, the firms' unfamiliarity with the conventions of the game, that led them to take a somewhat lackadaisical view of time. On the other hand, the document they were drafting was highly technical and complex, and a great deal depended on the accuracy of its language. Even by the lightning clock of Wall Street, twenty-four hours was hardly an eternity.

Then, too, Hugh Liedtke and the other leading executives of Pennzoil seemed to believe that their deal with Gordon, the company, and the museum was essentially concluded, that what remained was merely the fine print of a formal document. On Wednesday, while his lawyers struggled to write that document, Liedtke, in his Waldorf apartment, accepted congratulatory phone calls from executives at Exxon and Amoco. In the afternoon, he met with Gordon at the Pierre to discuss their new partnership. Gordon suggested that the two of them fly to California together and "walk down the halls of the building" to introduce themselves to the employees. Gordon wanted to assure the employees that their futures were secure and that the company would be moving positively ahead.

"I think that's a good idea and I'd like to do it as soon as possible," Liedtke told Gordon. "But I think the decent thing to do would be to let Mr. Petersen have time to get his things together and get out of there. He's in the process, as I understand it, of doing that, so it seems to me that to wait two or three days would be the thing to do under the circumstances, rather than embarrass him further."

Indeed, Petersen had flown back to California the night before. His future with Getty Oil was now being measured in days. Apart from Petersen, Liedtke and Gordon discussed other top company executives, that afternoon, and they listed who they might like to keep and who they would fire for lack of trustworthiness.

For Gordon Getty particularly, it was a sweet moment. In his Pierre Hotel suite overlooking Central Park, as a cold mist fell on the city, the Getty scion contemplated the spoils of his victory. Maligned for so many years by his family and by the company's shifting management, Gordon finally was empowered over all of them. Naïvely, he believed that Getty Oil Company belonged to him.

A "MANLY" PLACE

For perfectly understandable reasons, the great majority of Americans in the early 1980s regarded the nation's large oil companies as the more or less interchangeable parts of a monolithic, nearly omnipotent enterprise known colloquially as Big Oil. To the average consumer of gasoline and motor oil, the differences between Exxon, Texaco, Chevron, Gulf, Shell, Mobil, and the rest seemed largely cosmetic—a matter merely of corporate logos, advertising jingles, and celebrity spokesmen. Gordon Getty was typical: when Pennzoil announced its tender offer in December 1983, all Gordon knew about the company was that it employed a legendary golfer, Arnold Palmer, as its television pitchman. The public's perception was rooted not so much in ignorance as in experience. At the gas pump, there were in fact no appreciable differences among the large oil companies. Their prices rose and fell more or less in tandem, their products were of similar type and quality, and their services were virtually identical. When change visited the industry—when prices rose or fell sharply because of OPEC, or when gasoline retailers suddenly eschewed traditional services in an effort to hold prices down—the large companies seemed to respond as if they were one. Indeed, many among the public believed that behind their Madison Avenue-designed façades, the big international concerns *were* a single enterprise, a conspiratorial oligopoly. In some areas of the oil business, particularly the refining and domestic distribution of oil products, federal and state government investigators had brought lawsuits alleging that Big Oil was, in fact, more collusive than competitive. The lawsuits failed to make their case. But while the Seven Sisters and their lesser siblings might be accused of cooperation on "macro" issues such as pricing and distribution, their control over the worldwide industry was profoundly undermined by OPEC, and in the 1980s they were fighting bitterly among themselves for control of declining domestic reserves.

In this contest for survival in a shrinking industry, played out largely beyond the public's view, the individual character of the large companies was clearly delineated. There were the shrewd aggressors, such as Boone Pickens' Mesa Petroleum and Hugh Liedtke's Pennzoil. There were family concerns like Getty Oil, weakened by generational change and by ill-advised diversification programs. There were the giant descendants of the Rockefeller Standard Trust, companies such as Exxon and Chevron that were untouchable in the raging takeover wars because of their size and relative efficiency. And then there was Texaco, the third-largest oil corporation in the country, long regarded as an aloof outsider to the oil fraternity—and a company which decided, on Wednesday, January 4, in the aftermath of Geoff Boisi's telephone call to president Al DeCrane, that it might like to remake its image.

If Gordon Getty had been asked that Wednesday what he knew about Texaco, he might have answered that his impressions of the company were derived mainly from Bob Hope, who for years had stood before the "Texaco Star" on television, relentlessly promoting its products and services. To the public, Texaco was one of the most visible of the large oil companies, since its principal strength, relative to its competitors, was its ability to sell gasoline. Texaco had for years been considered a leader in the "refining and marketing" or "downstream" side of the oil business, which was generally given short shrift by the other oil giants. With its modern refineries, omnipresent gas stations, and aggressive advertising, Texaco had made significant gains in this least profitable side of the oil business. Like the other Seven Sisters, Texaco's overall success rested on its ability to find and develop vast oil and natural gas reserves around the world, but to the public and even within the industry, its identity derived mainly from the sale of gasoline to consumers.

It was an unusually closed and autocratic company, dogged in the oil patch by a reputation for imperiousness, parsimony, and reactionary management. Texaco, as one financial journalist put it, was "the company that the rest of the industry loved to hate." It had been founded in 1902 at Spindletop, the great Texas gusher, and developed quickly into one of the world's leading oil producers, managing all the while to remain independent of the Standard Oil empire that swallowed so many growing companies. From the beginning, Texaco, known originally as the Texas Company, was torn by struggling factions in the oil patch and on Wall Street. The original partners were Joe "Buckskin" Cullinan, a Texas oilman, and Arnold Schlaet, a New York financier. As the company grew rich, the two battled for control; when the New Yorkers finally won and moved the company's headquarters to Manhattan, Cullinan raised a skull-and-crossbones flag above the company's Houston offices. But the gesture was to no avail. Over the next fifty years, Texaco was run by a succession of authoritarian chief executives who hoarded power tightly in New York and routed every decision through the company's Chrysler Building executive offices. Most prominent among them was the appropriately named Augustus C. Long, who held the chairman's title during the 1950s and 1960s, and who came to personify Texaco's despotic reputation and its remoteness from the fraternal brotherhood of the Texas oil business. Long's motto, they said in Texas, was "To hell with everybody else."

Despite the shocks caused by OPEC and despite the looming crises of declining oil reserves and Wall Street-instigated takeovers, little had changed at Texaco by 1980, when the regime of John K. McKinley came to power. The company's headquarters had been moved from Manhattan to the affluent suburb of White Plains, New York, where it was established on a sprawling, fortresslike corporate estate. McKinley himself reflected Texaco's enduring imperial culture. A tall, severe-looking man with thin lips, coal-black eyebrows, and large, protruding ears, he projected power and steely rationality. Some of his subordinates feared his rebukes, which were frequent and direct, and to them McKinley seemed like a cold, utilitarian schoolmaster sprung from the pages of Charles Dickens. In keeping with Texaco tradition, only a small handful of top executives enjoyed McKinley's confidences: Al DeCrane, the former Marine who became president when McKinley became chairman and chief executive; and James Kinnear, a Naval Academy graduate with extensive oil operations experience and, compared to his colleagues, an unusually approachable personality. Within the company and without, this group, known as "the triumvirate," was regarded by many as a kind of Politburo, with McKinley unquestionably in the role of premier. And though McKinley tried to decentralize some aspects of Texaco's operations, encouraging his division presidents to make their own decisions, he was unwilling or unable to shake off the customs of his company, which held that a chairman and chief executive should rule his corporate empire with an iron fist.

Certainly, that ethic was in keeping with John McKinley's own upbringing. His father, Virgil, an industrial management professor at the University of Alabama, was forty-six when McKinley was born. A strict man, Virgil McKinley was also a Baptist Sunday School teacher and an avid hunter, an avocation he passed on to his son. Though he saw most corners of the world, John McKinley remained at heart an Alabaman, a "very manly guy," as one of his friends put it, a Southerner imbued with the stiff discipline of the local football coach in Tuscaloosa, the legendary Paul "Bear" Bryant. As a captain during World War II, McKinley saw combat action in Europe and earned the Bronze Star. Upon his return to the United States, he joined Texaco as a chemical engineer and stayed for more than thirty years, rising through the company's hierarchy. His mentor, beginning in 1960, was Maurice Granville, who became chairman and chief executive in 1971. Granville promoted his protégé from the Texaco petrochemicals division to the post of president, and for nine long years, McKinley waited for his opportunity to finally take charge. Granville, like Augustus Long and the others before him, jealously guarded his decision-making authority before retiring in 1980. By then, it was clear that Texaco was facing a number of serious threats to its core businesses.

Since Granville had never effectively responded to the upheaval in the oil industry caused by OPEC, John McKinley came to power at a critical moment in Texaco's history. The company's downstream operations—its refining and marketing divisions—were collapsing under the pressure of aging plants and higher oil prices, which squeezed profit margins at the retail gas pump. More ominously, Texaco's basic oil and gas reserves were disappearing at an alarming rate—the company was running out of oil even faster than its besieged competitors, and it was having poor luck in exploration. Unleashed after nine years as Granville's second in command, McKinley moved decisively during the first years of his regime. He shut down half of Texaco's domestic gas stations, six of its fourteen refineries, and he modernized four other refineries. Willing to accept the hard truth about the company's rapidly depleting reserves, he approved major write-downs of previously bloated natural gas reserve estimates. And most boldly of all, he threw some $6 billion at Texaco's exploration-ists, hoping to turn up a dramatic new oil strike that would reverse the outward flow of the company's basic reserves.

A number of McKinley's reforms, though autocratically imple-mented, were nonetheless effective. The refining and marketing divi-sion, under Jim Kinnear's immediate supervision in Houston, Texas, staged an impressive turnaround. But by the fall of 1983, when news of dissension and turmoil at Getty Oil began to leak into the finan-cial press, Texaco's recovery was far from complete. Despite the bil-lions spent on exploration, Texaco, like its competitors, remained in what Boone Pickens would call a state of liquidation. It was selling its reserves much faster than it could replace them. Not only had the company failed to turn up any major discoveries, its average per-barrel "finding cost"—the amount of money required to discover a single new barrel of oil—was running as much as 50 percent above the industry mean. Under McKinley, Texaco had to spend between sixteen and twenty dollars per barrel in exploration costs, com-pared to an industry average of about twelve dollars. These high costs largely reflected the accounting consequences of an ambitious exploration program undertaken by McKinley. Still, there was a heightened mood of expectation and hope inside the company. Late in 1983, McKinley's hopes rested with an ambitious, highly expen-sive, collaborative oil exploration project known as "Mukluk," off the coast of Alaska. But the well turned out to be the most expensive dry hole in history, and when news of the failure reached Texaco's head-quarters in White Plains, McKinley knew that he would have to pass a large exploration write-off along to his stockholders. McKinley said later that the fiasco at Mukluk played a "subconscious" part in his decision-making during the first days of January 1984.

McKinley maintained a home in Tuscaloosa, Alabama, and he was there with his wife on Wednesday, January 4, when Al DeCrane called from White Plains to report on his latest conversation with Geoff Boisi. The relationship between Texaco's chairman and its president was formal, guarded, and unemotional, as were most of the relationships among top company executives. DeCrane, a youthful-looking, black-haired, bespectacled executive with an emphatically dispassionate manner, was in the midst of a subtle succession struggle with James Kinnear, Texaco's Houston-based vice-chairman and, on paper at least, DeCrane's equal in the Texaco hierarchy. Since DeCrane was in New York, however, working closely with McKinley, most company insiders figured that he had the inside track to the chairmanship when McKinley retired. McKinley, of course, was offering no guarantees.

The question of whether or not Texaco should bid for control of a rival oil company as large and rich as Getty Oil was a delicate one for DeCrane, even apart from its implications for the tangled politics of corporate succession. Certainly, DeCrane had to bring Boisi's suggestions about Getty Oil's availability immediately to McKinley's attention. But he could hardly presume to speak for the Texaco chairman. Hostile takeovers were a sensitive subject at Texaco headquarters. For decades the company had made it an informal rule, as a matter of both business practice and moral principle, that it would never make an unsolicited or unwanted takeover offer for another company. Texaco was perfectly willing to involve itself in a "friendly" merger at the polite invitation of another company's management. But it refrained from alienating the affections of other chief executives by attempting to acquire that which a seller was unwilling to part with.

Since all they knew about the situation at Getty Oil was what they read in the newspapers and what DeCrane gleaned from his brief conversations with Boisi and one or two other Wall Street bankers who wished to represent Texaco in an acquisition, it was hard for Texaco's top executives to be sure that Wednesday what kind of situation they were presently in. A policy of noninvolvement in hostile takeovers had been more easily adhered to in decades past, during the long era of unbridled prosperity and easy comradeship in the oil industry. But during the early 1980s, with Wall Street-funded aggressors such as Boone Pickens suddenly on the prowl, the mood in the oil patch was changed. There was less certainty, less stability, less trust. The merger bankers on the Street, with their deeply ingrained financial incentives, were the conduits of critical information. For Texaco, the acquisition of Getty Oil at the price levels being suggested by Goldman's Geoff Boisi—something over $120 per share—would represent a dramatic and inexpensive expansion of the company's reserves. If it acquired Getty, Texaco would virtually double its domestic oil reserves at a price somewhere around five dollars per barrel.

Such a bargain could not easily be ignored. But DeCrane and McKinley had been in this situation before, and they had been badly burned. Just over two years earlier, in July 1981, Seagram's, a diversified conglomerate best known for its whiskey, had made a hostile bid for Conoco, an oil company somewhat smaller than Getty Oil. Under siege, Conoco's chief executive, Ralph Bailey, had contacted McKinley to see if Texaco might be interested in rescuing his company from Seagram's clutches. Bailey knew that Texaco was after cheap oil reserves. McKinley told Bailey that he was only interested in making an offer if Bailey and his board of directors wanted to receive it; the Texaco chairman would do nothing "unfriendly." McKinley said further that if Bailey was willing to accept, Texaco was prepared to offer $85 per share, in cash, for all of Conoco's stock, a price higher than Seagram's original offer. A short time later, however, Bailey called back to say that he preferred not to make a deal with another oil company. Instead, he told McKinley, he was going to accept a takeover offer from Du Pont, the chemical giant, for somewhat less than $85 per share—and not all of it in cash. Bailey never said why he preferred to accept an inferior offer from Du Pont, but McKinley suspected it was because there was a greater chance that Bailey could retain his job if he was swallowed by a company with no oil expertise. There was some disappointment at Texaco over this missed opportunity, especially since McKinley could easily have won control if he had pressed his superior offer in an unfriendly way. Still, despite the disappointment, the Texaco chairman reendorsed his opposition to hostile deals. At the same time, though, he vowed that his company would work harder to close a merger if an opportunity as favorable as Conoco ever presented itself again.

Thus, the news on Wednesday that Sidney Petersen and the Getty Oil board of directors were looking for assistance from a "white knight" such as Texaco to rescue it from Gordon Getty and Pennzoil was greeted with a special sense of urgency in White Plains. Here, in the aftermath of the Conoco failure, was an opportunity for John McKinley to complete the turnaround at Texaco that he had been pursuing since his ascension to power some four year earlier.

"I think that if we wish to make a bid for Getty Oil, prompt action should be taken," DeCrane told McKinley when he called the chairman at his Alabama home on Wednesday morning, moments after he had been assured by Boisi that despite the press release's references to an "agreement in principle," Pennzoil and Gordon had not yet closed a deal.

"We're having studies made about Getty Oil's finances," DeCrane continued. "When will you be up here?"

"I'm flying up this afternoon," McKinley answered. "You go ahead and continue the investigations of all aspects of a bid. I'll meet with you when I arrive."

There was a Texaco corporate jet waiting for McKinley at the University of Alabama's airport. He arranged for a pilot to fly him up to White Plains at noon. Before he left, however, McKinley spoke with his golfing partner at Goldman, Sachs, cochairman John Weinberg, to be certain that what DeCrane was reporting to him was true. McKinley wanted to know whether what Boisi had said was accurate, that there was no deal between Getty Oil and Pennzoil and that Sid Petersen and his directors would like to receive a friendly offer from Texaco.

Weinberg said that was correct.

So John McKinley drove out to the Tuscaloosa airport, climbed aboard his waiting jet, and flew off to Texaco's headquarters in White Plains. It would take about forty-eight hours to close a deal of this magnitude. No one at Texaco wanted to let this one slip away.

22

BRUCE THE MOOSE

What Texaco needed that afternoon was an investment banker. McKinley knew as he flew north to White Plains that a kind of Wall Street feeding frenzy had erupted around Getty Oil—he knew it because bankers and lawyers were calling DeCrane, himself, and other Texaco executives every few minutes, seeking information, offering unsolicited advice, and above all hoping to be retained at the usual rates. Of the leading merger houses on the Street, there were only two (not counting dreaded Drexel Burnham Lambert, home of the hostile takeover artists, which McKinley would not have hired if it was the last firm on the planet) that were not already retained by one of the parties to the deal. Goldman, Sachs was already down to Getty Oil; Salomon Brothers to the museum; Lazard Frères to Pennzoil; and Kidder, Peabody to Gordon Getty. Of the two major firms still available, Morgan Stanley & Company, led by the semilegend Robert Greenhill, one of the early procreators of merger mania, was the obvious candidate to represent Texaco.

Like Goldman, Sachs, Morgan Stanley catered to the board rooms of the Fortune 500; like Goldman, too, it was regarded as a polite, stately, and elegant firm; and perhaps most importantly, John McKinley had developed close personal relationships with some of its leading bankers. In fact, one Morgan partner and his wife had visited socially with the McKinleys in Tuscaloosa over the Christmas holiday; it was through this friend that McKinley first began to hear that Getty Oil might come into play for Texaco. But McKinley, not wanting to surrender Texaco's decision-making to an advisor, delayed retaining Morgan Stanley until he had returned to White Plains and met with DeCrane late Wednesday afternoon. By then, it was too late. When a Texaco executive telephoned Morgan Stanley's offices around dinnertime, he learned that the firm was no longer available—it had been retained by someone else. The Texaco executives assumed correctly that the "someone" referred to by one of Morgan's senior merger partners during that telephone conversation was Chevron, which, McKinley had been told earlier in the day, was also preparing to make a bid for Getty Oil. The news reemphasized to McKinley and DeCrane that they were in a hotly competitive situation, one reminiscent of the Conoco deal. It also forced them to turn to the last major merger firm still available, First Boston Corporation, an investment house which, despite its name, was headquartered in Manhattan, and with which Texaco had no prior business relationship. More particularly, it pushed John McKinley and Al DeCrane into the eager arms of thirty-six year old Bruce Wasserstein, cohead of First Boston's aggressive merger division, and a *Wunderkind* even amid the precocity of modern Wall Street.

On the face of it, they were poorly matched. In background, personal style, and business philosophy, Wasserstein had little in common with the staid, disciplined leaders of Texaco's corporate empire. Far from being a combat veteran or military academy graduate, he had worked for Ralph Nader during the 1960s and dabbled in journalism and antipoverty work. His suits were wrinkled, he was overweight, and he was unrestrainedly verbose. Raised in Brooklyn in an intellectual, prosperous, and socially ascendant Jewish family, Wasserstein was above all else a prodigy. He matriculated at the University of Michigan at age sixteen and entered Harvard Law School at nineteen. Four years later, he had obtained not only his law degree, but a master's in business administration and a fellowship that allowed him to study economics at Cambridge University in England. After toying with less conventional careers, "Bruce the Moose," as he had been affectionately nicknamed on the streets of Brooklyn, accepted a job as an associate attorney at Cravath, Swaine & Moore, perhaps the most powerful corporate law firm in Manhattan. Told that he would become a partner in just a few years, Wasserstein was assigned by the firm in 1976 to assist First Boston's Joseph Perella, then head of the house's M&A division, with a relatively small merger deal Suddenly, Wasserstein was in his element—deal-making. The pace of mergers, the gaming, the money, the sense of power and control—all of it appealed to Wasserstein. Perella, the son of an Italian immigrant who had been hired by First Boston's Anglo-Saxon partners to bolster the firm's fading reputation, saw in Wasserstein's brilliance and innate aggression an important opportunity for his firm. He offered to double Wasserstein's fifty-thousand-dollar salary at Cravath and give him immediate responsibility in the First Boston merger division. Wasserstein accepted. Within five years, he was cohead of the department with Perella and had lifted First Boston into the major leagues of the merger game.

The attributes which led to Wasserstein and Perella's stunning success were precisely the opposite of those cultivated on the executive floors of Texaco headquarters. The First Boston bankers were aggressive, unruly, creative, egotistical, and openly emotional. As one journalist described it, "Wasserstein realized that the ability to structure a deal, to coin a memorable phrase that defined a strategy, to exhibit an unshakable sense of self-confidence when you presented your plan to the board of directors—and an uninhibited zeal for self-promotion when you won—were far more important traits than the old-line investment bankers' ability to cultivate a trim appearance and a comforting manner on the phone." Wasserstein was not alone in this realization—Marty Siegel, Gordon Getty's dashing retainer from Kidder, Peabody, was another prominent merger banker who relied on personality and self-promotion to win corporate clients—but Wasserstein extended the strategy to unprecedented lengths. Like Siegel, he made the blue-chip bankers at conservative houses such as Goldman, Sachs and Salomon Brothers uncomfortable. He lacked refinement. He seemed so interested in *money*.

On the morning of Wednesday, January 4, Wasserstein was awakened in a Houston hotel room, where he was staying on a short business trip, by a telephone call from one of his partners in New York. His partner told him about the press release that had just come over the news wire declaring that Pennzoil, Gordon Getty, the museum, and Getty Oil had reached "an agreement in principle." Wasserstein had been tracking Getty Oil's troubles for months, waiting for an opportunity to find a client and step into the fray. Now he realized that he would have to act quickly.

Throughout the day, Perella and Wasserstein worked the phones—Perella in Manhattan, his partner in First Boston's Houston office. They were searching not only for a client but for information. Wasserstein spoke twice to Marty Lipton, with whom he was friendly, and also with Larry Tisch. Six weeks earlier, when Tisch was named to the Getty Oil board, Wasserstein had taken the financier to lunch in Manhattan and pumped him for information about Getty's problems. He had stayed in touch since then, monitoring the shifting negotiations.

"Is there a deal here?" Wasserstein asked Tisch that Wednesday morning.

"No, not yet."

"Well, what I don't understand here is how the public is being treated."

"There are lots of things to be worked out here," Tisch replied. "I don't quite understand it, either."

"Listen, is there going to be a tender offer, a merger? What's the form of it?"

"Frankly, I don't know if it's worked out yet," Tisch answered.

"Let me ask you, if you don't have a deal yet, if I came in with someone who was willing to offer more and include the public, is that something that you would listen to?" Wasserstein asked.

"It all depends."

Wasserstein thanked Tisch and concluded their conversation. That was all the encouragement he needed. He swiftly began "chumming" for clients, eagerly telephoning executives at Mobil, Texaco, Phillips, and other oil companies, assuring them all that Getty Oil was there for the taking if only they would move quickly and aggressively. In Manhattan, Perella talked in rapid succession with investment bankers, arbitrageurs, stock analysts, and Wall Street lawyers, attempting in just a few hours to obtain a sophisticated understanding of the personalities and motives of Getty Oil's key executives and stockholders. By early evening, Perella felt that he was reasonably well informed. When Texaco, spurned by Morgan Stanley, finally called to say that it would retain First Boston, Perella said that he would immediately send a "team" of bankers, analysts, and merger lawyers to White Plains for a briefing. It was essential, both Perella and Wasserstein emphasized, that Texaco be prepared to act within twenty-four hours. They urged McKinley to arrange a Texaco board

of directors meeting for Thursday so that final authorization of a bid
for Getty Oil could be granted before Pennzoil or some other suitor
closed a deal.

It was nearly 11 P.M. by the time Perella and his colleagues arrived
at Texaco's suburban headquarters. McKinley had gone home, leaving the matter in DeCrane's hands. Wasserstein was on his way up
from Houston, but it would be nearly dawn before his jet landed at
tiny Westchester County Airport, just a few miles from the Texaco
complex. Until Wasserstein arrived, Perella would have to take the
lead for First Boston. Unlike Wasserstein, who described his mood
in the midst of nerve-racking, frenetic takeovers in terms of Bud-
dhist calm and serenity, Perella was a tense and moody man who did
not wear pressure well. Once, in the middle of a late-night merger
negotiation, Perella had been forced to leave a meeting in order to
have his acupuncturist relieve an intolerable pain in his back. Still,
Perella was confident, highly experienced, and well prepared to
advise Texaco's executives about their play for Getty Oil.

They met in a large conference room on the top floor of Texaco's
squat, concrete building. It was in some aspects an awkward gathering, since none of the principals had ever met. DeCrane said later
that he felt no tension between himself and the young, aggressive
bankers who arrived from First Boston, but it was clear from the
start that the advisors and the advised were operating under different assumptions. DeCrane was uncertain, for example, whether
Perella understood Texaco's longstanding policy that it would not
participate in hostile takeovers. Of course, it was not immediately
clear what relevancy that policy had in the present situation, since
the parties at Getty Oil were virtually paralyzed by animosity. Given
the recent history of Gordon Getty's relations with Sid Petersen, was
it possible for anyone to approach the company in a "friendly" manner? The question was never asked by DeCrane that night. In his
view, First Boston was retained merely for its expert advice, not to
formulate strategy. He assumed that First Boston knew about Texaco's decision in the Conoco deal. As DeCrane saw it, the purpose of
the eleven o'clock meeting with Perella was to review the information about Getty Oil gathered during the day by First Boston and
to hear the recommendations of the experts. If First Boston had its
own, aggressive ideas about how to attack Getty Oil and secure an
agreement, fine, the firm was entitled to express its opinions. But Al

DeCrane was not about to cede authority to mere retainers, especially ones with whom he had no prior experience. Advisors did not
make decisions. That was not how things were done at Texaco.

That Perella and his colleagues did not fully appreciate the peculiar corporate culture of their newfound client was evident from the
beginning of their presentation to DeCrane and the handful of Texaco finance men gathered in the conference room that night. Perella
began by laying out the situation, as it was presently understood by
himself and Wasserstein, in the excited tones of a wartime mercenary. DeCrane said little. He sat at the table and recorded Perella's
points on his notepad.

"Larry Tisch is the key board member, the key public shareholder," Perella said. "Wasserstein has talked to Tisch and he was told
that Tisch would look for a higher deal. Goldman, Sachs is mad and
embarrassed. They claimed it wasn't a fair value at $112.50. Goldman
has not reported that price in a fairness letter. They're embarrassed
that the board has been willing to go further and actually negotiate
at that price despite their unwillingness to give a fairness letter, and
they're mad at the museum for having said that it was prepared to go
forward at that price.

"The museum people felt that they were getting squeezed," Perella continued. "As they saw it, there was an outstanding tender offer
from Pennzoil that had the prospect of getting twenty percent of the
shares. And if Pennzoil did that, they would then be able to join with
Gordon, and that would put the museum in a squeezed minority
position. The museum feels that it needs to act. Lipton told Wasserstein that he thought there were about twenty-four hours in which he
was going to have to decide.

"We have learned that Gordon has talked about a sale at $125 per
share. Gordon is a buyer at a price and a seller at a price. Wasserstein
or one of our other partners has a contact who says that Gordon has
talked about where he is a buyer and where he is a seller, and that it
depends on the price. There's a can't-miss price at which Gordon will
be a seller. There are no signed documents. If you want to move, we'll
have to do it quickly."

Perella then ran down a list of possible competitors. Shell might
be interested in some of Getty Oil's properties, he said, but was not
considered a serious competitor for purchase of the entire company.
Chevron was a "definite yes"—they had retained an investment

banker, probably Morgan Stanley, and had been shopping on Wall Street that day for a merger lawyer. Mobil was a factor, Perella continued, and Gulf and Phillips were "possibly" interested.

"Well, you mentioned Mr. Getty," DeCrane intervened. "What about the company? What's their position?"

"One of our analysts has talked to Petersen, and he is defeated in his hope to retain control of the company. He said that he would entertain a sale," Perella answered.

There was some discussion about Pennzoil's option to buy 8 million Getty Oil shares at any time, an option that had been described in that morning's press release.

"That could be a way to take care of Liedtke," Perella said.

That is, it was predictable that the Pennzoil chairman would be upset if Texaco took Getty Oil away from him. By allowing Pennzoil to exercise its option to buy Getty Oil shares at the lower price of $112.50, Texaco could "take care" of Liedtke by letting him quickly sell those shares to Texaco at a higher price, clearing a handsome trading profit that would cover Pennzoil's expenses and soothe the chairman's ego. Perella also said, however, that the option was not enforceable until the deal with Getty Oil was final—and it was his view, of course, that the "agreement in principle" announced that morning was no agreement at all. Thus, as Perella saw it, if Texaco closed the deal and then wished to permit Liedtke to exercise his option, it would be simply buying Pennzoil off, not fulfilling any legal obligation.

Perella went on to say that if there was a problem with the deal, it probably involved Gordon Getty. Perella said that there was a question about whether, and under what circumstances, Gordon was permitted to sell the 32 million shares held by his family trust. According to the original trust document, Perella said, the trustee could only sell to "avoid loss" to the trust.

"So you might have to go the tender-offer route to merge him out or create concern that he will take a loss," Perella said. "The problem is that there seems to be no way to get Gordon on base first."

Perella had driven to the heart of the matter, and what he meant was this: if Texaco wished to buy all of Getty Oil's stock, it would have to outflank Gordon Getty. Gordon controlled 40 percent, the museum 12 percent, and the Getty Oil board 48 percent—the public's shares. Since Gordon could only sell if he faced a loss, Texaco might well have to force him into that position. If Texaco made an agreement with the museum and the Getty Oil board first, it would have secured more than 50 percent of the company's shares—enough to take control. It could then approach Gordon, explain that he was now in the minority, and threaten to squeeze him out at an unfavorable price if he did not agree to sell. Unquestionably, Gordon would then be facing a substantial loss. He would be legally permitted to sell. The problem, Perella implied, was that there was really no other way to go about it. If you approached Gordon first, if you tried to "get him on base," and offered to buy his shares at some price above $120, he might be legally unable to sell even if he wished to do so because he would not be facing a loss. Of course, despite the declarations that there was a "can't-miss" price at which Gordon would be willing to sell, neither Perella nor DeCrane nor anyone but Gordon knew whether, in fact, the Getty scion would be willing to surrender his joint bid with Pennzoil for control of the family company and sell his shares—at any price. Perhaps what Gordon wanted was not cash but power over Getty Oil. It was impossible for them to know. The advantage of Perella's strategy, his plan to make a deal first with the museum and the directors and then force Gordon into a sale, was that it rendered Gordon's ambitions moot, whatever they might be. Faced with the imminent prospect of a squeeze, Gordon would have no choice. He would have to sell. He would be the juice.

Al DeCrane would later claim that this strategy was never embraced by himself or John McKinley because it violated Texaco's policy of strictly avoiding unfriendly takeovers. To some, this claim by Texaco's top executives was plausible. To others, it was not. What is certain is that Perella articulated the "squeeze" strategy during his nocturnal meeting with DeCrane, that DeCrane and another Texaco executive in the conference room wrote down Perella's points, and that no one explained to Perella that his proposal violated the precepts of Texaco policy—they assumed Perella understood.

Without contradiction from their client, it was only natural that Perella, and later his partner Wasserstein, would describe Texaco's strategy options in the most direct, ruthless, and bloody terms. To begin with, such language reflected the flavor of their Wall Street culture. Moreover, First Boston's reputation and success in the merger business had been built on such clear-eyed, unsentimental analysis. To the freewheeling Wasserstein, particularly, a takeover was not an exercise in formalism, like a game of chess or croquet. As a child, Wasserstein rewrote the rules of his family's Monopoly game, passing out properties to the players before the dice were thrown, thus transforming the game into a test of gumption, strategy, and greed. It was the same for him now in the merger business. He and Perella lacked—or disdained—the refinement that would permit them to describe the amoral, even anarchic tactics of a takeover in language suitable for gentlemen.

Around two-thirty in the morning, Al DeCrane went home. Before he left, he instructed his team of Texaco finance men to continue their evaluation of Getty Oil's finances, based on publicly available documents and information supplied by First Boston, and to prepare for a meeting with himself and McKinley first thing in the morning. The Texaco directors were scheduled to convene for a special meeting at the White Plains headquarters building the next afternoon. If by then McKinley had reached a decision to go forward with a bid for Getty Oil, the directors would be asked to ratify his proposal at the board meeting. DeCrane told his finance men that McKinley would have to reach some conclusion in the morning, before the directors arrived.

Thursday broke clear and cold in peaceful Westchester County. By seven they were all assembled in the conference room once more: Wasserstein, in from Houston, DeCrane, McKinley, and, of course, Perella and the finance men who had never left the Texaco compound. Wasserstein was introduced to his new clients. He reported that before their arrival he had telephoned Marty Lipton at his Manhattan apartment—Wasserstein had not awakened the attorney even at such an early hour, since Lipton had been up at three, reviewing Pennzoil's draft of a final merger agreement—and that Wasserstein had confirmed that he was now working for a client, whose name he could not reveal, and that his client might have some interest in bidding for all of Getty Oil's stock. Lipton had said that he would be available to discuss the matter later, when he reached his office. As he reported this conversation with the museum's attorney to DeCrane and McKinley, Wasserstein emphasized, as he had done at every opportunity during the past twenty-four hours, that time was of the essence. Lipton was under tremendous pressure. He might sign an agreement with Gordon and Pennzoil at any moment.

For more than an hour, and with consultation from Wasserstein and Perella, McKinley and DeCrane reviewed the financial documents that had been prepared overnight by their subordinates. Using various assumptions about the amount of Texaco's offer, ranging as high as $130 per share, they examined the price per barrel that Texaco would be paying for Getty Oil's vast reserves. They talked about Getty's nonoil subsidiaries such as ERC and ESPN and about how much they would fetch on the market; McKinley had no interest in perpetuating Sid Petersen's diversification program and the Texaco chairman intended to quickly sell all of Getty Oil's nonoil assets if he bought the company. At a wide range of prices, it looked like a sweet deal.

What seemed to preoccupy John McKinley in the frantic hours before he met with his board of directors was not so much the financial advisability of acquiring Getty Oil—the deal was a good one for Texaco—but rather the willingness of the Getty Oil parties to receive his offer. So far, McKinley had involved himself only indirectly in the contacts with Lipton, Tisch, Petersen, and the others. He was relying on the representations of First Boston, which stood to make some $10 million if Texaco went ahead with its acquisition and less than $1 million if it didn't. Naturally, Wasserstein and Perella were urging McKinley to go forward. It wasn't that McKinley didn't trust his new bankers; it was that he didn't know them—he hadn't played golf with them or taken them hunting in the Alabama wetlands. They did not belong to his clubs; they did not share his culture. And so in the hours before noon, when McKinley made his most critical decisions, the Texaco chairman seemed to rely in his own mind on assurances from men of his own rank, his own station in corporate life.

A significant factor in his mind, for example, was the willingness of his friends at Morgan Stanley to represent Texaco in the deal on Wednesday, before the firm was hired by Chevron. Morgan Stanley understood Texaco, McKinley thought, and they wouldn't have solicited the company if the deal was improper. Similarly, McKinley was comforted by assurances from Marty Lipton and Larry Tisch (he had worked with Lipton in the past) who said that everyone involved, with the probable exception of Hugh Liedtke, would welcome rescue from a white knight. But McKinley did not call Gordon Getty himself. For an assessment of Gordon's willingness to sell, the Texaco chairman relied on Larry Tisch, who had been nominated to the Getty Oil board by Gordon but who had spoken against his sponsor at the marathon directors meeting earlier in the week.

Just before noon, McKinley telephoned Marty Lipton directly. He told the attorney that Texaco was the client Bruce Wasserstein had been hinting about all morning.

"We are about to have a directors meeting," McKinley said. "I am going to recommend to my board that we make a specific proposal regarding the acquisition of Getty Oil at a price materially higher than the current Pennzoil proposal. I don't know how long our meeting will run. We want to make sure that before you sign an agreement, you're aware of what our proposal is. If necessary, we'll abbreviate the meeting to the degree we can, but we do want to make this proposal to you. And in any event, we will be in touch with you by late this afternoon. If it is necessary, we are willing to communicate earlier."

Lipton replied that he would listen to Texaco's offer before he signed any final documents with Pennzoil and Gordon. He reiterated that the deal was still open, that Texaco was welcome to bid. As much as anything else, Lipton's assurances persuaded McKinley that the offer he was contemplating was proper. Marty Lipton, after all, had done much to invent the field of modern merger law. He was the father of the poison pill, consultant to the Securities and Exchange Commission, author of congressional legislation, the man of a thousand mergers. If Lipton said the deal was proper, then surely it was. Sid Petersen said so. Larry Tisch said so. John Weinberg, McKinley's golfing partner at Goldman, Sachs, said so. All of Texaco's own lawyers said so, including Morris Kramer, a partner of Joe Flom and a well-known merger specialist.

John McKinley decided to go forward.

The meeting with his board of directors that afternoon was largely uneventful. The Texaco finance men presented a number of hastily prepared charts and graphs. The directors, who included such corporate luminaries as retired IBM chairman Frank Cary and Capital Cities chairman Thomas Murphy, asked questions about debt levels, financing, the impact of fluctuating interest rates and oil prices, the amount of oil being acquired and at what price, possible antitrust and international trade considerations, and so on. At one point, Texaco's general counsel, William Weitzel, told the board that Texaco had been approached by Goldman, Sachs and others who said that Getty Oil was looking for offers. Weitzel said that all of the information in his possession suggested the matter of Getty Oil's future was still open. Morris Kramer, a senior partner with Skadden, Arps, the Wall Street law firm, confirmed Weitzel's assessment. Based on Wasserstein's recommendation, McKinley asked his directors for authority to make an offer up to $125 for all of Getty Oil's shares—a total of more than $9 billion, which would make the deal the biggest corporate merger on record. At ten minutes before five in the afternoon, the directors voted unanimously to authorize McKinley's proposal.

Wasserstein was in a waiting area outside the Texaco board room when the doors opened and McKinley stepped out.

"What should we do now?" McKinley asked.

Wasserstein had no idea what the correct answer was, since McKinley had not told him what the directors had decided. For all he knew, the board had turned down the proposal. So he said nothing and simply followed the chairman into his expansive suite of offices nearby. He sat down in a chair across from McKinley's desk.

McKinley picked up his telephone and called Lipton. "Marty, our board has approved making a firm proposal with our conditions to you. The way we would like to handle this is Bruce and a team of our people will be arriving at your office to discuss this with you. Have you signed anything yet?"

"No," Lipton answered.

"I assumed you would not sign anything until you heard my proposal."

Suddenly, alerted that the deal was on, Wasserstein was ecstatic. He and First Boston were about to make a deal to dwarf all others. McKinley placed a few more calls: one to John Weinberg at Goldman, Sachs, to inform him that Texaco was going to make an offer and would like to meet with Getty Oil's representatives in Manhattan later that evening; one to Sid Petersen, to say the same thing; and one to Larry Tisch, from whom McKinley hoped to obtain Gordon Getty's phone number. Gordon was still staying at the Pierre, and Tisch said that he would contact him there to see if he would be willing to receive a call from McKinley. The Texaco chairman said that he, Al DeCrane, and vice-chairman Jim Kinnear (who had been summoned to White Plains from Houston earlier that day) were leaving immediately for Manhattan, about an hour's drive away. Before the night was over, the future of Getty Oil would be decided, one way or another.

23

DENOUEMENT

All day, John McKinley had been worried that if Texaco did not move quickly enough, Marty Lipton and the representatives of Getty Oil management might sign a final agreement with Pennzoil and Gordon before Texaco was able to present its higher offer. As it happened, the concern over this possibility, expressed at regular intervals by Wasserstein and Lipton, was mainly, if not entirely a canard, an attempt to pressure Texaco into action. Although they represented parties on opposite sides of the takeover deal, Wasserstein and Lipton shared a strong desire to have *some* deal involving Texaco take place, and soon—Lipton because he wanted a higher price for the museum than the $112.50 put up by Pennzoil, and Wasserstein because his fees depended on Texaco's consummation of a takeover.

The truth was, however, that there was no serious prospect on Thursday that Pennzoil's final merger documents would be signed by anyone. On Wednesday, there had been no negotiations because the Pennzoil attorneys failed to deliver their drafts until late in the evening. On Thursday, Getty Oil's lawyers, led by Bart Winokur, responded in kind. Despite numerous phone calls from the panicky Pennzoil lawyers, who were beginning to hear rumors about possible interest in Getty Oil by Texaco, Chevron, and other large companies, Winokur and his team of attorneys declined to meet until six in the evening. The reason, Winokur said, was that he and his colleagues were studying complex legal and financial issues which

Pennzoil's lawyers had inexplicably failed to address in their draft. All afternoon, fearing that Winokur was only filibustering while Goldman, Sachs sought a white knight to take the company away from Pennzoil, Hugh Liedtke's lawyers pressed for a meeting. They were worried that an outsider might enter the bidding. In California that afternoon, a court hearing had been called by the beneficiaries of Gordon's family trust—the Georgettes, and the children of J. Paul Jr. and Ronald Getty. Having read in the newspapers about Gordon's takeover alliance with Pennzoil, the beneficiaries were seeking a temporary restraining order barring Gordon from going ahead with the deal until it was reviewed by his family. Tim Cohler had been dispatched to Los Angeles to argue that the order should not be granted, but the Pennzoil attorneys were afraid that if it was, their final documents might not be signed for days.

Pressed for a meeting on Thursday afternoon, Bart Winokur said he wasn't ready—over the telephone, he ticked off a list of important issues that were not addressed in Pennzoil's documents and said that he wanted to draft responses before sitting down for face-to-face negotiations. Particularly, Winokur said he was concerned about a number of complicated issues surrounding the sale of Getty Oil's ERC insurance subsidiary. Under the complex formula devised at the Inter-Continental Hotel by Marty Lipton, the sale of ERC would determine the final price paid to shareholders—Geoff Boisi had withheld his fairness opinion pending the outcome of negotiations over that formula. Desperate to make some progress, Pennzoil's lawyers finally suggested that they set aside the ERC problem until later and meet to see if they could reach agreement on the other problems raised by Winokur. A meeting was set for six o'clock at the Paul, Weiss law offices in Midtown. Winokur and the other Getty Oil lawyers agreed to attend.

Patricia Vlahakis, like Winokur, had spent the day in her office on Park Avenue reviewing Pennzoil's documents and drafting responses for negotiation. She, too, had concerns about a number of tax and legal issues that had not been addressed in Pennzoil's first draft. Around five-thirty, informed by Pennzoil's lawyers about the six o'clock meeting at Paul, Weiss, Vlahakis gathered up her things, shut the door to her office, and rode the elevator up to Marty Lipton's floor. She found her mentor and senior partner in his office and told him that she was leaving for a negotiating session with Pennzoil at Paul, Weiss.

"I don't want you to go to that meeting," Lipton responded. "There is a team of people from Texaco on their way down here from White Plains. I need you to stay and participate in the meetings with them this evening."

Vlahakis had heard reports from Lipton earlier that an outside bid for Getty Oil was possible, but she had not known that a serious offer was imminent. She asked him what she should do about the negotiations with Pennzoil.

"Call them and tell them you're not coming. See if you can talk with them about some of the points over the phone."

Vlahakis returned to her office and made the call. Bill Griffith, the Pennzoil attorney she spoke to, said that no one was available to discuss the issues with her by telephone. Vlahakis said that she could not attend the meeting at Paul, Weiss.

By the time Vlahakis returned to Lipton's floor, the bevy of lawyers, bankers, and executives from Texaco had arrived. After a few moments of mingling and introductions in Lipton's expansive office, the group, including Lipton, Texaco vice-chairman James Kinnear, and general counsel William Weitzel, sat down for a catered dinner.

"I've been authorized by Harold Williams, the museum president, to meet with you," Lipton began. He handed Kinnear and Weitzel a sheet of paper. William Weitzel was a balding, intense, genial man who had been recruited to Texaco from a career in criminal prosecution in order to upgrade the corporation's legal department. Befriended early on by McKinley, who lived nearby him in Connecticut, Weitzel advanced quickly and became a member of Texaco's tight inner circle when his friend and mentor became chairman in 1980. He was ultimately responsible for Texaco's legal strategy.

The sheet of paper passed out by Lipton contained a list of contract provisions. "These items are absolute necessities for any type of agreement with the museum," Lipton declared. He went through the list, explained what each item was and why it was necessary. The first question was price—how much was Texaco willing to pay? There followed some technical provisions concerning how the museum would be paid for its shares and whether it would be paid regardless of Texaco's arrangements with Gordon and the company. Finally, there was an entry that read, "Indemnity—will the museum be fully indemnified against any claims by or through Getty, Pennzoil, and the Sarah C. Getty Trust?"

"What do we need an indemnity for?" Weitzel asked. If it was granted, Texaco would assume all responsibility for any lawsuits against the museum arising from the deal, including its legal fees.

"The museum has had a long history of disagreements and upsets and lawsuits involving the museum shares and Gordon's shares and the company," Lipton answered. "There are a lot of bad feelings out there and there is constant litigation. My client needs an indemnity as an essential element for his peace of mind. You don't have any exposure on this indemnity that I know of, except maybe some legal fees, but I have to have it because when my client finishes making a deal with anybody, he is going to want to have some peace of mind that he's finally through with all this squabbling. Whether he makes a deal with Texaco or Pennzoil or anybody else, he's going to require an indemnity."

Weitzel made no commitment. He was trying to test Lipton, to see which of these points were really "essential terms" and which could be negotiated. And despite his worries about the museum's "peace of mind," what Lipton seemed most concerned about was the price Texaco was willing to pay. No matter how Kinnear and Weitzel tried to avoid the subject, Lipton returned to it.

"Are you prepared to give your price?" Lipton wanted to know.

"No, we are not." Texaco had decided that Gordon should hear the price first—without him, there could be no deal. Gordon, not the museum, was the question mark.

Lipton was angry. "You know, there's no point in us discussing this unless you are going to give me a price."

"We're not. Look, you've got like ten or twelve percent of the stock. Gordon Getty has like forty percent. Any price we give you will just become a floor price when we talk with Mr. Getty. So we're not giving you a price until we see Mr. Getty."

It was apparent to Weitzel that Lipton was going to try every trick he could think of to learn Texaco's price. It seemed to Weitzel that Lipton launched into "some theatrics" in order to force them to respond. Lipton would walk out of his office, saying that there was no point in having further discussions, and Weitzel and Kinnear would have to follow him into the hallway and persuade him that they should at least talk about the items on Lipton's list other than price. And so, pouting and reluctant, Lipton would return to his office, only to bring up the question of price again and storm into the hall. Eventually, Lipton gave up and the meeting concluded.

As soon as Weitzel and Kinnear left to consult with their advisors in the conference room, Bruce Wasserstein came in to visit with Lipton. Lipton asked him if he knew what price Texaco was going to offer. Not so shy as his client, Wasserstein volunteered that Texaco would be offering at least $120 per share, probably more, but that he could not be certain of the exact number. Thus informed, Lipton sought out Wasserstein's clients and began to lobby them for an offer price of $125 per share. Again and again, Lipton insisted to Weitzel and Kinnear that if Texaco offered anything less than $125, the deal would never go through.

"There's a real urgency about this," Lipton said. "There is concern among the Getty Oil directors and advisors that Gordon and Pennzoil will make some type of deal that will end up being less advantageous to the shareholders than what was in the press release. The board therefore feels some pressure to negotiate with Pennzoil. At the same time, they're really unhappy with the price and they encouraged Goldman, Sachs to look for other bids. You need to move quickly if you want to bid. And if you'll come up with a price of $125, I'm authorized to enter into an agreement with you right now."

Despite Lipton's impressive histrionics, Weitzel resisted. He and Kinnear refused to discuss a final price until after they had met with Gordon.

"Well, Gordon Getty is going to be in bed. If you want to see him, you'd better get over to see him soon," the Texaco executives were told. Gordon was often asleep before ten, they were informed, and it was already eight-thirty.

Toward that end, Weitzel and Kinnear twice telephoned John McKinley at the Carlyle Hotel on Madison Avenue, where they had dropped the chairman off on their way to Lipton's office. They wanted to know if he had yet been able to arrange a meeting. The first time, McKinley said that he had gotten in touch with Gordon but that nothing had been arranged because Gordon had to locate and summon all of his advisors to the Pierre Hotel. The second time, McKinley said that a meeting had been set for nine o'clock.

Weitzel and Kinnear stood up and told Lipton that they would see him later, after their critical meeting with Gordon. Some of Texaco's advisors stayed behind at Lipton's offices to continue their discussions.

STEVE COLL

In a car chauffeured by a Texaco driver, Weitzel and Kinnear rode over to the Carlyle. They went up to McKinley's room, briefly reported on their negotiations with Lipton, and then left together for the Pierre Hotel. They arrived in the ornate lobby precisely at nine, were joined by Wasserstein, and then rode the elevator to Gordon's floor. Tom Woodhouse of the Lasky firm was in the elevator car as they went up, but none of the Texaco executives knew him, and it wasn't until all of them knocked on the same door that they were introduced.

With Tim Cohler at the court hearing in California, Gordon's only advisors that night were Marty Siegel and Tom Woodhouse. Their first session with the Texaco executives lasted about one hour. For the second time in five days, the chairman of a major American oil company had come pilgrim-like to Gordon Getty's two-room suite at the Pierre in the hope that he might enrich his enterprise through Gordon's cooperation. The contrast between John McKinley and Hugh Liedtke was vivid, however. Whereas on Sunday, Liedtke had been relaxed, open, and direct, putting Gordon at ease with stories about his early days in the oil patch with Gordon's father, McKinley seemed reserved and somewhat uncomfortable. He tried to warm Gordon up by talking to him about Texaco's charitable sponsorship of the Metropolitan Opera's radio broadcasts. When that conversation ebbed, the Texaco chairman emphasized that he had come with only the most friendly intentions. It was not clear, though, whether the message was getting through to Gordon, even though McKinley believed it was.

"We only want to do something if you want an offer from us and you feel you're in a position to receive an offer from us," McKinley said.

"I'd like to receive an offer—a nice, high one," Gordon answered. "At one price, I'm a buyer. At another price, I'm a seller."

This was in keeping with the advice of Gordon's investment banker, Marty Siegel. Siegel had told Gordon that there was a "range of values" for Getty Oil, beginning at the low end at about $110 and topping out at about $130 per share. It was Siegel's advice, simply stated, that Gordon should buy low and sell high. At $112.50, the Pennzoil price, Gordon was a buyer—he would take control of Getty Oil. At some price closer to the high end of Siegel's range, Gordon might agree to sell his family trust's shares.

Several problems kept cropping up during Gordon's first and somewhat awkward session with McKinley that night. One question was whether Gordon was free to sign any agreement at all because of the temporary restraining order obtained by his relatives late that afternoon in California. (Cohler had telephoned before McKinley's arrival to say that he had been unable to block the order, that he expected it would be lifted sooner rather than later, but at the moment Gordon could not sign any agreement with anyone.) Similarly, there were questions about the "Dear Hugh" letter Gordon had signed earlier in the week with Pennzoil, wherein he had promised to seek the removal of Getty Oil's board of directors if it failed to approve the joint takeover with Pennzoil. In answer to questions from McKinley and Weitzel, who knew nothing about the letter, Tom Woodhouse produced a copy for their review. Woodhouse pointed out that before Gordon had signed the letter, he had inserted the phrase "Subject to my fiduciary obligations" before each binding clause, which meant that if Texaco's offer was high enough, Gordon might have a legal responsibility as trustee of his family fortune to accept Texaco's money.

"It's my understanding that you would be free to and indeed should receive any higher offers," Woodhouse advised Gordon after reviewing the letter with Weitzel.

"That's my understanding, too," Gordon replied.

Gordon and McKinley began to fence back and forth, each attempting to get the other to name a price first. Their conversation went on in fits and starts for perhaps half an hour. Gordon was becoming frustrated. In the midst of this sparring, there was a knock on the door and Larry Tisch was ushered into the suite. Tisch had been summoned by Gordon from an uptown restaurant, where he was celebrating a friend's birthday; the balding financier was still in his tuxedo. Informed of Texaco's overtures, Tisch began to mediate, encouraging both Gordon and McKinley to identify a fair price.

"The Getty Oil board is feeling very pressured by the Pennzoil tender and I think it's in the interest of both Gordon and the company to see if there's a higher price available," Tisch said.

Still, McKinley would not name his price; he was still attempting to force Gordon to mention a number first. Thus stalemated, someone finally suggested that the two sides caucus separately to see if they could arrive at a solution. Gordon had mentioned earlier that his wife, Ann, was asleep in the bedroom, so McKinley and his Texaco colleagues agreed to retreat to the Pierre's lobby for their meeting. Around ten o'clock, they left the suite.

When the door was shut behind them, Marty Siegel picked up the telephone and called Marty Lipton at his office. So many times before, in critical situations, Lipton had been able to find the common ground and negotiate a solution.

"We'd like you to come right over to the Pierre," Siegel said. "There's been a meeting between Gordon and McKinley and it did not go well. We think it might be helpful if you came over."

Lipton said that he was on his way.

In an elevated alcove of the Pierre's lobby, the Texaco executives and advisors sat around a coffee table and tried to determine what they should do next. There was a discussion about Gordon Getty's character, as it pertained to bargaining over price. The question was whether the psychology of the meeting suggested that McKinley would be better off just shooting his wad, offering his highest price from the start, or whether he should offer a lower price and let Gordon try to bargain.

"I personally read Mr. Getty as being a sort of genteel person who would not like to haggle. I think we would be best off just giving him whatever is the best price that we are willing to offer," Weitzel advised. It wasn't clear to Weitzel what that best price was. The directors had authorized a maximum of $125, but it wasn't clear whether McKinley would go that high.

"I think you should offer the $125," Weitzel urged McKinley. "I think from my conversations with Lipton that it would probably be acceptable to the museum, and also, I don't think this is a situation where haggling will be successful."

McKinley, however, was not giving a clue as to his intentions. He was only asking the others for their opinions.

In the middle of this discussion, Marty Lipton walked into the Pierre lobby. He spotted Wasserstein and the Texaco executives and approached their table.

"We met with Gordon, but it's not clear to us that he wants to receive a proposal from us. We're concerned about what his position is, whether he would be receptive to an offer," Lipton was told. As the museum's attorney listened, it seemed to him that Texaco's executives were deeply confused by their meeting with Gordon and that they were uncertain what to do next or what Gordon would like them to do next.

"Based on the conversations I've had in the past with him, I think he would be interested in receiving a proposal," Lipton finally said. "I think it's best that I go upstairs and talk to the people in Mr. Getty's suite."

When Lipton arrived, he greeted his close friend Larry Tisch. The Texaco executives believed that Tisch was Gordon Getty's friend, but that was not how Tisch regarded his presence at the Pierre that night. He had met Gordon no more than three times; he did not consider the Getty scion to be his friend. It was Marty Siegel who had summoned Tisch from the uptown birthday party, and it was Marty Lipton to whom Tisch felt loyalty. Neighbors in Manhattan, veterans together of other takeover wars, Lipton and Tisch were close confidants.

Briefed on Gordon's impasse with McKinley, Lipton proposed a solution. He asked Gordon whether, assuming McKinley offered an acceptable price, he would be willing to sign a document saying that except for the restraining order imposed by the California courts, Gordon would like to sell all of his shares to Texaco. With such a written assurance from Gordon, Lipton said, Texaco could close its deal with the museum and the company and then buy Gordon's shares when the court order was lifted. After discussing the idea with Tom Woodhouse, Gordon said that Lipton's proposal was acceptable. The question now was price. They went back and forth for a while, but finally, Gordon agreed that if the price was $125 per share, he would accept Texaco's offer.

Armed with that declaration, Lipton and Tisch left Gordon's suite and returned to the hotel lobby. The Texaco group was still sitting at its table, talking.

"Have you all got a price that you're willing to give Mr. Getty?" Lipton asked as he approached them.

"Yes," McKinley answered.

"What is it going to be?"

"Well, I was thinking of something along the lines of $122."

"That just won't do it," Lipton insisted. "Gordon is never going to agree to that."

Tisch joined in. "That's not going to be enough. You need to do $125 if you're going to get his agreement."

"If I were to go to $125, what do you think would be the reaction of the Getty Oil directors?" McKinley asked Tisch.

"I've spent a couple of days with those people and I am confident that the Getty board would fully support an acquisition by Texaco if you're offering all shareholders $125 per share. I think you ought to go upstairs and say $125 because anything less won't do it."

The badgering of McKinley continued even in the elevator. By the time they reached Gordon's door, none of them was entirely certain what the Texaco chairman would do.

When they entered, there was at first some general conversation unrelated to price. Finally, McKinley turned to Gordon.

"I am prepared to make an offer since you said you would be happy to receive one. I've given it a lot of thought as to what the price should be. I had been thinking of a price of about $122.50." McKinley paused and curled his lips into a half-smile. "But I have gotten some indications here that there is another price that would be more agreeable to you, and so I am prepared to offer—"

Before McKinley could finish his sentence, Gordon burst in. "I accept!" he declared. The suite erupted in laughter. Gordon calmed himself. "Oh. You are supposed to give the price first."

"Yes," McKinley said. "I am prepared to go to $125."

"Fine," Gordon replied. "Fine. Thanks. I accept."

There ensued a discussion of the document earlier proposed by Lipton, wherein Gordon would declare his intention to sell to Texaco but for the order imposed by the California courts. As the others talked, Lipton sat down on a couch and began to write the document out by hand. As Marty Siegel watched him, he thought back to a similar scene some months before, at the Lasky offices in San Francisco, where Lipton had written out the plainly worded standstill truce in his own hand. That agreement had lasted just a few weeks. Siegel hoped this one would be more enduring.

When Lipton was finished, Tom Woodhouse telephoned his partner Tim Cohler in California, explained what had transpired, and read him Lipton's draft. Cohler suggested a few changes which were negotiated with Lipton, and then a new copy was written out. Finally, around eleven-thirty, the document was ready for Gordon's signature.

The Getty scion hesitated. "Moses Lasky has been my family's lawyer for many years," Gordon said. "In my mind, he knows more about the history of the family trust than anybody else alive. With something this important, I would feel more comfortable if Mr. Lasky had reviewed it." Turning to Tom Woodhouse, Gordon said several times that his decision to consult Lasky, who had remained in San Francisco since the Pennzoil tender was announced, was in no way a reflection of his opinion of Woodhouse's abilities. Whether he did or not, Woodhouse assured his client that he took no offense.

They telephoned Lasky at home and at his office and found that he had gone out to dinner and that no one knew where he could be reached. They left urgent messages, but it was not until well after midnight when Lasky returned the calls, listened to the document drafted by Lipton, and said that he thought Gordon was doing the right thing. Thus assured, Gordon signed the document and made arrangements to begin final negotiations with Texaco the next day. They had, after all, reached only an agreement in principle, or something like it.

Later on, there would be a great deal of discussion about Gordon Getty's state of mind that Thursday night at the Pierre Hotel. The central question was whether the conversations and negotiations that passed in his suite that evening constituted a "squeeze" of the sort Bart Winokur had warned about one year before. Had Gordon been forced to sell to Texaco? It depended entirely on who one asked. John McKinley, for one, adamantly insisted that if Gordon had not wished to receive an offer from Texaco, then he and his team of executives and advisors would have walked away from the entire deal—that he would only have bought Getty Oil if all three parties agreed to sell. That was in keeping, McKinley said, with Texaco's policy of only making friendly acquisitions.

For his part however, Gordon had the strong impression that he had no choice but to sell to Texaco—that if he didn't, McKinley would make his deal with the directors and the museum, locking up 60 percent of the company's stock, and then would squeeze Gordon out. Gordon would be the juice. McKinley never said he would do so; in fact he said the opposite. Gordon merely drew the inference. Gordon said later, for example, that he had no idea whether his takeover agreement with Pennzoil was still in effect that night—all he knew was what his lawyers told him. And everyone around him advised that he should sell. Of course, even if Gordon had wanted to sell, it was essential for everyone involved that he at least *appear* to have no choice in the matter. The provisions of the trust document held that the family's Getty Oil stock could only be sold to avoid a loss. And so as it had from the beginning of Getty Oil's difficulties, the question of Gordon's motives, his ambitions, remained in doubt.

"I wasn't in every room at every time," Gordon Getty said later, attempting to explain his critical decision that Thursday night. "The Getty board, many of them were treating me as an enemy at that time and wouldn't necessarily tell me what they knew. Getty management, even more so. What little I did know—I wouldn't have known independently if I was free to deal with Texaco when Texaco came along. I wouldn't have dealt with them without my attorney's advice on the matter. My attorneys told me that they thought I was free, but they weren't sure of it and they wouldn't advise that I deal with Texaco without the indemnification [against future lawsuits] from Texaco. And if I were free to deal with Texaco, however, I had a pretty clear fiduciary duty to deal with them because it was clearly in the interest of the [family] trust to make the Texaco deal as opposed to the Pennzoil deal. And besides, I probably no longer had the option of making the Pennzoil deal at that point in time, with the museum and the board lined up in a different way and the Texaco deal being clearly in the interests of all stockholders other than the trust—it meant that the Pennzoil deal was probably no longer obtainable once Texaco came along. So if I was free to accept the Texaco offer, I certainly should. And so I did."

And with that, Gordon Getty ended his family's century-old ownership of Getty Oil Company; indeed, he ended Getty Oil Company itself. But he did not, as it turned out, manage to sweep away his troubles.

24

BIG BOYS

It was a sleepless weekend for most of them, and by Sunday it was over. John McKinley had won; Getty Oil belonged to Texaco. Really, the suspense was over by dawn on Friday, just eight hours after Lipton, Tisch, Wasserstein, McKinley, and the rest of them cleared out of Gordon Getty's suite and returned to Lipton's midtown offices. All through the night, Lipton sat face to face with Texaco's lawyers and executives, negotiating a final agreement to sell the museum's shares. Lipton got virtually everything he asked for, including an indemnification against all future lawsuits arising from the deal. The bespectacled attorney assured Texaco that it faced ho serious liability by offering this guarantee, except perhaps for some legal fees that might arise if the museum was forced to defend nuisance lawsuits. He showed them Pennzoil's "Memorandum of Agreement" with Gordon Getty and said that it did not represent a binding contract. Lipton did not, however, produce the notes of Getty Oil's marathon board meeting at the Inter-Contintental; nor was he asked to do so. In Lipton's adamant view, the board's 15–1 vote to approve the $112.50 offer from Pennzoil was merely an authorization to negotiate, not a final deal. There was nothing for Texaco to worry about, Lipton said. They should just sign the documents.

And this was Marty Lipton, after all, a kind of roving corporate statesman, renowned not merely for his ability to consummate deals, but for his integrity and his vision of the merger business. Even that night, there was developing among Texaco's leading executives a deep respect for Lipton, a dependence upon him. It was not merely Lipton's reputation. It was his position in the deal. As representative of the Getty Museum, Lipton was forced to mediate the bitter resentments between Sid Petersen and Gordon Getty, resentments which predated Lipton's involvement in Getty Oil's affairs by more than a year. To many of those involved, and particularly to the Texaco executives, Lipton had acquitted himself beautifully. At the critical turning points—in London, in San Francisco, at the Inter-Continental—he had managed to forge a solution, even if it was only temporary. Now Lipton was again in the middle. Summoned by Marty Siegel, he had come that Thursday night to the Pierre and had pushed both Texaco and Gordon to an agreement. When he returned to his law offices after midnight, he continued his work, quickly negotiating a final document with Texaco that would become the prototype for agreements between Texaco and Getty Oil, and between Texaco and Gordon. Lipton had accomplished in less than twelve hours what Pennzoil had failed to accomplish in more than two days: he had closed the deal. Lipton and his client would come to view this triumph as a by-product of the attorney's long experience in mergers and acquisitions; Hugh Liedtke and his advisors would regard Lipton's success rather differently.

Indeed, for Pennzoil's executives and advisors, the denouement was devastating. Arthur Liman, the Manhattan lawyer who had done so much, he thought, to close a deal with Getty Oil's directors at the Inter-Continental, arrived at his office Friday morning to find that Texaco had issued a press release over the broad tape declaring that it had made a deal to buy the museum's shares for $125, that Getty Oil's directors had "approved in principle" a similar transaction for the public shares, and that Gordon Getty supported the takeover. Stunned and angry, Liman picked up his telephone and called Marty Siegel, Gordon's investment banker.

"Martin, the announcement on the tape has just been read to me," Liman said.

"Arthur, I'm sorry," Siegel replied.

"Marty, I am not going to be the messenger to Liedtke this time. You better call Hugh Liedtke and tell him yourself about this and not slink off."

Liman said later that he did not telephone Marty Lipton, the man with whom he had so successfully negotiated in the hallways of the Inter-Contintental, because he was too upset.

Apoplexy was the mood in Hugh Liedtke's Waldorf apartment as well. When Liman telephoned to report on his conversation with Siegel, it became clear to Pennzoil's chairman that Gordon had betrayed him—either that, or Gordon had been forced into betrayal by Texaco and Marty Lipton. At first, Liedtke had hoped that there was still a chance to rescue Gordon from Texaco's clutches and to renew their joint takeover bid. When he heard from Liman, he knew there was no hope: Gordon had been thrown over. After a discussion with his top executives, Liedtke decided that the only way to frighten off Texaco was through a direct threat to the Getty Oil board of directors. In addition, if he was now going to lose Getty Oil to Texaco, Liedtke wanted to be compensated for his trouble: he wanted to exercise the 8-million-share option, the one Joseph Perella of First Boston had earlier identified as a way to "take care" of Liedtke if Texaco won out. If Texaco honored the option, Pennzoil could at least earn many millions in trading profits on the deal. Just after noon, Liedtke dispatched from his suite the following telegram, addressed to the directors of Getty Oil Company in Los Angeles:

"Gentlemen: We expect you to comply with the terms of your agreement with Pennzoil Company approved by your board by a 15–1 vote only three days ago, including specifically the option granted to Pennzoil to purchase eight million Getty treasury shares at $110 per share. If you fail to keep your agreement, we intend to commence actions for damages and the shares against Getty Oil Company, your individual board members, the Getty Trust, the Getty Museum, and all others who have participated in or induced the breach of your agreement with us. In your evaluation of your course of action, we trust that you will consider not only your obligations to us but also the significant antitrust issues presented by the Texaco offer, your obligation to those who have made significant investment decisions in Pennzoil securities based on your public announcement as well as the future well-being of your employees. Very truly yours, J. Hugh Liedtke, chairman of the board and chief executive officer, Pennzoil Company."

When Liedtke's message arrived, however, the Getty oil directors were not available to consider its contents. They were at that moment in the midst of a "telephonic board meeting," a conference call linking directors scattered about the country in Los Angeles, New York, Chicago, Phoenix, Philadelphia, Austin, Tulsa, and Riverside, California. The purpose of the meeting was to give approval to the deal with Texaco—a kind of approval different from what the directors believed they had given Pennzoil earlier in the week.

"Would acceptance of the Texaco offer preclude consideration of any higher offers?" Getty Oil director Henry Wendt asked at one point during the hour-long conversation.

"Texaco contemplates that its agreement with the company would prevent the company from seeking further offers or disclosing any proprietary information or discussing the possibility of any other offers with others," Geoff Boisi answered. "Texaco now has a lockup on the museum shares. McKinley expects that no further action will be taken to frustrate the deal."

McKinley also expected, as it happened, that no steps would be taken to "take care" of Hugh Liedtke. The 8-million-share option would not be honored, he said—there was no deal with Pennzoil to require it. Of course, that view was shaped by the advice McKinley received from his own lawyers, from Marty Lipton, from the representatives of Sid Petersen and the Getty Oil directors. *Everyone* McKinley talked with told him that there was no deal with Pennzoil. That Liedtke had focused on the option in his telegram seemed to some evidence that Pennzoil's chairman himself didn't believe that he had a deal, that he was interested primarily in a profit for his trouble. In any event, both McKinley and Sid Petersen elected to ignore the threats in Liedtke's telegram that Friday. Indeed, Petersen decided to preempt those threats: his general counsel, Dave Copley, advised that Getty Oil file suit in Delaware seeking judicial confirmation that there was no deal with Pennzoil. That way, subsequent lawsuits would likely be tried in Delaware, a state renowned for sophisticated judges and a legal system favorable to corporations. Petersen authorized the strategy and a lawsuit was filed that Friday afternoon.

While Texaco's triumvirate—McKinley, DeCrane, and Kinnear—shuttled back and forth between Manhattan and White Plains, negotiations proceeded largely without complication throughout the weekend. McKinley and Petersen, the two chief executives, spoke at length about severance pay for all of those Getty Oil employees who would inevitably be considered "redundant" by Texaco once the merger was completed. At the Pierre, Gordon and his attorneys spent much of their time negotiating with the rest of Gordon's family and their lawyers, trying to persuade them that Texaco's offer was a good one, and that there was no choice but to accept it. Late Friday, the California judge before whom the Georgettes and other beneficiaries had brought their complaints about Gordon ruled that if everyone in the family could come to an agreement, Gordon was free to sign with Texaco. After hour upon hour of long-distance conversations, including one between Gordon and his brother J. Paul Jr. in London, the family at last acceded to the deal in the early morning hours of Sunday. Gordon signed the final documents, which in language and intent closely mirrored those negotiated by Marty Lipton, and the deal was done. He, too, had an indemnity against future lawsuits, as did all of the executives, directors, and representatives of Getty Oil Company. Where once they had been bitterly opposed, suddenly Gordon and Sid Petersen shared the same interests—they both wanted to be protected by Texaco.

For each of them, a long and consequential battle was finished. Sid Petersen's career was over. He would float softly into early retirement in Los Angeles, jostled gently by the ropes of his golden parachute. Similarly, Gordon would retreat to the luxurious isolation of his social and musical worlds in San Francisco and New York. The Broadway mansion was as comfortable as ever. Ann was busy shopping for an apartment in New York. Life would go on. In fact, since under the terms of Texaco's takeover the value of Gordon's family trust would be converted to just over $4 billion in cash, and since Gordon's yearly share of the interest from that sum would rise from about $30 million to more than $100 million, life would go on rather nicely. The lawsuit filed against him by his nephews and nieces over the issue of his sole trusteeship remained. But with so much cash now in the family's possession, there was no reason to believe that the problems could not be solved. There was enough money to go around.

So, too, for the advisors, the Wall Street game-players for whom the Texaco takeover represented a summit of achievement. In the era of big deals, it was the biggest deal ever. Ten billion dollars. The amount just rolled off an investment banker's tongue, with the emphasis placed on the hard consonant sound of "b" as in "billion." For Geoff Boisi's efforts, Goldman, Sachs earned a record $18.3 million in fees. Marty Siegel made some $15 million for Kidder, Peabody. Salomon Brothers, Marty Lipton's banker, earned about $4 million. And the boys from First Boston, Bruce Wasserstein and Joe Perella, managed to take home approximately $10 million for seventy-nine hours of work, or just over $126,582 per hour.

"You can consider the fees in this deal as tips," Marty Siegel quipped to the newspapers.

But by Sunday afternoon, when the papers were all signed and the principals were immersed in their rituals of congratulation, Hugh Liedtke was still stiffed. He had not a penny. He had no barrels of oil. And he was very angry about it.

It was not clear afterward who had initiated the effort, but early the following week an attempt was made to placate Pennzoil's chairman, who had come to resemble an irate bulldog in both spirit and appearance. Liedtke had spent the weekend in Manhattan, watching football in his Waldorf apartment, and brooding. He was too mad to return to Houston. Finally, he received a call from Jim Glanville, his investment banker from Lazard Frères, who was embarrassed about the way things had turned out—Lazard was the only major Wall Street firm involved in the deal to walk away empty-handed. When he telephoned, Glanville reminded Liedtke that he was close to the McKinley family; they were neighbors in affluent suburban Connecticut. McKinley had telephoned, Glanville said, and the banker wanted permission to return the call. Liedtke said that he could, but that he should say very little about Pennzoil's plans and strategies. If he met with Texaco's chief executive, Glanville should simply listen.

They met first on Sunday evening at McKinley's home. Glanville arrived with his wife, then sequestered himself with the Texaco chairman. They talked briefly.

"Texaco bears no hostility toward Lazard or Pennzoil," McKinley emphasized.

"We're all big boys," Glanville replied.

The two friends talked about Pennzoil's complaints and about the regulatory and antitrust hurdles Texaco had yet to overcome in Washington before its deal could be formally closed. Glanville said that unlike Texaco, an integrated oil giant, Pennzoil had no significant antitrust problems, and moreover, because of Liedtke's personal connections and his company's history, Pennzoil wielded great influence in Washington. If Texaco would consider some kind of cooperative venture, Pennzoil's political power might be very helpful, Glanville said. After discussing several other topics, McKinley indicated that he might like to meet with Liedtke to see if he could smooth any ruffled feathers. Glanville said that he would see what he could do.

After phone calls back and forth, a date was set for Wednesday, January 11, in Washington D.C. A suite was rented at the historical Hay-Adams Hotel, across from the White House. Liedtke asked two of his executives to fly up from Houston; McKinley also brought along a pair of aides to the meeting. On the plane ride from Houston, Baine Kerr, the Pennzoil president, wrote out a proposal on a single sheet of paper. His idea for a compromise with McKinley was simple. Pennzoil had been prepared to buy three-sevenths of Getty Oil for $112.50 per share. Now the price had gone up to $125. Pennzoil would put up the same amount of cash it had originally offered, only now, at the new price, it could afford only about three-eighths of Getty Oil. Under Kerr's proposal, Texaco would agree to sell three-eighths of Getty to Pennzoil at $125 per share.

"In my view, it is much better for Texaco and Pennzoil to look for ways to work together than it is to look for ways to disagree," McKinley said when the meeting began. "We can think of a number of ways in which Texaco could be helpful to Pennzoil. One way might be for us to sell Pennzoil some of our ownership in the Hueso field on favorable terms."

The Hueso field was an oil reserve in which Texaco and Pennzoil jointly participated.

"If you're not interested in that," McKinley continued, "there might be other ways in which Texaco could be helpful to Pennzoil."

Sitting across the room, Hugh Liedtke was unimpressed. His flaccid face was creased in concentration. Now he leaned forward and spoke his mind to the chairman of Texaco.

"*Hueso* is the Spanish word for bone," Liedtke said. "Pennzoil is not interested in being thrown a bone. The only thing that we are interested in is some approach that would permit us to have the benefit of our bargain, which was an ownership interest in Getty Oil."

Liedtke asked Baine Kerr to distribute copies of his handwritten proposal drawn up on the plane the day before.

"I don't think Texaco would be interested in doing anything like this," McKinley said when he had perused the document. It was out of the question—Liedtke was asking for the moon. McKinley urged him to "seriously consider" his offer to be helpful to Pennzoil in some reasonable way. And with that the meeting ended. McKinley and his executives flew back to their corporate estate at White Plains; Liedtke went home to Houston on a Pennzoil jet.

So the issue was joined. John McKinley, the "manly" leader of the nation's third-largest oil corporation, believed that he had done nothing wrong, that he owed Pennzoil nothing. Indeed, he was already being lionized in the national business press for having "outfoxed" Gordon Getty and for rescuing Texaco from its years of corporate drift brought on by declining reserves. Suddenly, Texaco was an aggressive, vital, expanding oil giant, no longer the Seven Sisters' mean-spirited spinster. For his part, J. Hugh Liedtke was badly stung. For all his successes in the oil business, for all his financial innovations and takeovers and spin-offs—for all of Pennzoil's spectacular growth—he had fallen short in the one deal that would have put him over the top. For Hugh Liedtke, there could never be another deal like Getty Oil again. The company was so rich, and so divided against itself—it had been a once-in-a-lifetime opportunity. Now it was gone.

Hugh Liedtke had two choices.

On the one hand, he could learn to accept defeat. He could return to Houston, to the management of his business and to the preparations for his retirement. There was his family—the companionship of his wife, the antics of their friends, the grandchildren everywhere. There surely was plenty of money. More and more, there would be time for cruises in the Caribbean, fishing trips to the ranch in Arkansas, vacations in Europe.

On the other hand, Hugh Liedtke could stew in his own juices. He could become more and more angry over the loss of Getty Oil to Texaco. He could become obsessed. He could become determined to take revenge on all of those who had done him wrong: Texaco, Marty Lipton and the museum, Getty Oil management, the investment bankers, even Gordon Getty, his former partner. He could try to make them pay.

Those who knew Hugh Liedtke well understood which course he had to follow.

PART FOUR

A JURY OF THEIR PEERS

SORE BACK LAWYER

Houston, Texas, is a vertical city, a monolith with a sprawling, dirty base. From the air, its disordered expanse of freeways, warehouses, barrios, and suburbs seems to flow in tributaries to the center, feeding downtown's great clump of bare, shining skyscrapers. The modernity of this downtown skyline—its progressive architecture, its dizzying heights, its network of subterranean tunnels linking shops and offices—is a source of pride for the city's boosters. To them, the skyline is a symbol of Houston's passage from a steamy, backwater frontier town along the bayou to a climate-controlled, cosmopolitan capital of the New South. But the city's gleaming architecture is also suggestive of a second transformation: a consolidation of power and wealth. Stoked by the boom in oil and gas prices during the 1970s, Houston's downtown establishment erected monuments to itself as much as to a new civic image. Long a close-knit fraternity, the downtown business and political leaders grew in the direction of their city: upward into the azure Texas sky.

More than in most American cities, Houston's downtown establishment was dominated by its large law firms. It was a cultural as well as economic phenomenon. Through rapid cycles of boom and bust, in an atmosphere of fast dealing, open competition, and precipitous fiasco, the major law firms became over the years bastions of stability and influence. Oilmen came and went, their businesses flourishing and suffocating like flowers in the seasons, but the lawyers prospered in spring and fall alike. The client of a major downtown firm might pass through the firm's specialized departments as if propelled by natural law: as the business bloomed, the corporate department would handle its charters and stock offerings; as the company became entangled in commercial disputes, the litigation department would try its cases in court; and finally, when the cycle was played out, partners in the bankruptcy department awaited with consoling words and the appropriate Chapter 11 papers. Over a lifetime, an individual client might repeat this cycle two or three times with different businesses, and through every phase the wealth and power of the law firm grew. Psychologically, the lawyers at the big firms represented the antithesis to Houston's wild, risk-taking ethic. They were cautious men, well trained, cerebral, detached. In a city that sometimes resembled a casino, they were the only ones in town who never rolled the dice. Instead, they stood quietly beside the table, ever so often raking off a pile of money.

In January 1984, when an embittered Hugh Liedtke returned home without a single barrel of oil to show for his bid to take control of Getty Oil, there were three exceptionally large and powerful law firms headquartered in downtown Houston: Fulbright & Jaworski, Vinson & Elkins, and Baker & Botts, Liedtke's firm for more than twenty-five years. In those first days after Pennzoil's defeated takeover attempt, gossip circulated in the legal establishment that Liedtke blamed his lawyers for his uncharacteristic failure in New York, and that he was so angry that he might take his lucrative business away from Baker & Botts. This hopeful gossip, as it turned out, was unfounded, although Liedtke did shake up his own team of in-house legal advisors: Pennzoil general counsel and former Baker & Botts partner Perry Barber left Liedtke's employ for a job heading his old firm's Washington office. But the ties between Liedtke and his downtown law firm ran too deep to be severed by this setback, particularly since Liedtke directed much of his anger at Texaco, not his own advisors. Still, there was a sense in those first weeks of January that Baker & Botts now had something to prove—to its client, to its rivals in the Houston legal establishment, and to the smug Wall Street lawyers and bankers who had vanquished the firm in Manhattan.

In any takeover, failed or successful, lawsuits spring up quickly. They are almost always employed as short-term tactical devices. In the way a baseball manager might argue with the umpires over

a close call at third base, lawyers beseech judges to issue preliminary injunctions or temporary restraining orders to stall or reverse
takeover events. And during the tense, chaotic maneuvering that
surrounded Texaco's successful bid to take Getty Oil away from
Pennzoil and Gordon Getty during those first days of January, a
number of such tactical lawsuits had indeed been set in motion. In
Delaware, where many large companies are incorporated because of
favorable tax laws and a sophisticated court system, Getty Oil had
filed suit seeking a judge's declaration that there had been no contract between Pennzoil and the Getty Oil directors. Pennzoil countered by suing in the same forum Texaco, Getty Oil, Gordon Getty's
family trust, and the museum. The suit asked for an injunction that
would prohibit Texaco from completing its deal with Getty Oil, Gordon, and the museum. Pennzoil wanted Getty Oil's rich assets "held
separate" from Texaco until the dispute over who the oil properly
belonged to was resolved. At the same time, Pennzoil initiated and
sponsored private antitrust suits in Oklahoma and Rhode Island
seeking to have the Texaco merger blocked on competitive grounds.
In Washington, Liedtke tried to deliver on his indirect threats about
Pennzoil's political power; he hired a prominent lobbyist to persuade
Congress's antitrust subcommittees that Texaco's acquisition of Getty
Oil should be enjoined.

What was important about all of these legal maneuverings, as
it turned out, was the chaotic atmosphere they engendered. There
were lawyers flying in all directions—to Delaware, New York, Tulsa,
Washington, Providence, and Los Angeles, where the Getty family beneficiaries were still attempting to intervene in the deal. New
law firms were being retained left and right—firms whose partners
were not intimately familiar with the long and sordid history leading to Texaco's final bid for Getty Oil. So-called "accelerated discovery" programs were suddenly under way, with each side trying
to subpoena as many documents and take as many depositions in
the shortest possible time. In this flurry, legal strategists on nearly
every side assumed, based on their experience in similar situations,
that few of these lawsuits would ever advance to trial. These were
typical tactical cases, it was thought, the inevitable postscript to a
high-stakes merger game. The important question that January was
whether Congress or one of the judges involved would issue an
injunction holding up Texaco's merger with Getty on antitrust or

breach-of-contract grounds—an eventuality thought to be unlikely. As one of the lawyers involved put it later, "It was the typical kind of lunacy in these sorts of takeover litigation cases where you hope you're smart enough not to screw up. This was a really tough case because you had so many different interests: Getty Oil, the museum, Gordon's trust, Pennzoil, Texaco, and so on. You never knew what the hell everybody was going to do."

To press his interests in this legal free-for-all, Hugh Liedtke had assigned Houston-based Baker & Botts partners John Jeffers and Irv Terrell, as well as some partners from the Paul, Weiss firm in New York, to the several cases now under way. Liedtke's lawyers scrambled like mad rabbits from city to city, taking depositions, reviewing "discovered" documents, filing motions, and arguing hearings before judges. In mid-January, Jeffers and Hugh Liedtke flew together to New York in a Pennzoil jet—Liedtke was about to have his deposition taken in the Delaware lawsuit. Liedtke outlined his strategy to Jeffers: the Pennzoil chairman wanted, if possible, to have Texaco's merger with Getty Oil blocked on breach-of-contract grounds by the Delaware court. If that effort failed, however, he was not going to "forgive or forget" about what Texaco and Getty Oil's executives and advisors had done to him in Manhattan.

"I'd like, if possible, to have a damage suit in which Joe Jamail would be the lead counsel," Liedtke said. "Joe is a friend of mine; he's never represented me, but I think he's a great damage suit lawyer and he has a great reputation for his ability with juries. I'd like to have him."

John Jeffers thought that his client's idea made good sense. The richly flamboyant Jamail was known in Houston as the "king of torts." He was renowned throughout the city for the outrageous judgments he won from juries in personal-injury and other plaintiffs' damage suits. He happened also to be the leading antagonist of Houston's three giant corporate law firms, including Jeffers' Baker & Botts, which tended to represent corporate defendants in the local damage suits brought by Jamail and his brethren in Houston's populist, highly colorful, and vaguely disreputable personal-injury plaintiffs' bar. An alliance between Jamail and the staid downtown firm of Baker & Botts would be unusual indeed. At the moment, however, winging to New York with one of his firm's most important clients, John Jeffers was less concerned about any potential discomforts of partnership with Jamail than he was about serving Hugh Liedtke.

The immediate difficulty, as Jeffers and his partner Irv Terrell saw it, was that obtaining an injunction in Delaware was a nearly insurmountable legal challenge. Under the law, such an injunction could be issued only if a judge was convinced that no other remedy was available to the injured party. That is, Pennzoil would have to prove to the Delaware judge that only by stopping Texaco's merger with Getty Oil could Pennzoil be "made whole." Thus, there were two barriers to overcome: first, Jeffers and Terrell would have to prove that their client had been wronged, that Texaco and the Getty Oil board of directors had breached a contract with Pennzoil; and second, they would have to demonstrate that the only way to compensate Pennzoil for this wrong would be to stop Texaco from merging with Getty. It was this latter test that was most difficult to meet. Even if the Delaware judge found that Pennzoil's contract had been broken and that Liedtke was entitled to compensation, it did not follow that no other remedy was available. Pennzoil could sue for damages—money— and then use that money to buy enough oil to replace the barrels lost to Texaco. Hugh Liedtke's attorneys tried to argue in Delaware that Getty Oil was a unique and irreplaceable target, that its oil reserves were so rich and politically secure that no amount of money could compensate for their loss, but the judge was, not surprisingly, unimpressed. He ruled on February 7 that Pennzoil's case for breach of contract appeared strong to him, but that the damage remedy was indeed adequate to satisfy any injury Hugh Liedtke might have sustained in New York.

Having failed to secure an injunction, the Baker & Botts lawyers were now confronted with a serious problem. Their client was determined to pursue a jury trial for damages, and wanted his friend Joe Jamail to run the show. But the lawsuit against Texaco, Getty Oil, the museum, and Gordon was pending in the Delaware courts. The lawyers also knew that Joe Jamail would be uninterested in trying any lawsuit in Delaware—Texas-born and -bred, rich, and successful, Jamail did not eagerly travel out of state, especially to a place like Wilmington—Delaware's unglamorous legal capital. Even more germanely, the Delaware Chancery Court, where corporate disputes were heard, had evolved from the ancient English distinction between law and equity cases. And under Delaware equity court rules, it would be very difficult for a plaintiff to have his case heard by a jury, and even if a jury was impaneled, its verdict was not binding on the judge. Similarly, there were no provisions in the Delaware courts for awarding "punitive" damages. So the Baker & Botts lawyers tried to determine if there was some way they could move their lawsuit to a Texas state court, where Jamail would be in his element and where the court rules were more favorable.

It was then, during the second week of February 1984, that the Baker & Botts lawyers discovered what one attorney involved later described as the "ten-billion-dollar boo-boo."

The mistake was a product of the chaotic atmosphere surrounding all the lawsuits and accelerated discovery programs sprouting up during the early weeks of 1984. And it was the result, in all probability, of a critical, if subtle, distinction between the types of law firms involved in this legal pandemonium.

During the crucial two weeks following Pennzoil's 20 percent tender offer for control of Getty Oil, Hugh Liedtke's attorneys from Baker & Botts had been criticized by their counterparts in the large Wall Street firms for their lack of familiarity with the protocols of modern merger-making. The Baker & Botts lawyers specialized in corporate lawsuits, not mergers. They had some experience in deal-making, but they could hardly match the resumés of such Wall Street giants as Marty Lipton's Wachtell, Lipton, Rosen & Katz, or Texaco's firm, Skadden, Arps, Slate, Meagher & Flom. Even Pennzoil's special New York retainer, Arthur Liman of Paul, Weiss, Rifkind, Wharton & Garrison, was known more for his criminal defense work than for his merger expertise. Liman's New York law partners were respected for their abilities in drawn-out corporate litigation battles, not especially for their negotiating skills in fast-breaking merger deals. The fact was that Hugh Liedtke had no Wall Street specialists in his stable of legal advisors, and there were some who believed this was a central reason behind his defeat at the hands of Texaco. But now it was precisely Liedtke's dependence on his hometown corporate litigation experts at Baker & Botts that turned things to Pennzoil's advantage. Unlike the Wall Street merger lawyers, Liedtke's attorneys did not think of lawsuits as short-term tactical devices. To them, a lawsuit was something to be won or lost. It was a game one played to the very end.

After the judge in Delaware turned down their request for an injunction, the Pennzoil lawyers checked the court files in Wilmington, and what they found pleased them greatly. Getty Oil Company, the museum, and Gordon Getty's family trust, had each "answered" Pennzoil's breach-of-contract lawsuit—that is, they had filed papers denying Pennzoil's charges and asserting counterclaims of their own. But Texaco, represented by the takeover specialists at New York-based Skadden, Arps, had asked for an extension, and as of Thursday, February 9, they had not yet filed a response. This was not because an answer was a complex or difficult brief to prepare—an experienced attorney could dictate an adequate one in thirty minutes. The Skadden, Arps lawyers explained later that they did not answer Pennzoil's suit because they thought it was not necessary under Delaware law, that once a discovery program was undertaken, an answer was not needed. But it was also true that the Skadden, Arps lawyers did not ordinarily worry about answering lawsuits filed against their clients. They were in the takeover business, where lawsuits were like rockets: they took off in a fast and fiery explosion and then faded quickly from view. Only a handful ever survived beyond the preliminary injunction stage.

"Their whole mind-set is the preliminary injunction, and then it's over," John Jeffers said later, speaking of Wall Street legal specialists generally. "In some ways, it's a wonderful life, because all your cases are over in six weeks and you go on to the next thing. Nothing consumes your life for four or five years like it does for us mortal trial lawyers. I had a friend at one of the takeover firms, and I can remember him bragging about how he never had to file an answer because his cases were all over before the answer date. I think that's sort of what happened here."

More precisely, what happened was that on Thursday, February 9, Jeffers and his partners at Baker & Botts dismissed their case against Texaco in Delaware and refiled it the same day in state court in Houston. They took advantage of something known in legal shorthand as "Delaware rule 41," which permitted a plaintiff to dismiss his lawsuit "without prejudice" and refile it elsewhere as long as the defendant had not answered the original complaint. Since the lawyers for Getty Oil Company, the museum, and Gordon's family trust *had* filed their answers to the Delaware suit by the appropriate date, Baker & Botts could successfully employ this maneuver only against Texaco. In its lawsuit against the other defendants, Pennzoil was stuck in Delaware—without a jury, without Joe Jamail, and without punitive damages. Texaco alone would have to face a jury trial in

Houston. It was not everything the Baker & Botts lawyers might have wanted, but for Hugh Liedtke, it was enough.

Embarrassed and outraged, Texaco and its Wall Street lawyers scrambled to block Pennzoil's ploy. But a Delaware judge ruled that Liedtke was well within his rights. The attorneys at Skadden, Arps tried to explain to John McKinley and Texaco's other top executives that their failure to answer in Delaware was an innocent error, that they followed reasonable assumptions and analysis, but the firm's embarrassment was compounded by the fact that all of the other Delaware defendants had avoided Pennzoil's trap by routinely filing their answers. Only Texaco had been hauled down to Houston to face justice in the Texas state courts.

As winter yielded to spring, the question remaining was whether Texaco would additionally face the peculiar courtroom skills of Joe Jamail once a trial in Houston got under way. Despite repeated entreaties from his friend Hugh Liedtke, Jamail had not yet decided whether he would take on the case—complex corporate disputes did not excite him. Jamail figured that Liedtke was just smarting from a business deal gone sour and that his wounds would mend soon enough. So he kept putting Liedtke off. He told his friend to try to put the loss of Getty Oil behind him.

Later on, Hugh Liedtke and his attorneys would talk a great deal about notions of honor and morality as they pertained to the case of *Pennzoil v. Texaco* and to the Byzantine entanglements at Getty Oil which preceded the lawsuit. They would describe their grievances against John McKinley, Sid Petersen, and the directors and advisors at Getty Oil in simple, virtuous language—the righteous, patriotic vocabulary of frontier myth. They talked about "handshake" deals and about the raw, honest culture of the Texas oil patch, where a man's word was more important than his signature. Drawing on the powerful, coded, century-old rhetoric of Southern and Western populism in American politics, they talked in sinister tones about the concentrated power of New York lawyers and investment bankers.

To anyone intimately familiar with the eighteen-month-long battle for control of Getty Oil, in which manipulation, deceit, ignorance, ego, and greed propelled the action from nearly every quarter, the application of such starkly moral concepts to the story seemed to require a long leap of the imagination. As Liedtke and his lawyers repeated this rhetoric about honor and morality, however, they seemed more and more to believe its every tenet. Liedtke, particularly, portrayed himself as a straight-dealing, plain-talking, white-hatted Texan who stepped into Manhattan that New Year's Day of 1984 with the naïve expectation that folks there would do him right. With his philosophy degree from Amherst, his MBA from Harvard, and his law degree from the University of Texas, the Pennzoil chairman was perhaps overeducated for this role. But he was not cynical, either—at some important level, Liedtke clearly *did* believe in honor, morality, family, and the Republican Party. The question always was, as it is for every man, to what degree did these ideals comport with reality? To what degree were they relevant in a $10 billion hostile takeover battle? To what degree had Liedtke followed his professed moral precepts through the course of his own long and ambitious career in the oil business?

The important issues had perhaps as much to do with class and culture as they did with abstract notions of business ethics. In his effort to secure a jury trial in Houston and to enlist Joe Jamail to his cause, Hugh Liedtke seemed to understand this point. While Liedtke's career was divided in important ways between Texas and the Northeast, between entrepreneurialism and corporate consolidation, between the populist oil patch and the powerful Republican establishment, Joe Jamail embodied the unfettered, anti-authoritarian, incontinent spirit of Houston, Texas, the city in which he was born and raised. Liedtke wanted Jamail to take on his case against Texaco not simply because Jamail had a superb record in local jury trials, but because if anyone was capable of recasting the ethically convoluted, technically complex, economically gargantuan dispute over control of Getty Oil into a Texas morality play, it was Jamail. Joe Jamail would not have to plan such a strategy rationally, he would not have to think it out and write it down in outline form—he would know intuitively how to do it.

He would know because it was the way he saw the world. It was the way he lived. The son of Lebanese immigrants to Texas, Jamail was a short, compact man with a prominent nose, strong eyes, and an explosive, deeply charismatic ebullience. He drank vodka like it was water, ogled women across the state, drove his black Jaguar at excessive speeds, cussed routinely, partied regularly with country singer Willie Nelson, and otherwise lived in easy companion with the most exaggerated Texas myths. He was fifty-eight years old when Hugh Liedtke first asked him to consider trying the case of *Pennzoil* v. *Texaco*, and he was slowing down only at the margins of his life—cutting back on the cigarettes, postponing the drinking sessions until later afternoons, and turning over some of his cases to the younger partners at his small, personal-injury, "sore back" firm in downtown Houston.

One morning when it was all over, when Wall Street and Washington and executives at the nation's largest corporations wanted to know who Joe Jamail was and where he had come from, the aging trial lawyer sat in a wooden rocking chair beside the floor-length window in his skyscraper office in Houston, sipped from a tall glass of iced tea, and told the story of his life in words only the most skillful provincial novelist could hope to produce:

"My father had a confectionary store. You can't see it from here now because the building was way down on the end of Main Street. There's an old picture we had of it somewhere. They made cotton candy and divinities and shit like that. He also had the very first taxi company, which was run by mules. It was called Old Jitneys. I don't remember any of this, but these are the tales my grandmother and great aunt used to tell.

"My father was a big, handsome man. He and his brother started in the old market of Houston. You can see the spot from here. And he used to have a little table in there. Well, they grew, and finally they got a store and they built it up to where it was one of the biggest chains in the city. When they finally sold them, they had twenty-eight food stores in Texas. So he was very successful.

"I went to grade school here and then I went to a Catholic high school for boys. I graduated from St. Thomas High School on a Sunday in 1943. I was sixteen. I was still young to get out of high school, and my mother was just insisting that I not go off to any kind of war. My brother had enlisted, my oldest brother, and he was a naval aviator in training overseas. There were four boys and one girl in the family. I'm second to the oldest. Anyway, my family told me when I got out of St. Thomas that I'm going to Texas A&M. All the Jamails go to A&M. Shit, I hated A&M. I'd been at boys' school all my goddamn life, after grade school. I didn't like it. Anyway, they took me up there on a Sunday, and I escaped on Wednesday. I just ran away from that sonovabitch and hitchhiked to Austin and enrolled at the University of Texas as a premed student taking biology, zoology, German—hard shit. And I never went to class. So I got five F's.

"So I came home. But before I came home, I had gone over and taken my physical and decided to join the Marine Corps. You had to get your mother and father's permission if you were seventeen like I was. So I came home and I forged my mother and dad's names and got this old drunk druggist to notarize it for fifty cents. And I was gonna go on off to war. It's a cruel thing to do to your parents. So finally, right before I left, I went in and told 'em. My dad was thoroughly pissed off at me, but he just looked right at me.

"He says, 'Well, all I can tell you is that I've done what you're going to do, I've been to war, and it's not fun. You may think it is, but you're going to wish you had never done it. There's no point in me getting angry at you—you're going to be mad enough at yourself. Try to be a good Marine.'

"And my mother, of course, was just beside herself. I think she installed a stained-glass window in every Catholic Church in Harris County praying for my safe return. This was cruel. My mother and I were close. My father and I were close, too. My father just died last year. He was ninety-four.

"Well, I regretted the Marines every fucking day, almost. I went over the hill every time I had a chance. My record looked like they took a bottle of red ink and dumped it on the sonovabitch. But I got out honorably discharged, served it, did it all in stride. So I'm out of that sumbitch and I'm not yet twenty. So I laid around here drunk for about two weeks, just hunting pussy all over town. Goofy. One day I get in about six in the morning, drunk. So my dad comes in.

"He says, 'You gotta get up.' And I said, 'I just got in.' He said, 'I know. You got to go. You're worrying your mother. And I'm not going to put up with your being drunk. Two weeks is enough. And don't give me that war shit—I've done that. I've been there, boy, you got that?' I was 'boy' to him until he died.

"He thought I ought to go to school. He said, 'You can either help to run my business or you can go to school. You're not going to lie around here drunk.' So he gave me three hundred dollars, which was a lot of money. He said, 'Take one of them cars and go off, go somewhere and think about it.'

"So I started out for New Orleans—that's where I really wanted to go. I made and then blew about three thousand dollars in a gambling dive down in Galveston on the way. I had a lot of money, then in two nights I blew it. Just whores and the rest of it. I stopped in Lafayette,

Louisiana. It got late and I went in this bar. I remember it vividly—it was called the Buckhorn Bar. And I fell in love with the bar lady, a big, well-endowed lady. So I get about half-drunk, get me a room, and spend the night there. And I get talking to this guy who knew my family. He was a lawyer—name was Kaliste Saloon. He's now a judge. He got to shooting the shit with me, and he says, 'Stick around here tomorrow and I'll show you my office.' So we went over to his office the next morning, and I watched him on the phone doing all this stuff, lawyering.

"I said, 'Pretty neat action. This guy's got a pretty good racket.' So he took me to see the Southwest Louisiana Institute, where I could go to school. I enrolled. There were a lot of pretty young girls down there—the ratio was about two to one in the men's favor—and all of them were Cajun, goddamn pretty girls. I went to school there for a year. And then, goddamn, I kind of caused a scandal. I moved some old girl I knew, a singer, into my room with me. They didn't do that in them days.

"I remember I took my English exam in the Buckhorn Bar. It was given by a fine, drunk professor who was expelled, I think, from one of the better schools in the East, and he just found himself a little place down in Lafayette. And he'd hustle them little girls. It was just beautiful to watch. Great big fellow, just Shakespearean. He gave me my English exam in the Buckhorn Bar and proclaimed that I had made an A and I now needed to buy a round. Which I did.

"But after the scandal, I got the word from my family, 'Get out of Lafayette.' So I had to hoof it. I drove straight to Austin and enrolled in the summer session at the University of Texas, where I stayed for the rest of my schooling. I didn't have anywhere to go, so I just walked over to the law school. I never took the entrance exam. It was a problem later. First year, I was on probation. I failed torts. I did as bad as you could fuck it up. But I was saved because I passed contracts. I came back that summer to Houston and I thought about not going back to school, but I said, 'Bullshit.' And I went back and I just changed my way of studying and thinking and then burned them up. I made good grades and finished probably in the upper twenty-five or thirty percent. But the first year was almost a disaster.

"I took the bar exam in May of 1952. I was still not even done with school—I needed another semester and a half. But if you were a veteran, you could take the bar with sixty hours of classes or so.

I took it on a dare. We were sitting around there drinking. I was kind of hoorah-in'. This was like on a Thursday. So some of my buddies said, 'Okay, loudmouth, why don't you go take the fucking bar exam if you're so smart.' So we bet a hundred dollars—me against four buddies—that I could take the sumbitch and pass it. And the hundred dollars would be used to buy beer for each other.

"I hadn't studied. I hadn't done any of the application shit. Nothing. I rushed to Houston on Saturday morning to see if I could apply. The chairman of admissions just kind of laughed at me because I was so fucked up. But they said it was okay.

"I studied over the weekend. A couple of professors were really nice. The word got around that this fucking nut was going to do this. And I sailed into that sumbitch, and I made a 76 on the bar exam. Seventy-five is passing. So I'm a lawyer. I didn't know anything about taxation. But when you're loose, you can play.

"I was offered a job at the big downtown firm of Fulbright & Jaworski. I was the only guy they hired that year. I was there about a month. They introduced me to some of the senior men, very conservative bunch of shit. You can't sign your name to anything. So I walked out and called the man who hired me and said, 'We both made a big mistake. I been to war and law school and all kinds of shit and I ain't doin' this.' So I opened a small office with two other guys: Fred Jamail, a cousin, and Myron Love. Most of my classmates wrote me off. It wasn't socially acceptable to do what I did. But I had a couple of friends at Baker & Botts and Vinson & Elkins, and they'd come over and we'd go eat hot dogs. I admired them for doing that.

"I knew all along that I wanted to be a trial lawyer. After this first firm, which I was at only for a couple of months, I worked as a prosecutor for about a year and then I joined another small trial firm.

"The first case I tried after I got out on my own that got a great deal of notoriety was a case called *Glover* v. *City of Houston*. This man was driving one night and he hit a tree over here behind Rice University, off Main Street. The city claimed that what he hit was a 'tree island esplanade.' I claimed it was a goddamn nuisance. This man hit a curb, jumped the curb, went nineteen feet, knocked a keep-right sign down—he's in the grass now—went another twenty-two feet, hit the tree. Later, he died. I represented his widow. He had alcohol in his blood—enough, they claimed, to make him intoxicated. I subpoenaed the mayor of Houston and put him on the stand. I asked the mayor about why he put the tree there. I got a lot of notoriety. The jury went out and gave us everything I sued for, which was a lot of money in those days. Well, it just blew everybody's mind. There was coverage everywhere. Nobody thought you could sue a city, first off, and then there was the business about him hitting a tree. And the press was very kind to me. The thing went all over the country.

"And I heard from my old torts professor, who had moved on to teach torts at the University of Pennsylvania. When I failed his class my first year of law school, this professor had told me that I ought to quit, that I shouldn't stay in law school. He said at the time, 'You're not ever going to make a lawyer.' Well, now he wrote me a letter that said, 'I have just read with interest about the Glover case. I told you that you would never make a lawyer and I meant it.'

"Later on, I tried so many colorful cases. I was blessed. My first love is damage suits. My father didn't like this shit I was doing, you know, suing businesses, being a 'sore-back lawyer.' He was oriented the other way. So was my mother.

"I like to help people, though. Listen, I could hire out tomorrow to the business world. They come in here every day. Every day. Banks. Every bank in town has tried to get me. But why do that? I'm not into that. I'm more into one-on-one. And I don't need any more money. I think people are by and large getting the shaft. And what they need is good lawyers like me."

Hugh Liedtke understood this much in the winter of 1984: if Joe Jamail could be persuaded to try the case of *Pennzoil* v. *Texaco* before a Houston jury, if he could be convinced that Pennzoil had "gotten the shaft" during its attempt to take control of Getty Oil, then John McKinley and his battery of Wall Street lawyers and advisors would face a kind of reckoning unknown in the equity courts of Delaware or in the elegantly appointed suites of Manhattan's finest hotels, where the deal for Getty Oil had been made and lost. They would have to explain themselves to Joe Jamail.

Liedtke's relationship with Jamail was strictly social. Their children attended the same private school in Houston. They had met at a birthday party in the early 1970s. Drinking, fishing, traveling, playing dominos—they found that they enjoyed each other's company immensely, and so did their wives, both tolerant, expressive, gregarious women. To Baine Kerr, Pennzoil's president and the former corporate partner at mammoth Baker & Botts, Liedtke's relation-ship with Jamail seemed "a good change for Hugh. It was a chance to get around somebody who is totally outside the corporate mold. Hugh relaxed with him, got away from the big wheels of business, which after a time get pretty damn boring." So it was in the context of friendship, not the oil business, that Liedtke urged Jamail to take his case. He told his friend that he felt sorely hurt, angry, betrayed, and appalled at what had happened to him in New York. He said that he wanted to bring Texaco to account.

In March, the two of them went fishing at Liedtke's sprawling Arkansas ranch. They were out on a boat together when the Pennzoil chairman reiterated that he wanted Jamail to be his lead trial lawyer. The suit had already been moved to Houston. Jamail would not have to leave town but for a few dispositions.

"You still fumin' about that?" Jamail asked. "I am tired of hearin' about this. Goddamn it, quit it."

"Joe, it's just a fact that they're wrong. And more than that, it's not honorable. They violated my contract."

"Do you still want to do this?" Jamail asked, seriously.

"Yeah."

"I'll do it. Let's go get a drink."

"I guess we've got a done deal now, don't we?" Liedtke asked.

"We do," Joe Jamail replied.

THE LONER

By the summer of 1984, the excited publicity surrounding the takeover of Getty Oil Company had faded away. Pennzoil's various attempts to block Texaco's merger with Getty had failed. In White Plains, the triumphant team of Texaco executives led by John McKinley was busy with complex, ambitious programs designed to integrate Getty Oil's operations into its own. Getty's nonoil operations were sold off (ERC, the insurance company, fetched $1.075 billion) and Getty Oil's old Los Angeles headquarters operation was dissolved into Texaco's Western regional division. More than one thousand "redundant" Getty Oil managers and employees lost their jobs. In July, Getty's top executives, now known among their disgruntled subordinates as the "divine nine" because of the lucrative golden parachutes they had secured, formally retired. Sid Petersen retreated to his corner Tudor home near the big movie studios in Burbank. The oldest among the deposed Getty Oil regime were still in their fifties, but of the divine nine, only young Steadman Garber eventually accepted a full-time job with another corporation. Petersen dabbled with some oil investments and concentrated on his work with the Los Angeles Philharmonic.

Gordon Getty, led by his soaringly ambitious wife, became increasingly visible in the monied artistic and literary societies of New York and San Francisco. His family fortune was still tied up by the beneficiaries' lawsuit instigated by Sid Petersen and filed against him in November 1983. The judge in the case ordered that the cash proceeds from the stock sale to Texaco be temporarily invested in short-term U.S. government bonds until a settlement of the family lawsuit was reached. Whatever its disposition would be, Gordon's fortune would be considerably enriched. And protected by Texaco's indemnity, Gordon Getty was not terribly concerned about the lawsuits filed in Delaware and Houston by Pennzoil.

Indeed, the case of *Pennzoil* v. *Texaco* had sunk by mid-1984 into the great sea of routine business litigation, far from the public's view. The Wall Street bankers and lawyers so prominently involved in the deal were now off chasing new and bigger mergers; the Texaco-Getty merger, the largest in American history when it occurred, was soon supplanted in rank by a deal between Gulf and Chevron, a merger instigated by a Boone Pickens takeover raid. Even among the principal participants in the Pennzoil lawsuit, there did not seem to be much interest or excitement. John McKinley and Texaco's other top executives said later that Baker & Botts' successful jurisdictional maneuver, leading to the shift from Delaware to Houston, focused their attention on the suit and caused them to initiate a search for a Houston-based law firm to handle the matter. But there was so much else to do in White Plains during those frantic first months following the merger, and besides, all of Texaco's lawyers—including the respected Wall Street advisors such as Marty Lipton who had been involved in the deal—assured McKinley that Pennzoil's case was a sure loser on the merits.

Slowly, then, the once public resentments and conflicts between executives and shareholders at Getty Oil, Texaco, and Pennzoil, were absorbed and pursued in proxy fashion by the companies' Houston-based lawyers. It might be expected that once the attorneys took over, the mood of anger and confrontation extant at the time of the takeover would be diffused, replaced by cool, lawyerly analysis and negotiation. Such an expectation, however, could not account for the peculiar personality of Pennzoil lead counsel Joe Jamail, and perhaps more importantly, it could not account for the tangled personal history of Richard Miller, the man chosen by Texaco to try its case in Houston.

John Jeffers and Irv Terrell, the Baker & Botts partners assigned to Pennzoil's case from its inception, had wondered all along whether they could work successfully with a trial attorney such as

Joe Jamail, whose career and personality contrasted sharply with the upright traditionalism of their large downtown firm. Jeffers and Terrell were second-generation Houston professionals, affluent, well-schooled, well-trained, driven by their careers. Jeffers' father had been an attorney at the downtown firm of Vinson & Elkins, where he enjoyed a long and successful practice. A squat, polite, emotionally restrained man with distinctive furry eyebrows resembling those of the late Soviet premiere Leonid Brezhnev, the younger Jeffers attended private high school, Yale University as an undergraduate and then law school at the University of Texas. He joined Baker & Botts upon graduation and trained as a trial lawyer specializing in complex corporate disputes. He was, it was said admiringly, a solid corporate lawyer—thorough, cautious, cerebral. His partner Terrell, at thirty-eight just a few years his junior, shared Jeffers' upbringing and professional orientation, if not his personality. A tall, expressive, high-strung man with a talent for calculated belligerence, Terrell had built an impressive career at Baker & Botts by concentrating on defense-oriented trial work. His early training had come from representing insurance companies on the defense side of local personal injury cases, where he did battle with Joe Jamail's colorful brethren in the plaintiff's bar. Later, he graduated to complex commercial disputes. At the time of his involvement in the Pennzoil lawsuit, Terrell had never before handled a plaintiff's case; in twelve years of practice, he had only worked on the defense side of civil lawsuits.

Despite some initial apprehension, Jeffers and Terrell were early and pleasantly surprised by the ease with which they formed a working partnership with Joe Jamail, that great and wild antagonist of the downtown law firms. Neither of them had ever tried a case against Jamail, but Jeffers' father had known Jamail during the latter's incipient period as a Houston muckraker, and Jamail recalled the elder Jeffers fondly. From that basis, he lavished trust and independence on his younger partners—he would need their corporate expertise in a trial as complex as *Pennzoil* v. *Texaco*, and besides, Jamail was not about to travel across the country taking depositions and reviewing documents during the months-long discovery phase of the case. For their part, Jeffers and Terrell knew that Jamail was the most successful jury lawyer in Texas, if not in the country, and when they found that his legendary ego was tempered by humor and a willingness to divide the workload into equal thirds among them, their doubts about Jamail quickly dissolved.

Apparently pleased with their own partnership, the interest of all three Pennzoil attorneys turned to their opponent, veteran Houston trial lawyer Richard Miller, a man whose life and career were intimately entangled with their own.

Richard Miller and his small, elite Houston trial firm of Miller, Keeton, Bristow & Brown were retained by Texaco early in 1984 after a search conducted by the company's Houston legal department. There was no question that local counsel was required for the case; it would be the height of foolishness to try a local Texas jury suit with lawyers imported from New York. In the past, much of Texaco's commercial litigation in Houston had been handled by Baker & Botts, which of course was unavailable for the Pennzoil case. Texaco interviewed attorneys at the other two major downtown firms, but settled in the end on Miller, who came very highly recommended. Beyond his obviously impressive legal career, Miller was a man well suited to the authoritarian imperatives at Texaco headquarters. Like Texaco chairman John McKinley, Miller was distinctive for his "manly" attributes.

His mother died when he was born, and for that and other reasons, Dick Miller regarded his father as the most influential person in his life. A commercial feed manufacturer who ran a small plant in Tulsa, Oklahoma, Miller's father was a severe man who taught his son that "the most important thing is to be able to count on yourself," as Miller put it later. Thus, Miller was encouraged as a boy to involve himself in individual rather than team sports, to develop in himself the spirit of the "individual warrior." It was a lesson that Miller embraced, one he later tried to impress upon his own son. An eleventh-grader in the midst of World War II, Miller quit high school to enlist in the Marines, where he served for three years. When he returned home, he attended the University of Tulsa for two years before transferring to Harvard College in the fall of 1948. He took undergraduate courses for a year and then, his intellectual gifts obvious to his professors, he "talked" his way into Harvard Law School, from which he graduated in 1952. That fall, he came to Houston and accepted a position with Baker & Botts, where he stayed for more than thirty years.

Miller had known all along that he wanted to be a trial lawyer, and he devoted himself to his profession with an uncommon singleness of purpose. Trial work attracted him because it was the aspect of a legal career that was romanticized in the popular imagination. It was the field where a man could count on himself, where he could do battle to a verdict with another attorney, *mano a mano*, on a field of intellectual combat. "What you finally learn," Dick Miller said, "is that really good trial lawyers don't do the work for the client. They do it for themselves." At least, that was Miller's motivation, and his drive to excel and win was obvious to everyone who came in contact with him. His partners called him "a type triple-A plus," because to them he seemed so tightly wound, a loner propelled by some mysterious force to achieve the nearly impossible standards he set for himself and others. The Baker & Botts partners who worked with Miller remarked uniformly that no one could be as good a lawyer as Miller thought he should be—not even Miller himself could meet his own exacting standards.

He was an erect, trim, imposing, punctiliously dressed man with a severe, pocked face, thinning hair, and icy blue eyes. He lived by the credo that personal image and first impressions were key not only to professional success but to authority over others; he advised his younger partners to spruce up their appearances. His white shirts were monogrammed and crisply starched, his suits were perfectly tailored, and his shoes were polished to a Marine Corps shine. There was about Dick Miller the air of a man in full control of every detail, every nuance—a power born of the relentless drive for mastery. He was, in a phrase Miller regarded as the ultimate compliment, a "tough hombre."

His thirty-year career at Baker & Botts was luminous, if also marked over time by an estrangement from his colleagues at the firm. Beginning with small personal-injury cases and graduating to complex business litigation, he tried more than three hundred civil lawsuits to verdict, working nearly always on the defense side. He rose to become head of the litigation department, the heart and soul of the firm, and was a key member of its management committee. His success derived not from his relationships with his partners or his clients, who tended to regard him as a distant, alienated figure, but from his unceasing devotion to his work, to winning. "The difference between winning and losing is mental attitude," Miller said. "Given equal ability, the guys who win are the guys who refuse to lose. That's true in everything that I know anything about. When you go to trial

on a case, it's just you against him. You look across the counsel table
and you know how tough the guy is in his head. And that's what
counts." the most important emotion in any lawsuit, Miller believed,
was fear—the fear of the lawyers, the fear of the witnesses, the fear
of the clients. To win was to conquer one's own fears and exploit the
fears of others, particularly those of the opposing attorneys. Unlike
many trial lawyers, Dick Miller was never afraid to take his cases to
trial. He did not worry that he might later be embarrassed by losing
a verdict larger than an earlier settlement offer. He said himself that
the best lawyers could win any case. And Dick Miller clearly believed
that he was one of the best lawyers. The evidence of his own career
supported that belief—he was a winner.

By the early 1980s, the estrangement of Dick Miller from his
partners at Baker & Botts had grown to the point where it was
known to even the firm's youngest associates. It wasn't a matter of
shouting matches in the hallways or fist-pounding confrontations
at the management committee meetings; it was a subtle, powerful
tension, the perhaps inevitable alienation of an individualist from
the large institution that harbored him. In Miller's view, the problem was that an institutional, downtown law firm such as Baker &
Botts could not accommodate legal superstars like himself once they
reached the peak of their powers. Miller wanted to charge hourly
fees much higher than those commanded by the firm's senior partners, but the management committee rebuffed him. Just as important, Miller knew that there was an institutional cycle to a career at
Baker & Botts. By the time he reached his late fifties, it was expected
that Miller would begin to step aside some and make room for the
younger partners such as John Jeffers and Irv Terrell who were ready
to take on the firm's biggest cases. But Dick Miller was not about to
allow himself to be eased out to pasture. He felt that his best years as
a trial lawyer were still ahead of him. "It was a combination of factors," he said later, explaining his decision to leave the firm in September 1983. "It became personally unacceptable to me to continue
to work for a lot less money than I could achieve somewhere else,
and it also became unacceptable to me to be pushed aside, if that's
the right word, or to share. I'm willing to make my own way. I'm not
only willing, I'm going to insist on it."

From Miller's desire for stardom and control, the law firm of
Miller, Keeton, Bristow & Brown was born. With another defector

from Baker & Botts, Daryl Bristow, Miller joined forces with Richard Keeton, himself a refugee from the downtown firm of Vinson & Elkins, and also Robert Brown, who came from a mid-sized Houston firm. Combining Miller's reputation for outstanding trial work with Keeton's ability to build lasting relationships with clients, their idea was to establish an elite, expensive, boutique trial firm to handle uniquely complex and difficult lawsuits—the "Bet your company case," as one of the partners put it soon after the firm was formed. On its face, it was the sort of law firm perfectly suited to handle Texaco's defense against Pennzoil.

Actually, Dick Miller accepted the case reluctantly. He was in the midst of a trial in Midland, Texas, when Texaco first contacted the firm about retaining his services. Miller told his partners that he wasn't interested—he was busy and he wasn't sure that he wanted to get into a big case against his former partners at Baker & Botts. What was more, Miller was friendly with then-Pennzoil general counsel Perry Barber. But his new partners urged him to reconsider; the Texaco trial would be an enormously lucrative opportunity for their fledgling firm. "You're not partners with those guys anymore," they told Miller. "You're partners with us. If Pennzoil was such a good friend of yours, why didn't they ask you to try the case for them?" This last point hit home with Miller. He had forfeited a substantial partnership interest in Baker & Botts as a penalty for going into competition with the firm in Houston. Miller decided to take on the case.

Throughout 1984, during the discovery phase of *Pennzoil* v. *Texaco*, Dick Miller was opposed in the lawsuit not primarily by Joe Jamail, who was busy trying a personal-injury suit in Waco, Texas, but by Baker & Botts partners John Jeffers and Irv Terrell, both of whom had worked for Miller during his tenure as head of their firm's litigation department. Terrell, particularly, regarded Miller as an important figure in his career—not a mentor, exactly, since Miller did not cultivate close relationships with his partners, but a teacher, an example. Important elements of Terrell's style as a trial lawyer—his aggressiveness, his calculated belligerence toward opposing attorneys, his toughness in settlement negotiations—were drawn from Dick Miller's example. But Terrell did not embrace Miller's ascetic life-philosophy, his notions about the "individual warrior" as trial attorney. While rarely accused of sentimentality, Terrell was an open, accessible man, tuned to the shifting emotions of those around him. And while he had learned from Miller, their relationship had been strained. They had worked on a long trial together, back when Terrell was a young associate at the firm, and Terrell had not forgotten the sting of Miller's personal rebukes or his former boss's inability to share work and credit for the case with his colleagues. John Jeffers, too, had worked closely with Miller in the past and harbored few fond memories of the experience. He was a different sort of lawyer from Miller and Terrell; intimidation was not his style. Jeffers' cerebral approach often permitted him to deflect Miller's attempts at intimidation—he did not allow himself to be ruffled. But Terrell and Miller were cut from the same cloth, and when they found themselves on the opposite sides of depositions as discovery in *Pennzoil* v. *Texaco* got under way, the hostility between them was palpable. It seemed to both Jeffers and Terrell that Miller tried to bully his former partners with an intensity and malice even beyond his ordinary methods, as if to prove that his former apprentices could never hope to match his own powers. So implacable did the tensions between them become that Miller once offered to settle the feud with his fists. Terrell rationalized the anger between them by saying that it was his own deliberate strategy to provoke Miller into a fury that might cloud his opponent's judgment during depositions. But it was clear that at some raw, emotional level, Terrell wanted a piece of Miller, too.

The resentments that flowed between the former partners were so deep that they sometimes caught the clients in the case by surprise. The deposition of Texaco president Al DeCrane, for example, taken at Texaco's White Plains headquarters on April 26, 1984, degenerated into a shouting match between Miller and Terrell, much to DeCrane's consternation. After baiting each other with snide comments through several hours of questioning, Miller and Terrell finally blew up over Miller's persistent insinuations that Terrell had unfairly tricked him a few days earlier by having a Houston judge sign an order authorizing an accelerated schedule of depositions. Miller also accused Terrell of withholding documents from the witness.

"This is going to lead us into another discussion of you calling me up and calling me dirty names," Terrell finally said, referring to a phone call from Miller at the time the Houston judge signed his order.

"I haven't called you anything but chickenshit. That's all I ever called you, and there has never been any evidence to the contrary,"

Miller replied angrily. "I am only talking about what you did with reference to that order."

"He got beat by the Houston court and he hasn't gotten over it," Terrell explained to the others in the room. Then, to Miller: "You can't get over it and that's why you keep getting so upset. And you are going to get beat again."

"We will see. Do not raise your voice. I do want the record to show that in the hearing that we had, the judge told you to show me that order before—"

"I have got the transcript and that's an absolute falsity."

"Do you recall me asking him if I was entitled to see the order?"

"That's not what you said."

"That's what he said."

"No, it wasn't."

"That's about the most unfair, unethical conduct I am familiar with in this case," Miller exploded. "What bothered me was that you sneaked over to the courthouse with that order without show-ing it to me. The court told me that I was entitled to see it and you know it."

"That's not true, but you will get over it," Terrell answered, pro-voking Miller further. "Losing is tough, but you will get over it."

"I will never get over being treated unfairly."

"You will get over it. Do not worry about it."

"It's just like the business of this document here that you stick in your file after you take some little dab at it," Dick Miller said, waving an exhibit in his hand.

John Jeffers intervened. "If we keep having all this posturing about fair, I will go on to tell about the time you set the watch back."

"Remember that?" Terrell asked Miller, referring to a long-ago railroad trial in which Miller had allegedly turned back his wrist-watch in a courtroom demonstration that was designed to impeach a witness testifying about how long it took for a train to get from one place to another.

"Let me tell you something," Miller seethed. "You are my friends, but if you call me a liar, we are going to see who can whip who."

"All right," Terrell said. "That will be fine. I am sure we will get to it in the course of this case. We are getting to everything else."

"We will see," Miller continued, pressing his threat. "As old and decrepit as I am."

"If you can't solve it as a lawyer, you are going to beat me up. Is that what you are saying?" Terrell asked.

"I am not going to let you or anybody else call me a liar. You can remember that."

"I will remember that. And I would not let you ever call me a chickenshit again. Do you understand that?"

"I already called you one."

"So I guess you are even. We will have to fight it out one of these days, right?"

"I would like for you to finish this deposition and treat this witness fairly," Miller concluded.

They sounded at times like prepubescent schoolyard rivals. It was not unusual for trial attorneys to bait each other at depositions, in the way heavyweights posture for the cameras at a prefight weigh-in, but the vitriol between Terrell and Miller exceeded the bounds of propriety, even as defined by lawyers. Richard Keeton, battling with Joe Jamail at the videotaped deposition of John McKinley in White Plains, called Jamail a "chickenshit" over the manner in which Jamail was questioning his client. But when Jamail retorted by swearing at Keeton and threatening to walk out of the deposition, there was a humorous, collegial undertone to their debate, a sense of two old boys from Houston having fun with each other. McKinley himself had to smile as he listened to the lawyers snipe back and forth—it was a good show. But no such playfulness extended to the exchanges between Miller, Terrell, and Jeffers. There was a venomous animosity between them, an undercurrent of genuine hatred. Miller on the other hand was oddly respectful when he was around Jamail; he said that Jamail was more or less his equal in the warrior-sport of trial-lawyering, and at times Miller seemed reluctant to draw his foe into combat. But it was clear that Texaco's lead counsel did not feel so magnanimous about Jeffers and Terrell, his former partners and students. He was determined to bully them; in depositions he seemed almost obsessed by their presence.

And so the pretrial phase of *Pennzoil* v. *Texaco* proceeded in the same mood of anger and confrontation that had shaped the takeover events giving rise to the case. Jeffers and Terrell pushed hard to bring the suit to trial; they feared that Pennzoil's still-active Delaware case against Getty Oil, Gordon Getty's trust, and the museum might be argued before the Houston jury trial involving Texaco got under way.

Miller tried to delay discovery in the Houston case, but he failed to slow things down appreciably. In July 1985, just nineteen months after Texaco's takeover of Getty Oil, a trial date was set in Houston state court before Judge Anthony Farris.

In May 1985, Pennzoil president Baine Kerr met in Houston with Texaco vice-chairman James Kinnear to talk about a possible negotiated settlement of *Pennzoil* v. *Texaco*. With an expensive trial now just weeks away, it was natural for the two parties to see if they could make a deal. It was equally natural for Kerr and Kinnear to do the talking—they were both easy-going men disinclined to fits of rage or stubbornness when talking about the case. The same could not always be said about their two superiors, Hugh Liedtke and John McKinley. Kerr proposed a simple transaction: Pennzoil would buy from Texaco, at the equivalent of its last offer price of $112.50 per share, three-sevenths of the oil and gas reserves formerly owned by Getty Oil. It was actually a less generous offer than the one made by Hugh Liedtke in Washington, D.C., in the immediate aftermath of the takeover, but Pennzoil was presumably willing to adjust its price if Texaco was interested in negotiation. Informed of Kerr's offer, however, John McKinley said that the proposal was "impossible." He would rather take the case to a jury.

Setting aside the emotional components of a possible settlement, which were significant, McKinley was prepared to go to trial in the early summer of 1985 because of the advice he had received from Dick Miller and Texaco's other, New York-based attorneys. Miller told the Texaco chairman that while one could never be absolutely certain about what a given jury might do, it was his opinion that the likely worst case in a trial of *Pennzoil* v. *Texaco* would be a verdict along the lines of $250 million to $500 million against Texaco—this despite the fact that Pennzoil was asking for $14 billion in damages. Miller said that even if there was a "complete runaway" jury, Texaco would be hit with a verdict no larger than about $2 billion. The largest civil verdict ever was just $1.8 billion, in the 1980 Chicago trial of *MCI* vs. *AT&T*, and that award had been drastically reduced on appeal. The pretrial settlement proposed by Baine Kerr would require Texaco to sell oil and gas reserves to Pennzoil worth more than $3 billion at current prices. Simply as a matter of dollars and cents, then, it was easy for McKinley to reject a settlement. In a settlement, there would be the inevitable implication that Texaco had done something wrong, and that made McKinley's decision even easier. The Texaco chairman adamantly believed that so far as he was aware, no one in Texaco's employ, including the company's highest-ranking executives, had done anything illegal or immoral during the taking of Getty Oil. Miller assured him that there were no "smoking guns," that McKinley knew all the facts. And so the chairman and his directors decided to go to trial.

Dick Miller was characteristically confident that he could win his case, which would be tried, by mutual agreement of the parties, under New York law. (The contract Pennzoil alleged was "tortiously interfered" with by Texaco was made in New York.) In Delaware, a sophisticated chancellor had reviewed the facts and said that while the evidence that Pennzoil had made a binding contract with the Getty Oil directors was relatively strong, the evidence that Texaco had knowingly and intentionally interfered with that contract was weak. John Jeffers and Irv Terrell had used the chancellor's opinion as a guidebook during the pretrial discovery, working to develop the interference side of their case more than the contract side. For them, an unfortunate consequence of the peculiar circumstances which had brought only the case against Texaco to Houston was that Pennzoil now had a doubly difficult standard to meet before the jury. Not only did Pennzoil have to prove that it had reached a binding, valid contract with the Getty Oil board at the conclusion of its wild, marathon meeting at the Inter-Continental Hotel on January 2 and 3, 1984, it had to further demonstrate that Texaco had knowingly, deliberately, and wrongfully interfered with that contract. Dick Miller told his own clients at Texaco headquarters in White Plains that on the contract side of the case, he believed that Pennzoil's evidence was weak. But Miller emphasized that even if Joe Jamail could somehow convince the jury that a valid contract had existed, he would have a nearly impossible time persuading anyone that Texaco had improperly interfered with that contract. Of course, that was precisely what the Texaco executives themselves believed—it was what they had to believe.

One event before the commencement of the trial shook the faith of Texaco's top executives. Dick Miller had said repeatedly that what concerned him about trying *Pennzoil* v. *Texaco* against Joe Jamail was not so much his opponent's ability as a trial lawyer—Jamail was a formidable jury lawyer, to be sure, but Miller considered himself to be Jamail's equal. Rather, Miller was concerned about Jamail's deep political connections. Everyone in Houston, it seemed, was a friend of Joe Jamail's. He had recently represented the locally powerful Cullen family in a much-publicized will contest. He boasted close friendships with politicians of every ideological stripe. Through a long and prosperous career, as a result of both his gregarious personality and his generous campaign contributions, Jamail had managed to befriend hundreds of judges across the state of Texas. It was Miller's opinion that Jamail's impressive trial record stemmed as much from his ability to cultivate a "friendly" atmosphere in court as from anything else. After hearing gossip for months about Jamail's supposedly close relationship with Judge Anthony Farris, a veteran Republican jurist, Miller discovered shortly before trial that Jamail had contributed ten thousand dollars—an amount Farris described as a "princely sum"—to the judge's campaign fund. The contribution had been made during the pretrial phase of *Pennzoil* v. *Texaco*. Ordinarily, such a contribution would have no bearing on a trial because state court rules made it unlikely that a judge assigned to a case during its discovery phase would also preside at trial. But in the spring of 1985, the rules were changed, and Farris was assigned to the trial of *Pennzoil* v. *Texaco*. Miller filed a motion seeking Farris' removal because of Jamail's contribution, but an appellate judge turned him down, leaving Texaco's counsel in an awkward position. Having failed in his effort to throw Farris out, Miller now had to try his case before him. At the least, it was an uncomfortable predicament.

For his part, Joe Jamail was feeling positively giddy as the trial date neared. He kept telling his friend Hugh Liedtke that he was going to "win this damn thing," and there was something about Jamail's enthusiasm that inspired faith. Jeffers and Terrell and the young associates working on the case at Baker & Botts had the details of the case—its thousands of pages of depositions and documents, the videotaped testimony of out-of-state witnesses, the various precedents under New York law concerning the validity of a contract—well in order. Required now was Joe Jamail's spirit, his magic with the jury. In the spring of 1985, Jamail at last began to meet daily with Jeffers and Terrell to discuss the progress of their discovery work and to prepare a trial strategy. Jamail was clearly in charge, but the three worked easily together, often retiring in the evenings to Jamail's favorite watering hole out by the Gulf Freeway, where their

discussions were fueled by alcohol. The sometimes playful, intoxicated mood of their preparations, contrasted vividly with the late-
night work at Miller, Keeton, Bristow, & Brown's downtown offices,
where the sober, determined Miller set a deadly earnest tone.

The night before opening arguments in *Pennzoil* v. *Texaco*, Joe
Jamail was holed up in his immense house, writing. Just before sundown, his friends Willie Nelson and Darrell Royal, ex-football coach
at the University of Texas, happened by in a white stretch limousine.
After a few moments of mad pounding on the door, Jamail let them
in. The trio stayed up most of the night, drinking and carrying on.
"Now *that's* how you get ready for an opening argument," Jamail said
later, grinning broadly. It worked for him as it would work for no
one else. Jamail's considerable intellect was often underestimated by
his opponents, as was his capacity for steely-eyed seriousness. But
in reflective moments, he acknowledged that he was driven essentially by his instincts, his intuitive perceptions of human strengths
and frailties. As he had in countless cases before, Jamail intended to
apply those instincts in the trial of *Pennzoil* v. *Texaco*. "The way to
win," he kept saying, "is to keep it simple."

27

PROMISES

Houston in July feels like a hot compress on the back of one's neck. Ninety degrees is a cold snap. The eyes sting, breath shortens, and the mind wanders woozily through the day, yearning for cool clarity.

While the air conditioning cranked along gamely, there was no relief from lethargy in the wooden chambers of the downtown state courthouse during those first days of July 1985. What the jurors remembered later was a sense of slow, creaking anticipation, as if they had been informed that they were six weeks pregnant. It was hard not to feel some excitement, too—the hallways were crowded with the executives and retainers of two of the country's largest oil companies, and all the warnings from the judge about a protracted trial suggested something important was at stake—but the pace was excruciating. The panel from which the final jurors and alternates would be chosen was one hundred strong the first day, and it included dozens who wanted nothing but to escape the courtroom, to go back to home or office, away from the rambling exhortations of the gray-suited lawyers. It was not a place that anyone would pick to spend the summer.

The selection of the jury, known as voir dire, was the first signal that the trial of *Pennzoil* v. *Texaco* would be extraordinary. It went on for five days; it was the longest voir dire that any attorney involved could remember witnessing. In part, the problem was the projected length of the trial. The judge said that it would take six weeks, an estimation that could be safely doubled. It was hard to find sixteen ordinary Houstonians—twelve jurors and four alternates—able to commit themselves without prior notice to a months-long trial. But mainly, it took so long because Joe Jamail wanted it to. Nothing about the case was more important to him than the jury. It is the advantage of the plaintiff in Texas state court that he may ask the first questions of the jury panel to determine if anyone is prejudiced against him. It was Jamail's practice to use this opportunity as a kind of first-draft opening argument. When he stepped before the panel that Wednesday morning, July 10, 1985, he was prepared to voice the essential themes of his case again and again, without interruption, until he was confident that he had made an indelible impression on the jurors he would select.

"There are going to be a lot of issues that you are going to hear, but after you sift through all the issues, only one thing is going to be clear to you," he declared at the beginning. "And that is, this is a case of promises—and what those promises meant to Pennzoil, what they meant ultimately to Texaco."

On and on Jamail went, describing the basic factual outline of Pennzoil's case, employing again and again words like "morality" and "honor" and "handshake deal." He pointed to his "friend" Hugh Liedtke, seated in the audience, and told the panel that this case had gone to trial because his friend had been betrayed by "a conspiracy between Texaco and a group of New York investment bankers and New York lawyers," a conspiracy so rancid it "is going to waken you about that kind of business morality and that kind of business world." Early on, he read to the panel from a transcript of a local television news interview granted by Dick Miller before the trial. Asked if he thought a handshake deal was a legally binding agreement, Miller had replied, "Yet if they want to say that there is some old tradition in the oil field, huh, Jesus Christ, they were in New York."

Jamail went on: "The statement that I just read to you—Mr. Miller as spokesman for Texaco made it—is the position Texaco takes that somehow the promises and the morality of the marketplace are different in New York than they are here."

Then, in typical style, Jamail recast his argument in the form of a rhetorical question, superficially phrased to weed out panelists who might be potentially prejudiced against Pennzoil, but at heart designed to reinforce his theme: "My question to you: Is there anybody on this panel who has an opinion at this time or a feeling at this time that is in agreement with the statement that I just read to you that Mr. Miller says is Texaco's position in this, that a handshake in New York is meaningless? If there is any one of you that has any such opinion, I need to know that. . . ."

Predictably, no hands went up. "I take it you do not," Jamail said.

Jamail and his partners had decided that they were looking for jurors with stability in their lives, people who looked like they expected commitments to be honored. They did not want cynics or transients on the jury. Following a general rule of plaintiffs' trial work, they did not want evangelists, either, because, as Irv Terrell put it later, "they like to leave both sides where they are because God will take care of them later, which doesn't help the plaintiff." Assessing such fundamental personal qualities on the basis of appearance and the answers to a few rhetorical questions was a deeply intuitive art, and one for which Joe Jamail was justly renowned. Each side had only six "strikes," or opportunities to remove panelists without proof of prejudice. Any number of panelists could be removed by the judge "for cause" if they revealed a predisposition to favor one side over the other. If Jamail or Miller intuitively disliked a particular panelist, they tried first to persuade the judge to remove the juror for cause. Here Jamail was most clearly in his element. A panelist about whom there was some question would be invited to approach the bench, where he or she could be quietly interviewed by Jamail, Miller, and the judge. Time and again, through gentle and persuasive questioning, Jamail led prospective jurors to admit some hidden prejudice. Unlike Miller, who tended to be argumentative at the bench, Jamail cajoled the panelists—his tone was friendly, understanding, like a priest in confession.

"He said he would not be a very good juror for us because of the way he feels," Jamail said at one bench conference, which concerned a juror who had relatives in Texaco's employ.

"Yes," the panelist agreed. "I think I would be a poor risk for your side. That's my opinion."

"Because of the feelings you now have?"

"Yes, sir."

"Closeness to Texaco?"

"My concern is that I might be swayed by those relationships, yes, sir."

"With Texaco?"

"Yes, sir."

"And because of that relationship, we would have to do some-thing to overcome it on behalf of Pennzoil."

"Certainly. Certainly."

"Yes. And that would reflect in your attitude while you were on the jury, if you were on the jury?"

"Subconsciously, it might, yeah."

"You believe it would, don't you?"

"I am concerned about it. Concerned about it."

With that, the judge struck the juror from the panel.

Of the sixteen who were finally chosen, there was only one about whom Jamail had any doubts. She was a nurse named Laura John-son, and it seemed to Jeffers and Terrell that Jamail's doubts were residue from his long experience in personal-injury cases; a "sore-back lawyer" never wants a medical professional on his panel. The three lawyers talked back and forth about whether they wanted to use one of their precious strikes against her, and finally Jeffers and Terrell told Jamail that he should make his own decision, that they would stand by it. Jamail went off to the bathroom, thought about it a while, then returned to say that the nurse would be fine. There was a nearly religious intensity about Jamail during the jury selection phase. Each choice seemed a kind of satori for him.

In the end, it was the kind of jury one would see described in a promotional film about the American justice system: stalwart, work-ing and middle-class, racially and ethnically diverse. There was a forklift salesman, an independent businesswoman, an oil company secretary, a janitor, a retiree, a letter carrier, an employee of the city of Houston. They were, as a group, remarkable for being ordinary. Certainly, none of them had ever come in intimate contact with the class of men on whom they would now be asked to pass judgment.

Pennzoil's affirmative case, which lasted nine weeks, depended pri-marily on the live courtroom testimony of three witnesses: Baine Kerr, Arthur Liman, and Hugh Liedtke. All three of them recounted, in extended narratives, the tale of Pennzoil's attempt to take con-trol of Getty Oil during the first days of January 1984. Kerr testified for seven days, Liman four, Liedtke for eight. They talked about why Getty Oil was such an important target, describing its rich oil, gas,

and mineral assets scattered around the globe. They talked about
the divided ownership of the company, the relative stock positions
of Gordon Getty, the museum, and the public. They said that they
didn't know too much about the internal disputes and problems at
Getty Oil following the death of Lansing Hays in May 1982. But their
impression was, they testified, that the cause of all the trouble, and the
reason Getty Oil was put into play, lay with chairman Sid Petersen.
The Pennzoil witnesses, particularly Liedtke, wrapped Gordon Getty
in the legends of Texas oil culture—Gordon was only trying to take
his daddy's place at the head of the family company, he said. Hugh
Liedtke was going to help Gordon overcome the entrenched, morally
bankrupt management led by Petersen and protected by his coterie
of Eastern-dominated bankers and lawyers. But Pennzoil was foiled
in this noble attempt by the lawyers' tricks and deceits, he said.

Setting aside its relationship to reality, Pennzoil's tale was a
powerful and compelling one, mythological in scope and appeal.
Its details were vivid and neatly in place, reinforced by the oft-
repeated themes of betrayal and honor drawled by Jamail from his
first moment before the jury. With the witness examinations divided
evenly between them, each of the three Pennzoil attorneys played a
critical role. Jamail set the tone, speaking always about morality—
not as a kind of Christian abstraction, but as it related to social class
and culture in Texas and New York. Terrell was the enforcer, the
cynical conscience. At the counsel table, he kept his attention on the
jurors, rolling his eyes and shaking his head mockingly whenever
Dick Miller or Texaco's representatives offered a rationale for their
entrance into the Getty Oil deal. And Jeffers played the professor, the
teacher. Much of the evidence Pennzoil presented during its affirmative case—contract drafts, damage estimates, stock exchange agreements—was excruciatingly complex and dull. Jeffers presented this
evidence in a dogged, plodding manner; his style bored some jurors,
but it lent an important rational foundation to the emotional aspects
of Pennzoil's presentation.

The crucial documentary evidence had been available to both
sides for more than a year. To prove that it had reached a binding
contract with the Getty Oil directors on the evening of January 3
at the Inter-Continental Hotel, Pennzoil offered, in addition to the
narrative testimony of Kerr, Liman, and Liedtke, three documents
fundamental to the deal: the "Memorandum of Agreement" signed

by Gordon, Pennzoil, and the museum after the meeting between Liedtke and Gordon at the Pierre Hotel on New Year's Day; the so-called "Copley notes" taken by Getty Oil general counsel Dave Copley at the marathon Inter-Continental board meeting, wherein he recorded the conversations and votes of the directors; and the press release issued by Getty Oil on the morning of January 4, which described the basic terms of an "agreement in principle" arrived at the night before between the directors, Gordon, and Pennzoil.

Several other important, contemporaneous documents pertaining to the contract issue were offered by Pennzoil as well: a January 2, 1984, fee letter from Goldman, Sachs to Sid Petersen, setting out the terms of Goldman's compensation in a deal with Pennzoil; a handwritten note made by Steadman Garber in Los Angeles during a conversation with Getty Oil executives in New York, in which Garber recorded the words, "board agreed but for Chaunce that deal should be done;" and an affidavit by Gordon Getty's banker, Marty Siegel, prepared at the request of Gordon's lawyers shortly after the Inter-Continental meeting, in which Siegel declared that "the Getty Oil board of directors approved a corporate reorganization transaction. . . ."

These documents were the heart of Pennzoil's evidence. They were the same documents that had led the chancellor in the Delaware lawsuit to declare eighteen months earlier that Pennzoil's contract case seemed likely to be proved in court. And to this base Pennzoil's lawyers added new evidence, developed during the discovery phase in the spring and summer of 1984, suggestive of Texaco's "interference" with its contract.

The most powerful of these documents were the handwritten notes taken by Al DeCrane at his meeting with First Boston's Joseph Perella in the early morning hours of January 5. Recording Perella's comments about how Texaco should proceed in its acquisition, DeCrane had noted that his company might have to "stop the train" and then "take care" of Hugh Liedtke by allowing Pennzoil to exercise an option for 8 million shares.

Jamail and Terrell also spoke frequently to the jury about the legal indemnities provided by Texaco to the Getty Oil board, the museum, and Gordon Getty, absolving them from liability for their conduct in the deal. Disingenuously, Pennzoil's lawyers implied that the indemnities were the reason that only Texaco, and not the museum,

Gordon, or the Getty Oil directors, had been brought before the
Houston jury to answer for the betrayal of Hugh Liedtke—as Jamail
put it, Texaco had "bought this lawsuit" when it granted the indemnities. Since Judge Farris ruled that Dick Miller would not be permitted to counter this assertion by informing the jury that Pennzoil was
suing Getty Oil, the museum, and Gordon's trust in Delaware, the
impression stuck. (This was one of several key rulings by Farris on
the admissibility of testimony and evidence which Texaco claimed
were biased and improper.) The indemnities became an important
focus of the Pennzoil attorneys' moral outrage. A kind of syllogism
of evil was developed around them: Texaco granted the indemnities;
therefore, it knew that it was doing something wrong; therefore, it
assumed responsibility for the wrongs of those it chose to protect.

As the trial slogged onward through July and August, however,
it was not so much the details of Pennzoil's fundamental documentary evidence that seemed to pique the jury's interest. It was
the demeanor of the rich and important witnesses paraded before
them. There, too, Jamail and his partners worked to strike a balance
between accessible, emotional testimony and declarative, narrative
accounts of Pennzoil's unfortunate experience in Manhattan during
the first week of January 1984. Baine Kerr told the colorful story of
Pennzoil's corporate history: its founding by George Bush and the
Liedtke brothers in the dusty Texas oil fields (his version tended to
downplay the role of family and social connections in the company's
early growth); its rapid ascent into a multibillion-dollar enterprise;
and above all, its culture of wildcatting entrepreneurism and its
deep roots in the Texas oil patch. Arthur Liman, who was effectively
presented as an exception to Jamail's rule that "New York lawyers"
were untrustworthy, testified in vivid, almost novelistic detail about
his dealings with Marty Lipton, Gordon, and the Getty Oil directors. Most provocative of all was his description of that moment at
the Inter-Continental on the evening of January 3 when the bankers and lawyers burst through the doors of Sutton Room II and one
of them—it was Marty Lipton or Marty Siegel, Liman thought—
declared, "Congratulations, Arthur, you've got a deal." Liman's testimony that he subsequently entered Sutton Room II and shook hands
with a number of Getty Oil directors accorded perfectly with Jamail's
earliest thematic speech to the jury about the Texas honor of a handshake deal.

And finally, among the key live witnesses, there was Hugh Liedtke, the Texas oilman with the face and spirit of a bulldog, a witness so perfectly suited to his role before the jury that he almost seemed to be a caricature drawn from Joe Jamail's imagination. All of the witnesses, including Liedtke, were thoroughly coached and prepared by their lawyers, but when the Pennzoil chairman was on the stand, he exuded such natural stubbornness and honesty that his testimony seemed utterly spontaneous. Occasionally, Liedtke seemed to surprise even Jamail with his answers—several times he rejected the premise of his own lawyer's question. The friendship and affinity between witness and examiner was obvious, however; their dialogue was no more forced than a conversation over dominos and beer. In one telling exchange, Jamail asked Liedtke to compare his own managerial methods with those of Texaco's executives. He wanted Liedtke to comment on the failure of McKinley, DeCrane, and Kinnear to examine the Copley notes before going ahead with their acquisition.

"Based on your experience, sir, if you were going to negotiate a transaction of this magnitude, would a request by Texaco to see the January second Getty board meeting notes, January second and third, be unreasonable or reasonable?" Jamail asked.

"I can't imagine anybody acting without having thoroughly investigated all of the things that you've mentioned," Liedtke declared. "I would think that the top management of the company would have examined those documents—each of them themselves and each one of them having done it. People don't get that place in a corporation without doing their homework."

"Would you as an oil executive, acting responsibly, have gone forward to make a contract with someone if you had not reviewed all of these things?"

"No, of course not."

"Why wouldn't you?"

"Mr. Jamail, I would consider that about as arrogant and unethical a thing to do as I can possibly imagine."

Dick Miller's cross examination of Liedtke was fiercely determined—it was his most passionate examination of the entire trial. It was characteristic of Miller, who measured men by their inner drive, their warrior spirit, that he thought of Hugh Liedtke as the soul of *Pennzoil* v. *Texaco*. In preparing for Jamail's affirmative case, Miller had asked himself this: Who is responsible for bringing this case? Who has the strength of personality to bring this case and resist settlement? Who's ego is sustaining this case? It was certainly not the mild-mannered Baine Kerr, Pennzoil's president, Miller thought. It was not Baker & Botts. It was not Jamail. The answer, Miller believed, was Hugh Liedtke.

During his decades-long career at Baker & Botts, Miller had never worked closely with Liedtke, but since Pennzoil was a major client of his firm, he had seen the chairman up close. Miller felt that he knew Hugh Liedtke, the way a hunter knows his game. From his experience and his peculiarly intense instincts, Miller had come to believe that Liedtke was a manipulative, cynical financier—hardly the honest, drawling wildcatter from the oil patch that he portrayed himself to be. The concrete evidence that Miller possessed to support his view was the difficulty Liedtke had with the Securities and Exchange Commission a decade before, during one of Pennzoil's complex financial restructurings—Liedtke had settled the case by agreeing to forfeit his improper profits. But Judge Farris ruled that Liedtke's past difficulties were not admissible in the present case. And so Miller had only his powerful instincts to follow during his cross examination. He believed that Liedtke's bid for 20 percent of Getty Oil and his subsequent alliance with Gordon Getty painted a shadier portrait of the Pennzoil chairman than the one proffered by Jamail.

Jeffers and Terrell sensed Miller's obsession with Liedtke; it was apparent in their former partner's entire approach to the trial. In his asides to the jury during examinations, and in his voir dire and opening arguments, Miller portrayed Hugh Liedtke as a manipulative, cynical mastermind who planned to "use" Gordon Getty to acquire three-sevenths of Getty Oil's assets at a bargain price. Miller had to tread carefully here, because it would be detrimental to his case if he cast Gordon, in Boone Pickens' phrase, as the puppy to Hugh Liedtke's sledgehammer—then Miller would have a hard time arguing that Gordon had sold his stock to Texaco freely and willingly. But Miller made his point: by insisting on the one-year "out" clause in his power-sharing deal with Gordon, Liedtke had belied his assertion that he was nobly trying to restore Gordon Getty to the throne of his family company. Miller emphasized the "hostile" aspects of Pennzoil's 20 percent tender offer and the pressure it put on the museum and the Getty Oil board. Jeffers and Terrell came to believe that Miller's obsession with Liedtke's role in the case had a great deal to do with the former Baker & Botts partner's desire to defeat his old firm and one of its most important clients—that Miller's legendary devotion to winning had an extra dimension in this case. Miller himself did not see it that way; he said that the emphasis he placed on Liedtke derived solely from his view that Pennzoil's chairman was the driving force behind the entire lawsuit.

Miller's cross-examination of Liedtke went on for days. He pressed the Pennzoil chairman on every possible topic, from Liedtke's motives in bidding for Getty Oil to his opinions about Petersen and McKinley, to his failure to sign a definitive agreement with the Getty Oil directors. But the more persistent the questioning, the more stubborn Liedtke became. Even if he was caught in an obvious and harmless error, Liedtke refused to yield to Miller.

"Well, George Getty died in 1973?" Miller asked at one point while questioning Liedtke about a *New York Times* article presented to the witness.

"No, George Getty did not die in 1973." On this point, Liedtke was in fact mistaken. It hardly mattered; George Getty was not relevant to the case. But Liedtke would not back down.

"When did he die?" Miller asked.

"I don't recall."

"How do you know he didn't die in 1973?"

"Well, because so many of the statements that the reporter's made here, Mr. Miller, have been inaccurate. I don't think I want to accept that one until you show me. If you show me that one, I'll accept it. I would think Mr. Getty died in 'seventy-six, so probably George did die around that time, but Jack Roth was—"

"Around what time?"

"Around 'seventy-three or 'seventy-four, right in that time frame. But that does not change the fact that what I told you is accurate."

On other occasions, Liedtke got the better of his questioner. When Miller pressed the witness as to why, having discovered that Texaco had taken Getty Oil away from him, Liedtke sent a threatening telegram to the Getty Oil board but did not communicate with Texaco.

"Here you are on the sixth of January," Miller intoned dramatically. "You wake up and find out that somebody has stolen seven and a half billion dollars from you, and you don't even get in touch with them."

"Well, suppose I'm in the banking business and somebody's stolen the Brink's truck," Liedtke replied. "Do I call the robbers or do I call the police?"

"Well, I'd have to say that's a clever remark, no doubt about it," Miller said, his tone so sarcastic that Jamail stood to object.

It was also during Dick Miller's cross-examination of Hugh Liedtke that the Great Zipper Incident—or the Great Zipper Trick, depending on who one believes—took place. It is the goal of every trial lawyer to curry favor and sympathy with the jury, and so he must seize every opportunity to humanize himself to the panel. Dick Miller conceded afterward that he was long a student of trial lawyer trickery, but he insisted that the zipper incident was not deliberately concocted. What happened was this: Miller returned from a short break in his cross-examination of Hugh Liedtke with his fly wide open. He resumed his questioning. One of the jurors began to giggle. Another juror joined in, then another, until the box was nearly shaking from suppressed convulsions. Finally, Miller's partner, Robert Brown, passed Miller a note that read, "Your pants are unzipped."

"I am told I need to make some repairs," Miller told the judge. "May I be excused momentarily?"

"You can make repairs anytime, Mr. Miller."

When Miller returned, he smiled to the jury and said, "Well, I thought somebody would have spoken a little bit louder."

It was the adamant and quite angrily held opinion of Joe Jamail that Dick Miller had come into court with his fly unzipped on purpose, in order to impress the jury with his vulnerable, likable humanity. Jamail was convinced of this because he himself had used the same trick on occasions in the past—in fact, Jamail went so far as to accuse Miller of stealing the idea from him. Miller seemed offended not so much by that accusation, which he denied, but by the failure of Pennzoil's lawyers to laugh with him at the joke.

The man notably absent from Houston state courtroom 151 during the long months of the Pennzoil presentation was Gordon Getty. In the story told by Joe Jamail, Hugh Liedtke, Arthur Liman, and the rest, Gordon was a singularly important character. Indeed, he was central to Pennzoil's sweeping themes about honor and morality.

And yet he remained an essentially mysterious figure. It was said that Gordon wanted to run his father's company, and that he had challenged the management practices of Sid Petersen, particularly Getty Oil's diversification into nonoil businesses. For this, Pennzoil's attorneys argued, Gordon was treated with disdain, malevolence, and skullduggery by Petersen and his band of Wall Street retainers. Jamail referred again and again to the Getty Oil board meeting of November 1983, when the directors asked Gordon to leave the room while they voted to intervene in the family lawsuit Petersen and Getty's outside counsel Bart Winokur had helped to organize. The moniker "Back Door Bart" was skillfully concocted to describe Winokur's role. But Pennzoil's descriptions of Gordon Getty and his relations with Getty Oil's management were sharply limited. There was no detailed testimony about Gordon's behavior in London in October 1983, for example, or about his dealings with Petersen and Winokur during the previous eighteen months. The Pennzoil attorneys skillfully portrayed Gordon as a victim—not helpless, not in any way immature, but rather, like Hugh Liedtke himself, unable to defeat the power and manipulations of Wall Street's best and brightest lawyers and bankers.

Gordon testified only by videotaped deposition; he was beyond the subpoena range of the Texas state courts, and he was unwilling to voluntarily appear because of his entanglement in family litigation. So his presence at the trial, while critically important, was strangely distorted—he could be evaluated only by his television performance. On the days Gordon's deposition was shown, the courtroom was packed; everyone wanted to see and hear the famous Getty scion. Gordon did not disappoint his audience. His distinctive character was evident even in this limited medium. He smiled and mugged for the camera hilariously. When asked about a specific exhibit, he would hold the paper up and shove it toward the camera like a comedic TV talk-show guest. In serious moments, his eyebrows knitted, his bony fingers draped across his cheek, and he seemed a portraiture of exaggerated concentration.

The substance of his testimony was crucial in one aspect. For Pennzoil to prove that Texaco had interfered with its contract, it had to convince the jury that Gordon had been forced to sell his family trust's stock. On the evening of January 5, 1984, when Gordon was visited at the Pierre Hotel by John McKinley, Gordon and Pennzoil were partners. If Gordon testified that he had made his deal with Texaco out of his own free will, voluntarily and without coercion, then Pennzoil's interference case would be severely undermined. It was important to Pennzoil that the "squeeze" scenario be credibly presented to the jury—that is, the jury had to believe that after forging a hasty alliance with Petersen for the company and Lipton for the museum, Texaco forced Gordon to sell out his 40 percent. In this scenario, if Gordon failed to sell, Texaco would squeeze him out at an unfavorable price—Gordon would be the juice. The question was, how did Gordon himself feel about the sale to Texaco? Facing the family lawsuit in California challenging his control of the Getty fortune, he had to be careful about not only what he said, but how he said it. At his videotaped deposition, John Jeffers, who was handling the questioning, had not been sure what Gordon's answer would be.

"Would it be fair to say that when Texaco showed up at this meeting, its representatives, Mr. Lipton for the museum, and you found out that the museum was going to sell to Texaco, that you felt you had no choice but to do so?" Jeffers finally asked after a lengthy build-up.

"I think that's a fair statement," Gordon answered.

That was all Pennzoil needed from him. Gordon's reply might on its face be ambiguous. (What did he mean, that he had no choice? Was he threatened? Did he ask what would happen if he chose not to sell? Why not?) But the opening was wide enough. Through it, Joe Jamail and his two partners pulled the basic premise of their client's case. Together, Gordon and Pennzoil had been victimized by Texaco and its Wall Street proxies. Gordon's treatment at the hands of Petersen, Winokur, and the rest, was morally outrageous. The way Pennzoil's attorneys told it, it was a story as plain as black and white.

Indeed, that was how Gordon himself privately viewed his involvement in the affairs of Getty Oil over the company's final eighteen months—during that entire time, he had done nothing wrong, he said. His trip to London in October 1983 was a waste of time, he conceded, and thus reflected a slight miscalculation on his part, but his behavior was at all times perfectly appropriate, even admirable. It was Gordon Getty's self-image that was presented to the jury by Pennzoil in the Harris County Courthouse that summer of 1985. Whatever its relation to reality, it was the view of Gordon that best served Hugh Liedtke's case. If a dissenting opinion was to be offered to the jurors, it would have to come from Texaco.

28

OF SHARKS AND BEAR HUGS

After two months of testimony, Pennzoil rested its case against Texaco on Wednesday, September 18, 1985. The last witness, examined by Jamail, was Texaco chairman John McKinley, who had been subpoenaed by Pennzoil when he arrived in Houston to attend the voir dire jury selection in July. Texaco's executives said later that they had anticipated this maneuver by Pennzoil's lawyers and were prepared to have one or more of the company's officers testify as "adverse" witnesses during Pennzoil's affirmative case. But as the end-note to his presentation, Jamail's cross-examination of McKinley, which immediately followed Hugh Liedtke's testimony, dramatically emphasized the aggressive challenge of Pennzoil's accusations.

It is a time-worn adage of jury trial lawyering that a defendant must be at least "even" with his opponent when the plaintiff rests his case. Otherwise, the theory goes, the defensive witnesses will have too much ground to make up with the jury. Another time-worn adage, which negates the utility of the first, is that trial lawyers see precisely what they want to see in the faces of the jury. So it was hardly surprising that when Pennzoil rested, Joe Jamail, Irv Terrell, and John Jeffers believed that they were way ahead, while Dick Miller and his partners thought that they were at least even, if not ahead themselves.

In theory, it is desirable for any defendant to put on as few witnesses as possible, so as to avoid damaging cross examination. Such a strategy is only possible if the defendant's case has been effectively presented during cross-examination of the plaintiff's witnesses. In Texaco's case, this had not been accomplished by Miller and his partners—not because their cross-examinations were ineffective, but because the Pennzoil witnesses told a highly selective version of the events in New York in January 1984. Texaco had little choice but to call a parade of witnesses to the stand: Texaco executives who would testify that they had been invited into the friendly deal by Getty Oil's Sid Petersen; Getty Oil directors who would testify that they had made no binding contract with Pennzoil; and Wall Street lawyers and bankers who would say that negotiations with Pennzoil had never been concluded because there were so many "open points" in the proposed joint takeover by Gordon and Hugh Liedtke.

Joe Jamail and his partners had expected all along that the defense's first witness would be Al DeCrane, Texaco's president. When they thought about their own case, the Pennzoil attorneys realized that its weakest aspect was the proof of Texaco's deliberate "interference" with Pennzoil's alleged contract. In depositions, the cool, cerebral DeCrane had testified confidently about the circumstances surrounding Texaco's entrance into the deal and about his company's friendly intentions toward Getty Oil management. Immaculately dressed, exuding the authority of his office, DeCrane was articulate and unflappable. He faced one difficulty as a witness: the embarrassing notes he had taken early on the morning of January 5 during his meeting with the First Boston bankers. But DeCrane handled the notes as well as anyone could expect. He emphasized that his scribblings reflected the opinions of Texaco's new team of investment bankers that night, not the views of DeCrane, McKinley, or the Texaco directors. He said that Texaco would never have taken control of Getty Oil unless all the Getty interests, including Gordon, wanted to be rescued from Pennzoil by a white knight.

So when Texaco's attorneys stood in the courtroom on the morning of Thursday, September 19, and called Bart Winokur to the stand, the Pennzoil lawyers were shocked. Winokur had been the target of their most vitriolic rhetoric during the first half of the case. He was not a Texan. He had no legitimate connection to the oil business. He was just a lawyer—one of the storied Eastern lawyers at whose feet Jamail laid the blame for Pennzoil's betrayal.

Later on, there would be a great deal of debate about the strategic decisions made by Dick Miller and his partners during the first weeks of September, as they prepared for the opening of Texaco's defense. Miller would say that each decision reflected a consensus between himself, his partners, the lawyers from Texaco's general counsel office, and even Texaco's top executives. The Texaco executives, for their part, would say that they were merely following the expert advice of their lead trial counsel. Miller himself detested management by consensus; trial work to him was the ultimate test of individualism. When devising strategy, he pushed his client hard to follow his lead. Miller and his client shared an inclination to authoritarian decision-making; they were like magnets pushing against each other.

In White Plains, McKinley, DeCrane, and general counsel Weitzel were to some degree isolated from Miller by layers of hierarchy in the Texaco legal department, but they made their opinions clear nonetheless. In discussions about the order of defense witnesses, McKinley asked if it wouldn't be best to lead with a witness from Texas—Getty Oil president Robert Miller, perhaps, or Getty Oil director and former chairman Harold Berg. But Miller was looking for a different kind of witness. He wanted someone who could provide the jury with an overview of Getty Oil's predicament at the time of Pennzoil's hostile tender offer, someone who could vividly describe the intense pressure the directors faced from Gordon and especially Hugh Liedtke. Through the summer, while Pennzoil's case was presented, Miller told Sid Petersen that he would be Texaco's first witness. Petersen would testify that Liedtke was in effect holding a gun to his head, that Liedtke and Gordon were trying to steal Getty Oil at an unfair price, and thus Texaco's friendly rescue of the company was heroic. Then Miller changed his mind and settled on Winokur, who was more confident and articulate than Petersen—Winokur was an accomplished storyteller, and he could testify about a wider range of topics than Petersen, including the "open points" in Getty Oil's negotiations with Pennzoil.

Miller discounted the notion that a Texaco executive like DeCrane should testify first. Miller believed that to begin with an attack on the interference side of Pennzoil's case would be to tell the jury, in effect, "Maybe there was a contract, but we didn't know it at the time." Such a position was untenable, he thought. And besides,

Miller, McKinley, DeCrane, Winokur, Marty Lipton, and everyone
else involved in Texaco's defense adamantly believed that there was
no contract under New York law, that an "agreement in principle"
was no agreement at all. They had merely to convey this certainty to
the jury.

And so Bart Winokur took the stand, much to the delight of Joe
Jamail, Irv Terrell, and John Jeffers. Their only concern about Winokur centered on his obvious skills as a storyteller; they worried that
if the jurors found Winokur to be a fully credible witness, they might
be seduced by the tale he told. It was in some ways ironic that Bart
Winokur's credibility should become such an important issue at the
trial. After all, the feeling of Gordon Getty and his lawyers, justified
or not, that Winokur was duplicitous and manipulative, had led to
much of the dissension that put Getty Oil into play in the first place.
Now Winokur would be required before a Houston jury to defend
not only his dealings with Pennzoil, but Getty Oil management's
relations with Gordon Getty as well.

Isolated in semiretirement in Los Angeles, Sid Petersen was disappointed that he had not been called to testify by Texaco. Petersen
and the other deposed Getty Oil executives felt that Texaco treated
them with a measure of condescension and disdain. There was an
atmosphere of corporate machismo about it all, a sense that Texaco's executives were the victors and Getty Oil's managers the vanquished, this despite the "friendliness" of the merger and the soft
landings afforded the divine nine by their golden parachutes. Texaco
seemed to them unwilling to defend the Getty Oil Company in the
trial against Pennzoil. Petersen and his colleagues offered time and
again to explain the convoluted, angry, and morally ambiguous history of management's dealings with Gordon Getty following the
death of Lansing Hays. But Miller and Texaco's in-house attorneys
seemed uninterested. They had to be careful about attacking Gordon
Getty in court, because if they portrayed him as an incompetent or a
fool, they lent credence to Pennzoil's theory that Texaco had put the
squeeze on Gordon.

At the same time, however, it was clear to Petersen, his former
colleagues, and their attorneys, that Pennzoil's case was strengthened
by its selective attacks on Petersen and Winokur. Pennzoil's lawyers
pilloried "Back Door" Bart Winokur and the Getty Oil directors
for their deceits at the November 1983 board meeting. But Texaco

did nothing to counter, or at least modify, this impression by raising questions about Gordon's behavior in London or during the fall of 1982, when the Getty scion disclosed internal company information to potential predators such as Corby Robertson. The portrayal of Gordon's dealings with Petersen and Winokur was one-sided, described almost entirely by the terms of Joe Jamail's skillful advocacy and moral rhetoric.

Much to the consternation of Sid Petersen, this imbalance was not righted by the testimony of Bart Winokur; if anything, the imbalance was aggravated. The direct examination was conducted by Miller's partner J. C. Nickens, and it seemed designed to make two basic points about the case: first, that in the context of mergers and acquisitions protocol, Pennzoil was the hostile predator, the "shark;" and second, that the "agreement in principle" reached with the Getty Oil directors on the evening of January 3 was not binding because a number of important, outstanding issues had yet to be resolved. To the first point, Winokur introduced the jury to the imaginative jargon of modern Wall Street merger experts, and he tried to describe Pennzoil's place in this vocabulary.

"What situation does the phrase 'bear hug' describe?" Winokur was asked early in the first of his six days on the stand.

"Well, it's when a target company is approached by a potential acquiring company that in effect pretends to make love, so to speak, hugs the acquiree. The term 'bear hug' is meant to imply, unlike a hug from a normal human being that you can disengage from, the bear is a lot stronger, and once he hugs you, you're stuck."

"And in terms of your understanding of that phrase, did it describe the Pennzoil tender offer?"

"Let me just clarify that. I think he was referring to the proposed transaction as a bear hug," Winokur said, meaning a Getty Oil director's characterization of Pennzoil's offer. "The tender offer he would have described as a gun at the head."

"Now, you're familiar with the term in this business, 'shark'?"

"Yes."

"To what does that term refer?"

"That usually refers to one who begins a hostile tender offer or sometimes not the one that begins it, but once the blood is in the water, the man who comes along to take advantage of the wounded target."

"You mentioned another phrase. Is this phrase 'blood in the water' a phrase that's used in the merger and acquisition business?"

"Yes."

"To what does it refer?"

"It refers to a situation where a target company has been wounded, in effect has bled, and as we all know in that situation, when sharks are around, as soon as there is blood in the water, they immediately close in on the victim."

"One last phrase here, Mr. Winokur. Are you familiar with the phrase 'in play'?"

"Yes."

"What does that phrase refer to in the merger and acquisition business?"

"It usually refers to a situation where attention has been called to a potential victim so that the sharks are beginning to congregate or gather around for the kill."

Winokur's colorful and detailed direct testimony about the pressures Getty Oil's directors faced from Pennzoil and about the fitful negotiations with Baker & Botts following the Inter-Continental hotel meeting did successfully recast Hugh Liedtke's role in the Getty Oil takeover. But the testimony left Winokur vulnerable on two counts. By emphasizing the "open points" in the negotiations between Getty Oil and Pennzoil, Winokur was himself open to the charge that he was merely engaging in obstructionism, holding off a final deal with Liedtke until Geoff Boisi could hastily line up a new buyer for the entire company. Perhaps more importantly, so far as the jury was concerned, Winokur's direct testimony fundamentally challenged Joe Jamail's moral view of the case. Winokur was saying that to the degree morality was involved in the takeover, it was Hugh Liedtke who was the villain—to adopt Winokur's deeply mixed metaphors, Liedtke was the shark with the gun at Getty Oil's head, or else he was the bear standing in the bloodied water, waiting to hug Sid Petersen. The imagery might be convoluted, but the point was clear: if anyone had exhibited questionable ethics in the deal, it was Pennzoil. This left Winokur in a nearly impossible position. Challenged on cross-examination, he would have to defend not only his own ethical conduct, but the morality of Sid Petersen, the Getty Oil directors, Marty Lipton, and the executives of Texaco. By emphasizing Pennzoil's moral culpability, Winokur was inviting a direct attack on his own personal credibility.

He got that, in spades. Irv Terrell took the cross-examination, and he was unrelenting. Terrell understood that he and the witness were not standing on level ground in the eyes of the jury. Here was Winokur, Harvard-educated, Jewish, boyish-looking, bright, brash, and articulate, attacking the credibility of Hugh Liedtke, that dog-faced monument to everything that was good and right about the Texas oil business. The contempt on Terrell's face was chilling, and the gangly lawyer made it a point to communicate his feelings to the jury at every opportunity. So often did Terrell shake his head sarcastically or scrunch his face into an expression of extreme skepticism, it became a running objection by Texaco's attorneys.

"Well, you left Mr. Katz there and Mr. Katz knew that you were going to go meet with Texaco?" Terrell asked while questioning Winokur about his negotiations with Pennzoil on the night of Thursday, January 5. Katz was an attorney representing Getty Oil; Terrell was referring to Winokur's participation in the all-night negotiations following McKinley's meeting with Gordon at the Pierre.

"Well, he knew that I was going over because there was a possibility that we might get an offer from Texaco. He knew because I had said to him, 'Look, nobody knows what's going to happen there. We have got to try and see if we can come up with an agreement.

"But you didn't tell Pennzoil, did you?"

"Of course not."

"Well, Mr. Katz certainly didn't tell Pennzoil, to your knowledge, did he?"

"Well, I wasn't there. I don't know what—I would hope he didn't."

"Huh," Terrell grunted sarcastically.

Nickens shot to his feet. "Your honor, I must object again. Once again, Mr. Terrell is making some comment about the testimony. I doubt that the reporter was able to pick up the 'huh' that Mr. Terrell made, but it's improper and he should not be allowed to make comments on the witness's testimony, even if he doesn't like it."

"Ms. Court Reporter, did you pick up the 'huh'?" Judge Farris asked.

"Yes, sir, I did."

"The objection is sustained on the 'huh.'"

What concerned the Texaco attorneys as Winokur's cross-examination wound on was not so much Irv Terrell's hostile body language or his guttural asides, which were to be expected, but rather the attitude of Judge Farris toward Winokur. It was Dick Miller's opinion that Farris was signaling to the jury, by his expressions and comments, that he did not believe Winokur's testimony. There had been earlier references by Farris to the appearance at trial of "storied" lawyers from New York and Philadelphia, remarks seemingly in tandem with Jamail's themes about the cultural and moral chasm between Wall Street and Texas. Then, just before a break in Winokur's testimony, the judge admonished Winokur for "slipping" in his legal opinions about the case, which had been ruled inadmissible testimony. When the jury was cleared from the courtroom, Miller approached the judge and engaged him in a heated argument.

"The witness is not familiar with practice rules here in Texas and I know him personally," Miller told Farris. "He is an honorable man and I know he would not do that, slip something in. The jury now believes, because of the comment the court made, that the witness has deliberately attempted to evade the rules of evidence and somehow to say something unfair, improper, which puts the witness in a very bad light in front of the jury. I have seen Mr. Terrell and Mr. Jeffers grinning at the jury over there and making these motions as they are wont to do. It puts the witness in a very impossible position . . . I suppose he is at a very considerable disadvantage because he talks a little funny, if I can say so, and I know he won't take umbrage at that, but for there to be a suggestion that the witness has slipped something in—"

"Mr. Miller, are you quite through lecturing me?" Farris exploded.

"I didn't mean to be lecturing you."

"That's what you have been doing and I will have no more of it. Understood, sir? You want to make a bill of exceptions for the record, make it right now."

"I only want the court to instruct—"

"Do you want to make a bill, sir?"

"No, I want the court to instruct the jury to disregard the court's comment, and I shall request it."

"I will not do it, and I will further say, counsel with this man tonight, because I will unload tomorrow morning if that happens again. And I want that answer stricken. You are going to have to ask that question again. If you want to make a bill on that, do it now."

"Well, what kind of bill—"

"Any kind you wish, Mr. Miller. I will not be lectured to."

"Sir, I was not lecturing you and I must take exception to your honor's remark—"

"All right. Take exception."

"I intended my remark to—"

"We are recessed for today."

"—to be courteous and polite to your honor as always."

The following day, Friday, September 20, Farris was informed that Winokur's testimony would be interrupted for several days because the witness had to return to Philadelphia to observe the Yom Kippur religious holiday. Ordinarily, Farris, who was recovering from a heart attack, worked half-days on Friday mornings and Monday afternoons. When he heard that Texaco's attorneys wanted to extend Winokur's testimony into Friday afternoon, Farris was visibly angry. In the presence of the jury, he made a brief speech about the disruption caused by Winokur's schedule.

"As I understand it," Farris said, "I have been asked to work this afternoon so that we would meet the needs of the witness in returning to his home in Philadelphia. This has caused a great amount of consternation from the jurors, all of them, now in their twelfth week. As I understand it, the holiday called Kol Nidre starts Tuesday at sundown. Yom Kippur—Y-o-m, K-i-p-p-u-r—is all day Wednesday. The witness cannot be here from approximately sunset Tuesday through Wednesday and cannot be back here before Thursday. In view of the great unrest among the jurors now in their twelfth week at six dollars a day, I feel that it is unfair to ask them to give up their Friday afternoon, which they had counted on, to allow this witness to have a better schedule. The witness will just have to return and finish whatever schedule he has here, whether it be on cross or direct."

By the end of his testimony, Winokur's alienation from the judge and jury was undeniable. His otherness, in class and culture and religion, had been emphasized explicitly and implicitly. At some level, Dick Miller seemed to understand this, as in his odd remark to Farris that Winokur talked "a little funny." (Winokur had no lisp or distinctive accent, but he spoke brashly, with the confidence of an Ivy League debater.) But no one on the Texaco side believed that Winokur's testimony had been damaging. If anything, they thought, it was an important step forward, a shift in control over the trial's moral tone. Winokur's manner and appearance might be different from Pennzoil's key witnesses, but he was undeniably bright and articulate—surely, the points he made were appealing to the jury. Besides, as to the issue of Winokur's cultural and geographical credentials, how important could that be? Miller and his partners stood behind every Texaco witness. And surely, if indeed it mattered, there was no man at the trial more Texan than Dick Miller.

THE ALIENS

Geoff Boisi, the lanky and sometimes nervous merger banker from Goldman, Sachs, followed Bart Winokur to the stand. Having chosen to lead Texaco's defense with the testimony of Getty Oil's Wall Street advisors, it was only appropriate that Miller should next call Boisi to testify. Beginning in July 1983, when Gordon first proposed an LBO takeover of Getty Oil, Winokur and Boisi had been a nearly inseparable team, advising Sid Petersen from day to day on strategy and tactics. It had been Boisi's firm that established $120 per share as the minimum fair price for Getty Oil's stock, and it was Boisi who fought off Hugh Liedtke's bid by inviting Texaco into the deal—even as the Getty Oil directors were meeting at the Inter-Continental to consider Gordon Getty's joint takeover offer with Pennzoil.

Miller was personally enamored of Boisi. Though relatively young, he exuded a stability and personal integrity that Miller found absent in the flashier, better-known Wall Street bankers involved in the deal, such as First Boston's Bruce Wasserstein and Kidder, Peabody's Marty Siegel. Miller shared the opinion of Boisi's allies in the deal that the young banker had behaved heroically at the Inter-Continental, refusing to issue a fairness letter despite pressure from such eminent American financiers as Larry Tisch and Harold Williams, who supported Pennzoil's $112.50-per-share offer. Miller's idea was that Boisi would bolster Winokur's testimony about the egregious pressure, the "gun at the head," put on the Getty Oil directors by Gordon and Pennzoil.

Boisi would also testify that all of the Wall Street experts involved in the deal, including those representing Pennzoil, knew—or should have known—that an "agreement in principle" was nothing more than an agreement to agree, and that in practical terms it represented an invitation to outsiders to bid for the company.

Someone had to persuade the jury of this last point. Someone had to convince them that the language they saw in the January 4 press release, the words "agreement in principle," did not mean what they might appear to mean. Somehow the jury had to be persuaded to accept the rules of the Wall Street merger game. It had to accept that language had implications different there from its meaning in a forklift factory out by the Gulf Freeway or on a downtown Houston used-car lot. Of course, this was precisely what Joe Jamail had been warning the jurors about from the opening of trial, that a parade of New York lawyers and bankers would try to convince them that a deal in Manhattan was not the same as a deal in Houston. From the very beginning, he had put the Eastern witnesses on the defensive. If the Wall Street experts were to persuade the jury that their special use of language was legitimate, that the rules of their merger game were credible and fair and honest, they had to *sound* credible themselves. They had to be confident, plain-spoken, direct. They had to persuade the jury of their own personal integrity. By adopting the heartland imagery of the handshake deal, Arthur Liman, who had testified just two months before Texaco's defense began, had succeeded in this, and he was a New Yorker, a lawyer, and Jewish besides. So it was not impossible for the likes of Winokur and Boisi to succeed. But their demeanor was critically important.

Miller was confident that Boisi's personal integrity would impress the jury. But Irv Terrell, who again drew the cross-examination assignment, felt that Boisi was vulnerable because he was a naturally high-strung man. Terrell decided to put the witness under as much personal pressure as he could muster. By attacking Boisi again and again, by hounding and pressing and challenging, Terrell hoped to exploit the banker's innate nervousness, to make him sweat and stammer before the jury. On the facts, Boisi was most exposed in two areas: his participation in Getty Oil management's "conspiracy" against Gordon Getty, as Pennzoil was now describing it, and his telephone calls on January 3 and 4 to Texaco, Chevron, and other third parties while negotiations with Pennzoil were under way.

"And you felt that was an honest thing to do?" Terrell asked menacingly at one point, questioning Boisi about the Getty Oil November board meeting where Gordon was invited to leave the room while the directors voted to intervene in the family lawsuit against him.

"Well, any—he was going to be—it was going to be communicated to him, so he knew what was going to happen."

"That's fine as an explanation. Could I have a yes or no? Did you feel that was an honest thing to do?"

"I guess I do."

The challenge to Boisi—the challenge to all the Wall Street witnesses—was to explain the precepts of their profession generally, and their actions in the Getty Oil deal particularly, in confident, concise, and accessible language. None of them could afford to sound defensive. But since "the other side" of Getty Oil management's dealings with Gordon Getty—the examples of Gordon's own questionable behavior—was never explored in direct examination, Terrell and his partners were free to exploit with impunity, and in isolation, the most dramatic examples of management's maltreatment of Gordon. Then, when the cross-examination moved on to the detailed issues that were crucially important to Pennzoil's case, such as the meaning of an "agreement in principle" and the ethical appositeness of Geoff Boisi's telephone calls on January 3 and 4, the Wall Street witnesses were already on the defensive. Terrell and his partners could ask their questions in language that rang with broad moral implications. The Wall Street witnesses, whose experience with language centered on the formulation and use of precise, narrow, morally neutral definitions, found themselves in an exceedingly difficult position. They had to respond to the questions by attempting to dissect and redefine words that contained universal moral meaning. Asked if they accepted the commandment "Thou shalt not steal," they had to answer, "Yes, but it's important to understand what stealing means on Wall Street."

"My question to you is, do you have to use good faith?" Terrell asked Boisi in one critical exchange on the morning of Thursday, October 10. "Are you required to use good faith to see whether you can implement the details of the agreement in principle?"

"Well, you put a word in there, 'required."

"That's the word I put to Mr. Petersen. That's the word I'm putting to you."

"Okay. I'm trying to answer that—with that caveat. When one talks about required, when you are dealing with a public company, you also not only have to operate in good faith, which I think people should do all the time—I hope that I do—but in addition to that, you have a fiduciary responsibility. Whether you are a chairman of the board or whether you are an investment banker for the company, you can be working in good faith to an agreement in principle you've been developing. But that doesn't mean that you don't have a responsibility to look into other proposals that perceptibly would be better than the agreement in principle that you have on the table."

"Listen to? Or go out and shop for, solicit them? Listen to other proposals or shop for them?"

"Well—you, you use whatever word you want. I don't understand your question."

"Well, you used the word, you have a 'responsibility' to listen to other offers. Do you have a responsibility to go out and solicit other offers?"

"Well, now you are getting into specific words again. I don't know—what is your definition of solicit?"

"What you did on the fourth."

"Well, what I did on the fourth was I called somebody to thank him for his cooperation the day before and to indicate to him that, out of courtesy, a public announcement was going to be made. And in the context of that conversation, a question was asked of me as to whether or not a binding agreement had been developed. And my answer was no. And then the second question was, well, in that case, if somebody came in and made another offer, would you have to listen to it? My answer was yes. I don't regard this as soliciting."

"So your evidence is that when you talked to Mr. DeCrane on the fourth, you did not solicit an offer. It was merely a courtesy call. He was the one who made the offer, is that right?"

"Well, he didn't even make an offer on that day. He was asking for information. I gave him information. . . . And it was apparent to me from the conversation that I had with Mr. DeCrane that that clearly was still a possibility in his mind, if not a probability. So when he asked me the question about where the transaction stood, it was also clear to me that he understood the implications of what went over the Dow Jones wire with regard to the agreement in principle."

"You've given your explanation. Was the answer to my question yes or no? Did you solicit him? Did you solicit him the morning of the fourth; yes or no?"

"Well, yeah, I'm asking you—"

"Yes or no."

"I would say no."

"All right. Were you soliciting when you called Chevron and the Saudi government that same day?"

"No, I was doing the same thing I did with Mr. DeCrane. I was calling them because I had spoken to some of them the day before, to the Saudi government."

"All right. So people you called on the fourth and fifth were just courtesy calls. They weren't to solicit? That's your evidence?"

"No, that's not what I said at all. That is not what I said at all."

"Were you—"

"What I said—what I said was the first telephone call on the third, excuse me, on the fourth was out of the courtesy call to several different people."

There was a surreal quality to these examinations, a sense that lawyer and witness were speaking in two different languages. In his answer to Terrell's question about negotiating in "good faith," Boisi even seemed to acknowledge the point. He conceded that he hoped everyone acted in good faith all the time, out of a general sense of morality and fairness, but Boisi then went on to qualify his answer by explaining that this moral precept coexisted with a "fiduciary" responsibility. Thus, Boisi implicitly acknowledged that financial and moral imperatives might well come into conflict. There was no real way around it. In the language of his own world, Wall Street's world of complex, high-stakes merger-making, the distinctions Boisi drew were perfectly understandable, even necessary. But in a Houston, Texas, courtroom before twelve ordinary, working-class citizens, the subtlety was lost. It sounded like double-talk.

No more dramatically was this linguistic chasm evident than in Joe Jamail's cross-examination of Marty Lipton, which began one week after the close of Boisi's testimony. There had been a long and vigorous debate within the Texaco defense team about whether to call Lipton to the stand at all. Dick Miller, for one, opposed the idea. He knew that the Pennzoil lawyers had targeted Lipton. Unlike all the other key Texaco witnesses, Lipton had not been deposed by the Pennzoil lawyers, and Miller correctly surmised that this was because

Jamail wanted to spring his questions for the first time in open court, before the jury. "They set us up," Miller told Texaco's lawyers and executives. But at Texaco headquarters in White Plains, there was an inexorable momentum in support of Lipton's appearance at trial. Lipton was the preeminent merger expert, perhaps the best-known corporate lawyer in the country. Texaco felt that Liman's testimony could not go unrebutted. As Miller put it later: "It became impractical not to put him on. Texaco board members were his friends. He had represented Texaco in the past. The perception was that it would be intolerable to try the case and lose without Marty Lipton testifying on your behalf. I didn't see it that way. I didn't think we needed him. I didn't want to worry about what would happen if we lost—I want to win."

Texaco executives said later that while Miller initially opposed calling Lipton, it was he who made the final call. They said that an important element of the debate centered on Patricia Vlahakis, the young lawyer who had worked with Lipton during the Getty Oil deal. Vlahakis had been scheduled to testify live, but at the time of trial she was pregnant and under a doctor's orders not to travel. She testified by video deposition, but the effect was not the same. So the decision was made to call Lipton.

Rotund, bespectacled, Semitic in appearance, Lipton was preceded into courtroom 151 by his reputation not only as an attorney but as the celebrated representative of a specific class and culture in modern American society. If the jurors had not heard of him before trial, they had learned a great deal about him during three and a half long months of testimony. He was the father of the poison pill, the man of a thousand mergers, the most respected and feared attorney on Wall Street. It was Lipton who had insisted that Texaco provide legal indemnities to protect the museum's peace of mind when the deal was done. It was Lipton who had been so active at the Inter-Continental board meeting, negotiating compromises and scribbling out the terms of detailed transactions on his notepad. It was Lipton who had been summoned to the Pierre Hotel at that key moment on the evening of January 5 when John McKinley was stalemated in his discussions with Gordon Getty, and it was Lipton who handwrote the letter of intent that sealed the sale of Gordon's stock to Texaco. From the moment of his entrance into Getty Oil's affairs, he had been at the center of the company's destiny.

It was telling that Pennzoil's attorneys were eager to cross-examine Lipton not because they knew him personally or because they believed that he was a man of dubious personal integrity. They wanted Lipton to testify because of what he represented. They understood that Lipton could not help but feel uncomfortable on the stand in courtroom 151, questioned for the first time by that great muckraking, populist advocate, Joe Jamail. The decision not to take Lipton's deposition, to target him as a live witness, as John Jeffers put it later, "was not directed to him as a person so much as to my experience that when a lawyer like that or an investment banker is able to give his testimony by deposition, it's a very comfortable experience for him because he'll be in his own office or his lawyer's office, with five or six lawyers around him objecting and harassing the examiner at every turn. . . . But to make Lipton sit in front of a jury, where he's unprotected, where it's just him and the examiner and the jury and the judge, it's going to be a different story."

Joe Jamail made a five-hundred dollar bet with his old friend Jim Kronzer, who had been an early partner of Jamail's back when he was getting started as a Houston "sore back lawyer," that Texaco would decide in the end to call Lipton to the stand. On Thursday morning, October 17, when Lipton rose from the audience and walked to the witness box, Jamail turned to Kronzer and said, smiling, "Now. Pay now."

The semantic dilemma which had lurked just beneath the surface of Irv Terrell's examinations of Bart Winokur and Geoff Boisi was drawn fully into the open by Joe Jamail during his cross-examination of Marty Lipton. Indeed, Jamail's first question that Thursday afternoon dove straight to the heart of Lipton's predicament.

"Mr. Lipton, you seem to be a man who uses his words precisely. Do you?"

"I try to."

And try he did. But the more Lipton struggled to defend his language against Jamail's attacks, the more he became entangled in contradiction. Paradoxically, the more articulate Lipton was, the less clear became his meaning. Jamail employed words and ideas in the way they were used by ordinary Houstonians. Lipton spoke the language of a New York specialist.

Referring to negotiations between Marty Siegel and Arthur Liman leading up to the "Memorandum of Agreement" signed by

Gordon Getty and Hugh Liedtke, Jamail asked, "They would know what was essential to those two if they were going to run the company, wouldn't they?"

"Well, I would think not really. I would think neither Mr. Getty nor Mr. Siegel would know that. And they would need expert advice in the oil and gas business to work out a real agreement with respect to that."

"You mean they can't agree without hiring a bunch of experts to tell them what it is they think and want to do?"

"I think that the Getty Trust and Kidder, Peabody and Mr. Siegel would need considerable expert help in working out any agreement along those lines, yes."

"Are you suggesting that Mr. Cohler and Mr. Woodhouse are not expert help?"

"Well, I think both Mr. Cohler and Mr. Woodhouse are lawyers who have considerable expertise, but I think for that kind of arrangement, lawyers who specialize in the oil and gas business and who understand joint operating agreements and things like that would be essential to work out any kind of agreement at all."

"Mr. Lipton, I want to be real sure that I understand this. Are you saying that two people cannot agree unless they hire a bunch of lawyers to tell them they've agreed? Is that—"

"No."

"—what you are telling us?"

"I'm not saying that at all, Mr. Jamail. I'm saying that two people who are contemplating an agreement with respect to a ten-billion-dollar transaction would be awfully foolish to do it on the basis of an outline and the absence of experts' advice. I would think that they would want to very carefully, with experts, negotiate every aspect in trying to envisage every possible problem and enter into a formal, definitive, signed agreement that specifies what the relationship is going to be."

"Mr. Lipton, are you saying that you have some distinction between just us ordinary people making contracts with each other and whether or not it's a ten-billion-dollar deal? It's a different standard in your mind?"

"Yes, indeed."

"I see. So if it wasn't a bunch of money involved in this Getty-Pennzoil thing, it could be an agreement?"

"Well, if there was five or ten dollars involved, I guess you might say that. But even if it was a five-million- or a one-million- or a ten-million-dollar transaction, I would think it would be downright foolish not to have experts' advice and a formal agreement."

"Well, I didn't ask you about being foolish, now. We've got Mr. Cohler. He's a lawyer, isn't he?"

"Yes."

"Mr. Woodhouse, he's a lawyer, isn't he?"

"Yes."

"Are you saying that they could misadvise or did misadvise Mr. Getty?"

"No, I'm not saying that at all. All I'm saying is that in a transaction of that kind, I would expect that Mr. Getty would have other lawyers. Every time I've been involved in a transaction that involves oil and gas business and operating agreements and so on, I've consulted with experts in that field."

"I'm sure the legal profession would be very grateful to you for creating all this business, but that is not the point. The point is that people can agree without lawyers, can they not?"

"Yes."

It is a general rule that lawyers do not make good witnesses for precisely the reasons Marty Lipton demonstrated—they pay too much attention to detail. They worry over narrow definitions while losing sight of larger themes. By declaring that "Yes, indeed" there was a distinction in his mind between contracts carried out by ordinary people and a ten-billion-dollar transaction, Lipton was only voicing what seemed an obvious truth to him. In effect, he was declaring the reason for his professional existence. But he could not see that Jamail was asking about something else entirely. Jamail was not talking about contracts per se—the actual documents written out and signed during a transaction. He was asking about the *reason* contracts existed—the social, legal, and moral obligations implied by them. Certainly, Marty Lipton understood such concepts as well as anyone. But in his world, the word "contract" had been stripped of its abstract quality, its underlying meaning. It was defined only in practice, as an accumulation of case precedent and appellate opinion narrowing and enhancing its meaning in infinite progression, the way the number pie is calculated by a computer set permanently to the task.

As the cross-examination progressed, Jamail took an increasingly personal tack. He sensed that Lipton was uncharacteristically afraid and that the jurors were measuring the witness by the standards Jamail had set at the beginning of trial. Faced with Jamail's battling demeanor, Lipton's attempts at precision became increasingly intense.

"This escrow agreement prepared by your partner would ensure that you had some advantage over the other shareholders, financial advantage?" Jamail asked at one point, referring to a draft agreement prepared by Patricia Vlahakis.

"You said Ms. Vlahakis was my partner. She's my associate."

"Excuse me. I strike that. The rest of that statement is true, is it not?"

"I don't think so. I'm sure if we go back I can get you the answer to the question."

Here Lipton had crossed an important line. By taking pains to point out that Vlahakis was not his partner, he had given his obsession with exactness a human face. Jamail sensed that the jurors would be offended. The jurors were secretaries, office managers, custodians—the boss that awaited them when the trial was over wielded a very real power over their lives. Though his remark about Vlahakis was inadvertent, a product of his desperate verbal jousting with Jamail, Lipton had carried his "expert" use of language into a realm the jurors intuitively understood.

Jamail took advantage of Lipton's error at important moments in the examination, using it to underline the lawyer's testimony.

"If the board approved it, they were bound, weren't they?" Jamail asked, referring to the first vote on the "Memo of Agreement" at the Inter-Continental board meeting.

"If the board approved this? No, I don't think the board or the company was in any way bound if the board approved this."

"Well, sir—"

"They didn't approve it, but even if they had approved it, I don't think they would be in any way bound by this document."

"Well, sir, is this just a game that was going on up there for two days? Nobody is bound but Pennzoil?"

"No, absolutely not. It was not a game at all. It was a very serious thing involving, you know, close to ten billion dollars."

"Well, sir, do you consider—you have told us that the museum would not be bound, the company would not be bound, nobody would be bound even if the board approved this plan. Is that right?"

"That's correct, sir."

"Mrs. Vlahakis is your colleague, as you put it, associate."

"Yes, sir."

And again, just moments later, Jamail capped off a similar exchange by remarking, "We are talking about in this discussion with Ms. Vlahakis—as you have pointedly told us was your colleague and not your partner—and we are talking about plaintiff's exhibit number two. . . ."

In the end, even Dick Miller accepted that it had not gone well—one had only to look at the faces of the jurors as the cross-examination neared its conclusion to be certain that they disapproved of Marty Lipton. Obviously, it did not follow that the jurors disapproved of Texaco, and from this Miller and his client took hope. They had promised the jury during voir dire that each of Texaco's four leading executives would take the stand to testify freely and openly about their involvement in the acquisition of Getty Oil. Even the Pennzoil attorneys readily conceded that Texaco's top executives, particularly president Al DeCrane, general counsel William Weitzel, and vice-chairman James Kinnear, would provide strong and effective testimony refuting the notion that Texaco had interfered with Pennzoil's contract. When Lipton stepped off the stand, the question remaining was whether that testimony would come too late.

"YOU WILL DECIDE THE ETHICS"

Judge Anthony Farris, a conservative former Marine who liked to announce to the jury that the trial would reconvene at "0900 hours" in the morning, succumbed to the heart ailment that had been plaguing him for months and withdrew from *Pennzoil* v. *Texaco* late in October 1985. In part because Farris could tolerate only a modest courtroom schedule, the trial had dragged on for nearly four months, and there was no end in sight. Dick Miller had yet to call his most important witnesses, Texaco's top executives, and he had scheduled a number of Getty Oil directors to testify even before DeCrane, Weitzel, and Kinnear took the stand.

With Farris so seriously ill that he was unable to involve himself in any aspect of the case, a retired Lebanese-Texan judge from San Antonio, Solomon Casseb, was appointed to preside over the remainder of the trial. Arguing that Casseb could never hope to familiarize himself with the record in the case—the trial transcript alone now numbered well over ten thousand pages—Miller moved for a mistrial. Predictably, Casseb denied the motion. He intended to finish the case. A natty dresser who apologized in open court for failing to bring his best clothes with him from San Antonio, Casseb listened to one day of summary arguments from Jamail, Miller, and their partners, and then plunged ahead with the trial. Casseb even declared that he would not read the testimony already presented in court, as if such abstention would somehow enhance his impartiality.

He did, however, insist that the pace of the trial be rapidly accelerated—no more ninety-minute lunches and half-day recesses would
be permitted.

As a result of Casseb's stern prodding, the daily trial transcripts
began to thicken; three and even four witnesses testified in a single day, some live, some by deposition. The case, which had begun
in a mood of heat-induced lethargy, began to acquire a whirlwind
energy, as if someone had pushed the fast-forward button. Confident that the appearances of Winokur, Boisi, and Lipton had turned
the momentum in their favor, the Pennzoil lawyers tried merely to
prevent slippage in their position. They felt now like relief pitchers
called in to protect a ten-run lead; the challenge was simply to not
blow the game.

A series of strong Texaco witnesses took the stand: Henry Wendt,
the handsome, confident pharmaceuticals executive; Larry Tisch,
the self-made titan of American finance; Chauncey Medberry, the
retired Bank of America chairman. Medberry represented the old
Getty Oil directors loyal to J. Paul Getty, Wendt the more recent
appointees of Sid Petersen, and Tisch the nominees of Gordon Getty.
All of them testified that they had made no contract with Pennzoil.
Medberry was the least effective; his memory was frail and John Jeffers confused him repeatedly on cross-examination. But Wendt and
particularly Tisch were unflappable and unintimidated. Jamail cross-
examined Tisch, and he approached him in a manner far different
from his examination of Tisch's close friend Marty Lipton. Rather
than attacking, Jamail coaxed and goaded gently. And when he did
try to draw the witness into his thematic traps, Tisch was ready.

"You're not friends with Gordon Getty?" Jamail asked.

"No, sir."

"Did Gordon Getty think you were his friend?"

"Define 'friend' and I'll answer the question."

"Sir, I can't define the New York friendship—"

"There's no difference between a friend in Texas and a friend in
New York, sir."

Dick Miller recognized that after the cross-examination of Lipton he had ground to make up. At times, he felt that he was battling
not only Pennzoil's attorneys, but his own client and the judge as
well. The performances of Wendt and Tisch encouraged him. But
even at the defense's lowest moments during Lipton's testimony,

Miller continued to express optimism to his client—his only caveat was concern about the demeanor and evidentiary rulings of the judge. At the beginning of the trial, Miller had felt that the jurors did not care much for Farris' military bearing, but by the time Texaco's case opened, he thought the judge had won the jury's sympathy and that his attitude influenced the jurors' perceptions of the witnesses.

During the ten-day hiatus in late October, following Farris' collapse and before Casseb took charge, Miller traveled to White Plains to attend a Texaco board of directors meeting. Miller told the Texaco directors that he was optimistic, but he reiterated his concern about the lingering impact of Farris' skeptical demeanor toward key Texaco witnesses such as Winokur and Lipton. In addition to the reports from Miller, McKinley and DeCrane heard daily evaluations from vice-chairman Jim Kinnear, who had been selected as Texaco's official "corporate representative" at trial and who attended every day of testimony. Kinnear reported that the jurors seemed to like Dick Miller and that Texaco's witnesses, particularly the impressive Wendt and Tisch, seemed to be controlling the momentum of the case. Kinnear said that he was concerned about some of the evidentiary rulings—particularly the decision by Farris that information about Pennzoil's Delaware lawsuits could not be imparted to the jury—but he expressed optimism that Texaco would win the lawsuit outright.

On both sides, evaluation of the trial's progress was influenced by an inevitable kind of self-fulfilling prophecy. Since McKinley, DeCrane, Kinnear, and Weitzel adamantly believed that they had done nothing wrong, that Texaco had nothing to apologize for, they believed that the jurors would share their perceptions of the case. And since Jamail, Jeffers, and Terrell were equally confident that Pennzoil's version of the Getty Oil deal was prevailing in court, they reported consistently to Hugh Liedtke that he would win the verdict; the only question, they said, was the amount of damages the jury would award.

The testimony of Texaco's top executives, beginning on November 5, was something of an anticlimax. Jim Kinnear was ushered on and off the stand in a single afternoon. He seemed to have been called only to fulfill Miller's original promise to the jury, during voir dire, that each important Texaco executive would testify in person before them. William Weitzel, who had negotiated the indemnity agreement with Marty Lipton in the early morning hours of Friday,

January 6, followed Kinnear. Weitzel had been impressive in depositions, and besides DeCrane, he was the defensive witness that the Pennzoil attorneys had most feared going into trial. Now they were not so worried; by saving the Texaco executives until the end, they believed, Miller had allowed Pennzoil to control the tone of the trial—Weitzel and DeCrane could not hope to undo the damage done by the Wall Street witnesses. There was a moment during John Jeffers' cross-examination of Weitzel when the Texaco executive exploded in anger at Jeffers' sarcastic implication that Weitzel agreed to the indemnity because he knew that a wrong was being committed. Weitzel said later that his eruption was calculated, that he wanted to impress the jury with his strong feelings about the case, but Jeffers and his partners thought the incident only strengthened their standing with the jurors. DeCrane's appearance proceeded without incident. His direct testimony, a long narrative recounting the deliberations and negotiations of Texaco's top executives from the time they first heard that Getty Oil might be available for acquisition, was smoothly and confidently delivered. On cross-examination, Irv Terrell badgered DeCrane about the handwritten notes he took during the meeting with First Boston's bankers, but DeCrane argued convincingly that neither he nor McKinley followed the banker's recommendations.

At last, early on the afternoon of Tuesday, November 12, the examination of the trial's last live witness drew to a close. In a final show for the jury, Terrell and Miller batted DeCrane back and forth in short "recross" and "redirect" examinations, each attorney jockeying to get the last word.

"Mr. DeCrane," Terrell intoned grandly, "if this jury believed that people had come in here and lied to it under oath, you'd want the full power of the court to redress that, wouldn't you? Wouldn't you?"

"I don't think anyone has lied that I'm aware of."

"If they have and the jury believes they have, you would want the full power of the court and the jury to put an end to that, wouldn't you?"

"I believe that justice and truth should be what we would seek in this whole proceeding."

"Thank you. That's all we have."

Miller stood up. "Would that apply to Liedtke?" he asked.

"That applies to everybody."

"That's all."

Terrell rose. "Would it apply to Mr. Lipton?"

"It applies to everyone."

"Mr. Boisi?"

"To everyone."

"Thank you."

So ended the testimony in *Pennzoil* v. *Texaco*. In all, thirty-three witnesses had appeared in person or by deposition, including several of the most celebrated names in American finance. And yet, almost everything about the trial remained obscure, hidden from the public. The national business press had not bothered to cover the proceedings; there had been some early stories about the gargantuan size of the damages being sought by Pennzoil, but news about the case quickly disappeared. It was just another contract case, the standard fare of commercial litigation. The takeover of Getty Oil, which had produced bold headlines and excited profiles of the participants, was long forgotten. And since nearly everyone outside of Pennzoil's towering headquarters building in downtown Houston seemed to believe that Texaco would prevail, the trial held only cursory interest among those Wall Street deal-makers who had everything to win or lose by its outcome.

On the day following DeCrane's departure from the witness stand, the lawyers began their critical arguments before Judge Casseb to hammer out the precise language of the judge's charge to the jury. It was the unusual practice of the Texas state courts that the charge, in which the judge describes to the jury the legal standards governing a case, would be written down and distributed to the jurors during their deliberations. In most states, the charge was read out orally by the judge when the jury retired; thus, its impact dissipated once the jurors reached the deliberation room and began to talk about what they had seen and heard in court. In Texas, the charge was like a blueprint for the jurors, a series of carefully worded questions that provided a specific, limited framework for deliberations. Naturally, there was deep concern on both sides of the case about exactly what the charge would say. Both Pennzoil and Texaco retained legal scholars to help them draft language that would favor their presentation of the legal and factual issues at trial. To save time, each side submitted its preferred draft to Judge Casseb and then prepared for oral arguments where the final compromise language would be decided from the bench.

The arguments, which lasted a day and a half, went badly for Texaco. Casseb ruled consistently for Pennzoil. Richard Keeton, who took the lead for Texaco, tried to persuade the judge that he should define the terms of Pennzoil's alleged contract. "We have in four months not been able to get any plaintiff or any representative of plaintiff to tell us what were the terms of the contract," Keeton argued. "If they want to go with the 'Memorandum of Agreement' or the $112.50 price modification, which is the thrust of most of their questioning, that is one way. But we have to draw a circle around what is the contract or proposed contract that this jury is then going to consider." But Pennzoil's lawyers countered with arguments that "the ultimate issue in this case" was not the exact terms of a contract but "whether the parties, all four of the parties, intended to be bound to an agreement." Such was the language submitted in Pennzoil's proposed jury charge.

In fact, to Texaco's deep consternation, the word "contract" never appeared in the final charge language. Instead, Casseb accepted Pennzoil's proposed use of "agreement," with its obvious linguistic ties to the "agreement in principle" at the center of the case. The question of whether or not that agreement in principle announced in the January 4 press release was a binding contract was the single most important factual and legal issue at trial. If Casseb employed the word "contract" in his charge, he would be asking the jury to decide whether an agreement in principle was a binding contract. But by using the word "agreement," he was in effect fudging the issue, Texaco argued. It was a semantic question with billion-dollar implications.

"All through this case there has been testimony that an agreement in principle is some sort of an agreement, but it is not a binding agreement," Keeton desperately argued. "There has been the use of the word 'agreement.' We are talking about a tortious interference with the contract. To focus on the word 'agreement' is to absolutely not let the jury understand the nature of all the testimony by every witness that's come up who has either talked in terms of the words 'binding agreement' or has talked in terms of contract. . . . And by putting this not only very weak word, but a word that by itself has many meanings, you have made a change that makes it virtually impossible for this defendant to get a finding when the evidence is itself very, very clear that the issue at a minimum is contested. But you have chosen a word that does not let the jury understand that."

The same chasm in the use and implications of language that had so affected the testimony of Texaco's Wall Street witnesses had again taken on central significance in the case. Texaco wanted the charge to employ precise, narrow terms—the morally neutral language of the specialist. Pennzoil pressed for broad words that resonated with social and ethical meaning. A "contract" was usually a document, a corporeal entity that might or might not be legally enforceable, depending upon its adherence to specific, encoded rules and standards. An "agreement" was a state of mind, or, as one of Pennzoil's lawyers put it, "an intention to be bound." The existence of an agreement in a specific case depended not so much on the presence of objective, quantifiable elements, but on human motivations, human intentions. As it had been during important moments of testimony at trial, the debate between the two sides seemed to occur on separate levels that did not intersect. One either accepted Pennzoil's view that what mattered in the taking of Getty Oil was a canvass of human psychology—ambition, greed, betrayal, honor—or one accepted Texaco's view that only specific legal standards of "contract" and "interference" were truly important. The witnesses who tried to argue Texaco's position were ensnared by the predicament inherent in their argument, namely, that morality mattered less than law— as Boisi had put it, that "good faith" was subordinate to "fiduciary" responsibility.

Pennzoil defended its position before Casseb by arguing that simply because the Wall Street bankers and lawyers did not understand this contradiction, that did not let them off the hook. It was fine for Winokur, Boisi, Lipton and the rest to believe, in keeping with the rules of their merger game, that an agreement in principle was no agreement at all. But as the charge Casseb accepted put it, "It is not necessary that the actor appreciate the legal significance of the facts giving rise to the contract. If he knows those facts, he is subject to liability even though he is mistaken as to their legal significance and believes that the agreement is not legally binding or has a different legal effect from what it is judicially held to have."

Casseb himself seemed to understand that with regard to the complex legal standards governing the issues in the case, it was possible that Pennzoil's insistence on broad, inclusive language was unsupported by precedent. "I would like to go on record in stating that I am at a disadvantage because I did not read the full parts of this evidence," he announced in the midst of the hotly contested arguments over the jury charge. "And I guess I'm going to have to assume the consequences of it because I guess it will be my error if any error is committed." Nonetheless, assured by Jamail that "we think we've met our burden" with regard to the legal plausibility of Pennzoil's proposed charge, Casseb plunged ahead. He decided on a charge that excluded the word "contract."

Another important element of the charge arguments concerned damages. Pennzoil was seeking $14 billion; $7 billion in actual damages and $7 billion in punitive damages. During its affirmative case, the Pennzoil lawyers had put on two witnesses to support its claim for actual damages: a Pennzoil accountant named Ronald Lewis, and a retired oil executive named Thomas Barrow. Employing extravagant economic models and colorful charts, the two had argued that Pennzoil was entitled to monetary compensation equal to the long-term value of oil and gas reserves equivalent to those allegedly snatched from its grasp by Texaco. Barrow offered three formulas for this calculation. The first was a "replacement costs" theory arguing that if Pennzoil had acquired three-sevenths of Getty Oil, it would have bought oil and gas reserves at about $3.40 per barrel, whereas if it had to find that same amount of oil and gas, it would cost $10.80, and so Pennzoil was entitled to the difference. Barrow's second model compared the proposed purchase of Getty Oil on a per-barrel basis with other purchases of oil companies. His third was a "present value" model which compared Pennzoil's per-barrel proposed purchase price with the long-term estimated revenues that would flow from Getty Oil's reserves, making assumptions about the future world price of oil and the cost of production. All three models showed an impressive bottom line owed to Pennzoil—approximately $7 billion in cash.

In a characteristic act of courage or bravado, depending on how one looked at it, Dick Miller had elected not to put on any rebuttal testimony about damages during Texaco's defensive case. He felt that damage rebuttal only weakened his case, since by arguing for lower damages Texaco would inevitably seem to be conceding some culpability. Miller felt that the cross-examination of Barrow, which had been handled by Richard Keeton, had been so effective that the jury would never accept any of the witness's three models. The huge numbers involved did not daunt Miller; after all, he had been retained for his ability in the "bet-your-company" genre of civil litigation.

Neither were Texaco's top executives unduly concerned about the lack of damage rebuttal. Jim Kinnear had conducted extensive research designed to attack the assumptions made by Barrow, but his work was employed only in Keeton's cross-examination, not in Kinnear's own direct testimony. Chairman John McKinley said later that he was only following the advice of his attorneys, but since he shared many of Miller's "manly" attributes, the argument that damage rebuttal only contributed to the appearance of weakness likely held an emotional appeal as well. McKinley said later: "The advice we got was, 'Look, you don't owe them anything, and it is a poor tactic of law to present damage testimony because then people start looking in between the two numbers for a compromise figure.' Plus, as we came down to the end of the trial, we had a new judge pressuring us to finish quickly. . . . Any fair judgment would recognize that their damage claim was in defiance of common sense, we thought." Miller had developed a countertheory to the damage models argued by Barrow—that Pennzoil was entitled only to the value of the stock it sought to purchase, not the oil and gas assets conveyed by ownership of the stock—and he tried to have this theory included in Judge Casseb's jury charge.

"Their contract was to obtain stock," Miller's partner J. C. Nickens argued to the judge. "And if they were deprived of the bargain of that stock, then they were deprived of the difference of the value of that stock on the date they were to acquire it and what they would have paid for it." That bottom line, Texaco had calculated, was only about $500 million. But Joe Jamail told Casseb, "The test is that the jury may make a reasonable estimate of the damages based on all relevant data, the expert testimony, including opinion evidence," and once again, Pennzoil prevailed. The charge reflected Jamail's position.

Texaco's top executives were staying at the Four Seasons Hotel in downtown Houston on the day the final charge was delivered to both parties. When Miller brought it to the Texaco suite, the mood for the first time was one of deep discouragement and concern. Kinnear thought the charge "was obviously a directed verdict for Pennzoil." Miller, too, was upset, but he again expressed to his client that "he felt very strongly that it was going to be all right," as McKinley later put it.

If the Texaco executives could not fully appreciate that the charge memorialized Joe Jamail's populist, moral view of the issues at trial, they had only to wait for the closing arguments for confirmation that Pennzoil and Texaco were presenting to the jury starkly different ideas about the significance of the taking of Getty Oil Company.

The closing arguments began on Thursday morning, November 14, 1985. Each of the three Pennzoil lawyers handled a section of the argument; it was characteristic of Miller's approach to trial work that only he spoke for Texaco. Jeffers and Terrell spoke first, then Miller. Under Texas rules, Joe Jamail would have the final word before the jury.

Jeffers, the cerebral orator, spoke mainly about contract issues and damages. It was Terrell who struck up in earnest the relentless themes first framed by Joe Jamail during voir dire four months before.

"You're going to be able to do something that I, in my lifetime, will never be able to do as a lawyer," Terrell told the jurors as he stood behind a lectern a few feet from the box. "You will decide the ethics. You will decide whether you can go out and take somebody else's deal just because you're bigger and stronger, you've got a lot of muscle, you've got a lot of lawyers, you've got investment bankers. And above all, what have you got? You've got indemnities.

"These people do these things and they have no personal responsibility. And I'm telling you that if you speak out, they will hear you. Not just these men—they'll hear you for sure—but the whole business community. But if you don't care about the way corporations treat each other, and I know there are people who believe in that, then you don't have to do anything."

Terrell centered his attack on Lipton and Boisi, referring to them by name more often than to Texaco's executives. He reiterated Pennzoil's argument that Texaco was wholly responsible for the conduct of its Wall Street witnesses because it had provided them with legal indemnities. "Lipton is a man who not only is proud of the fact that he got this higher price and he got protection for his client, this indemnity, but he wants to sit here and tell you that Arthur Liman's been his friend for twenty-five years," Terrell said. "Mr. Liman, before Mr. Lipton testified, he spoke of Mr. Lipton as his friend. But if ever somebody denied somebody three times, that was it. Lipton did, to Liman. I mean, you take your pick between these two men. I know who I believe." And about Boisi: "Now if you believe that Geoff Boisi made 'courtesy calls' on the fourth and fifth, we need to talk about a car I'd like to sell you because it's just incredible."

Terrell ended with a plea suggestive of a call for class revolt, as if the trial of *Pennzoil* v. *Texaco* had been a microcosm of some struggle for liberation by ordinary Americans against their ruling class. "It doesn't matter what is in this charge that you have in your hands unless you do something with it. It's yours to use or not use," he said. "I suggest to you that you use it so that everybody, whether we're a big deal oil company or a medium-sized oil company, whatever kind of person we are, whether we're the chairman of the Philadelphia museum board of arts or whatever, that we all live by the same rules, that we're responsible for our actions. And that's all I have to say. Just don't let them get away with these indemnities. Please don't. Thank you."

After a fifteen-minute break, Dick Miller took the floor. Watching his former mentor pace before the jury in characteristic fashion, Irv Terrell, who had been exceedingly nervous during his own argument, thought that Miller, too, appeared to be tight as a drum. That afternoon, Miller quoted Justice Oliver Wendell Holmes and Sherlock Holmes and then confused the two. He told a story about Alice in Wonderland. The next morning, Friday, when Miller continued his argument, he corrected his confusion of the two Holmeses and told the jury that his partners had "pointed out to me I ought to get to the point and ought to quit acting like I know everything."

When Miller was composed, however, he was impressive. His argument contained two separate threads. First and foremost, he argued that there simply was no contract between Pennzoil and the Getty Oil directors, and that there certainly was no interference from Texaco. "We did not crash this party," Miller declared. "We were invited to the party. We didn't look them up. They looked us up. . . . This has got to be the first case in the history of mankind where the white knight got sued by the dragon. And that's just exactly what happened."

But Miller also sensed that he had to somehow rebut the urgent moral pleadings of Jamail and Terrell. At times, he did this by rejecting outright their contention that anything important was at stake in the case. "It's got to be one of the dullest cases that's been tried," he said, adding that the "most exciting thing in the case was when I came into the courtroom with my fly unzipped."

At other times, though, Miller returned to the earlier themes he developed during his emotional cross-examination of Hugh Liedtke, arguing that if anyone was a villain in the deal, it was Pennzoil. "It's a company run by lawyers who know a lot about this business, who understand takeovers and who understand power and the force of money and the sense behind the attack and who, as they looked at the saga of the Getty Oil Company unfolding, could see, could sense the weakness of that company and the fact that its leadership was in disarray because of this internal dispute—and who were willing to take advantage of it, saying, 'There's an opportunity there for us.'"

Miller also defended the integrity of Lipton, Winokur, and especially Boisi, pointedly accusing Terrell of cowardice because he attacked the banker's integrity when Boisi was absent from the courtroom. "I can't believe that anybody who saw that guy, who saw him testify, could do anything except believe him," Miller declared.

"They didn't have a contract," Miller closed, "never had a contract, and what they have got is a company that's run by three lawyers who have got this lawsuit and they are trying to hit a big gusher here in court. That's what this lawsuit is about."

After a break for lunch, Joe Jamail rose to conclude Pennzoil's presentation. At the Pennzoil counsel table, and in the first row behind it where Hugh Liedtke, Baine Kerr, and other Pennzoil executives sat, there was a keen sense of excitement and anticipation. Alone before the jury, with no witnesses or objections or documents to soften the impact of his brawling, muckraking, ebullient personality, Jamail was at the peak of his powers. He hauled the lectern right over to the jury box, so that he was almost in their laps.

Miller had used the word "contract" throughout his closing argument, attempting to mitigate the effect of the wording in the charge, but Jamail turned immediately to the issue. "For Mr. Miller to stand here and attempt to change the court's charge, the wording in it, by inserting things that he likes, is typical. It's what they've done from the beginning of the case."

"Judge Casseb is one of the most honored and brilliant judges in America. If he had wanted to say to you, 'contract,' he would have said it."

"Miller," Jamail went on, "told you a lot of old lawyer's stories. I hope I don't take up your time doing that. I will tell you a lawyer's truism, though: 'When the law is on the lawyer's side, he talks about the law. When the facts are on the lawyer's side, he talks about the facts. When he has neither, he just talks—and I guess tells Alice in Wonderland stories."

In its specifics, Jamail's argument essentially ignored Texaco, concentrating instead on the trio of witnesses Miller called to the stand at the opening of his defensive case. He began with Winokur. "You remember him, 'Back Door' Bart?" Jamail asked the jurors. "Snuck in the back door when they got Gordon Getty out of the room? Kicked him off or tried to instigate a lawsuit to kick him off the board of trust of his own family trust? Instigated, funded a lawsuit to remove or in the alternative to appoint a cotrustee who could dominate him. That's really good faith and that's a lot of fiduciary.

"They really laid a whole lot of fiduciary on Gordon Getty. And that's what you are dealing with. And he stands here and wants to talk about morality? Not today."

Warming visibly, Jamail quoted Lipton's testimony about the "different standard" in the lawyer's mind between a multibillion-dollar deal and a contract between "ordinary" people and then turned the issue into a broad attack on merger lawyers and investment bankers, whom Jamail openly characterized as conspirators against the people. "That's the specialized group you had to deal with that would have injected themselves into our business community and into our law, calling themselves merger and acquisition lawyers, carving up corporate America to their liking. And nobody loses. Those investment bankers and the lawyers that comprise the merger and acquisition field, they get together. They're all within a couple of miles of each other. One wins one day and another wins another day, and the investment bankers win all the days—and they win with these indemnities. . . . You can send a message to corporate America, to the business world, because it's just people who make up those things.

"It isn't as though we are numbers and robots. We are people. And you can tell them that you are not going to get away with this. . . . I know you are going to do the right thing. You are people of morality and conscience and strength. Don't let this opportunity pass you."

And with that, Joe Jamail turned and walked back to his counsel table. The trial of *Pennzoil* v. *Texaco* was finished. No one in the courtroom—not Jamail, not Miller, not John McKinley, not Hugh Liedtke—knew how the twelve jurors felt about their four-month ordeal, or whether they cared at all about the two huge oil corporations that had taken them away from their jobs and even their families for week after monotonous week of testimony and argument. What had taken months and millions of dollars in legal fees to present would now require just hours to decide. The lawyers and clients on both sides told each other that they trusted in the jury's fairness and wisdom. It was what they had to believe. There was no other choice.

31

CITIZENS

When the Door to the jury deliberation room was closed that Friday afternoon, the feeling inside was volcanic. Week after week, month after month, through moments of high drama and passages of unspeakable tedium, the twelve jurors had been proscribed from discussing the trial among themselves. They had followed this order more or less exactly. Between the women, there had been talk during the trial about which lawyer or witness was the best-looking (Marty Siegel, who testified by videotape, was the witness who garnered the most approval; Dick Miller led the lawyers), and between the men, there had been similar contests concerning the women in the courtroom, although there were fewer candidates for them to choose from. But although they had been thrown into intimate contact with one another, the jurors had never been able to openly discuss the trial. They knew all about each other's personal lives: children, spouses and ex-spouses, job stresses, births and deaths. They knew each other's personalities, habits, and eccentricities. But none of them knew how the others felt about the long, emotional trial they had witnessed together.

Now, suddenly, they could talk. Feelings and words exploded. Everyone was speaking at once; some of them were crying, some laughing. There was so much to be said, so much to be shared, it seemed at first that it might take days just to settle everyone down.

Among the twelve jurors, there were eight whites and four

blacks, and at least one of the white jurors had been concerned going
into the deliberation room that this might be a factor in the discussions ahead. There had been some tension on the jury during the
last weeks of trial. It had begun when Judge Casseb took over the
case and vowed to speed up the pace of the proceedings. His first
step was to eliminate the half-day holidays on Monday mornings
and Friday afternoons which had been established at the beginning
by Judge Farris. Farris had instructed the jurors to schedule all of
their pressing personal appointments, with doctors and dentists and
so on, during those half-days; no other time off would be granted.
When Casseb took charge and eliminated the holidays, some of the
jurors had outstanding appointments which had been scheduled
during Farris' reign. Casseb said that he was sorry, but he could not
permit any more holidays. Then Theresa Ladig, a single parent, had
asked Casseb if he would recess the trial early on Halloween so she
could take her boys trick-or-treating, as she had promised them, and
Casseb agreed. A few days later, one of the two black women on the
jury asked permission to attend a parent-teacher conference at her
children's school. But Casseb said no. The black woman complained
to the other jurors that Casseb was prejudiced, that he had favored
Theresa's request over her own for racial reasons. Thereafter, the once
cordial, if hardly intimate, relations between blacks and whites on
the jury had been infused with tension. An emotional and difficult
subject had been broached. There was no open bickering or arguing
between the jurors—after all, it was Casseb, not Theresa Ladig, who
was accused of prejudice—but there was a new discomfort among
them, a sense that sides had been taken.

Some of the white jurors perceptively attributed this racial tension to the emotional exhaustion and frayed nerves that they recognized in themselves after so many months of trial. But during those
first moments in the jury room, there was unspoken concern about
whether the issue would shape the deliberations. An early vote was
taken on the threshold issue of whether or not there had been a contract, or "agreement," as the charge put it, between Pennzoil and the
Getty Oil directors. The vote was 7–5 in Pennzoil's favor. All four of
the blacks, and one white woman, a bookkeeper named Susan Fleming, voted for Texaco. Given the tensions during the last weeks of
trial, the sharp racial division in the vote seemed ominous. Israel
Jackson and Ola Guy, two of the black jurors, announced promptly

that they did not believe there was a contract and that they weren't going to change their minds about it, either. They said that they really didn't want to discuss it.

In the election of the jury foreman, an effort had been made to diffuse the racial issue. Jim Shannon, a white public relations specialist who worked for the city of Houston, nominated Fred Daniels, a black postal worker, to be foreman. Daniels, a quiet man who sometimes passed out flyers advertising events at his church to the other jurors, was elected by acclamation but declined to serve. Still, to some of the white jurors, the gesture seemed to have an effect; Daniels was the first to change his vote to Pennzoil's side, and the only one to do so that Friday afternoon. Next, Shirley Wall, an older white woman who had been popular with many of the jurors during the long months of trial, was nominated to be foreman, and she, too, was elected by acclamation. She also declined to serve, however, citing her fear of public speaking. Finally, Richard Lawler, a white, thirty-one-year-old salesman of heavy industrial equipment and a man of even temperament and obvious leadership ability, was nominated, and he agreed to take the job.

One of Lawler's first actions was to ask the judge for permission to go home. He and some of the other jurors had the impression that they were expected to continue their deliberations right through the weekend, if necessary, until they reached a verdict. Lawler thought that what he and the jury really needed was rest, a chance to sort through their thoughts and feelings about the case. Then they could come back on Monday and discuss the issues in a more rational manner. The outpouring of emotion, the questions about race, the mood of confused impasse—all of it would be behind them. Lawler and the others were surprised when Casseb readily granted his request. Shortly after 4 P.M., the jurors went home.

Lawler himself spent the weekend with a friend, digging for crabs along the shores of the Gulf of Mexico, south of Houston. It was an ideal environment in which to sort through his feelings about the case. There was no question in his mind that Pennzoil was right, that Texaco and its Wall Street lawyers and bankers had arrogantly stolen Getty Oil from Hugh Liedtke. But he wanted to sort through his intuitive reactions. He wanted to develop a rationale that he could articulate to the other jurors and to the world at large; he understood that the jury's decision, whatever it was, would be closely scrutinized when the case was over. What bothered Lawler above all was the indemnities granted by Texaco to the museum, Gordon, and the Getty Oil board of directors. It seemed to him that Texaco *knew* that it was doing something wrong, but that its executives had decided that the prize of Getty Oil's rich assets was worth any risk of future legal exposure, and so they had agreed to the indemnities. This assessment was bolstered by the fact that the indemnities had first been proposed by Marty Lipton, the master merger lawyer, whom Lawler regarded as the least credible witness in the case. He felt that Lipton was a nearly sinister force behind the deal between Texaco and Getty Oil. On the contract issue, Lawler thought that the documentary evidence was overwhelming—the "Memo of Agreement," the press release, and the Copley notes all added up to a firm deal, in his view. It was not as if Lawler was naïve about business affairs. He entered into commercial contracts all the time, selling forklifts and other heavy industrial equipment. Perhaps, as he put it later, he was not "at the heights" of American finance, but "in my industry I could not deal that way very long." Texaco's three key Wall Street witnesses—Winokur, Boisi, and Lipton—had impressed him as people who cared little, if at all, about the moral implications of their work. Lawler felt that in their enthusiasm for merger-making, they perpetuated a harmful practice that emphasized money and assets over people.

With both Lawler and Jim Shannon, who had participated actively in the frenzied deliberations on Friday, Miller's attack on Hugh Liedtke, apparently intended to suggest a moral culpability at least equal to that of his own Wall Street witnesses, was entirely unsuccessful. Shannon and Lawler both recognized that Liedtke was hardly the innocent oilman whom Pennzoil's attorney sometimes tried to portray. Lawler saw in Liedtke the familiar characteristics of a Texas "hard-nosed businessman," one who "knew how to make a dollar, knew how to hold on to a dollar, and knew which direction he was going—a man of purpose." Shannon had an even stronger view that Liedtke was "a Russell Long type or an LBJ type. . . . Hugh Liedtke makes J. R. Ewing and Blake Carrington pale by comparison." But simply because they recognized that Liedtke was a savvy, well-connected, perhaps even ruthless oilman, it did not follow that they held him personally responsible for Pennzoil's opportunistic entrance into the contest for control of Getty Oil, in the way they held

McKinley responsible for the actions of Winokur, Boisi, and Lipton. Neither did the jurors hold a particularly sympathetic opinion of Gordon Getty. Lawler said later that if he owned an oil company, he would rather have Sid Petersen in charge, "more than Gordon Getty, who really became a weak point as far as Pennzoil's story was concerned. Anyone with any sense would have realized that Gordon would have become a figurehead in the organization and the true men running it would have been Hugh Liedtke and Baine Kerr." But as it was presented at trial, the whole issue of Gordon Getty's combative relations with Getty Oil management seemed to Lawler "a nice sidebar issue, but it had very little to do with why we were there."

When the jurors returned to the courthouse at eight-thirty Monday morning, the mood of emotional turmoil which had characterized their discussion on Friday had passed. They were refreshed, calm, and ready to proceed. The vote was retaken on the first issue in the charge, the threshold question that asked, "Do you find from a preponderance of the evidence that at the end of the Getty Oil board meeting of January 3rd, 1984, Pennzoil and each of the Getty entities, to wit: the Getty Oil Company, the Sarah C. Getty Trust and the J. Paul Getty Museum intended to bind themselves to an agreement that included the following items, A, B, and C?" (The alphabetized items were the terms of Pennzoil's proposed power-sharing arrangement with Gordon Getty). The vote, which had been 8–4 when deliberations recessed on Friday, was now 9–3 in Pennzoil's favor; Velinda Allen, one of the black women on the jury, had switched sides. Under Texas law, only a 10–2 vote was required in a civil case such as *Pennzoil* v. *Texaco*, so the jury was now just one vote from a verdict. The discussion moved quickly and fairly calmly, with Lawler, Shannon, and Shirley Wall arguing most vigorously for Pennzoil. Fairly quickly, Ola Guy, a black woman who worked as a housecleaner, was converted. She had never argued strongly for Texaco's position; her comments were generally confined to the assertion that "Pennzoil is bad, too."

Suddenly, then, the vote was 10–2 in Pennzoil's favor, on both the contract and interference issues. Lawler, for one, was unsatisfied—he wanted a unanimous verdict before returning to the courtroom. The discussion continued, and for the first time it moved on to the issue of damages. The question of actual damages was easily dispensed with: $7.53 billion, one of the numbers suggested by

Pennzoil's expert witness Thomas Barrow, was quickly agreed upon by the majority. But now Ola Guy, the most recent convert to Pennzoil's side, wasn't sure if she wanted to award any damages at all. The Pennzoil supporters reviewed with her the damage testimony presented by Barrow.

"What other standard can we apply?" they asked logically.

Guy relented; the vote went 10–2 on actual damages. Still, Susan Fleming, the bookkeeper, and Israel Jackson were holding out, with Fleming doing most of the talking for the opposition. But since 10–2 was sufficient for a verdict, Lawler moved down the list of questions in the charge; next to be considered was the issue of punitive damages. Here the jurors reached another impasse. A vote was taken: seven voted for the full $7.5 billion in punitive damages sought by Pennzoil, the two holdouts voted for nothing, and the rest voted for some number in between. Shannon wrote a question mark on his ballot.

The debate became heated, although this time the pressure was coming from Pennzoil's most ardent advocates, Shirley Wall and Laura Johnson, who said that they were unwilling to award anything less than the full amount of punitive damages. The discussion went round and round. One issue was whether Texaco had acted in "wanton disregard," as the charge put it, of Pennzoil's rights. There was some question about exactly what that phrase meant, so it was decided that a note should be passed out to the judge asking for clarification.

When Casseb read the note to the lawyers, who were waiting dutifully in the courtroom, Jamail and his partners were ecstatic. It was a promising sign indeed that the jurors were haggling over punitive damages; they must have already decided the issues of contract and interference. After a brief discussion with Miller and Jamail, Casseb typed up a definition taken from a Texas manual on jury charges, which characterized wanton disregard as "reckless, heedless disregard to the rights of others." He sent the definition back into the jury room.

After a break for lunch, the debate over punitive damages continued among the jurors well into the afternoon. Some of the jurors pressed for a compromise formula that could somehow be rationalized—they did not want to decide on an arbitrary number. There was a great deal of discussion about the indemnities and about the role of Winokur, Boisi, and Lipton in the deal. Someone—there were conflicting recollections later about exactly who—proposed that the jury find for $3 billion in punitive damages, $1 billion for each of the three Wall Street witnesses. But again, there was disagreement. Just after 2 P.M., Lawler decided to send out another question to Judge Casseb. "To what extent is Texaco liable for the actions of Lipton, Winokur, and Boisi?" the note inquired.

The Pennzoil lawyers could scarcely contain their glee. When he read the note, Casseb said that there was nothing he could tell the jurors, that he would send in a message telling them to be "guided by the instructions in the charge and the evidence, period." Jamail agreed with the judge's position.

"And a request for anything additional, I guess, is denied?" Miller asked.

"At this time," Casseb replied.

"At this time?" Miller repeated.

"No objections?"

"No objections to this," Jamail said.

"This is fine with us, your honor," Miller agreed.

It later became apparent that Miller did not immediately grasp the implications of the jury's question. Overnight, while the jury was in recess—everything had been decided on a 10–2 vote but the punitive damages—Miller realized, after discussions with his partners and his client, that the jury's question was dangerous indeed. When court reconvened early Tuesday morning, he pleaded with Casseb to correct the previous day's answer with a message that read, in part, "The Court now instructs you that a party is only responsible for the actions of its own employees, agents, or representatives acting within the scope of their employment." Having defended their integrity so vigorously at trial, Miller was now prepared to throw his Wall Street witnesses overboard. It was not Winokur, Boisi, and Lipton who were on trial; it was Texaco.

"It's exactly because of the indemnities and the confusion that has been injected into this record that we think this instruction should be given," Richard Keeton argued. "Because on at least ten occasions in the record it has been stated—if not directly, at least implied—that this is a suit on the indemnities, and therefore, Texaco is liable for anything that any of the Getty entities did by virtue of the indemnities."

"What counsel for Texaco wishes now is for this court to argue the case in the jury room," Jamail replied succinctly. Casseb denied Miller's request without comment.

Meanwhile, inside the jury room, the debate was rapidly concluding. Reluctantly, the Pennzoil advocates holding out for the full $7.5 billion in punitive damages agreed to the compromise, $3 billion formula, which would bring the total award to Pennzoil to $10.53 billion, by more than fivefold the largest civil verdict in American history. A final vote on all the questions in the charge was taken, and to the surprise and delight of Lawler, Susan Fleming and Israel Jackson switched their votes—the verdict was now unanimous on every count. Some of the jurors speculated later that the articulate Fleming had merely been playing devil's advocate all along. In any event, she now expressed no doubts about her final decision.

At precisely 11 A.M. on Tuesday morning, November 19, 1985, the twelve jurors filed back in to courtroom 151. Lawler, the foreman, was choked with emotion. He had not realized that he would be required to stand and read a portion of the verdict. He kept thinking about Dick Miller, the attorney he liked most of all at the trial. Several of the other jurors had similar, strong feelings; as they returned to the jury box, they could not bring themselves to look at Miller. It was as if they were informing their spouse that they had fallen in love with someone else. Lawler knew that the verdict would be a terrible blow to Miller's career. He felt sorry for him. He thought that Miller was a terrific lawyer, but that he'd simply drawn a bad case.

Liedtke and Kerr were there, of course, sitting in the first row behind Jamail, Jeffers, and Terrell. Among Texaco's top executives, only Jim Kinnear, the vice-chairman and official corporate representative, was in attendance; McKinley and the others were back in White Plains. The courtroom was packed with journalists and sophisticated financial speculators poised to relay word of the verdict to their brokers on Wall Street.

"Have you all reached a verdict in this case?" Casseb asked.

"We have, Your Honor," Lawler answered.

The judge read out the questions from the charge pertaining to contract and interference, asking whether the jury had found that an agreement had been reached between Pennzoil and the Getty Oil directors, and whether Texaco had "knowingly" interfered with that agreement.

"We do," Casseb declared in response to each question, reading the answer Lawler had written on the sheet before him.

"What sum of money, if any, do you find from a preponderance of the evidence would compensate Pennzoil for its actual damages, if any, suffered as a direct and natural result of Texaco's knowingly interfering with the agreement between Pennzoil and the Getty entities, if any?"

"The answer is: $7.53 billion."

Casseb asked how many of the jurors had agreed to that figure. All twelve raised their hands. Excited discussion rose from the audience.

"I want order in the court, please," Casseb demanded.

He read the question about punitive damages contained in the charge. "What sum of money, if any, is Pennzoil entitled to receive from Texaco as punitive damages?"

"Answer: $3 billion." Again Casseb polled the jury, and again, all twelve silently raised their hands.

After a brief speech thanking the jurors for their diligent devotion, and after setting a date with the lawyers for a hearing on whether the verdict should be formally entered, Casseb released the jury from its duty. A mob scene ensued. The jurors moved quickly back into the deliberation room to gather up their things and await some protection.

Jim Kinnear pressed into the hallway to find a pay telephone, from which he called John McKinley's private office number in White Plains to tell him the bad news. Texaco's chairman was stoical. After discussing the matter with general counsel William Weitzel, he asked Weitzel to make an announcement over the intercom system at corporate headquarters.

When the jurors reentered courtroom 151, this time flanked by a phalanx of marshals, they were warmly embraced by Joe Jamail and the other Pennzoil attorneys.

Dick Miller approached Theresa Ladig and told her that he was obviously shocked by the verdict. "I tried very hard to watch your face to see which way you were swaying," Miller told her.

"I know you were. That's why I tried not to show anything," she answered.

Surging, impromptu press conferences were formed in the hallways. Embracing warmly, Liedtke and Jamail were ecstatic. In a brief, calm statement, Kinnear vowed to appeal. Then the Texaco vice-chairman followed Jim Shannon out of the building, listening as the juror spoke to a flock of television and print reporters. He approached Shannon and asked him about the verdict. When Shannon told him that he had by and large liked the Texaco executives who testified, but that he could not abide the actions taken by Winokur, Boisi, and Lipton, Kinnear immediately concluded, as he put it later, that the jurors "didn't know what they were doing."

As they gathered their belongings in the jury room after the verdict was read, the jurors had decided to meet later that day for lunch at a Mexican restaurant far from the courthouse. After pushing through the crowds and shaking the packs of reporters who trailed them for blocks as they walked to their cars, the twelve finally reconvened over enchiladas and margaritas that Tuesday afternoon. It was a warm and happy occasion. The ordeal was behind them. Richard Lawler was presented with a modest gift in appreciation for his efforts as foreman. The idea of a reunion was proposed and endorsed. For all the tedium and tension and challenge, they had come through it together. They had passed judgment on a world that was in some ways far removed from their understanding and experience, but that in other, perhaps more important ways, was very close to home. Texaco lawyers and executives would later attack the integrity of some of the jurors and complain that all of them lacked the sophistication required to understand the issues in the case. But the jurors themselves never doubted their decision for a moment. They had been asked to decide right and wrong, and they had done it. The doubts expressed in the deliberation room had reflected concern over whether *anyone* could claim moral superiority from the tangled history presented—"Pennzoil is bad, too," as Ola Guy had put it—but that serious wrongs had been committed was never in question. So they easily accepted Joe Jamail's urging that out of this case, a message should be sent to "corporate America." Someone, the jurors said, had to pay.

THE FALL OF THE MERGER MANIACS

So devastating was the effect of the $10.53 billion verdict, which began almost immediately to collect interest at the staggering rate of $3 million a day, that Texaco was pushed to the brink of a bankruptcy filing just weeks after the jury delivered its judgment. It was saved only by the friendly intervention of a federal judge in New York, who at Texaco's request declared unconstitutional a Texas state law requiring defendants, before appealing, to post a bond equal to the amount of the judgment against them. Rather than posting a $12 billion bond, which Texaco executives claimed would force an immediate bankruptcy filing, the judge allowed the White Plains–headquartered giant to put up $1 billion as evidence of its good faith during appeal. As a legal matter, the intervention of a New York federal judge into a Texas civil case was dubious—Pennzoil attorney Larry Tribe later denounced the maneuver before a sympathetic U.S. Supreme Court as a "Fortune 500 exception to federalism"—and as a practical matter it only exacerbated the perception in Texas that Texaco somehow considered itself above the law.

Settlement negotiations began quickly and seemed promising at first. Meeting in neutral cities such as Tulsa, Oklahoma, and Nashville, Tennessee, settlement teams from Pennzoil and Texaco discussed in detail a swap of oil and gas reserves that would give to Hugh Liedtke the assets taken by Texaco. There was talk, too, about a friendly merger between Texaco and Pennzoil that would include a top position in the new company for Liedtke. (In the first hours after the verdict was handed down, excited analysts speculated that the easiest way for Texaco to avoid a bankruptcy filing would be for the company to launch a hostile takeover attempt against Pennzoil.) But plummeting worldwide oil prices during the first weeks after the verdict complicated the negotiations. In fact, so far did oil prices fall early in 1986 that it began to appear that Pennzoil was far better off with the cash awarded by the jury than it would have been if it had acquired three-sevenths of Getty Oil. Texaco vice-chairman Jim Kinnear even calculated that if Pennzoil's bid for Getty Oil had succeeded, Hugh Liedtke's company would have wound up with a negative net worth by the end of 1986. Instead, because of its courthouse windfall, Pennzoil was one of the few large oil companies not deeply shaken by the oil price collapse. Texaco faced a double whammy: plummeting prices and a multibillion-dollar civil judgment.

In January 1986, the settlement talks ended when Texaco presented the Pennzoil board of directors with a merger offer far below Liedtke's expectations. The Pennzoil chairman responded by publicly attacking Texaco's management for the first time since the verdict, calling its offer "almost laughable" and declaring that McKinley and his executives were running their company as a "fiefdom." Liedtke said that he didn't see "a chance of doing anything except litigating." McKinley, stunned at Pennzoil's response to his merger offer, said that he was "surprised at Pennzoil's characterization of our settlement discussions. Texaco has been dealing in good faith in all settlement negotiations."

Thrust into a demanding period of crisis management, McKinley and his executives never conceded that they had done anything wrong. The adjectives they employed most frequently to describe their predicament were "absurd" and "outrageous." A battery of public relations and legal firms was retained to press Texaco's appeals in courts and in the forum of public opinion. Editorial comment about the case was roughly divided along regional lines; Northeastern newspapers took up Texaco's cause, while a number of Texas papers sided with Pennzoil, particularly in response to Texaco's implicit attacks on the integrity of the Texas legal system. In the appeals process, Dick Miller's role in the case was predictably diminished; rumors began to circulate among the downtown Houston law firms that Miller, Keeton, Bristow & Brown was on the verge of dissolution. Texaco retained the renowned Manhattan litigator David Boies, of Cravath, Swaine & Moore, to lead its appeal effort, focusing the attack on Judge Casseb's jury charge and the evidentiary rulings made by Farris early in the trial.

Stoical to the end, the Texaco executives in White Plains fortified the bulwarks and led their defense unyieldingly. Under heavy pressure, however, the unified front presented at trial in courtroom 151 began to fracture. A new wave of lawsuits, promulgated mainly by Texaco shareholders who saw the value of their stock plunge in the aftermath of the verdict, strained the binding force of Texaco's much-maligned indemnities. The museum sued Texaco in California, seeking to have the alleged terms of its indemnity enforced. The old Getty Oil directors, themselves under siege from class-action shareholder lawsuits, sought to defend themselves with some independence from Texaco and complained that McKinley's lawyers had failed to defend Getty Oil's integrity during the Houston trial. In White Plains, the pressure on the Texaco board of directors mounted. Late in 1986, chief executive John McKinley retired and the directors appointed Jim Kinnear in his place. Al DeCrane, whom many expected to be named to the top slot, was relegated to the post of chairman and promised to work cooperatively with Kinnear. McKinley said that he recommended Kinnear over DeCrane for the top job because of the former's extensive operating experience in the oil business. (DeCrane was trained as a lawyer.) But it was also true that Kinnear was the Texaco executive least involved in the Getty Oil merger, and he was regarded both inside and outside the company as an open, accessible, and flexible leader, at least relative to DeCrane and McKinley.

Early in 1987, Texaco was devastated by the long-awaited appellate decision in the Texas state courts: the panel upheld all but $2 billion of the original $10 billion judgment, leaving Texaco liable for a total of $9.1 billion, with interest, more than enough to bankrupt the company if the judgment was enforced. When the U.S. Supreme Court weighed in two months later with its opinion on the appellate bond issue—ruling unanimously for Pennzoil—Texaco's worst fears were realized. During a frenzied week in April, 1987, Texaco's executives tried to negotiate a settlement with Pennzoil and simultaneously asked the Texas courts to exempt it from the state's bond requirements. Both efforts failed. In settlement talks, Texaco offered

$2 billion in cash; Liedtke insisted on $4 billion. The Pennzoil chairman was stunned when, instead of attempting to narrow the settlement gap, Texaco filed for bankruptcy protection. The stocks of both companies plummeted. By the spring of 1987, the old adversaries were still slugging at one another, only this time under a bankruptcy judge's supervision.

Meanwhile, Gordon Getty, the man so much at the center of the events leading up to Texaco's expensive predicament, was himself deeply embroiled in litigation. *In the Matter of the Sarah C. Getty Trust*, the suit filed against him by his relatives back in November 1983, with the support of Getty Oil management, dragged on and on, resembling with increasing exactness the fictional probate suit *Jarndyce v. Jarndyce* described in Charles Dickens' legal satire, *Bleak House*. The "family settlement" proposed in 1984, in which the vast Getty fortune would be divided into four separate trusts—one for Gordon, one for J. Paul, one for the heirs of George Getty, and one for the heirs of Ronald—was stalled by tax problems and family bickering. The actual fortune, billions strong, continued to sit in its court-ordered form of U.S. Treasury bonds, generating hundreds of millions of dollars in annual interest. And since the dozens of lawyers involved in the case took their millions in fees out of the interest payments, none of the Getty clients had an urgent financial incentive to expedite a settlement; indeed, it was conceivable early in 1987 that the question of Gordon's right to serve as sole trustee might actually be resolved in an embarrassing public trial.

Gordon himself seemed not to be bothered by the prospect. Dividing his time between his Broadway mansion in San Francisco and his new Fifth Avenue apartment in New York, he devoted himself mainly to the creation and performance of his musical compositions. He felt no sadness over the loss of Getty Oil. "I have no feeling on that score," he declared in an interview late in 1986. "I assure you my father wouldn't have, either. My father loved nothing better than buying in a low market and selling in a high market. He did it just as fast as he could without any twinge of remorse over getting rid of a long-held asset.

"Now, I don't think I made any wrong moves," Gordon continued, reflecting on the long course of his dealings with Sid Petersen, Hugh Liedtke, and John McKinley. "That trip to London was certainly a waste of time, but I don't think it was a setback. I don't think there were any setbacks that I can identify in the years of the trust's relationship with Getty Oil. I can't think of any lost ground."

The specific "message to corporate America" intended by the jurors in *Pennzoil* v. *Texaco* was perhaps lost amid the surging publicity and legal campaigns conducted by Texaco and its adversaries in the immediate aftermath of the trial; because of the astronomical size of the judgment, the issues discussed during those campaigns had far more to do with money and law than with the ethics or economic appositeness of the great era of Wall Street merger-making in the 1980s. Still, whether it was a cause or merely a symptom, the verdict did seem to signal the end of a heady, speculative phase in Wall Street's most bullish cycle since the go-go years of the late 1960s.

Even before the shocking, takeover-driven insider-trading scandal first uncovered by the arrest of a young Wall Street merger banker named Dennis Levine in May 1986, there were signs that some of the merger game's leading players had recognized that the frenzy was out of control. Marty Lipton, for example, whose large law firm and equally considerable personal reputation had risen in tandem with the takeover boom, testified before Congress in April 1985 that "takeover abuses have become a pressing national problem." Worried that debt generated by mergers would lead eventually to crisis, Lipton lamented, "Unfortunately, the future has no political constituency. . . . While different in form, what we face today is not different in substance from what happened in 1928 and 1929. Leverage produces great results on the way up, but no economy ever goes in a straight line, and high leverage inevitably produces a crash when an economy turns down." Cynics on Wall Street responded to Lipton's warning by blithely accusing the lawyer of hypocrisy—Lipton had already cashed in on the merger boom, so where did he get off trying to plug the flow of latecomers to the game?

With the indictment on insider-trading charges of the celebrated takeover arbitrageur Ivan Boesky late in 1986, however, a sudden chill swept through the great Wall Street investment banking houses. The game, it now seemed, was up. Throughout the 1980s merger boom, Boesky had been the Street's leading speculator in takeover stocks, often buying huge blocks of shares in advance of a takeover announcement and then making tens of millions when the merger was consummated. Boesky attributed his prescient stock purchases to dogged "research" into upcoming takeovers and to his own genius for trading, which he compared in an interview to the artistic talent of Renoir. It turned out, however, that Boesky was merely buying illegal inside information from prestigious Wall Street merger bankers.

Before his dramatic fall, Boesky published a book entitled *Merger Mania* in which he detailed the trading formula he supposedly used to make money speculating on takeovers. In the book, he provided a blow-by-blow account of his trading in Getty Oil stock during the fall of 1983, trading which eventually reaped him more than $50 million in profits. Following his guilty plea, Boesky pledged to cooperate with the Securities and Exchange Commission in its ongoing investigation of Wall Street speculators and investment bankers. At least one of the bankers prominently involved in the taking of Getty Oil, the dashing Marty Siegel, quickly received a subpoena. Within weeks, Siegel was singing. He told federal investigators that he had been for years accepting suitcases full of cash from Boesky in exchange for passing inside information about takeovers to the speculators. The details of their relationship were appalling—the increasingly paranoid Siegel standing in hotel lobbies awaiting Boesky's swarthy bag men, coded phrases passed between the two by telephone, secret year-end meetings in a Manhattan coffee shop called to square their annual accounts. It turned out that Siegel had tipped Boesky about Getty Oil virtually as soon as he was retained by Gordon Getty in the fall of 1983, thus ensuring the speculator's huge profits in the deal. As the government's investigation continued, it promised to eventually lay bare, once and for all, the conduct of Wall Street's most controversial bankers and lawyers during the period of their ascendancy over American finance and industry.

Siegel's fall was portrayed and easily comprehended in the terms of classical tragedy. A young man, gifted, handsome, ambitious, arrives on Wall Street, achieves enormous success, but is destroyed by his own insatiable greed. Certainly, that overlay fit the story. But there were indications that Siegel's fall was far more complex than that—it was suggested, for example, that his relationship with Boesky took hold not merely to shore up overdrawn personal accounts, but to further Siegel's career as a merger specialist. With Boesky rushing in advance to Siegel's deals, huge blocks of stock fell into hands friendly to the investment banker. It was this systemic connection, the sense that legitimate and scandalous practices in Wall Street merger banking were not easily distinguished, that began to unsettle the country as news about insider trading unfolded. So it had been sixty years earlier, in the 1920s era of stock pools and bear raids on the Street. To clean up the mess then, Roosevelt appointed one of Wall Street's most notorious manipulators, Joseph P. Kennedy, to head a new regulatory agency. More appalling than the idea itself was the fact that it actually worked: Kennedy did energetically clean up his brethren. Slowly, the influence of Wall Street over American business ebbed, and amid the poverty of the Depression, the most scandalous practices were eradicated. By 1987, it was apparent that the cycle had been renewed: the regulators were in ascendance over Wall Street and in time normalcy would be restored to the relations between industry and finance. All of that would come too late for the Getty Oil Company and for Texaco as well. Like Marty Siegel, Texaco had tried to take something and by doing so nearly destroyed itself. (Unlike Siegel, Texaco transgressed unwittingly.) Both stories were versions of the central metaphor of the times: Wall Street, for a decade hungrier and hungrier, finally consumed by its own appetite.

EPILOGUE

They were sitting in the Manhattan offices of Trans World Airlines Inc. chairman Carl C. Icahn one morning in December 1987, when one of Icahn's Wall Street lawyers started explaining exactly how the biggest lawsuit in U.S. history would play out in the bankruptcy court and how the U.S. Supreme Court would rule. Joe Jamail, the Texas "sore back lawyer" who won the case for Pennzoil at trial and who figured to pocket as much as $400 million if the suit was ever resolved, listened for three or four minutes, which is about how long he could listen to something he didn't want to hear.

They had come to Icahn's office to cut a deal: Jamail, Pennzoil chairman J. Hugh Liedtke, and a handful of the other lawyers involved in the case. After wallowing in Texaco's Dickensian bankruptcy proceedings since the previous April, *Pennzoil v. Texaco* had again come to life, and once more the puckish Jamail was at the center of things. Carl Icahn, an enormously successful corporate raider who had gained control of TWA Inc. in a hostile takeover, had decided there was potential for profit in Texaco's travails. After the stock market collapse in October 1987, he had purchased about 15 percent of Texaco's stock at fire sale prices from Australian investor Robert Holmes à Court. Icahn's plan was to use his clout as a major stockholder to force a settlement between Texaco and Pennzoil. Once freed from the uncertainties of its unprecedented legal troubles, Icahn figured, Texaco would watch its stock price rise gloriously, and he would make millions. If that didn't happen, then Icahn could always attempt to buy Texaco himself. But to cut the deal that was essential to his plans, Icahn needed Pennzoil's Liedtke and Jamail.

And now Jamail was saying that he had heard enough, that he was leaving. "I'm done. Let's go, Hugh," he drawled to Liedtke. "I've heard all the shit I'm going to hear."

"Don't get mad," Icahn told Jamail. "That's not going to solve anything."

"I'm not mad. I'm just bored."

"Where are you going?"

"I'm going to get a cold beer."

"It's only eleven o'clock in the morning," Icahn observed.

"Now, look, you can't be my guardian," Jamail answered, his voice animated with a playful malice. "I'm going to get a cold beer. And you're invited."

"All right," Carl Icahn said. "Let's go."

They found a tavern, threw back a few beers, and began to talk. Jamail sketched out a scenario for Icahn: he suggested that the lawsuit could probably be settled for less than $3.5 billion. He urged Icahn to visit Texaco and press for a deal. "You're the big, bad bogeyman now, not me," Jamail told Icahn, whose reputation for launching hostile takeovers had indeed seemed to spook Texaco in recent weeks.

Meeting several times over the next ten days with Liedtke and Texaco chief executive James Kinnear, Icahn began the shuttle diplomacy that on December 18, 1987, produced a signed $3 billion settlement of the Pennzoil lawsuit. Once the settlement was approved by Texaco's bankruptcy judge, the payment was made—in cash, by wire transfer—on April 7, 1988, the same day Texaco emerged from bankruptcy protection. On that day, *Pennzoil v. Texaco* officially ended.

The impetus for Texaco's historic settlement was a stunning decision by the Texas Supreme Court in November 1987 to uphold all of Pennzoil's $10 billion judgment without a formal hearing. The Texas high court justices did review thousands of pages of legal briefs submitted by the parties, but they were apparently so convinced of Pennzoil's righteousness that they declined to hold oral arguments in the matter. At first Texaco was merely outraged, railing in public and to the press that the Texas state court system was fundamentally corrupted by campaign contributions and open graft. Soon, however, the company began to see that anger would do little to solve the enormous problems created by the Texas Supreme Court's decision. For one thing, the ruling sparked Icahn to make his huge purchases. For another, it left only one chance for Texaco to win its case on appeal—at the U.S. Supreme Court.

Under the U.S. court system, matters of law and justice are sharply divided between state and federal courts. The U.S. Constitution, with its familiar amendments and guarantees, governs most of the important federal law. But the Pennzoil case had been filed and then tried in Texas state court. Afterwards, appeals had been made, and turned down, in the Texas Court of Appeals and at the Texas Supreme Court. When it lost before the Texas high court in November 1987, Texaco could obtain a hearing before the U.S. Supreme Court only if it could show that an important federal issue was at stake—for example, if it could show that Texaco's constitutional rights had been violated. Nearly all the factual and legal issues debated at the trial of *Pennzoil v. Texaco* were beyond the U.S. high court's jurisdiction because they involved matters of state law. The Supreme Court would agree to hear the case only if four of its justices were convinced that a compelling constitutional issue needed to be addressed. And while Texaco's lawyers ably dredged up a number of federal issues to present to the court, most observers expected the high court to turn the company's appeal down. (Only about 3 percent of petitions to the U.S. Supreme Court are heard by the court's nine justices.) If the Supreme Court declined to hear Texaco's appeal, then the Pennzoil judgment would be final. In all likelihood, Texaco, the country's third-largest oil company, would have to be liquidated in order to satisfy Pennzoil's claim.

So when Carl Icahn, spurred by beer and conversation with Jamail, began shuttling between Texaco's corporate estate in White Plains and Hugh Liedtke's Waldorf apartment in Manhattan that December, Texaco's executives were willing to listen, as they had never been before. By paying $3 billion to Pennzoil, Texaco was able to preserve itself, at least for a time, as a profitable and independent—albeit considerably smaller—oil company. Though it faced a takeover threat from Icahn when it emerged from bankruptcy, the company was also able to restructure itself as a leaner and less vulnerable organization.

Lawyers on all sides of the case made out handsomely. As part of the final settlement agreement, Pennzoil and Texaco agreed to absolve everyone involved in the taking of Getty Oil—Gordon Getty, the former Getty Oil directors, Marty Lipton and Harold Williams of the museum, the lawyers at Skadden Arps who forgot to file Texaco's answer in Delaware, the investment bankers at First Boston and Goldman, Sachs, Texaco's officers and directors, and, naturally, all of the lawyers for all of the parties—from any future liability arising from the case or the events that preceded it. For a brief time, lawyers representing Texaco shareholders objected to this arrangement, arguing that Texaco could recover much of its $3 billion payment by suing its lawyers and investment bankers for malpractice, but quickly these dissenters were taken care of as well—the shareholder lawyers were permitted to file with the bankruptcy court an application for fees not to exceed $10 million.

Upon receipt of his $3 billion, J. Hugh Liedtke decided to retire from day-to-day involvement in the affairs of Pennzoil Co., saying he wished to spend more time fishing and with his grandchildren. After the court hearing in White Plains, N.Y., where Texaco's bankruptcy judge, Howard Schwartzberg, pronounced his final blessing on Pennzoil's unprecedented award, the dog-faced Liedtke stood before the courtroom's jury box for a few moments and reflected on his accomplishment. "It hasn't exactly been pleasant over these last four years," Liedtke said. "But it was something that had to be done."

BIBLIOGRAPHICAL NOTE

The use of recollected and reconstructed dialogue in works of narrative nonfiction, while increasingly widespread, is in many ways problematic. First off, there is, or should be, the question of accuracy. In the absence of verbatim transcripts or detailed, contemporaneous notes, it is impossible for any journalist to recreate precisely a conversation that occurred outside his earshot months or years in the past. Memories, even the best ones, are inherently distorted. It is a primary human trait to filter the past through a prism of self-esteem, recalling nuance and detail which by their very precision cast the teller in the best possible light. No one vaguely remembers being a hero. But memories of cowardice or duplicity or malice—memories we all possess—are often shrouded and muddled. This is the essence of nationalism, of course, but it is also a plague on the work of journalists.

The obvious solution, taken by some scholarly historians, is to forego the use of dialogue altogether, unless it was transcribed contemporaneously. There are many reasons why modern journalists reject this approach, not the least of which are commercial. The strict constructionist is often a boring storyteller. Slogging through his books, the reader must wonder whether the scholar found his style only after practiced suppression of his imagination. So one must acknowledge the truth: a great many modern journalists write books the way they do, and publishers publish them, in large part because they all want the books to be widely read.

I point this out not because I think it is evil, but because so many journalists these days go to such absurd lengths to justify their use of reconstructed dialogue on moral and professional grounds. There is the standard disclaimer: "The author does not represent that the dialogue herein reflects the exact words used by the participants, but he does assert that the conversations are accurate in substance and spirit." Nowadays, journalists don't go much further than that; by their brief disclaimers they seem to feel that they have fulfilled some legal obligation to their readers, and now the reader is on his own—*caveat emptor*.

A few years back, before this disclaimer proliferated like a warning label on a popular product, authors occasionally tried to explain themselves a little. David McClintick, whose wonderful, best-selling book about the scandal at Columbia Pictures Industries gave birth to a thousand jacket blurbs declaring "Told in the style of *Indecent Exposure*," ventured that his reconstructed dialogue captured the truth *"more* accurately than paraphrase would. Human beings do not speak in paraphrase." (His emphasis.) Interesting, but in Tony Kornheiser's memorable phrase, I have trouble getting in a full upright and locked position on that one. How can a work of nonfiction that deliberately alters the available facts, however slightly, be more accurate than one that doesn't? Perhaps such a work could be more truthful, in the sense that Dickens holds more truth about nineteenth-century England than any history does, but McClintick does not make that lofty claim. Nor should he. He is writing journalism, not a novel, and not a "docudrama," that insipid and deceptive television hybrid. Theodore Dreiser, in thinking about a sensational murder case of his day, decided that the basic facts would make for a story of tremendous resonance. So he wrote *An American Tragedy*, a novel. If he had lived in our time, he might well have written a work of narrative nonfiction, complete with reconstructed dialogue, and then sold the miniseries rights to one of the networks.

So the author has to make choices. They are not easy, but it is important to think them through. And it seems to me that if a journalist decides, as I have, to employ reconstructed dialogue in the text of his narrative, then he has redoubled his obligation to the reader. The real problem with the modern journalistic genre is not that writers put quotation marks around words that would otherwise be presented as paraphrase. That, in itself, is essentially an artistic choice, an attempt to convey the life and corporeal energy of human action. By employing a simple cosmetic device, the journalist endows historical events with the feeling of truth—a feeling the reader intuitively appreciates. The choice to use quotation marks is influenced in part by commerce, in part by the cinematic tenor of our times, in part by a desire to coax resonance from the flat historical record— that is, it is a choice made for both good and bad reasons. Still, the choice belongs to the author, even when the author is a journalist. The important thing is that having made the choice, the author should justify himself to the reader. He should not treat the reader with condescension, or, as is more common, ignore the reader altogether with a dismissive disclaimer.

The important thing, I mean to say, is sourcing. Where did this dialogue come from? Who remembered it that way? What contemporaneous and documentary evidence is there to support the recollection? What rules did the author follow with sources? What standards did the author adhere to in the writing? What is surprising about contemporary works of narrative nonfiction, many of them written by excellent journalists, is that authors so rarely answer these questions for the reader, and if they do, their answers are sometimes appalling. There are prominent journalists who do not disclose in their books that they have made contractual arrangements with sources to share in the profits from publication and future sale to the movies. Why is that not scandalous? There are many nonfiction authors who do not write any endnotes at all, leaving the whole of their history unattributed. Some of these same authors work for newspapers that require them, with apparent contempt for the art of their writing, to attribute virtually every piece of information they publish to some source, even if the source is confidential. Why does a book contract liberate them from this policy?

Then there is the issue of fact-checking. It is perhaps impossible in a book-length work about a complex subject not to make factual errors. One can only hope to minimize them. To this end, some authors submit their manuscripts to trustworthy sources for review in advance of publication. The sources identify mistakes for the author. If there is disagreement over whether a passage is correct or not, the source may marshal evidence to persuade the author of his view, but the author is free to make his own decision. To a limited extent, I have used this method myself. While preparing an earlier book, I submitted the manuscript to one trustworthy source on each side of the conflict that I was writing about. The sources identified some embarrassing errors, argued with me about my interpretations, and questioned some of my assumptions. I found it a useful process, though regrettably and inevitably, it did not leave my book entirely error-free. Still, a journalist's decision to submit his work to a source in advance of publication, however trustworthy the source, cannot be made casually. Legally and ethically, it is a complicated decision, I think. One must weigh independence against accuracy, integrity against thoroughness.

Sometimes, for example, a source will insist on the right to see the manuscript as a condition of granting an interview. This, too, is a complicated issue. While working on my first book, I refused all such requests. In the course of researching this book, I turned down several more requests, but eventually granted one to Texaco, with the caveat that they could see only those portions of the manuscript pertaining to the company. I ceded no obligation to them other than to listen to their comments, but still, I do not feel entirely comfortable about my decision. If I had turned them down, I would have been denied a number of important interviews. But the compromise we arrived at, like many compromises, was unsettling. In meetings with two other sources who have nothing to do with Texaco, I read passages from my manuscript out loud and asked for comment. Somehow, this felt like a better arrangement, although clearly it was not materially different from my agreement with Texaco. Still, sitting at the table with my arms wrapped around the manuscript, I felt better. The book was mine. There are nonfiction authors, not ghostwriters, who routinely enter into written agreements with sources—agreements which permit the sources to dictate changes to the author's manuscript. One institution I contacted in the course of researching this book even had its lawyer send me a standard contract letter that would have granted it the right to make changes in my manuscript—it was a standardized form, I was told, because so many other authors signed it. These are serious journalists, seriously reviewed. I cannot understand why publishers do not insist such arrangements be disclosed to their readers.

Now, then, to the dialogue recorded in this book. So far as I have been able to determine, and I have worked very hard at it, the people who appear in this book really did say these things to each other, difficult though it may be to believe at times. It is true, as the standard warning label has it, that they did not necessarily use the exact words inside the quotation marks—except when those words are taken from transcribed proceedings. But the words I attribute to the characters in the book did not come from my imagination—they came from the sources listed in the Notes. As can be deduced from a careful reading of these endnotes, I tried to follow certain rules. For obvious reasons, I gave first preference to contemporaneous documents: handwritten notes, dictated memos to file, minutes, interoffice memos, and so on. Such documents say what they say; there is little bias about them. Absent such documents, I relied secondly on the sworn testimony of the participants, under the theory that people are less likely to perjure themselves under oath than they are likely to lie to journalists. Absent documents or testimony, I relied thirdly on the recollections of persons willing to be interviewed on-the-record. I do not discount the importance of confidentiality in journalism, but I embraced the theory that people are less likely to lie on-the-record than on background. I realize that this theory is debatable, but since it appeals to common sense, I prefer it to the competing notion that people are more likely to be truthful when they are not accountable for what they say. And lastly, I relied on interviews with confidential sources. I wish I could say that these interviews play no significant role in the narrative. I cannot. What I can say is that there is not one important conversation in this book sourced exclusively to confidential interviews. If the reader wonders where a particular conversation or discussion comes from, in virtually every case he or she can turn to the back and find a name or two or three attached to it. And then, presumably, the reader can begin to make an independent judgment about possible biases, whether mine or those of my characters. A substantial portion of the sworn testimony cited in the endnotes is not publicly available, but some of it will eventually be released. In any event, I have managed to get hold of it from those ubiquitous confidential sources.

In the interests of both full disclosure and personal sentiment, it should be known that my wife, Susan, was in many ways an equal partner in the research of this book. She traveled with me as well as on her own, researched the Getty family's history, obtained and sorted through legal and government documents, and even conducted a few interviews—all of this while raising our young daughter without significant outside help. However this book is judged, hers was an amazing feat.

NOTES

Chapter One

<u>5–7</u>

The account of Hays' last days is primarily from author's interview with Spencer Hays, supported by confidential interviews with three former partners in Hays' firm.

<u>7–8</u>

Gordon's trust income: the exact amount varied with Getty Oil dividend payments. On June 15, 1982, the trust received a $20,673,307.20 quarterly dividend check, of which one-third belonged to Gordon.

<u>8–9</u>

Memorial service eulogy: from handwritten notes retained by Spencer Hays and made available to the author.

<u>12–13</u>

Gordon's board room demeanor: from interviews with twelve former Getty Oil executives and directors, including former chief executives Sid Petersen and Harold Berg. Gordon Getty said in an interview with the author that the stories about his absent-mindedness are "all true," except one which had it that he composed opera scores in his mind during board meetings. "At a dinner party, maybe," Gordon said. "But never at a board meeting."

<u>13</u>

"Well-rounded and seasoned": letter from George Getty to J. Paul Getty, June 17, 1965.

13

"Your musical compositions": cited in Robert Lenzner, *The Great Getty* (New York, 1985), p. 151.

15

Ann's view of her role and Gordon's view of his father as a formidable lion: from televised interview on ABC's "20/20" broadcast, August 30, 1984. Also from author's interview with Gordon Getty.

15

Gordon's feelings about Lansing, and "You're going to have to go it alone" conversation: from author's interview with Gordon Getty.

15

"You left one word off your list" conversation: from author's interviews with Gordon Getty and Spencer Hays.

16

Value of trust: Getty Oil's stock price was fluctuating around $50 per share. The trust owned 31.8 million shares.

18

"Gordon is going to be around" meeting, and Hays' remarks: from February 9, 1981, memo to file by Robert H. Smith, executive vice-president of Security Pacific National Bank.

Chapter Two

21

"What is your luxury?": from "20/20" interview, August 30, 1984.

22–24

Ronald's biography: from *The Great Getty*; Russell Miller, *The House of Getty* (New York), 1985; and author's interviews with former Getty Oil executives. Executor fees and price of Italian house: from *The Economist*, November 14, 1984.

25

"I would be very pleased": cited in *The Great Getty*, p. 151.

25

"Keep hammering Gordon": Lenzner reports J. Paul telling his lawyer, "Keep killing my son." Lasky said in an interview with the author that "hammering" was the word his client employed.

26

Letter from J. Ronald Getty to Gordon Getty, May 18, 1982. Letter from Gordon Getty to J. Ronald Getty, May 28, 1982. Letter from

Horst Osterkamp to Gordon Getty, June 28, 1982. Letter from Moses Lasky to Gordon Getty, July 12, 1982.

27

What Gordon believed: from author's interview with Gordon Getty.

Chapter Three

29-31

What Petersen thought to himself: from author's interview with Sid Petersen. Gordon's comment about his ERC vote: from author's interviews with Petersen and former Getty Oil director Norman Topping.

30-31

Petersen's biography: from author's interviews with Petersen and former Getty Oil executives.

31-33

Decision to promote Petersen over Miller, and resentment of Petersen's new status: from author's interviews with former Getty Oil executives and directors. It should be noted that much of the bitterness about Petersen expressed in interviews with the author was perhaps colored, at the time of the interviews, by resentment over severance and retirement benefits awarded to different groups of former Getty Oil executives. Petersen received the most lucrative benefits.

34

What bothered Gordon: from author's interview with Gordon Getty.

35

"Those of us in management" conversation: from Petersen's deposition testimony in *For the Matter of the Declaration of the Trust of Sarah C. Getty Dated December 31, 1934*, civil action P685566, Los Angeles County Superior Court. The conversation is recounted in Volume I of Petersen's deposition, pp. 1910–1912, taken September 24, 1984. Gordon's comments concerning "forty percent is forty percent" are from author's interview with Gordon Getty.

36

What Copley felt: from confidential interviews by the author with two sources familiar with Copley's thinking.

36-37

Meeting with Copley, Lasky, and Cohler: from Copley's deposition testimony in *For the Matter. . . .* The meeting is described in Volume VIII of Copley's deposition, pp. 1523–1528, taken September

19, 1984. Tone of the conversation is from author's interview with Tim Cohler.

38–40

Dinner meeting between Petersen, Lasky, and Cohler: from Petersen's deposition testimony in *For the Matter* . . ., Volume I, pp. 1901–1906. Also from author's interview with Tim Cohler.

40–41

Change in committee assignments: from author's interviews with Sid Petersen and Norman Topping.

40–42

Gordon's investigation of Getty Oil: from author's interviews with Gordon Getty, Sid Petersen, Norman Topping, and confidential interviews with former Getty Oil executives.

42–44

July conversation in Texas: from Petersen deposition in *For the Matter* . . ., Volume I, pp. 1916–1917, and from author's interview with Sid Petersen.

45

"Classic case of the paranoia of the rich": Wendt remarks from exhibit 169 to Petersen deposition in *For the Matter* . . ., Petersen's handwritten notes from July 1982. Notes and testimony in Volume II of the deposition, pp. 2019–2026.

Chapter Four

47–50

Phoenix cab ride: conversation recounted in Petersen's deposition in *For the Matter* . . ., Volume I, pp. 1919–1920. Also from author's interview with Sid Petersen.

50

Gordon Getty said later: from author's interview with Gordon Getty.

50–51

Valuations of Getty Oil: letter from Fayez Sarofim to Harold Williams, August 26, 1981. Analyst report from Hamershlag Kempner & Co. to Harold Williams, May 18, 1982.

52–55

Pickens' critique: from author's interview with T. Boone Pickens, Jr. Cogent explanation of royalty trusts in *Fortune*, December 26, 1983.

55–56

Portrait of Evey: from author's confidential interviews with former Getty Oil executives and directors.

57–58
What Petersen thought: from author's interview with Sid Petersen.

57– 58
Cullen fortune and family history: *Wall Street Journal*, September 2, 1983.

58
Telephone conversation with Medberry: from Petersen's deposition in *For the Matter . . .*, Volume II, pp. 2040–2042.

58
Robertson's proposal: "Confidential Presentation to . . ." document, 18 pages, dated October 14, 1982, produced from the files of Corbin J. Robertson in *For the Matter. . . .*

60–61
Telephone conference call: from Petersen's handwritten notes of October 21, 1982, produced as exhibit 171 to Petersen's deposition in *For the Matter. . . .* Notes and testimony in Volume II of the deposition pp. 2037–2040.

62
"I have completed a review": from Getty Oil Memo from C. Steadman Garber to Sid Petersen, August 18, 1982.

63–64
Early royalty trust studies: from author's interviews with Tim Cohler, Sid Petersen, Gordon Getty, and former Getty Oil executives.

Chapter Five
66–67
December 23 meeting: from author's interviews with Tim Cohler and Sid Petersen. Letter from Gordon Getty to Sid Petersen, December 24, 1982.

68–69
What Petersen thought: from Petersen's deposition testimony, op. cit., and author's interview with Sid Petersen.

69–70
Winokur's biography: from Winokur's deposition in *For the Matter . . .*, Volume I, pp. 5–7, and from author's interviews with three confidential sources close to Winokur.

71–72
Hays & Landsman merger with Dechert Price, and Winokur's rise: from author's interviews with three confidential sources close to

Winokur. "You don't need to be here" conversation: from a confidential source.

72

Ivy League swagger: from author's interviews with former Getty Oil executives.

72

Meeting in Petersen's office: from deposition testimony of Dave Copley in *For the Matter . . .*, taken November 29, 1983, pp. 429–430.

73–74

"I called Corbin" conversation: from handwritten notes of Sid Petersen, January 6, 1983, produced as exhibit 174 to Petersen's deposition in *For the Matter. . . .* Notes and testimony about the conversation in Volume II of the deposition, pp. 2055–2072.

75

Arrival at Bonaventure: from author's interview with Tim Cohler. What Cohler thought is also from author's interview with Cohler.

75

Despite significant differences of opinion over its tone, accounts of the substance of the Bonaventure meeting provided by the participants in interviews with the author and deposition testimony are in accord. The dialogue recorded here is extracted from the following sources: author's interview with Sid Petersen; author's interview with Gordon Getty; author's interview with Tim Cohler; deposition testimony of Sid Petersen in *For the Matter . . .*, Volume I, pp. 1952–1960; deposition of Dave Copley in *For the Matter . . .*, Volume IX, pp. 1651–1661; deposition testimony of Bart Winokur in *For the Matter . . .*, Volume I, pp. 20–43.

81

"During our conversation": letter from Gordon Getty to Corbin J. Robertson, January 12, 1983.

82

"I take this opportunity": letter from Moses Lasky to Gordon Getty, dated January 16, 1983.

83–84

Business was a matter of intuition: from author's interview with Gordon Getty.

Chapter Six

87

The Georgettes contacted Petersen: from author's interview with Sid Petersen. Petersen's view of the Bonaventure meeting as a turning point and as the impetus for an examination of the trust document from his deposition testimony in *For the Matter . . .*, Volume I, pp. 1955–1960.

88

January 20 meeting with Landry: from excerpted deposition testimony of Dave Copley in public file of *For the Matter . . .*, Los Angeles County Superior Court.

89

Petersen's phone call to Flamson: from Petersen's handwritten notes of February 2, 1983, produced as exhibit 180 to his deposition in *For the Matter. . . .* Notes and testimony about the call in Petersen's deposition, Volume II, pp. 2100–2105.

90–92

February 9 meeting with Security Pacific executives: from excerpted Copley deposition testimony in public file, op. cit.

92–93

Contact with Bank of America: ibid.

93–94

J. Paul Jr.'s hospital stay: from affidavit of his London physician in *For the Matter . . .*, public file.

94–95

J. Paul Jr.'s biography: from *The Great Getty* and *The House of Getty*. "I am proud of my little family": from J. Paul Getty, *As I See It: The Autobiography of J. Paul Getty* (Englewood Cliffs, N.J., 1976), pp. 130–131. "A tie-dyed velvet outfit": cited by Lenzner, *The Great Getty*, p. 157.

95

What Petersen believed about remaindermen: from author's interview with Sid Petersen.

95–97

Copley's trip to London: from excerpted Copley deposition testimony in public life, op. cit.

Chapter Seven

99

What Gordon Getty concluded about Petersen and Winokur: from author's interview with Gordon Getty.

100

"And he isn't much good at that": remark from Petersen's deposition in *For the Matter . . .*, Volume I, p. 1962.

100

Gordon's thinking about hiring an investment banker: from author's interview with Tim Cohler.

100–102

Management concern about investment banker: from deposition testimony of Bart Winokur in *For the Matter . . .*, Volume I, pp. 43–49; author's interview with Sid Petersen.

102–103

Goldman, Sachs profile: *Business Week*, November 22, 1976; *Institutional Investor*, November 1984; *Wall Street Journal*, December 3, 1982.

103–104

First meeting with Goldman recounted in Winokur deposition testimony in *For the Matter . . .*, Volume I, pp. 49–59.

104–105

Finance men's attitude toward Goldman: from author's interviews with former Getty Oil executives.

105–107

Meeting between Whitehead, Petersen, and Gordon Getty in San Francisco and subsequent conversation in limousine: from Petersen's handwritten notes of March 18, 1983, produced as exhibit 183 to Petersen's deposition in *For the Matter. . . .* Notes and testimony in deposition, Volume II, pp. 2112–2125. Under questioning, Petersen explained the tenor of his conversation with Whitehead in the limo: "By the time they listened to Gordon Getty talk for two hours—by the time anybody listens to Gordon Getty talk for two hours—they come away with the idea that any corporation that he might be responsible for or in charge of has a problem."

107–108

Wulff reports: "Oil and Gas Valuation" Donaldson, Lufkin & Jenrette, dated February 1, 1983, and "Research Bulletin," also dated February 1, 1983.

108–109

"Going after a puppy": from author's interview with Boone Pickens.

108–110

Pickens profile: from author's interview with Boone Pickens. Also from *Fortune*, December 26, 1983.

110–112

Pickens' phone call to Gordon Getty and Beverly Wilshire meeting: from author's interview with Boone Pickens. Also from author's interview with Mesa executive David Batchelder.

112

Pickens' proposal: ibid. Also, author's interviews with Sid Petersen and former Getty Oil executives.

113

Pickens wrote to Petersen: letter from Boone Pickens to Sid Petersen, dated June 3, 1983.

113–116

Century Plaza meeting: from author's interviews with Boone Pickens, Sid Petersen, David Batchelder, and former Getty Oil executives.

Chapter Eight

117

Golden parachutes: Petersen's employment contract, dated May 16, 1983, 20 pages, provided for an annual salary of $565,000, plus benefits and termination pay in the event of a change in control at Getty Oil.

118

April 27 meeting with Isaacs: from excerpted deposition testimony of Dave Copley in *For the Matter . . .*, op. cit.

119–123

April 28 meeting with Security Pacific officials, and subsequent conversations between Nutten and Warren, Nutten and Gother, and among Nutten, Copley, Winokur, and O'Melveny & Meyers attorneys: all from deposition testimony of Wesley Nutten, III, taken November 29, 1983, in *For the Matter . . .* and excerpted in the public file of that case. Nutten's account is corroborated by deposition testimony of Dave Copley.

123–124

Meetings with Hufstedler: from deposition testimony of Seth Hufstedler, taken November 28, 1983, in *For the Matter . . .* and excerpted in the public file of the case. Also from deposition testimony of Wesley Nutten, op. cit.

125–126

Meeting with Isaacs from excerpted deposition testimony of Wesley Nutten in *For the Matter . . .*, op. cit.

127–128
Petersen's thinking in early summer of 1983: from author's interviews with Sid Petersen, former Getty Oil executives, and a confidential source familiar with Petersen's thinking.

128
"Of course, it was a challenge for me" quote: from author's interview with Gordon Getty.

Chapter Nine
131
Getty Oil directors not informed: from author's interviews with Sid Petersen and former Getty Oil board members. Corroborated by minutes of the company's July board meeting.

133
Petersen felt ambivalent: from author's interviews with Sid Petersen and a confidential source familiar with Petersen's thinking.

134–137
Origin of the LBO takeover idea, what Gordon told Cohler, and Cohler's call to Petersen: from author's interview with Tim Cohler. Concern about board-meeting vote corroborated in deposition testimony of Bart Winokur in *For the Matter . . .*, Volume I, pp. 96–98.

137
Petersen suspicious of Williams: from videotaped testimony of Sid Petersen in *Pennzoil* v. *Texaco*, presented July 30, 1985. Also from author's interview with Sid Petersen.

137
Williams' enigmatic tenure as SEC chairman: *Dun's Review*, 1979; *Wall Street Journal*, November 20, 1978.

137–138
"I met with Harold last week" conversation: from author's interview with Tim Cohler.

138
Gordon's objections to "black books": from author's interview with Tim Cohler and Winokur's deposition testimony in *For the Matter . . .*, Volume I, pp. 92–96. Cohler and Woodhouse meet with Williams: from author's interview with Tim Cohler.

139–142
This account of the board meeting is taken directly from the minutes, dated July 8, 1983. It accords with the recollections of participants.

143–144

The impolite comments here, including Medberry's "You mean we spent . . ." and Teets' exchange with Gordon about "maximizing values" are not recorded in the minutes, but were attested to in the author's interviews with Sid Petersen, three confidential sources in attendance at the meeting, and are referred to in Winokur's deposition testimony in *For the Matter . . .*, Volume I, pp. 102–105.

145

Gordon's conversation with Petersen immediately after the board meeting: from author's interview with Sid Petersen and from Petersen's deposition testimony in *For the Matter . . .*, Volume I, p. 1968.

Chapter Ten

147–149

Meeting between Cohler, Woodhouse, and Williams, and subsequent meeting between Cohler, Williams, and Gordon Getty: from author's interview with Tim Cohler.

149

Conversation between Cohler and Winokur: from author's interview with Tim Cohler and deposition testimony of Winokur in *For the Matter . . .*, Volume I, pp. 105–112. Winokur testified that in addition to requesting a study by Goldman, Sachs, Cohler remarked that Williams "had stated that it was inconceivable to him that he would ever be a minority shareholder in a company when Mr. Getty was the majority shareholder."

149–151

Biographical details about Boisi: from his testimony in *Pennzoil* v. *Texaco*, October 9, 1985.

151–152

Getty Oil career managers' feelings about Winokur, Boisi, and Cohler: from author's confidential interviews with former company executives.

152–157

This account of the July 20 meeting is from author's interview with Tim Cohler and from Winokur's deposition testimony in *For the Matter . . .*, Volume I, pp. 126–144. One substantive discrepancy in their recollections: Cohler recalled that Winokur raised the idea of a stock buy-back that would put Gordon Getty in a majority position, while Winokur testified that Cohler wanted to discuss the topic.

157–159
Conversation between Cohler and Boisi: from author's interviews with Tim Cohler and Geoff Boisi.

159–162
Dialogue here is primarily from author's interview with Tim Cohler, but also from Winokur's deposition testimony in *For the Matter . . .*, Volume I, pp. 142–148. Winokur's testimony corroborates the substance of the discussion as recollected by Cohler.

Chapter Eleven
163–164
Petersen's thoughts about the Getty Oil "family:" from author's interviews with Sid Petersen and a confidential source familiar with Petersen's thinking.

164–168
The substance and sequence of these conversations were confirmed by three sources: author's interview with Tim Cohler; deposition testimony of Sid Petersen in *For the Matter . . .*, Volume I, pp. 1973–1977; and deposition testimony of Bart Winokur in *For the Matter . . .*, Volume I, pp. 149–169. Dialogue was extracted from all three sources, as well as from handwritten notes of Sid Petersen produced as exhibit 188 to Petersen's deposition, Volume II, pp. 2153–2155. Goldman's valuation of Getty Oil at $120 confirmed in testimony of Henry Wendt in *Pennzoil* v. *Texaco* trial transcript, October 15, 1985, p. 17343.

169–170
Conversation between Cohler, Gordon Getty, and Lasky: from author's interview with Tim Cohler.

170
Second meeting between Petersen, Winokur, Copley, Cohler, and Lasky: from author's interview with Tim Cohler; deposition testimony of Bart Winokur in *For the Matter . . .*, Volume I, pp. 170–173; and Petersen's deposition testimony in *For the Matter . . .*, Volume I, pp. 1978–1979.

170–172
Conversations between Cohler and Copley, and subsequently between Cohler and Winokur: from author's interview with Tim Cohler. Substance of Cohler's conversation with Copley confirmed in deposition testimony of Sid Petersen in *For the Matter . . .*, Volume I, p. 1991.

172–175

Pebble Beach board meeting description: from deposition testimony of Sid Petersen in *For the Matter* . . ., Volume I, pp. 1986–1988; Petersen deposition testimony, Volume II, pp. 2156–2164; author's interview with Sid Petersen; author's interview with a confidential source present at the meeting; testimony of Henry Wendt in *Pennzoil* v. *Texaco* on October 29, 1985; and Winokur deposition testimony in *For the Matter* . . ., Volume I, pp. 179–181.

175–178

Telephone call from Winokur to Lasky: from author's interview with a confidential source. September 18 meeting in Philadelphia: from author's interview with Tim Cohler and Winokur's deposition testimony in *For the Matter* . . ., Volume I, pp. 179–189.

179–180

Gordon's lunch with Medberry and conversations with Lasky and Cohler: from October 4, 1983, memo to file by Moses Lasky titled "Re: Sarah C. Getty Trust."

180–181

What Lasky wrote: letter from Moses Lasky to Gordon Getty, October 1, 1983.

181

Meeting at Broadway mansion: from Lasky, October 4, 1983, memo to file.

181

Telephone conversation between Lasky and Winokur: from Winokur's deposition testimony in *For the Matter* . . ., Volume I, pp. 195–199, and from author's interview with Tim Cohler.

Chapter Twelve

183

Telephone conversation between Lasky and Winokur: from Lasky's memo to file of October 4, 1983, and Winokur's deposition testimony in *For the Matter* . . ., Volume I, pp. 203–205.

183–185

Account of board meeting: from the minutes dated October 2, 1983. Also from author's interview with two confidential sources in attendance.

185

Second telephone conversation between Lasky and Winokur: from

Lasky's memo to file of October 4, 1983, and Winokur's deposition testimony in *For the Matter* . . ., Volume I, pp. 203–205.

186–190

Timing of Lipton's involvement and biographical details: from author's interview with Martin Lipton.

190

Slept off jet lag: from author's interview with two confidential sources.

190–193

Substance of these negotiations: from Lasky's memo to file of October 4, 1983, and Winokur's deposition testimony in *For the Matter* . . ., Volume II, taken January 23, 1985, pp. 217–234. As to the state of mind of Gordon's attorneys at the conclusion of this meeting, Lasky wrote in his memo, "I stated to [Getty Oil's] representatives that we would recommend this deal to Gordon Getty. . . . I think that in London, the company went as far as it could go short of allowing Gordon as trustee to become owner of a majority of the stock without any limitation on his voting power."

193–194

Conversation between Gordon and his attorneys: from Lasky's memo to file of October 4, 1983. "We told Gordon several times that the deal with [Getty Oil] was the best solution," Lasky wrote.

194–195

Phone call from Cohler to Winokur: from Lasky's memo to file of October 4, 1983, and from Winokur's deposition testimony in *For the Matter* . . ., Volume II, pp. 234–237.

195–198

Meeting with Lipton: from Winokur's deposition testimony in *For the Matter* . . ., Volume II, pp. 244–255.

198–200

Meeting at Claridge's between Lasky, Lipton, Gordon, and Cohler: from Lasky's October 13, 1983, "Supplement" to October 4, 1983, memo to file.

200–201

Reconvened meeting between Winokur, Lipton, Petersen et. al.: from Winokur's deposition testimony in *For the Matter* . . ., Volume II, pp. 254–259.

201

Conversation between Gordon and his attorneys: from Lasky's October 13, 1983, "Supplement" to memo to file.

Chapter Thirteen

202–203

Car ride with Treves: from deposition testimony of Dave Copley in *For the Matter* . . ., excerpted in public file, and from Copley's deposition testimony in *Pennzoil* v. *Texaco*, taken January 18, 1984 and May 14, 1984.

203–204

Airplane trip: from author's interview with two confidential sources.

204–205

Siegel profile: from *Institutional Investor*, June 1985, and author's interviews.

205–206

Siegel's hiring: from videotaped deposition testimony of Marty Siegel in *Pennzoil* v. *Texaco*, presented August 20, 1985; author's interview with Tim Cohler; author's interview with a confidential source.

207

Siegel met with Gordon: from Siegel's videotaped deposition testimony in *Pennzoil* v. *Texaco*.

207

Telephone conversation between Cohler and Winokur: from Winokur's deposition in *For the Matter* . . ., Volume II, pp. 270–271.

207–208

Meeting between Lipton, Boisi, and Winokur: from Winokur's deposition testimony in *For the Matter* . . ., Volume II, pp. 262–267, 271–275.

209–210

Preliminary standstill negotiations: from author's interviews with Marty Lipton, Tim Cohler, two confidential sources, and from Winokur's deposition testimony in *For the Matter* . . ., Volume II, pp. 262–267.

210

Petersen flew from Bakersfield: from author's interviews with two former Getty Oil executives.

210–211

"My conversations with Marty Lipton" meeting between Gordon Getty, his attorneys, and Marty Siegel: from deposition testimony of Tim Cohler in *For the Matter* . . ., excerpted in the public file.

211

Conversation between Gordon, Petersen, and Williams: from Petersen's deposition testimony in *For the Matter* . . ., Volume II, pp. 2175–2176, and from author's interview with Sid Petersen.

212

"Mr. Getty is unwilling to sign any piece of paper" and following conversation: from Winokur's deposition testimony in *For the Matter . . .*, Volume II, pp. 289–291.

212–213

Topics of negotiation: from handwritten standstill agreement dated October 19, 1983.

213–215

Circumstances of standstill signing and conversations: from author's interviews with Marty Lipton and Sid Petersen, and from Winokur's deposition testimony in *For the Matter . . .*, Volume II, pp. 295–298.

Chapter Fourteen

216–217

Fee dispute between Gordon and his attorneys: from deposition testimony of Tim Cohler in *For the Matter . . .*, excerpted in the public file. Conversation between Lasky and Winokur: from Winokur's deposition testimony in *For the Matter . . .*, Volume II, pp. 300–303.

217–218

J. Paul Jr. telephoned Gordon and Ann: from affidavit of J. Paul Getty, Jr. in public file of *For the Matter. . . .* That Paul Jr. cried: from *Fortune*, January 21, 1985, citing deposition testimony of Gordon Getty in *For the Matter. . . .* Letter from Paul Jr. to Gordon cited in *Fortune*. Letter from Caroline Getty to Gordon Getty, October 21, 1983.

218

"Since the trust has so much money already" conversation: from *Fortune*, January 21, 1985, citing Gordon Getty's deposition testimony in *For the Matter. . . .*

218–220

Letter from Gordon Getty to Caroline Getty, J. Paul Getty, Jr., et al., November 1, 1983. Letter from Gordon Getty to J. Paul Getty, Jr., November 3, 1983.

221

Paul Jr.'s interest in lawsuit: from excerpted deposition testimony of Paul Jr. and Vanni Treves in public file of *For the Matter. . . .* Telephone conversations between Lasky and Copley and then Lasky and Winokur: from Winokur's deposition testimony in *For the Matter . . .*, Volume II, pp. 312–313.

<u>222</u>

Mark Getty's meeting with Vanni Treves: from affidavit of Mark Getty in public file of *For the Matter.* . . .

<u>222–225</u>

This account of the November 11, 1983, board meeting is from the minutes; deposition testimony of Dave Copley in *Pennzoil* v. *Texaco*; deposition testimony of Sid Petersen in *Pennzoil* v. *Texaco*, presented July 30, 1985; testimony of Geoff Boisi in *Pennzoil* v. *Texaco*, August 2, 1985; and, as cited in the text, from author's interviews with three confidential sources.

<u>225</u>

Scene of filing: from Hufstedler deposition testimony in *For the Matter* . . ., excerpted in public file and from memorandum prepared by Lasky, Haas law firm.

<u>226–227</u>

Lipton's reaction and telephone conversations: from consent agreement signed by Williams and Gordon Getty and dated December 5, 1983; deposition testimony of Bart Winokur in *For the Matter* . . ., Volume II, pp. 315–317; author's interviews with Marty Lipton and two confidential sources.

<u>227</u>

Directors recruited by Ann: from author's interview with Gordon Getty.

<u>227</u>

Williams furious: deposition testimony of Harold Williams in *Pennzoil* v. *Texaco*, presented November 1, 1985; deposition testimony of Bart Winokur in *For the Matter* . . ., Volume II, pp. 325–330.

<u>228</u>

Gordon still composing: from author's interview with Gordon Getty.

<u>228–229</u>

Consent signing: from testimony of Martin Lipton in *Pennzoil* v. *Texaco*, October 17, 1985; deposition testimony of Harold Williams in *Pennzoil* v. *Texaco*, presented November I, 1985; consent agreement signed by Harold Williams and Gordon Getty and dated December 5, 1983.

Chapter Fifteen

<u>233–238</u>

Profile of Liedtke and Pennzoil: from testimony of Hugh Liedtke in *Pennzoil* v. *Texaco*, August 26, 1985; testimony of Baine Ken in

Pennzoil v. *Texaco*, July 18, 19, and 22, 1985; *Business Week*, December 7, 1986; author's interviews with Baine Kerr, Joe Jamail, Irv Terrell, and John Jeffers.

238–239

Liedtke read *New York Times* article: from testimony of Hugh Liedtke in *Pennzoil* v. *Texaco*, August 27, 1985.

239–240

Early planning meetings, and "I don't want anything with $120 on it walking around" conversations: from deposition testimony of Clifton Fridge in *Pennzoil* v. *Texaco*, presented August 21, 1985, and from testimony of Hugh Liedtke in *Pennzoil* v. *Texaco*, August 26, 1985.

240–241

Meeting with Glanville: from Glanville's deposition testimony in *Pennzoil* v. *Texaco*, taken August 2, 1984. "Getty Oil's troubles began": from Hugh Liedtke's testimony in *Pennzoil* v. *Texaco*, September 4, 1985.

242–244

December 19 board-meeting description and conversation: from testimony of Hugh Liedtke in *Pennzoil* v. *Texaco*, August 26, 27, and September 4, 1985; testimony of Baine Kerr in *Pennzoil* v. *Texaco*, July 18, 1985; minutes dated December 19, 1983.

Chapter Sixteen

245

What Gordon believed about hostile takeovers: from author's interview with Gordon Getty.

245–246

Gordon's reaction to Pennzoil bid, and what he knew about Pennzoil: from Gordon Getty's deposition testimony in *Pennzoil* v. *Texaco*, presented August 22, 1985. "I remember that he thought the Pennzoil tender was a very helpful and promising development," Gordon testified. ". . . I agreed with him."

246

Conversation between Gordon and Marty Siegel: from deposition testimony of Marty Siegel in *Pennzoil* v. *Texaco*, presented August 19, 1985, and deposition testimony of Gordon Getty in that case, presented August 22, 1985.

247–249

Glanville background, meetings between Glanville and Lipton, telephone conversation between Glanville and Williams: from deposition testimony of James Glanville in *Pennzoil* v. *Texaco*, taken August 2, 1984, and testimony of Martin Lipton in *Pennzoil* v. *Texaco*, October 17, 1985.

249–250

Liedtke conversation with Gordon: from testimony of Hugh Liedtke in *Pennzoil* v. *Texaco*, August 26 and 27, 1985. Liedtke's call to Berg: from Liedtke's testimony of September 6, 1985. Berg's call to Copley: from author's interview with Harold Berg. Stuart's call to Bill Liedtke: from Hugh Liedtke's testimony, August 26, 1985.

250

Boisi said $100 per share would lead to full subscription: from deposition testimony, of Sid Petersen in *Pennzoil* v. *Texaco*, presented July 30, 1985.

251

Attempt to negotiate a unified front: from Petersen's deposition testimony, ibid.

251–252

Perspective of Lasky firm lawyers after filling of beneficiaries' lawsuit: from author's interview with Tim Cohler and two confidential sources familiar with the thinking of his partners.

252–253

Meeting between Gordon and Williams at Broadway mansion: from deposition testimony of Gordon Getty in *Pennzoil* v. *Texaco*, presented August 22, 1985; deposition testimony of Harold Williams in *Pennzoil* v. *Texaco*, presented November 1, 1985; testimony of Martin Lipton in *Pennzoil* v. *Texaco*, October 17, 1985.

253–254

Progress of negotiations: from handwritten notes of Dave Copley produced in *For the Matter . . .*, beginning "The following is based on the discussion among Boisi, Galant, O'Donnell, and Winokur, and Lipton and Vlahakis on the afternoon of December 28, 1983. . . ."

254

Gordon flew to New York: from deposition testimony of Tim Cohler in *Pennzoil* v. *Texaco*, presented August 1, 1985.

255–257

Meeting between Siegel, Glanville, Liman, Cohler, and Woodhouse: from deposition testimony of Marty Siegel in *Pennzoil* v. *Texaco*, presented August 19, 1985; deposition testimony of James Glanville in *Pennzoil* v. *Texaco*, taken August 2, 1984; testimony of Arthur Liman in *Pennzoil* v. *Texaco*, August 5, 1985. Telephone conversations with Liedtke: testimony of Siegel, Glanville, Liman, and testimony of Hugh Liedtke, August 26, 1985. Liedtke's conversations with Sarofim: Ibid.

257–259

Saturday meeting at Wachtell offices: from testimony of Bart Winokur in *Pennzoil* v. *Texaco*, September 27, 1985; deposition testimony of Stuart Katz in *Pennzoil* v. *Texaco*, presented October 31, 1985; handwritten notes of Dave Copley dated December 31, 1983.

259–260

Gordon's nomination of directors: from deposition testimony of Marty Siegel, op. cit.; author's interview with Gordon Getty; author's interview with investor Warren Buffett.

260–262

Saturday meeting: from Winokur and Katz testimony, Copley notes, op. cit., and testimony of Laurence Tisch in *Pennzoil* v. *Texaco*, November 4, 1985. Call from Siegel to Glanville: from testimony of Hugh Liedtke, August 26, 1985.

Chapter Seventeen

263

An eerie scene: from Liedtke's testimony in *Pennzoil* v. *Texaco*, August 26, 1985. Arrival of Kerr, Barber, and Goodrum from testimony of Baine Kerr, July 18, 1985.

264

Conversation at the Waldorf: from testimony of Liedtke and Kerr, ibid., and testimony of Arthur Liman in *Pennzoil* v. *Texaco*, August 5, 1985.

265–268

Meeting between Hugh Liedtke, Gordon Getty et al. at the Pierre: from testimony of Liedtke and Kerr, op. cit.; deposition testimony of Marty Siegel in *Pennzoil* v. *Texaco*, August 19, 1985; deposition testimony of Gordon Getty in *Pennzoil* v. *Texaco*, August 22, 1985.

269–271

Conversations at Lipton's New Year's Day party; phone talks between Liman, Glanville, and Lipton; and conversations among Liedtke and his advisors at the Waldorf concerning Lipton's reliability come primarily from testimony of Arthur Liman in *Pennzoil* v. *Texaco*, August 5, 1985. Also from Lipton's testimony of October 17, 1985 and Liedtke and Kerr's testimony, op. cit.

<u>272</u>

Monday meeting at Wachtell, Lipton offices: from *Pennzoil* v. *Texaco* deposition testimony of Petersen; Winokur trial testimony, September 19 and 27, 1985; deposition testimony of Patricia Vlahakis in *Pennzoil* v. *Texaco*, presented September 24, 1985; and from author's interviews with two confidential sources. What Cohler told Petersen is from Petersen's deposition testimony.

<u>273</u>

"You know we think that's inadequate" conversation: from testimony of Bart Winokur in *Pennzoil* v. *Texaco*, September 19, 1985.

<u>273–275</u>

Waldorf meeting between Glanville, Barber, Winokur, Boisi, and Galant: from Winokur testimony, ibid.; testimony of Geoff Boisi in *Pennzoil* v. *Texaco*, October 9, 1985; and deposition testimony of James Glanville in *Pennzoil* v. *Texaco*, taken August 2, 1984.

Chapter Eighteen
<u>277</u>

Seating arrangements at board meeting: from testimony of Martin Lipton in *Pennzoil* v. *Texaco*, October 17, 1985; deposition testimony of Dave Copley in *Pennzoil* v. *Texaco*, taken May 14, 1984; author's interview with Harold Stuart.

<u>277–278</u>

Circumstances of Williams' signing memo of agreement: from deposition testimony of Patricia Vlahakis in *Pennzoil* v. *Texaco*, presented September 24, 1985; testimony of Martin Lipton, October 17, 1985.

<u>278–279</u>

This and following accounts of the full Getty Oil board proceedings inside Sutton Room II—as opposed to various caucuses and private discussions that took place during recesses of the official meeting—are from the so-called "Copley Notes" produced in *Pennzoil* v. *Texaco*. During the board meeting, Getty Oil general counsel Dave Copley took detailed, handwritten notes of the discussion, recording the comments of the directors and advisors in sequence. Soon after the two-day meeting was concluded, Copley typed his notes into a word-processing system at the New York offices of Dechert Price & Rhoads. According to the testimony of Copley and a Dechert Price attorney who helped him arrange for word-processing services, Copley's original notes were then revised twice before a final version was produced. Copley testified that the changes he made were merely cosmetic, involving spelling, grammar, and the imposition of legalistic, business-speak language to summarize portions of the raw transcript. The final version is full of polite euphemisms, along the lines of "Mr. Getty indicated that Mr. Wendt was incorrect," when one imagines that perhaps Mr. Getty told Mr. Wendt to go stuff himself. We will never know—Copley destroyed the original handwritten notes. As to the substance of the dialogue recorded in the final version of the Copley Notes—the "sanitized" version, as Pennzoil's attorneys liked to call it—a variety of those present at the meeting later testified that the notes were remarkably accurate. In a few cases, where Copley's final version did purport to record the exact words spoken, participants at the meeting disagreed with the precise language attributed to them, but testified that the words were accurate in substance. In any event, I have relied in large part on the precise language set down in the final version of Copley's notes for much of the dialogue in Chapters Eighteen and Nineteen, substituting synonyms only occasionally, when Copley's euphemisms seem entirely unbelievable. For example, if Copley's "sanitized" notes are to be believed, none of the participants ever uttered the word "deal" during the entire twenty-five-hour meeting; instead, they always said "transaction." I find this implausible, and so have occasionally substituted "deal" into the dialogue. This is not an attempt to comment on the legal implications of the "transactions" under discussion, but is rather an innocuous—I think—effort to restore some semblance of reality to Copley's language.

In interviews and in testimony, those present at the Inter-Continental Hotel on January 2 and 3 later recalled conversations and exchanges not recorded in the Copley Notes. Most of these conversations were not recorded because they took place outside of Sutton Room II, during recesses, when the board was not officially in session. A few exchanges reliably testified to but not recorded in the Copley Notes did take place during the official meeting. It seems clear that they were not recorded, or did not survive word-processing, because the words were profane and angry, although it may also be that Copley simply did not hear everything that was said.

280

This caucus session is from testimony of Bart Winokur in *Pennzoil* v. *Texaco*, September 19, 1985.

280–281

Conversations: from the Copley Notes.

281

What Siegel thought: from videotaped deposition testimony of Marty Siegel in *Pennzoil* v. *Texaco*.

282–287

Discussion: from the Copley Notes.

287

The "chocolate cake" incident: from author's interviews with Geoff Boisi and a confidential source.

288–289

Negotiations over the $10 debenture from testimony of Arthur Liman in *Pennzoil* v. *Texaco*, August 7, 1985; testimony of Geoff Boisi in *Pennzoil* v. *Texaco*, October 9, 1985.

289–294

Discussion: from the Copley Notes.

294–295

The directors' reaction to the reading of the "Dear Hugh" letter is not recorded in the Copley Notes. That there was a hailstorm of profanity and Teets' off-color remarks are from the author's interviews with three confidential sources. Tisch's remark about "very bad form" is from testimony of Bart Winokur in *Pennzoil* v. *Texaco*, September 27, 1985. Larkin's comment that the "old man is rolling over in his grave": from author's interview with Harold Stuart.

Chapter Nineteen

296–297

Discussion: from the Copley Notes.

298

Note slipped under Glanville's door: from testimony of Bart Winokur in *Pennzoil* v. *Texaco*, September 19, 1985; testimony of Geoff Boisi, October 9, 1985; Boisi note produced in *Pennzoil* v. *Texaco*.

299–302

Boisi's phone conversations: from testimony of Geoff Boisi in *Pennzoil* v. *Texaco*, October 9, 1985; deposition testimony of Geoff Boisi in *Pennzoil* v. *Texaco*, taken July 12, 1984 and presented August 2, 1985; deposition testimony of Al DeCrane in *Pennzoil* v. *Texaco*, presented August 13, 1985.

302–304

Liman's negotiations with Lipton and Liedtke: from testimony of Arthur Liman in *Pennzoil* v. *Texaco*, August 7, 1985; testimony of Martin Lipton, October 17, 1985; Copley Notes.

304

Board meeting reconvenes briefly: from Copley Notes.

304–305

Negotiations between Liman, Lipton, and Boisi: from testimony of Martin Lipton in *Pennzoil* v. *Texaco*, October 17, 1985; testimony of Arthur Liman, August 7, 1985.

305–306

Discussions in caucus: from testimony of Bart Winokur in *Pennzoil* v. *Texaco*, September 19, 1985.

306–307

Board discussion: from the Copley Notes.

307–308

Liman's conversation with Liedtke: from testimony of Arthur Liman in *Pennzoil* v. *Texaco*, August 7, 1985.

309–310

Liedtke's mood and conversation with Ann Getty: from testimony of Hugh Liedtke in *Pennzoil* v. *Texaco*, August 27, 1985.

Chapter Twenty

312

Why only Patricia Vlahakis was available to work on press release: from author's interview with Martin Lipton.

312–313

Scene of confusion at Paul, Weiss offices: from deposition testimony of Patricia Vlahakis in *Pennzoil* v. *Texaco*, presented September 24, 1985; testimony of Bart Winokur, September 20, 1985; author's interview with three confidential sources.

313

"You're stuck with Gordon Getty" conversation: from deposition testimony of Richard Howe in *Pennzoil* v. *Texaco*, presented November 5, 1985; author's interview with a confidential source.

313

Vlahakis was feeling frightened: from author's interview with Patricia Vlahakis.

314

"If you don't get off the phone" conversation: from testimony of Patricia Vlahakis presented September 24, 1985.

314–315

Handwritten draft of press release, and subsequent conversation between Vlahakis and Winokur: from testimony of Patricia Vlahakis presented September 24, 1985, and testimony of Bart Winokur September 20, 1985, op. cit.

315–316

Goodrum comment, and Vlahakis conversation with Lipton: from Vlahakis' testimony, September 24, 1985, op. cit.

316–317

Press release produced for *Pennzoil* v. *Texaco* and issued by Getty Oil on January 4, 1984.

317

What Boisi believed about an "agreement in principle": from testimony of Geoff Boisi in *Pennzoil* v. *Texaco*, October 10, 1985.

319

Boisi's call to DeCrane: from deposition testimony of Geoff Boisi in *Pennzoil* v. *Texaco*, presented August 2, 1985; Boisi's testimony, October 9, 1985; DeCrane's testimony in *Pennzoil* v. *Texaco*, November 8, 1985.

320

"The fat lady has not yet sung": from Petersen's deposition testimony in *Pennzoil* v. *Texaco*, taken January 17, 1984.

320

Delay in document-drafting: from testimony of Patricia Vlahakis presented September 24, 1985 and testimony of Bart Winokur, September 20, 1985, op. cit.

321

Liedtke conversation with Gordon: from testimony of Hugh Liedtke in *Pennzoil* v. *Texaco*, August 28, 1985.

Chapter Twenty-one

323–325

Texaco history and profile: from *Los Angeles Times*, January 19, 1986; *Wall Street Journal*, January 11, 1984, November 27, 1985; *Fortune*, March 17, 1986; author's interviews with John McKinley,

Al DeCrane, Jim Kinnear, William Weitzel, and former Texaco executives.

327

DeCrane called McKinley from testimony of Alfred DeCrane in *Pennzoil* v. *Texaco*, November 8, 1985.

328

Texaco's dealings with Conoco from testimony of John McKinley in *Pennzoil* v. *Texaco*, September 17, 1985.

329

Conversation between DeCrane and McKinley from testimony of John McKinley, September 10, 1985; deposition testimony of Al DeCrane in *Pennzoil* v. *Texaco*, presented August 13, 1985; DeCrane testimony, November 8 and 10, 1985.

Chapter Twenty-two

330–331

Contacts between Texaco and Morgan Stanley from testimony of John McKinley, September 10, 1985, op. cit.; testimony of Al DeCrane November 8 and 10, 1985, op. cit.

331–332

Profile of Wasserstein and First Boston from *Esquire*, May 1984; deposition testimony of Bruce Wasserstein in *Pennzoil* v. *Texaco*, presented October 30, 1985.

333–334

Conversation between Wasserstein and Tisch, and early work of Wasserstein and Perella: from Wasserstein deposition testimony in *Pennzoil* v. *Texaco*, presented October 30, 1985.

334

Description of Perella: from *Esquire*, May 1984.

334

DeCrane said that he felt no tension between Texaco and First Boston: from author's interview with Al DeCrane.

334–338

Meeting between Texaco executives and First Boston bankers: from deposition testimony of Texaco associate comptroller Patrick Lynch in *Pennzoil* v. *Texaco*, presented August 12, 1985; testimony of Al DeCrane, November 11, 1985; DeCrane's handwritten notes of the meeting produced in *Pennzoil* v. *Texaco*.

<u>338</u>
Wasserstein rewrote Monopoly rules: from *Esquire*, May 1984.
<u>338–339</u>
Meetings at Texaco headquarters on the morning of January 5: from DeCrane testimony, November 11, 1985, op. cit.; Wasserstein deposition testimony, presented October 30, 1985, op. cit.; DeCrane deposition testimony, presented August 14, 1985, op. cit.; DeCrane's handwritten notes, op. cit.
<u>339</u>
Morgan's willingness to represent Texaco a significant factor in McKinley's mind: from author's interview with John McKinley.
<u>340</u>
McKinley's call to Lipton: from Wasserstein deposition testimony, presented October 30, 1985, op. cit.; testimony of John McKinley in *Pennzoil* v. *Texaco*, September 11, 1985; author's interview with John McKinley.
<u>340–341</u>
Texaco board meeting of January 5: from McKinley testimony, September 11, 1985, op. cit.; DeCrane testimony, November 11, 1985, op. cit.
<u>341</u>
Wasserstein's attitude, and McKinley's calls: from deposition testimony of Bruce Wasserstein, presented October 30, 1985, op. cit.; testimony of John McKinley, September 11, 1985, op. cit.

Chapter Twenty-three
<u>343–344</u>
No prospect that an agreement would be signed Thursday, and Winokur's reasons why he wasn't ready: from testimony of Bart Winokur in *Pennzoil* v. *Texaco*, September 26, 1985.
<u>345</u>
Vlahakis' conversation with Lipton, and decision not to go to Paul, Weiss: from deposition testimony of Patricia Vlahakis in *Pennzoil* v. *Texaco*, presented September 25, 1985.
<u>345–346</u>
Meeting between Lipton, Weitzel, and Kinnear: from testimony of William Weitzel in *Pennzoil* v. *Texaco*, November 6, 1985; also from Lipton's testimony, October 17, 1985, and Kinnear's testimony, November 5, 1985.

347

Wasserstein told Lipton that Texaco would offer at least $120: from Lipton's testimony, October 17, 1985, op. cit.

348–350

First session of McKinley's meeting with Gordon Getty at the Pierre: from testimony of Jim Kinnear in *Pennzoil* v. *Texaco*, November 5, 1985; testimony of William Weitzel, November 6, 1985, op. cit.; deposition testimony of Martin Siegel, presented August 20, 1985; deposition testimony of Gordon Getty in *Pennzoil* v. *Texaco*, presented August 23, 1985; testimony of John McKinley, September 12 and 13, 1985.

350

Siegel's call to Lipton: from testimony of Martin Lipton, October 17, 1985, op. cit.

350

"I personally read Mr. Getty as being a sort of genteel person" conversation between Weitzel and McKinley: from testimony of William Weitzel, November 6, 1985, op. cit.

350

"We met with Gordon, but it's not clear to us" conversation: from testimony of Martin Lipton, October 17, 1985, op. cit.

351

How Tisch regarded Gordon Getty: from testimony of Laurence Tisch in *Pennzoil* v. *Texaco*, November 4, 1985.

351

"Have you all got a price that you're willing to give Mr. Getty?" conversation: from testimony of William Weitzel, November 6, 1985, op. cit. Corroborated by Lipton testimony, October 17, 1985, and Tisch testimony, November 4, 1985, op. cit.

352

"I accept!" declaration by Gordon, and following dialogue: from testimony of William Weitzel, November 6, 1985, op. cit. Corroborated in substance by Lipton, Tisch, and McKinley testimony, op. cit.

354

What Gordon thought about Texaco's offer, quote beginning "I wasn't in every room at every time": from author's interview with Gordon Getty.

Chapter Twenty-four

355

Indemnity negotiations between Texaco and Lipton: from testimony of William Weitzel in *Pennzoil* v. *Texaco*, November 6, 1985, and testimony of Martin Lipton in *Pennzoil* v. *Texaco*, October 17, 1985.

356

"Martin, the announcement on the tape has just been read to me" conversation between Liman and Siegel: from testimony of Arthur Liman in *Pennzoil* v. *Texaco*, August 7, 1985.

357

Mood in Waldorf suite, and Liedtke's thinking: from testimony of Hugh Liedtke in *Pennzoil* v. *Texaco*, August 27, 1985. Text of telegram produced in *Pennzoil* v. *Texaco*.

358

Telephone board-meeting discussion: from Getty Oil secretary Robert E. Haffe's notes of the meeting.

358

Everyone McKinley talked to told him there was no deal with Pennzoil: the trial and deposition testimony in *Pennzoil* v. *Texaco* makes this clear; McKinley said the same in an interview with the author.

358

Decision to file suit in Delaware: from deposition testimony of Sidney Petersen in *Pennzoil* v. *Texaco*, presented July 30, 1985.

358–359

McKinley talked to Petersen about employees: from testimony of John McKinley in *Pennzoil* v. *Texaco*, September 17, 1985. Gordon negotiated with his family: from deposition testimony of Tim Cohler in *Pennzoil* v. *Texaco*, presented August 1, 1985.

360

Bankers' fees, and "You can consider the fees in this deal as tips" quote: from *Wall Street Journal*, January 17, 1984.

360

Liedtke stayed in New York: from Liedtke's testimony of September 9, 1985, op. cit.

360–361

Glanville calls Liedtke, and meets with McKinley in Connecticut: from deposition testimony of James Glanville in *Pennzoil* v. *Texaco*, taken August 2, 1984; deposition testimony of John McKinley in *Pennzoil* v. *Texaco*, taken July 10, 1984. Recalling the meeting at his home with Glanville, McKinley testified: "He said that we are all big boys. He said that Pennzoil does not have the wherewithal to buy all of Getty. He was basically complimentary of Texaco's activity."

McKinley also recalled that Glanville told him that he was personally disappointed because Lazard Frères had had difficulty concluding several mergers they had attempted.
361–362
Settlement meeting in Washington, D.C.: from McKinley's deposition testimony, ibid.; also from deposition testimony of Perry Barber in *Pennzoil* v. *Texaco*, taken October 12, 13, and 14, 1984, and
author's interview with Baine Kerr.

Chapter Twenty-five
367
Liedtke hired a prominent lobbyist: from author's interview with
Stephen Ross, former staff attorney with the House antitrust
subcommittee.
368
Conversation between Liedtke and Jeffers: from author's interview
with John Jeffers.
369–370
Pennzoil's early legal strategy: from author's interviews with John
Jeffers and Irv Terrell.
370
Skadden, Arps attorneys explained later: from *Wall Street Journal*,
December 20, 1985.
374–378
Jamail's autobiography, beginning with "My father had a confection-
ary store": from author's interview with Joe Jamail.
378–379
Liedtke's relationship with Jamail: from author's interviews with Joe
Jamail and Baine Kerr.
379
"You still fumin' about that?" conversation between Jamail and
Liedtke in Arkansas: from author's interview with Joe Jamail.

Chapter Twenty-six
380
Top Getty Oil executives known as the "divine nine": from author's
interviews with two former Getty Oil executives.
381
Jurisdictional maneuver focused Texaco executives' attention on

lawsuit: from author's interviews with John McKinley, Al DeCrane, Jim Kinnear, and William Weitzel.

381–382

Biographical details about Jeffers and Terrell, and early relationship with Jamail: from author's interviews with John Jeffers and Irv Terrell.

383

Texaco's search for Houston counsel: from author's interview with William Weitzel.

383–386

Miller's biography, and relationship with Baker & Botts: from author's interviews with Dick Miller, Baine Kerr, John Jeffers, and Irv Terrell. "The most important thing is to be able to count on yourself"; "What you finally learn"; and "It was a combination of factors" quotes: from author's interview with Dick Miller.

386

Miller reluctant to take on case, and conversations with Barber and his partners: from author's interview with Dick Miller.

386–387

How Terrell and Jeffers regarded Miller: from author's interviews with John Jeffers and Irv Terrell.

387–388

Colloquy: from deposition transcript of Al DeCrane in *Pennzoil* v. *Texaco*, taken April 26, 1984.

389

Keeton called Jamail "chickenshit," and McKinley had to smile: from videotaped deposition of John McKinley in *Pennzoil* v. *Texaco*.

389–390

Pretrial settlement discussions: from author's interview with Baine Kerr and three confidential sources.

390

What Miller and other attorneys told McKinley, and why he was prepared to go to trial: from author's interview with John McKinley.

391–392

What Miller thought about Jamail: from author's interview with Dick Miller. That Farris described Jamail's contribution as a "princely sum": from *Fortune*, January 21, 1985.

392

Jamail told Liedtke he was going to "win this damn thing": from author's interview with Joe Jamail.

392–393
Drinking session the night before opening arguments: from author's interview with Joe Jamail. "Now *that's* how you get ready for an opening argument" and "The way to win is to keep it simple" quotes: also from author's interview with Joe Jamail.

Chapter Twenty-seven
394
What the jurors remembered later: from author's interviews with Jim Shannon, Richard Lawler, and Theresa Ladig.
395
"There are going to be a lot of issues that you are going to hear" and following quotes: from *Pennzoil* v. *Texaco* trial transcript, July 9, 1985.
396
What the Pennzoil lawyers were looking for: from author's interviews with Joe Jamail, Irv Terrell, and John Jeffers.
396–397
Colloquy with juror: from *Pennzoil* v. *Texaco* trial transcript, July 11, 1985.
398–399
Terrell's mannerisms at trial, and jurors views of Jeffers: from author's interviews with Jim Shannon, Richard Lawler, and Theresa Ladig.
400
Texaco "bought this lawsuit": from *Pennzoil* v. *Texaco* trial transcript, November 15, 1985.
401
Jamail's examination of Liedtke: this and similar exchanges can be found on pp. 10219–10247 of the *Pennzoil* v. *Texaco* trial transcript.
401–402
Miller felt that he knew Liedtke: from author's interview with Dick Miller.
402
That Jeffers and Terrell sensed Miller's obsession, and what they came to believe about Miller's attitude toward Liedtke: from author's interviews with John Jeffers and Irv Terrell.
403
"Well, George Getty died in 1973?" exchange: from *Pennzoil* v. *Texaco* trial transcript, September 5, 1985.

403
"Here you are on the sixth of January" exchange: from *Pennzoil* v. *Texaco* trial transcript, September 9, 1985.
404
Zipper incident: from author's interviews with Dick Miller, Joe Jamail, and Theresa Ladig. Courtroom dialogue: from *Pennzoil* v. *Texaco* trial transcript, September 5, 1985.
406
"Would it be fair to say" exchange: from *Pennzoil* v. *Texaco* trial transcript, August 23, 1985.
406
That was how Gordon himself privately viewed his involvement: from author's interview with Gordon Getty.

Chapter Twenty-eight
407
Texaco's executives said they anticipated subpoena: from author's interviews with John McKinley and William Weitzel.
408
Pennzoil attorneys expected DeCrane to be first Texaco witness: from author's interviews with Joe Jamail, John Jeffers, and Irv Terrell.
409
Miller said that decisions reflected a consensus and that he did not care for consensus: from author's interview with Dick Miller. Texaco executives isolated from Miller by layers of hierarchy: from author's interviews with McKinley, DeCrane, Weitzel, and Kinnear. It should be noted that at the time of these latter interviews, Texaco's executives and directors were facing lawsuits by company shareholders alleging that Texaco had mismanaged the *Pennzoil* v. *Texaco* litigation. Thus, it is hardly surprising that Texaco's executives would claim that they left all of the important decisions to their lawyers. One former Texaco manager involved with the case claimed in an interview with the author that McKinley et al. were intimately involved in "micromanagement" of the case and did not cede the important decisions to their attorneys. This manager was not part of the Texaco executives' inner circle, however.
409
Miller told Petersen he would be the first witness: from author's interview with Sid Petersen.

409–410

Miller discounted notion that DeCrane should go first: from author's interview with Dick Miller.

410

Petersen was disappointed: from author's interview with Sid Petersen.

411–412

Winokur testimony: from *Pennzoil* v. *Texaco* trial transcript, September 19, 1985.

413

Winokur-Terrell exchange and Nickens' objection: ibid.

414–154

Miller's argument with Farris: ibid.

415

Farris' Yom Kippur remarks: from *Pennzoil* v. *Texaco* trial transcript, September 20, 1985.

Chapter Twenty-nine

417

Miller was personally enamored of Boisi: from author's interview with Dick Miller.

418

Terrell felt that Boisi was vulnerable: from author's interview with Irv Terrell.

419

Boisi-Terrell exchange: from *Pennzoil* v. *Texas* trial transcript, October 9, 1985.

419–421

Boisi cross-examination: from *Pennzoil* v. *Texaco* trial transcript, October 10, 1985.

422

Debate over whether to call Lipton: from author's interviews with Dick Miller and William Weitzel. "They set us up" and "It became impractical not to put him on" quotes: from author's interview with Dick Miller.

423

"Was not directed to him as a person" quote: from author's interview with John Jeffers. Jamail's bet: from author's interview with Joe Jamail.

423–425

Jamail's cross-examination of Lipton: from *Pennzoil* v. *Texaco* trial transcript, October 17, 1985.

426

Jamail sensed that Lipton was uncharacteristically afraid: from author's interview with Joe Jamail. Exchanges following: from trial transcript, October 17, 1985.

427

Miller accepted that it had not gone well: from author's interview with Dick Miller.

Chapter Thirty

429

Tisch exchange with Jamail: from *Pennzoil* v. *Texaco* trial transcript, November 4, 1985.

429–430

Miller felt he was battling judge and sometimes his own client: from author's interview with Dick Miller. That Miller continued to express optimism: from author's interviews with John McKinley, William Weitzel, and Al DeCrane.

430

Miller met with Texaco board, and what he told them: from author's interview with William Weitzel.

431

Now Pennzoil attorneys were not so worried about DeCrane: from author's interviews with John Jeffers and Irv Terrell.

431

Views of Weitzel's eruption under cross-examination: from author's interviews with William Weitzel, John Jeffers, and Irv Terrell.

431–432

Closing trial colloquy: from *Pennzoil* v. *Texaco* trial transcript November 12, 1985.

433–435

Arguments about the charge, and quotes: from trial transcript November 13, 1985.

436

Decision not to put on damage testimony: from author's interviews with Dick Miller, John McKinley, and William Weitzel. "The advice we got" quote: from author's interview with John McKinley.

436

"Their contract was to obtain stock" argument: from *Pennzoil* v. *Texaco* trial transcript, November 13, 1985.

436

Scene at the Four Seasons: from author's interviews with John McKinley and James Kinnear.

437

"You're going to be able to do something" and following quotes: from *Pennzoil* v. *Texaco* trial transcript, November 14, 1985.

437

What Terrell thought about Miller: from author's interview with Irv Terrell.

438–439

Quotes from Miller's argument: from trial transcript, November 14 and 15, 1985.

439–440

Quotes from Jamail's argument: from trial transcript, November 15, 1985.

Chapter Thirty-one

442–447

This account of the jury's deliberations, and all quotes attributed to the jurors are from author's interviews with Jim Shannon, Richard Lawler, and Theresa Ladig. Some portions were confirmed by author's interviews with John Jeffers, Irv Terrell, and Dick Miller, who conducted interviews of their own with the jurors.

447–448

Casseb's response to the first note: from the jurors; and courtroom colloquy over the second note: from *Pennzoil* v. *Texaco* trial transcript, November 18, 1985.

448

That Miller changed his mind overnight, and discussion with Casseb: from trial transcript, November 19, 1985.

449

Final deliberations, and feelings of the jurors as they returned to courtroom: from author's interviews with Jim Shannon, Richard Lawler, and Theresa Ladig.

449–451

Courtroom scene and exchanges: from trial transcript, November 19, 1985, and author's interviews with Jim Shannon, Richard Lawler, Theresa Ladig, John Jeffers, Joe Jamail, Irv Terrell, Dick Miller, and James Kinnear.

Chapter Thirty-two

452

"Fortune 500 exception to federalism": from author's notes taken at Supreme Court argument.

452–453

Settlement talks: from author's interviews with Baine Kerr and John McKinley; *Wall Street Journal*, daily coverage in December 1985 and January 1986.

454

Reasons for Kinnear's selection: from author's interview with William Weitzel.

455

"I have no feeling on that score" and following quote: from author's interview with Gordon Getty.

456

Testimony of Martin Lipton before a subcommittee of the House of Representatives' banking committee, April 3, 1985.

INDEX

ABOUT THE AUTHOR

Steve Coll is a staff writer at the *New Yorker*, the dean of the Columbia Journalism School, and the bestselling author of seven books. Previously he served as president of the New America Foundation and worked for two decades at the *Washington Post*, where he won the Pulitzer Prize for Explanatory Journalism for a four-part series on the Securities and Exchange Commission during Ronald Reagan's presidency. The award-winning series became the basis for *Eagle on the Street* (1991), coauthored with David A. Vise. Coll's other books include New York Times Notable Book *The Deal of the Century* (1998); *Ghost Wars* (2004), winner of the Pulitzer Prize for General Nonfiction; *The Bin Ladens* (2009), winner of the PEN/John Kenneth Galbraith Award for Nonfiction; and *Private Empire* (2012), winner of the Financial Times and McKinsey Business Book of the Year Award.

STEVE COLL

FROM OPEN ROAD MEDIA

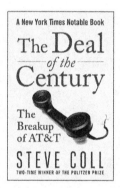
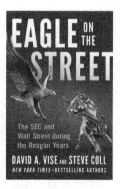
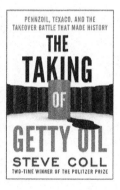

INTEGRATED MEDIA

Find a full list of our authors and
titles at www.openroadmedia.com

FOLLOW US
@OpenRoadMedia

CPSIA information can be obtained
at www.ICGtesting.com
Printed in the USA
BVOW06s1454040218
507191BV00001BA/19/P